FOREST EVER FOREST

by CHRIS BROUGHTON

Dedicated to my father
Allen Victor Broughton
1932 - 1999

Published in 2001 by:
Tricky Red Publications
PO Box 6729
Nottingham
NG1 3JE

Illustrations by **Martyn Swinscoe**

Design and Artwork by:
Swinscoe Communications
190 Mansfield Road
Nottingham
NG1 3HX

Repro by:
Blue Brick Design
Nottingham

Printed by:
Progressive Printers (Nottm.)
Westbury Road
Basford
Nottingham
NG5 1EJ

ISBN: 0-9540699-0-0

CONTENTS

CHAPTER

ACKNOWLEDGEMENTS •
FOREWORD BY GARRY BIRTLES •
PREFACE •
INTRODUCTION BY ROBERT BANKS •
FOREST EVER FOREST, ALL OUR HOPES ARE WITH YOU 1
OH, WE'RE BETTER THAN UNITED AND WE'RE LOUDER 2
THAN THE KOP
WHENEVER YER SAD, WHENEVER YER BLUE, WHENEVER 3
THE FOREST ARE PLAYING
TIPTOE THROUGH THE POPSIDE, WITH ME 4
HERE A NOD, THERE A NOD, EVERYWHERE A NOD-NOD 5
WE'LL SUPPORT YOU EVERMORE, WE'LL SUPPORT YOU EVERMORE 6
CITY GROUND, OH MIST ROLLING IN FROM THE TRENT 7
WE ARE THE BEST TEAM IN THE LAND, THIS NO-ONE CAN DENY 8
WE'RE ON THE MARCH WITH CLOUGHIE'S ARMY 9
WE ARE THE NUTTERS, THE NUTTERS FROM NOTTS 10
BRIAN CLOUGH AND PETER TAYLOR 11
TELL MI MAM, MI MAM, I DON'T WANT NO TEA, NO TEA 12
SHE WORE, SHE WORE, SHE WORE A SCARLET RIBBON 13
WE ARE THE EUROPEAN CHAMPIONS 14
WE'VE BEEN TO EUROPE, WE'VE WON THE CUP TWICE 15
THERE'LL ALWAYS BE AN ENGLAND, AND ENGLAND SHALL BE FREE 16
ARE YOU WATCHING JIMMY GREAVES? 17
WHO'S YER FATHER, WHO'S YER FATHER, 18
WHO'S YER FATHER – REFEREE?
FOR EVER AND EVER, WE'LL FOLLOW OUR TEAM 19
LET'S ALL LAUGH AT DERBY, LET'S ALL LAUGH AT DERBY 20
FIVE HO, FIVE HO, IT'S BACK TO NOTTS WE GO 21
THERE'S A CIRCUS IN THE TOWN, IN THE TOWN 22
AND NOW YER GONNA BELIEVE US, WE'RE GONNA WIN THE LOT 23
TOTTENHAM – WE ALWAYS BEAT TOTTENHAM 24
WE ALL AGREE, WALKER IS WORTH MORE THAN DERBY 25
WE'RE THE PRIDE OF NOTTINGHAM 26
GOODBYE ALL, GOODBYE ALL, WE'RE SAYING GOODBYE TO IT ALL 27
WHEN HE GETS THE BALL, HE SCORES A GOAL, GARY-GARY CHARLES 28
HE'S GOTTA PINEAPPLE ON 'IS 'EAD 29
ONE TEAM IN EUROPE, THERE'S ONLY ONE TEAM IN EUROPE 30
OH SANDY-SANDY, SANDY-SANDY-SANDY-SANDY AN-DER-SON 31
WELL I NEVER FELT MORE LIKE SINGING THE BLUES 32
BIG FAT RON'S RED AND WHITE ARMY! 33
I KNOW I AM, I'M SURE I AM, I'M FOREST 'TIL I DIE 34
WE ALL LIVE IN A FLAT IN HYSON GREEN 35
FACTS NOT MYTHS 36
THE A TO Z OF TRENT END CHANTS AND ANTHEMS 37
SOURCES OF REFERENCE •
SUBSCRIBERS •

ACKNOWLEDGEMENTS

Thanks to Sue for your patience, tolerance and understanding over the last four years, and for putting up with being not only a 'football widow' most Saturday afternoons, but also an 'author's widow' the rest of the time. I couldn't have done it without your support.

Thanks also to my brother Graham, and friends John Farley, Lee Hannah, Andy Oakley and Pete Buxton, for reading the first draft of this book and providing me with honest and constructive feedback. Thanks also for your ongoing support and encouragement.

A big, big thank you to my old friend Garry Birtles for writing the Foreword; to my colleague and friend Robert Banks for writing the Introduction; and to my good friend Martyn Swinscoe for designing the front cover, providing the brilliant illustrations, typesetting the finished manuscript, and dealing with the Printers; not to mention his marketing input.

I would also like to thank the Secretaries of West Bromwich Albion FC, West Ham United FC, Ipswich Town FC, Newcastle United FC, Wimbledon FC, the Notts FA, and Arnold Town FC, for responding promptly to my requests for statistical/historical information.

Many thanks to Nottingham Forest FC for their kind permission to re-produce numerous extracts from the official Forest Review and to the Nottingham Evening Post/Football Post for kindly allowing me to reproduce a number of articles and letters from past publications.

Thanks also to my son Thomas and his friends Scott West, Dean Farley, James Harris, Jonathan Pack, Chris Pack, Anoop Kanabar, Phil Broughton and Kev Gent for standing outside the City Ground prior to the game against QPR on 31st March 2001 and distributing thousands of leaflets on my behalf.

For their generosity in helping me market this publication, I would also like to thank the following:

Michelle Wilson of the Nottingham Evening Post.
Brian Tansley of BBC Radio Nottingham.
Mick Coll of the Barbers Shop, Attenborough Lane, Attenborough.
Mark and Mandy Jackson of the Sandwich Bank, Attenborough Lane, Attenborough.
Mike West of West's News, Radcliffe Road, West Bridgford.
Rocco and Concetta Carrelli of the Bridgford Restaurant, Radcliffe Road, West Bridgford.
Teresa Summerfield of Teresa's Sandwich Bar, Pavillion Road, West Bridgford.
Richard and Pete Abrahams of The Bakery Wine Bar, Beeston.
Steve, Dave and Pete Willans of the Southbank Bar, Bridgford Road, West Bridgford.
Aram Ashtari of the Hubble Bubble Bar, Pavillion Road, West Bridgford.
Paul and Cheryl Dooley of the Larwood & Voce Tavern, Trent Bridge, West Bridgford.
Tony Exton of the Nottingham Forest Sportsmans Social Club, Pavillion Road, West Bridgford.
Paul and June DeAth of The Magpies, Meadow Lane, Nottingham.
John Whitelaw and Jayne Hardy of the Trent Navigation, Meadow Lane, Nottingham.
And, last but by no means least…Big John Webster of 'The Peoples Republic of Shirebrook' for enticing half the population of North Notts to buy this book.

Without the help and support of all the above, this book would never have got off the ground (so you can blame them if you like!).

FOREWORD BY GARRY BIRTLES

WHEN CHRIS Broughton called my mobile phone, my immediate thought was that it was something to do with Nottingham Forest, and sure enough it was. For people who don't know Chris as I do, he is one of the most passionate and staunchest Forest fans you could wish to meet, and a friend of mine for many years standing.

As we rattled on passing the pleasantries, asking about old friends, and flicking our way through the trials and tribulations of the current Forest campaign, Chris, who when talking about his beloved Forest is very hard to stop in his tracks, finally came to the point of the call. He explained that he was writing a book, a graphic history of his experiences travelling home and away as a supporter since the 1966/67 season and asked me if I would write the foreword. I obviously had not seen the book or any of it's contents but did not hesitate in saying yes straight away because as a supporter first and then as a player, I lived through a lot of the ups and downs Chris and his fellow friends and supporters went through.

After explaining the ins and outs of the contents of the book, Chris told me there would be some illustrations to graphically show some of the stories and these would be drawn by another friend of mine Martyn Swinscoe, a year younger than me but a fellow pupil of the Alderman White School, Bramcote and also a fabulous artist (drawing and drinking!) He used to help us less gifted artists with our course work for exams.

My story and my involvement with Nottingham Forest is well documented, but it all started way back for me as a fifteen-year-old on trial at Aston Villa as a left winger. I went to the West Midlands club on trial for a month and hardly performed like a John Robertson (but then who did?), so it was the short trip back down the A38 to Nottingham to find a job and start playing football locally again. My father Ray, who was an eternal taxi driver for myself and team-mates and a constant source of encouragement through all the early years of my development, was employed as a floorlayer. So when I went to the job centre and a vacancy for a floorlayer appeared, I jumped at the chance. On the football front I started playing for Long Eaton United on Saturdays thanks to the chairman of the club John Raynor, another very important person in my progress to the ranks of pro football. Eventually I was asked by Dave Hailwood, the player-secretary of Sunday side Long Eaton Rovers to play for them, and as several of the Long Eaton United lads played for them, I agreed.

At this time the involvement on the social side of things was centred around our local hostelry in Chilwell called the Cadland, where all the Rovers lads and many others regularly amassed for lively drinking sessions. The 'Cad' was the focal point locally but people came from miles around, such was the pub's reputation, and it was here that I was lucky enough to strike up friendships with the best bunch of lads imaginable, a great laugh, great drinkers, fabulous card players and of course Forest fans; and these friendships are still there to this day.

On one of many nights out in Nottingham we ended up at the Palais de Dance, one of the places to be seen in Nottingham, and with a revolving dance floor that regularly flung slightly tipsy dancers on to the floor. On that fateful night a petition was doing the rounds in the club asking people to sign up to get Brian Clough as the new manager of Forest. I duly signed and Clough became the manager in 1975, and two years later I had signed on myself.

In the 78/79 season when things really took off for me personally in a big way, I was worried what the reaction would be towards me from all the lads in the pub, especially my lifelong friend Martyn Northfield who had been best man at my wedding. At first things seemed as though they had changed, as much for the lads as for me. I was probably trying too hard to remain one of the lads, and people were saying they were only drinking with me because I was a footballer. What crap! It was soon sorted out and we got back to doing what we did best: drinking and having a laugh (thanks to Ralph Kent, a constant source of hilarity, not just to me but to everyone. He was, and still is, completely bonkers.)

I have an eternal debt of gratitude to all the lads who drank with me in the good times and the bad times and who are still mates to this day. We had some fabulous times along the way, celebrating some great victories always in the Cadland and at parties afterwards, and a lot of people mentioned in this book and a lot who aren't, kept my feet on the ground and stopped me becoming the big headed, arrogant footballer that we see so much of today. If I did step out of line, I was soon put back in my place by the constant Mickey taking; so to every one of you, and there are many, I can't thank you enough.

It was an absolute pleasure, and still is.

WHEN MY next door neighbour and friend Steve Reid decided to sever his last remaining link with Nottingham Forest FC by selling off his programme collection way back in 1984, he unwittingly planted a seed in my mind which has taken almost seventeen years, and much blood, sweat and tears, to mature into a 400-page novel.

Having collected programmes only randomly up to this point, since first watching the 'Reds' in season 1966/67, I decided there and then, this was my opportunity to put things right and bought from him his entire collection, lock, stock and barrel. Since that day I have collected every single Forest Review and my complete collection goes right back to the aforementioned season.

I knew right back in 1984 that one day I would have to do something constructive with this wealth of information, and that a book of some description would eventually emerge. However, as with any project of this magnitude, it is always a question of getting around to it when the time is right.

A number of things are responsible for fuelling my appetite for this book; my passion for my hometown of Nottingham being one of them. My love of Nottingham and Nottingham Forest FC is so intense, only the merest criticism of either by anyone, makes my blood boil. When walking or driving through Nottingham, I feel happy, contented and proud. It is without question a wonderful place to be and to live, and I expect every one else to feel the same way as I do, or else!

Towards the end of 1985, a long and drawn out argument between Forest and Derby supporters developed via the Letter's Page of the Football Post. At the time, preliminary discussions were taking place within the game about the setting up of a breakaway Premier League in England and various ideas regarding what the criteria for joining this elite group of clubs was likely to be, were bandied around. Naturally, most of the big clubs, including Forest, were eager to stake their claim.

Laughingly, Derby Secretary Stuart Webb publicly declared that the Third Division 'Rams' – playing to gates of 10,000 at the time – should be the East Midlands' sole representatives, should the Premier League eventually get off the ground. This naturally caused a bit of a stir in Nottingham (well something as highly amusing as this would, wouldn't it?) and a couple of juicy letters from Forest supporters were published in the Football Post the following Saturday. And, to put it mildly, they were less than complimentary about our 'grass-eating' friends.

For several weeks after, we had to put up with one wild claim after another – and this was our Football Paper, not theirs – from Derby supporters who, at the very least, could be accused of living in cloud cuckoo land. Apparently, Derby was the 'hotbed of football' in this country, had support which 'rivalled that of Manchester United, Liverpool and Newcastle', and what's more, Nottingham 'wasn't even on the footballing map' as far as they were concerned.

The arguments raged on, but eventually I'd had enough and decided to settle the issue with some hard-hitting facts, gleaned from my rapidly expanding programme collection. This put a stop to it straight away, but my penchant for Forest statistics had been further re-enforced and every fixture, result and attendance has been meticulously recorded since, with the aim of sharing this information with the rest of the world at some stage in the future.

When I was invited to work in the Sales & Marketing department of my employer's head office in Manchester in 1993, I jumped at the opportunity. Although this temporary secondment was initially expected to last only two weeks, I ended up spending eighteen months there, writing distance learning material and training courses as part of our Training & Development team. There, my appetite for writing grew stronger and stronger and in addition to this, I was now proficient in the use of a word processor. The prospect of a book about Forest was now becoming more and more of a reality.

Over the years, an abundance of books about the 'Reds' have emerged, each one providing a wealth of statistical and historical information for the die-hard supporter to chew over. Players and managers have also had their say. One thing which has been sadly lacking though, is a fan's-eye view of proceedings down on Trentside during this period. And that's where I come in.

I consider myself very fortunate indeed to have lived through unquestionably the most successful period in the Club's history. I can imagine in a hundred years' time supporters asking: ''I wonder what it was like in those days?'' Even now I hear many of Forest's younger generation of supporters asking the very same question. The reference books will provide them with all the statistics, but won't enable them to smell or to feel what it was really like. By taking all these facts and figures and wrapping my own experiences around them, I have tried to bridge this gap and to capture the true spirit of the era. And in any case, I couldn't possibly go to my grave in thirty or forty years' time (fingers crossed), without having got it all off my chest first!

Football has undergone massive changes during my lifetime – some of them for the better, some of them for the worse. It has also been blighted throughout by the phenomenon of hooliganism. But what the game has brought into my life is almost immeasurable. I have visited virtually every town and city in this country on numerous occasions and travelled the length and breadth of Europe as well. I have also made scores of friends along the way. But, most importantly, I have enjoyed every single moment.

Those unfortunate people, who have no interest in football, will never appreciate the emotional roller coaster ride which the game brings into your life. During ninety minutes of football, you can experience almost every emotion known to mankind, from abject despair one minute, to total and utter jubilation just minutes later. And, just to sum up what life as a Forest supporter is like; since I started writing this book in April 1997, Forest have been relegated from the Premiership, promoted, relegated again, nearly relegated from Division One, and nearly promoted back to the Premiership again. There is never a dull moment when you support Nottingham Forest FC, believe me.

I hope you enjoy reading this book half as much as I've enjoyed writing it. And watch out for the sequel in another thirty years' time. Here's hoping anyway.

INTRODUCTION BY ROBERT BANKS

(Author of: "An Irrational Hatred of Luton" and "West Ham 'Til I Die")

I'VE ALWAYS had a soft spot for Nottingham Forest. I'm not going to tell you exactly where it is, but it developed a long time before Chris Broughton honoured me with the task of writing the introduction for this marvellous book.

I'm a West Ham fan. Since the age of six I have followed the Hammers all over the country, and in the process produced two books of my own, charting my adventures as a football fan. Perhaps that's why I can identify with the purpose of this book. There will be Forest fans who remember every detail just as well as Chris does, and will enjoy seeing them from a different perspective. There will also be people who don't recall the detail, and will be eager to have their memories jogged. There will also be younger fans who weren't even born when Forest went through their halcyon period of the late-70's, who will read this and feel as though they had been there all along.

My liking for Forest developed in the late-70's. Forest won the title the year West Ham were relegated, and I remember how refreshing it was to see a different team challenging the then invincible Liverpool side. People may deny it now, but that Liverpool team was almost as universally detested as the Manchester United of today. I watched Trevor Francis diving in at the far post to win the European Cup for Forest in 1979, but bizarrely, in the twisted manner reserved only for football fans, my clearest memory of that night is Barry Davies' three-changes-of-underpants commentary, "That's what I wanted to see Robertson do!"

At that time Forest were ground breaking in many ways, as a football club, as well as the way in which Clough's team approached the game. I was at an age when I was impressed by silly things like a shiny kit made by Adidas, and a simple but effective club badge. I know Chris has his own thoughts on that badge, but for me it made Forest one of the first clubs to have a "trademark" and was an icon for good football, and the only challenger to our own pair of crossed hammers in symbolising the club's roots and what it stands for – loyalty from it's local fans.

I know from experience that Forest fans are a loyal bunch. I was at the FA Cup semi-final in 1991. Taking part in the half hour long chanting of: "Billy Bonds' claret and blue army!" I know it still rankles with some Forest fans that the game is remembered for that fact more than their emphatic 4-0 victory. But I know, had the tables been turned, Forest fans would have done the same. For most football fans, simply being there used to be more important than performances, SKY TV revenues or Christmas tree formations. For some - a sadly dwindling band - it still is.

Reading this book re-enforces that point. If you have never been to a game, or not been for a while, it will make you understand what all the fuss is about when football fans gather in the canteen on a Monday morning to discuss the weekend's action. Genuine football fans, of any club, will identify with this book, because it demonstrates the wonderful memories the game can provide, and the firm friendships that can be forged through a mutual love of the best game in the world.

This book has been a labour of love for Chris, and I'm delighted for him that it has finally seen the light of day after many years of hard work. He has gone to extraordinary lengths to make sure everything about it is perfect, and I'm sure you'll gather that from it's appearance alone. It's been worth the effort. It's not often an historical document is published with such a deeply personal slant, that will be universally accepted. If A.J.P. Taylor had written it, he'd be up for the Nobel gong.

If you are a regular at The City Ground, read this book and it will revive some vivid memories. I swear you'll be able to smell the onions on the burger stand.

"FOREST EVER FOREST, ALL OUR HOPES ARE WITH YOU"

MY EARLIEST recollections of the game of football and in particular Nottingham Forest FC, are as a small boy growing up in Arnold on the outskirts of Nottingham in the early-1960s. Although I was born in the St.Anns area of the City at the end of 1957, my family moved to Arnold in 1961 when I was three years-of-age.

One of my favourite pastimes as a small boy was to visit the King George V Recreation Ground on a Saturday afternoon with my older brother Graham and pals to watch Arnold St.Marys play in the Central Alliance Premier League. As they were a semi-professional club, a small admission fee was required to gain entrance into the ground. However, there were too many holes in the fence surrounding the pitch to make paying to get in a viable proposition for a gang of scruffy little toe-rags like us. In any case, on the rare occasions when we were unable to sneak in and watch the game for free, we could always view the proceedings from our vantage point at the top of the slide on the park adjacent to the ground.

It was during these frequent visits to Arnold St.Marys that I first really became aware of Nottingham Forest FC. Some of the 'more mature' members of our gang had previously accompanied their fathers or older brothers to matches and were therefore familiar with many of the popular terrace chants of the time, and in particular, those of Forest's notorious Trent Enders. Terrace chanting was in it's infancy then and had probably originated on Liverpool's Kop End or Manchester United's Stretford End, where the early hits of rock and pop groups such as the Beatles or the Rolling Stones would be mimicked by swaying masses of young, mainly male supporters who had congregated on the terraces. The words and lyrics would be adapted to coincide with the names of the most popular players in the team or with the town or city with which they were associated. Many of these songs were adopted by the fans as club anthems; some of which have been passed down through generations of supporters and can still be heard to this day.

One of the earliest Trent End anthems, "Forest Ever Forest", is still sung today although, somewhat frustratingly, the first verse seemed to vanish into thin air about fifteen years ago, never to be heard of again. Sung to the tune of "Land of Hope and Glory", it goes:

Forest ever Forest,
All our hopes are with you,
True supporters forever,
'til our days are through,
La-la-la-la-la-la;

Through the seasons before
us, Down through history,
We will follow the Forest,
Onto victory,
La-la-la-la-la-la!

The Trent End of the early-to-mid-sixties was, not surprisingly, inhabited predominantly by 'Mods' and 'Rockers', who had collectively earned themselves a reputation for being "witty, enthusiastic and noisy" within the confines of the ground, and "rowdy, aggressive and somewhat unruly" outside. As with any other large provincial city, Nottingham had then, as it still has today, a substantial working-class population who, after a hard week's labour, were looking to let off some steam. The football grounds of the 1960s provided them with the perfect environment to do just that and consequently the previously unheard of phenomenon of football hooliganism gradually began to emerge.

One of Nottinghamshire's main industries at the time was Coal Mining, with most of the pits being situated in the north of the County and collectively employing upwards of 40,000 people, mainly young men. Many of these would converge on the City Ground on a Saturday afternoon, so it wasn't surprising that Forest's Trent Enders soon earned themselves a reputation for being tough and uncompromising. In fact, one of their favourite pastimes in those early days was to throw visiting supporters into the River Trent after the game;

particularly if Forest had lost! They would taunt opposing supporters throughout the game with chants of: *"You're goin' in the Trent, You're goin' in the Trent, You're goin' in the Trent,"* or with, for example: *"United-United, Can you swim? United, Can you swim?"*

I have vivid memories of catching a Corporation bus into town with my parents one Saturday afternoon, which was packed full of swearing, chanting, Forest supporters, on their way to a game. Many of them were wearing pit helmets, which had been painted red and white, and had slogans and the names of players emblazoned across them. Many of these young men were extremely rough looking and some of them had the initials ''NFFC'' tattooed on the fingers of one hand and ''ACAB'' on the other. (Just in case you don't know, this stands for: ''All Coppers Are Bastards''). And although I was only about six at the time, I remember being fascinated by this rather frightening bunch of reprobates.

People may be forgiven for thinking that football hooliganism is a phenomenon of the 1980s or 90s - merely an aspect of modern day living. But believe me, soccer violence has long since celebrated it's thirtieth birthday. It's incredible to think that some of it's original perpetrators are today not too far away from drawing their old age pensions! Admittedly, the violence of the 1960s and early-70s had more of a spontaneous nature about it, and the hooligans were less sophisticated, less sinister, and certainly far less organised then their modern day counterparts. Nevertheless, the problem has undeniably been around for a very long time now. The following is an extract from the Forest Review for the game against Birmingham City on Tuesday, 13th September 1966:

''SOCCER'S PUBLIC wants rugged, tough, play-it-hard stuff; I see no reason why it should not be so. I feel they want to see both sides battle until they drop.''

Strong words from a Football League manager before his side's local derby game ten days ago. What reaction his remarks caused can best be gauged by the fact that the actual game ended with two players getting their names taken, one being sent off the field and fights breaking out on the terraces between rival sets of fans! Whilst we are not suggesting that this statement was made with any other than the best intentions in mind it seems, either directly or indirectly, to have incited both players and spectators to 'have a go'.

In case you are wondering why we have mentioned the affairs of other clubs in this programme it is because we feel strongly that hooliganism on the terraces – all too prevalent these days more's the pity – is caused by a minority of long-haired scruffy youths who find comfort and a false courage in a crowd and try to cause fights amongst rival factions bringing discomfort and sometimes injury to the innocent bystander and disgrace to the good name of football.

We, at the City Ground, have for many years cherished a reputation for sportsmanship on the field and off, but in recent seasons, an unruly element have been causing trouble mainly at the back of the River Trent end goal and despite several appeals to their good sense, they continue to tarnish our image. Some appallingly bad behaviour was noticed on the visit of Chelsea two weeks ago.

Has a familiar ring to it, doesn't it?

IN 1966, we left Arnold and moved to Chilwell, which is situated in the south of the County, almost on the Notts/Derbys border. At this time I was still waiting to attend my first Forest match, and by now, at the age of eight, I was itching to do so. However, unlike many of my friends, I had parents who weren't remotely interested in football and, even in that day and age, they were not about to let an eight-year-old go it alone. My only hope was my brother Graham, who was two years older than me, and whose interest in Forest was growing as rapidly as mine.

The season of 1966/67 was a particularly memorable one for Nottingham Forest FC and it was almost impossible not to get caught up in the general euphoria and expectation surrounding the Club and the City at that time. Despite a fairly uninspiring start to the season, they did have a particularly promising side, with an ideal blend of youth and experience, and it soon became obvious that this wasn't going to be just another season of mediocrity and under-achievement for Nottingham's premier football team.

A total of six wins, three draws, and six defeats in their first fifteen games had placed them in an unimpressive eleventh position in the First Division table going into the home game with Sunderland on Saturday, 12th November 1966. They then embarked on a thirteen-match unbeaten run in the League commencing with a 3-1 win over Sunderland and ending with a 1-0 defeat away to Manchester United on Saturday, 11th February 1967. This impressive spell included no less than eight victories and five draws and elevated them to third position in the table behind Liverpool and Manchester United respectively. They'd also set off on an exciting FA Cup run and were regularly playing to packed City Ground crowds in excess of 40,000.

The Cup run began on Saturday, 28th January, with a 2-1 third round home victory over Second Division Plymouth Argyle in front of a crowd of 34,005. They were then drawn at home again in the fourth round, where they entertained First Division Newcastle United on Saturday, 18th February. Goals from Frank Wignall, John Barnwell and Joe Baker secured them a 3-0 victory in front of a crowd of 45,962 and saw them safely through to the fifth round.

Once again they enjoyed the rub of the green and were drawn at home to Third Division Swindon Town. The game took place on Saturday, 11th March, and rather surprisingly, ended in a goalless draw in front of a crowd of 45,878. The replay at Swindon's County Ground took place the following Tuesday and once again honours were even. Peter Hindley scored Forest's goal in a 1-1 draw. This led to a second replay, this time at neutral Villa Park, on Monday, 20th March, when at the third attempt, the 'Reds' finally progressed through to the quarter-final stages, courtesy of a 3-0 victory in front of a massive 52,596 crowd. The scorers on this occasion were Barry Lyons, Joe Baker and John Barnwell. Rumour has it, that before the kick off – which incidentally was delayed due to crowd congestion – there was a traffic jam stretching all the way back along the A453 from Birmingham to Nottingham!

Sandwiched between these two fifth round FA Cup replays, Forest entertained West Ham United in a vitally important League match at the City Ground on Saturday, 18th March. They went into this game still in third position in the table with a total of 39 points from 31 games played, behind Manchester United in first place and Liverpool in second place, both of whom were on 43 points from 31 played (this was at a time when only two points were awarded for a victory, as opposed to the three which are awarded today). And not only was this a vitally important match for Nottingham Forest FC in their quest for their first ever League Championship title, but it was also one of some significance for me personally, as it was my first ever at the City Ground.

The game itself turned out to be no showpiece, but it was everything that I'd ever imagined. Television coverage in those days was restricted almost entirely to highlights, with the only live matches being exclusively FA Cup, European Cup, or World Cup Finals. The atmosphere of a live English First Division game was therefore, something which I was not as yet familiar with. I attended the match with my brother Graham and a mate called Phil Chad – a Brummie who lived across the road from us in Chilwell. Predictably, we headed straight for the Trent End enclosure and, as was the norm in those days, paid the admission fee of two shillings and sixpence (equivalent to twelve and a half pence in today's decimal currency!) at the turnstiles. The line-ups that day were:

	FOREST	**WEST HAM**	
1	Peter Grummitt	Jim Standen	1
2	Peter Hindley	Jack Burkitt	2
3	John Winfield	Billy Kitchener	3
4	Terry Hennessey	Martin Peters	4
5	Bobby McKinlay	Paul Heffer	5
6	Henry Newton	Bobby Moore	6
7	Barry Lyons	Peter Brabook	7
8	John Barnwell	Ron Boyce	8
9	Joe Baker	Peter Bennett	9
10	Frank Wignall	Geoff Hurst	10
11	Ian Storey-Moore	John Sissons	11
	Sub: John Brindley	Sub: Harry Redknapp	

This particular Forest side is without doubt one of the most accomplished I've watched during my time as a supporter, and some thirty-odd years later, the names still roll off the end of the tongue: Ian Storey-Moore, Frank Wignall, Terry Hennessey, Henry Newton, John Barnwell and, the hero of them all, Joe Baker – the undisputed 'King of the Trent End'. Never in all my years as a Forest supporter has any other player – and I include the likes of Stuart Pearce, John Robertson, Duncan McKenzie, Ian Storey-Moore and Trevor Francis in this equation – ever received anything like the kind of sheer adulation and hero-worship that was bestowed upon 'our Joe'. The Trent End composed more songs about him during his time at the Club than the Beatles had hit records. A variation of 'Molly Malone', one of their favourites was:

In Nottingham fair city,
Where the girls are so pretty,
I first set my eyes,
On sweet Molly Malone;

As she wheeled her wheel-barrow,
Through the streets broad and narrow,
Crying JOE-JOE-JOE-BA-KER!
JOE-JOE-JOE-BA-KER!

You may also note some familiar names on the West Ham team-sheet that day, not least the three members of Sir Alf Ramsey's World Cup winning team in Geoff Hurst, Martin Peters and Bobby Moore. The Trent End taunted this talented trio mercilessly throughout the game with chants of: *"Ramsey's Bum Boys!"* Baker himself scored Forest's winning goal, sweeping in a deflected shot past goalkeeper Jim Standen and into the Trent End goal, earning them a vital 1-0 victory in front of a crowd of 31,426. It may not have been a classic game, but in my book it had definitely been well worth the long wait.

This victory against the 'Hammers' was the first in a sequence of eight straight wins for the 'Reds', six of which were in the League, and the last of which was against Aston Villa at the City Ground. They went into this game against lowly Villa in second position in the table with 49 points from 36 games played, and only three points behind leaders Manchester United, who'd played one game more. The Championship was an issue which still had to be resolved and Forest did themselves no harm whatsoever, with a fine 3-0 victory over their Midlands counterparts. The goals were scored by Barry Lyons and Ian Storey-Moore (2), in front of a crowd of 41,468.

This run of eight straight wins for the 'Reds' also included two in the FA Cup, the first of these being the previously-mentioned fifth round replay against Swindon Town, and the second of which took place on Saturday, 8th April 1967 – undoubtedly one of the most exhilarating Cup ties that Forest have ever been involved in. This was the famous quarter-final tie against Everton, which took place at the City Ground.

As there was more chance of me falling head over heels in love with a Derby fan, than there was of us obtaining tickets for this match, we had to settle for a transistor radio and our own imaginary FA Cup quarter-final battle played out on Inham Nook 'Rec' in Chilwell. Anyone who is fortunate enough (and old enough!) to have witnessed this epic Cup tie against the 'Toffeemen', will tell you the same story - that of a pulsating, passionate encounter, which swung firstly in

Everton's favour, then Forest's, then back again in Everton's direction, and finally at the death, Forest's way again.

Everton took an early first-half lead through Jimmy Husband, and right up until half-time, the game seemed to be going their way. However, Forest came to life after the break and, after intense pressure on the Everton goal, found themselves drawing level, and then going 2-1 in front, with both goals coming from the inspirational Ian Storey-Moore. But, seemingly well in command, and with only twelve minutes left on the clock, they allowed Everton back into the game and Jimmy Husband popped up again to score their equalising goal. The contest now seemed destined to end in a draw and an inevitable replay at Goodison Park.

However, Storey-Moore had other ideas, and in the final minute scored the last of his three goals, and dramatically, at the third attempt. His first effort was blocked by keeper Andy Rankin, with the striker then heading the rebound onto the crossbar and finally nodding a second rebound into the back of the net. This sent the partisan crowd of 47,510 into raptures and the Everton players and supporters into the depths of despair. This was Moore's first ever hat-trick in a Forest shirt and one which must rank as the most significant in the Club's history.

Forest had booked themselves a semi-final slot for the first time since 1959, the year in which they'd last lifted the Cup by beating Luton Town 2-1 in the Final at Wembley. However, they'd paid a heavy price for this victory over the 'Scousers', with Joe Baker having limped off during the first half of the game with a serious leg injury. And unfortunately, this would prevent him from taking any further part in Forest's monumental season.

Without their injured goal-scoring star, they lost 2-1 to Spurs in the semi-final at Hillsborough on Saturday, 29th April, with Terry Hennessey scoring their consolation goal in front of a crowd of 55,000. Consequently, their dream of a League and Cup double was now over. By the time they entertained Manchester City at home the following Tuesday evening, they were some five points behind leaders Manchester United, with only three games left to play, and with an inferior goal average. Their faint hopes of a first-ever League Championship trophy had also therefore, almost certainly disappeared.

They ended the season as 'Runners-up' to United and consequently, a campaign, which had initially promised so much, had eventually delivered so little. However, they could now only go from strength to strength, surely? They had an excellent side, a capable and popular manager in Johnny Carey, and had enjoyed massive support from the Nottingham public. During the season, they had attracted no less than nine City Ground attendances in excess of 40,000. These were:

DATE	OPPOSITION	COMPETITION	SCORE	ATTENDANCE
01-10-66	Manchester United	League	4-1	41,854
14-01-67	Leeds United	League	1-0	43,849
04-02-67	Tottenham Hotspur	League	1-1	41,822
18-02-67	Newcastle United	FA Cup 4	3-0	45,962
25-02-67	Leicester City	League	1-0	47,188
11-03-67	Swindon Town	FA Cup 5	0-0	45,878
27-03-67	Burnley	League	4-1	41,586
08-04-67	Everton	FA Cup 6	3-2	47,510
15-04-67	Aston Villa	League	3-0	41,468

The average League attendance for the season was a healthy 31,282, with the highest being the 47,188 who saw them defeat East Midlands neighbours Leicester City 1-0 on Saturday, 25th February. The lowest in the League was 20,482 for the visit of Arsenal. Boosted by some impressive FA Cup attendances, the average overall was an impressive 32,675. The highest attendance of the season in all competitions was, not surprisingly, the 47,510 who attended the epic Cup quarter-final tie against Everton in April.

In my opinion, the season of 1966/67, proves beyond any shadow of a doubt, that in footballing terms at least, the City of Nottingham was 'alive and kicking', long before the celebrated arrival of a certain Mr.Brian Clough, almost a decade later.

SEASON 1966/67 – STATISTICS

FOOTBALL LEAGUE DIVISION ONE – FIXTURES

Date	Opposition	Venue	Competition	Score	Attendance
Aug 20	**Stoke City**	H	League	1-2	21,848
24	Chelsea	A	League	1-2	27,501
27	Sheffield United	A	League	2-1	16,047
30	**Chelsea**	H	**League**	0-0	22,199
Sept 3	**West Bromwich Albion**	H	**League**	2-1	21,871
6	**Fulham**	H	**League**	2-1	22,135
10	Leeds United	A	League	1-1	35,634
13	**Birmingham City**	H	**LC 1**	1-1	19,271
17	**Newcastle United**	H	**League**	3-0	21,732
20	Birmingham City	A	LC 1 – Replay	1-2	21,510
24	Tottenham Hotspur	A	League	1-2	34,405
Oct 1	**Manchester United**	H	**League**	4-1	41,854
8	Leicester City	A	League	0-3	39,970
15	**Liverpool**	H	**League**	1-1	32,887
26	West Ham United	A	League	1-3	22,982
29	**Blackpool**	H	**League**	2-0	22,083
Nov 5	Liverpool	A	League	0-4	40,534
12	**Sunderland**	H	**League**	3-1	24,962
19	Aston Villa	A	League	1-1	18,165
26	**Arsenal**	H	**League**	2-1	20,482
Dec 3	Manchester City	A	League	1-1	24,013
10	**Sheffield Wednesday**	H	**League**	1-1	22,540
17	Stoke City	A	League	2-1	23,312
23	Everton	A	League	1-0	34,084
26	**Everton**	H	**League**	1-0	36,227
31	**Sheffield United**	H	**League**	3-1	27,683
Jan 7	West Bromwich Albion	A	League	2-1	21,975
14	**Leeds United**	H	**League**	1-0	43,849
21	Newcastle United	A	League	0-0	37,079
28	**Plymouth Argyle**	H	**FA Cup 3**	2-1	34,005
Feb 4	**Tottenham Hotspur**	H	**League**	1-1	41,822
11	Manchester United	A	League	0-1	62,727
18	**Newcastle United**	H	**FA Cup 4**	3-0	45,962
25	**Leicester City**	H	**League**	1-0	47,188
Mar 4	Blackpool	A	League	1-1	14,003
11	**Swindon Town**	H	**FA Cup 5**	0-0	45,878
14	Swindon Town	A	FA Cup 5 – Replay	1-1	28,008
18	**West Ham United**	H	**League**	1-0	31,426
20	Swindon Town	(Played at Villa Park)	FA Cup 5 – 2nd Rep	3-0	52,596
25	Sheffield Wednesday	A	League	2-0	42,213
27	**Burnley**	H	**League**	4-1	41,586
28	Burnley	A	League	2-0	17,695
Apr 1	**Southampton**	H	**League**	3-1	37,731
8	**Everton**	H	**FA Cup 6**	3-2	47,510
15	**Aston Villa**	H	**League**	3-0	41,468
19	Sunderland	A	League	0-1	26,215
22	Arsenal	A	League	1-1	36,196
29	Tottenham Hotspur	(Played at Hillsborough)	FA Cup Semi-Final	1-2	55,000
May 2	**Manchester City**	H	**League**	2-0	33,352
6	Southampton	A	League	1-2	25,305
13	Fulham	A	League	3-2	20,417

HOME ATTENDANCES

	AGGREGATE ATTENDANCE	HIGHEST ATTENDANCE	LOWEST ATTENDANCE	AVERAGE ATTENDANCE
League:	656,925	47,188	20,482	31,282
League Cup:	19,271	19,271	19,271	19,271
FA Cup:	173,355	47,510	34,005	43,338
All Competitions:	849,551	47,510	19,271	32,675

FINAL LEAGUE TABLE - DIVISION ONE

Position	P	W	D	L	GF	GA	Pts
1. Manchester United	42	24	12	6	84	45	60
2. Nottingham Forest	**42**	**23**	**10**	**9**	**64**	**41**	**56**
3. Tottenham Hotspur	42	24	8	10	71	48	56
4. Leeds United	42	22	11	9	62	42	55
5. Liverpool	42	19	13	10	64	47	51
6. Everton	42	19	10	13	65	46	48
7. Arsenal	42	16	14	12	58	47	46
8. Leicester City	42	18	8	16	78	71	44
9. Chelsea	42	15	14	13	67	62	44
10. Sheffield United	42	16	10	16	52	59	42
11. Sheffield Wednesday	42	14	13	15	56	47	41
12. Stoke City	42	17	7	18	63	58	41
13. West Bromwich Albion	42	16	7	19	77	73	39
14. Burnley	42	15	9	18	66	76	39
15. Manchester City	42	12	15	15	43	52	39
16. West Ham United	42	14	8	20	80	84	36
17. Sunderland	42	14	8	20	58	72	36
18. Fulham	42	11	12	19	71	83	34
19. Southampton	42	14	6	22	74	92	34
20. Newcastle United	42	12	9	21	39	81	33
21. Aston Villa	42	11	7	24	54	85	29
22. Blackpool	42	6	9	27	41	76	21

AWAY ATTENDANCES

	AGGREGATE ATTENDANCE	HIGHEST ATTENDANCE	LOWEST ATTENDANCE	AVERAGE ATTENDANCE
League:	620,472	62,727	14,003	29,546
League Cup:	21,510	21,510	21,510	21,510
FA Cup:	135,604	55,000	28,008	45,201
All Competitions:	777,586	62,727	14,003	31,103

"OH, WE'RE BETTER THAN UNITED AND WE'RE LOUDER THAN THE KOP"

ON THE strength of their achievements during the previous campaign, Forest went into the season of 1967/68 full of expectations, and to say the least, optimistic about their chances of acquiring some silverware for the first time since lifting the FA Cup in 1959. And three wins and a draw in their first four games did nothing to dampen their enthusiasm or that of their supporters. Having opened their account on Saturday, 19th August, with a 3-1 win over Sheffield United at Bramall Lane, they were then held to a 3-3 draw at home to newly-promoted Coventry City the following Tuesday, in front of yet another impressive City Ground crowd of 44,950. They followed this up by beating Arsenal 2-0 at home the following Saturday in front of a crowd of 33,977, and then went on to beat Coventry 3-1 in an early return game at Highfield Road the following Tuesday.

Unfortunately, they began to lose their way a little then, losing their next two games 2-0 away to Manchester City and 1-0 at home to Liverpool, and in doing so, embarked on a long and inconsistent vein of form. Whilst their home form was pretty impressive – six wins and a draw in their next seven fixtures at the City Ground – they seemed incapable of producing anything like this kind of consistency on their travels. In fact, their next away victory in the League wouldn't be until 30th December, when they defeated Stoke City 3-1 at the Victoria Ground.

Prior to this success in the Potteries, their poor away form had consisted of a 1-0 second-round League Cup victory at Fourth Division Scunthorpe United, a 1-0 Inter Cities Fairs Cup victory in Germany over Eintracht Frankfurt, and seven defeats and two draws in the League. Although the win over the Germans had given them an aggregate 5-0 victory in the Fairs Cup, they lost out to Swiss side FC Zurich in the second round. Having won the first leg 2-1 in Nottingham, the Forest players were naively preparing themselves for extra time in the second leg in Zurich, having lost the tie 1-0, only to be informed they had in fact lost on the 'away goals' rule.

By the time they entertained Leeds United at home on Saturday, 25th November, they'd been dumped out of the League Cup 3-0 by Burnley at Turf Moor in the third round, were out of Europe, and were lying in a disappointing ninth position in the First Division table. What's more, they were also beaten 2-0 by Leeds that day, in front of a crowd of 29,569.

DESPITE their frustrating League form, the 'Reds' had nevertheless been playing to some packed City Ground audiences, with the average home League attendance after eight games being an impressive 38,469! During this period, they attracted their biggest ever City Ground crowd of 49,946 for the visit of League Champions Manchester United on Saturday, 28th October 1967 – still a Club record to this day. This game against the star-studded 'Red Devils' is one that will live in my memory for ever and a day, and one which I feel honoured and privileged to have witnessed. Maybe it had as much to do with me being only nine-years-old at the time, as it did with the actual quality of the football served up by Forest that day. But memories of both the game and the occasion itself are firmly ingrained in my mind.

Not only was the Forest side packed full of all my own boyhood heroes such as Joe Baker, Ian Storey-Moore, Terry Hennessey et al, but the United side included such living legends as Denis Law, Bobby Charlton and George Best – without a doubt, the greatest collective trio of footballers the British Isles has ever produced. To actually see all these players together in the flesh, on the same pitch, at the same time, was almost beyond the realms of fantasy for someone of my tender years – especially when my only concerns in life at that time were the game of football and Nottingham Forest Football Club.

I watched this encounter from the 'Kids Pen' in the Trent End, accompanied as ever by our Graham and our mutual Brummie sidekick, Phil Chadd. And what a game it turned out to be. Two goals from the magnificent Joe Baker and another from Frank Wignall put Forest into a commanding 3-0 lead, and despite a spectacular consolation goal from the delightful right foot of George Best, United were only ever going to be second best to the 'Rampant Reds' that day. Their array of stars were, to put it mildly, completely outplayed and Forest finished the game comfortable and worthy 3-1 winners in front of an ecstatic City Ground crowd. Throughout the game, the Trent End reverberated to one of it's favourite songs; a throwback to the previous campaign, when the two clubs were battling it out for the League title:

> *Oh, we're better than United,*
> *An' we're louder than the Kop,*
> *We're second in the League,*
> *An' we should be at the top!*
>
> *La-la-la-la, La-la-la-la-la…*

After this game the rest of the season could only ever be an anti-climax, and at least as far as Forest were concerned, this certainly turned out to be the case. They were knocked out of the FA Cup at the fourth round stage, losing 2-1 to Leeds United at Elland Road in front of a crowd of 51,739. And in fact, their form over the final nineteen League games of the season, consisted of just four wins, four draws and two defeats at home, and no wins, two draws and seven defeats – including 6-1 drubbings at both Wolves and Liverpool – on their travels.

The Forest management tried desperately to improve the Club's fortunes on the field and in December brought in the mercurial talents of Jim Baxter from Sunderland for a then Club record fee of £100,000. But sadly, at the age of only 28, his best days were already behind him. A player with an immense pedigree, Baxter had joined Sunderland in 1965 after five incredibly successful years with Glasgow Rangers. During this time he'd won many international caps for Scotland, Scottish League Championship medals in seasons 1960/61 and 1962/63, and Scottish Cup medals in both 1962 and '63. He'd also sampled European action with the Glasgow giants in both the European Cup and the Cup Winners' Cup competitions.

However, he'd also earned himself a reputation for hard living off the pitch and this was now unfortunately beginning to take it's toll out there on the field of play. Consequently, he never really displayed his true abilities to the Forest faithful, although I do recall him scoring a goal of exceptional quality in the 2-2 draw at home to Southampton on Saturday, 10th February 1967. I had a bird's-eye view of it from my position just behind the wall at the bottom of the old East Stand terracing, level with the edge of the penalty area.

The ball was played up to him as he stood just outside the box with his back to the Trent End goal and slightly to the right of the area. He cushioned it perfectly on his chest, flicked it up into the air with his left foot, then spun around and crashed an unstoppable right-foot volley into the top left hand corner of the net. *"Come on without, Come on within, You'll not see nothing like the Mighty Jim,"* sang the Trent End as they enthusiastically celebrated the City Ground's undisputed goal of the season.

ALTHOUGH Forest finished the season in a somewhat disappointing eleventh position in the First Division table, I wasn't too downhearted, as I was now firmly established as a 'regular' down at the City Ground. I was now a 'true' supporter of Nottingham Forest Football Club and extremely proud to be so.

And despite their slightly disappointing season, the average League attendance at the City Ground was again a creditable 32,548. The highest was, not surprisingly, the record-breaking 49,946 for the visit of Manchester United, with the lowest being the 20,658 for the visit of Fulham. Furthermore, there'd been no less than sixteen gates in excess of 30,000, out of a total of twenty-five home games in all competitions. Not a footballing City – Nottingham? What a load of old codswallop!

SEASON 1967/68 – STATISTICS

FOOTBALL LEAGUE DIVISION ONE – FIXTURES

Date		Opposition	Venue	Competition	Score	Attendance
Aug	19	Sheffield United	A	League	3-1	29,223
	22	**Coventry City**	**H**	**League**	**3-3**	**44,950**
	26	**Arsenal**	**H**	**League**	**2-0**	**33,977**
	29	Coventry City	A	League	3-1	41,212
Sept	2	Manchester City	A	League	0-2	29,547
	5	**Liverpool**	**H**	**League**	**0-1**	**39,352**
	9	**Newcastle United**	**H**	**League**	**4-0**	**30,151**
	13	Scunthorpe United	A	LC 2	1-0	13,235
	16	West Bromwich Albion	A	League	1-2	21,136
	20	Eintracht Frankfurt	A	ICFC 1 – 1st Leg	1-0	4,500
	23	**Chelsea**	**H**	**League**	**3-0**	**34,871**
	30	Southampton	A	League	1-2	26,724
Oct	7	Burnley	A	League	1-1	18,400
	10	Burnley	A	LC 3	0-3	14,421
	14	**Sheffield Wednesday**	**H**	**League**	**0-0**	**37,983**
	17	**Eintrach Frankfurt**	**H**	**ICFC 1 – 2nd Leg**	**4-0**	**27,090**
	25	Tottenham Hotspur	A	League	1-1	40,928
	28	**Manchester United**	**H**	**League**	**3-1**	**49,946**
	31	**FC Zurich**	**H**	**ICFC 2 – 1st Leg**	**2-1**	**32,896**
Nov	4	Sunderland	A	League	0-1	29,158
	11	**Wolverhampton Wanderers**	**H**	**League**	**3-1**	**36,522**
	14	FC Zurich	A	ICFC 2 – 2nd Leg	0-1	15,300
	18	Fulham	A	League	0-2	22,413
	25	**Leeds United**	**H**	**League**	**0-2**	**29,569**
Dec	2	Everton	A	League	0-1	44,765
	9	**Leicester City** **(Abandoned – ice)**	**H**	**League**	**0-1**	**24,041**
	16	**Sheffield United**	**H**	**League**	**1-0**	**30,501**
	23	Arsenal	A	League	0-3	32,512
	26	**Stoke City**	**H**	**League**	**3-0**	**37,577**
	30	Stoke City	A	League	3-1	21,415
Jan	**6**	**Manchester City**	**H**	**League**	**0-3**	**39,581**
	13	Newcastle United	A	League	0-0	43,274
	20	**West Bromwich Albion**	**H**	**League**	**3-2**	**34,298**
	27	**Bolton Wanderers**	**H**	**FA Cup 3**	**4-2**	**37,299**
Feb	3	Chelsea	A	League	0-1	33,483
	10	**Southampton**	**H**	**League**	**2-2**	**27,318**
	17	Leeds United	A	FA Cup 4	1-2	51,739
	24	**Burnley**	**H**	**League**	**1-0**	**26,110**
Mar	13	Leeds United	A	League	1-1	32,508
	16	**Tottenham Hotspur**	**H**	**League**	**0-0**	**37,707**
	19	**Leicester City**	**H**	**League**	**2-1**	**30,403**
	23	Manchester United	A	League	0-3	61,978
	30	**Sunderland**	**H**	**League**	**0-3**	**24,543**
Apr	6	Wolverhampton Wanderers	A	League	1-6	28,198
	12	West Ham United	A	League	0-3	36,589
	13	**Fulham**	**H**	**League**	**2-2**	**20,658**
	16	**West Ham United**	**H**	**League**	**1-1**	**22,189**
	20	Sheffield Wednesday	A	League	0-0	28,805
	22	**Everton**	**H**	**League**	**1-0**	**23,809**
May	4	Leicester City	A	League	2-4	25,605
	11	Liverpool	A	League	1-6	38,850

HOME ATTENDANCES

	AGGREGATE ATTENDANCE	HIGHEST ATTENDANCE	LOWEST ATTENDANCE	AVERAGE ATTENDANCE
League:	716,056	49,946	20,658	32,548
	(Includes abandoned fixture versus Leicester City)			
FA Cup:	37,299	37,299	37,299	37,299
ICFC:	59,986	32,896	27,090	29,993
All Competitions:	813,341	49,946	20,658	32,533

FINAL LEAGUE TABLE - DIVISION ONE

Position		P	W	D	L	GF	GA	Pts
1.	Manchester City	42	26	6	10	86	43	58
2.	Manchester United	42	24	8	10	89	55	56
3.	Liverpool	42	22	11	9	71	40	55
4.	Leeds United	42	22	9	11	71	41	53
5.	Everton	42	23	6	13	67	40	52
6.	Chelsea	42	18	12	12	62	68	48
7.	Tottenham Hotspur	42	19	9	14	70	59	47
8.	West Bromwich Albion	42	17	12	13	75	62	46
9.	Arsenal	42	17	10	15	60	56	44
10.	Newcastle United	42	13	15	14	54	67	41
11.	**Nottingham Forest**	**42**	**14**	**11**	**17**	**52**	**64**	**39**
12.	West Ham United	42	14	10	18	73	69	38
13.	Leicester City	42	13	12	17	64	69	38
14.	Burnley	42	14	10	18	64	71	38
15.	Sunderland	42	13	11	18	51	61	37
16.	Southampton	42	13	11	18	66	83	37
17.	Wolverhampton Wanderers	42	14	8	20	66	75	36
18.	Stoke City	42	14	7	21	50	73	35
19.	Sheffield Wednesday	42	11	12	19	51	63	34
20.	Coventry City	42	9	15	18	51	71	33
21.	Sheffield United	42	11	10	21	49	70	32
22.	Fulham	42	10	7	25	56	98	27

AWAY ATTENDANCES

	AGGREGATE ATTENDANCE	HIGHEST ATTENDANCE	LOWEST ATTENDANCE	AVERAGE ATTENDANCE
League:	686,723	61,978	18,400	32,701
League Cup:	27,656	14,421	13,235	13,828
FA Cup:	51,739	51,739	51,739	51,739
ICFC:	19,800	15,300	4,500	9,900
All Competitions:	785,918	61,978	4,500	30,227

"WHENEVER YER SAD, WHENEVER YER BLUE, WHENEVER THE FOREST ARE PLAYING"

FOREST BEGAN the season of 1968/69 in less than impressive fashion, drawing three and losing one of their first four opening League games. However, things were very shortly to 'hot up' for the 'Reds', but sadly, for all the wrong reasons. They went into the home game against top-of-the-table Leeds United on Saturday, 24th August, lying in sixteenth position in the First Division table.

A pre-match article in a popular boys' football magazine which had previewed the forthcoming fixture a week earlier, rather prophetically ran the headline: *"LEEDS ABOUT TO SET FOREST ON FIRE"*. And with half-time approaching in the game and the score standing at 1-1, a thick cloud of black smoke was seen coming out of the top of the Main Stand by spectators on the opposite side of the ground in the East Stand. The alarm was raised and the stand quickly and calmly evacuated before the fire really began to take a hold. Fortunately, there was no loss of life or in fact any serious injuries amongst the crowd of 31,126, although the blaze completely destroyed the dressing rooms, offices, boardrooms, and not surprisingly, much of the seating in the stand itself. Sadly, it had spread so quickly that all the Club's records, trophies and mementoes had also gone up in flames. Most of the players had also lost personal effects such as wedding rings and other items of jewellery.

As the City Ground would be out of action for the foreseeable future, Forest needed a temporary home, and to their credit, neighbours Notts County were quick to offer the use of their Meadow Lane facilities. Forest were to play their next six home games down at 'the Lane' and the first of these was a second round League Cup tie against West Bromwich Albion on Tuesday, 3rd September. Although I hadn't attended the Leeds game and hadn't therefore witnessed the events of that day, I was however amongst the crowd of 23,970 who turned up at Meadow Lane to see the 'Reds' lose their first encounter at their temporary headquarters by three-goals-to-two. And in failing to overcome Albion, they set a precedent for the remainder of their short stay on the 'wrong side of the Trent'. Although I stood on the 'Lane End' that evening, Forest's Trent Enders set up their own temporary home at the side of the stadium in the County Road Stand and as usual, made themselves heard throughout the game. Barry Lyons and Ian Storey-Moore scored Forest's goals.

Ironically, their very next League fixture was also against the 'Baggies' the following Saturday, although this time at the Hawthorns. Forest exacted swift revenge though with a 5-2 victory – their first of the season – with the goals coming from Sammy Chapman, Joe Baker (2), and Ian Storey-Moore (2). This inspired the ever-imaginative Trent Enders to leave the ground at the end of the game singing: *"Roses are red, Violets are blue, Nottingham 5 - Albion 2."*

Forest failed to win any of their six League and Cup fixtures at Meadow Lane and by the time they returned to the City Ground to face Arsenal on Saturday, 16th November, were languishing in 20th position in the table. They had a total of only 11 points from 16 games, with their only victory to date being the one at West Brom. Although the City Ground was now back in business, neither the Main Stand, nor Forest as a team were, and once again they went down 2-0 to the 'Gunners' in front of a restricted crowd of 24,450.

On 2nd December, Forest sacked their popular manager Johnny Carey and replaced him with former Leicester City manager Matt Gillies, who had left the 'Foxes' just a month earlier. Under his guidance, the 'Reds' then managed to scrape together nine more victories in the League over the remaining 26 games of the season, including a surprise 2-0 victory over Liverpool at Anfield – their last victory there – and ended the season in a disappointing 18th position. With only 33 points on the board in total, they were just three points above the relegation zone.

This had been a depressing season all round for the 'Reds', what with the Main Stand fire, a lowly position in the League, and being dumped out of both the League Cup and FA Cup at the first attempt – the latter courtesy of a thumping 3-0 third round defeat away to Second Division Preston North End. In addition to this, some of their star performers had looked decidedly mediocre, in particular striker Joe Baker, who'd managed to find the net on only four occasions during a total of 31 League appearances. The writing suddenly seemed on the wall for Forest and sadly, the team which had only recently threatened to win the League and Cup double, was about to be prematurely dismantled by the Club's management. The only bright spot of the season had been the form of striker Ian Storey-Moore, who was rapidly emerging as the most influential player in the team, despite a lengthy absence through injury during the second half of the season. He was even beginning to threaten Joe Baker's mantle as the undisputed 'King of the Trent End'.

DESPITE all of this, I was still enjoying every single moment of being a Forest supporter, and in particular, that of being a Trent Ender. The Trent End was a magical place to be as a twelve-year-old boy, especially when it was full to it's 9,500 capacity, with singing, chanting, swearing, pushing, shoving, aggressive, witty, Forest supporters. At this point in time, it would be fair to say the Trent End was inhabited mainly by 'long-haired, scruffy youths', many of whom wore leather jackets with cut-off denims over the top. These were peppered on the back with small metal studs and emblazoned with 'Hells Angel' slogans.

Their favourite pastime during the game would be to fight amongst themselves, and quite often with the police - and usually for no apparent reason. Their repertoire of songs and anthems was almost unending and these would be interspersed with rhythmic clapping and chanting, or bouncing up and down en-masse. What a sight this must have been for the spectators on the other sides of the ground? Other than the many 'Joe Baker' anthems, two very popular songs during the late sixties were:

Whenever yer sad,
Whenever yer blue,
Whenever the Forest are playing;

If we're out o' luck,
We fight like fuck,
T' keep the Trent End swayin'!
Ooh, Ooh, Ooh, Ooh, Ooh, Ooh,
Ooh, Ooh, Ooh, Ooh, Ooh, Ooh.

We don't care we're Forest fans,
Doo-da, Doo-da,
We don't care we're Forest fans,
Doo-da, Doo-da-day;

On the piss all night,
On the piss all day,
We don't care we're Forest fans,
Doo-da, Doo-da-day!

However, the face of the Trent End was about to change, albeit gradually, as a new and different kind of cult began to emerge, mainly in the South of the country. My earliest recollection of this exciting 'Skinhead cult', was when Forest played Chelsea at home on Tuesday, 8th April 1969. I was sitting on the top deck of a 'Corpo' bus making it's way slowly down Arkwright Street through the football traffic, heading towards Trent Bridge. Suddenly, a gang of about 100 Chelsea supporters came swarming across the road in front of us and across the junction with London Road. To a man, they were dressed in rolled up denim jeans, braces, checked shirts, and casual denim jackets; with shiny 'Doctor Marten' boots completing the uniform. And every single one of them was sporting a haircut that can only be described as 'down to the bone'. This was a phenomenon that was about to take the country by storm.

At around the same time, another very interesting situation was developing just down the road in Derby – although at eleven-years-of-age, the significance of all this was completely lost on me. Under the guidance of a certain Brian Clough and his partner Peter Taylor, Derby County Football Club (hereafter referred to as 'the Sheep'), captained by former Spurs defender Dave Mackay, were storming their way towards the Second Division Championship, and about to embark on the most successful period in their history. However, at that particular moment in my life, the town of Derby (hereafter referred to as 'Shitesville') – a whole fifteen miles away from Nottingham - might just as well have been situated on another planet as far as I was concerned.

DESPITE a very poor season, Forest's average home League attendance was a reasonable 25,202, and this included no less than five that were in excess of the 30,000 mark. The highest was a massive 41,892 for the visit of Manchester United, with the lowest being the 17,651 who turned out at Meadow Lane for the visit of Newcastle United.

SEASON 1968/69 – STATISTICS

FOOTBALL LEAGUE DIVISION ONE – FIXTURES

Date	Opposition	Venue	Competition	Score	Attendance
Aug 10	**Burnley**	**H**	**League**	**2-2**	**30,298**
14	Chelsea	A	League	1-1	36,515
17	West Ham United	A	League	0-1	31,114
20	**Sheffield Wednesday**	**H**	**League**	**0-0**	**27,819**
24	**Leeds United**	**H**	**League**	**1-1**	**31,126**
	(Abandoned – Main Stand Fire)				
28	Newcastle United	A	League	1-1	34,613
31	Everton	A	League	1-2	45,951
Sept 3	**West Bromwich Albion**	**H** *	**LC 2**	**2-3**	**23,970**
7	West Bromwich Albion	A	League	5-2	23,377
14	**Coventry City**	**H** *	**League**	**0-0**	**22,260**
21	Tottenham Hotspur	A	League	1-2	37,386
Oct 5	**Stoke City**	**H** *	**League**	**3-3**	**21,519**
8	**Newcastle United**	**H** *	**League**	**2-4**	**17,651**
12	Sunderland	A	League	1-3	25,575
19	**Ipswich Town**	**H** *	**League**	**1-2**	**21,148**
26	Manchester City	A	League	3-3	32,937
Nov 2	**Wolverhampton Wanderers**	**H** *	**League**	**0-0**	**19,490**
9	Leicester City	A	League	2-2	26,828
16	**Arsenal**	**H**	**League**	**0-2**	**24,550**
23	Queens Park Rangers	A	League	1-2	18,857
30	**Liverpool**	**H**	**League**	**0-1**	**25,175**
Dec 7	Southampton	A	League	1-1	17,957
14	**Sunderland**	**H**	**League**	**1-0**	**18,007**
21	Ipswich Town	A	League	3-2	18,739
28	Stoke City	A	League	1-3	20,452
Jan 4	Preston North End	A	FA Cup 3	0-3	20,008
11	Wolverhampton Wanderers	A	League	0-1	24,659
18	**Leicester City**	**H**	**League**	**0-0**	**27,776**
Feb 1	Arsenal	A	League	1-1	35,585
15	Liverpool	A	League	2-0	42,306
25	**Leeds United**	**H**	**League**	**0-2**	**36,249**
Mar 1	Burnley	A	League	1-3	11,884
4	**Queens Park Rangers**	**H**	**League**	**1-0**	**21,035**
8	**West Ham United**	**H**	**League**	**0-1**	**24,303**
11	**Southampton**	**H**	**League**	**1-0**	**19,031**
22	**West Bromwich Albion**	**H**	**League**	**3-0**	**20,546**
24	**Manchester City**	**H**	**League**	**1-0**	**24,612**
31	**Manchester United**	**H**	**League**	**0-1**	**41,892**
Apr 5	Manchester United	A	League	1-3	51,952
7	Sheffield Wednesday	A	League	1-0	26,001
8	**Chelsea**	**H**	**League**	**1-2**	**30,413**
12	**Tottenham Hotspur**	**H**	**League**	**0-2**	**22,920**
19	Coventry City	A	League	1-1	37,772
25	**Everton**	**H**	**League**	**1-0**	**26,629**
30	Leeds United	A	League	0-1	46,508

* Fixtures played at Meadow Lane during rebuilding of Main Stand

HOME ATTENDANCES

	AGGREGATE ATTENDANCE	HIGHEST ATTENDANCE	LOWEST ATTENDANCE	AVERAGE ATTENDANCE
League:	554,449	41,892	17,651	25,202
	(Includes abandoned fixture versus Leeds United)			
League Cup:	23,970	23,970	23,970	23,970
All Competitions:	578,419	41,892	17,651	25,148

FINAL LEAGUE TABLE - DIVISION ONE

Position	P	W	D	L	GF	GA	Pts
1. Leeds United	42	27	13	2	66	26	67
2. Liverpool	42	25	11	6	63	24	61
3. Everton	42	21	15	6	77	36	57
4. Arsenal	42	22	12	8	56	27	56
5. Chelsea	42	20	10	12	73	53	50
6. Tottenham Hotspur	42	14	17	11	61	51	45
7. Southampton	42	16	13	13	57	48	45
8. West Ham United	42	13	18	11	66	50	44
9. Newcastle United	42	15	14	13	61	55	44
10. West Bromwich Albion	42	16	11	15	64	67	43
11. Manchester United	42	15	12	15	57	53	42
12. Ipswich Town	42	15	11	16	59	60	41
13. Manchester City	42	15	10	17	64	55	40
14. Burnley	42	15	9	18	55	82	39
15. Sheffield Wednesday	42	10	16	16	41	54	36
16. Wolverhampton Wanderers	42	10	15	17	41	58	35
17. Sunderland	42	11	12	19	43	67	34
18. Nottingham Forest	**42**	**10**	**13**	**19**	**45**	**57**	**33**
19. Stoke City	42	9	15	18	40	63	33
20. Coventry City	42	10	11	21	46	64	31
21. Leicester City	42	9	12	21	39	68	30
22. Queens Park Rangers	42	4	10	28	39	95	18

AWAY ATTENDANCES

	AGGREGATE ATTENDANCE	HIGHEST ATTENDANCE	LOWEST ATTENDANCE	AVERAGE ATTENDANCE
League:	646,968	51,952	11,884	30,808
FA Cup:	20,008	20,008	20,008	20,008
All Competitions:	666,976	51,952	11,884	30,317

"TIPTOE THROUGH THE POPSIDE, WITH ME"

FOREST BEGAN this campaign minus their star striker Joe Baker who they'd rather controversially sold to Sunderland for £50,000 during the close season. Joe was the second of the 'stars of 66/67' to have left the Club by this time; the first being Frank Wignall, who'd joined Wolves a year earlier. Several more of their prized assets would also be allowed to leave though before the season was out.

By the time they took on Chelsea at the City Ground on Saturday, 22nd November, this somewhat depleted Forest side was sitting in an uncomfortable 16th position in the table, having taken only 16 points from their first 20 League games. Their below-par season to date had consisted of only 3 wins, 10 draws, and 7 defeats, and they were yet to achieve their first victory on their travels. However, for some reason, all this seemed of little consequence to the majority of Forest's Trent Enders, who at this point in time appeared to have their minds focused on just one thing - the following Saturday's fixture against their newly-promoted neighbours, Derby County.

"If yer all goin' to Derby, Clap yer 'ands," they sang over and over again throughout this 1-1 draw with Chelsea. And it seemed from the response, just about everyone was. Forest had been allocated 8,000 terrace tickets for the game - all for the Popside enclosure - and a measly 20 (yes twenty!) for the seats.

During the game against Chelsea, I was intrigued by the 'anti-Derby' sentiments, which were emanating from the swaying Trent End choir all around me. "Where on earth did all this hatred and resentment come from?" I wondered. I hadn't even heard of Derby County until the end of the previous season, yet alone had time to start falling out with their supporters. One after another, the songs came pouring out:

Tiptoe through the Popside, With a razor, An' a sawn-off shotgun, Tiptoe through the Popside, With Me!

Dave Mackay running dairn the wing, You will 'ear the Trent End sing, YA-FAT-BASTARD! YA-FAT-BASTARD! YA-FAT-BAST-AR-ARD!
'Ear worra say now!

If y'all 'ate Derby clap yer 'ands, If y'all 'ate Derby clap yer 'ands, If y'all 'ate Derby, All 'ate Derby, All 'ate Derby clap yer 'ands! SHEEP-SHEEP-SHEEP-SHAGGERS! Baaaaaaaaaaaaah!

Derby, Derby, 'ave ya gorra puff? Yes sir; yes sir, Brian Clough! Derby, Derby, 'ave ya gorra queer? Yes sir; yes sir, John O'Hare!

Derby, Derby, 'ave ya gorra a woman? Yes sir; yes sir, John McGovern! Derby, Derby, 'ave ya gorra Queen, Yes sir; yes sir, Lesley Green!

And these were just a selection of the songs being sung over and over again throughout the ninety minutes. Anyway, I had my ticket, and I was off to my very first away match. I could hardly wait! The Forest Review for the Chelsea game had carried this wonderful preview of the forthcoming encounter. Under the heading: *"IT'S DERBY NEXT WEEK!"* it perfectly captured the excitement leading up to the game:

CHAPTER 4

• *Next Saturday, 29th November, is the date that all fans of Derby County and ourselves have eagerly awaited - almost, one might say, since the back-end of last season when promotion for our neighbours was a certainty. Here, at last, is the opportunity for the two clubs to meet again in the First Division; an event that hasn't happened for many a long year.*

• *In fact, one has to go back to the 1905/06 season to find the last occasion we met in this grade. Then, as so often happens in 'derby' games, the scores were level at both grounds. It was 0-0 at the City Ground and 2-all at the Baseball Ground.*

• *County have had a magnificent start to the season and one has nothing but sincere admiration for the way the management, the players, staff and supporters have buckled down to the exacting sphere of football that is the world's best competition...the First Division of the Football League!*

• *So it's all roads leading to the Baseball Ground next Saturday. Consult the RAC route map in this 'Review' if you are not certain of how to get to their ground. A word of warning to the 8,000 Nottingham fans (our share of Derby's all-ticket allocation) travelling to the game!*

• *The route from Nottingham will be crowded with traffic and, although it's only a 15 miles journey, give yourself ample time to negotiate the route to get there well in time to take your place on the terraces.*

• *Car parking facilities (see the route map for these) in the vicinity of the ground are sparse; you'll be well advised to leave your car at home on this occasion. Take the train, or the bus. Travel how you will...but be warned...take care...we'll see you there!*

I was one of the many thousands who appeared to have taken the Club's advice and travelled on the train and was on the first of many 'specials', which had been chartered for the purpose. Typically, football specials would carry upwards of five hundred supporters in those days, usually packed tightly like sardines into the most ancient and dilapidated of British Rail's rolling stock. Still, we cared little about this as we poured out of the carriages and onto the platform at Derby Station. The sound of: *"FOREST! FOREST! FOREST!"* echoed right through the building as the massed army of fans rushed up the stairs, through the gates and onto the streets outside. *"WE HATE DERBY! WE HATE DERBY!"* chanted the mob as we were met by dozens of police - many on horseback - waiting to escort us to the ground.

There is something incredibly exhilarating about being part of a 500-strong army of hyped-up and noisy football supporters, making your way through the streets of a foreign town - particularly that of your sworn enemy - escorted by scores of nervous and anxious-looking police officers. The sheer size of the crowd is quite overwhelming and seems to stretch back as far as the eye can see. This was the first time I'd sampled this particular experience, and the adrenaline was simply gushing through my veins.

We arrived at the ground at least an hour before kick off, and after queuing for what seemed like an eternity, we finally made it through the turnstiles and onto the Popside terracing. The Baseball Ground was completely enclosed and in sharp contrast to the wide-open spaces of the City Ground. Apart from the Popside itself - which was a very modern looking stand - the rest of the ground was very old and 'wooden' in it's appearance. The upper tier of the Popside was an all-seated area, with the lower tier all-standing. The terraces stretched right back underneath the stand and there was a dividing fence with a gangway down the middle. This ran all the way down from the refreshment area at the back, to the small perimeter wall at the front.

We made our way towards the half-way line and took up our places about a third of the way up the terracing. Very quickly the stand began to fill up on both sides of the dividing fence and soon we were caught in the middle of a swaying mass of fans. It seemed like the whole of the Trent End had transported itself en-masse to the Baseball Ground and the travelling 'Red & White Army' were intent on letting the people of Derby know they'd arrived. On the other side of the fence, the Derby fans were also beginning to mass in equally large numbers and a war of attrition was starting to break out. The Trent Enders taunted their rivals with an array of amusing little ditties, such as:

When Derby g' dairn agen, agen, We'll sing, we'll sing, When Derby g' dairn agen, agen, We'll sing, we'll sing;

When Ian Moore scores a goal, Ya can shove yer 'ector up yer 'ole, An' we'll all go mad, When Derby g' dairn agen!

I was bo-orn, Under a Trent End goal, I was bo-orn, Under a Trent End goal;

Boots are made f' kickin', A razor's made to slash, I've never seen a Derby fan, I didn't want t' bash!

I was bo-orn, Under a Trent End goal, A Trent End, Trent End goal.

Between then and kick off, the ground filled up rapidly towards it's 38,000 capacity. It seemed every minute or so, another train-load of Forest supporters would arrive and come spilling into the ground. Once again, I was quite overwhelmed by the sheer hatred they seemed to have for the Derby supporters. However, it also has to be said, they appeared to hate us just as much in return. As the two teams hadn't met each other competitively for many decades, I wondered if this mutual hatred had been caused by some form of genetic disorder, passed down through the generations. Perhaps the antagonism originally began with our great-grandfathers way back in season 1897/98, when we whooped the 'Rams' 3-1 in the FA Cup Final at Crystal Palace!

The two teams came out to a crescendo of noise from the passionate and vociferous crowd. Having experienced this almost unique atmosphere on many occasions since, I defy anyone to tell me the more high-profile Merseyside or Manchester 'derbies' could possibly be more passionate or intense affairs than a Forest-Derby encounter, particularly when both teams are competing together in the top flight. On this occasion, the BBC's Match of the Day cameras were there to record the action and Forest's excellent 2-0 victory - their first away win of the season. This was the stuff dreams are made of - well, at least as far as I and 8,000 other Forest supporters were concerned anyway. Goals from Ian Storey-Moore and Barry Lyons, one in each half of the game, sent the travelling red and white hordes home in ecstatic mood.

However, the scenes outside after the match were very ugly indeed, as hundreds of rival supporters fought running battles with one another throughout the streets leading from the ground to the railway station. The sound of breaking glass, the roar of rampaging youths, and the wail of police sirens, could be heard coming from every direction, as bottles, bricks and all manner of missiles were hurled from one side of the road to the other. It was a massive relief to finally arrive back at the station and get safely back on board the train home to Nottingham. That said, this was an experience I wouldn't have missed for the world.

THE draw at home to Chelsea, followed by this victory at Derby, set Forest off on an eleven-match unbeaten run in the League, which consisted of six wins and five draws. During this unbeaten sequence of games, they entertained Sunderland at home on Saturday, 24th January. This fixture gave the Forest faithful an early opportunity to welcome Joe Baker back to the City Ground. Joe was already proving to be a popular figure on Wearside, despite the fact his best years were already behind him. Sportswriter Tony Pritchett of the Sheffield Telegraph had written the following article about Joe earlier on in the season. Under the heading: *IT'S THE MAGNETISM OF JOE BAKER*, it perfectly describes the magical relationship which Baker had forged with the supporters during his time in Nottingham:

"Popularity is a funny thing. How is it that some players have this magic crowd appeal and others - maybe better players, better clubmen - never seem to have that same aura about them......the flair which instantly identifies them with the fan on the terrace?

It might be a good idea, some time, to run a competition to find the most POPULAR Forest team of the last ten years.

Not the most successful, mind you, the most popular. What set me thinking about this was a recent trip to Sunderland with Sheffield Wednesday.

Really, it was like going down to the Trent End all over again except that the Sunderland crowd don't make as much noise as those marvellous Forest kids.

I'm talking, of course, about the impact Joe Baker has had on the crowd at Roker Park.

To be honest, Joe hasn't been a sensation at Roker and in the match I saw, he didn't make much of an impression.

But Joe, always 'King' here in Nottingham, has struck up that personal something with the fans. That old familiar chant of "Joe, Joe, Joe Ba-ker" which was born on Trentside, now echoes around Wearside.

And on the way to the ground the walls are daubed with Joe's name. Pick of the lot was a huge drawing of the World Cup and the legend in paint, "Joe, Joe Mexico."

Baker always had magnetism, didn't he? I remember the day when Jim Baxter came. The fans gave Jim a regal welcome but then Trentside took up the chorus "Joe's still the King; Joe's still the King; Ee aye addio, Joe's still the King."

Some players, no matter how hard they graft, no matter how many goals they score or make, never win this kind of adulation.

As I said, popularity is a funny thing!"

BY the time Forest took on the 'Sheep' in the return League fixture at the City Ground on Saturday, 14th March, they were in a comfortable twelfth position in the table, with 35 points from 34 games played - some 17 points clear of the relegation zone. Unfortunately, they lost this particular encounter with their 'woolly-backed' neighbours by three-goals-to-one, in front of another massive crowd of 42,074. So, a season which had also once again seen the 'Reds' dumped out of the FA Cup by Second Division opposition - they lost 2-1 away to Carlisle United - was now beginning to peter out. Their appalling away record was largely to blame for their mediocre campaign; in 19 matches, they'd won just twice, drawing nine and losing ten. And they'd scored a meagre 22 goals, whilst conceding 43 in return.

Furthermore, two more of their established stars had left the Club before the season was out: cultured Welsh international wing-half, Terry Hennessey joined the 'Sheep' in a £110,000 deal; and stylish midfielder, John Barnwell, moved onto Sheffield United. However, the arrival of forward Peter Cormack from Hibernian had gone some way towards appeasing the now very disgruntled supporters. Not only had we had to contend with last season's shock dismissal of manager Johnny Carey, but also new manager Matt Gillies was now systematically dismantling the exciting team the amiable Irishman had built up around him.

Cormack made his debut during Forest's last away fixture of the season at West Brom - a game which Graham and I decided to attend. We travelled to the West Midlands on one of three Trent buses that departed from Mount Street Bus Station on Maid Marion Way. I was still only twelve-years-old at the time and was most impressed by my travelling companions that day. The bus was full of Skinheads who seemed like mature adults to me, but on reflection, were probably only about eighteen. They seemed a right bunch of hard nuts as they made abusive gestures towards passers-by through the windows and fought running battles with one another down the aisle of the bus. And 'by eck', some of 'em were even smoking and drinking beer out of cans!

As we arrived at the Hawthorns, the buses dropped us all off outside the Hawthorns Pub, which is situated at the opposite end of the ground to the Visiting Supporters' Enclosure. It was a warm and sunny spring day and the car park area in front of the pub was already filled with beer-swilling Forest supporters. Although the inhabitants of our bus had been mainly young Skinheads, many of Forest's Trent Enders - and in particular the hard-core hooligan element - still consisted at the time of long-haired Rockers of the early-to-mid-twenties age group. The so-called 'leader of the Trent End', was a chap called Kenny Stevenson, a small but tough-looking Hell's Angel, who had shoulder length, blond hair.

Many of Forest's more mature supporters will remember him as the fella in the Trent End who, until fairly recently, used to announce his arrival in the ground before each game by imitating the sound of an air raid siren. Well that person is Kenny Stevenson and as far as I'm aware, he's still a regular down at the City Ground today. (*When Forest visited Barnsley in a First Division fixture during the 1993/94 season, I spotted him in a bar in the town centre before the game and went over to talk to him. He didn't know me from Adam, but I was curious to know why his famous impression was no longer evident down at the ground. He duly responded by treating the whole of the bar to an ear-piercing rendition, which just about shattered everyone's eardrums!*)

About five minutes after we arrived at the Hawthorns, Kenny and his gang were involved in a major skirmish with about fifty West Brom Skinheads, who suddenly appeared out of nowhere, amidst a hail of beer glasses, bottles and bricks. The police were quickly on the scene, and fortunately for us, the situation was brought swiftly under control before any innocent bystanders got caught up in the melee.

Once inside the safety of the ground, I began to enjoy the pre-match atmosphere - particularly the chanting and rhythmic clapping of the hundreds of West Brom Skinheads beginning to mass on the Birmingham Road terracing at the opposite end of the stadium. There is a long-running dispute between the fiercely rival supporters of West Brom and Wolves over which club was the first to play the Harry J.Allstars hit 'The Liquidator' before each of their home games. Well I can vouch for the fact Albion played this track before this game in 1970 - and it had only been released a year earlier. I can distinctly remember the fans clapping and singing along to it.

Despite Peter Cormack's debut that day, greeted by a chorus of: ''Na-na-na-na, Na-na-na-na, He-he-hey...Peter Cormack!'' from the travelling band of a thousand Forest fans, the 'Reds' were soundly beaten by four-goals-to-nil in front of a crowd of 20,691. As the final whistle blew and we made our way out of the ground, both Graham and I were slightly bemused by the fact the bulk of the Forest supporters were hot-footing it off, rather sharpishly, in the opposite direction to us, as we made our way back up the road to where the buses had dropped us off before the game.

However, we were shortly to discover there were two very good reasons for this. Firstly, the actual coach park was in completely the opposite direction to the one in which we were going (the driver had simply dropped us off outside the pub prior to the game after some 'gentle persuasion' by about twenty thirsty Skinheads). And secondly, half the Skinhead population of the 'Black Country' - many, many, hundreds of them believe me - were heading up the street in our direction, intent on giving the Forest supporters a send off they'd remember for the rest of their lives. Eventually, we did manage somehow to find our way back to the buses unscathed - although this was undoubtedly more down to luck than judgement - and we were soon safely on our way back home to good old Nottingham.

THE hooligan element in football was now beginning to emerge more strongly than ever before - a situation which was causing both the Police and the Football Authorities a great deal of concern. Earlier on in the season, Forest Chairman, Jack Levey, had made the following impassioned appeal to fans:

> "We at the City Ground are always delighted with the vociferous - often humorous - volume of support we receive at our home games. It is gratifying and a definite stimulant to players, but, when a minority resort to constant ill-timed obscene chants and verbal attacks on visiting players, supporters and officials, it is time to call a halt to such disgraceful behaviour.
>
> I appeal to these groups of people (one hesitates to call them 'supporters') who cause this kind of trouble - PLEASE, PLEASE DON'T DO IT!
>
> It gives our club a bad name, it loses us much needed support, it isn't funny, it certainly is no credit to the individuals themselves and, as far as Nottingham Forest is concerned, we are more than prepared and determined to take every step to prevent it."

Unfortunately, judging by some of the events I'd witnessed during the course of the season, this appeal had fallen completely on deaf ears. However, despite Forest's unwelcome hooligan element - not to mention their mediocre form in the League - their average home attendance was still a creditable 25,406. This included six gates in excess of 30,000, the highest of which was the 42,074 who witnessed the 3-1 home defeat at the hands of the 'Sheep'.

SEASON 1969/70 – STATISTICS

FOOTBALL LEAGUE DIVISION ONE – FIXTURES

Date		Opposition	Venue	Competition	Score	Attendance
Aug	9	Ipswich Town	A	League	0-0	19,310
	12	**Stoke City**	**H**	**League**	**0-0**	**22,740**
	16	**Leeds United**	**H**	**League**	**1-4**	**34,290**
	20	Stoke City	A	League	1-1	20,028
	23	Arsenal	A	League	1-2	30,290
	26	**West Bromwich Albion**	**H**	**League**	**1-0**	**22,924**
	30	**West Ham United**	**H**	**League**	**1-0**	**27,097**
Sept	3	Barrow	A	LC 2	2-1	8,919
	6	Wolverhampton Wanderers	A	League	3-3	33,166
	13	**Southampton**	**H**	**League**	**2-1**	**23,200**
	16	Coventry City	A	League	2-3	26,038
	20	Sunderland	A	League	1-2	16,044
	23	**West Ham United**	**H**	**LC 3**	**1-0**	**20,939**
	27	**Crystal Palace**	**H**	**League**	**0-0**	**23,394**
Oct	4	Liverpool	A	League	1-1	44,859
	11	**Manchester City**	**H**	**League**	**2-2**	**30,037**
	15	**Oxford United**	**H**	**LC 4**	**0-1**	**20,734**
	18	Manchester United	A	League	1-1	53,702
	25	**Burnley**	**H**	**League**	**1-1**	**19,771**
	29	Leeds United	A	League	1-6	29,636
Nov	1	Everton	A	League	0-1	49,610
	8	**Tottenham Hotspur**	**H**	**League**	**2-2**	**24,034**
	15	Newcastle United	A	League	1-3	24,307
	22	**Chelsea**	**H**	**League**	**1-1**	**23,808**
	29	Derby County	A	League	2-0	38,225
Dec	**6**	**Sheffield Wednesday**	**H**	**League**	**2-1**	**19,039**
	13	Southampton	A	League	2-1	20,153
	20	**Wolverhampton Wanderers**	**H**	**League**	**4-2**	**15,921**
	26	**Arsenal**	**H**	**League**	**1-1**	**38,915**
	27	West Ham United	A	League	1-1	31,829
Jan	**3**	**Carlisle United**	**H**	**FA Cup 3**	**0-0**	**23,419**
	6	Carlisle United	A	FA Cup 3 - Replay	1-2	12,840
	17	Crystal Palace	A	League	1-1	22,531
	24	**Sunderland**	**H**	**League**	**2-1**	**19,544**
	31	**Liverpool**	**H**	**League**	**1-0**	**30,838**
Feb	7	Manchester City	A	League	1-1	27,077
	21	Burnley	A	League	0-5	11,185
	28	**Everton**	**H**	**League**	**1-1**	**29,174**
Mar	7	Chelsea	A	League	1-1	38,280
	14	**Derby County**	**H**	**League**	**1-3**	**42,074**
	21	Sheffield Wednesday	A	League	1-2	23,787
	27	Tottenham Hotspur	A	League	1-4	36,947
	28	**Newcastle United**	**H**	**League**	**2-2**	**21,360**
	31	**Manchester United**	**H**	**League**	**1-2**	**39,228**
Apr	4	West Bromwich Albion	A	League	0-4	20,691
	7	**Coventry City**	**H**	**League**	**1-4**	**15,569**
	10	**Ipswich Town**	**H**	**League**	**1-0**	**10,589**

HOME ATTENDANCES

	AGGREGATE ATTENDANCE	HIGHEST ATTENDANCE	LOWEST ATTENDANCE	AVERAGE ATTENDANCE
League:	533,546	42,074	10,589	25,406
League Cup:	41,673	20,939	20,734	20,836
FA Cup:	23,419	23,419	23,419	23,419
All Competitions:	598,638	42,074	10,589	24,943

FINAL LEAGUE TABLE - DIVISION ONE

Position	P	W	D	L	GF	GA	Pts
1. Everton	42	29	8	5	72	34	66
2. Leeds United	42	21	15	6	84	49	57
3. Chelsea	42	21	13	8	70	50	55
4. Derby County	42	22	9	11	64	37	53
5. Liverpool	42	20	11	11	65	42	51
6. Coventry City	42	19	11	12	58	48	49
7. Newcastle United	42	17	13	12	57	35	47
8. Manchester United	42	14	17	11	66	61	45
9. Stoke City	42	15	15	12	56	52	45
10. Manchester City	42	16	11	15	55	48	43
11. Tottenham Hotspur	42	17	9	16	54	55	43
12. Arsenal	42	12	18	12	51	49	42
13. Wolverhampton Wanderers	42	12	16	14	55	57	40
14. Burnley	42	12	15	15	56	61	39
15. Nottingham Forest	**42**	**10**	**18**	**14**	**50**	**71**	**38**
16. West Bromwich Albion	42	14	9	19	58	66	37
17. West Ham United	42	12	12	18	51	60	36
18. Ipswich Town	42	10	11	21	40	63	31
19. Southampton	42	6	17	19	46	67	29
20. Crystal Palace	42	6	15	21	34	68	27
21. Sunderland	42	6	14	22	30	68	26
22. Sheffield Wednesday	42	8	9	25	40	71	25

AWAY ATTENDANCES

	AGGREGATE ATTENDANCE	HIGHEST ATTENDANCE	LOWEST ATTENDANCE	AVERAGE ATTENDANCE
League:	617,695	53,702	11,185	29,414
League Cup:	8,919	8,919	8,919	8,919
FA Cup:	12,840	12,840	12,840	12,840
All Competitions:	639,454	53,702	8,919	27,802

"HERE A NOD, THERE A NOD, EVERYWHERE A NOD-NOD"

AT THE start of the 1970/71 season, I was just beginning my second year at the Henry Mellish Grammar School in Bulwell. Although this was an all-boys school and had a reputation locally as being full of middle-class snobs from the Nottinghamshire suburbs, nothing could have been further from the truth. The majority of it's pupils were in fact from very ordinary backgrounds and many - myself included - were from broken homes. My only claim to any academic fame was that I'd passed the 'eleven-plus' exam, making me eligible to attend any one of three grammar schools, including Mellish. Despite it's reputation, I went on to discover on more than one occasion, it was just as rough as any other school.

The headmaster at the time was a rather pompous individual whose nickname was 'Jed'. He was loathed and despised by just about everyone at the school, including most of the teachers. He considered himself a 'good Christian' - preaching "goodwill to all mankind" during morning assembly - and then spending the rest of the day treating everyone as if he'd just scraped them off the bottom of his shoe. As far as I was concerned, he was nothing more than an arrogant, condescending, hypocritical bully, who made life unbearable for anyone who failed to aspire to his own so-called 'high moral values'.

In view of the ordinary backgrounds of most of us, there were many football supporters at the school (this was at a time when the game was still a traditionally working-class pastime) and thankfully most of us were either Forest or County supporters. Not surprisingly though, there were also the usual number of 'shirt' supporters who'd affiliated themselves to the nation's more successful clubs such as Manchester United, Liverpool or Leeds United. And, though I hate to admit it, there was even the odd - and I mean ODD - Derby County supporter.

Personally, I have never quite been able to come to terms with this breed of 'supporter'. It's my belief that associating yourself with your own local team is born out of the strong sense of pride and patriotism you feel for your home town or city - the place in which you were born and bred. And this is the reason why most true football supporters care so passionately about the team they support. How anyone can claim affinity to Manchester United when the city is hundreds of miles from their home is beyond me. Most of these individuals are, as far as I'm concerned, nothing more than disloyal, unpatriotic, glory-hunters. What's more, most of them would probably disappear straight back into the woodwork at the first sign of failure on the part of their adopted team.

Nothing annoys genuine football supporters more, than the sight of young people wandering the streets of Birmingham, Nottingham, Leicester etc. wearing Manchester United or Liverpool shirts. Even more galling, when challenged, are their rather pathetic attempts to justify their association with these clubs. For example: "Well I've supported them all my life," or "my grandparents originated from there." Many of these 'supporters' have never even set foot in Manchester or Liverpool, let alone been to Old Trafford or Anfield. I often wonder just how many admirers these two clubs would have attracted from outside their respective cities, had it not been for the long periods of success they've enjoyed over the last three decades or so?

On the other hand however, I accept that both of them enjoy massive support from within their own catchment areas, and I have no argument whatsoever with anyone from Greater Manchester who supports United, or for that matter, anyone from Merseyside who supports Liverpool. However, as far as I'm concerned, anyone who is born and bred in Leicester should support Leicester City; anyone who is born and bred in Birmingham should support Aston Villa or the 'Blues'; and anyone who is born and bred in Derby...should support Chesterfield! *(Being a complete and utter hypocrite though, I have absolutely no problem at all with anyone who supports Forest - no matter where they're from!)*

I WAS now at the stage where I very rarely missed a match down at the City Ground, although being quite young still; my away excursions were fairly limited. However, there were a number of older pupils at our school who hadn't missed a match home or away for several seasons. One of these was Kev Marks, a fifth former who came from the Arnold area and was a well-known face in the Trent End. Along with his sidekick 'Norwich' - also a Trent Ender - 'Marksy' was one of Nottingham's original graffiti artists. His name and the initials 'NFFC' were plastered on almost every billboard in town, especially those along Arkwright Street and London Road - the main routes to the City Ground. Marksy was one of the original 'Townies' and would always be spotted whenever and wherever Forest played. He's now well into his forties and no longer a regular at matches - although I do still spot his face occasionally at the odd important or obscure away match, for example, when Forest are drawn at a previously unvisited venue in the Cup.

The face of the Trent End had changed quite dramatically now. The 'long-haired, scruffy' types were now in the minority and considerably outnumbered by the more fashionable and clean-cut gangs of 'Skinheads'. This was a fascinating cult to me, not least for the fact that our Graham - now 15-years-old - was a member of one of Nottingham's original Skinhead gangs in Long Eaton, which is situated just three miles down the road from where we lived in Chilwell. It had really taken off in a big way there. Although 'L.E.' is just over the border in Derbyshire, it has a Nottingham post code and is traditionally a 'Forest' stronghold, as are many of the other market towns along the Notts/Derbys border, such as Ilkeston, Heanor, Ripley, Shirebrook etc.

Graham and his chums would spend two or three nights a week down at the Youth Centre, which would rock to the sound of Tamla Motown music and was packed to the rafters with Skinheads - both male and female - aged between 15 and 18. Every one of them would dress in the designer clothes associated with the cult. Anyone wearing anything other than the original labels would be laughed out of town.

Typically, during the summer months, the lads would dress in checked Ben Sherman shirts, red braces, Levi or Wrangler jeans rolled up to just below the knee, Doctor Marten 'Airwair' boots, and red or lime green socks. Some also wore Levi or Wrangler denim jackets, or alternatively Harrington jackets which came in a variety of different colours and had a distinctive reversible tartan lining, so they could be worn either way round.

Other acceptable attire amongst the lads consisted of Granddad's vests, Fred Perry sports shirts, and Slazenger sweaters. For the more formal occasions, two-tone Levi 'Sta-prest' trousers, black blazers, and Doctor Marten shoes, Brogues or Loafers, would be donned. A red hankie was worn in the breast pocket of the blazer and this would be fastened into place with a gold tie-pin. Many 'Forest Skinheads' would also wear the 'NFFC' badge on the breast pocket of their blazers.

During the winter months, blue Crombie coats with black velvet collars were added to the uniform, plus Trilby hats (also known as 'Bluebeats'), and black brollies with sharpened metal tips. An alternative to the Crombie style of coat, was the equally impressive-looking Sheepskin, most likely to be worn during the very cold weather.

The most popular dance music amongst the Skinhead fraternity was the distinctive sound of Tamla Motown, which has it's origins in the American City of Detroit. Some of the most popular records in the discos of this era were the likes of 'Dancing in the Street' by Martha Reeves and the Vandellas, 'Tears of a Clown' by Smokey Robinson and the Miracles, 'Stoned Love' by the Supremes, and many other excellent numbers. Even today, this particular brand of music guarantees a full dance floor at even the most boring of wedding receptions or Christmas parties.

The Skinheads of the late-1960s and early-70s formed themselves into distinct gangs, which were referred to locally as 'Mafias', for example, 'Long Eaton Mafia', 'Stapleford Mafia' or 'Ilkeston Mafia'. But despite the occasional minor skirmish between rival groups, there was in fact a great deal of interaction between them. It was not unusual, for example, for members of the Long Eaton Mafia to attend other discos such as 'Pandora's Box' in Bramcote, or 'The Shed' or 'The Soul Shack' in Beeston, or for members of the Stapleford or Bramcote gangs to attend the soul nights held down at the Long Eaton Youth Centre. The main reason for the comradeship that existed between these otherwise rival Skinhead groups, was undoubtedly their mutual affinity to Nottingham Forest Football Club. After all, they were brawling side by side with one another most Saturday afternoons down on Arkwright Street.

Although still only 13, I was beginning to wear all the Skinhead gear myself and would tag along with Graham and his friends to the Youth Centre. I would gaze in awe at these immaculately-dressed youths throwing themselves acrobatically around the dance floor, in between swapping stories with one another of their many exploits down at the City Ground, or of their frequent confrontations with their Hell's Angel counterparts the 'Long Eaton Road Rats'. The young girls amongst the group would wear pretty much the same type of gear as the lads, although occasionally they'd swap their jeans and braces for two-tone suits and would usually wear 'Monkey boots' rather than Doc Martens.

The Long Eaton Mafia was several dozen strong. And as far as I can remember, the main characters were Kev Taylor, Mossy, Jammy, Big John, Titch Stokes, Adrian Sheldrick (also a well-known face down at the City Ground), Long Eaton Snowy, Stabbo Snowy, Gaz Smith and Mick Coll - all Forest supporters - and a big bald-headed chap called Martin Hall, who was much older than the rest of the group and a Derby supporter. He was also rumoured to be the 'main man' down at the Baseball Ground.

'Trent End Boot Boy!'

FOREST'S opening game of the season was against Coventry at the City Ground and they won this entertaining contest 2-0 with goals from Barry Lyons and Ian Storey-Moore, in front of a crowd of 25,137. Unfortunately, the game was marred by violent clashes between hundreds of rival Forest and Coventry Skinheads who rampaged across the East Stand terraces. During the fracas ammonia was sprayed and a number of people had to be treated by the St.John's Ambulance Brigade as a result. Although at the time, there was no official segregation of fans at the City Ground in terms of fences or Visitors' Enclosures, the hooligan problem had prompted the Club to allocate large areas of terracing on the East Stand to visiting supporters. Only a thin blue line of police would separate them from the home supporters.

However, at many home matches, Forest's hooligan element somehow managed to infiltrate the visiting group of supporters and fighting would suddenly break out in the very middle, right under the gaze of the police. They'd quickly respond by ejecting or arresting the main culprits. Immediately any trouble erupted in this way, there would be a mass stampede in the Trent End, with hundreds of fans rampaging across the terraces in an attempt to get near to the trouble. Some would even charge through the passageway running underneath the stand, eventually bursting through the small gate at the end and out onto the East Stand terracing.

The subsequent attempts by the police to restore order would usually result in violent clashes in the middle of the Trent End. A giant circle of fans would form around the police and as they moved in to make their arrests, they'd be attacked by a chanting, spitting, baying mob. Pointed helmets could be seen hurtling through the air, each one greeted with loud cheers and cries of: ''A-G, A-G-R, A-G-R-O, AGGRO!'' This would be followed by hundreds of youths whistling the theme tune to 'Z-Cars' or chanting: *''Harry Roberts is our mate; is our mate; is our mate; Harry Roberts is our mate; He kills Coppers!''*

Despite the rather violent tendencies of the Trent Enders of this era, they were very passionate about the 'Reds'. In fact the sheer intensity of their support must have given Forest the edge in many of their home fixtures. The humour and immense wit of these supporters was also second to none. One of their most amusing pastimes during games, was to mimic a somewhat demented soul who'd been attending home matches for many years and who always stood on the East Stand terraces near to the Trent End. They'd affectionately nicknamed him 'Noddy', due to his tendency to rock backwards and forwards throughout the game, whilst leaning over the crash barrier behind which he always stood.

The entertainment level of the game would normally determine the ferocity of his nodding. For example, a dull and boring game would be greeted with a very gentle rocking to and fro, whilst a tense and exciting affair would lead to frenzied, uncontrollable rocking backwards and forwards. The Trent Enders would wait for him to start nodding and then immediately serenade him with a chorus of:

Old Macdonald 'ad a farm,
Ee-aye, ee-aye-oh,
An' on that farm 'e 'ad a nod,
Ee-aye, ee-aye-oh;

With a nod-nod 'ere,
An' a nod-nod there,
'ere a nod, there a nod,
Everywhere a nod-nod;

Old Macdonald 'ad a farm,
Ee-aye, ee-aye, oh!

This was always accompanied by hundreds - possibly thousands - of nodding Trent Enders - a sight that always brought loud cheers of approval from other parts of the ground. Poor old Noddy was oblivious to it all though, completely in a world of his own. I'm sure he still attends matches at the City Ground even today, and I've spotted him on many occasions in the past, wandering the streets of his hometown, Long Eaton. With his ghostly grey features, lanky six-foot frame, and long grey gabardine mack, he looks not a day older than he did all those years ago.

DESPITE their opening day victory over Coventry, Forest's form up to the end of the year was less than impressive. By the time they entertained Luton Town at home in the third round of the FA Cup on Saturday, 2nd January, they were in a worrying 20th position in the table, having won just three League games out of a total of 22. Their away form was, as ever, appalling, with no victories at all in 11 games. Out of their dismal tally of 13 points, only 5 of these had been earned on their travels. In addition to this, they'd been dumped out of the Texaco Cup by Airdrie, the League Cup by Second Division Birmingham City, and had sold yet another of their star players, Henry Newton, to Everton for £150,000. In spite of all this, their average home League attendance to date, was a healthy 25,204.

To ignite their season, they needed a good run in the Cup, and after being held to a 1-1 draw by Luton - memorable mainly for the fact full-back John Winfield managed to pull down the Forest goal-posts after falling heavily into the back of his own net - this now seemed unlikely. However, they achieved an impressive 4-3 victory in the replay at Kenilworth Road - despite Malcolm Macdonald's hat-trick for the 'Hatters' - and were once again drawn at home to Second Division opposition in the fourth round, this time against Leyton Orient.

Rather surprisingly, the East Londoners held them to a goalless draw at the City Ground on Saturday, 23rd January. And although the first replay at Brisbane Road the following Monday had to be abandoned at half-time due to a waterlogged pitch, with the score standing at 0-0, Forest eventually progressed through to the fifth round, thanks to a 1-0 victory in the re-arranged fixture a week later. Their reward was a glamorous fifth round tie with Spurs at White Hart Lane on Saturday, 13th February. But despite the high expectations of the Club and the supporters, the 'Reds' were beaten by the odd goal in three, in front of a massive 46,336 crowd.

Despite the disappointment of this defeat, their moderately successful Cup run had given them a new lease of life and they went onto register another eleven victories in their final 20 League games. This included a 3-2 home victory over League Champions Everton - during which two-goal Peter Cormack was the star - a 1-0 away victory over Spurs (now why couldn't we do that in the Cup?), a 2-1 victory against the 'Sheep' at the 'BBG' (this was now becoming a habit), and a 3-1 victory over Manchester City at Maine Road. Furthermore, the excellent form of the now 'injury-free' Ian Moore was extremely pleasing for everyone at the Club. He notched no less than 14 goals during the second half of the season.

One of the most memorable games for me during the latter part of this season, was the visit to the City Ground of 'Champions elect' Arsenal, which took place on Tuesday, 13th April. This was memorable not so much for the result - an overwhelming 3-0 victory for the 'Gunners' on their way to a League and Cup double - but for the occasion itself. Forest's attendances in those days were such that, within the space of only a few days, the City

Ground could go from being relatively empty - as with the crowd of 23,032 for the game against West Ham the previous Saturday - to being packed to the rafters, as it was for this game against Arsenal, which attracted a massive crowd of 40,692.

As was usual in those days, I arrived at the ground very early and made my way to the middle section of the Trent End, taking up my normal position half-way down the terracing, directly behind the goal. By the time the teams took to the field, the Trent End was absolutely packed and in tremendous voice:

Bertie Mee sez to Bill Shankley,
'ave you 'eard of the North Bank - Highbury?
Bill sez no - I don't think so?
But I've 'eard of the Trent End Boot Boys!

La-la-la-la-la-la-la-la-la,
La-la-la-la-la-la-la,
La-la-la-la-la-la-la,
WE ARE THE TRENT END - BOOT BOYS!

During the chorus of this song, the whole end would bounce up and down in unison, eventually causing everyone to sway forward, crushing people behind barriers and against the perimeter wall at the front. This was a very frightening, but at the same time, exhilarating experience. As the crowd gradually managed to settle once again, the next chorus would begin:

We don't carry 'ammers,
We don't carry lead,
We only carry 'atchets,
T' bury in your 'ead;

We are true supporters,
Fanatics everyone,
We 'ate Derby County,
Spurs an' Everton!

NOTTINGHAM-BOOT-BOYS!
NOTTINGHAM-BOOT-BOYS!

The Arsenal players decided to have their pre-match warm up in front of the Trent End, much to the annoyance of the Trent Enders. Traditionally, the Forest team always warmed up at this end of the pitch and in turn, the name of every player would be chanted until acknowledged with a wave. Each acknowledgement would be greeted with a loud cheer and rapturous applause. Consequently, the Arsenal players were jeered incessantly throughout this five-minute period, with the young, long-haired Charlie George bearing the brunt of the abuse. His name was chanted over and over again, followed by wolf whistles, as he took turns in blasting the ball at goalkeeper Bob Wilson.

However, the last laugh was definitely on Charlie - at least as far as I was concerned anyway - as he hammered a thunderbolt of a shot inches over the crossbar...and straight into my ugly mush, almost knocking me senseless! I was seeing stars for the whole of the ninety minutes, although I was just about conscious enough to see a very impressive Arsenal side take the 'Reds' to the cleaners.

FOREST'S average League attendance, for what was a pretty unimpressive season all-round, was 23,322. The highest was the 40,692 for the aforementioned visit of the 'Gunners', with the lowest being a rather dismal 13,502 for the final game of the season against Stoke City.

'Noddy'

SEASON 1970/71 – STATISTICS

FOOTBALL LEAGUE DIVISION ONE – FIXTURES

Date	Opposition	Venue	Competition	Score	Attendance
Aug 15	**Coventry City**	**H**	**League**	**2-0**	**25,137**
18	**West Bromwich Albion**	**H**	**League**	**3-3**	**24,423**
22	Ipswich Town	A	League	0-0	19,150
26	Newcastle United	A	League	1-1	35,132
29	**Wolverhampton Wanderers**	**H**	**League**	**4-1**	**24,343**
Sept 2	Stoke City	A	League	0-0	13,951
5	Crystal Palace	A	League	0-2	26,510
9	Huddersfield Town	A	LC 2	0-0	18,165
12	**Manchester City**	**H**	**League**	**0-1**	**28,896**
14	**Airdrieonians**	**H**	**Texaco Cup**	**2-2**	**11,491**
19	Liverpool	A	League	0-3	40,676
21	**Huddersfield Town**	**H**	**LC 2 - Replay**	**2-0**	**15,818**
26	**Leeds United**	**H**	**League**	**0-0**	**31,475**
28	Airdrieonians	A	Texaco Cup	2-2	13,177
	(Aggregate score 4-4 - Airdrie won 5-2 on penalties)				
Oct 3	Arsenal	A	League	0-4	32,073
6	Birmingham City	A	LC 3	1-2	23,015
10	**Blackpool**	**H**	**League**	**3-1**	**16,618**
17	Coventry City	A	League	0-2	25,418
24	Huddersfield Town	A	League	0-0	17,121
31	**Tottenham Hotspur**	**H**	**League**	**0-1**	**25,301**
Nov 7	Everton	A	League	0-1	39,255
14	**Manchester United**	**H**	**League**	**1-2**	**36,373**
21	Burnley	A	League	1-2	13,013
28	**Derby County**	**H**	**League**	**2-4**	**30,539**
Dec 5	Southampton	A	League	1-4	19,016
12	**Chelsea**	**H**	**League**	**1-1**	**20,060**
19	**Ipswich Town**	**H**	**League**	**0-1**	**14,085**
Jan 2	**Luton Town**	**H**	**FA Cup 3**	**1-1**	**23,230**
9	West Bromwich Albion	A	League	1-0	20,015
11	Luton Town	A	FA Cup 3 - Replay	4-3	23,483
16	**Newcastle United**	**H**	**League**	**2-1**	**21,798**
23	**Orient**	**H**	**FA Cup 4**	**1-1**	**25,349**
25	Orient	A	FA Cup 4 - Replay	0-0	19,791
	(Abandoned at half-time due to waterlogged pitch)				
Feb 1	Orient	A	FA Cup 4 - Replay	1-0	18,530
6	**Southampton**	**H**	**League**	**2-0**	**18,009**
13	Tottenham Hotspur	A	FA Cup 5	1-2	46,336
17	Chelsea	A	League	0-2	19,339
20	**Burnley**	**H**	**League**	**1-0**	**20,873**
24	West Ham United	A	League	0-2	35,601
Mar 6	**Huddersfield Town**	**H**	**League**	**1-3**	**15,798**
10	Tottenham Hotspur	A	League	1-0	21,697
13	Manchester United	A	League	0-2	39,339
20	**Everton**	**H**	**League**	**3-2**	**21,643**
27	**Crystal Palace**	**H**	**League**	**3-1**	**16,507**
31	Derby County	A	League	2-1	34,857
Apr 3	Wolverhampton Wanderers	A	League	0-4	20,531
9	Manchester City	A	League	3-1	33,772
10	**West Ham United**	**H**	**League**	**1-0**	**23,032**
13	**Arsenal**	**H**	**League**	**0-3**	**40,692**
17	Blackpool	A	League	3-2	10,028
24	**Liverpool**	**H**	**League**	**0-1**	**20,678**
27	**Stoke City**	**H**	**League**	**0-0**	**13,502**
May 1	Leeds United	A	League	0-2	43,083

HOME ATTENDANCES

	AGGREGATE ATTENDANCE	HIGHEST ATTENDANCE	LOWEST ATTENDANCE	AVERAGE ATTENDANCE
League:	489,782	40,692	13,502	23,322
League Cup:	15,818	15,818	15,818	15,818
FA Cup:	48,579	25,349	23,230	24,289
Texaco Cup:	11,491	11,491	11,491	11,491
All Competitions:	565,670	40,692	11,491	22,626

FINAL LEAGUE TABLE - DIVISION ONE

Position	P	W	D	L	GF	GA	Pts
1. Arsenal	42	29	7	6	71	29	65
2. Leeds United	42	27	10	5	72	30	64
3. Tottenham Hotspur	42	19	14	9	54	33	52
4. Wolverhampton Wanderers	42	22	8	12	64	54	52
5. Liverpool	42	17	17	8	42	24	51
6. Chelsea	42	18	15	9	52	42	51
7. Southampton	42	17	12	13	56	44	46
8. Manchester United	42	16	11	15	65	66	43
9. Derby County	42	16	10	16	56	54	42
10. Coventry City	42	16	10	16	37	38	42
11. Manchester City	42	12	17	13	47	42	41
12. Newcastle United	42	14	13	15	44	46	41
13. Stoke City	42	12	13	17	44	48	37
14. Everton	42	12	13	17	54	60	37
15. Huddersfield Town	42	11	14	17	40	49	36
16. Nottingham Forest	**42**	**14**	**8**	**20**	**42**	**61**	**36**
17. West Bromwich Albion	42	10	15	17	58	75	35
18. Crystal Palace	42	12	11	19	39	57	35
19. Ipswich Town	42	12	10	20	42	48	34
20. West Ham United	42	10	14	18	47	60	34
21. Burnley	42	7	13	22	29	63	27
22. Blackpool	42	4	15	23	34	66	23

AWAY ATTENDANCES

	AGGREGATE ATTENDANCE	HIGHEST ATTENDANCE	LOWEST ATTENDANCE	AVERAGE ATTENDANCE
League:	559,577	43,083	10,028	26,646
League Cup:	41,180	23,015	18,165	20,590
FA Cup:	108,140 (Includes abandoned fixture versus Orient)	46,336	18,530	27,035
Texaco Cup:	13,177	13,177	13,177	13,177
All Competitions:	722,074	46,336	10,028	25,788

"WE'LL SUPPORT YOU EVERMORE, WE'LL SUPPORT YOU EVERMORE"

FOREST'S OPENING fixture of the season was against Liverpool at Anfield on Saturday, 14th August, where they suffered a 3-1 defeat in front of a crowd of 51,427. This was followed by a visit to Filbert Street the following Wednesday to take on neighbours Leicester City. This fixture was almost on the scale of a Forest-Derby clash, consequently there was guaranteed to be a sizeable following from Nottingham.

As this was in the middle of the school holidays, our Graham and I decided to make a day of it and caught a Barton's bus into town at around 11 o'clock in the morning. As arranged, we met up in town with our buddies from Chilwell, Tom Clough and Martyn Swinscoe. Although even in those days Tom was 'as hard as nails', 'Swinie' on the other hand, wasn't quite in the same category. In fact, he will probably go down in history as the only Forest supporter ever to have been beaten up at Preston North End!

First of all, we made our way down to the railway station to buy our tickets for the 'Forest Special' which was due to depart at around 5.45-p.m., some six hours later. Still, it was a hot and sunny day, and when you're a teenager, there aren't many better places to be in the middle of the summer holidays than 'down town'.

We spent part of the day window shopping in some of the fashion boutiques around at the time, such as 'Jeff's Fashions', the 'Metro Boutique', and 'Image', and stuffing our faces in 'Wimpys' Burger Bar' at the top of St.James' Street. (Wimpys was the 1970s' forerunner to McDonalds). We spent the rest of the afternoon chatting to other Forest supporters who were by this time beginning to mass in 'Slab Square'. One of these was a Skinhead from Clifton who our Graham had nicknamed 'Clifton Aggro', due to the fact that whenever there was a disturbance of any description down at a Forest match, he would always be there right in the thick of the action. He was about 16 or 17 at the time and sported a haircut that was 'down to the bone'. In the hot weather, he wore nothing other than rolled up jeans, Doc Marten boots and braces. He had the physique of a prize-fighter and the IQ of a gnat, therefore conversations with him tended to centre mainly around how many opposing supporters' noses he'd broken recently. However, he did once tell us he'd just bought the record 'Liverpool Lou' by the Scaffold, as he liked err...collecting 'football' songs? He hung around with a right motley crew as well, one of them being a lame chap who wore thick, black-rimmed glasses. In typical fashion, Swinie had rather cruelly nicknamed him 'Jim Jelly' due to the way he wobbled about when he was running.

At 5 o'clock we made our way down to the station and took up our places in the queue for the train. As always in those days, football supporters - being the absolute scum of the earth - weren't allowed to wait on the station platform like normal fare-paying passengers. No, we had to queue in the station concourse and be glared at for three-quarters-of-an-hour by a couple of dozen over-zealous British Rail Transport policemen. As the crowd built up in this area, ultimately spilling out onto Queens Road, the throng of several hundred youths began to chant loudly and this echoed impressively around the whole station. This caused 'normal' rail passengers to gaze open-mouthed as they made their way to their trains. ''Who were these beings from another planet, draped in scarves and banners?'' they seemed to be thinking, as they hurried on by.

CHAPTER 6

Eventually, the large wrought-iron gates keeping us out were pulled open by a couple of burley police officers and a stampede ensued down the stairs, across the platform, and onto the fifteen-carriage 'cattle-truck' that British Rail had so kindly laid on to transport us to the game.

As the saying goes: "If you treat people like animals, eventually they'll behave like animals." And unfortunately, as far as this particular occasion was concerned, a large proportion of the supporters who travelled on this train to Leicester did just that. Their behaviour was an absolute disgrace. We had barely left Midlands Station before the carnage began. Luggage racks were torn down, mirrors smashed, and seats slashed with razor blades. Graffiti was daubed everywhere, and the emergency cord must have been pulled at least a dozen times during what turned out to be a horrendous 60-minute journey. I had never in my life witnessed such sheer mindless vandalism and wanton destruction. It made me feel ashamed to be a Forest supporter.

What's more, immediately upon our arrival at Leicester, it was obvious that a large number of Forest's travelling supporters were hell-bent on causing trouble. I saw at least two youths brandishing knives amongst the 600 or so fans that spilled off the train and onto the station platform. And despite a heavy police presence, these same supporters went on the rampage throughout the streets of the town as they made their way towards the ground. There was also a considerable amount of brawling on the terraces during the game and, to cap it all, Forest's performance was absolutely abysmal. They went down 2-0 to their East Midlands rivals in front of a crowd of 32,079.

I wasn't looking forward to the journey back to the station after the game and, as we spilled out of the ground at the end, I couldn't help but wonder just what lay in store for us out on the dark and unfamiliar streets of Leicester. As none of us had a clue where we were going, we just followed the crowd. After walking for about five minutes, we crossed over a main road and climbed over a wrought-iron fence onto what is now known as Nelson Mandella Park. This is the big open park which stands between Welford Road and Waterloo Way. Here, the first of many serious skirmishes between the two sets of rival supporters took place. We just kept our heads down and ran as fast as we could across the park and then up a steep hill towards the station.

As we got nearer and nearer to the station, we were only too aware of the brawling that was taking place in the dimly lit streets just fifty yards or so behind us. The night air was filled with that awful sound of breaking glass, screaming and chanting youths, and the wail of police sirens. The train home was filled with battered and bruised supporters, and as we pulled out of the station, I was extremely grateful our little gang at least, had come through it all relatively unscathed. Tom and Swinie had both received a bit of a slapping as we were running through the park, but were both still in one piece. The following morning, the local news bulletins were dominated by accounts of the previous night's clashes and in particular the fact a Leicester City supporter had been stabbed and lay critically ill in hospital. A fifteen-year-old Forest supporter later served a lengthy prison sentence in connection with this incident.

THE defeats at Liverpool and Leicester were followed by a 1-0 victory at home to West Ham United on Saturday, 21st August. However, it would be another 12 games before they recorded their next victory in the League - this being a 1-0 success away to Huddersfield Town on Tuesday, 26th October. By this time the 'Reds' were already next-to-bottom of the table. I was still attending every home game, but my away excursions were limited mainly to local 'derbies' such as the one at Leicester. As Henry Mellish was a rugby-playing grammar school, Forest's home games on a Saturday would usually be preceded by a school match against one of the rival grammar schools in Nottingham such as High Pavement or Nottingham High School. A quick shower and a mad dash across town to West Bridgford always followed these games. However, as several members of our school team were also Forest supporters, we all used to travel down together.

Although Mellish operated a strict dress code, with the wearing of school uniforms mandatory, this rule didn't however apply to Saturdays - much to the obvious displeasure of Jed. His face was always a picture when we turned up for school games on a Saturday morning wearing our Skinhead gear. I was now also sporting my very own Skinhead haircut, having been dragged kicking and screaming into a Long Eaton barbershop by Graham and his pals during the summer holidays. I'd been held down whilst my long, curly, black locks were mercilessly hacked off by a sadistic, grinning barber. Mind you, this painful experience was made completely worthwhile by the look of absolute horror on Jed's face when I returned to school after the summer holidays. He'd repeatedly threatened me with suspension in the past because of the length of my hair and I remember gleefully muttering to myself: "Threaten me with expulsion now, ya pompous git!" when he first set eyes on my cropped hair.

Much to our constant amusement, the Skinhead fashion of the early-70s proved itself extremely compatible with the dress code that existed within our school. Wearing all the formal clothes associated with the cult could dramatically spice up our otherwise dowdy-looking uniforms. The naff grey trousers could be replaced with charcoal grey Levi 'Sta-prests', which looked even better with Doc Marten shoes or Brogues. A white Ben Sherman shirt and a fashionable black blazer completed the outfit. Even more satisfying, was that our school badge, which we were obliged to wear on the breast pocket of our blazers, could be rather ingeniously secured in place throughout the day using Velcro, and hastily removed - along with our school ties - the second we got through the school gates at the end of the day. This we would then replace with an 'NFFC' badge which fitted perfectly in it's place.

FOREST won just two more League games before the end of the year. The first was a 4-1 victory over fellow-strugglers West Brom at the City Ground on Saturday, 13th November, a game which saw a young Martin O'Neill make his goal-scoring debut. The second of these was a 1-0 home victory over Everton on Saturday, 11th December.

By the time they entertained League Champions Arsenal at the City Ground on Monday, 27th December, they were still second-from-bottom of the First Division table, with just 11 points from 22 games played. Only West Brom with 11 points from 22 games played, were keeping them off the bottom. They had by now also made their customary early exit from the League Cup, having lost 2-1 to Chelsea in a third round replay at Stamford Bridge. The visit of Arsenal once again drew the City Ground's largest crowd of the season - a massive 42,750. And not only did they see the 'Reds' put on a battling display in order to earn themselves a surprise 1-1 draw, they also witnessed one of the finest goals ever scored by a Forest player on Trentside.

During a first-half spell of Arsenal pressure in front of the Trent End goal-mouth, Ian Storey-Moore received a pass 25 yards inside his own half. After running some 75 yards with the ball at his feet, and beating several Arsenal players along the way, he then skilfully slotted it past the advancing Bob Wilson and into the net from eight yards out. The distance covered by the striker - seventy-four and a half yards to be precise - was confirmed later from official BBC footage of the game. This superb goal was one of the few highlights of an otherwise extremely disappointing season for Forest's long-suffering supporters.

Unhappy with the Club's lack of ambition though, Storey-Moore was also now getting itchy feet. On Saturday, 4th March 1972 - with Forest now anchored firmly to the foot of the table - he finally left the City Ground. He'd been at the Club for over ten years and scored more than 100 goals. Unfortunately, he became involved in a farcical tug of war between Derby County and Manchester United, who were both vying for his signature. In typical fashion, Brian Clough had paraded his latest '£200,000-plus signing' to the Baseball Ground crowd prior to their home game against Wolverhampton Wanderers. However, the Forest Committee - fearing a major backlash from their very disgruntled and angry supporters - vetoed the transfer. Amid much acrimony and ill feeling between the two East Midlands neighbours, 27-year-old Moore finally joined United. Ironically however, he went on to play only forty matches for them before his career was tragically cut short through injury.

As their miserable season drew to a close and relegation beckoned, a 'Gillies Out' campaign began to gather momentum amongst the few supporters who were still bothering to turn up at the City Ground. For the last four seasons, Forest had flirted with relegation, only to be rescued by the heroics of Storey-Moore during the dying stages of the campaign. However, with Moore having now gone and Peter Cormack making it clear relegation would only hasten his own departure from the Club, the 'Reds' seemed doomed.

Although they did manage to scrape together a total of four League victories during the second half of the season - including a thumping 4-0 home success over Coventry City - their form in general was such they became almost 'cannon fodder' to the majority of their opponents. They lost no fewer than 11 of their last 18 League games, including a humiliating 4-0 defeat at the hands of the 'Sheep' down at the 'BBG', and 6-1 defeats at both Tottenham Hotspur and Leeds United. They were also once again blown out of the FA Cup by lesser opposition, losing 3-1 away to Second Division Millwall in a third round tie at the Den. During this game, the travelling band of Forest supporters had their first taste of the South Londoners' infamous 'hospitality'.

Alas, after several years of trying, they finally achieved relegation to the Second Division after defeat in their final home game of the season. On Tuesday, 25th April, they suffered a 3-1 defeat in the Midlands derby with Wolves - a game they needed to win to stand any chance of staying up. This was an extremely painful and emotional experience for me and the majority of the 16,889 crowd, and as the players left the field at the end of the game, the sound of: *"We'll support you evermore,"* echoed defiantly around the half-empty stadium. As I left the ground with a tear in my eye and a lump in my throat, I couldn't help wondering just how long we were going to be watching Second Division football down at the City Ground. One thing was for sure though: there was absolutely no chance on this earth I'd be deserting this sinking ship.

This had been an appalling season for Forest - almost without exception - leading to an inevitable decline in attendances. However, despite the fact our 'nearest and dearest' of neighbours just 15 miles down the A52 had been in the process of winning the First Division Championship during the corresponding period, we still managed to pull in an average home League attendance of 21,433. This was a creditable figure, given such dire circumstances.

SEASON 1971/72 – STATISTICS
FOOTBALL LEAGUE DIVISION ONE – FIXTURES

Date		Opposition	Venue	Competition	Score	Attendance
Aug	14	Liverpool	A	League	1-3	51,427
	18	Leicester City	A	League	1-2	32,079
	21	**West Ham United**	**H**	**League**	**1-0**	**17,185**
	24	**Southampton**	**H**	**League**	**2-3**	**14,350**
	28	Crystal Palace	A	League	1-1	17,699
	31	**Stoke City**	**H**	**League**	**0-0**	**19,017**
Sept	**4**	**Sheffield United**	**H**	**League**	**2-3**	**27,041**
	7	**Aldershot**	**H**	**LC 2**	**5-1**	**8,380**
	11	Coventry City	A	League	1-1	20,380
	18	**Manchester City**	**H**	**League**	**2-2**	**21,488**
	25	Wolverhampton Wanderers	A	League	2-4	20,631
Oct	**2**	**Huddersfield Town**	**H**	**League**	**1-2**	**15,693**
	6	**Chelsea**	**H**	**LC 3**	**1-1**	**16,811**
	9	Ipswich Town	A	League	1-1	16,285
	11	Chelsea	A	LC 3 - Replay	1-2	24,817
	16	**Liverpool**	**H**	**League**	**2-3**	**20,945**
	23	Tottenham Hotspur	A	League	1-6	35,846
	26	Huddersfield Town	A	League	1-0	9,459
	30	**Derby County**	**H**	**League**	**0-2**	**37,170**
Nov	6	Chelsea	A	League	0-2	25,812
	13	**West Bromwich Albion**	**H**	**League**	**4-1**	**20,024**
	20	Newcastle United	A	League	1-2	24,583
	27	**Leeds United**	**H**	**League**	**0-2**	**29,463**
Dec	4	Manchester United	A	League	2-3	45,048
	11	**Everton**	**H**	**League**	**1-0**	**18,639**
	18	Sheffield United	A	League	1-2	27,663
	27	**Arsenal**	**H**	**League**	**1-1**	**42,750**
Jan	1	Manchester City	A	League	2-2	38,777
	8	**Crystal Palace**	**H**	**League**	**0-1**	**19,033**
	15	Millwall	A	FA Cup 3	1-3	17,940
	22	**Leicester City**	**H**	**League**	**1-2**	**27,250**
	29	Southampton	A	League	1-4	17,043
Feb	**12**	**Tottenham Hotspur**	**H**	**League**	**0-1**	**20,209**
	19	Derby County	A	League	0-4	31,801
Mar	4	West Bromwich Albion	A	League	0-1	16,702
	11	**Ipswich Town**	**H**	**League**	**0-2**	**9,872**
	14	**Chelsea**	**H**	**League**	**2-1**	**13,349**
	18	West Ham United	A	League	2-4	20,960
	25	**Coventry City**	**H**	**League**	**4-0**	**12,205**
	27	Leeds United	A	League	1-6	40,866
Apr	1	Arsenal	A	League	0-3	33,895
	8	**Newcastle United**	**H**	**League**	**1-0**	**12,470**
	10	Stoke City	A	League	2-0	13,907
	22	**Manchester United**	**H**	**League**	**0-0**	**35,063**
	25	**Wolverhampton Wanderers**	**H**	**League**	**1-3**	**16,889**
May	2	Everton	A	League	1-1	21,513

HOME ATTENDANCES

	AGGREGATE ATTENDANCE	HIGHEST ATTENDANCE	LOWEST ATTENDANCE	AVERAGE ATTENDANCE
League:	450,105	42,750	9,872	21,433
League Cup:	25,191	16,811	8,380	12,595
All Competitions:	475,296	42,750	8,380	20,665

FINAL LEAGUE TABLE - DIVISION ONE

Position	P	W	D	L	GF	GA	Pts
1. Derby County	42	24	10	8	69	33	58
2. Leeds United	42	24	9	9	73	31	57
3. Liverpool	42	24	9	9	64	30	57
4. Manchester City	42	23	11	8	77	45	57
5. Arsenal	42	22	8	12	58	40	52
6. Tottenham Hotspur	42	19	13	10	63	42	51
7. Chelsea	42	18	12	12	58	49	48
8. Manchester United	42	19	10	13	69	61	48
9. Wolverhampton Wanderers	42	18	11	13	65	57	47
10. Sheffield United	42	17	12	13	61	60	46
11. Newcastle United	42	15	11	16	49	52	41
12. Leicester City	42	13	13	16	41	46	39
13. Ipswich Town	42	11	16	15	39	53	38
14. West Ham United	42	12	12	18	47	51	36
15. Everton	42	9	18	15	37	48	36
16. West Bromwich Albion	42	12	11	19	42	54	35
17. Stoke City	42	10	15	17	39	56	35
18. Coventry City	42	9	15	18	44	67	33
19. Southampton	42	12	7	23	52	80	31
20. Crystal Palace	42	8	13	21	39	65	29
21. Nottingham Forest	**42**	**8**	**9**	**25**	**47**	**81**	**25**
22. Huddersfield Town	42	6	13	23	27	59	25

AWAY ATTENDANCES

	AGGREGATE ATTENDANCE	HIGHEST ATTENDANCE	LOWEST ATTENDANCE	AVERAGE ATTENDANCE
League:	562,376	51,427	9,459	26,779
League Cup:	24,817	24,817	24,817	24,817
FA Cup:	17,940	17,940	17,940	17,940
All Competitions:	605,133	51,427	9,459	26,310

"CITY GROUND, OH MIST ROLLING IN FROM THE TRENT"

IT WAS soon apparent to those involved with the Club, that life in the Second Division wasn't going to be simply a 'stroll in the park' for the 'Reds', as they opened their account with a 0-0 draw at home to Portsmouth on Saturday, 12th August. Furthermore, after a run of five seasons in or around the First Division relegation zone, not to mention consistently early exits from each of the domestic Cup competitions, the tolerance of the supporters had been stretched to the limit. This was reflected in the disappointing attendance of only 13,175 for the visit of 'Pompey' - and this was merely a sign of things to come.

Three wins, two draws and two defeats in their opening seven games put them in the surprisingly lofty position of eighth in the table. However, their tally of only five goals scored and a total of six conceded, spoke volumes for the 'entertainment value' of their performances to date. Attendances of only 9,591 for the visit of Oxford United, 10,659 for the visit of Brighton, and 9,495 for the visit of Luton Town, provided further evidence of the supporters' dissatisfaction with their team. What's more - on the back of a 3-0 defeat away to Queens Park Rangers on Saturday, 16th September - the visit of Cardiff City the following Tuesday, drew a desperately low crowd of only 6,414 to the City Ground - their lowest League gate since the visit of West Ham United on 2nd May 1955, which had attracted a mere 5,825 fans.

However, this was a period in the Club's history when they needed every bit of support they could muster. And I for one was determined not to miss a single home game, either in the Second Division - or at any other time in the future, if I could help it. Like any true football supporter, my whole life was then, as it still is today - albeit to a lesser extent - planned meticulously around the fixture list. Nothing is allowed to stand in the way of a Forest match - especially one that takes place at the City Ground. In fact, nothing infuriates me more, than those uncaring individuals who selfishly arrange their wedding days between the months of August and May, and then have the audacity to send me an invitation. Don't these inconsiderate so-and-sos appreciate that this is the football season for God's sake!

Anyway, not content with having turned us supporters into near suicidal wrecks, firstly by selling off all our star players, and then by subsequently getting us relegated, the Forest Committee decided, in their infinite wisdom, they would now cage us in like animals inside the City Ground. They planned to erect steel fences on the terraces to partition the Trent End off into three separate enclosures - and this was apparently 'all for our own protection'. And despite angry protests from hundreds of unhappy Trent Enders, these would be installed after the game against Millwall, due to take place on Saturday, 4th November.

Now, whether their intentions were entirely in the interests of ground safety, or just some kind of knee-jerk reaction to the continued bad behaviour of some Trent Enders, we will never really know. But it is a fact, some of the Committee had been extremely unhappy with the 'Gillies Out' demonstrations which had been taking place in that part of the ground in recent times, especially during the build up to his resignation in October. By the time Forest entertained the 'Lions', Dave Mackay had been installed as the new manager, but before this game, Club Chairman Jim Wilmer, made his feelings towards some of the supporters abundantly clear with these scathing remarks in the Forest Review:

CHAPTER 7

> *"To achieve success there must be efforts other than the appointing of new staff. I hope that there can be a mutual endeavour to improve both press and public relations. We know that relegation, poor games, increased admission and transport charges, some hooliganism inside and outside the ground and other factors have contributed to poor attendances. Let us, with the appointment of Dave Mackay, trust that a visit to the City Ground will once again be a worthwhile pleasure.*
>
> *I would like to see the "Trent Enders" give the same encouragement as they did in the 1960s. I feel sure the majority are true supporters and that henceforth they will ignore and discourage those who do not come to shout their support but only to disturb and provoke to the detriment of both team and spectators."*

Now without wishing to condone the unruly and unacceptable behaviour of Forest's hooligan element during this time, and whilst acknowledging that Mr.Wilmer was no doubt an honest and sincere man who had the Club's best interests at heart; I can't help but feel he was just somehow missing the point? Over a period of six seasons, Forest had gone from being 'star-studded Runners-up' in the First Division, FA Cup semi-finalists, and European contenders - to below average, Second Division, no-hopers. Along the way, they'd sacked highly popular manager Johnny Carey and sold off every one of their star players, including Joe Baker, Frank Wignall, John Barnwell, Terry Hennessey, Henry Newton, Jim Baxter, Ian Storey-Moore, and Peter Cormack (all internationals). They'd finished in 18th position in the table in season 68/69, 15th in 69/70, and 16th in 70/71, suffered an agonising relegation campaign in 71/72, and finally - as if to rub salt into our wounds - were looking more like Second Division relegation candidates, than First Division promotion hopefuls. And my God, was it painful.

Bill Shankley's legendary quote: "Football is not a matter of life or death...it's far more important than that!" perfectly sums up the sentiments of the true football supporter. The passion you feel for YOUR football club, and for YOUR town or city, is almost impossible to explain to the uninitiated. The anticipation you feel throughout the week leading up to an important game, is something all football supporters can identify with. And the amount of time you spend scrutinising the back pages of every tabloid newspaper or flicking through the Teletext pages just to find the merest snippet of information about your team, is enough to drive those who live with you completely round the bend.

What's more, the rush of adrenaline you feel when waking up on the morning of the game - especially if it's against one of your nearest rivals - is incredible. Then there's the absurd rituals you go through during the hours leading up to kick off. Putting on your lucky underpants; tucking into your lucky breakfast of black pudding and corn-flakes; pinning your lucky badge onto the lapel of your lucky jacket; parking your car on the lucky side of the car park (or if you've travelled down on the lucky Number 57 bus, drinking your lucky four and a half pints of lager); entering the ground through the lucky turnstile; making your way up to your very own lucky seat, via that lucky staircase of course. And all this, just to watch your decidedly unlucky team...get hammered by four-goals-to-nil!

"IF YOU put the fences up; We'll pull 'em down," sang the Trent Enders throughout the 3-2 victory against Millwall. However, this was all to no avail, and they were duly erected days later. And, true to their word, the Trent Enders tried their hardest on more than one occasion to remove the offending items of scrap metal. This prompted further appeals from the Club, such as this one before the game against Carlisle United on Saturday, 20th January:

"Sorry to see that our destructive friends (?) in the Trent End were at it again last Tuesday evening when the railings, erected for their own protection and to afford comfort to all Trent End patrons, were damaged. Come off it lads, this is costing the club money! At the same time, we would like to thank the majority of the Trent End partisans and indeed the rest of our supporters for giving the team such grand vocal support. The players appreciated it very much."

It would be fair to say the Committee and the Trent Enders were enjoying a kind of 'love-hate' relationship at this point in the Club's history. However, little did the Football Authorities of this time realise, just what catastrophic consequences the caging in of football supporters would go on to have many years later.

From a personal point of view, I had no intention of watching my football from the suffocating and undignified confines of a wrought-iron cage. I decided therefore to take up residence in any other part of the ground that happened to take my fancy on the day of the match. Sometimes this would be the fresh air and wide open spaces of the Bridgford End; whilst on others it would be under the shelter of the huge East Stand enclosure. Occasionally, I would even opt for the terraces at the front of the Main Stand. Unfortunately, most of Forest's hooligan element had also vacated the Trent End and consequently, a number of 'hooligan splinter groups' had cropped up in various parts of the ground. This made it very difficult for the police to maintain an acceptable level of crowd control - particularly for the bigger games. All in all therefore, the erection of fences in the Trent End had, in practical terms, proved counter-productive.

My penultimate match as a Trent Ender, had been for the visit of Swindon Town on Saturday, 21st October - prior to the fences being erected. And during this game, I'd committed the cardinal sin of leaving the ground some three minutes before the final whistle. How foolish of me. My only excuse for this unforgivable act of disloyalty was that it was a cold and windy day; there was a sparse and frustrated crowd of only 8,683 inside the ground; the team had put in yet another inept and lacklustre display; we were two-goals-to-nil down; and the clock was ticking away rapidly towards the 90-minute mark.

I'd had enough and left the ground muttering to myself all manner of treacherous things like: "That's it...that's the last time I'm comin' down 'ere to watch this load o' crap agen!"As I reached the other side of Trent Bridge though, I heard a faint roar coming from the distant crowd. "No...it couldn't be," I thought. "It must just have been the wind," I tried to reassure myself. "In any case, thi wunt o' scored if thid played 'til midnight," I tried once more to convince myself - unable to even contemplate the thought of missing a goal from my heroes.

As I reached the City Centre, I stood and gazed into a shop window, where the football results were just beginning to appear on the television screens lined up just a couple of feet in front of me. And there it was...right before my very eyes: "NOTTINGHAM FOREST 2 - SWINDON TOWN 2." Well I didn't know whether to laugh or cry - my sheer frustration at having left before the end of this amazing fight-back, tempered only by the fact that Forest had stolen an unlikely point.

Anyway, one thing this unfortunate little escapade did teach me is, " it is never over until the fat lady sings." What a pity then so many of my fellow Forest supporters seem to have such difficulty in grasping this rather simple concept. The game of football lasts for 90 minutes, and there are no rules in place, which prohibit the scoring of a goal either in the first or the final minute. Now I can sympathise fully with the unhappy supporter who leaves the ground two or three minutes early, when his or her team has played crap and is 4-0 down. What I can't understand, are the 'hordes' of supporters who seem to ritually leave the ground as much as ten minutes before the end, whatever the score-line, and whatever the entertainment value of the game. Moreover, they don't seem to differentiate in any way whatsoever, between a resounding 5-0 victory, courtesy of a vintage performance - or a 4-0 drubbing, during which the players have shown little or no effort and displayed not one ounce of pride. Just where are these individuals going in such a hurry? Have they got important meetings to attend, or planes and trains to catch? I think not. Do these same people buy tickets for the cinema and, just as the film is reaching it's climax, get up and leave? Or, go out to a restaurant and, just as the waiter is about to serve them with dessert, make their excuses and go? I doubt it! So, what is the problem with staying to the end of a game and applauding your team off the pitch? So what if your dinner's in the dog by the time you get home...or your misses won't talk to you for the rest of the evening? Cheering your team on right to the final whistle is far more important you know.

AS Christmas arrived, Forest were in 13th position in the table, with only 21 points from 22 games, and by now, the League Cup was also just a distant memory; we'd made our customary early exit from the competition at the hands of Aston Villa in round two. On Saturday, 23rd December, second-placed Blackpool visited the City Ground, and, if the form-book was anything to go by, the 'Reds' were in for another difficult game. However, a superb display saw them secure an unexpected 4-0 victory, with goals from Neil Martin, Doug Fraser, John Galley and the up-and-coming Duncan McKenzie. As I watched the game from the East Stand terraces, I couldn't have wished for a better 15th birthday present.

In the Forest Review for the game against Carlisle United on Saturday, 20th January, Secretary Ken Smales announced the Club was to run a competition - in conjunction with the Evening Post - for the design of a new Club badge. As the existing one was based on the Nottingham Coat of Arms, Forest didn't hold the copyright. This effectively meant any 'Tom, Dick or Harry' could produce goods bearing the Forest crest, without a penny going into the Club's coffers - a situation which could no longer be tolerated.

The closing date for the competition was 31st March, and they were looking for designs 'symbolic of Nottingham Forest' and which 'bore no likeness to the City Coat of Arms'. A panel made up of representatives from the Evening Post, the College of Art, and the Club, would decide the winning entry. Prizes consisted of £25 for the winner and £5 for the runner-up, and a £25 voucher from T.Bailey Forman for the best entry in an under-18 section.

In all, a total of 855 entries were received, some from as far afield as Australia and Germany. One entrant even submitted no less than 27 different designs - the sad bastard! Of these, 587 were received in the adult section and 268 in the junior section. The winning entry came from a 12-year-old Nottingham schoolboy. The now famous 'Tree' has been in place ever since, and, on the back of Forest's winning exploits in Europe many years later, is known throughout the world.

Call me a 'sentimental old fool' if you like, but I've always preferred the 'Coat of Arms' badge myself, as this perfectly symbolises my allegiance both to the Club and to the City. However, I do accept that the commercial implications to the Club are great, and besides, they continue to produce and market goods bearing the old badge even to this day. This allows supporters like myself to wallow in nostalgia, if we so wish.

However, as the 'Tree' itself is now becoming a little dated, perhaps it's time for another competition, preferably open to professional local artists, or Graphic Designers in and around Nottingham?

FOREST'S FA Cup exploits had again been short-lived. However, their third round exit at the hands of First Division West Brom, hadn't been without it's fair share of drama. Having earned a battling 1-1 draw at the Hawthorns on Saturday, 13th January, an exciting replay three days later had to be brought to an unexpected and abrupt end by the referee after 81 minutes. The City Ground suddenly became enveloped in a thick veil of icy fog which came drifting in rapidly from the banks of the River Trent. With the scores level at 1-1, the 19,168 crowd - Forest's biggest of the season - were just bracing themselves for extra time. However, they left the ground disappointed, with visibility down to just a matter of feet and no chance whatsoever of the game continuing.

The tie was hastily re-arranged for the following Monday, only for the two sides to battle out another draw - this time 0-0. So it was off to neutral Filbert Street for the second replay on Monday, 29th January, when Albion finally settled the tie with a 3-1 victory. There was only a small contingent of Albion fans amongst the predominantly 'red and white' crowd of 13,201.

Forest's League form up to the end of the season was at best, inconsistent. This was epitomised by consecutive 3-0 home victories over Sheffield Wednesday and Second Division Champions-elect Burnley at the end of March - followed by a 3-0 defeat at Orient, a 3-1 defeat at home to Middlesbrough, and Easter-Holiday defeats at both Preston North End and Blackpool. During this particular Bank Holiday weekend, several hundred Forest supporters went on the rampage along Blackpool promenade, enhancing their reputation as 'some of the worst in the country'.

One positive aspect of an otherwise disappointing campaign however, was the emergence of the young and talented Duncan McKenzie - a player of exceptional ability. He would soon develop into one of the most skilful, exciting and popular players ever seen down at the City Ground.

The 'Reds' ended the season in an uninspiring 14th position in the Second Division table - the mediocrity of this campaign leading to a rapid decline in the average League attendance to only 10,016. This included no less than 11 which were below the 10,000-mark, with the highest of the season being the 18,082 who turned up for the visit of Midlands rivals Aston Villa. However, this had been the fifth miserable season on the trot for the Club and it's long-suffering supporters. And, whilst I personally had every intention of sticking with them through thick and thin, it wasn't that difficult to understand why the level of support had diminished so dramatically.

SEASON 1972/73 – STATISTICS

FOOTBALL LEAGUE DIVISION TWO – FIXTURES

Date	Opposition	Venue	Competition	Score	Attendance
Aug 12	Portsmouth	H	League	0-0	13,175
19	Hull City	A	League	0-0	11,189
26	Oxford United	H	League	2-1	9,591
29	Brighton & Hove Albion	H	League	1-0	10,659
Sept 2	Carlisle United	A	League	2-1	7,624
5	Aston Villa	H	LC 2	0-1	17,655
9	Luton Town	H	League	0-1	9,495
16	Queens Park Rangers	A	League	0-3	12,528
19	Cardiff City	H	League	2-1	6,414
23	Aston Villa	H	League	1-1	18,082
25	Millwall	A	League	1-2	9,071
30	Sunderland	A	League	1-4	14,155
Oct 7	Huddersfield Town	H	League	1-1	7,931
14	Bristol City	A	League	1-1	13,861
21	Swindon Town	H	League	2-2	8,683
28	Sheffield Wednesday	A	League	2-1	21,807
Nov 4	Millwall	H	League	3-2	11,165
11	Cardiff City	A	League	1-2	12,765
18	Preston North End	H	League	0-1	10,832
25	Burnley	A	League	0-1	12,095
Dec 2	Orient	H	League	2-1	7,959
9	Middlesbrough	A	League	0-0	10,326
16	Fulham	A	League	1-3	8,255
23	Blackpool	H	League	4-0	10,078
26	Aston Villa	A	League	2-2	37,000
Jan 6	Oxford United	A	League	0-1	9,056
13	West Bromwich Albion	A	FA Cup 3	1-1	15,795
16	West Bromwich Albion	H	FA Cup 3 - Replay	1-1	19,168
	(Abandoned after 81 minutes due to fog)				
20	Carlisle United	H	League	2-1	6,866
22	West Bromwich Albion	H	FA Cup 3 - Replay	0-0	17,069
27	Luton Town	A	League	0-1	10,083
29	West Bromwich Albion (At Filbert St., Leicester)		FA Cup 3 - 2nd Replay	1-3	13,201
Feb 10	Queens Park Rangers	H	League	0-0	11,617
17	Portsmouth	A	League	0-2	11,151
24	Fulham	H	League	2-1	8,810
Mar 3	Huddersfield Town	A	League	1-1	7,473
10	Bristol City	H	League	1-0	8,680
13	Hull City	H	League	1-2	7,711
17	Swindon Town	A	League	0-0	10,066
24	Sheffield Wednesday	H	League	3-0	10,488
31	Burnley	H	League	3-0	12,552
Apr 7	Orient	A	League	0-3	6,373
14	Middlesbrough	H	League	1-3	9,258
21	Preston North End	A	League	1-2	7,701
23	Blackpool	A	League	0-2	8,322
24	Sunderland	H	League	1-0	10,306
28	Brighton & Hove Albion	A	League	2-2	9,709

HOME ATTENDANCES

	AGGREGATE ATTENDANCE	HIGHEST ATTENDANCE	LOWEST ATTENDANCE	AVERAGE ATTENDANCE
League:	210,352	18,082	6,414	10,016
League Cup:	17,655	17,655	17,655	17,655
FA Cup:	36,237	19,168	17,069	18,118
	(Includes abandoned fixture versus West Bromwich Albion)			
All Competitions:	264,244	19,168	6,414	11,010

FINAL LEAGUE TABLE - DIVISION TWO

Position	P	W	D	L	GF	GA	Pts
1. Burnley	42	24	14	4	72	35	62
2. Queens Park Rangers	42	24	13	5	81	37	61
3. Aston Villa	42	18	14	10	51	47	50
4. Middlesbrough	42	17	13	12	46	43	47
5. Bristol City	42	17	12	13	63	51	46
6. Sunderland	42	17	12	13	59	49	46
7. Blackpool	42	18	10	14	56	51	46
8. Oxford United	42	19	7	16	52	43	45
9. Fulham	42	16	12	14	58	49	44
10. Sheffield Wednesday	42	17	10	15	59	55	44
11. Millwall	42	16	10	16	55	47	42
12. Luton Town	42	15	11	16	44	53	41
13. Hull City	42	14	12	16	64	59	40
14. Nottingham Forest	**42**	**14**	**12**	**16**	**47**	**52**	**40**
15. Orient	42	12	12	18	49	53	36
16. Swindon Town	42	10	16	16	46	60	36
17. Portsmouth	42	12	11	19	42	59	35
18. Carlisle United	42	11	12	19	50	52	34
19. Preston North End	42	11	12	19	37	64	34
20. Cardiff City	42	11	11	20	43	58	33
21. Huddersfield Town	42	8	17	17	36	56	33
22. Brighton & Hove Albion	42	8	13	21	46	83	29

AWAY ATTENDANCES

	AGGREGATE ATTENDANCE	HIGHEST ATTENDANCE	LOWEST ATTENDANCE	AVERAGE ATTENDANCE
League:	250,610	37,000	6,373	11,933
FA Cup:	28,996	15,795	13,201	14,498
All Competitions:	279,606	37,000	6,373	12,156

"WE ARE THE BEST TEAM IN THE LAND, THIS NO-ONE CAN DENY"

A **QUIET** mood of optimism enveloped the City Ground at the beginning of what should have been Dave Mackay's first 'full' season in charge at the Club. An impressive run of pre-season results had seen Forest win six out of seven friendlies, including all three matches on their tour of Ireland. And a thumping 4-0 victory over Luton Town at the City Ground on the opening Saturday of the season, only heightened the levels of expectation now growing amongst the fans.

Just three defeats in their first twelve games saw them sitting in eighth position in the Second Division table by the time they drew 0-0 with Hull City at home on Tuesday, 23rd October. With a total of thirteen points accumulated prior to this game, they were five points behind leaders Middlesbrough. And had it not been for some rather indifferent form on their travels to date - which had brought them just four points in seven games - they'd have already been in a more challenging position.

Nationally, Football League attendances had shown a sharp decline during the previous season - a trend that had seen Forest's own City Ground average fall dramatically from 21,433 in season 1971/72 to just 10,016 a year later. Undoubtedly, relegation to the Second Division had accounted for the vast majority of these absent supporters, but the competition football was now facing from the leisure industry as a whole, was also beginning to take it's toll. At the end of season 1972/73, for example, Wolverhampton Wanderers finished in a creditable fifth position in the First Division table - four places higher than the previous season - and at the same time, experienced a drop of over 3,000 in their average League attendance.

However, there were a few encouraging signs Forest's promising form was beginning to woo back some of the missing supporters. They attracted gates of 13,452 for the visit of Sheffield Wednesday on Saturday, 8th September, and 12,958 for the visit of Preston North End two weeks later. Still, they had a long, long way to go before they'd see a return to anything like the levels of support they'd enjoyed in the past.

UNFORTUNATELY, the progress of the Club was about to receive a severe and completely unexpected setback as a direct result of events taking place some 15 miles down the road in the heart of 'sheep-shagging' territory. Old 'Big 'Ead' himself, Brian Clough, together with his sidekick Peter Taylor, had a massive fall out with Derby Chairman, Sam Longson, and walked out on the club. Naturally, this caused an outcry amongst the players and consternation amongst their dozens of supporters. And in an attempt to appease the confused and angry herd beginning to gather in the fields around the Baseball Ground, Mr.Longson decided to make a move for former club captain, Dave Mackay - still a somewhat heroic figure amongst these rather sad and inadequate creatures. And with loyalty not being high on the average football manager's agenda, the rugged Scotsman was off like a shot, leaving the 'Reds' without a manager for the third time in just five years.

When they entertained Aston Villa at home on Saturday, 27th October, Chairman Jim Willmer, made his feelings on the issue known to supporters in the Forest Review:

> *"The affairs of Derby County Football Club are of no concern to this club but it is, to say the least, unfortunate that, as the ultimate result of their recent trials and tribulations, we have become so adversely affected.*
>
> *Dave Mackay came to the City Ground on 6th November, 1972 and left on 25th October, 1973 to become manager of Derby County, with Des Anderson accompanying him in their dual managerial roles.*
>
> *It was the sincere wish of the Committee that he would remain with us until the goal which he was seeking had been netted and we returned to the First Division. However, it was not to be and we are indeed sorry, sad, and disappointed that after such a short period here he is leaving but as everyone must appreciate he could not, even with the best interests of our club at heart, have refused an opportunity in the advancement of his career which the new post offers."*

(Advancement my arse!)

Although Forest lost 2-1 to Villa, under the guidance of caretaker manager, Bill Anderson, they went on to win their next three games. A 1-0 victory at bottom-placed Crystal Palace on Saturday, 3rd November was followed by two successive home victories over Fulham (3-0) and Carlisle United (2-0) over the following weekends. But by the time they played Sunderland at Roker Park on Saturday, 24th November, Allan Brown - the former Luton Town, Torquay United, and Bury manager - had been installed as the new boss. This was in spite of calls from supporters to offer the job to Brian Clough, who'd only recently brought so much success to our sworn enemy down the road. However, having already pledged his future to Brighton & Hove Albion, Cloughie was never really in the frame.

Four draws, two victories and one defeat in Brown's first seven games at the helm - including a 1-0 Boxing Day success over Notts County at Meadow Lane in front of a crowd of 32,130 - meant Forest maintained their top-six status in the table. They'd now held this position since late October, and this gave them a realistic opportunity of mounting a serious promotion challenge during the second half of the season.

The third round of the FA Cup gave them a brief opportunity to concentrate their minds elsewhere, having been drawn at home to Third Division high-flyers Bristol Rovers. Somewhat controversially at the time, the Club announced the tie would be switched to a Sunday afternoon - the first time ever a competitive fixture at the City Ground would be staged on the Sabbath. Inevitably, this prompted a deluge of protests from the 'Sundays are sacred' brigade.

The fact a crowd of 23,456 - some 92.57 per cent higher than average - turned out for this fixture, provided ample proof, that a large percentage of Nottingham's footballing public, did indeed have an appetite for Sunday football. And although they may have sacrificed their traditional 'Sunday roast' for a cold and gristly meat pie, they were served up with a veritable feast of football. It was a thrilling, action-packed, end-to-end game, which eventually ended four-goals-to-three in Forest's favour. Two goals from Neil Martin, another from Sammy Chapman, and a penalty from George Lyall, led to 'loud rejoicing amongst the City Ground flock' and sent the majority of them home in 'joyous mood'.

They were drawn at home again in the fourth round - this time against First Division giants Manchester City. And, not surprisingly - in view of the success against Rovers - this was also pencilled in for Sunday, 27th January. This was a highly attractive tie and Forest were bracing themselves for a massive crowd. And what a fantastic occasion it turned out to be. Of the many hundreds of games I've witnessed during my thirty-odd years as a Forest supporter, there are some incredible encounters which stick out in my mind - not least many of those which took place during the Club's halcyon days of the late-seventies and early-eighties, when they were winning both domestic and European honours by the bucket-load. But this game against City will always remain right up there amongst the very best of them.

An enormous crowd of 41,472 packed into the City Ground to see Forest pit their wits against a side boasting the likes of Mike Summerbee, Colin Bell, Francis Lee, Rodney Marsh, and the legendary Denis Law. But in Duncan McKenzie, the 'Reds' had their very own rising star - arguably the most skilful player ever to pull on the famous 'Garibaldi'. Without question, he is the most gifted player I've ever seen in a Forest jersey. In fact, what Duncan couldn't do with a football, isn't even worth talking about. He was absolutely full of tricks, and despite his slight frame, was strong on the ball, good in the air, and a prolific goal-scorer. In today's game he'd undoubtedly be worth £10 million and be an integral part of any England set-up.

The game against City gave him the perfect stage on which to show off his skills - an opportunity he grasped with both hands - or, to be more precise, both feet. His performance was totally breathtaking and left the large crowd purring with admiration. One by one, the City defenders were left in his wake as he jinked first one way and then the other along the right flank, making his way towards the Bridgford End goal. And by the time he laid the ball back across the face of the goal for Ian Bowyer to sweep in his second and Forest's third, the pitch was littered with dazed and bewildered defenders. You could almost see the rings he'd drawn around them as he left them in his wake. In between the two he laid on for 'Bomber', he scored a spectacular goal of his own - a flying scissor-kick from a perfectly lofted Paul Richardson cross. And with George Lyall adding a fourth, the 'Reds' went on to record a famous 4-1 victory against all the odds. This was the greatest individual performance I've ever witnessed by a Forest player, and one which will stand out forever in the minds of the ecstatic 40,000-plus crowd.

FOLLOWING this epic Cup tie, Forest entertained high-flying Middlesbrough at the City Ground the following Saturday. With 41 points from 26 games played, and having conceded only 15 goals along the way, 'Boro' were the run-away leaders of the Second Division and destined ultimately for the top flight. With Forest in only seventh position in the table at this time, with 29 points from the same number of games, the visitors were expected to take both points. However, Forest had other ideas and, whilst continuing the excellent form they'd displayed in the Cup the previous Sunday, swept 'Boro' aside. They won a one-sided affair by five-goals-to-one, thanks to goals from Neil Martin, Ian Bowyer, John Winfield and George Lyall (2), in front of a more modest crowd of 18,799.

The Cup draw was once again kind to the 'Reds' and they were drawn at home in the fifth round to Second Division Portsmouth. Predictably, this game was also switched to a Sunday. Cup fever was once more beginning to grip the City and another large crowd was expected - especially as there would be a sizeable following from the South Coast. No less than 38,589 supporters packed into the City Ground on 17th February to see this game - an occasion which was marred by severe crowd trouble. Fights broke out before, during and after the game and involved literally hundreds of rampaging supporters. The thousands of visiting 'Pompey' supporters, who'd made the long trip north, had infiltrated various parts of the ground. This led to inevitable clashes on the terraces throughout the game. The impressive sound of the 'Pompey Chimes' rang out over and over again from every side of the ground - well except the Trent End that is!

After the two memorable encounters against Bristol Rovers and Manchester City, this tie proved to be a bit of an anti-climax. However, a 1-0 victory for the 'Reds' - courtesy of a Duncan McKenzie penalty - was all that mattered in the end, and we were in the last eight of the competition for the first time in seven seasons. And, having subsequently been drawn 'ha'way' to First Division Newcastle United, 14,000 travelling supporters were looking forward to a wonderful day out in the North-East on Saturday, 6th March.

It was back to League action for the time being though and a 0-0 draw at Millwall, was followed by a 2-1 home victory over Orient, and another goalless draw against Notts County, also at the City Ground. This 'derby' against the 'Pies' took place on 3rd March and drew another impressive crowd of 29,962. This was the first ever League fixture to take place at the City Ground on a Sunday.

Prior to the game against Orient, Forest Secretary Ken Smales, had opened up a rather unusual debate amongst the fans, when he posed the following question in the Forest Review:

"I wonder what you think to the idea of changing our name to just "Forest" like Arsenal, Everton, Orient etc.? Your views would be appreciated - just think, fans would not be able to sing "We hate Nottingham Forest".

Surprisingly, this outlandish suggestion actually seemed to appeal to a number of Forest supporters - at least if the letters' page of subsequent programmes was anything to go by. However, most of this support was based on the prospect of no longer having to listen to rival fans taunting us with chants of: *"Altogether now...we hate Nottingham Forest"*. Now as much as this song annoys me, I don't believe it reflects any kind of universal hatred of our beloved Club; it's just that the words fit very comfortably into the first line of the song. Hardly reason enough on it's own therefore to abandon a hundred-plus years of history by shortening the Club's name.

One interesting view expressed, was that if we became just 'Forest', we would no longer have to listen to the ill-informed referring constantly to us as 'Notts Forest' - something which infuriates all Forest supporters. Whilst my own personal view is that dropping the word 'Nottingham' from the Club's title would be nothing short of sacrilege, I do have some sympathy with this line of thought. Over the years, as my work has taken me all over the country, I've taken it upon myself at every possible opportunity, to put the record straight on this matter.

Personally, I'm at a loss to understand from where the confusion arises? Nottingham is a city and Nottinghamshire is a county. 'Nottm' is short for 'Nottingham' and 'Notts' is short for 'Nottinghamshire'. 'Nottingham' or 'Nottm Forest' represent the City of Nottingham - their ground being situated in West Bridgford - which is in the County of Nottinghamshire. And 'Notts County' - not 'Nottinghamshire County' - represent the County of Nottinghamshire and play their games at Meadow Lane - which is in the City of Nottingham. As the City of Nottingham is - technically speaking - situated in the County of Nottinghamshire - it could be argued, that Notts County play their home games both in the City and in the County. Now what's confusing about that?

BY the time the big day arrived, FA Cup fever was sweeping through Nottingham and Forest's army of fans was preparing to leave for the 350-mile round trip. Four special trains and a fleet of buses had been laid on to transport the 'Red Army' to the North-East. Although still only 16-years-old at this time, and in my final year at school, I was a frequent traveller to Forest's away games. A small gang of us - all from Chilwell - had become 'regulars' on the bus that travelled to all away matches from outside the Salutation Inn on Maid Marion Way. The main organiser of the 'Bus from the Sal' in those days was a chap called Simmo, and it would always be full of 'Townies'.

They were so-called because they always hung around in Nottingham Town Centre. They could always be found in the main pubs of that era, such as the Fountain, the Milton's Head, the Bodega, the Mint, or the Flying Horse. Although they originated from all areas of the City, they always met up in town and were all ardent Forest supporters. They also considered themselves an 'elite' group of people, rarely mixing with anyone who wasn't part of the click. At all Forest matches, particularly those away from home, they'd remain at a distance from the main body of Forest supporters. Without exception though, they'd always be right there in the middle of any crowd disturbances - no surprise really, as they were usually the main instigators.

Our small gang from Chilwell - which consisted of our Graham, Tom Clough, Swinie, Wags, Mick Coll, and Big Ollie (who actually came from Beeston) - were always hanging about in town. We'd long since been accepted by the 'Townies' and travelled all over the country watching Forest on the 'Bus from the Sal'. Although still a youngster, I was always allowed to tag along with them. Due to Chilwell's close proximity to Derbyshire - at least in the eyes of the 'Townies' - they would constantly refer to us as 'Sheep-shaggers' and taunt us with chants of: *"Chilwell-Chilwell-Derbyshire!...Chilwell-Derbyshire!"* What a bleedin' insult!

Although for most away games, there'd be only one coach from the Sal; on a good day, there were probably as many as two to three hundred 'Townies'. For the big occasions therefore, Simmo would lay on extra coaches, which would often be joined by others from places like Bulwell and Newark. Despite Nottingham being a fairly large City - currently the eleventh largest in England, population wise - everyone seems to know everyone else - or at least know someone who knows someone else. Consequently, most of Forest's travelling supporters of this era - often many thousands of them - would know each other, if not by name, then by sight at least. Some of the names and faces that stick out in my mind from those days and who were regulars on Simmo's coaches are: Eddie Sass, Rud, Spider, Tat, Johnny Harper, Gus, Donny, Porky, Meashy, Poss, Maddo, brothers Andy and Jez Cooke from Newark, Marksy, Denny Hendie, Steve Beardsley, Steve Pettit, Simon, Gary Banks, and many, many more. All of these are now well into their forties, but some are still regulars 'down the match'.

FOR some reason, the 'Chilwell boys' decided to travel by train to this quarter-final tie at Newcastle on Saturday, 9th March, and we departed from Nottingham's Midlands Station on the first of four 'specials' which had been laid on by the Club for this eagerly-awaited game. The wonderful thing about 'football specials' in those days was they always carried a buffet car and, unlike today's 'strictly dry' trains, served you with as much alcohol as you could manage to drink.

Consequently, by the time the train rolled gently into York Station - where it stopped inexplicably for about ten minutes - the majority of it's merry inhabitants were already well on their way to being 'pickled'. As it stood motionless inside the busy station, two to three hundred supporters hung out of it's doors and windows to treat the town's slightly bemused Saturday morning rail travellers to a ten minute rendition of: *"And it's Nottingham Forest; Nottingham Forest FC; We're by far the greatest team; The world has ever seen!"* Take it from me, the acoustics of a railway station are second to none and the sound of hundreds of slightly-

'Forest on tour'

intoxicated youths proudly singing their Forest anthem, made the hairs on the back of my neck stand to attention, as it echoed majestically around the station.

When we finally pulled into Newcastle's Manors Station, we were in extremely high spirits, and as we poured off the train and onto the platform, chants of *"FOREST! FOREST!"* almost lifted the roof off. Predictably, there was a heavy police presence, and after a delay of several minutes, we were marched briskly off in the direction of St.James' Park. We were surrounded by scores of 'old Bill' some on horseback, some with snapping, vicious looking dogs, and shadowed for the whole of the ten minute journey by four police vans filled with reinforcements.

It all seemed a bit over the top to me, but it wasn't too long before the significance of it all became apparent. As we passed by a pub on the left hand side of the road, about two hundred yards from the station, we were suddenly and unexpectedly bombarded with a hail of beer glasses, bottles and missiles, by a hundred-strong mob of Newcastle fans drinking in the street outside. The police moved in swiftly to arrest the most blatant offenders, many of whom seemed to be in their thirties or even forties. And, as if to even things up a little, any Forest fans displaying the slightest signs of retaliation, were also bundled into the back of an ensuing transit van.

As we reached the 'safety' of the ground, it had already dawned on me this day was going to be like no other I'd experienced during my time as a Forest supporter. Although we'd been allocated several thousand seats in the upper tier of the East Stand, the main bulk of our supporters - eight thousand or so - were standing on the wide-open spaces of the Gallowgate End. This, I would estimate, had a capacity of around fifteen thousand. As there was no official segregation, thousands of rival fans were effectively intermingled with one another - a recipe for disaster if ever I'd seen one. Not surprisingly, this whole end of the ground was one swaying mass of brawling, snarling supporters. I can only imagine it must have resembled a giant tin of wriggling maggots to those looking on from the opposite end of the stadium.

As they took to the field, the two teams received a tumultuous reception from the massive 52,551 crowd. The sound of: *"Ha'way-the-lads"* rang out impressively from all sides of the ground. The 14,000-strong army from Nottingham was submerged within a giant sea of black and white scarves, flags and tam-o'-shanters. However, after only ninety seconds of the game had elapsed, the only sound which could be heard around St.James' Park, was that of the jubilant 'Red Army' celebrating Ian Bowyer's opening goal for the 'Reds' - a header from a lofted through ball by Martin O'Neill. This was the signal for another spontaneous outbreak of violence on the part of the uncontrollable Geordies, as Forest supporters were once again attacked from every angle. The scenes were almost reminiscent of 'Custer's Last Stand'!

An equalising goal from United right-back David Craig on 26 minutes brought a temporary respite for Forest's beleaguered supporters. But the onslaught resumed two minutes before half-time when Liam O'Kane of all people, scored his first ever goal for the 'Reds', giving them a deserved 2-1 lead at the interval. When George Lyall increased the score to 3-1 in the second half from the penalty spot - after Duncan McKenzie had been fouled by Bobby Moncour - Forest's lead looked an unassailable one. What's more, Newcastle had also been reduced to ten men following Pat Howard's dismissal for dissent over the penalty award.

Once again, this was the signal for Newcastle's mindless fans to resort to violence. Two minutes later, they began to spill onto the pitch in their hundreds from the Leazes End of the ground, led by a bald-headed, 18 stone, 56-year-old bloke. *It's incredible to think if he's still alive today - although he was such a lard-bucket, I very much doubt it - at around 80 years-of-age, he'd surely be the oldest football hooligan in Britain, if not the world!*

As the hordes of 'fans' swept across the pitch towards the Gallowgate End - with one individual managing to punch Forest's Dave Serella in the face along the way - referee,

Gordon Kew, had little option but to lead both teams from the pitch. As Forest's embattled supporters stood waiting for the on-rushing Geordies to reach them, they suddenly had a change of heart and stopped ten or fifteen yards short of their destination. They soon began to drift slowly back towards the Leazes End. Perhaps this was due to the timely intervention of the police - many with dogs - who swarmed across the pitch in front of them determined to bring them to a halt. Or, maybe 'old lard-bucket' himself simply ran out of steam once he'd got past the half-way line, causing mass confusion amongst the ranks of these rampaging Geordie half-wits. Happily, the Tyneside Police eventually rounded up their rather geriatric ringleader after the game and his face was plastered on the front page of every tabloid newspaper the following day.

After a delay of some ten minutes, the teams took to the field once again and play resumed. Forest's shaken and rattled players managed to hold out for only a matter of minutes though, against the revitalised ten-man Geordies who were roared on by the passionate and volatile crowd. Once Terry McDermott had pulled a goal back from the penalty spot, following goalkeeper Jim Barron's nervous push on Malcolm Macdonald, suddenly the writing really was on the wall for the 'Reds'. John Tudor equalised minutes later with a diving header, opening the door for Bobby Moncour to score the 'winning' goal two minutes from time. This sent the crowd into a state of delirium.

And is if this wasn't bad enough, it was also pretty obvious to me the plight of Forest's travelling supporters wasn't yet over. All along the top of the wall at the back of the Gallowgate End, and down the stairways leading out of the ground, fans were perched like vultures waiting to pounce on their prey once the final whistle sounded. Furthermore, in the streets outside, clearly visible from the back of the open terracing, hundreds of presumably ticket-less youths had been massing since just after kick off. It was abundantly clear they had only one thing on their minds: violence! Consequently, the journey back to the station was a horrendous one, with running battles being fought out between the two sets of fans all along the way. Later, the mood amongst Forest's battered and bruised supporters standing around on the station waiting for the trains home, was one of shock, anger and utter disbelief at what had taken place.

Surely the FA wouldn't allow Newcastle to get away with this outrage? At the very least they'd be thrown out of the competition - possibly even heavily fined - and made to play their next half a dozen home matches behind closed doors? Forest's inevitable delegation to FA Headquarters in Lancaster Gate on Monday would return home with a sensible and positive decision from Ted Croker, Secretary of the Football Association, surely?...But not a bit of it - Newcastle's punishment: a replay - not at the City Ground, Nottingham - but at Goodison Park, Everton on Monday week. Absolutely incredible! I have seen some injustices during my time as a Forest supporter, but this Cup tie - riddled with controversy from start to finish - definitely takes the biscuit.

And despite vehement protests from both the Club and the fans, the FA wouldn't be swayed. Consequently, we had to resign ourselves to a further trip north, this time to the City of Liverpool. Once again we elected to go by train, and having skived the day off school, I made my way down to the station for my mid-afternoon rendezvous with the rest of the lads. Having bought our tickets, we took up our places in the already substantial queue of supporters snaking it's way around the foyer and out onto Queens Road. As we stood patiently waiting for the gates to open - thus causing the inevitable stampede - we compared notes with one another about our experiences at St.James' Park nine days earlier. And we were unanimous about one thing: we all hated the CHEATING GEORDIE BASTARDS!

The journey to Liverpool was another long and boozy affair. The most amusing part of the trip was when Wags pissed into John Loughton's half-empty can of beer whilst he'd gone for a 'Jimmy' himself. When he returned several minutes later, we all waited with baited breath for him to take a swig out of his can. Every time he was about to raise it to his lips, he would think of something else to say and put it back down on the floor of the carriage. The suspense was killing us, as we sat there nudging each other and sniggering like naughty little schoolboys. When he finally put it to his lips, he went for it big time and we all collapsed in a heap of laughter as he coughed, spluttered and sprayed an enormous mouthful of it out all over the carriage, drowning every one of us.

When we disembarked at Liverpool's Lime Street Station and boarded the fleet of double-decker buses waiting to take us to the ground, we were already decidedly the worse for wear. We'd been allocated the Gwladys Street End of the ground, with the Geordies occupying the Park End opposite. There were slightly more of them amongst the crowd of 40,681, although the numbers were certainly more even than those which we'd encountered at St.James' Park.

And we certainly weren't out-sung by the Geordies - no matter how passionate they are. As the two teams battled out an extremely tense and dour 0-0 draw, the sound of: *"Aye-Oh, Aye-Oh, We are the Trent End Boys; Aye-Oh, Aye-Oh, We are the Trent End boys; We are the best team in the land, This no-one can deny; We will follow the For-est!"* rang out from the 'red and white' end of Goodison. The Geordies responded with loud choruses of '*the Bladen Races*' and the sound of '*Ha'way-the-lads*' echoed round and round the stadium.

It was a long and tiring journey back home to Nottingham afterwards. And prior to leaving Liverpool, the local teenage population of the City said goodbye to us in their own inimitable way - by bombarding our buses with bricks, bottles and stones - hurled from every dimly-lit side-street and alleyway between Goodison and Lime Street Station.

The FA's reward for Forest and their long-suffering fans for this hard-earned draw was - would you believe - another replay at Goodison Park four days later. "Is there no justice in this world, or what?" This was the question being asked all over Nottingham. The cheating Geordie bastards meanwhile were laughing all the way to the semi-finals. Unable to skive another day off school, or to scrape together enough money to make a second journey to Goodison, I had to settle instead for the highlights on television later that evening.

Not surprisingly, we eventually lost this third and final tussle. A goal from 'Supermac' himself, who burst through the middle of the Forest defence to slam the ball home, gave Newcastle a 1-0 victory in front of a crowd of 31,373. But even this encounter was shrouded in controversy. Ian Bowyer had a perfectly executed twenty-yard free kick disallowed for 'ungentlemenly conduct'. And the reason? Well, team-mate Paul Richardson, had had the 'audacity' to run over the ball before 'Bomber' launched it firmly into the back of the net.

Although the cheating Geordies went on to reach the Final - courtesy of a semi-final victory over Burnley at Hillsborough - their opponents at Wembley were none other than the mighty Liverpool. And, as the saying goes: ''He who laughs last, laughs loudest.'' And I could swear the whole of Nottingham reverberated to the sound of laughter on Cup Final Day, as Kevin Keegan and his boys humiliated the second-rate Geordies, winning 3-0 in one of the most one-sided Cup Finals I've ever seen. Thanks a million Liverpool - we owe you one for that!

INEVITABLY, Forest's season petered out somewhat after this FA Cup fiasco in the North-East. They finished the campaign in seventh position in the Second Division table with 45 points from 42 games. They were however, only five points short of a promotion position. The season had certainly been a memorable one, and one which had again seen some large attendances at the City Ground. The average in the League was 14,415 - some 43.91 per cent up on the previous season. And, bolstered by the substantial FA Cup attendances, the average overall was a healthy 16,619. "Were the good times about to return to the City Ground ?" I wondered.

FOOTBALL LEAGUE DIVISION TWO – FIXTURES

Date	Opposition	Venue	Competition	Score	Attendance
Aug 25	**Luton Town**	**H**	**League**	**4-0**	**10,792**
Sept 1	Oxford United	A	League	0-1	7,861
8	**Sheffield Wednesday**	**H**	**League**	**2-1**	**13,452**
11	Hull City	A	League	0-0	8,134
15	West Bromwich Albion	A	League	3-3	14,779
18	**Swindon Town**	**H**	**League**	**2-0**	**11,031**
22	**Preston North End**	**H**	**League**	**1-1**	**12,958**
29	Bolton Wanderers	A	League	0-1	15,388
Oct 2	Swindon Town	A	League	0-0	6,353
6	**Millwall**	**H**	**League**	**3-0**	**11,387**
10	Millwall	A	LC 2	0-0	8,763
13	Orient	A	League	1-3	8,346
16	**Millwall**	**H**	**LC 2 - Replay**	**1-3**	**9,241**
20	Blackpool	A	League	2-2	8,101
23	**Hull City**	**H**	**League**	**0-0**	**10,392**
27	**Aston Villa**	**H**	**League**	**1-2**	**17,718**
Nov 3	Crystal Palace	A	League	1-0	22,075
10	**Fulham**	**H**	**League**	**3-0**	**10,530**
17	**Carlisle United**	**H**	**League**	**2-0**	**11,153**
24	Sunderland	A	League	0-0	22,252
Dec 8	Cardiff City	A	League	1-1	10,312
15	Middlesbrough	A	League	0-1	16,764
22	**Bolton Wanderers**	**H**	**League**	**3-2**	**9,498**
26	Notts County	A	League	1-0	32,130
29	Sheffield Wednesday	A	League	1-1	16,210
Jan 1	**Oxford United**	**H**	**League**	**1-1**	**15,079**
6	**Bristol Rovers**	**H**	**FA Cup 3**	**4-3**	**23,456**
12	**West Bromwich Albion**	**H**	**League**	**1-4**	**15,301**
19	Luton Town	A	League	2-2	11,888
27	**Manchester City**	**H**	**FA Cup 4**	**4-1**	**41,472**
Feb 2	**Middlesbrough**	**H**	**League**	**5-1**	**18,799**
10	Preston North End	A	League	1-2	13,486
17	**Portsmouth**	**H**	**FA Cup 5**	**1-0**	**38,589**
23	Millwall	A	League	0-0	8,833
26	**Orient**	**H**	**League**	**2-1**	**16,632**
Mar 3	**Notts County**	**H**	**League**	**0-0**	**29,962**
6	Newcastle United	A	FA Cup 6	3-4	52,551
	(Pitch invaded - result declared void)				
16	**Blackpool**	**H**	**League**	**2-0**	**15,724**
18	Newcastle United (Played at Goodison Park)		FA Cup 6	0-0	40,681
21	Newcastle United (Played at Goodison Park)		FA Cup 6 - Replay	0-1	31,373
23	Fulham	A	League	0-2	8,884
26	**Portsmouth**	**H**	**League**	**2-0**	**14,040**
30	**Crystal Palace**	**H**	**League**	**1-2**	**16,340**
Apr 6	**Sunderland**	**H**	**League**	**2-2**	**18,044**
12	Bristol City	A	League	0-1	13,125
13	Carlisle United	A	League	1-2	9,258
16	**Bristol City**	**H**	**League**	**1-1**	**12,756**
20	**Cardiff City**	**H**	**League**	**2-1**	**11,138**
24	Aston Villa	A	League	1-3	12,439
27	Portsmouth	A	League	2-0	11,765

HOME ATTENDANCES

	AGGREGATE ATTENDANCE	HIGHEST ATTENDANCE	LOWEST ATTENDANCE	AVERAGE ATTENDANCE
League:	302,726	29,962	9,498	14,415
League Cup:	9,241	9,241	9,241	9,241
FA Cup:	103,517	41,472	23,456	34,505
All Competitions:	415,484	41,472	9,241	16,619

FINAL LEAGUE TABLE - DIVISION TWO

Position	P	W	D	L	GF	GA	Pts
1. Middlesbrough	42	27	11	4	77	30	65
2. Luton Town	42	19	12	11	64	51	50
3. Carlisle United	42	20	9	13	61	48	49
4. Orient	42	15	18	9	55	42	48
5. Blackpool	42	17	13	12	57	40	47
6. Sunderland	42	19	9	14	58	44	47
7. Nottingham Forest	**42**	**15**	**15**	**12**	**57**	**43**	**45**
8. West Bromwich Albion	42	14	16	12	48	45	44
9. Hull City	42	13	17	12	46	47	43
10. Notts County	42	15	13	14	55	60	43
11. Bolton Wanderers	42	15	12	15	44	40	42
12. Millwall	42	14	14	14	51	51	42
13. Fulham	42	16	10	16	39	43	42
14. Aston Villa	42	13	15	14	48	45	41
15. Portsmouth	42	14	12	16	45	62	40
16. Bristol City	42	14	10	18	47	54	38
17. Cardiff City	42	10	16	16	49	62	36
18. Oxford United	42	10	16	16	35	46	36
19. Sheffield Wednesday	42	12	11	19	51	63	35
20. Crystal Palace	42	11	12	19	43	56	34
21. Preston North End	42	9	14	19	40	62	31 *
22. Swindon Town	42	7	11	24	36	72	25

* One point deducted for fielding an ineligible player

AWAY ATTENDANCES

	AGGREGATE ATTENDANCE	HIGHEST ATTENDANCE	LOWEST ATTENDANCE	AVERAGE ATTENDANCE
League:	278,383	32,130	6,353	13,256
League Cup:	8,763	8,763	8,763	8,763
FA Cup:	124,605	52,551	31,373	41,535
All Competitions:	411,751	52,551	6,353	16,470

"WE'RE ON THE MARCH WITH CLOUGHIE'S ARMY"

THE BIGGEST disappointment of the close season, was Duncan McKenzie's departure from the City Ground, following interest from a host of First Division clubs, including Derby County, Tottenham Hotspur, Birmingham City and Leeds United. After intense speculation in and around Nottingham, the Forest idol finally signed for Leeds on 6th August, in a deal worth £240,000. He became Brian Clough's first major signing for the Elland Road outfit - although Cloughie's own career at the club would last only forty-four days.

McKenzie's departure from Nottingham was a bitter blow for Forest supporters as they worshiped the ground he walked on. And despite the Club's best efforts to keep him, his leaving was an indication of just how low the fortunes of Nottingham Forest FC had now sunk. He was ambitious, and it seems, desperate to play in the top flight - and after all, who could blame him really? His sublime talents were wasted in the Second Division of the Football League. If only he'd known though, what the future had in store for Forest; I'm sure he'd have stayed put at the City Ground, and goodness only knows what he may have gone on to achieve in the game?

The 'Reds' began their season with an uninspiring 0-0 draw at home to Bristol City on Saturday, 17th August, in front of a crowd of 11,339. This was followed by a 3-0 defeat at Millwall the following Monday evening and a 2-0 defeat at Portsmouth the following Saturday. Not a very promising start to their 'promotion' campaign, to say the least. This was followed by a 2-1 win over Millwall at home on Tuesday, 27th August - in front of just 7,957 people - a 2-1 defeat at home to Oxford United the following Saturday, and a creditable 2-2 draw against Manchester United on Saturday, 7th September, in front of an Old Trafford crowd of 40,671 (yes Manchester United in the Second Division - how about that!).

The hooligan element amongst Forest's supporters were given an early opportunity to exact some revenge on their despised Geordie 'enemies' when the 'Reds' were drawn at home to Newcastle in the second round of the League Cup. However, possibly sensing they'd be on a hiding to nothing, the United fans stayed at home in droves on the night of Tuesday, 10th September, when the two teams met. Not surprisingly, there was a larger than usual turnout of Forest 'thugs' amongst the surprisingly low crowd of only 14,183 who witnessed this keenly-contested 1-1 draw.

Prior to the 3-0 defeat suffered by the 'Reds' in the replay at St.James' Park two weeks later, they managed to notch up their first away win of the season on Saturday, 21st September, when they beat Sheffield Wednesday 3-2 in a League game at Hillsborough. And aside from it being the first victory on their travels, this fixture is also memorable to me for three other reasons. Firstly, a very young Viv Anderson made his senior debut for the Club; secondly, the large travelling support from Nottingham tried to take Wednesday's 'Kop End' and were involved in running battles all over the terraces throughout the afternoon; and thirdly, about thirty-five of us from Chilwell travelled up to Sheffield in the back of a furniture van driven by Wags!

CHAPTER 9

Forest's form up to Christmas was such that, by the time they travelled to Hull City on Boxing Day, they were languishing in a mid-table position. This was unacceptable to an ambitious Club like Forest, and despite a 3-1 victory over the 'Tigers' - thanks to two goals from Neil Martin and another from recent signing Barry Butlin - there was a certain amount of unrest amongst supporters, who were beginning to fear a long period of stagnation on Trentside.

The straw that broke the camel's back, was the humiliating home defeat by neighbours Notts County the following Saturday. Goals from Les Bradd and Stevie Carter gave them a 2-0 victory in front of a disappointing 'derby' crowd of only 25,013. After a Committee meeting at the City Ground on 2nd January 1975, manager Alan Brown was given his marching orders. Inevitably, the supporters immediately clamoured for the appointment of Brian Clough - still out of work following his controversial sacking from Leeds four months earlier.

When the 'Reds' entertained First Division Tottenham Hotspur in the fourth round of the FA Cup at the City Ground on Saturday, 4th January, the 'we want Clough' campaign was really beginning to gather momentum. A crowd of 23,355 saw them come from behind to force a 1-1 draw, thanks to an equaliser from centre-half David Jones. Unbeknown to the Forest faithful, the Committee had already invited Clough along to the ground for an interview - although knowing Cloughie, I would imagine it was he who actually interviewed them! It's history now of course that the great man agreed to join the Club and he commenced duties on 6th January 1975 - a historic day for NFFC. It later transpired that Committee man Stuart Dryden had been the driving force behind this appointment.

He made an immediate impact on the team as well, as they secured an unexpected 1-0 victory over Spurs in the fourth round replay at White Hart Lane just two days later. Neil Martin scored the vital goal, but  inevitably it was Cloughie himself who stole all the headlines. This was followed by a 1-0 victory at Fulham's Craven Cottage the following Saturday. The positive response from the Nottingham public to his appointment was reflected in the 17,582 crowd that turned up at the City Ground to witness the 2-2 draw against Orient - his first home game in charge. This contrasted sharply with the season's average to date of just 11,633. What's more, after the misery of the previous six seasons down on Trentside, Cloughie's programme notes prior to this game, were like a breath of fresh air:

"When I was first asked to write this article my initial reaction was to say "No" because a football manager's job is not about writing notes for a match programme.

But it is the first opportunity I have had to introduce myself to you so here I am for the first - and last - time this season.

I know from the reaction there has already been to my arrival at the City Ground that something special is expected of me. But if you want wild promises of First Division football, big signings, and glamour in the near future...forget it!

I'm not making predictions outside saying that I will be trying my utmost to put the big and beautiful city of Nottingham back on the football map. The club has gone places in the past but so much has gone wrong, too many bad decisions have been made and not enough work put in.

One of the greatest tragedies to my mind is the way quality players have been allowed to leave the club over the last five or six years.

None of that would have happened had I been here unless there was a clear indication of the player not having his heart in the club.

It does not need a ready reckoner to assess that close on £1,000,000 worth of talent has left Forest for one reason or another.

There is no purpose at all in reflecting what might have been however, but take it from me - the transfer door is now firmly bolted as far as class players are concerned.

Of course, I was responsible for taking the last pearl from Forest's oyster when I signed Duncan McKenzie for Leeds. He is a fine player and one that I would give a lot to have with me now. I would also have loved to have had the job of sorting out the problems he obviously had here.

Nobody knows why he made his stand against Forest better than me. He must have been frustrated with what was happening and I can imagine his feelings were similar to yours. You had run out of patience because of what had gone wrong in the past and run out of hope for the future.

I will be trying to give you something to look forward to but there is no cash at the bank to buy players so hard work is the priority.

The first responsibility to improve things is mine but players must respond to me and show they are willing to work, listen, and learn.

There will be no pressure on them to win because results are not their worry. I want them to apply themselves to their profession and that happens to be football.

The players and I have had a successful start together at Tottenham and Fulham and not, in my wildest dreams, did I expect to kick-off with two wins. It was great to meet up with Bobby Moore at Craven Cottage last week. I still have tremendous admiration for him and was sorry he was not able to join me at Derby.

Today we are attempting to make it three wins in a row against Orient - a team who showed they are not short of ability in the Cup-ties with Derby. I understand they are the unluckiest team to be knocked out of the Cup for many a year.

So it will be far from easy for us because George Petchey has worked wonders at Orient. He has not bought any £100,000 players but they will be a tough side to beat.

You, the supporters, can help by encouraging the side. But as I have said in the local paper, I have no time for football "yobs" who come along to cause bother.

After Manchester United, Forest's hot-heads have one of the worst reputations in football and I aim to end that. My message is simply: "Get lost!"

To the well-behaved majority, I hope we have a successful time together and it is my intention to get to know you a lot better over the coming months.

I am not a manager who sits in his ivory tower all day long. I am a "half a beer and fish and chips" man.

I know I have got the name as soccer's "big mouth" but, deep down, I am an ordinary bloke doing a job of work!"

After their draw with Orient, they secured a 0-0 draw with Fulham, again at Craven Cottage, in the fourth round of the FA Cup. This was followed by a 2-0 defeat in the League at Oldham Athletic - their first under his leadership - so we quickly realised he was human after all. An impressive crowd of 25,361 turned up at the City Ground on Monday, 3rd February, for the replay with Fulham. The Londoners included both Alan Mullery and the legendary Bobby Moore in their line-up. And by this time, the Trent-Enders had already amended some of their favourite old anthems to celebrate Cloughie's arrival at the Club. This one in particular, echoed across Trentside right throughout the game:

> *We're on the march wi' Cloughie's ar-my,*
> *We're all goin' to Wem-ber-ley,*
> *An' we'll really shake 'em up,*
> *When we win the FA Cup,*
> *Cos Forest are the greatest football team!*

Unfortunately, this rather bold prediction on the part of the Trent-Enders turned out to be a little premature. A 1-1 draw with Fulham in this first replay was followed by an identical result back in West London in the second two days later. Consequently, it was back to the City Ground again for a third go at settling the tie on Monday, 10th February. But it was Fulham who finally progressed through to the fifth round with a 2-1 victory in front of a crowd of 23,240. This had been Forest's sixth game during a frantic period of only thirteen days. However, despite their exit from the Cup, the impressive attendances of late had put some much-needed money in the kitty, most of which would be allocated to the manager to spend in the transfer market.

Although upon his arrival he'd promised to end the recent exodus of quality players from the City Ground, he may have been unaware initially there were already players of great potential at the Club. Viv Anderson, Martin O'Neill, Ian Bowyer, John Robertson and Tony Woodcock, were all members of the squad at the time of his appointment. How many of these would have ever gone on to fulfil their true potential though without Clough's considerable influence, is open to debate.

Having completed the double signing of John McGovern and John O'Hare from Leeds United for a joint fee of £60,000, the nucleus of a promotion winning team was already in place. Significantly, he'd also secured the services of 59-year-old coach Jimmy Gordon who, like McGovern and O'Hare, had worked alongside him at Derby and Leeds. He'd recently been working as a store-man at Rolls Royce in Derby.

Forest's form for the remainder of the season was not that impressive. After their initial flurry under Clough, they went on to win only two more games in the League out of a total of sixteen. Of the six matches they lost during this period, one was a 1-0 defeat at home to Manchester United. Following instructions from Football League Headquarters, the United followers were allocated the Trent End for this game. This was the only enclosed section of the ground in which to accommodate these notoriously badly behaved supporters, who'd been marauding their way across the Second Division grounds of England in their thousands all season. This disgraceful behaviour was no doubt their way of dealing with the club's relegation from the First Division the previous season - a situation they were simply not prepared to accept. After all, they do have a divine right to be in the top flight...don't they?

"Thank you very much for the Trent End - Forest; Thank you very much; Thank you very, very, very much!" they sang throughout the game. The disgruntled Trent Enders had been banished to the East Stand en-masse. However, with the real possibility of crowd trouble, both inside and outside the stadium, many supporters had boycotted the game. Consequently, a disappointing crowd of only 21,893 witnessed United secure both points in a 1-0 victory on their march straight back to the First Division.

FOREST ended the season with an average attendance in the League of exactly 13,000. Their biggest was the 25,013 who witnessed the 2-0 defeat against Notts County, with the lowest being the 7,957 who turned out for the game against Millwall. Overall, however, their brief run in the FA Cup had boosted the average in all competitions to a slightly more respectable 14,365. However, in contrast to recent seasons, with Brian Clough now at the helm, we supporters at last had reason to feel optimistic about the long-term future of our much-loved Club.

SEASON 1974/75 – STATISTICS

FOOTBALL LEAGUE DIVISION TWO – FIXTURES

Date	Opposition	Venue	Competition	Score	Attendance
Aug 17	**Bristol City**	H	League	0-0	11,339
19	Millwall	A	League	0-3	7,533
24	Portsmouth	A	League	0-2	11,349
27	**Millwall**	H	**League**	**2-1**	**7,957**
31	**Oxford United**	H	**League**	**1-2**	**9,257**
Sept 7	Manchester United	A	League	2-2	40,671
10	**Newcastle United**	H	**LC 2**	**1-1**	**14,183**
14	**Hull City**	H	**League**	**4-0**	**9,437**
17	**Portsmouth**	H	**League**	**1-2**	**9,534**
21	Sheffield Wednesday	A	League	3-2	15,449
25	Newcastle United	A	LC 2 - Replay	0-3	26,228
28	**Sunderland**	H	**League**	**1-1**	**14,885**
Oct 2	Aston Villa	A	League	0-3	20,357
5	Southampton	A	League	1-0	16,042
12	**Norwich City**	H	**League**	**1-3**	**13,613**
19	West Bromwich Albion	A	League	1-0	13,868
26	**Bristol Rovers**	H	**League**	**1-0**	**11,495**
Nov 2	Bolton Wanderers	A	League	0-2	12,711
9	**Oldham Athletic**	H	**League**	**1-0**	**10,127**
16	Cardiff City	A	League	1-2	9,279
23	**York City**	H	**League**	**2-1**	**10,047**
30	Orient	A	League	1-1	5,217
Dec 7	**Fulham**	H	**League**	**1-1**	**10,057**
14	Bristol City	A	League	0-1	10,006
21	**Blackpool**	H	**League**	**0-0**	**8,480**
26	Hull City	A	League	3-1	12,278
28	**Notts County**	H	**League**	**0-2**	**25,013**
Jan 4	**Tottenham Hotspur**	H	**FA Cup 3**	**1-1**	**23,355**
8	Tottenham Hotspur	A	FA Cup 3 - Replay	1-0	27,996
11	Fulham	A	League	1-0	9,159
18	**Orient**	H	**League**	**2-2**	**17,582**
28	Fulham	A	FA Cup 4	0-0	14,846
Feb 1	Oldham Athletic	A	League	0-2	10,736
3	**Fulham**	H	**FA Cup 4 - Replay**	**1-1**	**25,361**
5	Fulham	A	FA Cup 4 - 2nd Replay	1-1	11,920
8	**Bolton Wanderers**	H	**League**	**2-3**	**11,922**
10	**Fulham**	H	**FA Cup 4 - 3rd Replay**	**1-2**	**23,240**
14	York City	A	League	1-1	7,666
22	**Cardiff City**	H	**League**	**0-0**	**12,806**
28	Oxford United	A	League	1-1	7,602
Mar 8	**Aston Villa**	H	**League**	**2-3**	**20,205**
15	Sunderland	A	League	0-0	30,812
22	**Manchester United**	H	**League**	**0-1**	**21,893**
25	Notts County	A	League	2-2	20,303
29	Blackpool	A	League	0-0	11,640
Apr 1	**Sheffield Wednesday**	H	**League**	**1-0**	**14,077**
5	Bristol Rovers	A	League	2-4	9,648
12	**Southampton**	H	**League**	**0-0**	**11,554**
19	Norwich City	A	League	0-3	24,302
26	**West Bromwich Albion**	H	**League**	**2-1**	**11,721**

HOME ATTENDANCES

	AGGREGATE ATTENDANCE	HIGHEST ATTENDANCE	LOWEST ATTENDANCE	AVERAGE ATTENDANCE
League:	273,001	25,013	7,957	13,000
League Cup:	14,183	14,183	14,183	14,183
FA Cup:	71,956	25,361	23,240	23,985
All Competitions:	359,140	25,361	7,957	14,365

FINAL LEAGUE TABLE - DIVISION TWO

Position	P	W	D	L	GF	GA	Pts
1. Manchester United	42	26	9	7	66	30	61
2. Aston Villa	42	25	8	9	69	32	58
3. Norwich City	42	20	13	9	58	37	53
4. Sunderland	42	19	13	10	65	35	51
5. Bristol City	42	21	8	13	47	33	50
6. West Bromwich Albion	42	18	9	15	54	42	45
7. Blackpool	42	14	17	11	38	33	45
8. Hull City	42	15	14	13	40	53	44
9. Fulham	42	13	16	13	44	39	42
10. Bolton Wanderers	42	15	12	15	45	41	42
11. Oxford United	42	15	12	15	41	51	42
12. Orient	42	11	20	11	28	39	42
13. Southampton	42	15	11	16	53	54	41
14. Notts County	42	12	16	14	49	59	40
15. York City	42	14	10	18	51	55	38
16. Nottingham Forest	**42**	**12**	**14**	**16**	**43**	**55**	**38**
17. Portsmouth	42	12	13	17	44	54	37
18. Oldham Athletic	42	10	15	17	40	48	35
19. Bristol Rovers	42	12	11	19	42	64	35
20. Millwall	42	10	12	20	44	56	32
21. Cardiff City	42	9	14	19	36	62	32
22. Sheffield Wednesday	42	5	11	26	29	64	21

AWAY ATTENDANCES

	AGGREGATE ATTENDANCE	HIGHEST ATTENDANCE	LOWEST ATTENDANCE	AVERAGE ATTENDANCE
League:	306,628	40,671	5,217	14,601
League Cup:	26,228	26,228	26,228	26,228
FA Cup:	54,762	27,996	11,920	18,254
All Competitions:	387,618	40,671	5,217	15,504

"WE ARE THE NUTTERS, THE NUTTERS FROM NOTTS"

DURING THE close season, Forest had signed the experienced left-back, Frank Clark, from his hometown club Newcastle United, after they'd handed him a free transfer. Another piece of the 'Clough jigsaw' was now therefore in place. Clark, who carried with him the dubious distinction of never having scored a League goal during his long career (over 400 games for the 'Magpies'), made his League debut in the opening match of the season against Plymouth Argyle at the City Ground on Saturday, 16th August. A goal by John O'Hare and an own goal from Argyle's Mickey Horsewill gave Forest a 2-0 victory in front of a crowd of 13,083.

Prior to this game, the City Ground had once again witnessed some violent crowd scenes as Forest and Plymouth fans fought running battles on the Bridgford End terraces. Several hundred Plymouth fans - their faces daubed with green and white paint - were ambushed by hordes of rampaging Forest supporters, who came at them from all directions. This prompted fans in the Trent End enclosure to come spilling onto the pitch in an attempt to join in the affray. The Plymouth fans were eventually led away to safety by the police, many being escorted away from the ground several minutes before the game itself had even kicked off.

Forest's unwanted and infamous hooligan element was now beginning to seriously test the patience of both Brian Clough and members of the Committee. Secretary Ken Smales was once again scathing of them in the Forest Review prior to the game against Notts County on Saturday, 30th August:

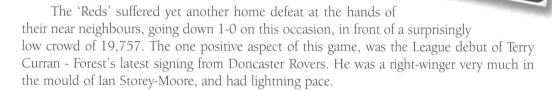

"The disgraceful scenes on our terraces at the Plymouth game have already been amply described in the press and the forthright comments of Brian Clough on the subject merely underline the thoughts of us at the City Ground.

Whatever the idiots who came onto the running track at the Trent End were thinking about I do not know. What were they trying to achieve? If they cannot behave themselves they should just stay away. We do not need their presence at the City Ground.

It's a brave man who will stand up to a crowd of hooligans but we all hope that the time will come when the message gets to the ruffians that they are not wanted and their antics do not help the team or the club in any way. It was obvious from the applause that Brian Clough received from the crowd . that everyone wants to see the end of this tiresome social phenomenon now prevalent at almost every ground in the country."

The 'Reds' suffered yet another home defeat at the hands of their near neighbours, going down 1-0 on this occasion, in front of a surprisingly low crowd of 19,757. The one positive aspect of this game, was the League debut of Terry Curran - Forest's latest signing from Doncaster Rovers. He was a right-winger very much in the mould of Ian Storey-Moore, and had lightning pace.

DURING the month of September, Forest's form in the League was atrocious. A 0-0 draw away to Chelsea on Saturday, 6th September, was followed by a 2-1 defeat at home to Hull City the following Saturday. Then, a 1-0 victory at Oxford United a week later, was followed by 2-1 defeats at home to both Charlton Athletic on Wednesday, 24th September, and Bolton Wanderers on Saturday, 27th September. They'd now lost their last four home games and registered just two wins in a total of eight games. They had however, progressed through to the third round of the League Cup, having achieved a 7-2 aggregate victory over Plymouth Argyle in the second round. Their opponents in the next round were First Division Manchester City, but unfortunately they went down 2-1 at Maine Road on Wednesday, 8th October, in front of a crowd of 26,536.

By the time they entertained West Bromwich Albion at the City Ground on Boxing Day, their form had improved somewhat and they'd crept up to thirteenth position in the table with a total of 21 points from 22 games. At this stage, they'd won 7, drawn 7, and lost 8, scoring 23 goals and conceding only 20 along the way. They lost this encounter with the 'Baggies' 2-0 in front of a crowd of 19,393.

In the third round of the FA Cup, they'd been drawn at home to Third Division Peterborough United, with the tie scheduled for Saturday, 3rd January 1976. However, as this clashed with Derby's home tie with Everton, Notts County's home tie with Leeds United, and Leicester's home tie with Sheffield United - all considerably more attractive - Secretary Ken Smales asked the FA to switch the game to New Year's Day. This seemed a perfectly reasonable request, given the circumstances, but the FA decided - for reasons known only to themselves - to turn down this initial request. Undeterred however, Forest appealed and eventually the FA relented.

The Club's request to bring forward the game by two days was wholly vindicated when, despite torrential rain all day, the tie attracted a City Ground crowd of 31,525 - Forest's biggest of the season. Not only did this impressive gate highlight the appeal of the FA Cup, but it also reflected the crowd potential down at the City Ground, which remained as big as ever. Unfortunately, the large crowd had to endure a dismal 0-0 draw; so it was off to Peterborough's London Road Ground for a replay on Wednesday, 7th January, via the Forest-Rail special - a train chartered by the Club for all their away matches that season. And it was sold out for virtually every game.

Unfortunately, Forest lost this replay 1-0, and as the disgruntled and angry supporters poured out of the stadium following this frustrating defeat, chants of: *"We're gonna smash your fuckin' town to bits,"* filled the air. During the game, the 'Reds' had done everything but score; however, the performance of Peterborough's goalkeeper, Eric Steel - formerly of Notts County - was outstanding.

This disappointing Cup defeat was followed by an equally uninspiring 1-0 defeat away to Hull City the following Saturday and a 3-1 defeat against Chelsea a week later at the City Ground. Once again, this game was marred by ugly skirmishes between large gangs of Forest and Chelsea supporters, which took place on the open terraces of the Bridgford End. The scenes which occurred before, during, and after the game were very disturbing and a complete embarrassment to both clubs. Commenting on the lower than average crowd which had subsequently turned out for the next home game against Blackpool on Saturday, 7th February, Ken Smales made the following observations in the Forest Review for the game against Oldham Athletic six weeks later:

"However, to revert to the Blackpool match, I must say that I was both surprised and disappointed with the poor attendance of 8,582. I know it rained during the Saturday morning but didn't it also rain heavily when we played Bristol City? I am also aware that we had not won at home since the end of November, but our following, both home and away, has been terrific, so what caused the sudden drop of about 4,500 (we were averaging about 13,300 prior to this game)?

Blackpool, with all due respect, are not the most attractive of visitors on a February day, but I think that it was the outbreak of hooliganism at the previous game v. Chelsea that could have deterred many from attending. Just what are we going to do with this unruly gang that continue to decimate our gates. Can't they see the harm that they are doing to the club and Brian Clough's hopes of building a First Division side?

So, once again, I must appeal to everyone to try to stop the hot-heads from leading their weaker-minded followers into causing disturbances near to and inside the ground. It looks as though more fences will be installed to protect those who really come to watch the game."

BY this time I was 18-years-old, working and, with a few quid in my back pocket, following Forest on most of their away excursions. I was also extremely proud not to have missed a single home match of any description for the last seven seasons! Forest's away support at this time was enormous and journeys up and down the country involved almost every mode of transport known to mankind. The official Forest Travel Club had in excess of 600 members, and this guaranteed the Forest-Rail special would be full to capacity every time it departed from Midlands Station. This was always supplemented by a fleet of coaches - most of them being privately organised affairs - minibuses, cars and vans. At the time, our little mob from Chilwell, travelled to most away games on the 'Man of Iron' bus from Stapleford, run by a chap called Trig.

One of the most amusing sights en-route to away matches in those days, was that of 'The Yellow Peril' chugging it's way up and down the motorway. It could be seen at most away games and was always full of raucous, beer-swilling, youths. It was an old 'box van' with seats and windows in the back - rather like one of those old fashioned, square-shaped ambulances - and was painted bright yellow and black. It originated from the Long Eaton area and was always full of familiar faces. It was a sight to behold and always raised a laugh amongst the travelling 'Red Army'.

Such was the size of their away support; many towns and cities which Forest visited were swamped by hordes of boozed-up supporters. Most pubs and bars in the vicinity of the ground would be packed with boisterous gangs of youths. *"We are the Nutters; the Nutters from Notts!"* was one of their proudest boasts. Others included:

Forest boys, we are 'ere,
Woo-ooh, woo-ooh,
Forest boys, we are 'ere,
Woo-ooh, woo-ooh;

Forest boys, we are 'ere,
T' SHAG YOUR WOMEN,
AN' T' DRINK YOUR BEER!
Woo-ooh-ooh, woo-ooh-ooh.

Oh wi come from Nottingham Forest,
With a shotgun on our knee,
Oh wi come from Nottingham Forest,
An' it's time for you to flee;

Oh Derby County,
It's time for you to run,
Cos wi come from Nottingham Forest,
With a fuckin' grett shotgun!

Despite the boisterous and sometimes volatile nature of Forest's away support at this time, it seemed some of the Club's hierarchy did at least appreciate their substantial numbers.

Ken Smales paid the following tribute to them in the Forest Review before the game against Sunderland on Wednesday, 17th March - a fixture which the 'Reds' won 2-1 in front of a crowd of 16,995:

"The Forestrail trip to Carlisle proved quite an eye-opener to me and, I suspect, to many others. Here were 500 supporters on a cold March day prepared to travel with a middle of the table side to play a club in a similar position when, across the Trent, there was a clash between two promotion candidates. Fifteen miles up the road was a Sixth Round FA Cup-tie and here we were with a full load heading towards Carlisle, nearly 200 miles away. They tell me that League Champions, Derby County, could only muster 350 supporters on their train to West Ham, so where does that put our followers in the away supporters league?"

However, despite this glowing tribute, the troublemakers continued to tarnish the reputation of the Club. Just three days after the Sunderland game, the 'Reds' travelled to York City and, once again, the behaviour of a large number of the 3,000 travelling supporters was an absolute disgrace. Rowdy scenes in the pubs around York were followed by misbehaviour in the streets around the ground. And, to cap it all, there was a mass pitch invasion during the game. Once again, there was an outcry amongst angry Club officials, members of the public, and supporters alike. The City Ground post-bag was full of complaints concerning the goings on at this game. The following letter - from K.J. Thompson of Long Eaton - featured in the Review for the game against Oxford United on Saturday, 10th April:

"Dear Mr. Smales,

I would like to comment about the support Forest got at York City the other weekend. I travelled on the Forestrail train with about 500 others and was looking forward to the match. However, I stepped out of York Station to see about 50 Forest "yobbos" get off a special bus and start thumping cars and anyone who got in their way.

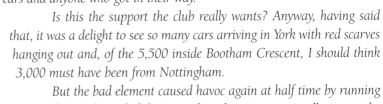

Is this the support the club really wants? Anyway, having said that, it was a delight to see so many cars arriving in York with red scarves hanging out and, of the 5,500 inside Bootham Crescent, I should think 3,000 must have been from Nottingham.

But the bad element caused havoc again at half time by running onto the pitch and fighting with police. Do we really want the reputation of Newcastle? Then as one of the "yobs" made his way over the wall back onto the terraces, a woman pushed him, obviously angry at the riotous scenes. He, I'm afraid to say, was a Forest fan and floored the woman. Talk about carry the red flag! I wonder what the woman thinks of Nottingham Forest Football Club now?

The team didn't show any of the skill that sent Sunderland home unhappy a few days earlier, and York were deserved winners.

Happily, there was no trouble on the train back to Nottingham, but the damage to Forest's name had been done."

AS a season that will be remembered more for the misbehaviour of a large number of supporters, than for the exploits of the team on the pitch, drew to a close, a Forest X1 played a Don Revie X1 at the City Ground on Monday, 26th April, in a testimonial match for long serving defender, Sammy Chapman. A crowd of 11,429 turned up to pay tribute to Sammy - a great favourite amongst supporters, due to his no-nonsense style of play. *"Six foot two; Eyes of blue; Sammy Chapman's after you! La-la-la-la, La-la-la, La-la,"* the Trent End would sing in an attempt to put the wind up opposition centre-forwards.

The Don Revie X1 included Derby players Bruce Rioch, Roy McFarland, Colin Todd and Archie Gemmill, along with Newcastle's Malcolm Macdonald, Sheffield United's Tony Currie, and Leicester's Frank Worthington. The Forest X1 included former City Ground idols Joe Baker and Duncan McKenzie. One supporter ran onto the pitch during the warm up, got down on his hands and knees and kissed Joe Baker's feet. And not surprisingly, the appearance of McKenzie in a Forest shirt once again, led to speculation he was about to return to the Club permanently. *"Bring back; Oh bring back; Oh bring back our Duncan to us - to us!"* sang a section of the crowd during the game, which incidentally, the Forest X1 won by three-goals-to-two. The rumours subsided when Duncan subsequently signed for Belgian side Anderlecht.

Forest finished the season in eighth position in the table, having won 17 and drawn 12 of their 42 matches. Their average home attendance in the League was 12,805, with the highest being the 19,757 who watched the 1-0 defeat by neighbours Notts County. The lowest was the 8,582 who turned up for the game against Blackpool. However, the 31,525 crowd for the FA Cup tie against Peterborough United, provided ample proof that the potential remained as big as ever. All it needed was a bit of success on the pitch, and this would signal the return of the missing thousands.

SEASON 1975/76 – STATISTICS

FOOTBALL LEAGUE DIVISION TWO – FIXTURES

Date		Opposition	Venue	Competition	Score	Attendance
Aug	16	**Plymouth Argyle**	H	**League**	**2-0**	**13,083**
	19	Rotherham United	A	LC 1 - 1st Leg	2-1	4,912
	23	Portsmouth	A	League	1-1	10,655
	27	**Rotherham United**	H	**LC 1 - 2nd Leg**	**5-1**	**7,977**
	30	**Notts County**	H	**League**	**0-1**	**19,757**
Sept	6	Chelsea	A	League	0-0	21,323
	10	**Plymouth Argyle**	H	**LC 2**	**1-0**	**8,978**
	13	**Hull City**	H	**League**	**1-2**	**12,191**
	20	Oxford United	A	League	1-0	5,318
	24	**Charlton Athletic**	H	**League**	**1-2**	**10,588**
	27	**Bolton Wanderers**	H	**League**	**1-2**	**10,780**
Oct	4	Bristol Rovers	A	League	2-4	7,698
	8	Manchester City	A	LC 3	1-2	26,536
	11	Fulham	A	League	0-0	10,149
	18	**Southampton**	H	**League**	**3-1**	**12,677**
	21	**Luton Town**	H	**League**	**0-0**	**12,290**
	25	Oldham Athletic	A	League	0-0	11,437
Nov	1	**Carlisle United**	H	**League**	**4-0**	**11,894**
	4	Blackpool	A	League	1-1	5,851
	8	Sunderland	A	League	0-3	31,227
	15	**Bristol City**	H	**League**	**1-0**	**11,583**
	22	Southampton	A	League	3-0	14,245
	29	**York City**	H	**League**	**1-0**	**13,108**
Dec	6	Orient	A	League	1-1	5,629
	13	**Portsmouth**	H	**League**	**0-1**	**11,343**
	20	Plymouth Argyle	A	League	0-1	10,545
	26	**West Bromwich Albion**	H	**League**	**0-2**	**19,393**
	27	Blackburn Rovers	A	League	4-1	10,720
Jan	1	**Peterborough United**	H	**FA Cup 3**	**0-0**	**31,525**
	7	Peterborough United	A	FA Cup 3 - Replay	0-1	17,866
	10	Hull City	A	League	0-1	6,465
	17	**Chelsea**	H	**League**	**1-3**	**14,172**
	31	Luton Town	A	League	1-1	8,503
Feb	7	**Blackpool**	H	**League**	**3-0**	**8,582**
	21	Bristol City	A	League	2-0	15,302
	24	Charlton Athletic	A	League	2-2	10,655
	28	**Oldham Athletic**	H	**League**	**4-3**	**11,509**
Mar	6	Carlisle United	A	League	1-1	7,153
	13	**Fulham**	H	**League**	**1-0**	**11,445**
	17	**Sunderland**	H	**League**	**2-1**	**16,995**
	20	York City	A	League	2-3	5,571
	27	**Orient**	H	**League**	**1-0**	**11,127**
Apr	3	Bolton Wanderers	A	League	0-0	22,415
	10	**Oxford United**	H	**League**	**4-0**	**11,259**
	13	Notts County	A	League	0-0	29,279
	17	West Bromwich Albion	A	League	0-2	26,580
	20	**Blackburn Rovers**	H	**League**	**1-0**	**13,006**
	24	**Bristol Rovers**	H	**League**	**3-0**	**12,127**

HOME ATTENDANCES

	AGGREGATE ATTENDANCE	HIGHEST ATTENDANCE	LOWEST ATTENDANCE	AVERAGE ATTENDANCE
League:	268,909	19,757	8,582	12,805
League Cup:	16,955	8,978	7,977	8,477
FA Cup:	31,525	31,525	31,525	31,525
All Competitions:	317,389	31,525	7,977	13,224

FINAL LEAGUE TABLE - DIVISION TWO

Position	P	W	D	L	GF	GA	Pts
1. Sunderland	42	24	8	10	67	36	56
2. Bristol City	42	19	15	8	59	35	53
3. West Bromwich Albion	42	20	13	9	50	33	53
4. Bolton Wanderers	42	20	12	10	64	38	52
5. Notts County	42	19	11	12	60	41	49
6. Southampton	42	21	7	14	66	50	49
7. Luton Town	42	19	10	13	61	51	48
8. Nottingham Forest	**42**	**17**	**12**	**13**	**55**	**40**	**46**
9. Charlton Athletic	42	15	12	15	61	72	42
10. Blackpool	42	14	14	14	40	49	42
11. Chelsea	42	12	16	14	53	54	40
12. Fulham	42	13	14	15	45	47	40
13. Orient	42	13	14	15	37	39	40
14. Hull City	42	14	11	17	45	49	39
15. Blackburn Rovers	42	12	14	16	45	50	38
16. Plymouth Argyle	42	13	12	17	48	54	38
17. Oldham Athletic	42	13	12	17	57	68	38
18. Bristol Rovers	42	11	16	15	38	50	38
19. Carlisle United	42	12	13	17	45	59	37
20. Oxford United	42	11	11	20	39	59	33
21. York City	42	10	8	24	39	71	28
22. Portsmouth	42	9	7	26	32	61	25

AWAY ATTENDANCES

	AGGREGATE ATTENDANCE	HIGHEST ATTENDANCE	LOWEST ATTENDANCE	AVERAGE ATTENDANCE
League:	276,720	31,227	5,318	13,177
League Cup:	31,448	26,536	4,912	15,724
FA Cup:	17,866	17,866	17,866	17,866
All Competitions:	326,034	31,227	4,912	13,584

"BRIAN CLOUGH AND PETER TAYLOR"

WITH THE exception of the first two seasons, my ten years as a Forest supporter had been littered with disappointment, and at times, downright despair. However, although I didn't know it at the time, my loyalty to the 'Reds' was about to be repaid many times over.

The arrival of Peter Taylor at the Club in July 1976, following two years in charge of Third Division Brighton, gave rise to a fair amount of optimism in and around Nottingham. Nevertheless, no-one could have predicted just to what extent the fortunes of Nottingham Forest Football Club were about to be transformed.

The re-unification of the Clough-Taylor partnership had certainly stirred the imagination of the bookies. At the start of the season, they were quoting Forest as 8-1 joint third favourites for promotion, along with Bolton Wanderers. Wolves were favourites at 4-1 and Southampton - the current FA Cup holders - were second at 6-1. Although Taylor's four-year contract at the City Ground was officially in the capacity of Clough's assistant, it was widely accepted in the game, their working relationship was based largely on the principal of equality. Taylor's primary responsibility was talent spotting, whilst Cloughie's was more along the lines of motivating and controlling the players and staff - and, quite probably, the Forest Committee for that matter! Clough was also virtually a one-man publicity machine. It seemed almost that his every remark or opinion - no matter how controversial - would be splashed across the back page of every tabloid newspaper.

The preliminary rounds of the Anglo-Scottish Cup dominated the early part of the season. Forest had been drawn in the same qualifying group as First Division duo West Bromwich Albion and Bristol City, in addition to Second Division neighbours Notts County. A 0-0 draw against the 'Magpies' at Meadow Lane on Saturday, 7th August, was followed by an impressive 3-2 victory at home to the 'Baggies' the following Wednesday, and an equally impressive 4-2 victory over Bristol City the following Saturday. This meant they were through to the first round proper, with both legs against Scottish First Division side Kilmarnock scheduled to take place in September; a tie they went on to win 4-3 on aggregate.

Their opening League skirmish resulted in a 2-2 draw away to Fulham at Craven Cottage on Saturday, 21st August. This was followed by a 1-1 draw at home to Charlton Athletic on Wednesday, 25th August, and a 3-1 defeat at home to a very impressive looking Wolves side the following Saturday. Their early season jitters began to diminish thanks to a 4-2 midweek victory away to Third Division Walsall in the second round of the League Cup. This was followed by a 1-1 draw away to Luton Town in the League the following Saturday, and a dramatic 4-3 home win over Hereford United in the League one week later - a game in which they came back from 2-0 down early on to take both points.

Their form then began to pick up dramatically, and apart from a few setbacks on their travels, was generally exciting and full of attacking flair - particularly at home. By the end of November, they'd stuck five past Carlisle United, six past Sheffield United, five past Burnley, and three past Blackburn Rovers, all at the City Ground. They were sitting in fourth position in the table behind Chelsea, Bolton Wanderers and Blackpool respectively. And, despite a 3-0 setback at home to Coventry City in the third round of the League Cup, they'd also progressed through to the Final of the Anglo-Scottish Cup, courtesy of a 4-1 aggregate victory over Ayr United in the second round.

With John Robertson and Terry Curran supplying the ammunition from the flanks, the newly-formed strike partnership of Peter Withe and Tony Woodcock was finding the back of the net with increasing regularity. The much-travelled Withe - still only twenty-five - had signed for £44,000 from Birmingham City. Eastwood-born Woodcock had forced his way into the first team reckoning with some impressive displays, following loan spells at Graham Taylor's Lincoln City and Fourth Division Doncaster Rovers. Withe's aerial ability and physical strength, combined with Woodcock's pace and skill on the ball, were proving a lethal combination in front of goal. Added to this, the skill and work-rate of the maturing Martin O'Neill - who eventually replaced the injured Curran out on the right wing - combined with the tenacity and experience of Ian Bowyer and the guile of John McGovern in the centre of midfield, had given the 'Reds' a strength and a balance they hadn't possessed in ages.

A 1-1 draw away to Orient in the first leg of the Anglo-Scottish Cup Final on Monday, 13th December, was followed by a resounding 4-0 victory for Forest two days later in the second leg at the City Ground. Two goals from full-back Colin Barrett, one from Sammy Chapman, and another from Ian Bowyer, were enough to give them a 5-1 aggregate victory in front of a crowd of 12,717. This earned the Club their first piece of silverware under the guidance of Brian Clough. Insignificant though this achievement may have been in the eyes of the footballing world, the players had now sampled the sweet smell of success and, as the saying goes: "Success breeds success."

ALTHOUGH the form of the team, and their attractive style of play, were the main talking points amongst supporters, the Club's infamous hooligan element continued to blight the 'Reds' - much to the consternation of manager Brian Clough. Major crowd disturbances had taken place on the East Stand terraces during the games against Wolverhampton Wanderers and Sheffield United earlier on in the season. This prompted the Club to allocate the Trent End to away fans for the visit of Chelsea on Saturday, 20th November. Unfortunately, this failed to prevent some serious trouble inside the ground during the game, which ended 1-1 in front of a crowd of 27,089. Nor was it sufficient either to deter the hooligan element outside, judging by the ugly scenes which occurred around the streets of Nottingham both before and after the game.

Despite the unwelcome troublemakers, the volume of support enjoyed by Forest, particularly away from home, was impressive, to say the least. The Boxing Day fixture against Bolton Wanderers at Burnden Park attracted a massive crowd of 32,630, many of whom were 'Travelling Trickies'. Most of these were crammed into the Great Lever Stand alongside the Bolton supporters, separated only by a five-foot high fence and a thin blue line of police. *"Ian Greaves' blue 'n' white army,"* chanted the Bolton fans before the game. *"Ian Greaves' Salvation Army,"* retorted Forest's travelling army of fans, quick as a flash. *"You're gonna get your fuckin' 'eads kicked in,"* responded the Bolton fans churlishly. *"You're goin' 'ome like Sandy Richardson,"* came the mocking reply seconds later. Peter Withe grabbed Forest's goal in a tense, but exciting 1-1 draw.

A New Year's Day fixture at Blackburn's Ewood Park sent the travelling hordes northwards for the second time during the festive season and once again the lads turned out in force. We travelled up to this game on the Man of Iron bus. As we were making our way to the ground following a pleasurable two hours in a pub nearby, we encountered the 600-strong army who'd travelled up on the Forest-Rail special and were being escorted from the station by the police.

One of them had apparently pinched a box full of party hats from a night-club the previous evening and distributed them throughout the train on the journey up from Nottingham. Consequently, the whole street was filled with denim-clad youths wearing Doc' Marten boots, Forest's scarves (yes - football scarves were acceptable attire in those days), and an assortment of fezzes, gold and silver crowns, and pirates' hats. Furthermore, as football specials were not yet 'alcohol-free' zones, the majority of them were already in full party mode.

An excellent 3-1 victory for Forest, with goals from Peter Withe, Tony Woodcock and Ian Bowyer, kept them in fourth position in the table, some five points behind the leaders Chelsea. This provided the perfect excuse for the travelling fans to extend their festive celebrations.

With the Christmas period now out of the way, it was time for the 'Reds' to turn their attentions to the FA Cup. They'd been drawn at home to Bristol Rovers in the third round on Saturday, 8th January and this game ended 1-1 in front of a crowd of 17,874. The replay at Eastville three days later also ended 1-1, and a second replay was necessary, this time at neutral Villa Park on Tuesday, 18th January. The 5,000 Forest supporters amongst the crowd of only 5,736, witnessed a resounding 6-0 victory for the 'Reds' from their vantage point high up on the Holte End - the only part of the ground open. Forest's goal-scorers were Tony Woodcock (2), Ian Bowyer, Peter Withe, Viv Anderson and John O'Hare.

Once again, they were drawn at home in the fourth round, and again to Second Division opposition in the form of Southampton. Anticipating a large crowd for this fixture, and a large following from the South Coast, the Trent End was again allocated to visiting fans. The game took place on Saturday, 29th January, and an enthralling encounter ended 3-3 in front of a huge crowd of 38,284. Unfortunately, the 'Reds' were beaten 2-1 in the replay at the Dell the following Tuesday, and their Cup ambitions were put on ice for another season.

However, the controversial decision to hand over the Trent End to Southampton fans for the City Ground tie caused an outcry amongst Forest's Trent End supporters. The Club was inundated with letters of complaint from disgruntled fans. The following letter, from a Miss W. Hallam of Derby, appeared in the Forest Review for the game against Luton Town on Saturday, 12th February:

"Once again a big crowd is expected for the Southampton game so, once again, the true fans of the Trent End have to move.

I would like to ask you if you think this is fair to someone like myself, who has stood in all weathers and through some bad times for twelve years at this end, to have to be put in another part of the ground as if we were the hooligans?

Surely now that the ground is fenced off in most parts the visiting fans could be kept together anywhere on the terraces?

I hope the club realises that they need the Trent End support for the lads on the field, anywhere else does not sound the same on account of there being a different type of roof over them. It is no good saying that the police are to blame, because the club could show the authorities the fencing arrangements which should make their job easier.

Please look after your fans, they stuck by the club through some very poor times, so prove to them that you are grateful instead of kicking them in the teeth every time the crowd is more than 15,000. Big attendances were dealt with in the past without any upset to the home fans. Remember the record crowd of almost 50,000, we were not kicked out of the Trent End in those days.

These are not only my feelings, everyone I spoke to about the Chelsea game had the same complaint. Remember, do this kind of thing too often and the fans may move out of the club altogether, then what would happen?"

BY the time they entertained neighbours Notts County at the City Ground on Tuesday, 8th March, Forest were sitting in eighth position in the table with 32 points from 27 games and were five points adrift of a promotion position. County were one place above them and had won the previous two League encounters between the two at the City Ground. And, disappointingly, they made it three in a row with a 2-1 victory, in front of a crowd of 31,004.

Despite this setback, the whole Club was about to breathe a collective sigh of relief, following the successful battle during February to keep Clough and Taylor at the City Ground. This followed an attempt by newly-appointed Derby Chairman, George Hardy, to take them back to the Baseball Ground following the departure of manager Dave Mackay, who they'd also poached from Forest four years earlier. After protracted talks with Forest Officials, their respective families, and close friends, the dynamic duo made the historic decision to stay with the 'Reds' - a decision that would ultimately change the whole history of the Club.

Although at this time I never missed a home game of any description, there were a few occasions when I was unable, for one reason or another, to follow them away from home. On these rare occasions, I'd tune into Nottingham's popular commercial radio station, Radio Trent. I'd listen intently to the pre-match analysis provided by Sports Editor Martin Johnson and the regular match updates from his young and enthusiastic understudy Clive Tyldesley - now a well-known TV commentator. Although primarily a Man United supporter, Clive had undoubtedly adopted Forest as his second team. His main role as a sports journalist was to cover all of their matches, home and away.

The following article by him, entitled: *"I WAS A STRETFORD ENDER"*, appeared in the Forest review for the game against Notts:

"Six years ago I was a Stretford Ender - a fully paid-up member of that fanatical horde which makes its presence felt wherever Manchester United play. The uniform consisted of two scarves - one red and white and knotted on the wrist, the other in the club colours of Glasgow Rangers decorated with a badge which read simply "I hate Leeds".

Uniforms inspire pride - and it was easy to be proud in Manchester. Visiting supporters were few and far between and the team retained a certain charisma even in their darkest days. The Stretford stronghold was rarely threatened. Twice a season half of Merseyside arrived in town. I used to go to the station when the specials rolled in. Suddenly an echoing noise would well up, then a loud, threatening chant and three or four hundred Liverpudlians cascaded through the foyer and out into the city - our city!

When we travelled away it was different. We were the aggressors. Residents came to their front doors to watch the swarm of famous hooligans go by. Pubs were closed and traffic was stopped so we could pass. Best of all, the local "yobbos" would gladly sacrifice their "Kop-end" for the afternoon, recognising the futility of a fight.

The collective force of a dozen train-loads of idiots lent a sense of power to the individual. The newspapers recorded our antics with outraged enthusiasm. We gained a reputation second to none. Whether it was Belgium or Oldham the headlines followed our every move. Unfortunately the fans became proud of the reputation, determined to enhance it on every trip. United got kicked out of Europe, the ground was closed for two games, a "derby" match was stopped by a pitch invasion - a unique list of violent "firsts" for the Stretford End.

One of my greatest thrills as a broadcaster was going back to Old Trafford as their guest. To sit in the press-box and to hear Tommy Docherty exaggerating wildly after a victory was a dream come true. We all heard a lot from "The Doc" in the build-up to last year's Cup Final. Here was a controversial character on the threshold of this major honour and all he was talking about was crowd control. The manager of a great football club begging a few stupid louts not to spoil the day. Of course he had also appealed many times before, but usually it was qualified with "they're the best fans in the world, but for a mindless minority". Hardly a week has gone by at Old Trafford in the last ten years without someone branding the Stretford End as "animals". But not until I heard Tommy Docherty say that half his staff's time was taken up by the fruits of crowd trouble, and that the fans were all anybody spoke to him about, did the penny drop in my head.

Nottingham Forest share a lot in common with Manchester United. Through lean years the club has maintained a First Division set-up. On the field a new man has come and is making progress towards turning the clock back ten years. He's even doing it with red-shirted wingers! On the terraces the support has remained young and vocal. Put in perspective, the loyalty of the travelling fans is just as impressive. But, unfortunately, the comparison has occasionally been stretched to include damage and arrests.

My job gives me the privilege of seeing more of this club than the average supporter. I've sat and waited whilst the Committee have debated the various solutions to the problem; I've 'phoned the chairman and vice-chairman at work for their reactions to police statements; I've seen Ken Smales and his staff up to their necks in complaints; I've heard John Carter and Mick Tinkley and the rest of the travel organisers defending the name of Forest fans in cases of extreme provocation or just sheer innocence; I've interviewed the manager and seen him suddenly become angry at the very mention of the word; and I'll never forget walking onto the station at Southampton with a couple of the players and being greeted by the sight of an almighty "barney" on the opposite platform. The two concerned came out with some real "red-card" language and very nearly went over and sorted it out themselves.

And now, to cap the lot, the all-conquering "Nutters of Notts" have stopped their first match nearly three years after Newcastle did it to us. The trouble at the Chelsea game doesn't really bear comparison to that at St.James's Park and it could well be that the first punch was thrown by a Londoner. But the result is the same and the players have come off worst.

So now we have a police inspector calling for the cancellation of certain matches. The inventors are back with their cumbersome "juveniles accompanied by adults" ideas - all the things designed to take the thrill out of going down to the City Ground with your mates to stand in a swaying crowd with scarf aloft and telling the rest of the football world what to do with their "we hate Nottingham Forest".

The novelty has gone out of hooliganism. Fans of Hartlepool and Darlington and even non-league clubs have had a go at it. We've all "taken" each other's Kops, we've thrown everything man has invented at each other, we've also employed every conceivable offensive weapon and, if we're very lucky, we've had our picture in the paper.

The only pinnacles left to climb are adult-only soccer matches and the complete closure of the City Ground. This looks a good time to gracefully retire and hang our boots up."

EXACTLY one week after the County game, Forest entertained Hull City at the City Ground - a game they won comfortably by two-goals-to-nil in front of a crowd of 15,116. Goals from the prolific duo of *"PE-TER-WITHE-AND-TO-NY-WOOD-COCK"* strengthened further their promotion credentials. The game also marked the senior debut of a certain young man from Chilwell named Garry Birtles, an acquaintance of mine and a regular in our local pub in Chilwell, the Cadland Inn. I'd known Garry for many years, and had played for Attenborough Colts Under Thirteen's side at the same time he was playing for the Under Fifteen's. He'd attended the Alderman White Secondary Modern School in Bramcote, which was also attended by most of my mates in that area.

Although considered a foregone conclusion in Chilwell that Garry would make the grade, he became disillusioned with the game, having been discarded by Aston Villa at the age of fifteen. By the time he left school at sixteen, he'd virtually hung up his boots. However, he was eventually persuaded by his pals in Chilwell to sign on for Long Eaton Rovers, the Notts Sunday Premier League side they all played for. Not only did this rekindle his appetite for the game, but it was also instrumental in him joining Long Eaton United who played their Saturday fixtures in the Midland League. He was playing for them when he caught the eye of a number of Football League clubs.

Having been tipped off Manchester United were showing more than a passing interest in this very promising local teenager, Cloughie - not wishing to have such talent pinched from under his nose - decided to check the situation out for himself. He went along personally to watch Garry in a League fixture at Enderby Town. And despite his famous quip that "the half-time Bovril was more inspiring than Garry's performance", he'd at least seen enough to offer him a three-month trial down at the City Ground.

However, as he came to the end of a fairly uninspiring three months, it seemed unlikely he'd be offered the full-time contract he yearned. He was almost resigned to returning to his old job as a floor-layer alongside his father, Ray. However, unbeknown to him, Peter Taylor had travelled incognito to his final reserve game at Coventry City and watched from the terraces. One piece of skill from Garry in the final minutes - when he controlled the ball, dragged it back with his left foot, and drifted effortlessly past a defender - convinced Taylor he was worthy of a full-time contract. Consequently, his boyhood dream of playing for the 'Reds' was about to be fulfilled.

WHEN they entertained Southampton at home on Tuesday, 22nd March, Forest were sitting in seventh position in the table with 34 points from 30 games. They were only six points adrift of a promotion position with twelve games to go. This was a rearranged fixture - the original on Wednesday, 16th February, had been abandoned after 47 minutes due to fog, with the score standing at 1-0 to Southampton. The 'Reds' weren't playing well at all in this game, having also lost their three previous fixtures. However, a 2-1 victory in the rearranged contest, courtesy of goals from Woodcock and O'Neill, provided the springboard from which they embarked upon a run of five straight victories. This included an impressive and vital 3-1 success over promotion rivals Bolton Wanderers in front of a City Ground crowd of 24,580 - a result which catapulted them into third position in the table. Now all they had to do was maintain or even improve upon this position over the final seven games of the season and they'd be well and truly back in the big time.

A 1-1 draw at promotion-chasing Notts County on Saturday, 9th April - watched by a Meadow Lane crowd of 32,518 - was followed by a costly and demoralising 2-1 defeat at top of the table Chelsea the following Saturday. Once again this fixture was marred by crowd disturbances between rival gangs of Chelsea and Forest 'thugs', with some particularly ugly incidents taking place on the London Underground.

With only five games to play, they were now in fourth position in the table, having swapped places with County. Victory in the home game against Cardiff City on Saturday, 23rd April was paramount if they were to achieve their promotion objective. However, despite bombarding the visitors' goalmouth for virtually the whole of the ninety minutes, they suffered an agonising 1-0 defeat and promotion now looked an unlikely possibility.

Some hope was restored the following Wednesday when they defeated Oldham Athletic by three-goals-to-nil at the City Ground, with goals from Bowyer, Woodcock and O'Neill. Due to work commitments - I was in London at the time - to my extreme annoyance and frustration, I was unable to attend. This was the only home game I'd missed during the Club's five long seasons in Division Two, and the first of any description for almost eight years.

This was followed by a disappointing 1-1 draw away to Bristol Rovers the following Saturday - a game I did attend along with thousands of other 'Travelling Trickies' - and a 2-1 victory at Plymouth Argyle the following Monday evening. This meant, as they went into their final game of the season at home to Millwall, they were sitting in third position in the table, but were by no means assured of promotion. The top of the table looked like this:

Position	P	W	D	L	GF	GA	Pts
1. Wolverhampton Wanderers	40	21	12	7	82	44	54
2. Chelsea	40	20	12	8	68	52	52
3. Forest	**41**	**20**	**10**	**11**	**76**	**43**	**50**
4. Notts County	40	19	10	11	64	56	48
5. Bolton Wanderers	38	19	9	10	70	49	47
6. Blackpool	39	15	16	8	55	41	46

Although mathematically speaking, both County and Blackpool were still in the promotion picture, a victory for Forest over Millwall would mean only Bolton, who had three games in hand, were all that stood between them and the First Division. A 1-0 victory over the 'Lions', thanks to an own goal from defender Jon Moore, in front of an ecstatic City Ground crowd of 23,529, meant the players had now done everything they possibly could to achieve promotion. And so had the fans. It was now entirely in the hands of Bolton, who were five points behind with three games left.

A 2-1 victory against Cardiff City in midweek left the Burnden Park outfit requiring three points from their final two games. By the time their game against Second Division Champions Wolves kicked off the following Saturday, the Forest team were airborne and heading for a well-earned rest on Cloughie's favourite holiday island of Majorca. When they landed at Palma Airport, they'd already been informed of Wolves' 1-0 victory, and the promotion celebrations were about to begin in earnest.

Although promotion hadn't been achieved in front of Forest's army of fans, virtually the whole of Nottingham had tuned into the Bolton-Wolves game on the radio. The City Centre was soon awash with dancing, singing youths. Although relegation five years earlier had been an emotional experience, the sheer euphoria of promotion was something that is almost impossible to describe. Yes at last - we really were back in the big time!

FOREST'S average home attendance during this promotion season had improved to a more respectable level. The average League attendance was 17,978, and the average overall was 17,132. The highest in the League was the 31,004 for the clash with neighbours and promotion rivals Notts County, and the lowest was the 12,081 who'd turned out for the visit of Hereford United. The highest overall, was the 38,284 for the fourth round FA Cup tie with Southampton. The footballing population of Nottingham was once again beginning to stir.

SEASON 1976/77 – STATISTICS
FOOTBALL LEAGUE DIVISION TWO – FIXTURES

Date		Opposition	Venue	Competition	Score	Attendance
Aug	7	Notts County	A	Anglo/Scot Cup (Qual)	0-0	11,258
	11	**West Bromwich Albion**	**H**	**Anglo/Scot Cup (Qual)**	**3-2**	**7,018**
	14	**Bristol City**	**H**	**Anglo/Scot Cup (Qual)**	**4-2**	**8,527**
	21	Fulham	A	League	2-2	9,437
	25	**Charlton Athletic**	**H**	**League**	**1-1**	**12,662**
	28	**Wolverhampton Wanderers**	**H**	**League**	**1-3**	**17,222**
	31	Walsall	A	LC 2	4-2	8,437
Sept	4	Luton Town	A	League	1-1	11,231
	11	**Hereford United**	**H**	**League**	**4-3**	**12,081**
	14	**Kilmarnock**	**H**	**Anglo/Scot Cup 1 - 1st Leg**	**2-1**	**8,911**
	18	Southampton	A	League	1-1	23,096
	21	**Coventry City**	**H**	**LC 3**	**0-3**	**15,969**
	25	**Carlisle United**	**H**	**League**	**5-1**	**12,479**
	28	Kilmarnock	A	Anglo/Scot Cup 1 - 2nd Leg	2-2	4,227
Oct	2	Hull City*	A	League	0-1	16,096
	9	**Sheffield United**	**H**	**League**	**6-1**	**17,801**
	16	Blackpool	A	League	0-1	17,089
	20	**Ayr United**	**H**	**Anglo/Scot Cup 2 - 1st Leg**	**2-1**	**9,138**
	23	**Burnley**	**H**	**League**	**5-2**	**15,279**
	30	Oldham Athletic	A	League	0-1	10,597
Nov	3	Ayr United	A	Anglo/Scot Cup 2 - 2nd Leg	2-0	3,326
	6	**Blackburn Rovers**	**H**	**League**	**3-0**	**12,972**
	13	Orient	A	League	1-0	5,921
	20	**Chelsea**	**H**	**League**	**1-1**	**27,089**
	27	Cardiff City	A	League	3-0	12,741
Dec	**4**	**Bristol Rovers**	**H**	**League**	**4-2**	**16,302**
	11	Millwall	A	League	2-0	9,307
	13	Orient	A	Anglo/Scot Cup Final - 1st Leg	1-1	5,058
	15	**Orient**	**H**	**Anglo/Scot Cup Final - 2nd Leg**	**4-0**	**12,717**
	18	**Plymouth Argyle**	**H**	**League**	**1-1**	**15,180**
	27	Bolton Wanderers	A	League	1-1	32,630
Jan	1	Blackburn Rovers	A	League	3-1	14,524
	8	**Bristol Rovers**	**H**	**FA Cup 3**	**1-1**	**17,874**
	11	Bristol Rovers	A	FA Cup 3 - Replay	1-1	12,357
	14	Charlton Athletic	A	League	1-2	8,021
	18	Bristol Rovers	(Played at Villa Park)	FA Cup 3 - 2nd Replay	6-0	5,736
	22	**Fulham**	**H**	**League**	**3-0**	**24,718**
	29	**Southampton**	**H**	**FA Cup 4**	**3-3**	**38,284**
Feb	1	Southampton	A	FA Cup 4 - Replay	1-2	29,401
	5	Wolverhampton Wanderers	A	League	1-2	30,661
	12	**Luton Town**	**H**	**League**	**1-2**	**18,225**
	16	**Southampton**	**H**	**League**	**0-1**	**16,189**
		(Abandoned after 47 minutes due to fog)				
Mar	2	Hereford United	A	League	1-0	7,503
	5	Carlisle United	A	League	1-1	7,603
	8	**Notts County**	**H**	**League**	**1-2**	**31,004**
	12	**Hull City**	**H**	**League**	**2-0**	**15,116**
	19	Sheffield United	A	League	0-2	30,370
	22	**Southampton**	**H**	**League**	**2-1**	**12,393**
	26	**Blackpool**	**H**	**League**	**3-0**	**16,658**
	29	**Orient**	**H**	**League**	**3-0**	**16,267**
Apr	2	Burnley	A	League	1-0	11,112
	6	**Bolton Wanderers**	**H**	**League**	**3-1**	**24,580**
	9	Notts County	A	League	1-1	32,518
	16	Chelsea	A	League	1-2	36,499
	23	**Cardiff City**	**H**	**League**	**0-1**	**20,646**
	27	**Oldham Athletic**	**H**	**League**	**3-0**	**17,139**
	30	Bristol Rovers	A	League	1-1	8,900
May	2	Plymouth Argyle	A	League	2-1	13,542
	7	**Millwall**	**H**	**League**	**1-0**	**23,529**

HOME ATTENDANCES

	AGGREGATE ATTENDANCE	HIGHEST ATTENDANCE	LOWEST ATTENDANCE	AVERAGE ATTENDANCE
League:	395,531	31,004	12,081	17,978
	(Includes abandoned fixture versus Southampton)			
League Cup:	15,969	15,969	15,969	15,969
FA Cup:	56,158	38,284	17,874	28,079
Anglo/Scottish Cup:	46,311	12,717	7,018	9,262
All Competitions:	513,969	38,284	7,018	17,132

FINAL LEAGUE TABLE - DIVISION TWO

Position	P	W	D	L	GF	GA	Pts
1. Wolverhampton Wanderers	42	22	13	7	84	45	57
2. Chelsea	42	21	13	8	73	53	55
3. Nottingham Forest	**42**	**21**	**10**	**11**	**77**	**43**	**52**
4. Bolton Wanderers	42	20	11	11	74	54	51
5. Blackpool	42	17	17	8	58	42	51
6. Luton Town	42	23	6	15	67	48	48
7. Charlton Athletic	42	16	16	10	71	58	48
8. Notts County	42	19	10	13	65	60	48
9. Southampton	42	17	10	15	72	67	44
10. Millwall	42	17	13	14	57	53	43
11. Sheffield United	42	14	12	16	54	63	40
12. Blackburn Rovers	42	15	9	18	42	54	39
13. Oldham Athletic	42	14	10	18	52	64	38
14. Hull City	42	10	17	15	45	53	37
15. Bristol Rovers	42	12	13	17	53	68	37
16. Burnley	42	11	14	17	46	64	36
17. Fulham	42	11	13	18	44	61	35
18. Cardiff City	42	12	10	20	56	67	34
19. Orient	42	9	16	17	37	55	34
20. Carlisle United	42	11	12	19	49	75	34
21. Plymouth Argyle	42	8	16	18	46	65	32
22. Hereford United	42	8	15	19	57	78	31

AWAY ATTENDANCES

	AGGREGATE ATTENDANCE	HIGHEST ATTENDANCE	LOWEST ATTENDANCE	AVERAGE ATTENDANCE
League:	349,398	36,499	5,921	16,638
League Cup:	8,437	8,437	8,437	8,437
FA Cup:	47,494	29,401	5,736	15,831
Anglo Scottish Cup:	23,869	11,258	3,326	5,967
All Competitions:	429,198	36,499	3,326	14,799

"TELL MI MAM, MI MAM, I DON'T WANT NO TEA, NO TEA"

FOREST MADE their return to the top flight of English football with only one new addition to their first team squad - Kenny Burns had arrived from Birmingham City during the summer for a fee of £150,000. A prolific goal-scorer for the 'Blues', partnering Trevor Francis up front, he was also renowned for his defensive capabilities. And it was with a central defensive role in mind that Clough and Taylor decided to move in for him. Although he'd earned himself a fearsome reputation both on and off the field, if Cloughie couldn't bring him into line, then quite simply, no one could.

Following a highly successful pre-season tour of Switzerland, Austria and West Germany, when Forest had won all five games, scoring no less than 18 goals and conceding only 4 in the process, confidence was running high throughout the Club. As they headed north for the opening League fixture of the season against Everton at Goodison Park on Saturday, 20th August, their army of travelling supporters was also in buoyant mood. We were also hoping to celebrate the Club's return to Division One with a victory.

Whilst the majority of the football world, and to be fair, most supporters, were expecting them to achieve at best a mid-table position by the end of the season, Clough and Taylor were setting their sights much higher. Taylor was even bold enough to predict European qualification was a distinct possibility.

And to say they took Everton by storm in this opening fixture is an understatement, to put it mildly. Their 3-1 victory - with goals from Peter Withe, John Robertson and Martin O'Neill - oozed class from start to finish. Not only did they win convincingly; but they simply destroyed the Merseyside outfit. The 7,000 'Travelling Trickies' amongst the crowd of 38,001, left Goodison knowing they'd witnessed the beginning of something special.

Judging by the rather disappointing crowd of only 21,743 that welcomed them back to the City Ground the following Tuesday evening though, it was evident the sheer quality of their performance at Everton hadn't yet filtered through to the rest of the Nottingham public. A 1-0 victory over Bristol City, thanks to a goal from Withe, proved ideal preparation for the eagerly-awaited return to Trentside the following Saturday of our arch enemies Derby County.

A slightly more impressive crowd of 28,807 saw Forest rip the 'Sheep' apart, and with two goals from Withe and another from Robertson, they ran out comfortable 3-0 winners. Far from looking like First Division newcomers, they were already looking like possible Championship contenders. The general view amongst the game's pundits however, was that their excellent start was more down to enthusiasm than anything else.

After a magnificent 5-0 midweek victory over West Ham at home in the second round of the League Cup - with goals from Bowyer (2), O'Neill, Woodcock and Withe - the 'Reds' were brought crashing down to earth the following Saturday when they took on Arsenal at Highbury and were soundly beaten by three-goals-to-nil. Following the match, the BBC's then resident Arsenal fan, Bob Wilson, incensed supporters by declaring: "Forest are a bubble which is about to burst." He even went as far as to suggest they'd probably now just sink into obscurity. As it turned out, he would live to regret this statement. At every conceivable opportunity in the future, Forest supporters threw his words right back in his face. *"If you 'ate Bob Wilson, Clap yer 'ands,"* became a very popular chant down at the City Ground, particularly when the Match of the Day cameras were present.

After this resounding defeat in North London, Kenny Burns was heavily fined by the Forest management for a head-butting incident, which had gone un-noticed by the referee during the game. The Match of the Day cameras had featured the whole incident. As they prepared for the forthcoming trip to Wolves the following Saturday, the press were widely reporting that Clough and Taylor were on the verge of signing Stoke City goalkeeper, Peter Shilton, for a fee of around £270,000 - a record for a goalkeeper.

CHAPTER 12

As usual, Forest took with them a sizeable following to Molineux. The Visiting Supporters' Section was situated within the massive South Bank End of the ground which, when full to it's capacity, probably held in the region of 15,000 to 20,000 fans. However, Wolves had not yet fully grasped the concept of crowd segregation and unfortunately the only thing separating the 5,000 Forest supporters from a mob of 10,000 snarling Wolves' fans, was a thin blue line of police. Not much of an obstacle at all to the football hooligan of the late 1970s! Consequently, the two sets of supporters spent the majority of the afternoon kicking the living daylights out of one another. *"Sammy Chung and his Golden Wonderers,"* chanted the Wolves fans during the first half of the game. This prompted an immediate response of: *"Sammy Chung and his Chinese Takeaway,"* from the travelling red and white hordes.

Once again the Match of the Day cameras were there to record the action (the match that is - not the kick-boxing competition taking place on the terraces) and the sporting population of England was treated to a glimpse of fast, free-flowing, football - Clough and Taylor style. When they went 3-0 up, following goals from Withe, Bowyer and Woodcock, Wolves looked dead and buried. However, the fighting on the terraces looked far from over, so Graham, Chambo and I decided to make an early exit, heading back to the safety of the car. We were absolutely convinced all three points were safely in the bag. To our horror though, by the time we got back to the car park, Wolves had already pulled one back. We then had to endure a nail-biting last few minutes of match commentary on the radio as the 'Golden Wonderers' pulled another one back and then went agonisingly close to equalising just seconds before the final whistle.

The signing of Peter Shilton was duly completed on Wednesday, 14th September, and he was immediately pencilled in to make his debut in the game against Aston Villa at the City Ground three days later. Football fever was now gradually beginning to spread throughout the City of Nottingham. It would take some time though to entirely convince the long-suffering supporters of Nottingham Forest FC the Club really was once again a force to be reckoned with, following so many years of decline. A crowd of 31,016 turned up to see Shilton make his debut in a comfortable 2-0 victory for the 'Reds', courtesy of goals from Woodcock and Robertson. They'd gone into this game in third position in the table behind Manchester City and Liverpool, having accumulated eight points from five games. The defeat at Arsenal had been the only blemish on their record to date.

Before they travelled to East Midlands neighbours Leicester City the following Saturday, Clough and Taylor were once again busy in the transfer market. They signed Archie Gemmill from Derby County in a £130,000 deal, with Forest's popular young goalkeeper John Middleton going in the opposite direction as part of the deal (poor sod!). Although Gemmill had not signed in time to make his debut at Filbert Street, this proved of no consequence, as Forest ran out easy 3-0 winners. The goals came from O'Neill, Woodcock and Robertson. Over 7,000 'Trickies' were amongst the crowd of 21,447 and consequently the atmosphere resembled that of a home game for the 'Reds'.

By the time they entertained Norwich City on Saturday, 1st October, they were sitting in second position in the table, with twelve points from seven games played. Manchester City - also on twelve points from the same number of games - were top of the division on goal difference. Gemmill made his debut in this game and the two sides fought out a keenly contested 1-1 draw. Kenny Burns scored his first goal for the Club in front of 23,741 fans.

This was followed in midweek by a further home fixture against Norwich's country cousins Ipswich Town. They were a very capable team at the time managed by the legendary Bobby Robson and captained by England full-back Mick Mills. On the morning of the game, Mills had committed the cardinal sin of criticising Forest's players in the national press - referring to them as "a bunch of has-beens." He was greeted with a torrent of abuse from the Trent End, the second he emerged from the tunnel: *"Mick Mills - Mick Mills - Shut-yer-mouth; Mick Mills - Shut-yer-mouth!"* they chanted incessantly. And they weren't the only ones to have taken umbrage either - the players turned on the style in a big way for this one, and took Ipswich to the cleaners. They romped home to a 4-0 victory with all four goals coming from the brilliant Withe. As Mills and his team-mates trudged dejectedly from the pitch at the end, having been completely humiliated, the sound of: *"Mick Mills - Mick Mills, What's the score?"* rang out across the City Ground. The crowd of 26,845 began to celebrate Forest's elevation to the very top of the First Division table.

After securing a 0-0 draw away to West Ham the following Saturday, their next game was also at home against second-placed Manchester City on Saturday, 15th October. And a crowd of 35,572 turned out to watch a tense battle fought out by two impressive teams, in a highly charged and intense atmosphere. And once more, the Match of the Day cameras were present. City took a first-half lead through Brian Kidd following a right wing corner from Peter Barnes. However, the 'Reds' equalised shortly afterwards with a goal from the excellent Woodcock. He'd recently scored a hat-trick on his England Under-21 debut against Finland. A brilliant run down the left flank by Robertson, who left two defenders in his wake with one turn of his hips, ended with a pinpoint cross for the young striker to tap in at the near post.

The second half was equally impressive with both teams having their fair share of the spoils, and as the game entered it's final stages, it seemed destined to end in a draw. However, with only minutes left, Robertson went on another decisive run down the left. Having beaten several players, he managed to get to the by-line and send in another low cross towards the unmarked Woodcock. He was just lining himself up to despatch the ball into the net when, at the very last second, Withe intervened. As he intercepted the ball on the edge of the six-yard box, not only was he surrounded by City defenders, but he also had his back to goal. This brought gasps of despair from the Forest crowd who were convinced he'd prevented a certain Woodcock goal. But, before they had time to draw breath, he spun around and despatched a low deflected shot under the despairing dive of goalkeeper Joe Corrigan and into the back of the net. The City Ground erupted with joy. A crescendo of noise welled up from the massive crowd, and upon the final whistle, both teams were given a deserved standing ovation as they left the field.

Following this dramatic victory, Cloughie surprised everyone by launching a scathing attack on the Nottingham public. In a tabloid newspaper, he accused them of:

- "Not turning up in sufficient numbers to warrant a top-class football team!"
- "Not getting behind the team!"
- "Being foul-mouthed and abusive!"

He also drew comparisons between the City and other towns such as Sunderland, Middlesbrough and - would you believe - Derby? He argued their respective grounds would have been packed to the rafters had they been enjoying similar levels of success to that of Forest. I do seem to remember him having a similar swipe at the Derby public though during his early days down at the 'Sheep-dip'.

Although the vast majority of Forest supporters were not overly upset by his remarks, the reputation of the Nottingham public had suffered in the eyes of those outside the City. Consequently, they've carried with them to this day, the slightly unfair reputation for being a 'little bit fickle'. From a personal point of view, I found this a bitter pill to swallow and feel Cloughie should have chosen his words more carefully. There had been many years of decline down on Trentside and once people lose the habit of going to football matches on a regular basis, it takes a long time to tempt them back. It's not simply a tap which can be turned on or off at will.

THE following Saturday, Forest travelled to London to take on Queens Park Rangers at Loftus Road, where goals from Ian Bowyer and Kenny Burns gave them another 2-0 victory in front of a crowd of 24,449. They headed back up the motorway to Nottingham still sitting proudly at the top of the First Division table. They were understandably in confident mood therefore, as they prepared to face their Second Division neighbours Notts County at home in the third round of the League Cup on Tuesday, 25th October. Other than in the County Cup, I'd never seen them beat Notts at the City Ground; the 'Pies' had won three and drawn one of these four encounters during my twelve years as a Forest supporter. You can imagine my delight therefore, when goals from Bowyer (2), Robertson (penalty), and Woodcock gave them a convincing 4-0 victory in front of a crowd of 26,931. As Peter Shilton was Cup-tied, 17-year-old Chris Woods made his senior debut for the 'Reds' in this game.

Since it's introduction in season 1960/61, this competition hadn't exactly been a lucky one for Forest; they'd never even progressed beyond the fourth round. However, following two resounding victories so far, supporters were beginning to wonder if this was going to be 'our season': *"Tell mi mam - mi mam, I don't want no tea - no tea, (Why not?) - We're goin' t' Wember-ley, Tell mi mam - mi mam,"* sang the Trent End during this victory over County.

Prior to the home fixture against Middlesbrough the following Saturday, Cloughie - who was now waging a one-man war against Forest's notorious Trent Enders - erected a large sign in the middle of the pitch which read: "GENTLEMEN NO SWEARING PLEASE! Brian." The Trent End - much to everyone's amusement (including the great man himself) - duly responded with chants of: *"What the FLIPPIN' 'ELL was that?"* when a Boro goal attempt whistled ten feet over the Forest bar! Already two points clear at the top of the table prior to this game, Forest's 4-0 victory - which included two stunning thirty-yard thunderbolts from Viv Anderson - further enhanced their title aspirations.

The following Saturday, they again headed south down the M1, this time to take on Chelsea, struggling in the bottom half of the table. A 1-0 defeat - only their second in 14 games - once again inspired the 'Doubting Thomas's'. But when fifteenth-placed Manchester United visited the City Ground a week later - already some ten points behind the 'Reds' - they weren't expected to ask too many questions of the League leaders.

As the game kicked off, the crowd of 30,183 was bathed in beautiful autumn sunshine. However, during the course of the first half - when United had unexpectedly taken the lead - the skies above were gradually beginning to darken. Then, with the second half only four minutes old, the visitors' lead was cancelled out by a suspiciously 'off-side' looking effort from defender Kenny Burns. Shortly afterwards, the heavens opened and the crowd was given an almighty soaking. Although I'd encountered many extreme conditions over the years, since abandoning my dry and relatively cosy position in the Trent End, I'd never experienced weather quite like this. Everyone in the ground was desperately seeking refuge from this veritable 'monsoon'. But fortunately, by the time 'wee Archie Gemmill' rose to head a superb winning goal almost from the edge of the box, following an excellent cross from Withe, the rain had almost subsided. And despite a missed penalty from 'Robbo' shortly afterwards, the game ended 2-1 to the 'Reds'. The drenched and frozen supporters left the ground with a warm glow inside them at least - apart from the small group of around two to three hundred United supporters. At the time, their away support was restricted to just a handful by the Football Authorities, owing to the previously mentioned poor behaviour on their travels during the preceding seasons.

Off the field, supporters had to endure a nail biting few weeks when Cloughie applied for the England job, following the sudden and unexpected departure of Don Revie. He was quite naturally 'the people's choice', but the FA - being the bunch of old farts that they are - were intimidated by his forthright and outrageous views - not to mention his unpredictable nature. He was considered an 'anti-establishment' figure, likely to rock the boat. Despite this, he was short-listed and invited to attend Lancaster Gate for an interview in December.

The Evening Post launched a local campaign to keep him - and Taylor - at Forest and, in addition to handing him a 12,000-strong petition pleading with him to stay, Forest supporters erected a sign at the side of the pitch before one home game which read: "BRIAN - NO LEAVING PLEASE! The gentlemen." As far as the day-to-day running of the Club was concerned though, it was very much a case of 'business as usual' for Cloughie.

Following the victory over Man United, Forest travelled to Elland Road on Saturday, 19th November, to take on mid-table Leeds. And although they lost 1-0 in front of a crowd of 42,925 - they did so in controversial circumstances. After keeper Peter Shilton had been left unconscious in the six-yard box following a goal-mouth scramble, the Forest defence cleared the ball up-field. However, despite their pleas for the game to be stopped, the referee inexplicably allowed play to continue. Consequently, when the ball was pumped back into the area, striker Ray Hankin was able to slot it into the back of the net unhindered, with 'Shilts' still spark out on the floor.

Incredibly, not only would this be Forest's last defeat of the season; but it was also the prelude to a record 42-match unbeaten run in the League which lasted almost 13 months and spanned two seasons. This is still a record in the top flight to this day and one that is unlikely ever to be beaten. Can you imagine the acclaim with which such an achievement would have been greeted, had it been put together by the likes of Man United, Liverpool or Arsenal? What a pity then Forest received such scant recognition at the time? And what's more, it hardly ever gets a mention today.

This controversial defeat at Leeds was followed a week later by a 0-0 draw at home to West Brom. They went into this game against Albion still top of the table, a position they'd now occupied since the victory against Ipswich on 4th October. Up to this point, they'd accumulated a total of 24 points from 16 games played, winning 11 in the process, and drawing 2. They'd also scored a total of 30 goals to date, whilst conceding only 11. The chasing pack at this stage consisted of Everton and Coventry, both on 22 points, West Brom on 21, and Arsenal on 20 - all from 16 games played. Despite a crowd of 31,908 for this game, Cloughie took yet another swipe at the Nottingham public for their 'lack of support.'

It was back to League Cup action during midweek, as Forest entertained Midlands neighbours Aston Villa on Tuesday, 29th November, in a fourth round tie. And another superb display of all-out attacking football, saw them easily overcome the visitors 4-2, with goals from Lloyd, Anderson, Withe and Woodcock. The attendance of 29,333 for a fourth round tie in this competition, was more than most clubs would have attracted.

Of all the wonderful feats of goalkeeping I witnessed during Peter Shilton's illustrious career with the 'Reds', there is one particular moment, which will live in my memory forever. This came about during their next League game against Birmingham City at St.Andrews on Saturday, 3rd December. I was amongst the 6,000-strong travelling army who'd made the relatively short journey to 'Brum', helping to swell the attendance to an impressive 29,925. Roared on by their large and noisy following, Forest coasted into a 2-0 lead, thanks to goals from O'Neill and Woodcock, and were strolling comfortably towards the final whistle. Then, following a cross from the right wing, which he cushioned perfectly on his chest, 'Blues'' striker Trevor Francis, spun around and smashed an 'unstoppable' right-foot volley towards the top corner of the net. Unstoppable, that is, to a mere human being - but not to Peter Shilton. He launched himself from the ground like an 'Exocet Missile' and incredibly turned the ball over the crossbar. The best save I've ever seen, without a doubt.

The next visitors to Nottingham were Coventry the following Saturday, who by this time had fallen back into fifth position in the table. Nevertheless, they were still only four points behind the 'Reds'. A crowd of 29,823 witnessed another positive result on home territory - their eighth in only ten games. Goals from O'Neill and skipper John McGovern gave them a 2-1 victory. Unfortunately though, Larry Lloyd suffered a broken bone in his foot, which resulted in him being sidelined for over a month.

ON Monday, 12th December, Forest supporters received the news they'd all been waiting for - the FA had decided to appoint former West Ham manager Ron Greenwood as the new England supremo. It was at this moment in time Cloughie effectively became 'the best manager England never had'. Whilst this may have been bad news for the rest of the country, it was great news for the City of Nottingham, and as they say: "Charity begins at home."

Despite his obvious disappointment, Cloughie immediately got on with the task of making Forest the greatest club side in the land. He acted swiftly to sign a replacement for the injured Lloyd, snapping up Dave Needham from QPR for a fee of £150,000. He'd only recently joined them from Notts County, but jumped at the chance of making a quick return to the East Midlands where he still lived. The fact the 'Reds' were riding high at the top of the First Division table may have also been instrumental in him coming home to Nottingham.

He was pencilled in immediately for his debut against Manchester United at Old Trafford the following Saturday - 17th December. Although United were a pale shadow of the once great side of the 1960s, to me the very name "Manchester United" still had a magical ring about it. What's more, the thought of visiting Old Trafford - the 'Mecca' of English football - for the very first time, made my spine tingle.

For this very special occasion, we chose the Forest-Rail special as our mode of transport. The princely sum of £4.00 included both the cost of travel and a ticket for the game. A trip to Manchester was indeed a daunting prospect, not least for the fact the United supporters carried with them a fearsome reputation. As mentioned several times already, after many years of destruction and mayhem on their travels, they'd been banned from attending matches away from Old Trafford.

I don't mind admitting as we pulled into Old Trafford station, I was more than a little worried. Much to my amazement though, we were met by only a handful of police and weren't even given an escort to the ground. You can imagine the scenes therefore, as five-to-six-hundred visiting fans were left to their own devices and allowed to simply wander unhindered through the streets of Salford. Needless to say, skirmishes took place between rival supporters along the way. Although I was frightened to death throughout the whole of the mile and a half journey, I was also mesmerised by the carnival-like atmosphere which prevailed in the streets around the stadium. Although I'd never been to Wembley at this time - vowing not to do so unless it was to see Forest - I could only imagine that the scenes around Old Trafford were comparable to those along Wembley Way on FA Cup Final Day.

As we reached the 'sanctuary' of the stadium and made our way through the turnstiles into the Scoreboard End, I encountered my first disappointment of the day - the size of the famous Stretford End at the opposite end of the ground. Having seen it a thousand times before on Match of the Day, it had always seemed an enormous construction to me. However, at approximately 2.00 p.m. on a Saturday afternoon, with only a handful of supporters inside the ground, it really wasn't that impressive at all. That's not to say I was in any way disappointed with Old Trafford itself though - as this truly was a magnificent stadium, even then. And, by the time the teams took to the field almost an hour later, there were no less than 54,374 people inside, including at least 4,000 from Nottingham - and I mean Forest supporters by the way.

Seconds before kick-off, a large gang of United thugs came charging into our end and all hell broke loose between the two sets of supporters. The United fans in the Scoreboard Paddock - a two-tier section of terracing situated above us and immediately to our left - enjoyed every second of it, and stood cheering on their 'brave' companions throughout. The police eventually ejected the intruders and calm was restored. Those in the Paddock then began to taunt a lad called 'Pecky' - a rather large Forest fan from Clifton - with chants of: *"One Billy Bunter, There's only one Billy Bunter."* But to his credit, he acknowledged them by climbing up onto the wall at the front and taking a bow. This was greeted with cheers of approval from Forest's travelling contingent and a round of applause from the Scoreboard Paddock. Nevertheless, they went on to taunt him for most of the afternoon.

As the game kicked off, the noise inside Old Trafford was unlike anything I'd experienced before - particularly when United were on the attack. At one point early on, following a corner at the Scoreboard End, the noise was so intense I had to stick my fingers in my ears - it was absolutely deafening. However, what then began to unfold out there on the pitch, could never have been imagined even in my wildest of dreams. Forest were simply magnificent. The football they played was breathtaking and United just couldn't live with them at any time during the whole of the ninety minutes. It was fast, exciting, one-touch football, the like of which most of the 54,000 crowd hadn't witnessed before.

Following several early chances, Forest went ahead through an own goal from Brian Greenhoff. This owed more to the tenacity of Tony Woodcock though, than to any shortcomings on the part of the unfortunate defender. Before half-time, Woodcock himself had put them two-up, crashing an unstoppable half-volley into the roof of the Stretford End goal, following brilliant approach play by Robertson and Withe. They began the second half in the same manner, with more breathtaking, free flowing football. Inevitably, following numerous goalmouth opportunities, they went three-up through Robertson and finally four-up through Woodcock again. Without exaggeration, the score could have been 10-0; such was their total domination of the game. With the United fans shell-shocked and silenced, the only sound that could be heard echoing around Old Trafford, was that of 4,000 jubilant Forest fans triumphantly declaring: *"An' now yer gonna bel-ie-ie-ve us...We're gonna win the League!"*

As the final whistle blew and Old Trafford emptied to the sound of: *"Your gonna get your fuckin' 'eads kicked in,"* from the departing United supporters, I began to wonder what lay in store for us in the streets outside. What's more, the Stretford End's chants of: *"You'll be dead by 5 o'clock,"* sent a shiver down my spine. Fortunately, the police kept us in the ground for at least twenty minutes after the whistle, while the crowds outside were dispersed. And then, in contrast to their low-key approach prior to the game, the 'escort to end all escorts' shepherded us safely back to our buses, vans, cars and trains. Despite the fact it was now some thirty minutes or so since the end of the game, every side-street along the way was filled with baying United supporters, just waiting for the slightest opportunity to pounce.

When the game was featured on Match of the Day later that evening, the quality of their performance caused quite a stir. Not only was the BBC's mailbag filled with admiring letters from an appreciative public - including one from the great Stan Cullis (manager of Wolves during the 1950s) - but the City Ground post-bag was absolutely bulging. And much of this correspondence was from United supporters, every bit of it complimentary. Just as significantly, this incredible performance had also silenced the few remaining doubters. No longer were the 'Reds' considered merely as 'Championship Pretenders'.

AS high-riding Forest went into their Boxing Day fixture against third-placed Liverpool; it was obvious the Nottingham public were now also convinced they were credible contenders for the title. A crowd of 47,218 packed into the City Ground for this top-of-the-table clash. Although I'd been there at the time of the record 49,946 attendance during season 1967/68, I'd forgotten just how packed this stadium really was with almost 50,000 people inside. Not only was going to the toilet a complete non-starter - not at all pleasant if like me, you'd had a couple of hours in the pub beforehand - but you were literally unable to move one way or the other throughout the whole ninety minutes. However, an exciting, but tense affair, between the country's two 'premier' teams ended 1-1, with Forest's goal coming from the trusty left boot of midfielder Archie Gemmill - an absolute thunderbolt from the edge of the area.

They then travelled to St.James's Park on Wednesday, 28th December, where goals from Needham and McGovern earned them a 2-0 victory against struggling Newcastle United. They followed this up with an impressive 3-1 victory against Bristol City at Ashton Gate on Saturday, 31st December, with goals from Needham, Woodcock and O'Neill. And whilst the rest of the Nottingham public were preparing for their New Year's Eve celebrations, several thousand Forest supporters - myself included - were negotiating the long journey home from the West Country. I was on one of two special trains laid on by the Club and was fortunate enough to arrive back in time to celebrate on home turf, what had been a wonderful year for the whole Club.

If Cloughie needed further evidence of the Nottingham public's willingness to support a successful side, then this came in the guise of another bumper 40,000-plus crowd for the next home game against Championship rivals Everton on Monday, 2nd January 1978. The attendance of 44,030, meant close on 100,000 people had flocked to the City Ground over the festive period alone. Hardly the sort of statistics you'd associate with an 'apathetic' public. Once again, the 'Reds' had to settle for a point in this game, with the ice-cool Robertson grabbing their goal from the penalty spot.

On Saturday, 7th January, Forest took a brief, but welcome break from the League and turned their attentions to the FA Cup - a trophy which they hadn't lifted since 1959, and one which had eluded Cloughie throughout his managerial career. They'd been drawn at home to Third Division Swindon Town, the team with whom they'd fought out that epic Cup battle back in the 1966/67 season. However, on this occasion, the 'Robins' proved no match for the 'Mighty Reds' and were swept aside at the first attempt. Two goals from Woodcock and one each from Withe and Robertson secured Forest's comfortable 4-0 victory, in front of a crowd of 28,953.

It was back to League action again the following week, with the 'Red Army' marching into 'Shitesville'. However, they were rather surprisingly held to a 0-0 draw at the 'Sheep-dip' by the middle-of-the-table 'Rams'. But despite this stalemate, they now had a total of 38 points from 25 games and were four points clear of second-placed Everton, who'd played the same number of games. Fourth-placed Arsenal would be the next visitors to Nottingham the following weekend, but in the meantime, the 'Reds' had an important League Cup quarter-final tie against Bury at Gigg Lane to attend to in midweek.

I travelled up to the North-West on one of two coaches from the Inham Nook pub in Chilwell and we arrived at the ground well before kick off. This gave us plenty of time to indulge in our customary pre-match ritual of five pints of lager and a good old sing song, followed by a cold meat pie and a Bovril in the ground just before kick off. As usual, there were thousands of 'Travelling Trickies' amongst the crowd of 21,268 who were packed into the tiny stadium. Apart from a few hundred in the seats, the bulk of the travelling support was crammed into an old wooden stand at one end of the ground.

As seems to be the norm inside most grounds in Lancashire - be they large Premiership stadiums or small Third Division venues such as Bury - the atmosphere inside Gigg Lane was electric. Realistically, there was only ever going to be one outcome to this completely one-sided encounter. The semi-final stage of the competition was bound to present Forest with a much sterner test, but this would be inevitable if they were to fulfil their long-awaited dream of a trip to Wembley. As already mentioned, I had vowed long before that my first ever trip to the 'Twin Towers' would be to see my beloved Forest and I wasn't prepared to set foot inside the famous old stadium under any other circumstances.

By the time they swept into a 3-0 lead against Bury, with goals from Bowyer, O'Neill and Robertson, the celebrations had already begun: *"Aye-Oh, Aye-Oh, We are the Trent End boys; Aye-Oh, Aye-Oh, We are the Trent End boys; We are the best team in the land, this no one can deny; We will follow the Fo-o-rest!"* sang 5,000 jubilant fans, whilst at the same time bouncing up and down on the flimsy wooden terraces. The stand was so old; the whole of the floor was flexing up and down like a springboard under the weight. Amongst our gang from Chilwell that evening, was a certain Mr Garry Birtles, who'd travelled up by car with a few of the lads from the Cadland. Although he'd not figured in a first team game since his debut against Hull City the previous season, he was still on the fringe of the first team, thanks to some consistently good performances in the Reserves.

It was back to League action the following Saturday with that home fixture against Arsenal. They'd previously inflicted upon Forest their heaviest defeat of the season at Highbury. The 'Reds' were back to full strength for this game with the return of Shilton, Needham and Gemmill - all of whom had been Cup-tied in midweek. And ironically, this particular trio were to play a significant part in a pulsating 2-0 victory, in front of a crowd of 35,743.

After intense early pressure on the Arsenal goal, Needham put the 'Reds' in front with an unstoppable header into the roof of the Trent End goal, following a right wing corner from Woodcock. Shilton then made a couple of excellent saves, in particular one from striker Alan Sunderland, enabling Forest to retain their one goal advantage. 'Wee Archie' then scored what must rank as one of the goals of all time on Trentside, effectively putting the game beyond Arsenal's reach.

Yet again, the BBC's Match of the Day cameras were there to record the action, with the following commentary from David Coleman brilliantly describing Gemmill's effort:

"Pat Rice, the Arsenal captain knowing full well that all they need is a goal...and that's Gemmill - he really stole that!...Withe...he's got support from Woodcock in the middle...there's two against two...Gemmill's arrived all the way from the back, and Withe hasn't seen him...he has now - 2-0!"

FOREST'S dramatic season continued with a fourth round FA Cup tie the following Saturday against high-riding Manchester City at home. Once again, this game ended in a 2-1 victory for the 'Reds', thanks to goals from John Robertson - a magnificent curling effort from 25 yards out - and Peter Withe, in front of a crowd of 38,509. With almost two thirds of the season now over, Forest were very serious contenders for all three of English football's major domestic honours. Not only were they some six points clear at the top of the table, but they were also due to play Leeds United in a two-legged League Cup semi-final, and were through to the fifth round of the FA Cup. They'd been drawn away to First Division QPR in this competition. The Saturday before the Leeds trip, they entertained Wolves at the City Ground and another impressive 2-0 victory, with goals from Woodcock and skipper John McGovern, earned them two more precious points in front of a crowd of 28,803.

Over 10,000 fans made the 70-mile journey from Nottingham to Leeds in the hope of cheering the 'Reds' onto Wembley. The atmosphere inside Elland Road, generated by a crowd of 43,222, was absolutely incredible. From the first whistle, it was apparent Forest hadn't travelled up there merely to secure a first leg draw. Their fast, counter-attacking football was breathtaking and they soon began to overwhelm a shell-shocked Leeds. Two goals from the superb Withe - the first an unstoppable header - the second a powerful low shot from six yards out - gave them an early 2-0 lead. The travelling hordes were going berserk and the only sound echoing loudly around the stadium, was that of the Trent End's latest anthem:

Although Leeds did manage to pull one back before half-time, John O'Hare - making his first senior appearance of the season - put the game beyond doubt in the second half, with a low shot from 20 yards out, following a neat one-two with Bowyer.

As the final whistle blew, the travelling army of supporters began to celebrate what was surely an inevitable place for the 'Reds' in the League Cup Final at Wembley. Unfortunately, there were some ugly scenes outside afterwards, as rival supporters fought

City Ground,
Oh mist rolling in from the Trent,
My desire, is always to be here,
Oh City Ground;

Far have I travelled,
And much have I seen,
Goodison, Anfield,
The places I've been;

Maine Road, Old Trafford,
Still echo to the sounds,
Of the boys in the red shirts,
At the Ci-ty Ground;

City Ground,
Oh mist rolling in from the Trent,
My desire, is always to be here,
Oh City Ground.

running battles with one another in the streets around the ground.

At this point in time, life as a Forest supporter was not only an exciting and rewarding one, but it was also a very expensive one. No sooner had the euphoria of this victory over Leeds died down, than we were once again on the road in pursuit of further possible Cup glory. It was off to Loftus Road to take on QPR in the fifth round of the FA Cup on Saturday, 18th February.

Once again, over 5,000 fans made the 120-mile journey south to North-West London to see another tense and exciting Cup battle fought out on a bone hard and freezing pitch. And although the 'Reds' went behind to a first-half header from striker Martin Busby; roared on by their noisy travelling army, they laid siege to the Rangers' goal throughout the second half. But, despite throwing everything bar the kitchen sink at goalkeeper Phil Parkes, it seemed their hopes of a domestic treble were about to disappear.

However, with only seconds left on the clock, Gemmill broke clear down the left flank and sent over an inch-perfect cross for the on-rushing O'Neill. He aimed a glancing header into the far corner of the net, thereby earning the 'Reds' a replay, and at the same time sending the 'Red & White Army' into a state of frenzy. Their treble hopes were, after all, still very much alive.

The following Wednesday, it was back to League Cup action and the semi-final second leg tie against Leeds at the City Ground. This fixture had originally been scheduled for the week before, but had been postponed at the very last minute due to a frozen pitch. This angered the near 40,000 fans who'd undertaken a wasted journey to the ground. The Leeds fans in particular were furious and strongly criticised the Club and match officials.

With a sizeable following amongst the 38,131 crowd roaring them on, Leeds set about Forest straight from the kick off. And it was no surprise when they took a twelfth-minute lead, following an unstoppable thirty-yard strike from Frank Gray, which crashed into the roof of the net. Although the 'Reds' were soon on level terms, thanks to an effort from Peter Withe, in front of a very relieved Trent End, a mistake by Lloyd shortly afterwards let in winger Arthur Graham to put the visitors in front for a second time. They continued to press forward and shortly before the break, cultured midfielder Tony Currie, curled a vicious thirty-yard shot against the underside of the Forest bar. Had this effort been just two inches lower, the precious two-goal advantage built up in the first leg at Elland Road would have been cancelled out. The half-time whistle came as a big relief to both players and supporters alike.

Despite the Yorkshiremen's dominance of the first half, the 'Reds' proved a different proposition after the break and slowly began to take a grip of the game. This was the Forest we'd become accustomed to. Bowyer pulled them level on the night, O'Neill increased the lead to 3-2, and finally Woodcock added a fourth. This effectively put the tie beyond United's reach. The Forest crowd were ecstatic; it was the first time I'd ever heard the whole ground singing together in unison. The sound of: *"Tell mi mam - mi mam, I don't want no tea - no tea,"* rang out right across Nottingham. Yes, after all these years of living in hope, I really was finally going to see Forest playing in a major Cup Final at Wembley

As this game was at least another month away, Forest had more pressing matters to attend to. First of all, it was back to League action and a trip to Norwich City on Saturday, 25th February. They took the first half by storm in this game, running up a 3-0 interval lead, thanks to goals from Withe, Barrett and O'Neill. However, possibly as a result of fatigue, they went to pieces after the break and were lucky in the end to escape from Carrow Road with a point. Still, it was another precious step nearer to the title and they had also now stretched their unbeaten run to nineteen games.

The following Monday, it was time once again to do battle with QPR in the FA Cup. This encounter would decide who'd go into the last eight of the competition. And despite the visitors' less than substantial following, an impressive 40,097 people flocked to the City Ground to watch this fifth round replay. Once again though, it ended in a 1-1 draw, although on this occasion, only after extra time had been played.

Although John Robertson scored for Forest from the penalty spot, the game is probably best remembered for the Trent End's incessant taunting of Rangers' midfield star Stan Bowles. It had been widely reported in the press prior to the game that Stan's misses had recently left him, unable to cope any longer with his insatiable appetite for gambling. Consequently, chants of: *"Stan Bowles - Stan Bowles, Where's yer wife? Stan Bowles - where's yer wife?* rang out throughout the whole of the game.

On the toss of a coin, it was back to the City Ground again three nights later, in a bid to finally resolve matters at the third attempt. On this occasion, two goals from Woodcock and another from O'Neill ensured the 'Reds' ran out comfortable 3-1 winners, in front of another large crowd of 33,950. Once again during this game, the Trent Enders excelled themselves with another priceless ditty:

> *Tell mi mam - mi mam,*
> *T' put the champagne on ice,*
> *We're goin' t' Wembley twice,*
> *Tell mi mam - mi mam!*

Imagine my astonishment many years later, when I heard Middlesbrough fans chanting this very same song - word for word - when they were on their way to both the FA and League Cup Finals during season 1996/97. Now, either someone in the Northeast had just stumbled across these lyrics by sheer coincidence, or they've been doing the rounds for the last two decades. Anyway, on behalf of the Trent End, I hereby lay claim to this particular terrace song, backed up by the following quote from Secretary Ken Smales in the Forest Review for the game against Leicester City on Tuesday, 14th March 1978:

> *"There are signs that humour is returning to the terraces at the City Ground, although it must be said that this situation may only prevail just as long as we continue to win. "...put the champagne on ice, we're going to Wembley twice" was one example..."*

(Ever get the feeling Ken didn't like us by any chance?)

The Cup battle with Rangers was followed by a 2-0 League victory over West Ham at home on Saturday, 4th March. A goal from centre-half Needham and a Robertson penalty gave the 'Reds' another vital two points, in front of a crowd of 33,924. The following Saturday, it was back to FA Cup action again though and a quarter-final trip to West Brom. They were enjoying a relatively successful period in their history under the guidance of 'larger than life' manager Ron Atkinson. Their side boasted a number of quality players, such as Cyrille Regis, Derek Statham, Ali Brown and Willie Johnston. Although they occupied a position in the top half of the First Division table, the Cup represented probably their only real chance of winning some silverware this season. Consequently, they were not likely to be pushovers for Forest, despite the fact we were now unbeaten in our last 22 competitive games.

Around 10,000 Forest fans made the 50-mile trip to the Hawthorns and were packed tightly into the Smethick End of the stadium. From the first whistle it was clear the 'Baggies' were up for it, and they never allowed Forest to get into their stride. A rather fortuitous looping effort from Mick Martin put them 1-0 up in the first half, and a tremendous opportunist goal from Regis early on in the second increased their lead. Only then did the 'Reds' begin to show what they were made of; but despite laying siege to the Albion goal for the final half-hour of the contest - during which they had a Woodcock effort disallowed for off-side - it was just never going to be their day. Consequently, their long unbeaten run was now over...as was their quest for the treble.

As the travelling hordes spilled out of the Smethick End after the final whistle, some bright spark decided to set fire to a wooden kiosk situated just outside the stadium. The narrow footpath at the back of the stand was filled with thousands of fans trying to make their way out of the ground. Initially the flames and smoke caused a degree of panic amongst these supporters, who were crammed into the alleyway like sardines. A number of them climbed over a six-foot high fence, which led down to the back gardens of some nearby houses. Within seconds, hundreds of youths were clambering over and making their way down the steep embankment. One bewildered-looking resident, could only stand open-mouthed on his back doorstep, as an army of fans poured through his back garden, up his path, and out through his front gate. I could hardly contain myself as I tried to imagine what this must have looked like to his neighbours across the road!

Despite the disappointment of this FA Cup exit, Wembley fever was sweeping through the City of Nottingham as Forest prepared themselves for their League Cup Final battle against the Mighty Liverpool, due to take place on Saturday, 18th March. The Club's official allocation of tickets for this showpiece game was 30,000 - slightly more than the 12,500 allocation for the FA Cup Final against Luton Town in 1959 - although in reality many thousands would also be acquired through a variety of other sources.

Forest prepared for their trip to Wembley with an important League game against their relegation-threatened neighbours Leicester City at home on Tuesday, 14th March. Prior to this fixture, the top of the First Division table looked like this:

Position	P	W	D	L	GF	GA	Pts
1. FOREST	29	19	7	3	54	18	45
2. Everton	31	16	9	6	58	36	41
3. Manchester City	30	17	5	8	56	33	39
4. Arsenal	31	15	8	8	41	26	38
5. Liverpool	31	16	6	9	42	28	38
6. Coventry City	30	15	7	8	58	46	37

Whether it was the shock of losing their first game in what seemed like an eternity, or just pre-Wembley nerves, but once again Forest failed to turn on the style against the 'Foxes'. However, they did manage to scrape a 1-0 victory, courtesy of a Robertson penalty, in front of a crowd of 32,355. They therefore secured for themselves another two vitally important points. Although they were heading to Wembley with a depleted squad, due to Shilton, Gemmill and Needham all being Cup-tied, they took comfort from the fact they were now six points clear in the battle for the League title. They also still had a game in hand over second placed Everton.

AS we set off from the Cadland car park in Chilwell at 8.00-a.m. the following Saturday to make the long-awaited journey to the 'Twin Towers', we were filled with excitement and anticipation. Could we overcome the might of Liverpool without three key players? Would we reach Wembley in time for the kick off? And would the famous old stadium prove as awesome in real life as it had always seemed on the telly? These were the questions we were all asking.

Everyone had turned out for this game, and for the first time in ages, our entire gang from the 'good old days' was re-united. Graham, Wags, Mick Coll, Tom Clough, Swinie, Ollie, Chambo - they were all there for this one. We departed from the Cad' in a convoy of cars, vans and minibuses, all festooned with red and white scarves, flags and banners, each one proclaiming our allegiance to NFFC.

As we joined the M1 at junction 25, the sheer volume of Wembley-bound traffic overwhelmed me. Every mode of transport available to mankind seemed to be heading south from Nottingham. Before we'd even reached Leicester Forest East, we'd experienced several lengthy and frustrating hold-ups. However, this was nothing compared to the delays we were about to encounter just south of Leicester, as the M1 and M6 motorways merged. The latter was of course carrying similar volumes of Cup Final traffic from Liverpool.

As we sat there motionless in a seemingly endless snarl up of assorted vehicles, I was already beginning to wish we'd opted for one of the many special trains departing from Midlands Station that morning. Or even to have had the good sense to travel down on Friday, along with hundreds of other supporters. But, just as I was about to give up hope of getting there on time, we slowly began to gather momentum and the remainder of the journey remained relatively trouble free. As we finally got near to the stadium, we came across hundreds of drinking and chanting Forest supporters who'd already arrived in the Capital, and seemed to have taken over every single pub within a five-mile radius of Wembley. Having hastily parked up, we headed straight for the nearest pub where we indulged in a most enjoyable couple of hours.

When we set off down Wembley Way about twenty minutes before kick off, the sight of tens of thousands of Forest and Liverpool fans dressed from head to toe in red and white hats, scarves, banners and flags, was one to behold. The carnival-like atmosphere outside the stadium was exactly as I'd dreamt a million times before.

We'd been allocated the 'Tunnel End' and after making our way up a steep flight of steps; we eventually made it through the turnstiles. We then climbed a never-ending staircase leading to the top of a huge bank of terracing in the upper tier. As we got within yards of the entrance, the noise coming from within was deafening. As we spilled through and onto the top of the terraces, the sight of 100,000 flag-waving fans was breathtaking. In 1971, I'd attended the Rangers versus Celtic Cup Final at Hamden Park, Glasgow and was amongst an 'old firm' crowd of 130,000 people - most of whom were pissed as farts. However, as Forest and Liverpool took to the field this day at Wembley, the atmosphere was as good as I'd ever experienced in my lifetime.

The teams lined up as follows:

	FOREST	LIVERPOOL	
1	Chris Woods	Ray Clemence	1
2	Viv Anderson	Phil Neal	2
3	Frank Clark	Tommy Smith	3
4	John McGovern (Captn.)	Phil Thompson	4
5	Larry Lloyd	Ray Kennedy	5
6	Kenny Burns	Emlyn Hughes (Captn.)	6
7	Martin O'Neill	Kenny Dalglish	7
8	Ian Bowyer	Jimmy Case	8
9	Peter Withe	Steve Heighway	9
10	Tony Woodcock	Terry McDermott	10
11	John Robertson	Ian Callaghan	11
	Sub: John O'Hare	Sub: David Fairclough	

It would be fair to say Liverpool - the Bookies' favourites - were the better side on the day. In fact, they almost overwhelmed Forest's relatively inexperienced team. But then again, appearing in Wembley Finals was almost a habit for them. In contrast to this, it was a 'first' for almost the entire Forest squad. Roared on as they were from start to finish by their noisy and passionate 40,000-strong army, the 'Reds' held on throughout the ninety minutes and then again through extra-time. This was due in no small way to the heroics of 18-year-old Chris Woods in goal, as he bravely kept Dalglish and Co. at bay. Forest carved out very few chances during the whole 120 minutes, but were nevertheless, given a standing ovation upon the final whistle. Although we hadn't actually lifted the trophy in the famous old stadium, nothing was going to spoil an otherwise wonderful occasion for the Club; it's fans, and the City of Nottingham.

Old Trafford, Manchester was the designated venue for the replay, and so we were heading north the following Wednesday to see the two sides battle it out once again. This time our chosen mode of transport was the train and we clambered aboard one of the many specials laid on for the occasion. Liverpool had been allocated a larger share of the 55,000 tickets and it seemed the Kop End had transported itself en-masse to a temporary home on the famous Stretford End. However, the 26,000-plus Forest supporters amongst the crowd of 54,375, were determined not to be out-sung. Consequently, the atmosphere inside Old Trafford was electric.

An injury to skipper John McGovern had ruled him out of this replay and effectively stretched Forest's resources to the limit. The experienced O'Hare had taken his place in the centre of midfield, and on the substitute's bench, sat the previously untested Stephen Elliott. Despite this, Forest gave the Merseysiders a much stiffer test than in the first encounter at Wembley and overall, the game was much more evenly balanced. What's more, a score-line of 0-0 at half-time gave heart to players and supporters alike.

As the second half got underway, Forest - playing in all-yellow - were kicking towards their massed ranks of supporters in the Scoreboard End of the ground. The sound of: *"Come on you Yellows,"* rang out impressively all around Old Trafford. And the players seemed to grow in confidence and stature as each minute ticked by. With the half only seven minutes old, an inch-perfect pass put O'Hare clean through the Liverpool defence and left him with only keeper Clemence to beat. Just as he was about to enter the box, defender Phil Thompson deliberately and cynically cut him down from behind. And, despite vociferous protests from the Liverpool players - who were vehemently claiming he'd been outside the box when the initial contact was made - referee Pat Partridge stood firm and awarded the spot kick.

As the ice-cool Robertson stepped up to take it, the tension on the terraces at our end of the stadium was quite unbearable. Many supporters just couldn't watch as he took his customary four paces and calmly slotted the ball into the bottom left-hand corner of the net. The 'Red & White Nottingham Army' went absolutely berserk. I could hardly hear myself think; such was the noise.

The final thirty minutes of the game were full of nail-biting action. Firstly, 'Robbo' went agonisingly close to making it 2-0 with a thumping drive from the edge of the box, brilliantly saved by Clemence. And then Terry McDermott blasted a stunning twenty-yarder into the bottom corner of the Forest net, only for it to be ruled out for an alleged handball. This brought a further storm of protests from the irate Liverpool players, who claimed he'd controlled it on his chest as he bore down on goal.

But, despite intense pressure during the final stages of the game, the 'Reds' held firm. And this was due in no small way to the heroics of Kenny Burns in the heart of the defence - he was simply magnificent. Never had I witnessed such total commitment from anyone in a Forest shirt. He deserved the freedom of the City for his performance that evening - along with the rest of his team-mates of course. It was fitting he, in his role as acting captain, should be the one to go up and receive the trophy. As he proudly held it aloft in front of thousands of ecstatic supporters, he became the first Forest player to lift a major trophy since 1959, when Jack Burkitt had lifted the FA Cup. Take it from me, we were dancing in the streets of Manchester that evening.

The only blemish on this otherwise wonderful occasion, was the bleating and moaning of the mardy 'Scousers' after the game - particularly Phil Thompson and Emlyn Hughes. Thompson whinged on and on about the foul having been committed outside the box and that it had been a 'calculated professional foul' on his part. All I can say in response is, it's a bloody shame he wasn't sent off as well. Emlyn Hughes just whinged on about everything, as usual. Still, they weren't going to spoil our party. We headed home determined to celebrate a wonderful triumph and one which would be savoured by everyone associated with our great Club.

THREE days later, a crowd of 35,552 turned up at the City Ground to pay homage to the team and to see them proudly show off their bounty, prior to the game against Newcastle.

Despite the comfortable five-point lead they held at the top of the table, with twelve games still to play, there was no room for complacency. The pitch was by this time showing the strain of 23 competitive matches, and following a prolonged period of wet weather, resembled a potato patch. In spite of these appalling conditions, they managed to notch up another priceless win. A Robertson penalty and a scrambled effort from Anderson gave them a 2-0 success over the relegation-doomed Geordies.

A 2-2 draw away to Middlesbrough the following Wednesday, with goals from Woodcock and O'Neill, stretched their unbeaten run in the League to an impressive 16 matches. Their last defeat had been the controversial one at Leeds way back in November. This was followed by a 3-1 April Fool's Day victory over Chelsea at home, thanks to goals from Burns, Robertson and O'Neill, in front of a crowd of 31,262.

On Wednesday, 5th April, we set off for Birmingham to see them take on mid-table Aston Villa. Once again, we travelled to this game on the Forest-Rail special, which took us directly to Whitton Station, only a short walk from Villa Park. And as usual, the train was packed to the rafters. In recent years at least, this contest had become something of an eagerly awaited 'derby' game. As we stood patiently waiting for our police escort in the station concourse, the sound of the Trent End's latest anthem rang out:

You are my Forest,
My only Forest,
You make me happy,
When skies are grey;

You'll never notice,
'ow much I love you,
Please don't take,
My For-est away!

La-la-la-la-la,
La-la-la-la-la,...

Forest were played off the park that night. However, Championship-winning sides are built upon the ability to defend resolutely when asked to and then clinically catch the opposition on the break. And that is exactly what happened on this occasion. They withstood everything Villa could throw at them for 88 minutes, only for Woodcock to plunder the winning goal with his head in the dying seconds. This had been more or less their only serious attempt on goal all evening. As the thousands of travelling fans packed tightly into the North Stand began to celebrate another decisive victory, the home fans left the ground quite rightly proclaiming: "We wuz robbed!"

On the very same evening, Everton - our only serious challengers for the title - were losing 1-0 at Goodison Park to arch-rivals Liverpool. This meant with eight games to go, Forest needed only six points to secure their first ever League Championship.

The first of these was secured the following Tuesday at Maine Road, when they battled out a goalless draw with Man City in front of 43,428 spectators. And their somewhat unimpressive form continued the following Saturday when they stumbled to an uninspiring 1-1 draw with Leeds at the City Ground. However, Peter Withe's first goal in 13 games, knocked another point off their target in front of a crowd of 38,662.

Due to their substantial Cup commitments throughout the season, Forest's backlog of fixtures had grown to significant proportions. The last few League games were consequently now coming thick and fast. The one against QPR on Tuesday, 18th April, was one of ten they were involved in during that month alone. This also included testimonial games for Derby's Henry Newton and Notts County's Les Bradd. However, a 1-0 victory over the 'Rs', thanks to a Robertson penalty, virtually assured them of the title in front of 30,339 ecstatic fans. Pragmatic as ever, Cloughie wasn't prepared to accept the title had been secured - not until it became a mathematical certainty anyway. And they still needed another point from their remaining five matches to put the matter completely beyond doubt.

On the back of this, a 10,000-strong army of supporters converged on Coventry for their next game four days later. And Saturday, 22nd April 1978 would prove to be a monumental day in the history of Nottingham Forest Football Club. Although City were riding high in the table themselves and boasted the 'fearsome' strike-force of Ian Wallace and Mick Ferguson, the 'Red & White Army' marched into Coventry convinced the 'Reds' would secure the one point they needed.

Once again though, their end of season dip in form meant it was 'backs to the wall' stuff all the way through to the final whistle. Shilton made several acrobatic saves to keep the rampant 'Sky Blues' at bay and the score at 0-0. The final whistle was the signal for mass celebrations at the 'red and white' end of Highfield Road. The thousands of fans packed into this stand were dancing around all over the place, hugging and kissing one another, and generally going berserk. Some even climbed up to the very top of the floodlights to hang up their Forest scarves and banners. A few hundred also managed to get onto the pitch, and as hundreds of rival supporters at the other end had done likewise, the police had to act swiftly to prevent a pitched battle taking place.

When the players finally left the pitch after several minutes of celebrating, the Forest supporters refused to leave the stadium. Highfield Road reverberated to the sound of *"Forest ever Forest"* long after the game had ended. Naturally, the celebrations spilled out onto the streets of Coventry and continued all the way back home to Nottingham. The City Centre was awash with red and white clad youths long into the early hours. No one wanted to go home that night and I'm sure many didn't. Many more like me, went home, but simply couldn't remember how, or even when! Still, you wait half your lifetime and more to see your team win a League Championship; and the majority of football supporters up and down the country never, ever get to fulfil this improbable dream. When it comes your way therefore, you have to savour every moment of it.

The partying had barely died down when the 'Reds' headed off to Portman Road the following Tuesday evening to take on Ipswich Town. With two trophies already safely in the bag, the end of season nerves subsided and their superior brand of football once again emerged. So much so that even full-back Frank Clark - still without a League goal in the whole of his long and distinguished career - decided to get in on the act. He scored an excellent goal as the 'Champions' came away with a comfortable 2-0 victory under their belts.

Before the final home game of the season against Birmingham City the following Saturday, the players were officially presented with the Championship trophy in front of an appreciative crowd of 37,625. For once, the pubs around the ground were actually empty before 3 o'clock, as even the most ardent of drinkers amongst Forest's army of supporters were eager to participate in this never to be forgotten experience. Having milked the applause, the players put aside their hard-earned medals and fought out a goalless draw with their Midlands counterparts. Although the game itself was hardly memorable, it was significant in that it confirmed Forest's unbeaten home status for the season in all competitions.

Immediately after their status as Champions had been confirmed at Coventry a week earlier, Clough and Taylor had taken the unprecedented step of negotiating for themselves a testimonial game in their own honour. This was staged at the City Ground on Bank Holiday Monday, 1st May 1978, two days after the Birmingham game. A Forest X1, based mainly around the current eleven, took on and beat a Derby County X1 by two-goals-to-one. A crowd of 18,272 turned up to pay homage to the pair and in the process give their respective bank balances a 'much needed' boost.

At the end of a season in which Cloughie had regularly maligned supporters for one reason or another, the Review for this game carried the following message from skipper John McGovern, under the heading *"THANKS A MILLION!"*:

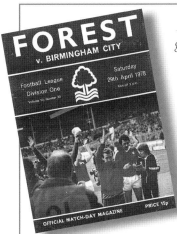

At the end of this season, unique for everyone at Nottingham Forest, it gives me great pleasure in saying "thank you" for your tremendous support.

There is a true saying in football that you are only as good as your last game. Hopefully, if the support we received continues in Europe, then every last game will be a memorable one.

One thing is certain, everyone at Nottingham Forest gave 100 per cent towards winning the League Championship and the Football League Cup.

We also expect 100 per cent in return from our supporters - and we think we get it!

Keep out of trouble, keep your voices in harmony, and thanks again from all the lads. See you in Europe!

WITH only two games left - both away - the only remaining challenge for the 'Reds' was that of extending their unbeaten run in the League to a staggering 26 matches. The first of these was against West Brom on Tuesday, 2nd May. Goals from Bowyer and Robertson (penalty) ensured honours were even. And following this exciting 2-2 draw, played on a warm spring evening, we were half-tempted to drop in again on our old friend who lives just over the wall, behind the back of the stadium. On this occasion though, we thought it best not to trudge through his back garden uninvited.

Their final game of the season - a 0-0 draw against Liverpool at Anfield two days later - kept their unbeaten sequence in tact and meant they'd finished the season seven points clear of their Merseyside rivals, who finished as Runners-up. Kenny Burns was one noticeable absentee from the Forest line-up - he was in London picking up the Sportswriters' Player of the Year Award. Several weeks earlier, Peter Shilton had picked up the PFA Player of the Year Award and Tony Woodcock the Young Player of the Year Award at the Hilton Hotel. This meant as a Club, Forest had just about grabbed every honour in the domestic game this season.

This had been a monumental year for Nottingham Forest Football Club, and one I - as a fanatical lifelong supporter - will never forget. Most football supporters (with the exception of 'Scousers' and 'Mancunians') never get to see their team achieve more than an occasional, fleeting glimpse of success. However, in one season alone, I'd witnessed my team capturing the League Championship and League Cup trophies, and seen them go an unbelievable 28 matches unbeaten at the City Ground in all competitions. What's more, they'd lost just four out of a total of 55 competitive matches overall, and hadn't been beaten at all in the final 26 League fixtures home or away!

Furthermore, their exciting brand of football had won them countless admirers up and down the country and seen them playing to packed audiences week in and week out. City Ground attendances were also back to the levels of the late-1960s, with no less than 18 games attracting crowds in excess of 30,000. The highest of these was the 47,218 for the visit of Liverpool and the average overall in the League was 32,501. And what more could any football supporter wish for from their team? European success perhaps? But no, that kind of glory only ever comes the way of the Liverpools and the Manchester Uniteds of this world, doesn't it?

SEASON 1977/78 – STATISTICS

FOOTBALL LEAGUE DIVISION ONE – FIXTURES

Date		Opposition	Venue	Competition	Score	Attendance
Aug	20	Everton	A	League	3-1	38,001
	23	**Bristol City**	**H**	**League**	**1-0**	**21,743**
	27	**Derby County**	**H**	**League**	**3-0**	**28,807**
	30	**West Ham United**	**H**	**LC 2**	**5-0**	**18,224**
Sept	3	Arsenal	A	League	0-3	40,810
	10	Wolverhampton Wanderers	A	League	3-2	24,622
	17	**Aston Villa**	**H**	**League**	**2-0**	**31,016**
	24	Leicester City	A	League	3-0	21,447
Oct	**1**	**Norwich City**	**H**	**League**	**1-1**	**23,741**
	4	**Ipswich Town**	**H**	**League**	**4-0**	**26,845**
	8	West Ham United	A	League	0-0	26,126
	15	**Manchester City**	**H**	**League**	**2-1**	**35,572**
	22	Queens Park Rangers	A	League	2-0	24,449
	25	**Notts County**	**H**	**LC 3**	**4-0**	**26,931**
	29	**Middlesbrough**	**H**	**League**	**4-0**	**27,373**
Nov	5	Chelsea	A	League	0-1	36,116
	12	**Manchester United**	**H**	**League**	**2-1**	**30,183**
	19	Leeds United	A	League	0-1	42,925
	26	**West Bromwich Albion**	**H**	**League**	**0-0**	**31,908**
	29	**Aston Villa**	**H**	**LC 4**	**4-2**	**29,333**
Dec	3	Birmingham City	A	League	2-0	29,925
	10	**Coventry City**	**H**	**League**	**2-1**	**29,823**
	17	Manchester United	A	League	4-0	54,374
	26	**Liverpool**	**H**	**League**	**1-1**	**47,218**
	28	Newcastle United	A	League	2-0	41,612
	31	Bristol City	A	League	3-1	31,990
Jan	**2**	**Everton**	**H**	**League**	**1-1**	**44,030**
	7	**Swindon Town**	**H**	**FA Cup 3**	**4-1**	**28,953**
	14	Derby County	A	League	0-0	33,384
	17	Bury	A	LC 5	3-0	21,268
	21	**Arsenal**	**H**	**League**	**2-0**	**35,743**
	24	**Manchester City**	**H**	**FA Cup 4**	**2-1**	**38,509**
Feb	**4**	**Wolverhampton Wanderers**	**H**	**League**	**2-0**	**28,803**
	8	Leeds United	A	LCSF - 1st Leg	3-1	43,222
	18	Queens Park Rangers	A	FA Cup 5	1-1	26,803
	22	**Leeds United**	**H**	**LCSF - 2nd Leg**	**4-2**	**38,131**
	25	Norwich City	A	League	3-3	26,004
	27	**Queens Park Rangers**	**H**	**FA Cup 5 - Replay**	**1-1**	**40,097**
Mar	**2**	**Queens Park Rangers**	**H**	**FA Cup 5 - 2nd Replay**	**3-1**	**33,950**
	4	**West Ham United**	**H**	**League**	**2-0**	**33,924**
	11	West Bromwich Albion	A	FA Cup 6	0-2	36,506
	14	**Leicester City**	**H**	**League**	**1-0**	**32,355**
	18	Liverpool (At Wembley Stadium)		LC - Final	0-0	100,000
	22	Liverpool (At Old Trafford)		LC - Final Replay	1-0	54,375
	25	**Newcastle United**	**H**	**League**	**2-0**	**35,552**
	29	Middlesbrough	A	League	2-2	25,445
Apr	**1**	**Chelsea**	**H**	**League**	**3-1**	**31,262**
	5	Aston Villa	A	League	1-0	44,215
	11	Manchester City	A	League	0-0	43,428
	15	**Leeds United**	**H**	**League**	**1-1**	**38,662**
	18	**Queens Park Rangers**	**H**	**League**	**1-0**	**30,339**
	22	Coventry City	A	League	0-0	36,881
	25	Ipswich Town	A	League	2-0	30,062
	29	**Birmingham City**	**H**	**League**	**0-0**	**37,625**
May	2	West Bromwich Albion	A	League	2-2	23,523
	4	Liverpool	A	League	0-0	50,021

HOME ATTENDANCES

	AGGREGATE ATTENDANCE	HIGHEST ATTENDANCE	LOWEST ATTENDANCE	AVERAGE ATTENDANCE
League:	682,524	47,218	21,743	32,501
League Cup:	112,619	38,131	18,224	28,154
FA Cup:	141,509	40,097	28,953	35,377
All Competitions:	936,652	47,218	18,224	32,298

FINAL LEAGUE TABLE - DIVISION ONE

Position	P	W	D	L	GF	GA	Pts
1. **Nottingham Forest**	**42**	**25**	**14**	**3**	**69**	**24**	**64**
2. Liverpool	42	24	9	9	65	34	57
3. Everton	42	22	11	9	76	45	55
4. Manchester City	42	20	12	10	74	51	52
5. Arsenal	42	21	10	11	60	37	52
6. West Bromwich Albion	42	18	14	10	62	53	50
7. Coventry City	42	18	12	12	75	62	48
8. Aston Villa	42	18	10	14	57	42	46
9. Leeds United	42	18	10	14	63	53	46
10. Manchester United	42	16	10	16	67	63	42
11. Birmingham City	42	16	9	17	55	60	41
12. Derby County	42	14	13	15	54	59	41
13. Norwich City	42	11	18	13	52	66	40
14. Middlesbrough	42	12	15	15	42	54	39
15. Wolverhampton Wanderers	42	12	12	18	51	64	36
16. Chelsea	42	11	14	17	46	69	36
17. Bristol City	42	11	13	18	49	53	35
18. Ipswich Town	42	11	13	18	47	61	35
19. Queens Park Rangers	42	9	15	18	47	64	33
20. West Ham United	42	12	8	22	52	69	32
21. Newcastle United	42	6	10	26	42	78	22
22. Leicester City	42	5	12	25	26	70	22

AWAY ATTENDANCES

	AGGREGATE ATTENDANCE	HIGHEST ATTENDANCE	LOWEST ATTENDANCE	AVERAGE ATTENDANCE
League:	725,360	54,374	21,447	34,540
League Cup:	218,865	100,000	21,268	54,716
FA Cup:	63,309	36,506	26,803	31,654
All Competitions:	1,007,534	100,000	21,268	37,316

"SHE WORE, SHE WORE, SHE WORE A SCARLET RIBBON"

FOREST'S MAGNIFICENT Championship winning season was followed during the summer of 1978 by one of the most exciting and entertaining World Cup tournaments of all time. This took place in South America, and in truly exhilarating and cavalier fashion, was won by the host nation Argentina. Their side was packed full of highly-skilled, articulate and completely uninhibited players such as Mario Kempes, Ricardo Villa and Osvaldo Ardiles and was captained by the inspirational Daniel Passarella. On their way to the Final - which took place in the impressive River Plate Stadium in Buenos Aires - they swept all opposition aside.

Their opponents in the Final were Holland, and roared on by their passionate, hot-blooded fans, they strolled to a 3-1 victory in a volatile and intimidating atmosphere. The team's arrival onto the pitch before every game would be greeted by a spectacular ticker-tape reception, as would each of their goals. This became the hallmark of the competition.

So impressive were the Argentinians, the players became household names around the world virtually overnight. And by the end of the tournament many of them had been earmarked by Europe's top clubs as immediate transfer targets. Shortly before the start of our domestic season, Tottenham manager Keith Burkinshaw had pulled off one of the transfer coups of the decade, by signing both Osvaldo Ardiles and Ricardo Villa for a joint fee of around £750,000. And guess who Spurs were scheduled to play on Saturday, 19th August - the opening day of the season...? Forest at the City Ground of course.

Unlike Spurs, Forest had made no signings whatsoever during the close season. However, having won the Championship the previous season, it could be argued the current squad of players was more than capable of dealing with the new set of challenges which lay ahead. One rather unsettling rumour beginning to circulate however, was that Peter Withe - having had a difference of opinion with Cloughie - would soon be on his way out of the Club.

Following his four-goal performance against Ipswich at the beginning of the previous campaign, he'd gone on to register just nine more in a further 47 competitive matches. Despite this, his all-round contribution to the performance of the team had been immense and had endeared him to the Forest faithful. Furthermore, during their emphatic 5-0 demolition of Ipswich in the Charity Shield at Wembley on Saturday, 12th August, he'd looked as sharp and as robust as ever; scoring an excellent headed goal and making a telling contribution to the game.

This traditional curtain raiser to the season provided the backdrop for another wonderful day out for Forest's growing army of fans. The sun shone brightly over North-West London and the pubs around the stadium were packed full of thirsty and good-natured supporters; both sets of fans mixed freely together without a hint of trouble. And the quality of Forest's football was breathtaking. Martin O'Neill (2), Larry Lloyd and John Robertson scored the other goals in a one-sided affair in front of 64,438 fans. This sent a clear message to the rest of the First Division: Forest were not going to be 'one season wonders'.

HAVING renewed my season ticket for the Kop at a cost of £20, I set off eagerly for West Bridgford on the opening day of the season to see the 'Reds' do battle with the newly-promoted Londoners. I was also anxious to see the much talked about ground improvements which had taken place during the summer - apparently at such great expense. Not only had the entire City Ground terracing been dug up and replaced, but a new electronic scoreboard had also been installed at the back of the Bridgford End. Furthermore, to comply with UEFA regulations, a perimeter fence had been erected to prevent fans spilling onto the pitch during matches.

As I sat enjoying a pre-match pint outside the Town Arms on Trent Bridge (which later became the Aviary and is now called Casa), bathed in hot summer sunshine, the sheer number of Spurs fans making their way to the ground staggered me. It seemed the whole of North London had made the 120-mile journey to Nottingham to welcome their team back to the First Division. One train-load of fans escorted over the bridge by dozens of police must have numbered a thousand. It took about fifteen minutes to get them all across and, needless to say, there were a few skirmishes taking place. Sadly, there were numerous groups of boozed-up Forest supporters intent on having a go.

The Visitors' Enclosure at the City Ground was situated within the East Stand, and although this held around 3,000 when full to it's capacity, there were an estimated 9,000 Spurs fans amongst the crowd of 41,223. This was the largest away following I'd ever seen during my twelve seasons of watching the 'Reds'. The match wasn't all-ticket and consequently, once the ground was full to it's recently reduced capacity, the gates were closed, leaving thousands of disappointed supporters outside.

As the teams took to the field, a massive ticker-tape reception from the Spurs fans turned the City Ground into a 'Mini River Plate Stadium' and brought memories of the World Cup flooding back. Although O'Neill gave Forest a first-half lead, the Argentinians made a telling contribution to the game, with Ricardo Villa rounding off a fine individual performance by sliding in Tottenham's equaliser. Inevitably, with so many Spurs supporters inside the ground, the occasion was marred by spontaneous outbreaks of fighting which took place right along the East Stand throughout the course of the game.

Following an unimpressive goalless draw at Coventry three days later, it was off to North-West London again the following Saturday to see the 'Reds' take on Queens Park Rangers at Loftus Road. In contrast to the previous season's frost-bitten FA Cup encounter between the two sides in February, this game took place in red-hot summer sunshine. As we stood on the small open terracing at the School End of the ground prior to the game, a small group of Forest supporters climbed into the seats in the stand away to our left and began gathering up dozens of club newspapers which were draped over the back of the seats.

Once they'd gathered together a large bundle, they climbed back over the wall and made their way up to the rear of the Visitors' Enclosure, which by this time was almost full to it's 2,000 capacity. Only then did the purpose of this strange behaviour become clear, as they began ripping up the papers. As the teams took to the field, they were greeted by another ticker-tape reception. Once the excitement had died down and the teams were warming up in front of their respective fans, I noticed the whole of the terracing at our end of the ground had been left covered in a thick carpet of paper. This prompted a couple of pea-brained idiots to start bonfires on the concrete steps, causing a fair amount of discomfort to the rest of the travelling supporters.

This game ended in a goalless draw, as did the midweek League Cup tie against Oldham at Boundary Park three days later. Prior to the home game with West Brom the following Saturday, Cloughie was presented with the Bells Scotch Whisky Manager of the Year Award by Bells' Chairman Raymond Miquel - an accolade he richly deserved. Unfortunately for him - and the crowd of 28,239 - the 'Reds' could only muster another 0-0 draw - their fourth on the trot. On this occasion, they had youngster Steven Elliott leading the attack in place of the recently departed Withe. As mentioned earlier, he'd had one disagreement too many with Mr. Clough and as a result, had been palmed off to Second Division Newcastle United for a fee of around £250,000.

Not only was his departure a big disappointment to me, but I was also frustrated to see the blossoming talents of Garry Birtles overlooked; Cloughie obviously seeing more potential in the previously untried Elliott. However, he was largely unimpressive on his senior debut, as he was again in the 4-2 victory over Oldham in the League Cup replay at the City Ground some four days later.

With Forest sitting in tenth place in the table, having drawn all of their opening four League games - and in the process scoring only one goal - Cloughie finally decided to throw Birtles - and 16-year-old Gary Mills - into first team action against Arsenal at the City Ground on Saturday, 9th September. And this brave gamble paid dividends with both youngsters playing starring roles in Forest's impressive 2-1 success. Goals by Robertson (penalty) and Bowyer sealed their victory in front of a very relieved home crowd of 28,124.

Ironically, qualification for the European Cup had seen Forest drawn against the reigning Champions Liverpool in the first round. The first leg was scheduled to take place at the City Ground on Wednesday, 13th September and Birtles' display against Arsenal the previous Saturday had assured him of a place in the starting line-up for arguably the most important Cup game ever staged on Trentside. However, the fact Archie Gemmill had now recovered from injury meant Gary Mills was relegated to the substitute's bench.

An all-ticket crowd of 38,318 packed into the City Ground to witness this high profile encounter between England's two most talented teams. Although Forest were reigning League Champions, they were still considered inferior to the 'Mighty Liverpool' - at least, that is, in the eyes of the nation's soccer pundits. Liverpool's considerable experience in European football made them odds-on favourites to overcome European Cup novices Forest over the two legs. And their somewhat faltering start to the season only strengthened this argument.

However, no-one could have predicted the impact the young Birtles would have on this game. Not only did he score his first senior goal for the Club - and incidentally Forest's first ever in the European Cup - but he also ran the Liverpool defence - and in particular Phil Thompson - ragged throughout. Woodcock set things up for him during the first half, racing through the centre of Liverpool's defence and squaring the ball for him to side-foot it accurately into the bottom corner of the net from fifteen yards out. Not only was Garry ecstatic in scoring his debut goal, but the fact he'd scored it in front of the packed Trent End, the very place he'd stood many times as a young lad watching his own boyhood heroes, was real 'Roy of the Rovers' stuff.

He continued to be a thorn in Liverpool's side throughout the second half, although in fairness to them, they dominated for long periods without ever really looking like scoring. Then, just as the contest was entering it's final stages, and the visitors were beginning to view a 1-0 first leg deficit as acceptable, Birtles set off on a long and decisive run down the left flank. As he reached the by-line, he sent over an inch-perfect cross to the far post, where the unmarked Woodcock was now lurking. He headed the ball down perfectly for the on-rushing Colin Barrett, who smashed an unstoppable volley into the roof of the net. The City Ground erupted! As the final whistle blew and the players jumped all over one another in celebration, the near-40,000 crowd were unanimous in their praise. The sound of: *"One Garry Birtles...There's only one Garry Birtles...One Garry Bir-tles...There's only one Garry Birtles!"* echoed impressively around the ground.

HAVING secured a 1-1 draw against Manchester United at Old Trafford the following Saturday, the 'Reds' took on Middlesbrough at home a week later. Although this was a fairly mediocre affair which ended 2-2, Birtles scored his first ever League goal - and it was one of the finest individual efforts I've ever seen. Having picked up the ball just inside Middlesbrough's half, he pushed it first past one defender and, as he cut inside, through the legs of another. Then, as it bobbled along the edge of the box, he surged forward to crash an unstoppable half-volley into the back of the net with his favourite left peg. What a pity the television cameras weren't there to capture it on film.

In the Review for this game, the Club decided to wage war on the now notorious hooligan element amongst it's supporters. They published a blacklist of fans convicted by the courts following disturbances at the game against Arsenal two weeks previously. Not only did they print the names and addresses of ten convicted Forest supporters, but also the nature of their offences and the amount of the fines imposed. In each case this had been £400 plus costs; and when you consider the price of a terrace season ticket was just £20, it gives some indication of how seriously the courts were now viewing such offences. For reasons known only to themselves however, the Club chose only to single out those offenders with a

Nottingham address, whilst adding a footnote at the bottom of the page which read: "In addition to the above, there were seven offenders from London and one from South Wales."

The following Wednesday the 'Reds' travelled up to Anfield for the second leg of their European Cup tie against Liverpool. Despite their superb display in the first leg two weeks earlier, and their two-goal lead, the 'experts' were still predicting - some might even say hoping for - a Liverpool victory overall. Some of them even tried to justify their bias by suggesting Liverpool's greater European experience would give English football a far greater chance of securing it's third consecutive European Cup triumph.

What they hadn't taken into account though, was that Cloughie's whole footballing philosophy was based first and foremost on the principle of defending. His players had the ability to sit back comfortably, even under the severest of pressure, and then get men forward as quickly as possible from midfield to deliver the sucker punch. This strategy was tailor-made for the two-legged European competitions. What's more, a back-four that consisted of Viv Anderson, Larry Lloyd, Kenny Burns and Frank Clark, in front of a goalkeeper of Peter Shilton's stature was, to put it mildly, awesome! Needless to say, the 'Reds' came away from Anfield having fought out a well-earned 0-0 draw and of course a famous victory over the two legs.

The Final was scheduled to take place at the Olympic Stadium in Munich the following May and the Trent End were now predicting Forest's march to European glory. Their latest anthem rang out triumphantly around Anfield:

She wore, she wore,
She wore a scarlet ribbon,
She wore a scarlet ribbon,
In the merry month of May;

An' when I asked her,
Why she wore that ribbon?
She sez it's for the Forest fans,
Who's gooin' to Ger-ma-ny!

Ger-ma-ny, Ger-ma-ny,
Oh we're all pissed up,
An' wi gonna win the Cup,
Ger-ma-ny, Ger-ma-ny!

The following Saturday, the 'Reds' built upon this memorable European success with a 2-1 victory against Aston Villa at Villa Park. This was followed in midweek by a comprehensive 5-0 victory over Third Division Oxford United at the Manor Ground in the third round of the League Cup - a competition which was rapidly becoming Forest's favourite. And by the time they entertained Wolves at home on Saturday, 7th October, they'd climbed to sixth position in the First Division table, with ten points from eight games - five points behind early season pacemakers Liverpool.

A 3-1 victory for Forest, thanks to two goals from the rapidly maturing Birtles and another from the ever dependable O'Neill, in front of a crowd of 29,313, was then followed by another 3-1 success against Bristol City at Ashton Gate the following Saturday. Birtles again grabbed one of the goals, with Robertson netting the other two. As they began their preparations for the midweek trip to Greece to take on AEK Athens in the second round of the European Cup, their faltering start to the season was now nothing more than a distant memory.

And an excellent performance in their first competitive game on foreign soil for almost eleven years enabled them to build up a solid 2-1 first-leg lead. Once again Birtles was on the score-sheet, with skipper John McGovern grabbing the other - only his second competitive goal in ten months. Although he was the Club captain, and had been so right throughout Forest's meteoric rise, he was by no means the most popular of players amongst supporters. This wasn't due to any lack of ability or commitment on his part; but more a reflection of his less than emphatic physical presence. Consequently, he was a regular target for all the City Ground's terrace comedians.

One supporter who'd been entertaining the crowds all around him on the Bridgford End for many years, we had nicknamed 'Doctor Who', due to his long shock of thick, white hair.

He stood about six foot two, had large protruding teeth and was in his early-to-mid-fifties. During one particular game, McGovern attempted to thread a pass through the heart of the visitors' defence for the on-rushing Tony Woodcock. Unfortunately, his rather feebly struck effort got bogged down in the heavy mud and was easily intercepted by a defender. "Fuckin' 'ell McGovern...I've seen more penetration in a used Tampax!" came the thunderous roar from the middle of the Kop, where Doctor Who was standing, red-faced and foaming at the mouth; those all around him completely doubled up with laughter.

FOLLOWING their midweek European excursion, it was back to League action once again the following Saturday as Forest took on Ipswich Town at the City Ground. And, considering Forest were the current League Champions; were making good progress in the European Cup; and were now up to third position in the First Division table - I'd be the first to concede attendances at the City Ground to date were a little on the disappointing side. The average overall during the previous season had been 32,404; whilst the current average stood at 30,637 in the League and 30,024 overall. However, as a loyal and die-hard supporter myself for many, many years, I was beginning to get slightly irritated by the attitude of certain individuals within the Club towards the good citizens of Nottingham.

Since his arrival at the Club in January 1975, we'd had to put up with a fair amount of flak from the great man Cloughie for one reason or another. Now, Secretary Ken Smales seized upon the opportunity to have a go at us in a big way. His Forest Focus column in the Review for the Ipswich game was made up almost entirely of sarcastic comments about the local sporting public - the very people who put their hard-earned cash into the Club and made one sacrifice after another to 'keep the faith'. Talk about biting the hand that feeds you!

I'm sure in his defence he'd argue his comments were not aimed at the true supporters of the Club. However, who did he think was buying the Forest Review and reading his match-day comments week after week; none other than the very people who WERE attending matches and therefore lending their vocal and financial support to the 'Reds'. What's more, it's a slightly arrogant approach for any business to adopt towards it's potential customers - virtually demanding they come along and part with their money. I'm sure a little bit of market research wouldn't have gone amiss. After all, the Nottingham public had proven beyond doubt many years previously they were willing to support a top-class team. Why then, were some of them apparently so reluctant to do so now?

Some of the answers were already staring the Club in the face in their very own Review magazine. Week after week, the views of the disgruntled and stay-away fans were made abundantly clear. And whether you sympathise with them or not, some of the main concerns of these supporters - and the letters were by no means exclusively from Forest supporters - were:

• The poor facilities on offer within the City Ground. For example: wooden benches for seats in the East Stand; poor visibility from all areas of the terracing which had been made too shallow when being re-laid; huge pools of water and mud which lay across the entrances to the ground outside the East Stand.

• The fences erected around the perimeter of the pitch were seriously obstructing the view of many supporters who stood on the terraces - this being the majority, as there were only 8,500 seats in the ground, despite an overall capacity of 42,000.

• A recently erected advertising hoarding hanging from the top of the stand at the front of the Trent End, was seriously obstructing the view of a sizeable proportion of the Trent Enders. Many couldn't even see the new electronic scoreboard which had been erected at the back of the Bridgford End.

> • Cloughie's constant threats to shut the Trent End due to the bad language of a minority, were causing a great deal of unrest amongst the non-swearing majority of Trent Enders - many of whom were season ticket holders.

Although the entertainment value on offer was beyond question; no business - and make no mistake, football is essentially a business - can demand the general public turn up and hand over their hard-earned cash as a matter of course. The manager of the Theatre Royal or the Nottingham Ice Stadium, for example, would no sooner be found lambasting the population of Nottingham for poor attendances, than would the manager of Yate's Wine Lodge or McClusky's Night-club for not selling enough alcohol on a Friday or Saturday evening. Whatever makes football clubs believe they have a God-given right to capacity crowds week in, week out, goodness only knows? What clubs such as Forest should have been doing, is putting their own house in order and then setting out to entice the paying customer with modern, comfortable facilities - and not necessarily all-seater stadiums either - with a welcoming, customer friendly approach. With it's unrivalled night-life and expanse of leisure and sports facilities, Nottingham is not exactly bereft of things to do at a weekend; therefore, the best possible way to put bums on seats, is to ensure that yours is the best value for money product in town.

The die-hard supporters such as myself and many others, will generally tolerate most conditions - however good or bad - simply to watch their team play. And on a personal note, I would have waded ankle deep through a field of cow dung, to stand barefoot on a carpet of broken glass for two hours, just to watch Forest. But the less committed want good value for money, all-round, or else - and rightly so. What's more, the die-hard supporters want the Club to occasionally show some public appreciation of their support; and what better way to do that than through the pages of the Official Match-day Programme, or alternatively through the pages of the local evening newspaper. However, all the Club seemed to be focusing their attentions on were the stay-away fans; the relatively small number of Forest thugs; and the minority of Trent Enders who occasionally chanted obscenities - something which was by no means unique to the City Ground in any case.

Ironically, the very same pages of the Review were also filled with letters from all over the country congratulating the Club on the excellent behaviour of it's supporters on their travels. These included: one from a Hampshire Police Superintendent following their recent visit to Southampton stating how much he appreciated the "excellent behaviour" of Forest supporters; one from the Chief Constable of Bristol citing the "responsible attitude" and "good behaviour" of Forest supporters at the game against Bristol City; one from a St.John's Ambulance Officer following their visit to Oxford congratulating them on the "excellent way in which they behaved themselves"; and another from a pub landlord in Liverpool praising the behaviour of a group of young fans who came into his pub during the recent trip to Anfield: "It was a pleasure to have them and they were just great," he commented. I have to say also, these are the very Forest supporters who I can relate to - and they are a million miles away from the types certain individuals within the Club seemed determined to focus upon.

HAVING disposed of Ipswich 1-0 in front of a crowd of 28,911, the 'Reds' followed this up with a 0-0 draw at Southampton a week later. They then prepared themselves for another big night of European Cup action at the City Ground, with the second round of their second leg tie against AEK Athens coming up on Wednesday, 1st November. Once again the eyes of the nation were on Forest as they stepped out to represent their country on the European stage. Only a handful of Greeks were amongst the crowd of 38,069, who witnessed yet another sparkling display from the 'Rampant Reds'. They smashed five past keeper Lakis Stergioudas in a one-sided 5-1 victory. Dave Needham, Tony Woodcock, Viv Anderson and Garry Birtles (2) scored the goals; and Forest's performance sent shock waves through the rest of Europe. Even some of the English press were reluctantly accepting that the City of Nottingham might just be capable of following in the respective footsteps of Manchester and Liverpool in becoming the country's primary European football ambassadors.

Back-to-back games against Everton in the League the following Saturday and then the League Cup three days later followed this European encounter. The first of these clashes was at the City Ground and ended goalless in front of a crowd of 35,515. However, what the first game had lacked in goal-mouth action, the second more than made up for. This turned out to be a five-goal thriller in front of a Goodison Park crowd of 48,503. Forest's 3-2 victory, thanks to goals from Lloyd, Anderson and Woodcock, saw them through to the quarter-final stages of the competition. However, a torn cartilage sustained by Kenny Burns during the game would keep him out of action for more than two months.

The following Saturday, the 'Reds' travelled to White Hart Lane for an important League fixture against Spurs. Goals from Anderson, Robertson and Birtles in front of a massive 50,541 crowd, secured them an impressive 3-1 victory and two more precious points. And what's more, their unbeaten run in the League now spanned twelve months and numbered 40 games in all.

This was followed by further League action and a 0-0 draw at home to QPR the following Saturday. A 1-0 victory against Bolton Wanderers at Burnden Park a week later then earned them another two points. The all-ticket encounter with Chelsea scheduled for Saturday, 2nd December, was postponed due to a frozen City Ground pitch - not ideal preparation for their important top-of-the-table clash with leaders Liverpool at Anfield the following Saturday. In addition to this, they'd be without injured trio Kenny Burns, Martin O'Neill and Tony Woodcock for this 'clash of the titans'. Disappointingly, after a total of 42 League games unbeaten, they finally succumbed and went down by two-goals-to-nil. Terry McDermott scored both goals in front of an ecstatic Mersyside crowd of 51,469. They'd been longing to avenge the European Cup defeat at the hands of Forest back in September; not to mention the League Cup Final defeat back in March.

This magnificent unbeaten run was just one of many wonderful achievements by the Club at this time. And the rewards for the players were now coming thick and fast. When England took on Czechoslovakia in a friendly at Wembley on Wednesday, 29th November 1978, no less than three Forest players were in the starting line up; these were Peter Shilton, Tony Woodcock and - making his full international debut - Viv Anderson. 'Spider' - as he was affectionately known to Forest supporters, due to his long telescopic-like legs - became the first black player ever to represent England at full international level.

Before the end of the season, Forest would have no less than eight full internationals on their staff. These included: Kenny Burns, John Robertson and Archie Gemmill - all of Scotland; Martin O'Neill of Northern Ireland; and Shilton, Woodcock, Anderson and Trevor Francis - all of England. In addition to this, both John O'Hare (Scotland) and Larry Lloyd (England) had previously represented their countries at full international level.

After the disappointment of Anfield, Forest's next game was a League Cup quarter-final encounter with Second Division high-flyers Brighton & Hove Albion at the City Ground on Wednesday, 13th December. And the defeat against the 'Scousers' was soon forgotten as the 'Reds' romped to a 3-1 victory in front of a crowd of 30,672. John McGovern opened the scoring in the first half, with Brighton's Peter Ward (later to become a Forest player and an expensive flop) equalising, before goals from Robertson and Birtles put the game beyond doubt. The Trent End, whilst delighted with Forest's progression through to the semi-final stage of the competition, also had one eye on the forthcoming visit by Derby County to the City Ground on Boxing Day. They sent out this rather chilling message to the Baseball Ground faithful, via the recorded television highlights that evening:

'ark now 'ear,
The Trent End sing,
The Der-by ran away;

An' we will fight,
For evermore,
Be-cause of Box-ing Day!

Along with many other terrace chants of this era, this one is still doing the rounds, although it's been adapted to suit the individual clubs concerned. However, I can say without fear of contradiction, this particularly nasty little ditty has it's origins on the terraces of the City Ground.

Following a 1-0 victory at home to Birmingham City on Saturday, 16th December and a 0-0 draw away to Manchester City the following weekend, this eagerly awaited encounter with the 'Sheep' came and went without too many incidents. Tony Woodcock scored Forest's equaliser with a spectacular diving header in front of a delighted Trent End, in a fixture that attracted no less than 34,256 spectators. It could be said, as the year drew to a close, that 1978 had been a prolific one for the 'Reds'. The question was: "How would they follow that?"

THE scheduled New Year's Day clash with Leeds at Elland Road was postponed due to a frozen pitch, as was the FA Cup third round tie at home to Aston Villa on Saturday, 6th January. However, this tie was hastily rearranged for the following Wednesday and Forest began 1979 with a 2-0 victory, thanks to goals from Needham and Woodcock in front of a crowd of 29,550.

Having surrendered their long unbeaten run in the League at Liverpool back in December, they were beaten by two-goals-to-one by Arsenal at Highbury - not the luckiest of venues for Forest over the years - on Saturday, 13th January. However, they were still battling it out on no less than four fronts. They were riding high in the First Division table; were through to the fourth round of the FA Cup; the quarter-finals of the European Cup; and on Wednesday, 17th February, were due to play Third Division high-flyers Watford in the League Cup semi-final first leg at the City Ground.

At this time, Watford were managed by Graham Taylor, had a flamboyant Chairman in Elton John, and a prolific young striker by the name of Luther Blissett leading their attack. They came to Nottingham full of confidence, having already been to Old Trafford in the second round and disposed of Manchester United, with Blissett grabbing two excellent goals in a 2-0 victory. And by this time, the City Ground pitch was reminiscent of a freshly ploughed potato field and hardly conducive to the passing game of football the 'Reds' were renowned for.

Blissett himself fired the visitors into a ninth-minute lead, sending their travelling supporters into a state of frenzy. But, in addition to Forest's free-flowing style of play, Cloughie had also instilled into them a considerable amount of steel and determination. It was no surprise therefore; that they were soon on level terms again, with Birtles despatching a looping shot into the Trent End goal from the edge of the penalty area. And the score remained one-apiece until into the second half when Birtles blasted Forest in front with a deflected shot - again from the edge of the box. Robertson virtually assured them of their second successive trip to the Final with a stunning strike, following a poor clearance from goalkeeper Steve Sherwood. Although the majority of the 32,438 crowd left the ground in jubilant mood, with the second leg at Vicarage Road still to come two weeks later, no-one was taking anything for granted.

The severe weather conditions were once again causing havoc with the fixture list and the following Saturday's home game against Manchester United was called off. And one week later, it seemed the FA Cup fourth round tie at home to Fourth Division York City would suffer the same fate. However, a snow-covered pitch was surprisingly passed fit and a 3-1 victory to the 'Reds' ensued in front of a frost-bitten crowd of 25,228. Lloyd, McGovern and O'Neill grabbed Forest's goals.

On Wednesday, 30th January, I set off for Watford - my first ever trip to Vicarage Road

- hoping to see the 'Reds' through to Wembley again. To retain their two-goal advantage from the first leg, they simply shut up shop for the whole of the ninety minutes and cruised through to a decisive goalless draw. Forest's massive travelling support amongst the crowd of 27,656 spilled out of the ground in celebratory mood. In contrast to this, the home fans were very frustrated indeed, many of them bemoaning Forest's rather negative tactics on the night. But the record books show the 'Reds' were through to Wembley for a second year in succession - surely ample justification for their rather cautious (some would say 'professional') approach to the game.

With the Final scheduled for Saturday, 17th March - six weeks away - they could forget about defending their crown for a while and concentrate on the other three competitions they were still involved with. The first of these was their defence of the First Division Championship and an away fixture at mid-table Middlesbrough the following Saturday. And they came away from Ayresome Park with a 3-1 victory, thanks to two goals from Garry Birtles - his fourteenth and fifteenth of the season - and a penalty from John Robertson.

More bad weather and the postponement of the scheduled home games against Aston Villa and Norwich City and the away game at Wolves, meant their fixture with Bristol City at the City Ground on Saturday, 24th February, was their first competitive match for three weeks. However, their excellent form continued and a 2-0 victory, with goals from Needham and Birtles, further enhanced their chances of clinging on to their League title - although Liverpool were still sitting pretty at the top of the table.

The draw for the fifth round of the FA Cup had presented Forest with a home tie against Arsenal - not the easiest of opposition over the years - and although this originally fell victim to the weather, the game eventually took place on Monday, 26th February. And the 'Gunners' certainly brought with them to Nottingham their 'lucky Arsenal' tag as, despite laying siege to their goal, Forest were unable to break down their resilient defence. Both Robertson and Birtles struck the woodwork and goalkeeper Pat Jennings pulled off a string of world-class saves. Then Frank Stapleton delivered the sucker punch - firmly heading home Liam Brady's superbly placed free kick. This was Forest's first home defeat since the 1-0 victory by Cardiff City on Trentside way back on Saturday, 23rd April 1977 - 48 games before.

A 1-1 draw at Ipswich in the League the following Saturday - with Birtles once again on target - settled their nerves as they prepared for the following Wednesday's visit of Grasshoppers of Zurich for the first leg of their third round European Cup tie. Once more the eyes of the nation were upon them as they attempted to make progress through to the last four of the competition. And once again, they did the City of Nottingham proud, as they comfortably swept their Swiss opponents aside. Goals from Birtles, Robertson (penalty), Gemmill and Lloyd gave them a virtually unassailable 4-1 lead to take with them to the Continent two weeks later.

In the meantime, it was back to domestic action again and the small matter of a trip to Everton the following Saturday. There they grabbed a 1-1 draw, with defender Colin Barrett scoring their goal on his return to first team action following a five-month lay off through injury. A 2-1 League victory at home to Norwich followed four days later, thanks to a brace from Tony Woodcock. And then it was time for the League Cup Final against Southampton at Wembley Stadium the following Saturday. What a boring, mundane life we Forest supporters were leading at the time!

OF all my experiences watching the 'Reds', if I could re-live just one day in it's entirety, then it would undoubtedly have to be League Cup Final Day, Saturday, 17th March 1979. Given I've been fortunate enough to see Forest in no less than ten Wembley Finals (six League Cup, one FA Cup, one Charity Shield, one Simod Cup, and one Zenith Data Cup); two European Cup Finals; travelled the length and breadth of Europe watching them; and seen them win the Football League Championship - this may seem an unlikely choice. However, the whole day - from start to finish - was sublime.

At the time, I was employed as a Civil Servant in the Ministry of Defence at Chilwell Army Garrison. Along with myself, a number of my colleagues were regulars at the City Ground and we always stood together at the back of the Bridgford End, just in front of the house which overlooked the ground and is owned by the Club and used as it's Youth Team Hostel. Chris Hooper, Kev Salmon, Ian Adkin, Dave Tideswell and myself would travel to night matches together straight from work and would also meet up most Saturdays to indulge in some pre-match refreshments. Most of us were season ticket holders and hardly ever missed a game. Upon reaching this year's Final, we'd decided to organise our own coach to Wembley and managed to fill it in no time at all.

On the morning of the game, we awoke to a thin carpet of snow on the ground and freezing cold temperatures. Our coach - which we'd hired through Skills Coaches - was due to depart from the Cadland at 9.00-a.m. As I lived directly across the road, I was first to arrive at around 8.00-a.m. - or so I thought. As I walked around the back of the pub, I suddenly heard a loud chorus of: *"We're on the march with Cloughie's Army,"* coming from inside. "Chris...we're in 'ere," came a familiar voice from the doorway behind me. I turned to see Tom Clough beckoning me inside. Ken, the Landlord - never one to miss out on an opportunity to make a few bob - had very kindly opened up the Doghouse Bar so we could all 'shelter from the snow'. He was busy pulling pints like it was five minutes to closing time on a Friday night.

The coach arrived at around 8.45-a.m. and by the time the usual last minute arrivals had 'graced us with their presence', we'd already loaded up with gallons of ale and were ready to roll. We departed on time with the snow still falling heavily. Unlike the previous year, the journey south was unhindered, although the motorway was crammed full of red and white coaches, minibuses, transit vans and cars - not surprising, considering we'd been allocated a total of 34,000 tickets for this showpiece event. We arrived at the stadium well before midday, therefore giving the already intoxicated inhabitants of our coach a further three hours of drinking time before kick off. And not a minute of this precious time would be wasted either as we headed straight for the nearest pub, which of course was already full to the brim with singing, chanting Forest supporters. And incredibly, by this time, North-West London was bathed in glorious sunshine.

After a most enjoyable - and entirely trouble-free - three hours of merrymaking in the pubs and bars around Wembley, we finally made our way to the stadium just in time to see the teams walk out onto the hallowed turf. Much to everyone's surprise, Forest were led out by Peter Taylor, with Cloughie slipping almost unnoticed to his position on the bench, having walked briskly along the running track at the edge of the pitch. Apparently, he'd put in a request prior to the previous season's Final, for the two of them to lead the team out together. But having been refused permission, he'd decided to let Taylor do the honours this time around.

The teams lined up as follows:

	FOREST	SOUTHAMPTON	
1	Peter Shilton	Terry Gennoe	1
2	Colin Barrett	Ivan Golac	2
3	Frank Clark	David Peach	3
4	John McGovern (Captn.)	Steve Williams	4
5	Larry Lloyd	Chris Nicholl	5
6	Dave Needham	Malcolm Waldron	6
7	Martin O'Neill	Alan Ball (Captn.)	7
8	Archie Gemmill	Phil Boyer	8
9	Garry Birtles	Austin Hayes	9
10	Tony Woodcock	Nick Holmes	10
11	John Robertson	Terry Curran	11
	Sub: Ian Bowyer	Sub: Tony Sealy	

Although this Forest line-up was enough to strike fear into the hearts of most people, they were nonetheless without the injured Viv Anderson and Kenny Burns, and also recent signing Trevor Francis, who was ineligible. (*On Thursday, 8th February, he'd become the first £1 million player in the history of the game, when he joined the 'Reds' from Birmingham City. With Clough and Taylor initially reluctant to let him continue his summer playing activities in the North American Soccer League where he starred for Detroit Express, Coventry City had become favourites to sign him late on in the negotiations. However, in view of his immense talents, Cloughie finally relented and secured his historic arrival at the City Ground amidst a blaze of publicity*).

Once the pre-match formalities were over, the Final got under way with Forest attacking the 'Tunnel End'. The bulk of their near-40,000 following, were housed in the opposite end of the stadium. Alan Ball, who'd criticised Forest in the press prior to the game for their 'negative' style of play, not surprisingly incurred the wrath of the supporters early on, with chants of: *"Alan Ball - Wot a Wanker! Wot a Wanker!"* ringing out all over Wembley.

Despite a rather patchy start to the game by the 'Reds', Birtles went close on two occasions early on. Both efforts were headers, the first from a left wing cross by Robertson and the second from a deep, right wing cross by Barrett. After only sixteen minutes though, full-back David Peach put the 'Saints' ahead, following a neat one-two with Ball on the edge of the box. Although Forest never really got into their stride during the first half, they did put Southampton under a great deal of pressure during the last ten minutes.

As the second half got under way and the 'Reds' were attacking the goal behind which their supporters were gathered, they began to turn up the tempo and turn on the style. The fans responded magnificently, almost lifting the roof off the stadium. Our little gang from Chilwell was standing in the upper tier of Wembley's huge bank of terracing, packed in tightly amongst 40,000 singing, swaying supporters. The atmosphere was just awesome. As Archie Gemmill shot only inches wide of an upright, the sound of: *"Come on You Reds,"* echoed majestically around the stadium. When Forest won a corner out on the right; you could feel the massed ranks of supporters trying desperately to suck the ball into the back of the Southampton net!

With the second half only minutes old, Robertson hammered in a low cross-shot from the left, which was intercepted by defender Chris Nicholl, preventing it running through to the Southampton keeper Terry Gennoe. But, having dallied on the ball too long, it was stolen from him by Birtles, who promptly despatched it into the roof of the net from only two yards out. The stadium erupted with noise as Forest's army of fans went completely berserk. *"Aye-oh, Aye-oh, We are the Trent End boys,"* they sang, followed by a chorus of: *"Not-Not-Not-Not-Nottingham, Nottingham, Nottingham."* As Forest began to pile on the pressure, a low Birtles' cross from the left rolled straight under the body of Terry Gennoe and agonisingly along the goal-line before being hammered clear by Nicholl. This prompted a loud chorus of: *"We've got you on the run, We've got you on the run, We've got you on the run,"* from Forest's increasingly confident supporters.

In quick succession, Birtles had two 'goals' disallowed for offside, much to the frustration of players and supporters alike. In between these efforts, a booking for former Forest favourite Terry Curran prompted a chorus of: *"Ello, Ello, Forest reject, Forest reject,"* from the 'red and white end' of the stadium.

Eventually, having been put through by Woodcock, Birtles outstripped the Southampton defence and slipped the ball under the advancing keeper to put the 'Reds' 2-1 in front. After the euphoria had finally died down, the sound of: *"One Garry Birtles, There's only one Garry Birtles,"* echoed impressively around the stadium.

Then, having hardly had time to catch our breathe, the 'Reds' went 3-1 up as the revitalised Woodcock turned and slid the ball under the despairing dive of Gennoe, following a through ball from Gemmill. *"Easy-Easy,"* responded the Forest fans, who then treated the rest of the 100,000 crowd to their full repertoire of songs: *"We're on the march with Cloughie's Army, We've all been to Wem-ber-ley, An' wi really shook 'em up, When wi won the League Cup, Cos*

Forest are the greatest football team," followed by: *"City Ground, Oh mist rolling in from the Trent, My desire, Is always to be here, Oh Ci-ty Ground."*

With only two minutes left, Nick Holmes gave the 'Saints' the faintest hope of salvaging something from the game, as he crashed an unstoppable half-volley into the back of the net. However, the Forest supporters remained defiant. The sound of: *"We're gonna win the Cup, La-la-la-la-la, We're gonna win the Cup, La-la-la-la-la-la,"* rang out, followed by an ear-piercing chorus of whistles.

As the final whistle blew, the Forest players and fans were delirious. Not only were they the first team ever to retain the League Cup trophy, but they had also, by virtue of this result, already qualified for Europe the following season. As skipper John McGovern was handed the trophy by UEFA President, Doctor Artemio Franchi, Forest's travelling hordes saluted them with a chorus of: *"T' Mun-ich, T' Mun-ich, La-la-la-la-la-la-la, La-la-la-la-la-la-la!"*

Following the lap of honour by the players and their eventual departure from the pitch, we spilled reluctantly out of the stadium and jigged our way across the huge coach park outside. We searched for what seemed an eternity for our coach, which had become hidden amongst a sea of others. Having finally stumbled across it, we climbed aboard and immediately began to get stuck into our supply of beer. We were determined to celebrate every aspect of Forest's magnificent victory, in particular the exploits of our mutual friend from Chilwell, Garry Birtles. Just seeing your team win a Wembley Final is reason enough to celebrate - but when one of your own mates has scored two of the goals, the joy and elation you experience is impossible to describe.

We arrived back in Chilwell around 9.30-p.m. and naturally, everyone piled straight into the Cadland, which was packed solid. The party was in full swing and an hour later, who should come gliding into the pub, Winners Medal in hand, but our very own Mr. Birtles. The whole place erupted and he was treated to a five minute standing ovation, followed by a rousing rendition of: *"One Garry Birtles, There's only one Garry Birtles."* He was walking on air and, needless to say, the party went on long into the night. Somehow, on that particular evening, nothing else in life seemed to matter - just the game of football, Nottingham Forest FC, Garry's brace of goals, and winning the League Cup trophy. If only I could re-live this day again!

FOLLOWING this wonderful League Cup triumph, Forest quickly turned their attentions to the European Cup and a trip to the Swiss Capital, Zurich, for the second leg of their third round tie against Grasshoppers. With a comfortable 4-1 lead in hand from the first leg, for once, they could look forward to a major fixture in a confident and relaxed mood. As ever though, their attitude was spot on and they returned home with a 1-1 draw under their belts, thanks to a goal from Martin O'Neill. Remarkably, at the first time of asking, they were through to the semi-final stages of the biggest competition in Europe.

The following Saturday, it was back to League action, as they entertained Coventry at the City Ground. And their rich vein of form continued with a comfortable 3-0 victory in front of a 29,706 crowd. Once again the back-in-form Woodcock grabbed one of the goals; the others coming from centre-half Dave Needham and the trusty left boot of Birtles.

On Wednesday, 28th March, they entertained Chelsea at home in an all-ticket affair which had already twice fallen foul of the atrocious weather conditions. At the time, all Chelsea's away matches were all-ticket due to some consistently bad behaviour on the part of their fans during recent seasons. This could go some way towards explaining the particularly disappointing crowd of only 24,514 who turned out to see a sparkling display by the 'Reds', who put six past the visitors without reply. Martin O'Neill grabbed a hat-trick, ably supported by a brace from Woodcock and another from Birtles.

Another home fixture the following Saturday brought Bolton Wanderers to the City Ground. And with the visitors leading 1-0 with only a minute of the game remaining, it looked as if Forest's proud unbeaten home record in the League was about to come to an unlikely end. However, Trevor Francis picked the perfect moment to score his first goal for the Club - in what was his sixth appearance - when he headed home a last-ditch equaliser, much to the relief of the 29,015 crowd.

Forest's fourth home League game in the space of only eleven days, saw them demolish Aston Villa by four-goals-to-nil in front of a punch-drunk City Ground crowd of 27,056. An own goal from Allan Evans and one each from Woodcock, Francis and O'Neill, meant the 'Reds' had picked up a further seven points out of eight during this hectic period. It also meant they still had a realistic chance of retaining their League Championship title. This was further enhanced by an impressive 3-1 victory over Chelsea at Stamford Bridge the following Saturday, with Francis, O'Neill and Bowyer grabbing the goals.

European Cup fever returned to the City of Nottingham on Wednesday, 11th April, as Forest took on West German Champions 1FC Cologne at the City Ground in the first leg of the semi-final. An all-ticket crowd of 40,804 packed into the stadium to witness what turned out to be one of the greatest Cup ties ever staged on Trentside.

On an extremely heavy pitch, Forest had expected Cologne to approach this first leg tie with caution, in the hope of finishing off the 'Reds' in the second in Germany two weeks later. However, a blistering start by the visitors saw them capitalise on some uncharacteristically poor defending from Forest and clinically they moved into an early two-goal lead, with goals from Belgian striker Roger Van Gool and midfielder Dieter Muller. Van Gool was single-handedly running the 'Reds' ragged and only the heroics of Archie Gemmill, who tracked back sixty yards to halt his direct run on goal, prevented them from going 3-0 down. However, his timely interception proved very costly - at least as far as he was concerned - as he sustained an injury which would keep him out for the rest of the season.

Just how significant Gemmill's tackle on Van Gool would prove to be, no-one could have known at the time, but the game seemed to turn dramatically in Forest's favour from that moment on. First Birtles pulled one back before half-time with a powerful header, and then Needham saw his thumping header rattle the crossbar. They then began to take a firm grip of the game. Substitute Bowyer - on for the injured Gemmill - levelled midway through the second half, smashing a low right foot shot through a crowded defence from fifteen yards out.

When Robertson dived full length to magnificently head home Birtles' right wing cross to put the 'Reds' 3-2 up, the City Ground erupted in a way I'd never witnessed before. It looked as if they'd clawed their way back from the depths of despair to claim a famous victory, and despite Cologne's vital two away goals, would at least have the psychological advantage of a first-leg lead to take with them to West Germany. However, the Germans had one last trick up their sleeves as they threw on Japanese substitute Yasuhiko Okudera. And within a minute of entering the fray, he'd put a low shot under the body of Shilton to level the tie at 3-3. 'Shilts' would have easily saved this rather tame-looking effort ninety-nine times out of a hundred, but such was the drama of this tie, he made an uncharacteristic and costly error. The ultimate outcome of this semi-final tie was left very much in favour of the Germans.

What's more, this dramatic result left me in a complete dilemma. Having saved what little money I had for a possible trip to the Final in Munich, should I take a gamble on them still making it through, or should I realise my dream of following them to the Continent and blow my cash on a trip to Cologne? One thing was for certain: I couldn't afford both. What if I gambled on going to Cologne; saw them pull off an historic victory, only to be unable to make the trip to Munich? On the other hand, if I didn't opt for Cologne and they were beaten, would I ever have the opportunity of seeing them play in the European Cup again?

Two very important factors helped me make up my mind. Firstly, Forest had already qualified for Europe the following season, albeit the less prestigious UEFA Cup. And secondly, the confident manner Clough and Taylor were adopting towards the second leg. Although the world's press had no doubts whatsoever that Forest were as good as dead and buried, everyone at the Club - from the Dynamic Duo downwards - seemed convinced they could still go through. "That's it", I thought. "I'm saving my dosh for the Final!"

It was back to League action the following Saturday, and time for me to head for the Baseball Ground to watch my heroes take two more points from the 'Sheep'. Birtles and O'Neill grabbed the goals in an uninspiring 2-1 victory. I made the unfortunate mistake of travelling to the 'Sheep-dip' with my brother-in-law Alan and my father-in-law Herbert. Embarrassing moment number one came when we bumped into Tom Clough, Mart Northfield and a few of the lads outside the ground before the game. They promptly decided to describe to me in graphic detail; the punch up they'd just had with a gang of 'Sheep-shaggers' on the way to the ground. Hardly the sort of conversation you want to engage in when you've got the wife's father with you!

Embarrassing moment number two though, was entirely the result of some rather curious and unexpected behaviour on the part of my father-in-law himself, as we watched the game from the upper tier of the Popside, surrounded by 'Sheep-shaggers'. How we'd managed to end up in this part of the ground, I don't re-call, but we were at the opposite end to the bulk of the Forest supporters, and there wasn't a red and white scarf within a hundred yards of us. As Derby began to get on top early on in the game, hundreds of supporters around us rose to their feet. Very soon, the rather inane sound of: "DER-BY! DER-BY!" began to gather momentum. This incensed my fifty-odd-year-old father-in-law - a lifelong Forest supporter - to such an extent, he did no more than rise to his feet and bellow at the very top of his voice: "FOR-EST! FOR-EST! FOR-EST!" As Alan and I sank lower and lower into our seats in total and utter embarrassment, three hundred 'Sheep' hurled abuse at him - much to his absolute contempt. I have to admit, I was quite proud of him to be honest.

Our trip to the 'Sheep-dip' was followed immediately by two midweek games at home, one the following Monday and the other two days later. The first saw Leeds United steal a point in a 0-0 draw in front of a crowd of 37,397; and the second against Man United ended 1-1, this time in front of 33,074 people. Consequently, over 70,000 spectators had passed through the City Ground turnstiles in the space of just 48 hours.

Forest warmed up for the trip to Cologne by beating Birmingham City 2-0 at St.Andrews on Saturday, 21st April, with goals from Birtles and Robertson. This meant that since the turn of the year, they'd lost just two out of twenty-four games - both against Arsenal. No wonder the management, the players, and 6,000 travelling fans were in defiant mood as they headed out to Germany.

Having saved my cash for the 'inevitable' trip to Munich in May, I had to listen to the match live on Radio Trent - a nerve-racking experience at the best of times. A capacity crowd of 60,000 packed into the impressive Muengersdorf Stadium and 54,000 at least were convinced the Germans were already on their way to the Final. Thousands of leaflets had been circulating around the city prior to the game, advertising trips to Munich. The arrogance of these Germans!

With the 'Reds' fielding their strongest possible defensive formation of Anderson, Lloyd, Burns and Clark - in front of the mighty Peter Shilton - they proved far more difficult to break down than in the first leg in Nottingham. They resisted literally everything Cologne could throw at them. For those of us listening at home, the tension was almost impossible to bear. No matter who they're playing, listening to a game on the radio is always a harrowing experience. But the significance of this occasion made it a million times worse.

Although a 0-0 draw would have put Cologne through on the 'away goals' rule, the tie was still very much in the balance. And a goalless first half seemed to cast at least an element of doubt into the minds of the Germans. As Forest grew in stature after the break, they began to push forward in search of the victory they had to achieve if they were to make it through to the Final. On sixty-five minutes, a left wing corner from Robertson was flicked on at the near post by Birtles - a common tactic at the time - and Bowyer arrived unmarked to head the ball firmly into the back of the net from only a yard out. This sent the travelling army from Nottingham into a state of frenzy. Once again, the injury sustained by Gemmill in the first leg in Nottingham had indirectly influenced the outcome of this second leg: Bowyer probably wouldn't have been playing, had 'Wee Archie' been fit to take his place in the side.

The 'Reds' held out magnificently until the end and deservedly claimed their place in the Final - and at the first time of asking too. Throughout Britain and Europe, the 'experts' of the press had to eat humble pie and admit Forest were worthy of their place. They'd travelled a long, hard road since their first round, first-leg victory over Liverpool way back in September. But their whole approach to the competition had been positive and tactically brilliant. *"To Mu-nich, To Mu-nich, La-la-la-la-la-la-la, La-la-la-la-la-la-la!"*

A CROWD of 41,898 welcomed them home to the City Ground the following Saturday, when ironically, Liverpool were the visitors. Furthermore, the Championship issue still had to be resolved. Third-placed Forest were seven points behind top-of-the-table Liverpool, who had a total of 57 points already in the bag. However, with a game in hand and no less than seven still to play, there remained a glimmer of hope. The 0-0 score-line after ninety minutes certainly favoured the 'Scousers' though. And Forest were left in the ludicrous position of having to cram in no less than six League matches in just nineteen days to bring their domestic campaign to a conclusion. Hardly ideal preparation for their European Cup Final encounter with Swedish Champions Malmoe on 30th May.

A 1-0 defeat at Wolves two days later further dented their challenge, and as they faced up to a home game with Southampton two days after, the defence of their League title was not the only thing falling apart. Contractors Norwest Holst had only two days earlier moved into the City Ground and begun to demolish the East Stand, to make way for the brand new 'Executive Stand'. This was to be constructed during the close season. Consequently, a restricted crowd of only 20,388 saw them grab a 1-0 victory over the 'Saints', thanks to a strike from Trevor Francis.

Disappointingly, their 1-1 draw at Norwich the following Saturday, when Woodcock scored his fourteenth goal of the season, meant that with only three games to go, they were eight points behind Liverpool. The title race was therefore effectively over - at least as far as Forest were concerned. Mathematically, only West Brom could catch Liverpool now, although with three games left, Liverpool needed just one more point to be absolutely certain.

A 3-1 victory at home against Man City on Wednesday, 9th May - with goals from Birtles, Bowyer and Woodcock, in front of another restricted crowd of 21,104 - was followed by a 2-1 victory at Leeds the following Tuesday, with goals from Gary Mills and unfortunate United defender John Hawley. When Trevor Francis scored the only goal in a 1-0 victory over West Brom at the Hawthorns on Friday, 18th May, the 'Reds' had effectively pipped the 'Baggies' to the Runners-up position by just one point. This was the final League encounter of the English domestic season.

There was now just one thing dominating the minds of the local population in Nottingham - the European Cup Final, twelve days later. We'd been allocated no less than 17,000 tickets for the Olympic Stadium, but an estimated 25,000 fans were expected to make the long, but eagerly awaited journey to the Bavarian Capital.

A TOTAL of eight special trains left Midlands Station on the morning of Tuesday, 29th May, bound for Germany. I teamed up with Chambo, my brother-in-law Alan, and work-mates Dale Dudley and Russ Thompson to make the journey. We were on the first train and this departed at around 10.00-a.m. - our destination Dover. To cope with the immense volume of supporters making the trip, the trains headed for a variety of cross-Channel destinations such as Folkestone, Ramsgate, Dover and Felixstowe. From there, a number of ferries would transport the 'Red & White Army' to various French ports including Dunkerque, Calais and Boulogne.

We arrived in Dunkerque in the middle of the afternoon and were immediately herded like sheep from the terminal to an adjoining railway station. We then had to endure a two-hour delay, firstly whilst waiting for another train-load from Nottingham to arrive; and secondly whilst local railway officials messed around trying to conjure up a single train big enough to transport all of us across the Continent.

When it eventually arrived and we clambered aboard, we were horrified by the conditions on board; they were, to say the least, basic. We were crammed into little compartments, each seating around eight at a push. The seats were made of plastic and rock-hard, there were no refreshments available and, unbelievably, no running water anywhere on the train, including the toilets. Still, we only had another 500 miles to travel from here! We finally rolled out of the station at around 5.00-p.m., and the long and arduous journey had begun.

As we headed off in a south-easterly direction, we settled down in our seats, opened up a few beers, and speculated about what lay in store for the 'Reds' the following evening. Inevitably, every time the train slowed down to pass through a station or came to a halt in a built-up area, hundreds of youths would hang out of it's doors and windows and hurl abuse at startled local residents: *"Fuckin' Frog Bastards!"* or *"Garlic Eatin' Whops!"* being about the most articulate examples. *And we wonder why foreigners hate us?*

By the time darkness arrived, most of us were considerably the worse for wear - especially the inhabitants of our compartment - and it was time to get some shut-eye. As we were crammed in like sardines, this was easier said than done. Having sat on these bone-hard, bum-numbing seats for several hours now, I decided my only option was to kip on the luggage rack - and this was made of steel meshing. Despite this, it was beginning to look more and more appealing by the minute. So up I clambered and off to sleep I went, leaving the others to fight it out over the remaining luggage rack.

I awoke just twice during the night. The first time when the train rolled quietly into Strasbourg, on the French-German border, and sat silently in the station for several minutes. The second when it jolted suddenly in the middle of the night and I rolled straight off the rack, plummeting four feet downwards onto a very startled - and heavily winded - Russ, who was lying flat out immediately below me. Needless to say, he wasn't amused.

By dawn, we were deep into the heart of Germany. I awoke to the sound of early morning rush hour as we rolled gently through the busy industrial town of Stuttgart, approximately 120 miles west of Munich. By early morning, we were bathed in bright spring sunshine - not so much as a cloud in the sky. It was apparent, even at this early hour; today was going to be an absolute scorcher.

At around 9.00-a.m., after numerous inexplicable and frustrating delays along the way, we finally pulled into the beautiful and historic City of Munich. As literally hundreds of us poured from the train, we were met by scores of armed police, many with dogs, who led us briskly out of the station and onto the streets outside. The game wasn't due to kick off until

8.15-p.m., therefore we had plenty of time to recover from our horrendous twenty-four-hour jaunt across Europe.

We grabbed some food and refreshments from a nearby store and made our way into a pleasant little park just a short walk from the station. There we sat enjoying the early morning sunshine and indulging in a much needed breakfast. At the same time, we plotted our itinerary for the rest of the day. As you can imagine, a trip to the city's famous Bier Kellers figured prominently on our list. Feeling suitably refreshed; we left the park and headed off towards the centre of town. And, even though it was still only early in the morning, the streets were already filled with travelling supporters from Nottingham. And most of these were heading in one direction - towards the Bier Kellers.

A while later we came across Munich's equivalent of Nottingham's Old Market Square - the Marianplatz. Although much smaller than 'Slab Square', it had a fountain in the middle and was surrounded by shops, restaurants and bars. The whole area was filled with hundreds of Forest supporters, most of whom were stripped to the waist. Many of them were cooling off by throwing themselves into the fountain, much to the amusement of the local inhabitants. There was a carnival-like atmosphere and this owed much to the strength of the local Bavarian beer. This had been consumed in great quantity by the thirsty hordes throughout the course of the morning. Many supporters had been in the city for several days already and had probably been pouring it down their necks since the minute they arrived.

Naturally, we were anxious to join in the fun, and after several litres of the 'amber nectar', were right there in the thick of the action. Both Radio Trent and Radio Nottingham were in the centre of the square, relaying the festivities directly home to Nottingham and generally helping to stoke up the atmosphere. As the day wore on, the crowd got bigger and bigger, the singing grew louder and louder, and the locals became more and more fascinated by the visiting 'heathens from afar'. And my vision became more and more impaired by the minute.

After a most enjoyable six-hour binge in the sunshine, we decided it was time to head for the Olympic Stadium, situated about three miles away on the outskirts of the city. This had been purpose built for the 1972 Olympic Games and had subsequently become the home of famous Bundesliga side Bayern Munich. As it was still four hours before the big kick off, we decided to take a slow walk; partly to take in the sights of this truly magnificent city and partly in an attempt to sober up. As we made our way towards the outskirts, the sheer volume of Forest supporters who'd made the long journey amazed me. Forest's official ticket allocation of 17,000 had been snapped up in no time at all, and in addition to this, virtually every Travel Agency in the East Midlands had been advertising all-inclusive package deals. Furthermore, hundreds of 'squaddies' from the British Army on the Rhine had also travelled to the city to cheer the 'Reds' on. In contrast to this, there was hardly a Malmoe fan in sight.

Notwithstanding the sheer beauty of the city, the local female population were a little bit special too - apart from their hairy armpits that is - and it's reputation as one of Europe's premier fashion centres was quite obviously well-earned. Although we were here strictly for the beer and the football, the sight of these scantily clad Bavarian beauties, out enjoying the 90-degree sunshine, certainly added some glamour to the proceedings.

As we got further away from the centre and nearer to the Olympic complex itself, the architecture of the city changed quite dramatically from the very ancient, to that of the very modern - in fact it became almost 'space age' in parts. The impressively modern Olympic Tower looked out proudly across the whole city, and the Stadium itself - with it's fibreglass, dome-shaped roof - was like something from another planet. There was an indoor Olympic pool adjacent to the Stadium and the whole complex was surrounded by a giant park which also boasted a large man-made lake.

When we arrived, there were thousands of Forest supporters within the grounds of the complex. They were spread out like ants as far as the eye could see. There were even a few hundred Malmoe fans around by this time. Naturally, scores of people had turned the lake into a giant outdoor swimming pool, in an attempt to cool off and escape from the scorching afternoon sun. Numerous games of water polo were taking place at the water's edge.

When early evening arrived, we clambered to the top of a steep grass-covered mound, cracked open our last few cans of lager, and sat watching open-mouthed as thousands upon thousands of red and white clad supporters arrived at the stadium. It was quite obvious large quantities of the local brew had been consumed during the course of the day - well we had to keep cool somehow? And when we finally made our way towards the turnstiles about an hour before kick off, we sensed the German Authorities were determined not to allow any alcohol within a hundred yards of the stadium. What's more, the police on duty outside, even seemed to be turning away those supporters suspected of having had one too many. "Good God", I thought, "there won't be many inside the ground at all at this rate!"

Having managed to cleverly conceal our own highly-intoxicated state, we entered the Stadium more or less unchallenged and took our places right at the back of the huge bank of terracing at the 'Forest' end. This huge 80,000-capacity complex was awash with red and white flags, scarves, hats and banners - not to mention Union Jacks and a multitude of Garibaldi shirts. It was enough to bring a tear to your eye.

As kick off drew nearer, our end of the Stadium - or to be more precise, our half - began to fill up almost entirely to it's capacity. In contrast, the 'Malmoe' end remained only sparsely populated. When the teams eventually made their way out onto the pitch, a crowd of 57,500 was inside. Only about 7,000 or 8,000 of these were sporting the sky blue colours of Malmoe.

The Forest line-up, for the greatest occasion in the Club's entire history, was:

Gemmill and O'Neill had fought a desperate battle to be fit for this Final, but in the end both had to settle for a place on the bench. At the time, Malmoe were managed by Englishman Bobby Houghton (Harry Bassett's assistant at the City Ground many years later). It seemed he'd brought them to Munich with only one thing on their minds: to close Forest down and deny them as little time and space as possible. Forest were red-hot favourites, but despite being renowned for their flair and imagination, found it almost impossible to break down the Swedes' blanket defence.

Consequently, what should have been a showpiece event, was reduced to little more than a game of cat and mouse, with only the 'Reds' showing any desire to go forward. Shortly before the break however, they got the reward their positive approach deserved, when Trevor Francis launched himself superbly at the far post to head home Robertson's deep left wing cross. The scenes on the terraces behind that goal were incredible.

The remainder of the game was hardly memorable - almost a non-event in fact. However, as McGovern stepped up to receive the trophy at the end and proudly hoist it aloft, this was of little consequence to the travelling hordes - and to the millions watching at home on television. This triumph had not simply been achieved on a hot and balmy night in May. It had been carved out on a cold September evening in Nottingham when Forest had cast aside the mighty Liverpool; and then on an historic night in April when they'd clinched a famous victory against all the odds in the second leg of the semi-final in Cologne. European Cups are not captured on the strength of one performance alone - be it in the first round of the competition, or in the Final itself. No, they are won by slogging it out head-to-head, home and away with the best teams in Europe, over a gruelling period of six, long months. Let's take nothing away from Forest - they fully deserved to be crowned 'Kings of Europe'.

As the players began their lap of honour, tears were rolling down my face. All around the stadium, grown men and women wearing red and white shirts were hugging and kissing one another, or standing alone blubbering. I couldn't help casting my mind back to all those cold and miserable nights down at the City Ground only six or seven years before, watching Forest take on the likes of Oxford United and Leyton Orient in front of crowds of only 10,000. At that time, a return to the top flight of English football had seemed an unlikely possibility - let alone being crowned CHAMPIONS OF EUROPE!

As soon as the celebrations died down, we had to make a swift exit from the stadium - as unfortunately we had a train to catch. We had to make our way quickly back to the station, as, much to everyone's annoyance, the 'specials' were due to depart within an hour of the final whistle. Having almost broken the four-minute mile, we were amongst the first to arrive and consequently, managed to board the first of four trains which would transport thousands of the travelling hordes back home to England. We quickly pulled the blinds down in our compartment and held the door firmly shut from the inside. There was no way on this earth we were going to put up with any more than five stinking carcasses in a confined space like this all the way back to Boulogne.

As we sat looking out across the station at the Malmoe-bound trains on the opposite platform, it became apparent that, having spent all day drinking in the boiling hot sun, we were already beginning to dehydrate. And there were no refreshments available on the train - not even any running water in the washrooms. What's more, we faced the prospect of a minimum fifteen-hour, non-stop journey back to Boulogne. Suddenly we began to panic.

Fortunately, we noticed that the Malmoe fans on the ultra-modern, refreshment-laden trains opposite, were downing beer as if it was going out of fashion. "Ere mate," shouted Russ through the open window of the train to a small group of Swedes milling about on the platform: "Come 'ere a minute midduck." And, much to our surprise, over they trotted. "Beer? Lager? Drink?" he shouted, as we all pointed longingly towards their beer-swilling compatriots. "Ah - beer - you want beer?" one of them responded. "Yes! Yes! Yes!" we pleaded frantically. "We get you some beer," they promised and headed briskly across the platform towards their train. "That's the fuckin' last we'll see o' them then," we all agreed, falling dejectedly back into our seats. What we hadn't reckoned on though, was that these were Swedish football supporters - not English! To our amazement, two minutes later, they returned as promised, arms filled with beer. And, like children feeding monkeys at the zoo, they passed the stuff through the window to us one can at a time. And despite our efforts to pay for them, they wouldn't take a penny. They were obviously completely oblivious to the fact - but without a doubt, these Good Samaritans saved our lives that night!

The journey back to Boulogne was a long and tiring one. The conditions on board the train were horrendous, with many people sleeping on the floor, or in the toilets. As predicted, there were no refreshments of any description on offer, and the carriages were crammed full of thirsty and hungry supporters. What's more, there were no breaks whatsoever between Munich and our destination in Northern France, late on Thursday afternoon. When we finally boarded our Nottingham-bound trains in Folkestone, following a short but refreshing trip on the cross-Channel ferry, we were totally and utterly exhausted.

Ours was the first train to leave Folkestone, and we breathed a collective sigh of relief - at last we were on the final leg of our journey. Back home, the team - and just about the whole population of Nottingham - were about to enjoy a Civic Reception. This started off at County Hall, and then made it's way through the streets of the City to the Old Market Square. The team were transported in an open-topped bus, with an estimated 200,000 people lining the route. Tens of thousands more were waiting for them in 'Slab Square'. The frustrating thing about it all though, was that it was taking place whilst the vast majority of the travelling supporters were still making their way home from Munich. And to add insult to injury, we were travelling on the Club's own official transport!

As we trundled slowly through the small town of Folkestone, a multitude of red and white scarves, flags and banners hanging from every window, it seemed the whole local population had turned out to welcome us home. In just about every back garden and on every street corner, folks young and old, stood waving and giving us the thumbs up. We felt like soldiers returning home victoriously from some distant war. And all this attention made us realise just how important the game of football is to the people of this country. Our team had been ambassadors not just for the City of Nottingham - but for the whole nation.

We gathered momentum as we approached the wide-open spaces of the South-East Countryside. This filled us with hope of perhaps making it back home in time to catch the tail end of the celebrations. Sadly however, this was not to be. We eventually rolled into Nottingham at around 9.30, and although we made a mad dash to the Square, the whole thing had finished only minutes earlier. The bulk of the crowd had already dispersed. Having travelled non-stop for twenty-four hours; to miss out by only a matter of minutes was both frustrating and annoying. The Club had let us down badly I felt, although I was somewhat surprised by the lack of dissenting voices. I'm sure many other supporters must have felt the same way as I did.

THIS aside, we had once again enjoyed a wonderful season of success. Two more trophies to add to the rapidly-expanding collection; almost a million people passing through the City Ground turnstiles; no less than thirteen attendances in excess of 30,000; three in excess of 40,000; and an average overall of 30,446. Yes - this had been a magnificent nine months for everyone associated with our great Club. The only problem was - how the hell could we follow this?

SEASON 1978/79 – STATISTICS

FOOTBALL LEAGUE DIVISION ONE – FIXTURES

Date		Opposition		Venue	Competition	Score	Attendance
Aug	12	Ipswich Town	(At Wembley Stadium)		FA Charity Shield	5-0	64,438
	19	**Tottenham Hotspur**		H	**League**	**1-1**	**41,223**
	22	Coventry City		A	League	0-0	28,585
	26	Queens Park Rangers		A	League	0-0	17,971
	29	Oldham Athletic		A	LC 2	0-0	13,793
Sept	**2**	**West Bromwich Albion**		H	**League**	**0-0**	**28,239**
	6	**Oldham Athletic**		H	**LC 2 - Replay**	**4-2**	**18,669**
	9	**Arsenal**		H	**League**	**2-1**	**28,124**
	13	**Liverpool**		H	**Euro Cup 1 - 1st Leg**	**2-0**	**38,318**
	16	Manchester United		A	League	1-1	55,039
	23	**Middlesbrough**		H	**League**	**2-2**	**26,287**
	27	Liverpool		A	Euro Cup 1 - 2nd Leg	0-0	51,679
	30	Aston Villa		A	League	2-1	36,735
Oct	4	Oxford United		A	LC 3	5-0	14,287
	7	**Wolverhampton Wanderers**		H	**League**	**3-1**	**29,313**
	14	Bristol City		A	League	3-1	26,947
	18	AEK Athens		A	Euro Cup 2 - 1st Leg	2-1	36,000
	21	**Ipswich Town**		H	**League**	**1-0**	**28,911**
	28	Southampton		A	League	0-0	22,429
Nov	**1**	**AEK Athens**		H	**Euro Cup 2 - 2nd Leg**	**5-1**	**38,069**
	4	**Everton**		H	**League**	**0-0**	**35,515**
	7	Everton		A	LC 4	3-2	48,503
	11	Tottenham Hotspur		A	League	3-1	50,541
	18	**Queens Park Rangers**		H	**League**	**0-0**	**28,032**
	25	Bolton Wanderers		A	League	1-0	25,692
Dec	9	Liverpool		A	League	0-2	51,469
	13	**Brighton & Hove Albion**		H	**LC 5**	**3-1**	**30,672**
	16	**Birmingham City**		H	**League**	**1-0**	**25,224**
	23	Manchester City		A	League	0-0	37,012
	26	**Derby County**		H	**League**	**1-1**	**34,256**
Jan	10	Aston Villa		A	FA Cup 3	2-0	29,550
	13	Arsenal		A	League	1-2	52,189
	17	**Watford**		H	**LCSF - 1st leg**	**3-1**	**32,438**
	27	**York City**		H	**FA Cup 4**	**3-1**	**25,228**
	30	Watford		A	LCSF - 2nd Leg	0-0	27,656
Feb	3	Middlesbrough		A	League	3-1	21,330
	24	**Bristol City**		H	**League**	**2-0**	**28,008**
	26	**Arsenal**		H	**FA Cup 5**	**0-1**	**35,908**
Mar	3	Ipswich Town		A	League	1-1	27,188
	7	**Grasshoppers Zurich**		H	**Euro Cup 3 - 1st Leg**	**4-1**	**31,949**
	10	Everton		A	League	1-1	37,745
	14	**Norwich City**		H	**League**	**2-1**	**24,046**
	17	Southampton	(At Wembley Stadium)		LC Final	3-2	100,000
	21	Grasshoppers Zurich		A	Euro Cup 3 - 2nd Leg	1-1	17,800
	24	**Coventry City**		H	**League**	**3-0**	**29,706**
	28	**Chelsea**		H	**League**	**6-0**	**24,514**
	31	**Bolton Wanderers**		H	**League**	**1-1**	**29,015**
Apr	**4**	**Aston Villa**		H	**League**	**4-0**	**27,056**
	7	Chelsea		A	League	3-1	30,083
	11	**1FC Cologne**		H	**Euro Cup SF - 1st Leg**	**3-3**	**40,804**
	14	Derby County		A	League	2-1	30,156
	16	**Leeds United**		H	**League**	**0-0**	**37,397**
	18	**Manchester United**		H	**League**	**1-1**	**33,074**
	21	Birmingham City		A	League	2-0	22,189
	25	1FC Cologne		A	Euro Cup SF - 2nd Leg	1-0	60,000
	28	**Liverpool**		H	**League**	**0-0**	**41,898**
	30	Wolverhampton Wanderers		A	League	0-1	23,613
May	**2**	**Southampton**		H	**League**	**1-0**	**20,388**
	5	Norwich City		A	League	1-1	16,616
	9	**Manchester City**		H	**League**	**3-1**	**21,104**
	15	Leeds United		A	League	2-1	33,594
	18	West Bromwich Albion		A	League	1-0	28,210
	30	Malmoe FF	(At Olympic Stadium, Munich)		Euro Cup Final	1-0	57,500

HOME ATTENDANCES

	AGGREGATE ATTENDANCE	HIGHEST ATTENDANCE	LOWEST ATTENDANCE	AVERAGE ATTENDANCE
League:	621,330	41,898	20,388	29,587
League Cup:	81,779	32,438	18,669	27,259
FA Cup:	61,136	35,908	25,228	30,568
European Cup:	149,140	40,804	31,949	37,285
All Competitions:	913,385	41,898	18,669	30,446

FINAL LEAGUE TABLE - DIVISION ONE

Position	P	W	D	L	GF	GA	Pts
1. Liverpool	42	30	8	4	85	16	68
2. Nottingham Forest	**42**	**21**	**18**	**3**	**61**	**26**	**60**
3. West Bromwich Albion	42	24	11	7	72	35	59
4. Everton	42	17	17	8	52	40	51
5. Leeds United	42	18	14	10	70	52	50
6. Ipswich Town	42	20	9	13	63	49	49
7. Arsenal	42	17	14	11	61	48	48
8. Aston Villa	42	15	16	11	59	49	46
9. Manchester United	42	15	15	12	60	63	45
10. Coventry City	42	14	16	12	58	68	44
11. Tottenham Hotspur	42	13	15	14	48	61	41
12. Middlesbrough	42	15	10	17	57	50	40
13. Bristol City	42	15	10	17	47	51	40
14. Southampton	42	12	16	14	47	53	40
15. Manchester City	42	13	13	16	58	56	39
16. Norwich City	42	7	23	12	51	57	37
17. Bolton Wanderers	42	12	11	19	54	75	35
18. Wolverhampton Wanderers	42	13	8	21	44	68	34
19. Derby County	42	10	11	21	44	71	31
20. Queens Park Rangers	42	6	13	23	45	73	25
21. Birmingham City	42	6	10	26	37	64	22
22. Chelsea	42	5	10	27	44	92	20

AWAY ATTENDANCES

	AGGREGATE ATTENDANCE	HIGHEST ATTENDANCE	LOWEST ATTENDANCE	AVERAGE ATTENDANCE
League:	675,333	55,039	16,616	32,158
League Cup:	204,239	100,000	13,793	40,847
FA Cup:	29,550	29,550	29,550	29,550
European Cup:	222,979	60,000	17,800	44,595
All Competitions:	1,132,101	100,000	13,793	35,378

"WE ARE THE
EUROPEAN CHAMPIONS"

DOWN AT the City Ground, the impressive new stand was beginning to take shape. As the season drew nearer, the Club's hierarchy was still pondering a suitable name for it and canvassing opinion amongst supporters. Various suggestions had been bandied about, such as the 'Clough and Taylor Stand', the 'Europa Stand' and the 'Sherwood Forest Stand'. In the meantime, it would be referred to as the 'Executive Stand', owing to the thirty-six executive boxes housed within it's impressive structure. As it would be several months before construction was complete, there was no rush to make a final decision.

By the time the season got under way at Ipswich on Saturday, 18th August, there had been considerable activity on the transfer front. Scottish internationals Asa Hartford and Frank Gray had been acquired from Man City and Leeds respectively - the fee in each case in the region of half a million; Frank Clark had finally decided to hang up his boots and had joined Sunderland as assistant manager; 36-year-old goalkeeper Jim Montgomery had arrived on a 'free' from Birmingham City to act as understudy to Shilton; and young keeper Chris Woods - still to make his League debut - had joined QPR in a £250,000 deal. Sadly, in an attempt to reduce the average age of the team, Cloughie had also decided to offload the popular Archie Gemmill, who would shortly join Birmingham for a fee of £150,000.

It was a hot summer's day when we set off for Portman Road. The 'Red & White Army' were really out in force for this one and determined to let the local population of Suffolk know they were in town. *"We are the Euro-pe-an Champions,"* they proudly proclaimed. It had been a very boozy lunchtime in and around Ipswich prior to the game and the travelling hordes, basking in the mid-August sunshine, just about drank the town dry. A crowd of 27,237 packed into the neat, but compact stadium to witness a close and exciting tussle between two of the country's most attractive footballing sides. A solitary effort from Tony Woodcock gave the 'Reds' a useful 1-0 victory - and another glorious season had begun.

The opening home fixture was against Stoke City the following Wednesday evening and a restricted crowd of 26,147 saw Forest carve out another 1-0 victory, thanks to a well struck effort by O'Neill from the edge of the box. Whilst the new stand was under construction, the capacity would be limited to a maximum of 28,040. During the close season, the Club had sold no less than 18,500 season tickets. This included 12,000 for the seats - many reserved for the new stand - and 6,500 terrace tickets. The cost of a Main Stand ticket was £60, whilst one for the terraces was just £27 - not an extortionate price by any means, to watch the Champions of Europe in action.

The victory over the 'Potters' was followed by a 4-1 home success over Coventry the following Saturday, which in turn was followed by a 1-1 draw at Third Division Blackburn Rovers in the League Cup four days later. The 'Reds' were aiming to stretch their unbeaten run in this competition to an amazing three years and become the first club ever to reach the Final on three successive occasions.

On Saturday, 1st September, we were off to the West Midlands to see them take on West Brom. This was a fixture I always looked forward to for a number of reasons. Firstly, there was always an intense, but friendly atmosphere inside the Hawthorns - a stadium, which, at the time, was reasonably large and comfortable, with a good view from it's steep terraces. Secondly, there was always a sizeable following from Nottingham - probably because both teams were renowned for their attractive style of play. And finally, from my own viewpoint - whilst being absolutely 'Forest' through and through - the 'Baggies' have always been amongst my favourite 'other' teams - along with Chelsea, West Ham and Glasgow Rangers.

A crowd of 26,315 was present to witness a stunning display of power from the 'Reds'. When we travelled away in those days, we did so in the absolute knowledge that we would dominate the opposition. Such was the sheer confidence of the players in their own ability; this rubbed off onto everyone associated with the Club. And no matter who the opposition happened to be, there was almost an air of invincibility about Forest.

Although Albion took an early lead through Gary Owen, before the interval Forest had turned the game around completely and were leading 3-1. As they mounted yet another attack, Kenny Burns sent a fierce thirty-yard shot hurtling towards the top corner of the net, beyond the despairing dive of keeper Tony Godden. Amazingly however, with the ball literally in mid-flight, referee Neil Midgley blew his whistle for half-time - the irritating twat! And as the two teams trotted off down the tunnel, they left behind a bewildered crowd. Was the score 3-1 or 4-1? We didn't have a clue.

The half-time score flashes on the public address system failed to resolve the mystery, and as the teams came back out onto the pitch for the second half, no-one was any the wiser. *''Shilton, Shilton, What's the score? Shilton, What's the score?''* sang the travelling 'Red Army', as he paced up and down his area immediately in front of us, watching another Forest attack unfold at the opposite end of the field. Now I'm not suggesting he's thick or anything, but it must have taken him at least ten minutes before he finally cottoned on and put us out of our misery. He turned and held three fingers up to confirm we were indeed still only leading 3-1. Now as far as I'm concerned, referees who behave like this particular individual want shooting. How anyone can possibly measure a period of forty-five minutes down to the absolute milli-second, is beyond me? Referees should be under strict instructions not to bring matters to a close until the ball is out of play or at the very least in a neutral area of the field.

By the end of a pulsating game, in which Robbo turned the Albion defence inside out, Forest had increased their lead to 5-1. What's more, Birtles had notched his first senior hat-trick for the Club. The other goal-scorers were Larry Lloyd and Frank Gray. The journey back to Nottingham and the ensuing pub-crawl around town that evening were most enjoyable.

By the end of October, Forest had played a further nine League matches, winning three, drawing three, and losing three (each defeat away from home and questioning their 'invincible' tag). Consequently, they were sitting in a promising second position in the table behind Man United with seventeen points from thirteen games. Furthermore, they'd progressed through to the fourth round of the League Cup, after thrashing Blackburn 6-1 at the City Ground and following this up by beating Middlesbrough 3-1 at Ayresome Park in the third round. They'd also disposed of Swedish side Oesters Vaxjo in the first round of the European Cup - winning 3-1 on aggregate - and now held a comfortable 2-0 first-leg lead over the Rumanians Arges Pitesti in the second. A 2-1 victory in the second leg in Rumania on 7th November, saw them progress through to the quarter-final stages of the competition, scheduled to be played four months later.

On the negative side - at 23 years-of-age - Tony Woodcock decided he'd outgrown his hometown club and was determined to take his silky skills to the European mainland. He was about to leave for a short, but successful career with old West German adversaries 1FC Cologne. He completed his move after Forest's frustrating 1-0 home defeat at the hands of Brighton - a game which saw him substituted and Forest's incredible unbeaten run of 57 League games on home soil come to a disappointing and unexpected end.

Prior to Woodcock's rather surprising exit from the City Ground, recent signing Asa Hartford had also parted company with the 'Reds', having made just three first team appearances - against Ipswich, Stoke and Coventry. He returned to the North-West, joining Everton hours before Forest's second round League Cup tie at Blackburn. He'd been off-loaded without ever really getting a chance to establish himself at the Club. Mind you, this was typical of Clough and Taylor's often controversial style of management.

BY the time they entertained West Brom at home in the League on 12th January 1980, they'd already progressed through to the semi-final stage of the League Cup on the back of successive 3-0 victories over both Bristol City and West Ham in fourth and fifth round replays on Trentside. They'd also knocked Leeds out of the FA Cup, claiming a superb 4-1 success at Elland Road, and had signed controversial midfielder Stan Bowles from QPR for a fee of £250,000. Unfortunately, they'd slipped to a disappointing tenth position in the table, having now accumulated a total of 24 points from 23 games. A 3-1 victory over the 'Baggies' in front of 27,724 people however, was followed a week later by another win at Leeds - this time by a more modest two-goals-to-one.

This set them up perfectly for a remarkable sequence of four meetings with League-leaders Liverpool in the space of only four weeks. This commenced with a first leg League Cup semi-final tie at the City Ground on Tuesday, 22nd January. A Robertson penalty - in front of a crowd of 32,220 - gave them a vital 1-0 lead to take to Anfield for the second leg on February 12th.

The following Saturday, the Merseysiders were back in town, this time for a showdown in the fourth round of the FA Cup. And it has to be said, on this occasion, Liverpool were by far the better side. A first-half strike from Kenny Dalglish and a second-half penalty converted by Terry McDermott gave them a convincing 2-0 victory, this time in front of 33,277 people.

In between the two legs of the League Cup semi-final, Forest took on Barcelona (European Cup Winner's Cup holders from the previous season) in a two-legged European Super Cup Final. The first leg took place in Nottingham on Wednesday, 30th January, and despite being labelled by some as nothing more than a 'glorified friendly', the game drew a reasonable crowd of 23,807. It also proved a very attractive contest, despite a difficult and muddy playing surface. A header from striker Charlie George - enjoying a one-month spell on loan from Southampton - gave the 'Reds' a 1-0 lead to take with them to Barcelona's magnificent 90,000-capacity Campo Neuvo Stadium for the second leg six days later.

Roared on by a partisan crowd, Barcelona took a thirtieth-minute lead in the return leg, when Brazilian Carlos Alberto scored from the penalty spot. However, an equaliser before half-time from the head of Kenny Burns stunned the massive 90,000 crowd into silence. And Forest's recent experiences of European football held them in good stead as they battled their way through a tense second period unscathed. They even managed the luxury of a forty-sixth minute penalty miss by 'Robbo' after Bowles had been up-ended in the box. Consequently, another piece of silverware was winging it's way towards the City Ground trophy cabinet - the Club's sixth in the space of just three years!

With their spate of Cup ties having been only briefly interrupted by a 0-0 League draw with Bristol City at home on Saturday, 9th February, it was now time for 'Forest versus Liverpool - Part Three'. They headed north-west for the second leg of the League Cup semi-final the following Tuesday evening. And despite having been overwhelmed by the 'Scousers' in the recent FA Cup encounter, Forest went on to extend their aggregate lead to 2-0 by virtue of another Robertson penalty, awarded when O'Neill was brought down by keeper Ray Clemence. A classy overall performance looked likely to earn them a rare victory at Anfield, but a late equaliser by David Fairclough gave the tie a more respectable look. However, for a record third year in a row, we were heading to Wembley and another League Cup Final showdown, this time against Midlands rivals Wolves.

Only seven days later, Liverpool again managed to exact quick revenge on Forest at Anfield, when goals from Terry McDermott and Ray Kennedy contributed to a convincing 2-0 victory, this time in the League. As far as this season was concerned, honours between the two were just about even.

Forest's patchy League form of late continued, although successive 4-0 home victories over Man City and Tottenham saw them climb to a more respectable sixth position in the table. Just as encouraging, was the recent form of star striker Trevor Francis, who plundered a hat-trick in the win over City and a brace during the rout of Spurs. This set them up perfectly for two vitally important fixtures which, back-to-back, would make or break their season. The first of these was the League Cup Final on Saturday, 15th March, and the second the European Cup quarter-final second leg tie in East Germany against Dynamo Berlin four days later. Unexpectedly, they'd lost the first leg 1-0 at the City Ground two weeks before in front of a disgruntled crowd of 27,946.

ONCE again we'd organised our own coach for the trip to Wembley and this was scheduled to depart from the 'Cad' at 9.00-a.m. prompt. And once again Ken was busy pulling pints for the sixty-strong 'Chilwell Army' at 7.30 in the morning. Although a trip to the 'Twin Towers' in any competition - however insignificant - is always an exciting and eagerly anticipated one, the magic of our previous two visits just wasn't there on this occasion. Why, I don't know? The following from Nottingham was every bit as substantial and vociferous; the sea of red and white scarves, flags and banners just as eye-catching; and unlike before, the black and gold emblems of the Black Country hordes at the opposite end of the stadium provided a perfect contrast to those of our own. In spite of all this, the whole thing just seemed a little flat to me right from the minute we left Nottingham, to the minute we returned home tired and dejected thirteen hours later.

In retrospect, this may have been due entirely to the fact we suffered a disappointing 1-0 defeat on the day - made even harder to accept because on paper, Forest were a vastly superior side and clear favourites to retain the trophy. Or, it may have been simply the manner in which victory was handed to Wolves on a plate. When David Needham attempted to intercept a long and hopeful ball up-field by a Wolves defender, what he hadn't noticed, was Shilton already on his way out to gather it harmlessly up. Either he didn't shout for it - or Needham couldn't hear him above the noise of the crowd; but he succeeded only in heading the ball straight into the path of the onrushing Andy Gray, who gratefully side-footed it into the wide-open net. And what's more, Forest certainly played well enough to win the game on the day, creating by far the lion's share of the chances and generally dominating possession. It seemed though, right from the very first whistle, it wasn't going to be our day. But then that's football for you.

The 'Red & White Army' left the stadium in defiant mood; the sound of: *"We're gonna win the European Cup,"* and *"We'll be back agen next year,"* almost drowning out the celebrations of the Wolves supporters..And, disappointingly, for the first time during any of my trips to Wembley, I witnessed the sort of crowd trouble I'd only previously encountered at League fixtures up and down the country. All in all therefore, this wasn't a very memorable occasion.

For the record, the teams lined up as follows:

	FOREST	WOLVES	
1	Peter Shilton	Paul Bradshaw	1
2	Viv Anderson	Geoff Palmer	2
3	Frank Gray	Derek Parkin	3
4	John McGovern (Captn.)	Peter Daniel	4
5	Dave Needham	Emlyn Hughes (Captn.)	5
6	Kenny Burns	George Berry	6
7	Martin O'Neill	Kenny Hibbitt	7
8	Ian Bowyer	Willie Carr	8
9	Garry Birtles	Andy Gray	9
10	Trevor Francis	John Richards	10
11	John Robertson	Mel Eves	11
	Sub: John O'Hare	Sub: Colin Brazier	

WITHIN hours of their Wembley disaster, the players, officials, and a handful of supporters prepared themselves for an uninviting trip behind the 'Iron Curtain'. It was time to take on Dynamo Berlin in the second leg of the European Cup quarter-final. This competition now provided Forest with their only realistic opportunity of landing a trophy this season. However, firstly they had to become the first club ever in the history of the competition to overcome a first leg deficit on foreign soil.

Once again, half the population of Nottingham were glued to their radios listening to the live match commentary on Radio Trent. As mentioned previously, this is not my favourite pastime by any means. However, a blistering display by the 'Super Reds' - and in particular Trevor Francis - calmed my nerves, as they powered their way through to the semi-finals for the second year running. They had set about the Germans straight from the kick off and remarkably, were 3-0 up by the half-time interval. Two goals from Francis and a Robertson

133

penalty destroyed every bit of confidence the Berliners had built up during their efficient and victorious display in Nottingham. Although Frank Terletzki pulled one back for them in the 48th minute of the game, Forest's knack of hanging on to a lead wasn't about to desert them. They returned home with a superb 3-1 victory under their belts.

Following a rapturous reception from several hundred supporters waiting for them until the early hours of Thursday morning at East Midlands Airport, it was back to League action again the following Saturday and a visit to the City Ground by Southampton. As far as this competition was concerned, Forest were now only playing for their pride. They went into this game in 9th position in the table with 30 points from 31 games, 14 points behind leaders Liverpool, with only 11 games remaining.

A 2-0 victory over the 'Saints' was followed by a 1-0 defeat at Brighton; a 2-0 home victory over second-placed Man United; and a 3-2 defeat away to Villa. The draw for the semi-final of the European Cup had seen them pitched against Dutch Champions Ajax Amsterdam - three-times winners of the competition. Their pedigree was second-to-none. Not only had they been Champions of Europe on three occasions, they'd also been Dutch Champions no less than 18 times. They had also won their own domestic Cup competition on eight occasions, twice won the European Super Cup, and were even past winners of the World Championship Trophy. The first leg of the tie was to be played at the City Ground on Wednesday, 9th April, with the return in Amsterdam two weeks later.

A crowd of 31,244 - Forest's fifth largest of the season to date - turned up for this first leg tie. Although their League form had been somewhat inconsistent, this was after all the semi-final of the European Cup, and for ônce I shared Cloughie's frustration with the apparent complacency of the Nottingham public. They should have been there in much greater numbers. Although the early-season capacity had been restricted, owing to the construction of the new stand - which itself had been delayed due to some untimely industrial action within the construction industry - it had been in full use for quite some time now. However, attendances had been on the disappointing side all season, to say the least. It has to be said though, that in terms of it's global popularity, football as a spectator sport was just beginning to enter a period of decline - and not just in the East Midlands. Alarmingly, this depression would continue throughout the early-eighties.

Once again, the City of Nottingham witnessed a wonderful night of European football. The brilliant Trevor Francis caught the eye in particular, smashing Forest into a first-half lead against the Mighty Dutchmen, raising supporters' hopes of a second successive trip to the Final. This was scheduled to take place in Real Madrid's spectacular Bernabeu Stadium. Although their display was not exactly 'vintage Forest', they continued to dominate in the second half, but without creating too much in the way of goalmouth incident. However, in the sixty-first minute, Francis managed to secure the 'Reds' a penalty, when his persistency caused Ajax defender Cees Zwamborn to handle in the box. Robertson, with his customary calmness and accuracy, sent keeper Piet Schrijvers the wrong way, slotting the ball low into the right hand corner of the net directly in front of the jubilant Trent Enders.

Owing to a period of inclement weather, Forest's only competitive encounter between the two legs of this semi-final tie, was a home fixture with our 'grass-eating' friends from just down the A52 on Saturday, 19th April. And not only did full-back Frank Gray's perfectly driven free kick give us a sweet 1-0 victory in front of 32,266 people, it virtually sealed the 'Sheep's' relegation to the Second Division (snigger-snigger!). Prior to this, they'd accumulated only 28 points from 39 games played. And with only three matches remaining, they were in a precarious 20th position in the table. What's more, Everton, who were one place above them, had three points more and two games in hand. Meks ya just want t' weep, duntit!

AS I strolled down to Toton Park the following afternoon to watch Long Eaton Rovers in action, I was still contemplating our part in the 'Sheep's' demise and day-dreaming about our inevitable trip to the European Cup Final. So confident was I of a jaunt to Madrid at the end of May, I wasn't at this stage planning to go to Amsterdam for the second leg of the semi-final. I was intending to save my cash for a week in the Spanish sunshine.

Although Garry Birtles was primarily concerned with his own playing career at the time, he was also heavily involved in his spare time with the running of Long Eaton Rovers. Most of his buddies from Chilwell played for the club; and those who didn't, went down to watch them most weekends.

On this particular occasion, I struck up a conversation with one of the 'Cadland boys' Pete Castledine, who was planning to drive over to Amsterdam for the game in midweek. What's more, he had a spare seat in his car and it was mine if I wanted it. He was travelling over with Gaz Edwards and Vic Plumb - both Rovers' players - and even when taking into account the expected cost of my imminent trip to Madrid, I decided I could easily afford this one as well. So, as soon as the game was over, I shot off home for my Sunday Roast, and to give the misses the good news: I was buggering off to Holland for three days!

We left Chilwell at around 6.00-p.m. on Tuesday to catch the midnight ferry from Dover to Calais. This was strangely bereft of fellow Forest supporters - especially as an estimated 8,000-plus were expected to make the trip to the Dutch Capital. As we sped out of the deserted French Port in the early hours of Wednesday morning -following a bit of a session on the boat - our plan was to head for the town of Lille, where we would park the car up for a few hours and get some kip. We would then travel on to the French/Belgian border at around daybreak.

It was 2.00-a.m. when we finally parked up outside a plush-looking apartment block smack in the middle of town - about fifty miles from Calais. Having wriggled into my sleeping bag, I tried to get comfortable on the back seat of the car - not an easy task, considering there were four of us sharing the confined spaces of a Mark 4 Ford Cortina 1300L. Not that I would criticise this rather remarkable vehicle, which, despite it's rather modest engine capacity, had averaged a speed of at least 100-mph since leaving Nottingham.

After enduring thirty minutes of farting, belching and snorting from the restless occupants of this vehicle, Gaz Edwards finally decided he'd had more than enough for one night. He jumped out of the car, grabbed a large piece of plastic sheeting which he'd stored away in the boot and spread it out on the grass, smack outside the front entrance to the apartments. He then clambered inside his sleeping bag and wrapped himself up inside the plastic sheeting. He looked just like a piece of rolled up carpet. This caused uncontrollable laughter inside the car, as we tried to imagine the bewildered faces of local residents as they emerged from the flats early the next morning. As dawn broke, the outline of Gary's prostrate and vagrant-like figure began to emerge through the early morning mist. Unfortunately, we were up and gone long before the unsuspecting residents had even begun to rise from their beds - more's the pity.

The journey from here to Amsterdam took another four hours. Along the way we passed through the Belgian towns of Gent and Antwerp and the Dutch town of Rotterdam - home of Ajax's fierce rivals Feyenoord. Having indulged ourselves in a rather sickly breakfast of ham, eggs, croissants and cheese - washed down by a jug of sludge-like coffee - in a small Belgian café en-route, it was around 11.00-a.m. before we arrived in Amsterdam. Such was the significance of this game; the demand for tickets had prompted Ajax to alter the venue. They'd swapped their own 25,000-capacity stadium, for that of the Olympic Stadium nearby, which held 65,000.

Our first port of call was the Stadium itself, where we parked the car up for the duration of our stay in the city. As we hadn't booked any digs either, this would also double as our sleeping quarters for the evening - assuming we were unable to find anywhere more suitable to doss down. We jumped on a tram and headed off into the centre of the city. There were already hundreds of Forest supporters in town and almost every bar and café along the route had been taken over by beer-swilling youths with Nottingham accents.

We had some sightseeing to take care of before going on the razzle ourselves and had planned to meet up with a few of our buddies in Amsterdam's famous red-light area - an attraction which no visitor to the city should miss - or so we had been reliably informed. And what an incredible place it turned out to be? Shop windows filled with scantily-clad women - many of whom would not have looked out of place on the catwalks of Paris or Milan. Live sex shows going on all over the place; not to mention a multitude of shops stashed full of porno books, magazines and sex aids. There were also numerous bars with erotic dancers flitting about in front of TV screens showing one blue movie after another.

What a far cry from Nottingham's own sleazy red-light district, situated as it is in the Forest Road area of the City. What's more, with prostitution being a strictly legal activity here in the more liberally minded Netherlands, the whole place seemed to have an air of respectability about it. And by all accounts, it's also a contributory factor in the comparatively low rate of sex-related crimes which Holland experiences when compared to other less open-minded European cultures.

Naturally, the whole area was like a magnet to the travelling masses from Nottingham - and many of them weren't there simply for the sightseeing. Needless to say, the 'ladies of the night' did a roaring trade whilst the 'Reds' were in town. And at fifty guilders a time - equivalent to around ten pounds then - it's hardly surprising really. Inside each 'shop window' sat one, sometimes two, very attractive young women - some wearing provocative looking underwear, some in see-through negligees, some wearing almost nothing at all. Prospective clients would negotiate with them through a small open window and then, presumably having agreed a fee, would be allowed inside. The 'buyer' and the 'seller' would then disappear behind the curtains at the back of the shop. Five or ten minutes later the very happy looking punter would re-emerge grinning from ear to ear and slip quietly back into the flock of tourists thronging the streets outside.

During the many hours we spent in this part of town, we observed lots of red-and-white-shirted punters going in and out of these fascinating little parlours. Indeed, whilst wandering through the maze of alleyways and footbridges linking the streets and canals together, we even came across a couple of our own mates from Chilwell - 'Spook' and Sean Brown. They were only too eager to describe to us in graphic detail, the threesome they'd just enjoyed with a gorgeous young blonde, for a bargain 75 guilders. (They may just have been winding us up of course). However, by far the most amusing incident of the whole day, was the sight of a drunken, spotty-faced, sixteen-stone youth in a Garibaldi shirt, wandering out of a doorway, declaring to the world at the top of his voice: ''Shag in a brothel! Av 'ad a shag in a brothel! Shag in a brothel! Av 'ad a shag in a brothel!'' (Lost yer virginity in a brothel more like - judging by the state of ya!).

Having spent a wonderful afternoon in downtown Amsterdam - a truly exciting and vibrant city - the hordes from Nottingham began to head for the bars and cafés around the Olympic Stadium. We boarded a tram packed with rival Forest and Ajax supporters. They were trying their damnedest to out-sing each other. And whilst on the surface the atmosphere seemed reasonably good-natured, a feeling of uneasiness was beginning to well up inside me. As we got closer to our destination, the singing became louder and louder, and with everyone bouncing up and down in unison, the tram was almost lifted from it's tracks.

It was such a relief when we finally arrived at the stadium and escaped from the intimidating and suffocating conditions on board that tram. We immediately scuttled off to the nearest bar, only to encounter the same volatile atmosphere. Although we hadn't witnessed any trouble so far on our travels, there had reportedly been several skirmishes between the two sets of supporters in and around the city during the course of the day. Dutch football supporters can be every bit as loud and aggressive as their English counterparts, therefore I can only imagine the atmosphere at an Ajax versus Feyenoord game must be every bit as fierce and intense as a Forest-Derby or a Man U-Leeds game.

'Two lips from Amsterdam'

After more beverages had been consumed, we headed for the Stadium and took our seats amongst the 8,000-plus Forest supporters who had made the journey. The Stadium itself was a big disappointment. It was old and dilapidated with uncomfortable wooden benches for seats. There were also huge chunks of crumbling masonry all over the place. However, with a 65,000-strong crowd inside, the atmosphere was as good as any I'd experienced, and this only intensified as the Dutch Champions pinned Forest back in defence during the early part of the game. The Nottingham contingent made themselves heard throughout, as they had done all day in and around the streets of the city.

Forest were under the cosh for most of the ninety minutes to be honest, although Kenny Burns was at his brilliant best in front of a very commanding Peter Shilton, who also made a string of superb saves. In the midst of it all, they did have their moments. In fact Trevor Francis spurned a glorious opportunity to put the tie beyond doubt, failing to head home a simple opportunity from Frank Gray's perfectly flighted left wing cross. When Soren Lerby finally headed Ajax into a sixty-sixth minute lead following a corner, the noise reached fever pitch. It took every last ounce of strength the overworked Forest defence could muster to hang onto their precarious aggregate lead. However, hang on they did, and as the final whistle blew, the 'Red Army' began to acclaim another remarkable achievement. We were through to our second successive Final. It was time for some serious celebrating.

Not surprisingly, along with hundreds of others, we headed straight back to the red-light area. There we would carry on our partying long into the night. And, as exciting as the place was by day, it was positively pulsating by night. There were literally thousands of people thronging the streets, although like ourselves, most seemed to be nothing more than curious observers. There were however, a lot of genuine punters around as well.

There were loads of small bars in the area, most brimming with Forest supporters. And inside most, another commodity was on offer in abundance: drugs. Soft drugs such as Cannabis - openly available in Holland - were shoved under our noses throughout the night by scores of greedy pushers. And it was pretty obvious those of a harder nature were also readily available. Sensibly, I decided to stick to my usual cocktail of twenty Bensons washed down by several pints of lager.

It was well into the early hours when we finally stumbled back to the car. And in the state we were in, even the back seat looked pretty inviting. We'd all consumed copious amounts of alcohol during the course of the day - therefore we had no problem settling down for what was left of the night. And God-knows, we needed some rest before embarking on our long trek home.

After a relatively uneventful journey, we arrived back in Nottingham around 6.00-p.m. on Thursday - forty-eight hours after first setting off on our adventure. This had been a fantastic couple of days and an experience I'll never forget for as long as I live. And although I was back at work the following day, there was one consolation: it was 'POETS Day' (Piss Off Early Tomorrow's Saturday). The Civil Service's flexible working hours meant that mostly on a Friday, we could slope off down the pub for about two hours at lunchtime, and be on our way home by half past three. Whilst in the pub, I had a captive audience, as I relived every moment of the last two days in graphic detail. My work-mates were green with envy. And as the Final was only a month away, we also added the finishing touches to our planned excursion to Madrid.

THE 'Reds' followed up their semi-final exploits with a more mundane 0-0 draw away to Middlesbrough in the League the following Saturday. This was followed by a 2-0 home victory over Norwich City four days later and a 4-0 success over Crystal Palace on Saturday, 3rd May. To everyone's horror, during the game against Palace, Trevor Francis - who'd netted two of the goals during a sparkling individual display - fell to the ground unchallenged late on with what turned out to be a ruptured Achilles tendon. This was to keep him out until the following season, and tragically for him, out of the Final in Madrid. And, having sold Tony Woodcock to Cologne earlier on in the season, the 'Reds' would be going into this game against Hamburg with only one recognised striker - Garry Birtles.

They finished their League programme with a 0-0 draw at Arsenal the following Monday, a 1-0 victory over Everton at home the following Friday, and a 3-1 defeat at Wolves on Monday, 12th May. In doing so, they completed the season in a respectable fifth position in the table. When the squad flew out to Majorca to prepare themselves for the Final, they left behind them the injured Larry Lloyd, who'd sprained his ankle playing for England against Wales at Wrexham. They were also without the wayward Stan Bowles who, unhappy at his inability to command a regular first team place, had simply not bothered to show up at the airport. What a true professional Stan was eh? Fancy spurning the chance of figuring in a European Cup Final - even just a place on the substitute's bench - all because he wasn't getting picked automatically week in, week out. Most professional footballers would give their right arm for such an opportunity.

We'd long since decided upon our mode of transport to Madrid and had paid our deposit for a twelve-seater minibus from Cardays Van Rental on Pavillion Road, just outside the City Ground. This was situated immediately behind the car wash, which is still there to this day. Ten of us would be sharing the long journey: myself, Chambo, Chris Hooper, Ian Adkin, Sam Ash, Deano, Russ Thompson, my brother-in-law Alan, our Graham, and my little brother Pete - aged just 13 at the time.

The capacity of the Bernabeu Stadium was around 125,000. However, as Nottingham is in the region of 1,000 miles away from the Spanish Capital - as is the German City of Hamburg - there would be no shortage of tickets on this occasion. Despite the distance though, we managed to sell around 12,000. The Germans on the other hand, sold only around 5,000 and would therefore be heavily outnumbered.

Having collected our vehicle from Cardays on the Saturday afternoon, we prepared ourselves for what was sure to be a long and arduous journey. And, having assured our rather fretful mother for the umpteenth time we'd take good care of our Pete, Graham and I loaded him into the back of the van at around 10 o'clock on the Sunday evening and set off on a grand tour of Nottingham picking up the rest of our travelling companions.

Although I'd now been supporting the 'Reds' for fourteen seasons and had followed them not only the length and breadth of this country, but also overseas to Europe, I had never felt as excited as I did that evening as we trundled around all over Nottingham. Everything about this trip was perfect. We were going to sunny Spain; travelling under our own steam; not restricted by anyone else's rules and regulations; were all good friends; shared the same sense of humour; enjoyed one another's company; and were off to see our beloved Forest play in the Final of the European Cup no less.

It was around midnight when we finally rolled out of Nottingham bound for Portsmouth. We'd booked ourselves onto the 9.00-a.m. ferry to Cherbourg on the Monday morning - a crossing of approximately four hours. Although all of us - with the exception of our Pete - could drive, only those over the age of 23 were covered to do so by the insurance. This excluded everyone except our Graham (aged 24) and Alan (aged 25) who had little option but to share this particularly daunting responsibility.

Having arrived in Portsmouth long before daybreak, the ten of us were soon bored out of our skulls and whiling away our time playing football on the deserted sea-front at Southsea. It was still another three hours before we were due to arrive at the ferry terminal; but by the time the score had reached 27-apiece, this particular pastime was becoming just a little tedious. We jumped back on the bus and headed for the docks. It would be more than two hours before we could board the ferry, so we just sat there in the car park making small talk and cracking jokes. Ian managed to keep us all amused by reading aloud the problem page of a magazine he'd just bought and had us rolling about all over the place by assuming the role of 'Agony Aunt'. He was dishing out all sorts of humorous advice to the rather inadequate individuals who'd written in telling the world all about their sad little hang-ups. As the tears

139

of laughter rolled down my face, it was obvious this was going to be one hell of a trip.

By 9.00-a.m. we were on board the ferry and making ourselves comfortable in the pleasant confines of the bar at the stern of the boat. As soon as we'd pulled out of the harbour - leaving behind the UK's antiquated and completely pointless licensing hours - the shutters came up and we were getting stuck into a lager breakfast. And we had a wail of a time. Consequently, by the time we sailed into Cherbourg four hours later, we were completely rat-arsed.

After we'd finally disembarked, we made our way through Customs and headed out onto the open roads of Northern France. By this time we'd been transformed into a bunch of obnoxious, xenophobic, lager louts! Whilst Ian was hanging out of the window shouting: ''I blow my nose in your general direction - you stupid French-type person you,'' to anyone unfortunate enough to pass by, the rest of us were bouncing up and down in the back singing: *"Forest boys we are 'ere, To shag your women and t' drink your beer,"* at the top of our voices. At the same time we were banging our fists on the windows like a pack of demented Neanderthals. Our Graham - the only sober one amongst us - was trying desperately to cope with driving on the right hand side of the road for the first time in his life, and with having sole responsibility for pointing us accurately in the direction of Madrid.

As we headed down the West Coast of France, one thing became abundantly clear: this was by no means going to be an inexpensive trip. The minibus was guzzling diesel faster than the ten of us were demolishing our crates of beer. And, with some serious drinkers on board - especially Russ 'Hollow Legs' Thompson - that was really saying something. What's more, unlike travelling on our own cost-free motorways in England, in both France and Spain, we had to pay expensive tolls just for the privilege. However, if we were to make it to Madrid in good time, we had little option but to ''put up and shut up.''

Rennes was the first town we came to of any significance, followed shortly afterwards by Nantes. There we had a short stay and replenished our rapidly diminishing food supply. By this time, all that was left of the pack-up we'd brought with us from Nottingham, were a few melted Kit-Kats, a couple of soggy bags of crisps and half a dozen beer-drenched sandwiches. As we headed south towards the quiet and picturesque coastal town of La Rochelle - our next port of call - the majority of us had just about recovered from our earlier drinking binge and were gradually getting back into the swing of things.

As we trundled along, undoubtedly the most amusing sight of the trip so far, was that of our Pete (13 years-of-age remember) nonchalantly leaning back in his seat, with a can of lager in one hand and a giant King Edward cigar in the other, trying his damnedest to keep up with the rest. However, he would soon pay a heavy price for this over-indulgence and ended up vomiting wretchedly out of the nearside window of the bus - much to everyone's amusement. Everyone that is, except our Graham who was absolutely seething with anger. He was still very sober and still trying to come to terms with driving on the right hand side of the road. ''Ooh look...I've just seen your Pete's spleen come flying past the window,'' announced Ian mockingly from the back of the bus, as Pete leaned right out, belching and gurgling the contents of his stomach out all over the hard shoulder at sixty miles per hour.

When we pulled into La Rochelle, he was sprawled out across the back seat sleeping like a baby. Having read the riot act to the rest of us for our extremely infantile behaviour, Graham settled down himself across the front seat to take a short, but well-earned rest. We left the two of them sleeping and went for a wander along the sea front. It wasn't too long before we came across a pleasant little café, where we sat down at the tables outside. And, having served us all with a glass of refreshingly cool beer, the owner sat chatting to us in fluent English, whilst we relaxed in the warm, early-evening sunshine. An hour or so later - having pointed us in the direction of a campsite nearby - he wished us all the best in the Final, and we set off at a leisurely pace back to the bus.

By eight o'clock, we'd erected our tents, cooked and eaten some grub, and were looking to amuse ourselves for the rest of the evening. Whilst Graham played nursemaid to the now very poorly Pete, we indulged in a game of football on the small field adjacent to the site. It wasn't until early the next morning we came to realise just how concerned Graham had been about our Pete that evening. Unbeknown to us, he'd been absolutely fuming because of our apparent indifferent attitude to the whole situation. Having assured him we'd been oblivious to Pete's plight, we promised unreservedly to keep a close eye on him for the remainder of the journey. Fortunately, despite being very hung-over, he was well on his way to a full recovery by the time we got on the road again at around nine o'clock that morning.

Graham had spent the whole of the journey so far in the driver's seat, so decided it was time to pass this responsibility onto the nervous-looking Alan. For the time being, Graham would assume the role of navigator. By late morning we were arriving in Bordeaux, which is about a hundred miles north of the French-Spanish border. This proved to be a busy little town with lots of traffic, and it wasn't long before Alan's inexperience behind the wheel began to shine through. Having almost gone the wrong way around a traffic island, the wrong way up a one-way street, nearly killed two pedestrians, and mounted the kerb three times, Graham decided it was time to come to everyone's rescue. He unceremoniously ejected Alan from the driver's seat and took to the wheel again himself. The rest of us just sat there motionless in the back, cringing at the sight of the long queue of frustrated, snarling Citroen owners backed up behind us. His timely intervention came as a huge relief to everyone and we were able to sit back and relax in the knowledge we weren't about to die in a head-on collision with a French juggernaut. Needles to say, Alan wasn't too keen on taking to the wheel again after this unfortunate little experience - and not surprisingly, the rest of us weren't that keen on him doing so either.

When we'd all calmed down enough, we were on our way again and Graham easily negotiated the town's rather complex and tricky one-way system. Mind you, being a Heavy-Goods mechanic and qualified HGV Class 1 lorry driver, this was hardly surprising really. As we turned left into a busy street, we unexpectedly came across two coach-loads of Forest supporters milling around outside a bar. We didn't stop to chat as it was apparent we still had a long journey ahead of us. And we were determined to get there in time to soak up as much of the pre-match atmosphere as possible.

It was now thirty-six hours since we'd set off from home and by this time the crowded and decidedly uncomfortable confines of the minibus were beginning to irritate. Where there had initially been laughter and excitement, there was now an atmosphere of tension beginning to develop. What's more, whilst the majority of us were quite up front - almost proud in fact - of our own individual exploits in the flatulence department - one decidedly smelly individual was however, determined to conceal his identity. This rather sneaky so-and-so had been silently dropping his high-intensity stink bombs one after another for several hours now. Due to his anonymity, he'd been appropriately nicknamed the 'Phantom Farter.' The trouble was, as the culprit was obviously too embarrassed to own up to these disgustingly nasty aromas, everyone was pointing the finger at everyone else. Alan seemed to be rapidly emerging as the main suspect, although he vehemently protested his innocence. Consequently, accusations, denials and counter-accusations, were flying around all over the place. One thing we had all agreed on though was this: when the identity of the 'Phantom' did finally emerge - he was in for a good kicking!

At the rear of the bus, between the back seats and the door, was a small compartment used for storing suitcases, luggage etc. And with all the holdalls, tents and sleeping bags thrown in and piled up on top of one another, it was beginning to look more and more inviting to me, as one uncomfortable minute after another ticked by. As I was now experiencing cramp in every part of my body, I decided I was going to give it a go. Having picked my moment, I clambered over the back seat - taking with me ample rations of food and drink - and flopped down eagerly into the middle of this makeshift bed. And after one and a half days of total discomfort, it was absolute heaven. The rest of the lads were green with envy. What's more, quite apart from the sheer comfort factor, there was the added bonus

I was now almost entirely shielded from the rather tedious antics of the 'Phantom Farter' who continued to cause consternation at the front.

By mid-afternoon, we'd arrived in the small town of Biarritz, just a few miles from the border with Spain. We had now entered Basque country. And with it's dusty streets, predominantly white buildings and seedy-looking Bullring, Biarritz looked every inch a Spanish town itself. We decided to replenish our food and drink supply once more before continuing our journey across the border and up into the Pyrenean Mountains. Much to our delight, we came across a small convenience store, where we were able to buy bottles of local plonk for the ridiculously low cost of only ten francs - the equivalent of about ten pence in English money at the time. In addition to this, we bought copious amounts of freshly baked French rolls and a variety of mouth-watering local cheeses. Having well and truly stocked up, we clambered back aboard the bus and headed for the hills. As we did so, a row erupted between Russ and myself, after I'd had the audacity to sit in 'his' seat.

From literally the moment we left Nottingham, he'd sat motionless in 'his' seat immediately behind our Graham. He'd moved only when it was absolutely necessary i.e. either to empty his bladder, or to stock up with more beer. Nobody had seen him eat so much as a morsel of food during the whole of the journey thus far. In fact we were convinced he existed exclusively on a diet of Carling Black Label. And he was such a lazy bastard; I could swear he was even consuming this intravenously. His beer supply was wedged under the seat in front of him and I'm convinced he had a tube running straight out of the top of his 'party six', up his trouser leg, through the inside of his Forest shirt, and into the main artery in his neck. Anyway, I couldn't be arsed to argue with him - the territorial bastard - and retreated unruffled to the back of the bus.

Having crossed the border into Northern Spain, we soon came across the City of San Sebastion. Along with it's neighbouring City, Bilbao, this is the main recruitment centre for the Basque Separatist Movement 'ETA'. As we climbed slowly into the Pyrenean Mountains, the long, winding road provided us with a bird's-eye view of the city. Large multi-storey tenement blocks dominated it's skyline, each one decorated from top to bottom with row after row of grimy washing. This gave the whole place an air of gloom and deprivation. Giant murals depicting gun-totting terrorists dressed in black berets adorned every building and 'ETA' propaganda was daubed everywhere. We were relieved to be heading away from the city and up into the mountains.

As we climbed higher and higher, we were beginning to feel more and more isolated. As darkness began to fall, we decided it was time to find a suitable resting-place for the evening. Eventually, we came across a small campsite at the edge of a small village high up in the mountains. We pulled onto the site, handed over our fee of around 1000 pesetas and immediately set about the task of constructing our tents.

Once we'd set everything up, we decided it was time for some grub. So out came the small Calor gas cooker we were carrying and on went the baked beans. By this time, it was almost completely dark and, obviously attracted by the flames from our stove; hundreds of flying, bullet-shaped beetles appeared all around us. Now I don't know whether this particular species of insect has it's origins in the Far East or something, but they were almost immediately throwing themselves in distinctively 'Kamikaze' fashion headlong into the bright blue flames of our cooker. Unfortunately some of them were sadly lacking in terms of their directional sense, succeeding only to dive headfirst into the large saucepan of Heinz's very best, which we were all by this time, drooling over. Still, as it turned out, they tasted remarkably like mushrooms, and therefore served only to enhance the quality of our meal.

As we sat munching away, we decided to crack open some of the wine we'd bought earlier on in the day. The first couple of bottles were passed around, and it was immediately obvious why they'd been so cheap - it was just like drinking watered down gnat's piss! ''Sod this for a game o' soldiers...Let's get the beer out instead,'' suggested Sam, as the offending bottles - most of them still unopened - were dumped unceremoniously into a giant waste-bin nearby.

Having demolished our feast of baked beans, French stick and Camembert cheese, washed down by three cans of Carling Black Label, we decided it was time to retreat to the warm and inviting confines of the minibus. There we would prepare our battle plans for the following day, reminisce about our past exploits 'down the match'...and get completely smashed! Graham though, in view of the many hours' driving which lay ahead the next day, decided to have an early night - as did the now 'strictly teetotal' Pete. They retreated to their respective tents, clambered into their sleeping bags, and fell promptly to sleep.

An hour or so later, having long since exhausted our full (and feeble) repertoire of jokes and anecdotes, we were well into some serious football talk. Who was going to perform tomorrow? How many Forest supporters would be there? Would many 'Krauts' bother to turn up? Would we be crowned Kings of Europe once again? These were all matters of some concern. We had just one problem though: we were rapidly running out of beer. And it wasn't as if there was a 'beer-off' just around the corner either. We were all beginning to panic when suddenly Ian declared: ''Hang on a minute...I know where there's some beer.'' He jumped out of the bus and crept off in the direction of Graham's tent. He returned two minutes later with a big grin on his face declaring: ''Like tekkin' candy from a baby!'' ''You bastard'' declared Chris, ''he was saving that for Madrid tomorrow'' his voice tinged with guilt. ''Tough shit'' retorted Deano from the back of the bus, ''He shuntav buggered off to bed then, should he...the miserable git!''

Naturally, within minutes we'd demolished Ian's ill-gotten gains and were beginning to despair yet again. ''Right then Russ,'' declared Chambo, ''there's only one thing for it. We'll 'ave to crack open the Whiskey.'' He then pulled out a bottle of 'duty-free', they'd invested in on the cross-Channel ferry. ''Only a swig each mind,'' he added, probably wishing he'd kept his big mouth shut. Another fifteen minutes and we were back to square one again, desperately searching for more alcohol. And we didn't mind in what form - just as long as it was alcohol. We were all scratching our heads and drawing blanks, when suddenly Deano cried out excitedly: ''I've got it...the wine.'' ''What wine?'' we responded. ''The stuff we chucked away earlier,'' he declared, throwing open the back door of the bus. And with that he jumped to the ground and shot off in the general direction of the waste-bin, the rest of us in hot pursuit.

Having scrambled through piles of rubble, we retrieved as many bottles as we could find in the darkness of the night. We were back on the bus in no time at all cracking them open one by one like a bunch of desperate winos. And amazingly, what had only three hours earlier been cast aside as mere gnat's piss; now tasted like vintage champagne!

The next thing I remember is waking up in my tent the following morning with the 'Mother of all hangovers'. However, having enjoyed a 'stimulating' cold shower, feasted on a good old-fashioned breakfast, and hurriedly packed away my tent, I was well on the road to recovery. In any case, once we got on the road again, I was going to clamber back into my comfortable 'hammock' at the back of the bus and get my head down once more. Anyway, today was the big one and I wasn't going to let anything spoil it - hangover or no hangover.

It was just after 9.00-a.m. when we finally left the campsite and got back onto the winding road that would take us to the other side of the Pyrenees. We were still 200 miles from the Spanish Capital, but reckoned if we 'got a bit of a bat on' should arrive around mid-afternoon. Apart from the two coach-loads of supporters we'd come across in Bordeaux the previous day, we hadn't encountered another red and white scarf or flag whatsoever during the whole of our journey. As we trundled our way through the mountains, we could see the road for miles ahead and it was almost winding it's way up into the clouds. And suddenly, there in the distance, about a mile ahead of us, we spotted the distinctly familiar outline of a red and white single-decker coach. ''No it couldn't be?'' proclaimed our Graham, his face pressed up against the windscreen, straining for a better view. ''Not a bloody Barton's bus up 'ere in the middle of the Pyrenean Mountains?''

Urged on by the rest of us, he wedged his foot to the floorboards, in an attempt to catch up with it as soon as possible. At first we seemed to be gaining ground rapidly, only to splutter almost to a halt on a sudden and steep incline. The coach then disappeared around a distant bend and we lost sight of it for what seemed an eternity. And just as we'd almost given up hope of catching it, so it suddenly and unexpectedly reappeared not more than two hundreds yards in front. Another two minutes passed and we had it firmly in our sights, inching closer and closer by the second. By this time it's red and white festooned occupants had spotted us creeping up behind and one by one, faces were appearing in the back window, each one pressed right up against the glass.

Having chosen his moment perfectly, Graham dropped it down a gear, and positively 'roared' past - hell, we were doing almost 30 miles per hour by this time! As we glided past, all you could see right along the length of the bus, was a row of bare, scrawny arses mooning out at us. A loud chorus of: *"We're gonna win the Eur-o-pe-an Cup,"* rang out through it's open skylights, accompanied by Graham on his horn. We were all hanging out of the windows like a bunch of loonies, much to the approval of our fellow travelling 'Reds', who cheered loudly and fell about laughing all over the coach. As they gradually disappeared out of sight behind us, jibes such as: ''For a minute there, I thought it was the 'Derby 5' veered off course'' were bandied about the minibus, much to everyone's contempt.

About five hours later, after a journey of over two and a half days, we finally reached the outskirts of Madrid. It was now 2.30 on the Wednesday afternoon. And whilst the travelling support from the East Midlands had been conspicuous by it's absence during the course of our journey, it was soon apparent Forest were going to have a substantial following in the Bernabeu Stadium. About fives miles outside the city, we came across a huge campsite, which had been taken over completely by travelling fans. There were hundreds already on site, with flags, banners and scarves draped across every tent and hanging from trees and bushes for as far as the eye could see. Reportedly, they'd been arriving in droves since the early hours of Tuesday morning.

Having pitched our own tents, we headed straight for the restaurant-come-bar, situated on the site. There we indulged in our first proper meal of the week - steak and chips with all the trimmings washed down with ice-cool beer. (Only later did it emerge the steak could well have been horse-meat!). This was absolute luxury after what we'd endured for the last few days. As the big kick off wasn't for another six hours, we had plenty of time for a well-earned rest. Following our meal, as we sat outside the bar in the hot afternoon sunshine, for the first time in more than forty-eight hours, I felt relaxed and refreshed and was at last looking forward to the game.

By late afternoon, the campsite was slowly beginning to empty as the merry hordes drifted off in the direction of the city. We decided it was time to go and jumped back on the bus. We headed out through the gates of the campsite just before 5.00-p.m. It was a warm and pleasant evening - exactly the sort you'd wish for on such an auspicious occasion. The centre of the city was chaotic to say the least, with eight lanes of traffic heading in all directions, lane control obviously never having been high on the town planners' list of priorities. It was like 'Wacky races' with everyone having total disregard for one another. The term 'Every man for himself' springs to mind.

Having skilfully negotiated the chaos, Graham managed to get us within a couple of hundred yards of the Stadium, where we parked up for the evening. All around us, the streets were filled with drinking, chanting supporters sporting Forest colours. Some of them had obviously been on the pop all day. In spite of this, they were generally well behaved, if a little boisterous. We were soon into the spirit of things and it wasn't too long before we were joining in the singing. We sat outside a pleasant little bar on the main road adjacent to the Stadium. There was a surprisingly heavy police presence and unfortunately, we were about to experience some rather heavy handed and completely unnecessary behaviour on their part.

About an hour before the game, they suddenly decided to clear the streets of supporters and, completely unprovoked, simply charged straight into us - many of them on horseback - waving their long and meaty looking batons around indiscriminately. They appeared to consider anyone in red and white fair game. There was mass panic right along the length of the street, with supporters of all ages and both genders caught up in the chaos. Whatever prompted them to act in this manner, God only knows, but it certainly left a nasty taste in my mouth and, I suspect, everyone else's. I'm sure everyone caught up in it, must have been equally as bemused and angry about the whole episode as I was. Unfortunately, we have seen on all too many occasions in the past that English football supporters represent easy prey for loutish Continental police forces - especially those in Spain.

Immediately after the melee had ended, we decided it was time to head for the safety of the Stadium and wandered off in the direction of the 'Forest' end. There were surprisingly few Hamburg fans around and those we did encounter on our short walk to the turnstiles proved very aloof and decidedly miserable, despite our best attempts to converse with them. They appeared very arrogant and had obviously been taken in by all the hype surrounding 'Mr. Curly Perm' and the prediction that underdogs Forest were about to lose their crown. ''Bollocks to 'em,'' we thought, as we got within spitting distance of the turnstiles.

We'd stockpiled an assortment of alcoholic refreshments, which we intended to take with us into the Stadium: jugs of wine; cans of lager; even a bottle of vodka. However, to our frustration, the Stadium Officials were having none of it and we had to resort to sitting on the pavement outside guzzling down as much as we could before going inside.

As we sat around, drinking ourselves stupid, one of our mates from Chilwell, Trev Woolley, suddenly and unexpectedly appeared out of the blue. Unable to persuade anyone else to make the trip with him, he'd made his way across Europe all on his lonesome. When we informed him we'd got two spare seats on our minibus, he couldn't believe it. He declined our offer of a lift back to Nottingham afterwards though, deciding instead to stick with the 'busload of right wallies' he'd travelled over with. And besides, he'd paid good money for his seat on that bus. He was keen to spend the rest of the evening in our company though and even kindly volunteered to help us polish off our booze. We all made our entrance into the Stadium together and took our places on the steep bank of terracing, where a few thousand travelling supporters had already gathered.

Although around 12,000 Forest supporters had made the long trip, there was only a meagre following from Hamburg. What's more, the overall attendance of 50,000 appeared minuscule within the vast expanses of the Bernabeu. There were huge empty spaces all around the Stadium. In my wildest of dreams, I couldn't imagine such a sparse crowd for a European Cup Final anywhere on the Continent today, what with corporate hospitality and complimentary tickets galore for the army of parasites which the game currently attracts. The wide-open spaces at this showpiece event were perhaps testimony to the world-wide 'popularity' of the game at this particular moment in time. Although I found it all very disappointing, it didn't seem to matter too much to the rest of the travelling hordes, who were more than making up for it with the noise they were generating during the build up to the game.

As the teams took to the field, the noise within the half-filled stadium was nevertheless deafening. With the pre-match formalities over, the players made their way over to our end of the ground to warm up. With star striker Trevor Francis missing through injury and midfielder Stan Bowles absent without leave, Hamburg - complete with England's curly-haired captain Kevin Keegan in their ranks - were strong favourites. However, with the likes of Shilton, Anderson, Burns, Lloyd (now recovered from injury), O'Neill, Birtles, Bowyer and

Robertson in their line-up, Forest weren't exactly short on quality and certainly not about to capitulate. They'd sweated blood to win this trophy twelve months earlier and had no intentions of giving up their crown without a fight. The full line-up was:

Peter Shilton

2 Viv Anderson 5 Larry Lloyd 6 Kenny Burns 3 Frank Gray

8 Ian Bowyer 4 John McGovern (Captn.)

7 Martin O'Neill 11 John Robertson

9 Garry Birtles 10 Gary Mills

Subs: John O'Hare, Bryn Gunn

Despite their status as defending Champions, without Francis, the 'Reds' were lightweight up front and were expected to play second fiddle to the cosmopolitan and star-studded German outfit. And sure enough, they were pinned back in defence almost from the first kick of the game. With a five-man midfield, striker Birtles cut a lonely figure up front. However, as usual, Burns and Lloyd were outstanding at the heart of the defence (whatever did they feed these two on - raw meat?). And on the rare occasions Keegan and Co. did manage to get through, 'Shilts' responded in magnificent fashion, the pick of his saves being an acrobatic leap to his left to turn over a thunderous drive from Hamburg captain Wolfgang Magath.

Having managed just one shot on goal - from the eager Birtles - during the opening fifteen minutes, the 'Reds' then came out of their enforced defensive cocoon in typical fashion on twenty minutes to fashion a 'smash and grab' 1-0 lead. Having picked up the ball wide on the left, just around the half-way line, Robbo jinked his way inside and played a neat one-two with Birtles ten yards outside the Germans' box. He loped forward another two paces, before curling in a decisive low shot beyond the despairing dive of keeper Rudi Kargus. When the ball found it's way into the bottom right hand corner of the net, he disappeared under a mountain of bodies and there was bedlam on the terraces all around me. The players and supporters went absolutely berserk. Unable to contain themselves, some supporters began to scale the six-foot high perimeter fence at our end of the stadium, but thought better of it when immediately confronted by machine gun wielding policemen.

From that moment on, it was pretty much 'backs-to-the-wall' stuff as far as Forest were concerned, with Keegan and Co. mounting one incisive attack after another. 'Shilts' made yet another stunning save, this time from Jurgen Milewski, and the 'Red & White Army' did their level best to lift the players. Some airhead at the back of the terraces did overstep the mark though; launching a big wooden stake in the direction of Keegan who'd ambled over to within a few yards of us to take a corner kick. It whizzed over the top of our heads and missed him by only a matter of inches. The half-time whistle came as a big relief to everyone (everyone dressed in red and white, that is) and the players trudged wearily off for a well-earned rest.

The second half began in much the same fashion - with the 'Reds' severely under the cosh. However, with the 'mighty Shilts' at his very best and the magnificent Burns brilliantly marshalling the overworked defence (oh what I'd give for a latter day equivalent of this fearsome Scotsman!), the nearest Hamburg came to an equaliser was when a sixty-fifth-minute half-volley from Manny Kaltz thundered menacingly against an upright. Shortly afterwards,

O'Hare was given a belated taste of European glory when he replaced the rapidly fading Mills, and with five minutes remaining, Bryn Gunn came on for the injured Frank Gray.

Incredibly though, in the dying minutes of the game, it was Forest who came closest to scoring and thus putting the issue beyond doubt, when Birtles was put clean through on goal - the one behind which the 'Red and White' hordes were gathered. But, having quite literally run himself into the ground, his tired and failing limbs caused him to dwell on the ball just long enough for a Hamburg defender to nip in and snatch it from under his nose at the very last second. If only he hadn't been so knackered, what a finale this would have been? Still, the spirit he showed right to the very last was typical of the whole team that night. And shortly after this last-ditch effort, the longest forty-five minutes I've ever endured finally came to an end. I was so relieved and elated, I just stood there on the terraces shaking with emotion and crying tears of joy. And I wasn't the only one, believe me.

After what seemed like an eternity, McGovern was finally hoisting the Cup aloft and the whole team were about to embark on their ritual lap of honour. They were saluted by their adoring army of fans as they did so. The whole thing was almost surreal and when the celebrations finally died down, we were all physically and mentally drained. As we poured out of the Stadium, the streets were filled with rejoicing fans, their red and white scarves, banners and flags held aloft in celebration. The City of Madrid was about to experience some serious partying by the looks of things. However, in view of the over-the-top policing we'd encountered earlier, we decided to give the centre of town a miss and retreated back to the sanctuary of our campsite a few miles away. There we were planning to indulge in a knees-up of our very own - we'd been reliably informed the bar was staying open right into the early hours of the morning.

As we crawled through the crowded streets of the city, we hung out of the minibus chanting: ''Robbo scored the only goal in Madrid - Oh Robbo!'' to the tune of 'Oh Geno', the latest hit by Dexy's Midnight Runners. Brilliantly topical we thought, and besides it seemed to be well received by the hordes of red and white clad supporters drifting slowly away from the Stadium. The bars around the city were already beginning to fill up and it was obvious many supporters wouldn't be going home until the next morning. When we finally made it 'home' about forty-five minutes after leaving the Stadium, many of our fellow 'campers' had already arrived back at the site and were getting ready for the party.

Having parked up, we immediately made our way to the bar, only to find it already bursting at the seams. We ordered our drinks - ice-cool lager - and quickly retreated to the patio outside where we gathered around a couple of tables and immediately began to relive every last moment of the game - every shot, every pass, every tackle, every save. And, so subjective is this wonderful game of ours, every one of us had our own unique perspective of what we'd just witnessed. Who'd played well and who hadn't; who'd contributed most and who had contributed little? One thing we all agreed on though: ''Robbo scored the only goal in Madrid...Oh Robbo!''

Having chilled out for about an hour in the cool night air, we retreated back into the rather claustrophobic atmosphere of the bar - ready to join in the party. This wasn't until we'd had yet another unexpected encounter with the local police though. As if determined to stop anyone enjoying themselves, a couple of stern-faced, gun-totting individuals had arrived out of nowhere and stormed inside the bar whilst we were still coming down to earth outside. We were convinced they were about to order the place closed for the evening, thereby leaving us in the wilderness and without so much as a lager-shandy with which to celebrate our historic victory. However, charmed by the wit and smooth talking of a couple of mature-looking individuals amongst the throng of supporters, they left as quickly as they'd arrived, even congratulating us on our victory as they departed.

Very soon, the party was in full swing. A couple of 'thirty-something' supporters were acting as cheerleaders and the singing went on long into the early hours. Every single Trent End anthem I'd ever heard - and believe me there are many - was blasted out over and over again by the 200-strong Forest choir. And although in reality the bar itself was fairly spacious; it was absolutely chock-a-block inside. Some individuals were standing on tables, some on chairs, whilst others were carried shoulder high, their fists punching the air. It was like being in the middle section of the Trent End on a match-day. I climbed up onto the bar where I plonked myself down next to some youth I'd never met before, but who could so easily have been my long lost brother, such was the rapport we immediately struck up with one another. One minute I was joining in with the seventeenth verse, of the fifteenth rendition of: *'Oh I love 'er swingin' tits'*...the next I was waking up in the back of the minibus, being frantically shaken by Chambo, who was screaming in my tab 'ole: ''Wake up ya lazy bastard - it's gone nine o'clock an' we're setting off in less than an 'our''

By ten o'clock we were showered, packed and back on the road again. And, having travelled for only a few minutes, we were already heading back up into the hills. As we slowly negotiated a bend at the top of a steep incline, just a few miles outside Madrid, we were flagged down by a couple of scruffy looking policemen who suddenly appeared in the middle of the road right in front of us. They were gesticulating frantically for us to pull over. Graham brought the bus to a halt on the grass verge and wound down the window. One of them stepped forward and mumbled something to us in Spanish. Naturally we hadn't a clue what he was rabbiting on about, although it was pretty obvious we'd not been stopped so they could engage us in idle chit-chat. Nor was this an attempt on their part to further Anglo/Spanish relations either. We were cobbing ourselves and praying they hadn't stopped us for a routine check of the tachograph, which incidentally hadn't been working since the moment we left Nottingham.

After several minutes of gesturing on his part - which was met by ten completely blank faces - he suddenly made himself abundantly clear with his demand - delivered in perfect English - for: ''Three thousand Pesetas.'' We looked at each other in horror. Shrugging his shoulders, Graham asked, in a rather high-pitched voice: ''Why...what for?'' With that, this rather shady-looking character walked slowly out into the middle of the road and made some sort of gesture we'd transgressed the double white lines, or something equally ludicrous. (Obviously a serious misdemeanour this and ironic really in a country which seemed to pay about as much attention to road safety as Billy Bunter did to healthy eating!) However, despite our futile protests, it was quite apparent our best course of action would be to cough up. Either that or end up banged away in some dingy little police station somewhere in the middle of nowhere for God knows how long and with God knows what gruesome consequences.

After digging deeply into our pockets, we just about managed to scrape together enough money - it's equivalent to around twelve pounds in our currency, and a lot of money then - and, somewhat reluctantly, Graham handed it over to this grinning slime-ball, purporting to be an upholder of the law. The problem facing us now, was this: would we have enough Spanish money left in the kitty to keep this gas-guzzling monstrosity filled up with diesel until we managed to get over the border and into France? Only time would tell.

''Fuckin' Spick Bastards!'' we exclaimed unanimously as we pulled away from the grass verge and back onto the road again. And as we looked back over our shoulders and through the rear window of the bus, we watched in amazement as these 'Reprobates from Hell' immediately flagged down another vehicle, which had presumably committed a similar 'offence'. And surprise, surprise...they just happened to be sporting red and white colours as well. Despite our anger and disgust, we didn't hang around to lend these latest unfortunate victims our moral support.

The journey home was sheer purgatory - not least for poor Graham, who did all the driving. We ended up having just enough Spanish dosh left to get us back into France, and by this time it was very late in the evening - well after midnight in fact. The tank was just about empty when we limped onto the forecourt of a small and deserted filling station somewhere in the South-West region. And, as this particular establishment was most definitely closed for the night, we had no alternative but to settle ourselves down and wait patiently for it to re-open early the next morning. Just to make matters worse, it was bloody freezing, and the 'Phantom' was on probably his best form of the whole trip. (It was many, many years later when Alan - everyone's prime suspect - finally owned up to being the guilty party. And God, was he proud of himself!)

The only enjoyable aspect of our return journey was the ferry crossing from Cherbourg to Southampton, early on the Friday evening. Naturally the whole four hours were spent in the bar, where we engaged in some friendly banter with a group of about a dozen youths from the Southampton area. Apparently, this was a regular pastime for them on a Friday - a return journey across the English Channel, without even setting foot on French soil. This enabled them to indulge in a non-stop eight-hour drinking binge - something which was otherwise impossible in the UK at that time, other than in the comfort of your own home. We had a great time talking football to them - providing them with a blow-by-blow account of our adventures over the last five days and generally having a right good laugh. Not surprisingly, we taunted one another about the great North/South divide. With our Nottingham accents, they refused to accept we were anything other than Northerners, despite our insistence Nottingham is neither in the North nor in the South, but simply in the Midlands. On the other hand, in view of their own rather distinctive Hampshire drawl, we got our own back by referring to them as 'Country Bumpkins' - much to their displeasure.

We eventually arrived back in Nottingham tired and exhausted at around three o'clock on the Saturday morning - thirty-odd hours incidentally after the victorious team had once again been feted at a Civic Reception in the City Centre. Tens of thousands had attended, although many supporters, like us, were still on our way home. By the time we'd trundled half-way round Notts dropping everyone off, it was 4.30-a.m. when Graham finally kicked me out of the minibus outside my flat in Chilwell. And, having desperately guzzled down a mug of piping hot tea, I was straight off to bed, where I slept uninterrupted for sixteen hours. This had been a truly wonderful and memorable week and again one I will never forget. It really sums up what being a football supporter is all about. Sadly though, only a lucky minority ever get to experience such an occasion. In fourteen years of supporting Forest, I'd seen and done probably ten times more than your average football supporter ever gets to see and do in a whole lifetime. And to be fair, if Forest were never to lift another trophy after this one, I'd experienced more than a fair helping of success in my lifetime - and I was still only 22.

AND so, another fantastic season in the history of Nottingham Forest Football Club had come to an end. A respectable fifth position in the First Division table, Runners-up in our favourite competition, the League Cup, and CHAMPIONS OF EUROPE FOR THE SECOND YEAR IN SUCCESSION. Despite all this, the average home attendance in all competitions was a disappointingly low 26,343, with the highest being the 33,277 for the FA Cup fourth round encounter with Liverpool. The lowest was the 20,462 who turned out for the fourth round League Cup replay against Bristol City in November. ''Was this 'Forest Fairytale' ever destined to end?'' I wondered. Whatever, I was determined to savour every last moment of it. ''Roll on next season!''

SEASON 1979/80 – STATISTICS

FOOTBALL LEAGUE DIVISION ONE – FIXTURES

Date		Opposition	Venue	Competition	Score	Attendance
Aug	18	Ipswich Town	A	League	1-0	27,237
	22	**Stoke City**	**H**	**League**	**1-0**	**26,147**
	25	**Coventry City**	**H**	**League**	**4-1**	**23,025**
	29	Blackburn Rovers	A	LC 2 - 1st Leg	1-1	20,458
Sept	1	West Bromwich Albion	A	League	5-1	26,315
	5	**Blackburn Rovers**	**H**	**LC 2 - 2nd Leg**	**6-1**	**21,244**
	8	**Leeds United**	**H**	**League**	**0-0**	**26,914**
	15	Norwich City	A	League	1-3	18,056
	19	**Oesters Vaxjo**	**H**	**Euro Cup 1 - 1st Leg**	**2-0**	**21,974**
	22	Bristol City	A	League	1-1	22,767
	25	Middlesbrough	A	LC 3	3-1	29,869
	29	**Liverpool**	**H**	**League**	**1-0**	**28,262**
Oct	3	Oesters Vaxjo	A	Euro Cup 1 - 2nd Leg	1-1	14,772
	6	**Wolverhampton Wanderers**	**H**	**League**	**3-1**	**27,569**
	10	Stoke City	A	League	1-1	28,514
	13	Manchester City	A	League	0-1	41,683
	20	**Bolton Wanderers**	**H**	**League**	**5-2**	**24,564**
	24	**Arges Pitesti**	**H**	**Euro Cup 2 - 1st Leg**	**2-0**	**24,828**
	27	Tottenham Hotspur	A	League	0-1	49,038
	30	Bristol City	A	LC 4	1-1	25,695
Nov	**3**	**Ipswich Town**	**H**	**League**	**2-0**	**24,593**
	7	Arges Pitesti	A	Euro Cup 2 - 2nd Leg	2-1	25,000
	10	Southampton	A	League	1-4	22,072
	14	**Bristol City**	**H**	**LC 4 - Replay**	**3-0**	**20,462**
	17	**Brighton & Hove Albion**	**H**	**League**	**0-1**	**25,837**
	24	Derby County	A	League	1-4	27,729
Dec	**1**	**Arsenal**	**H**	**League**	**1-1**	**27,925**
	4	West Ham United	A	LC 5	0-0	35,856
	8	Crystal Palace	A	League	0-1	34,840
	12	**West Ham United**	**H**	**LC 5 - Replay**	**3-0**	**25,462**
	22	Manchester United	A	League	0-3	54,607
	26	**Aston Villa**	**H**	**League**	**2-1**	**32,072**
	29	Coventry City	A	League	3-0	24,722
Jan	1	Everton	A	League	0-1	34,622
	5	Leeds United	A	FA Cup 3	4-1	35,945
	12	**West Bromwich Albion**	**H**	**League**	**3-1**	**27,724**
	19	Leeds United	A	League	2-1	29,816
	22	**Liverpool**	**H**	**LCSF - 1st Leg**	**1-0**	**32,220**
	26	**Liverpool**	**H**	**FA Cup 4**	**0-2**	**33,277**
	30	**Barcelona**	**H**	**Euro S C - 1st Leg**	**1-0**	**23,807**
Feb	5	Barcelona	A	Euro S C - 2nd Leg	1-1	90,000
	9	**Bristol City**	**H**	**League**	**0-0**	**23,421**
	12	Liverpool	A	LCSF - 2nd Leg	1-1	50,880
	16	**Middlesbrough**	**H**	**League**	**2-2**	**23,889**
	19	Liverpool	A	League	0-2	45,163
	23	**Manchester City**	**H**	**League**	**4-0**	**27,255**
Mar	1	Bolton Wanderers	A	League	0-1	16,164
	5	**Dynamo Berlin**	**H**	**Euro Cup 3 - 1st Leg**	**0-1**	**27,946**
	11	**Tottenham Hotspur**	**H**	**League**	**4-0**	**25,733**
	15	Wolves (At Wembley Stadium)		LC Final	0-1	100,000
	19	Dynamo Berlin	A	Euro Cup 3 - 2nd Leg	3-1	27,000
	22	**Southampton**	**H**	**League**	**2-0**	**27,675**
	29	Brighton & Hove Albion	A	League	0-1	25,128
Apr	**2**	**Manchester United**	**H**	**League**	**2-0**	**31,417**
	5	Aston Villa	A	League	2-3	29,156
	9	**Ajax Amsterdam**	**H**	**Euro Cup SF - 1st Leg**	**2-0**	**31,244**
	19	**Derby County**	**H**	**League**	**1-0**	**32,266**
	23	Ajax Amsterdam	A	Euro Cup SF - 2nd Leg	0-1	65,000
	26	Middlesbrough	A	League	0-0	17,021
	30	**Norwich City**	**H**	**League**	**2-0**	**21,242**
May	**3**	**Crystal Palace**	**H**	**League**	**4-0**	**24,529**
	5	Arsenal	A	League	0-0	34,632
	9	**Everton**	**H**	**League**	**1-0**	**22,122**
	12	Wolverhampton Wanderers	A	League	1-3	21,725
	28	Hamburg SV (At Bernabeu Stadium, Madrid)		Euro Cup Final	1-0	50,000

HOME ATTENDANCES

	AGGREGATE ATTENDANCE	HIGHEST ATTENDANCE	LOWEST ATTENDANCE	AVERAGE ATTENDANCE
League:	554,181	32,266	21,242	26,389
League Cup:	99,388	32,220	20,462	24,847
FA Cup:	33,277	33,277	33,277	33,277
European Cup:	105,992	31,244	21,974	26,498
European Super Cup:	23,807	23,807	23,807	23,807
All Competitions:	816,645	33,277	20,462	26,343

FINAL LEAGUE TABLE - DIVISION ONE

Position	P	W	D	L	GF	GA	Pts
1. Liverpool	42	25	10	7	81	30	60
2. Manchester United	42	24	10	8	65	35	58
3. Ipswich Town	42	22	9	11	68	39	53
4. Arsenal	42	18	16	8	52	36	52
5. Nottingham Forest	**42**	**20**	**8**	**14**	**63**	**43**	**48**
6. Wolverhampton Wanderers	42	19	9	14	58	47	47
7. Aston Villa	42	16	14	12	51	50	46
8. Southampton	42	18	9	15	65	53	45
9. Middlesbrough	42	16	12	14	50	44	44
10. West Bromwich Albion	42	11	19	12	54	50	41
11. Leeds United	42	13	14	15	46	50	40
12. Norwich City	42	13	14	15	58	66	40
13. Crystal Palace	42	12	16	14	41	50	40
14. Tottenham Hotspur	42	15	10	17	52	62	40
15. Coventry City	42	16	7	19	56	66	39
16. Brighton & Hove Albion	42	11	15	16	47	57	37
17. Manchester City	42	12	13	17	43	66	37
18. Stoke City	42	13	10	19	44	58	36
19. Everton	42	9	17	16	43	51	35
20. Bristol City	42	9	13	20	37	66	31
21. Derby County	42	11	8	23	47	67	30
22. Bolton Wanderers	42	5	15	22	38	73	25

AWAY ATTENDANCES

	AGGREGATE ATTENDANCE	HIGHEST ATTENDANCE	LOWEST ATTENDANCE	AVERAGE ATTENDANCE
League:	631,007	54,607	16,164	30,047
League Cup:	262,758	100,000	20,458	43,793
FA Cup:	35,945	35,945	35,945	35,945
European Cup:	181,772	65,000	14,772	36,354
European Super Cup:	90,000	90,000	90,000	90,000
All Competitions:	1,201,482	100,000	14,772	35,337

"WE'VE BEEN TO EUROPE, WE'VE WON THE CUP TWICE!"

DURING THE summer, Cloughie had once again delved into the transfer market with the purchase of Swiss international midfielder Raimondo Ponte from Grasshoppers Zurich for £250,000 and Scottish international centre-forward Ian Wallace from Coventry City for a whopping £1 million. Both were pencilled in to make their League debuts in the opening game of the season away to Tottenham Hotspur.

Not surprisingly, a large contingent from Nottingham made the trip south on a hot and sunny afternoon, desperate to catch a glimpse of the European Champions in action once again. With the stadium only a short walk from White Hart Lane Railway Station, we decided to catch the Forest Special from Midlands Station. This was packed full with around five or six hundred supporters, and as usual, we were greeted by a substantial police presence at the other end who were waiting to escort us to the ground. It was my first ever trip to Tottenham, and, as there had been some bad blood between the two sets of supporters in the recent past, I felt slightly nervous and apprehensive as we poured tentatively out of the station.

The mile or so walk to the ground proved relatively innocuous, although there were one or two hairy moments when we passed by a large pub on the right where about a hundred Spurs fans were sitting outside enjoying a pre-match drink. Although a handful of them did act in a fairly aggressive and threatening manner, they were quickly and effectively dealt with by the police. Once inside the ground, it was pleasing to see just how many 'Reds' supporters had made the trip south.

Although the behaviour of Forest's travelling supporters had improved dramatically in recent years - thanks mainly to Cloughie's one man crusade - they still had a small hard core of probably two to three hundred, determined to make a name for themselves. And on this particular occasion, they were very much out in force. Four coach-loads had departed from the 'Sal' early that morning to my knowledge. These particular excursions had by this time made a big comeback, although 'Simmo' - the original organiser in the early-seventies - had been superseded by a chap called Mick Randall. The regulars on these buses enjoyed quite a fearsome reputation around Nottingham and were referred to affectionately as 'Randall's Vandals'.

On this occasion, around two hundred of them came marching into the ground a couple of minutes after kick off, having made a late arrival from the pub. They'd also deliberately and quite provocatively made a detour around the back of the notorious 'Shelf Side' on the way, hoping for a confrontation with their Tottenham counterparts. The massive crowd of 43,398 packed inside White Hart Lane, must have wondered just how the hell Forest had managed to secure a second successive European title only three months earlier, such was the ineptitude of their performance. On the day they could count themselves very fortunate indeed to come away with only a 2-0 defeat.

The train journey back to Nottingham afterwards was a fairly mundane and uneventful one; the carriages loaded with dejected and disappointed souls. However, all this was to change suddenly and dramatically when we passed through Leicester Station about an hour and a half into our journey. The 'Sheep' - now a very ordinary Second Division outfit - had opened their account with a trip to Cambridge United that day, and as we rolled gently into the station, a couple of hundred 'Sheep-shaggers' were milling around on the platform, obviously waiting for a connecting train back to the 'Hovel'. As we rumbled slowly towards them at around five or ten miles per hour, they were blissfully unaware this was none other than the Forest Special heading their way, with between five and six hundred of their sworn enemy on board.

The second we began to roll past, a veritable barrage of missiles rained down on them from the train. Half-eaten sandwiches, meat pies, Cornish pasties, not to mention a hail of beer cans - mostly empty of course - could be seen hurtling through the air in their direction. At first they seemed startled and bewildered - somewhat disorientated even - and retreated several steps to escape the barrage. However, within just a few panic-stricken seconds, they'd gathered their senses, and, as it dawned upon them just what they were confronted with, surged forward and returned fire with a vengeance. Bottles, cans, half-eaten Mars Bars, all came screaming towards us. They lashed out at the side of the train with their boots as we sailed by and banged their fists on the windows. Some even tried to pull open the doors and clamber aboard.

By the time we'd travelled the length of the station - which probably took only a matter of seconds but seemed an eternity - the train was almost completely submerged in spit and gunge and we could hardly see out of the windows. At that precise moment, I couldn't help but marvel at the 'friendly' and 'good-natured' rivalry, which exists between our two clubs!

THE following Wednesday, Forest opened their City Ground account with a 2-1 victory over newly-promoted Birmingham City. Raimondo Ponte gave a sparkling display, scoring the second goal and generally running the City defence ragged. Birtles scored the other in front of a crowd of 26,561. Prior to this game, the new Executive Stand - already in use for most of the previous season - was officially, if rather belatedly, opened by manager Brian Clough.

During the run up to the season, the Club had sold a total of 15,921 season tickets, with receipts topping the £1 million mark for the very first time. Although on the face of it, a seemingly modest amount given Forest were Champions of Europe, this was in fact a reasonable tally considering the popularity of the game was by now very much on the downward trend. Attendances up and down the country were alarmingly low. For example, whilst Coventry could only muster a dismal 15,399 for the visit of Arsenal, on the same evening, Division One rivals Stoke City managed to pull in a paltry 10,722 for their opening fixture at the Victoria Ground.

By the end of September, a total of four victories, two draws and two defeats in their first eight League encounters, had seen Forest sitting in a comfortable fifth position in the table, some five points behind early season pacesetters Ipswich Town. Five-nil home victories over Stoke and Leicester were the highlights of the League programme to date, whilst a 7-0 victory over Fourth Division Bury at Gigg Lane in the third round of the League Cup, represented their most impressive result overall. Unfortunately, a 1-0 defeat away to Bulgarian Champions CSKA Sofia in the European Cup first round first leg on Wednesday, 17th September, meant only a two-goal victory in the second leg in Nottingham a fortnight later, would see them progress through to the second round.

Sadly, away from the field of play, violent clashes between rival groups of Forest and Middlesbrough supporters in the streets outside Ayresome Park following the League clash between the two clubs on Saturday, 6th September resulted in the death of 'Boro' supporter Craig French. Two youths from the Nottingham area later served lengthy prison sentences as a result of this incident. The curse of hooliganism was still gripping our national game, although at last, the general public and even a few politicians were beginning to grasp that it wasn't just a football problem, but a social one too. The incident at Middlesbrough occurred only three days after major disturbances at Peterborough United's London Road Stadium during Forest's midweek visit for a second round League Cup fixture. Apparently, a large number of Forest supporters had infiltrated the London Road End of the ground, and after violent skirmishes with the home supporters, were led around the side of the pitch by the police and shepherded into the Visitors' Enclosure at the opposite end.

On the pitch, the 'Reds' suffered a major disappointment when they were unable to break down a well-marshalled Bulgarian defence during the European Cup second leg tie against Sofia. They were dumped out of the competition, despite throwing everything bar the kitchen sink at the visitors for most of the game and were caught out by a classic breakaway goal. This left them needing to score at least three to stand any chance of going through, something they never looked like doing. Although they hadn't exactly relinquished their crown in style, they'd already enjoyed a two-year unbeaten run in the competition - a remarkable feat considering only three and a half short years before, they'd been struggling to find a way out of the Second Division.

The following Saturday, they entertained Man Utd at the City Ground, who were one point and four places behind them in the table. During the build up to this game, United had tabled an audacious £1 million bid to lure local hero Garry Birtles to Old Trafford. Although somewhat out of the blue, they'd probably been encouraged by Clough's apparent willingness, in the recent past at least, to offload quality players. We'd already seen the likes of Peter Withe, Archie Gemmill and Tony Woodcock leave the City Ground, giving the distinct impression no-one was considered in-expendable. In his programme notes prior to the game Clough made his thoughts on the matter abundantly clear:

"And another aspect of their visit here this afternoon is that Garry Birtles will continue to play well for us - as indeed he has all season. Being fully aware of Manchester United's £1 million bid for him, he'll no doubt be out to impress them."

Following United's 2-1 victory in front of a crowd of 29,801, he lambasted Birtles in the press for his own individual contribution to the game: "Birtles couldn't trap a bag of cement," he controversially declared. Naturally, Garry was extremely upset by these remarks and within only a matter of days was on his way up the M6 to sign on the dotted line. Consequently, what had appeared to be nothing more than a throwaway remark from our unpredictable manager; had seemingly prompted the departure of one of our most gifted players? Never had I seen Garry give anything less than one hundred per cent in a Forest shirt - something which, as a local lad and Forest supporter himself, he'd always worn with a great deal of pride.

Within two weeks, Peter Ward had been drafted in from Brighton & Hove Albion as his £450,000 replacement. Himself a product of amateur football in the East Midlands, the curly-haired striker had been a prolific scorer for the 'Seagulls' since being snapped up from Non-League Burton Albion during Peter Taylor's reign at the club. With Trevor Francis still struggling to recover from his serious Achilles tendon injury, for the time being at least, Forest's strike-force was now spearheaded by the relatively inexperienced Ward and the flame-haired Ian Wallace. And, following in the footsteps of the 'Withe-Woodcock', 'Woodcock-Birtles' and latterly, 'Birtles-Francis' partnerships, this latest pairing seemed little more than 'economy class' in comparison.

The once mighty 'Reds' were now looking decidedly ordinary, despite their ability to grind out narrow, if largely uninspiring victories in the League. Having been somewhat spoilt over the last few seasons; this was pretty hard to swallow. Not surprisingly, many of the European Cup bandwagon merchants, who'd attached themselves to the Club during this period, had already abandoned ship. And the extent to which this previously well-oiled machine had declined, was perhaps most graphically illustrated by the one-sided 4-1 defeat suffered at the hands of Second Division Watford in the fourth round of the League Cup on Tuesday, 28th October. In a nutshell, Forest were never at the races, and the large contingent from Nottingham trudged dejectedly out of Vicarage Road after the final whistle. The expression on everyone's face told much the same story: We had, without question, come to the end of a glorious era in the history of our Club.

On the bright side, one or two promising youngsters were beginning to emerge through the ranks and turning in some impressive performances in the Reserves. Nineteen-year-old keeper Steve Sutton had already been handed his senior League debut against Norwich City at Carrow Road in October, whilst at the tender age of eighteen, the impressive looking Colin Walsh made his League debut at Coventry on Saturday, 29th November. Perhaps Cloughie's apparent eagerness to dismantle his all-conquering team was influenced in no small way by his belief in these Forest youngsters?

Supporters were also cheered by the impending return to full fitness of Trevor Francis, who smashed an impressive hat-trick in the Club's 6-0 demolition of Non-League Grantham Town in a friendly on Wednesday, 10th December. He made his full return to first team action in the 1-0 defeat away to Valencia of Spain in the second leg of the European Super Cup Final on 17th December. Unfortunately, despite having won the home leg 2-1 at the City Ground three weeks earlier, the 'Reds' went down on the 'away goals' rule. The striker's return to fitness though, was considered far more important than the outcome of this contest, at least as far as the majority of supporters were concerned.

He marked his return to League action with the third goal in a 3-1 victory over Sunderland at the City Ground three days later. Raimondo Ponte and Colin Walsh were also on the score-sheet in a game which consolidated Forest's eighth position in the table. Despite their relative fall from grace, with 23 games behind them, they'd accumulated no less than 26 points and were only seven behind leaders Aston Villa.

THE Boxing Day fixture against Wolves at Molineux was certain to attract a large following from Nottingham. At least one of the 'Buses from the Sal' was now being organised on a regular basis by a lad called Alan Smedley from Chilwell, known locally as 'Beado'. Although I'd known him for many years, my neighbour who lived in the flat above me in Chilwell, Steve Reid - an avid Forest supporter since even before my time - was a close friend of his. Consequently, the two of us were always guaranteed a seat on the bus, and more often than not, Beado would allow us to travel free of charge. We were by no means 'Townies' ourselves, and as this mob still considered themselves a fairly elite group of people, it was most gratifying to know that between them they were subsidising our trips to away matches!

Beado usually organised his coach through local company Bartons, and the regular driver Neil, was a complete and utter nutcase. He drove like a man possessed and wasn't averse to taking the odd risk or two. For example, he'd think nothing of stopping suddenly right in the middle of a foreign town, just so the lads could pile off and engage in some fisticuffs with gangs of rival supporters. What's more, with alcohol being consumed in copious amounts during every journey - strictly legal at the time - those like me who were blessed only with 'sparrowesque' bladders, had absolutely nothing to fear. Rather than having to stop every ten minutes for a natural break, he actively encouraged us to stand on the steps at the front of the coach and pee straight into the stairwell, thus rendering 'stopping at the services' a pointless exercise.

At least four coaches had been laid on for the Boxing Day excursion, and fortunately for us, Bartons' Bus Depot was rather conveniently situated on Chilwell High Road. About thirty of us clambered aboard the first of these coaches in Beeston before all four headed off into town and the usual rendezvous point outside the Sal. As we cruised up Maid Marion Way and pulled up opposite the pub at about 10.00-a.m., we were staggered to find around three hundred youths milling around outside, all hoping to claim a seat. And there were less than two hundred up for grabs. Even though we managed to squeeze about seventy onto each coach, there were still several dozen disappointed and angry souls left behind as we set off on our way several minutes later.

The usual 'pit-stop' whenever we were travelling to the West Midlands in those days was Tamworth, and today would be no exception. And after a wonderful two and a half hours of drinking and bingeing, we were back on the road again and ready for action - football action that is of course (well at least as far as I was concerned anyway). As we approached Molineux, the majority of our travelling companions decided they weren't going to hang around waiting in the heavy football traffic outside the ground. They piled out of the doors and emergency exits and legged it straight across the dual carriageway, which runs directly behind the back of the South Bank. Not wishing to remain on the coach alone, we followed suit and within seconds were queuing up outside the Visitors' Enclosure. Rather conveniently, this just happened to be in the right hand corner of the South Bank (nowadays completely rebuilt along with the rest of Molineux and known as the Jack Hughes Stand).

Some of the 'Townies' decided they had time to engage in a bit of pre-match entertainment of their own making and waded into a large group of Wolves fans who were just emerging from the Molineux Public House. As usual the boys in blue quickly intervened and many of them didn't even get within fifty yards of the stadium. They were bundled unceremoniously into the back of a police van and whisked away to spend the rest of the day cooling off in the cells. Still, looking on the bright side, the coaches were sure to be a lot less crowded on the way home.

There was a following of at least five thousand from Nottingham amongst the sizeable festive crowd of 31,588. I was also pleasantly surprised to find, contrary to my many previous visits, Wolves had at last cottoned onto the idea of crowd segregation. The South Bank had been divided into two, although the Visitors' Section was somewhat smaller than the Home Supporters' Section. There were two large steel fences separating the two, with a gangway two-foot wide down the middle. This ran all the way from the top of the stand, right down to the perimeter wall at the bottom. Although only a matter of feet apart it ensured, unlike on previous occasions, the two sets of fans were prevented from kicking the living daylights out of each other. Perhaps a good thing really, considering there'd been some rather nasty clashes between the two at the League Cup Final earlier on in the year. There was obviously some bad blood on both sides of the fence, with chants of: *"Where were you at Wem-ber-ley?"* from within the Forest section, followed by: *"Run, Run, Whoever you may be, We are the boys of the Black Country,"* from the Wolves section in response.

One of the most irritating chants we Forest supporters have had to endure over the years is the very tedious: *"Altogether now...We hate Nottingham Forest..."* And even as far back as 1980, this was boring the arse off everyone connected with the Club. Consequently, we'd long since gone on the offensive and set about turning the tables on our rather small-minded rivals up and down the country at every opportunity. This was another perfect moment to take the initiative, and it went something like this:

Forest Fans: *"All together now...We 'ate Wolverhampton, We 'ate Wanderers too...Sssssshhhhhhh."*

Wolves Fans: *Five thousand blank expressions.*

Forest Fans: *" All together now...We 'ate Wolverhampton, We 'ate Wanderers too...Sssssshhhhhhh."*

Wolves Fans: *Five thousand even more blank expressions (the lights are on, but there's no-one at home!).*

Forest Fans: *"All together now...We 'ate Wolverhampton, We 'ate Wanderers too...Sssssshhhhhhh."*

Wolves Fans: *(At last the lights come on) "All together now, We 'ate Nottingham Forest..."*

Forest Fans: *"AND NOTTINGHAM FOREST 'ATE YOU, YOU BASTARDS!...Ahhhhhhh! (Completely drowning the Wolves fans out before they are able to get into their stride).*

Wolves Fans: *Five thousand blank expressions!*

When the teams took to the field, the travelling 'Red Army' immediately rounded upon Wolves' captain Emlyn Hughes, without doubt one of our most despised adversaries of all time. Although now at the twilight of his career, he'd been a crucial member of the Liverpool side beaten with such regularity by the 'Tricky Trees' during our halcyon days just two to three years earlier. Along with Phil Thompson, Terry McDermott and Graham Souness, Hughes could never come to terms with Forest's undoubted superiority. He was always on the back page of one tabloid newspaper or another whinging on about Forest's 'negative' tactics or how they'd once more been robbed of victory by the referee.

The sound of: *"ang yer boots up, 'ang yer boots up, 'ang yer boots up Emlyn Hughes,"* rang out from our section of the South Bank throughout the game, followed by chants of: *"You Scouse Bastard!"* And, as if to rub salt in to the wounds, Forest's display - and in particular that of the diminutive Raimondo Ponte - was absolutely superb. They completely demolished Wolves, and with two own goals, a Frank Gray penalty and a fourth from the superlative Swiss, they carved out an emphatic 4-1 victory. This had us all dancing out of Molineux at the end chanting: *"Jingle Bells, Jingle Bells, Jingle all the way, Oh what fun it is to see, Forest win away, Oh!"*

THE day after our Molineux invasion, the 'Reds' entertained Aston Villa at the City Ground. Trevor Francis and Martin O'Neill scored the goals in a 2-2 draw, in front of a large festive crowd of 33,900 - their biggest League gate of the season. The state of the City Ground pitch had improved considerably since the installation of a hot air balloon before the onset of winter. This was similar to the one pioneered by neighbours Leicester City, and not only had it enhanced the quality of the playing surface, it had also ensured an uninterrupted fixture list so far this season.

With the festive period over, it was FA Cup time once again, with Second Division Bolton Wanderers visiting Trentside the following Saturday for a third round tie. A superbly entertaining game, in which Trevor Francis (2) and Raimondo Ponte were the Forest scorers, ended 3-3 in front of 22,920 spectators. In the replay at Burnden Park three days later, a Francis goal in extra time, gave the 'Reds' a 1-0 victory. Their reward was the undisputed tie of the fourth round - Manchester United at home.

They continued their topsy-turvy League form with a 1-0 defeat at Ipswich, and by the time they lined up to face United on Saturday, 24th January, another one of the Club's seasoned campaigners, Ian Bowyer, had left the City Ground. Sunderland had snapped him up for a modest fee. The stadium was packed to it's capacity for this game and the vast majority of the 34,110 crowd went home happy. Trevor Francis headed home a left wing corner from Robertson to give the 'Reds' a vital 1-0 victory.

Once again, they came out of the hat first in the draw for the fifth round, this time pitting their wits against Second Division strugglers Bristol City, the tie to be played on Saturday, 14th February. In between these two Cup ties, 20-year-old Stuart Gray made his full League debut in the 1-1 draw against Manchester City at Maine Road. His no-nonsense style of play soon made him a popular figure on the City Ground terraces and he retained his place in the side for the visit of the 'Robins'. Goals from Robertson (penalty) and Wallace gave Forest a hard-fought 2-1 victory in front of a crowd of 26,742 and earned them a place in the quarter-finals of the competition for the first time in three years. And incredibly, they were drawn at home once again, with First Division leaders Ipswich Town providing the opposition.

A fortnight before this glamorous tie, they entertained Arsenal at the City Ground in a League game which stands out in my mind for two reasons: Firstly, Martin O'Neill had a superb game, scoring two goals in a comfortable 3-1 victory in front of 25,357 people; and secondly, he was sold to Norwich City immediately after the game. It is a well-known fact Cloughie and O'Neill didn't see eye-to-eye - but to be honest, several other players also enjoyed a similar relationship with the unpredictable manager. On Wednesday, 4th March - three days before the quarter-final tie - Larry Lloyd also parted company with the Club, joining Fourth Division Wigan as player-manager.

The biggest crowd of the season - 34,796 - packed into the City Ground for this eagerly awaited showdown with Ipswich. And what a sensational game it turned out to be, with the visitors storming into an early two-goal lead, thanks incredibly to two own goals from Viv Anderson. Remarkably, the 'Reds' pulled level before half-time, with replies from Francis and Walsh. Robertson then gave them a second-half lead with a calmly executed penalty, only for Dutchman Frans Thijssen to make things all square again before the end.

The 3-3 score-line resulted in a trip to Portman Road three days later for a replay. Thousands of 'Trickies' made the journey to East Anglia, only for many of them to be turned away at the turnstiles. Incredibly, the game wasn't all-ticket and 31,060 fans crammed inside the compact stadium. Unfortunately, a solitary goal from Arnold Muhren gave Ipswich a decisive 1-0 victory and Forest's FA Cup ambitions were in tatters once again. Ian Wallace had what appeared to be a perfectly executed 'goal' disallowed and then somehow managed to scoop an easy chance over the bar from only three feet out. Forest's front-line looked decidedly short on firepower at this stage of the season. Consequently, supporters were beginning to question the rather premature departure of the likes of Withe, Woodcock and Birtles over the course of the last three seasons.

When supporters welcomed Martin O'Neill back to Trentside during the visit of Norwich City on Saturday, 28th March, Forest's season was already pretty much over. They were in sixth position in the table, and with only seven games remaining, eight points behind leaders Ipswich, who'd played two games less. Apart from the 2-1 victory that day - with both goals coming from Francis - the only other bright spot was the debut of the Club's latest signing from Bayern Munich, Einer Jan Aas. The 25-year-old Norwegian defender - who incidentally was fluent in five different languages - had no problems settling in. He very quickly made his mark as one of the most cultured defenders ever to pull on the famous red and white shirt.

FOR the first time in four years, Forest ended the season without a trophy, although they did finish in seventh position in the First Division table. They were now entering a transitional phase, having come to the end of the most successful period in the Club's long history. Many of the old faces had gone, some fresh new talent had emerged through the ranks, and several experienced players had been drafted in to bolster the squad. The burning question amongst supporters was this: Having ended the season without a trophy, would we now be able to hang onto the brilliant and much-admired talents of Trevor Francis?

The average League attendance this season was 24,419, with the highest being the 33,900 for the visit of Champions-elect Aston Villa, and the lowest being the 19,690 for the visit of Middlesbrough - incidentally the lowest League gate at the City Ground since the visit of Oldham Athletic on 23rd April, 1977. It was also the first League attendance of below 20,000 during the whole of this period. The highest attendance overall was the 34,796 for the FA Cup quarter-final tie against Ipswich Town and the average in all competitions was 24,483. From a personal point of view, I had now missed just one home game (of any description) during the whole of the last twelve seasons. And what's more, I was determined not to miss any more - no matter what lay in store for us on Trentside over the coming seasons.

SEASON 1980/81 – STATISTICS

FOOTBALL LEAGUE DIVISION ONE – FIXTURES

Date		Opposition	Venue	Competition	Score	Attendance
Aug	16	Tottenham Hotspur	A	League	0-2	43,398
	20	**Birmingham City**	**H**	**League**	**2-1**	**26,561**
	23	Everton	A	League	0-0	25,981
	27	**Peterborough United**	**H**	**LC 2 - 1st Leg**	**3-0**	**16,117**
	30	**Stoke City**	**H**	**League**	**5-0**	**21,915**
Sept	3	Peterborough United	A	LC 2 - 2nd Leg	1-1	11,503
	6	Middlesbrough	A	League	0-0	17,119
	13	**Manchester City**	**H**	**League**	**3-2**	**23,184**
	17	CSKA Sofia	A	Euro Cup 1 - 1st Leg	0-1	65,000
	20	**Leicester City**	**H**	**League**	**5-0**	**27,145**
	23	Bury	A	LC 3	7-0	8,828
	27	Arsenal	A	League	0-1	37,582
Oct	**1**	**CSKA Sofia**	**H**	**Euro Cup 1 - 2nd Leg**	**0-1**	**25,813**
	4	**Manchester United**	**H**	**League**	**1-2**	**29,801**
	8	Sunderland	A	League	2-2	30,485
	11	Brighton & Hove Albion	A	League	1-0	17,391
	18	**West Bromwich Albion**	**H**	**League**	**2-1**	**25,096**
	22	**Leeds United**	**H**	**League**	**2-1**	**25,033**
	25	Norwich City	A	League	1-1	17,792
	28	Watford	A	LC 4	1-4	22,597
Nov	**1**	**Southampton**	**H**	**League**	**2-1**	**24,669**
	8	Liverpool	A	League	0-0	43,143
	11	Birmingham City	A	League	0-2	22,433
	15	**Tottenham Hotspur**	**H**	**League**	**0-3**	**25,400**
	22	**Ipswich Town**	**H**	**League**	**1-2**	**24,423**
	25	**Valencia**	**H**	**Euro S C - 1st Leg**	**2-1**	**12,246**
	29	Coventry City	A	League	1-1	15,151
Dec	**6**	**Crystal Palace**	**H**	**League**	**3-0**	**20,223**
	13	Leeds United	A	League	0-1	21,882
	17	Valencia	A	Euro S C - 2nd Leg	0-1	29,083
	20	**Sunderland**	**H**	**League**	**3-1**	**23,151**
	26	Wolverhampton Wanderers	A	League	4-1	31,588
	27	**Aston Villa**	**H**	**League**	**2-2**	**33,900**
Jan	**3**	**Bolton Wanderers**	**H**	**FA Cup 3**	**3-3**	**22,920**
	6	Bolton Wanderers	A	FA Cup 3 - Replay	1-0	22,799
	10	Ipswich Town	A	League	0-2	25,697
	24	**Manchester United**	**H**	**FA Cup 4**	**1-0**	**34,110**
	31	**Everton**	**H**	**League**	**1-0**	**25,631**
Feb	7	Manchester City	A	League	1-1	40,524
	11	Nacional Montevideo	N	World Club Championship	0-1	70,000
		(Played at National Stadium, Tokyo)				
	14	**Bristol City**	**H**	**FA Cup 5**	**2-1**	**26,742**
	18	Stoke City	A	League	2-1	17,303
	21	**Arsenal**	**H**	**League**	**3-1**	**25,357**
	28	Leicester City	A	League	1-1	26,608
Mar	**3**	**Middlesbrough**	**H**	**League**	**1-0**	**19,690**
	7	**Ipswich Town**	**H**	**FA Cup 6**	**3-3**	**34,796**
	10	Ipswich Town	A	FA Cup 6 - Replay	0-1	31,060
	14	**Brighton & Hove Albion**	**H**	**League**	**4-1**	**20,688**
	18	Manchester United	A	League	1-1	38,205
	21	West Bromwich Albion	A	League	1-2	19,532
	28	**Norwich City**	**H**	**League**	**2-1**	**22,353**
Apr	4	Southampton	A	League	0-2	22,712
	11	**Liverpool**	**H**	**League**	**0-0**	**27,363**
	18	Aston Villa	A	League	0-2	34,707
	20	**Wolverhampton Wanderers**	**H**	**League**	**1-0**	**19,711**
	25	Crystal Palace	A	League	3-1	13,352
May	**2**	**Coventry City**	**H**	**League**	**1-1**	**21,511**

HOME ATTENDANCES

	AGGREGATE ATTENDANCE	HIGHEST ATTENDANCE	LOWEST ATTENDANCE	AVERAGE ATTENDANCE
League:	512,805	33,900	19,690	24,419
League Cup:	16,117	16,117	16,117	16,117
FA Cup:	118,568	34,796	22,920	29,642
European Cup:	25,813	25,813	25,813	25,813
European Super Cup:	12,246	12,246	12,246	12,246
All Competitions:	685,549	34,796	12,246	24,483

FINAL LEAGUE TABLE - DIVISION ONE

Position	P	W	D	L	GF	GA	Pts
1. Aston Villa	42	26	8	8	72	40	60
2. Ipswich Town	42	23	10	9	77	43	56
3. Arsenal	42	19	15	8	61	45	53
4. West Bromwich Albion	42	20	12	10	60	42	52
5. Liverpool	42	17	17	8	62	46	51
6. Southampton	42	20	10	12	76	56	50
7. Nottingham Forest	**42**	**19**	**12**	**11**	**62**	**45**	**50**
8. Manchester United	42	15	18	9	51	36	48
9. Leeds United	42	17	10	15	39	47	44
10. Tottenham Hotspur	42	14	15	13	70	68	43
11. Stoke City	42	12	18	12	51	60	42
12. Manchester City	42	14	11	17	56	59	39
13. Birmingham City	42	13	12	17	50	61	38
14. Middlesbrough	42	16	5	21	53	61	37
15. Everton	42	13	10	19	55	58	36
16. Coventry City	42	13	10	19	48	68	36
17. Sunderland	42	14	7	21	58	53	35
18. Wolverhampton Wanderers	42	13	9	20	47	55	35
19. Brighton & Hove Albion	42	14	7	21	54	67	35
20. Norwich City	42	13	7	22	49	73	33
21. Leicester City	42	13	6	23	40	67	32
22. Crystal Palace	42	6	7	29	47	83	19

AWAY ATTENDANCES

	AGGREGATE ATTENDANCE	HIGHEST ATTENDANCE	LOWEST ATTENDANCE	AVERAGE ATTENDANCE
League:	562,585	43,398	13,352	26,789
League Cup:	42,928	22,597	8,828	14,309
FA Cup:	53,859	31,060	22,799	26,929
European Cup:	65,000	65,000	65,000	65,000
European Super Cup:	29,083	29,083	29,083	29,083
World Club Champ:	70,000	70,000	70,000	70,000
All Competitions:	823,455	70,000	8,828	28,395

"THERE'LL ALWAYS BE AN ENGLAND, AND ENGLAND SHALL BE FREE"

DURING THE close season, Cloughie had signed the blossoming talents of young midfielder Mark Proctor from Middlesbrough and had splashed out in a big way for Norwich City striker Justin Fashanu. He became the first black player in this country to be involved in a £1 million deal. However, speculation was rife in the press and also on the streets of Nottingham, that Trevor Francis would soon be off-loaded by the 'Reds'. Crowd favourite Raimondo Ponte had already packed his bags and gone, having been sold to Corsican side Bastia of the French League.

In a bid to increase the game's rapidly diminishing attendances, and to generally spice things up a little on the pitch, the Football League had increased the number of points awarded for a victory from two to three. It was hoped this would encourage the game's coaches and technical advisers to rid themselves of their hitherto negative approach and inspire a more attacking style of play. Along with the ever-increasing hooligan problem, and the economic recession, their over-cautious mentality was seen as the main reason for the worrying decline in the game's popularity.

Despite all of this, Forest had managed to sell over 14,000 season tickets during the summer, which in the circumstances wasn't at all bad really. This would be the Club's fifty-third season in the top flight since their formation in 1865. Along with Stoke City and neighbours Notts County - the oldest football club in the world - they'd been founder members of the Football League.

A crowd of 25,234 turned up at the City Ground to see them beat Southampton 2-1 in the opening fixture of the season on Saturday, 29th August. As ever, the first Saturday of the campaign was blessed with hot and sunny weather. Anyone planning a holiday in the UK would do well to note clear blue skies and boiling hot sunshine are the order of the day on this particular weekend. Alternatively, as mentioned previously, FA Cup Final weekend is also a pretty safe bet. And Trevor Francis showed the watching Match of the Day audience just what a hot property he was, with a blistering two-goal performance.

Sadly for us, this was to be his last City Ground performance in a Forest shirt. Immediately after the goalless draw at Manchester United two days later, he completed the second £1 million transfer of his career, when he signed for First Division rivals Manchester City. This meant that in the space of only twelve months, the Forest management had traded in the pace, skill and fluency of the Birtles-Francis partnership, for the rather pedestrian - and at times downright cumbersome - strike-force of Wallace and Fashanu!

It was hard to imagine even the most inexperienced of managers - let alone two of the most competent in the history of the game - dropping a clanger of this magnitude. But for them to consider all four strikers of similar value in monetary terms was beyond me. Admittedly, I have never played the game at this level, but I'd been kicking a ball about since my early childhood. What's more, I'd been watching the professional game week in, week out, for the last fifteen years. And as far as I'm concerned, you don't need to have played at a professional level, to be capable of spotting a misplaced pass or a badly timed tackle.

In Wallace's defence, despite his contribution outside the box being virtually non-existent, his reflexes inside were at times razor sharp. On Saturday, 5th September against Birmingham City at St.Andrews, he plundered an impressive hat-trick, but still managed somehow to end up on the losing side.

I travelled to 'Brum' that day on the 'Bus from the Sal'. However, whereas on numerous occasions in the past there'd been as many as three or four coaches departing from this venue, Beado was struggling to fill just one for this fixture. Not only had Forest's home support dwindled badly of late, but the previously impressive away following was now also in a serious state of decline. What's more, my usual travelling companion, Steve Reid, was also becoming more and more conspicuous by his absence. His excuses were coming thick and fast, but at the same time having a less plausible ring to them as each week went by. Apparently fit and healthy and positively raring to go the day before, he would be mysteriously struck down during the night by one debilitating illness or another. So severe in fact were these attacks, he would be rendered completely unable to walk. Consequently, 'poor old Pam', his misses, always had to come to the door on his behalf to deliver the bad news. Mind you, to be honest, I was almost as frightened of Pam as he was!

On the bright side, Steve's sudden and worrying bouts of illness - which he had of course always miraculously recovered from in time to play football the next morning - were indirectly responsible for me meeting up with and forging a lasting friendship with fellow Forest fanatic, John Farley - still one of my closest friends to this day. Having travelled on my own to Birmingham, John - a proper 'Townee' himself - just happened to sit next to me on the coach. We established an instant rapport, and as they say, the rest is history.

DESPITE the departure of Francis, in terms of results at least, the first three months of the season were fairly productive. By the time they entertained Arsenal at the City Ground on Saturday, 21st November, Forest were sitting in fifth position in the table, having accumulated a total of 23 points from 13 games. This included a total of six wins, five draws and only two defeats. However, their lack of firepower up front had seen them score only 16 League goals, whilst at the same time conceding just 13. To his credit, Wallace had found the net on no less than nine occasions, including a brace in a second round League Cup tie at Birmingham, increasing his tally against them to five already this season.

On the other hand, his partner Justin Fashanu had managed to score just twice, despite enjoying an uninterrupted 16-match run in the team. Consequently, his £1 million price tag - heavily influenced by a fluke goal for previous club Norwich City against Liverpool and captured on Match of the Day - was looking seriously over-inflated. He did however, bag his third of the season in this 2-1 defeat against the 'Gunners', in front of a crowd of 20,912.

The 'Reds' were also enjoying a reasonable run in the League Cup, having disposed of Birmingham by an aggregate 5-3 over the two legs of the second round tie. They'd also beaten Second Division Blackburn Rovers 1-0 in the third round at Ewood Park, and Fourth Division Tranmere Rovers by 2-0 on Trentside in round four. During this latest success, Cloughie had also paraded another foreign signing - midfielder Jurgen Roeber - formerly of Bayern Munich. He arrived at the City Ground following a short stint with North American Soccer League Club Calgary Bloomers. Seventeen-year-old centre-half Chris Fairclough also made his senior debut in this game.

After the 2-0 defeat by Liverpool at home on Saturday, 5th December, in front of just 24,521, Cloughie again went back into the transfer market to sign 33-year-old Arsenal defender Willie Young for a fee of £150,000. This became necessary after the classy Einer Aas - already firmly established as a crowd favourite - suffered a badly damaged ankle in the 3-2 victory at Sunderland in November. So severe was this injury, it would ultimately cut short the unfortunate Norwegian's career in the professional game.

The only thing standing in the way of Young making his Forest debut at Swansea on Saturday, 12th December, was the weather - possibly the severest encountered in this country since records began. The whole place had been suddenly and unexpectedly buried in a thick blanket of snow, accompanied by ice-cold Siberian winds. Virtually every amateur and professional fixture had to be postponed that weekend from Lands End to John O'Groats - everyone that is, except Swansea City versus Nottingham Forest. Miraculously, a small pocket of South Wales had somehow managed to escape the blizzards, and despite the Arctic temperatures, the pitch had also been passed fit. There was only one problem: how the hell would the players and supporters battle their way through the snowdrifts to reach the Vetch Field?

Only weeks earlier, the Club had unexpectedly arranged for the Forest-Rail special to be brought out of mothballs and announced that the team would be travelling by rail to this game, along with six hundreds supporters. And remarkably, despite the conditions, British Rail gave the thumbs up on the morning of the game and the train rolled out of Midlands Station as planned.

As ever, Beado had arranged a coach for this trip and this was due to depart from the Sal at around 8.30 in the morning. Although I was certain the whole trip wouldn't even get off the ground, I'd arranged to meet John as usual and felt obliged therefore to battle my way into town to meet him. As I sat half shivering to death on the bus, I was convinced no-one would even turn up at the Sal and very shortly I'd be on my way back home again to my nice warm bed. However, having eventually reached the Maid Marion Café at the top of Friar Lane, I was staggered to find the place packed to the rafters, with everyone already getting stuck into their bacon and egg butties. And there right amongst them, was the grinning face of Mr. Farley.

So impressive was this turnout given the atrocious conditions, Beado was determined not to turn away one of these brave and hearty souls. Somehow he managed to squeeze all 76 of us onto the usual 53-seater. Consequently, as the coach spluttered it's way up Derby Road at just after 9 o'clock, we were crammed in three to a seat wherever possible, with the remainder standing or sitting in the aisle. Being a couple of selfish bastards though, Farley and I had somehow managed to claim a whole seat exclusively for ourselves. As the grossly over-laden vehicle chugged it's way up to Canning Circus, I was still convinced we hadn't a prayer of reaching Swansea, so severe were the conditions outside. By the time we'd left the City Centre, a thick film of ice had already formed on the inside of the windows. Not only were the conditions on board extremely uncomfortable, with bodies strewn about all over the place, but it was now also impossible to see where we were going even. ''The things you do for love,'' I remarked to John, sarcastically.

Incredibly, having battled our way through snowdrifts and blizzard conditions all the way across England, we finally arrived in a clear and sunny Swansea at around 2.00-p.m. And after a couple of stiff drinks in a nearby pub, we made our way into the ground at approximately 2.45-p.m. Much to our amazement, there were already a few hundred Forest supporters inside the Visitors' Enclosure, and as we were effectively on 'foreign' soil, many had the Cross of St George daubed in paint on their faces and were wrapped up inside Union Jacks. Chants of: *''Wales - Wales - Wales,''* from the home supporters on the other side of the dividing fence, prompted an immediate response of: *''There'll always be an England, And England shall be free, If England means as much to you, As England means to me,''* from the travelling 'Red Army'. Despite the bitterly cold wind searing through the stands, I could already feel the temperature rising inside the Vetch Field.

Judging by the number of Forest supporters inside, we assumed the Forest-Rail special had already arrived in the city. However, a voice over the public address system minutes before the scheduled kick off, announced the Forest team had only just pulled into the station ten minutes earlier and the kick off would be delayed for several minutes. Only seconds afterwards, the first of six hundred supporters who'd also arrived by train with the players came pouring in through the turnstiles and onto the terraces. Suddenly a carnival-like atmosphere broke out.

The special train had pulled into Swansea Station at 2.45-p.m., and remarkably, following a short dash by coach to the ground behind a police escort, the players were changed and ready for action just minutes after 3.00-p.m. However, following a further delay while they messed around changing their studs to those more compatible with the frozen conditions, the game finally kicked off just eight minutes late. Impressive or what?

This last-minute dash to the stadium appeared to have had little effect on their stamina, as they turned in a very impressive performance in front of the watching Match of the Day cameras and a frost-bitten crowd of 17,559. A headed goal by Willie Young on his debut, following a left wing corner and a penalty from Robbo, gave the 'Reds' a useful 2-1 victory. This made the long and arduous journey seem worthwhile after all.

Surprisingly, there were a few fairly nasty incidents outside the stadium after the game, and as we headed home towards snowbound England, I for one wasn't disappointed to see the back of South Wales. By this time, the temperature was well and truly below freezing and there was again a thick coat of ice forming on the inside of the coach windows. Conditions on board were bloody awful. We were jammed in like sardines and generally freezing our nuts off. As I gazed around at everyone huddled together and shivering, I pulled the collar of my sheepskin coat right up behind my head and congratulated myself on the best two hundred quid I'd ever spent.

At around 9 o'clock, we stopped for a well-earned break in Worcester Town Centre. We were in desperate need of some alcoholic refreshment. As we piled off the coach and headed off down the main road which runs through the central shopping area, we found the whole place was just about completely deserted. There was a six-inch layer of snow everywhere and an ice-cold mist drifting eerily up from the ground. It was so cold in fact, when you breathed inwards; it felt like someone stabbing you in the chest with a knife. I looked up at John's face and was amazed to see his eyebrows and moustache, and even his hair, were all white and frozen. (According to the news on the radio the next morning, it had been one of the coldest days on record, with - coincidentally - temperatures in Worcester falling to an incredible minus twenty-seven degrees centigrade!).

After enjoying a couple of pints with the rest of the lads from our coach, John and I decided to set off on a mission. Match of the Day was about to begin and we were determined to get a piece of the action - whatever it took. Unfortunately in those days, pubs with televisions were about as common as 'Sheep-shaggers' with more than three brain-cells. Our only hope therefore, was one of the many small hotels situated along the main road into the town. And, for the first time since we'd met, I was about to witness the full force of Mr. Farley's silver-tongued charm - in all it's glory. And boy was I impressed.

As we made our way through the revolving door of a small, but expensive looking hotel, John made a bee-line for the reception desk, where he skilfully set about explaining our predicament to a sympathetic, if slightly bemused receptionist. Amazingly, having picked up the phone and summoned help, within a matter of seconds, we found ourselves being led briskly by the Front of House Manager in the direction of the residents' TV lounge on the first floor. There we were promptly served with sandwiches and as much alcohol as we could drink, whilst sitting in complete splendour watching our red-shirted heroes performing miracles on a twenty-six inch colour television.

When we eventually arrived back at the coach at around midnight, we were extremely well-oiled and ready for some serious shut-eye. The rest of the lads were very envious when furnished with the full details of our enjoyable little adventure - especially as we were the only ones who'd actually managed to see Match of the Day.

We finally arrived back in Nottingham at around 2.00-a.m., although it transpired afterwards the special train hadn't arrived back until 2.25-a.m. - eight and three quarter hours after pulling out of Swansea Station. It had suffered a two-hour delay after breaking down at Caerdydd Canalog (Cardiff Station). Thank heavens for the 'Bus from the Sal' is all I say.

The cold snap was so severe; the remainder of Forest's League programme for December was wiped out completely. This included the scheduled fixtures at home to Ipswich and

Notts County, and another Boxing Day special at Wolves. Consequently, we had to wait until Saturday, 2nd January 1982, before they played another competitive game. This was a third round FA Cup tie against Second Division Wrexham at the City Ground. Originally scheduled for the day before - New Year's Day - this had also been postponed at the last minute when the City Ground - not for the first time in it's history - suddenly became enveloped in a thick veil of icy fog, which had drifted in from the Trent. The three-week break had seriously affected Forest's form, and they were bombed out of the competition, losing 3-1 to the rampant Welshmen in front of a miserable crowd of just 15,649.

Forest's shortcomings up front, were now being matched by their rather lacklustre defence. At the age of only 28, Kenny Burns had been hived off to Leeds United three months earlier - and to rub salt in to our wounds, was playing some of the best football of his career. Just what had inspired Cloughie to part company with such an influential and classy player so prematurely, will always remain a mystery to me - especially as he was still very much in his prime? Having built a side capable of taking on and beating Europe's finest - with the consistent, and at times brilliant, Burns at the heart of it's defence - the maestro had now transformed Forest into a decidedly ordinary outfit.

Although we'd enjoyed a reasonably good run in the League Cup, this was also about to come to an end at the hands of Spurs at White Hart Lane in the fifth round. A fairly feeble looking Forest went down 1-0 in this tie on Monday, 18th January, in front of a crowd of 31,192. This meant that their only realistic objective for the remainder of the season, was a respectable position in the First Division table and an outside chance of qualifying for Europe the following season.

By the time they entertained the 'Pies' in the re-arranged League fixture at home on Saturday, 23rd January, they were occupying only a mid-table position, having accumulated 32 points from 19 games. A crowd of 26,158 saw relegation-threatened County plunder a vital 2-0 victory on this occasion, improving further their already impressive record at the City Ground. (Incidentally, the first competitive Forest versus Notts fixture, had taken place in 1866, making it the first real local 'derby' game and preceding the much higher-profile 'derbies' such as Liverpool v Everton and Man Utd v Man City etc.).

After a string of fairly mediocre displays, during which they picked up only 16 points from a possible 42, the 'Reds' then took on their black and white neighbours once again in the return League fixture at Meadow Lane on Easter Monday, 12th April. Goals from Ian Bowyer - now enjoying his second spell at the Club - and a young Calvin Plummer, gave them a 2-1 victory in front of a disappointing crowd of only 19,304.

As the players were warming up prior to this game, a large section of the Forest supporters - most of the crowd in fact - vented their frustration at a very forlorn-looking Justin Fashanu, with chants of: *"We're sick and tired of you - Fashanu, Fashanu,"* ringing out all around 'the Lane'. The lanky and awkward-looking striker had scored a meagre four goals all season in 30 League and Cup appearances. And what's more, he hadn't scored at all since the Division One clash at Sunderland on 25th November. And considering he was the man drafted in at such great expense to replace the highly-rated and multi-talented Trevor Francis, most supporters felt cheated and let down by the standard of his performances and his unacceptable goals per game ratio. To cap it all, he went on to make a further five appearances before the end of the season, without adding further to his tally.

THE final month of the season turned out to be an eventful one for the Club, both on and off the field. On 1st May, 21-year-old Peter Davenport - a scoring sensation in the Reserves - made his much-awaited League debut in the 2-0 defeat at Liverpool. He then scored his first senior goal for the Club in the 2-0 victory over Spurs at the City Ground on Wednesday, 12th May, in what was his fourth senior appearance. This victory brought to an end a sequence of ten consecutive League games on Trentside without a victory - much to the relief of the 15,273 crowd.

On Saturday, 15th May - the final day of the season - Forest travelled to Portman Road to take on Championship contenders Ipswich Town. Had Ipswich beaten Forest and other results gone in their favour, the East Anglian outfit would have been crowned Football League Champions. However, such was the growing apathy amongst Forest's disillusioned and dwindling band of supporters - don't some people have short memories? - there wasn't even a 'Bus from the Sal' for this game. Consequently, Farley and I had to travel to Suffolk by car.

It was a hot and sunny day, and when the teams took to the field, we were delighted to see 19-year-old Steve Hodge - another product of the youth set up - was about to make his senior debut on the left-hand side of midfield. And with the Nottingham-born player having a major impact on the game, in front of the watching Match of the Day cameras, Forest efficiently, if somewhat surprisingly, destroyed the home side's title aspirations with a stunning 3-1 victory. A perfectly executed hat-trick from the prolific Davenport, silenced the home crowd and gave Forest's small band of around a thousand travelling supporters a glimpse of what was to come in the future. As we headed home afterwards, we reflected upon what had been, for one reason or another, a very disappointing campaign for the 'Reds'. The performances of Hodge and Davenport though, filled us with optimism for the following season.

Off the field, assistant manager Peter Taylor - the other half of the 'Dynamic Duo' - announced he was about to retire from the game on the grounds of ill health. This was completely unexpected and came as a massive blow to all Forest supporters. We had the utmost respect for Taylor - a fellow Nottinghamian, and a sound bloke.

FOREST finished the season in a disappointing twelfth position in the table. And, for the first time since season 1976/77, the average League attendance at the City Ground failed to top the 20,000 mark. The highest was the 26,327 for the visit of West Ham United, with the lowest being the 15,037 for the visit of Swansea City. Although the decline on the pitch had undoubtedly contributed to this downturn in attendances, the general decline in the game's popularity was probably the biggest single factor. Check out these attendances at some of their away games during the course of this season:

• Sunderland v Forest at Roker Park on 25-11-81	- **17,419**
• Aston Villa v Forest at Villa Park on 28-11-81	- **26,847**
(Villa were reigning League Champions and on their way to winning the European Cup at the climax of the season!)	
• West Brom v Forest at the Hawthorns on 06-02-82	- **15,006**
• Wolves v Forest at Molineux on 16-02-82	- **11,195**
• Coventry v Forest at Highfield Road on 09-03-82	- **9,677**
• Leeds v Forest at Elland Road on 20-03-82	- **18,036**
• Arsenal v Forest at Highbury on 17-04-82	- **21,986**
• Everton v Forest at Goodison Park on 20-04-82	- **15,463**
• Ipswich v Forest at Portman Road on 15-05-82	- **19,974**
(Ipswich were playing for a possible League Championship trophy that day!)	

A comparison of Forest's home League attendances this season, with those of seasons 1967/68 and 1977/78, shows a drop of some 36.42% and 38.81% respectively. Similarly, a comparison of the average away attendances during the corresponding period shows a decline of 32.9% and 36.47% respectively. Sadly, the downward trend was set to continue throughout the game during subsequent seasons.

SEASON 1981/82 – STATISTICS
FOOTBALL LEAGUE DIVISION ONE – FIXTURES

Date		Opposition	Venue	Competition	Score	Attendance
Aug	29	**Southampton**	H	**League**	**2-1**	**25,234**
	31	Manchester United	A	League	0-0	51,496
Sept	5	Birmingham City	A	League	3-4	19,035
	12	**West Bromwich Albion**	H	**League**	**0-0**	**22,618**
	19	Stoke City	A	League	2-1	15,569
	23	**Sunderland**	H	**League**	**2-0**	**21,133**
	26	**Brighton & Hove Albion**	H	**League**	**2-1**	**19,220**
Oct	3	Tottenham Hotspur	A	League	0-3	34,870
	6	Birmingham City	A	LC 2 - 1st Leg	3-2	14,330
	10	Middlesbrough	A	League	1-1	15,043
	17	**Coventry City**	H	**League**	**2-1**	**20,101**
	24	Manchester City	A	League	0-0	34,881
	28	**Birmingham City**	H	**LC 2 - 2nd Leg**	**2-1**	**16,316**
	31	**Leeds United**	H	**League**	**2-1**	**25,272**
Nov	7	**West Ham United**	H	**League**	**0-0**	**26,327**
	11	Blackburn Rovers	A	LC 3	1-0	14,752
	21	**Arsenal**	H	**League**	**1-2**	**20,912**
	25	Sunderland	A	League	3-2	17,419
	28	Aston Villa	A	League	1-3	26,847
Dec	2	**Tranmere Rovers**	H	**LC 4**	**2-0**	**12,244**
	5	**Liverpool**	H	**League**	**0-2**	**24,521**
	12	Swansea City	A	League	2-1	17,559
Jan	2	**Wrexham**	H	**FA Cup 3**	**1-3**	**15,649**
	9	**Birmingham City**	H	**League**	**2-1**	**15,906**
	18	Tottenham Hotspur	A	LC 5	0-1	31,192
	23	**Notts County**	H	**League**	**0-2**	**26,158**
	30	**Stoke City**	H	**League**	**0-0**	**16,219**
Feb	6	West Bromwich Albion	A	League	1-2	15,006
	13	Southampton	A	League	0-2	21,350
	16	Wolverhampton Wanderers	A	League	0-0	11,195
	20	Brighton & Hove Albion	A	League	1-0	17,175
	27	**Middlesbrough**	H	**League**	**1-1**	**16,464**
Mar	9	Coventry City	A	League	1-0	9,677
	13	**Manchester City**	H	**League**	**1-1**	**20,927**
	17	**Ipswich Town**	H	**League**	**1-1**	**16,686**
	20	Leeds United	A	League	1-1	18,036
	27	West Ham United	A	League	1-0	24,633
Apr	3	**Everton**	H	**League**	**0-1**	**17,323**
	10	**Wolverhampton Wanderers**	H	**League**	**0-1**	**15,691**
	12	Notts County	A	League	2-1	19,304
	17	Arsenal	A	League	0-2	21,986
	20	Everton	A	League	1-2	15,463
	24	**Aston Villa**	H	**League**	**1-1**	**18,213**
May	1	Liverpool	A	League	0-2	34,321
	5	**Manchester United**	H	**League**	**0-1**	**18,449**
	8	**Swansea City**	H	**League**	**0-2**	**15,037**
	12	**Tottenham Hotspur**	H	**League**	**2-0**	**15,273**
	15	Ipswich Town	A	League	3-1	19,974

167

HOME ATTENDANCES

	AGGREGATE ATTENDANCE	HIGHEST ATTENDANCE	LOWEST ATTENDANCE	AVERAGE ATTENDANCE
League:	417,684	26,327	15,037	19,889
League Cup:	28,560	16,316	12,244	14,280
FA Cup:	15,649	15,649	15,649	15,649
All Competitions:	461,893	26,327	12,244	19,245

FINAL LEAGUE TABLE - DIVISION ONE

Position	P	W	D	L	GF	GA	Pts
1. Liverpool	42	26	9	7	80	32	87
2. Ipswich Town	42	26	5	11	75	53	83
3. Manchester United	42	22	12	8	59	29	78
4. Tottenham Hotspur	42	20	11	11	67	48	71
5. Arsenal	42	20	11	11	48	37	71
6. Swansea City	42	21	6	15	58	51	69
7. Southampton	42	19	9	14	72	67	66
8. Everton	42	17	13	12	56	50	64
9. West Ham United	42	14	16	12	66	57	58
10. Manchester City	42	15	13	14	49	50	58
11. Aston Villa	42	15	12	15	55	53	57
12. Nottingham Forest	**42**	**15**	**12**	**15**	**42**	**48**	**57**
13. Brighton & Hove Albion	42	13	13	16	43	52	52
14. Coventry City	42	13	11	18	56	62	50
15. Notts County	42	13	8	21	45	69	47
16. Birmingham City	42	10	14	18	53	61	44
17. West Bromwich Albion	42	11	11	20	46	57	44
18. Stoke City	42	12	8	22	44	63	44
19. Sunderland	42	11	11	20	38	58	44
20. Leeds United	42	10	12	20	39	61	42
21. Wolverhampton Wanderers	42	10	10	22	32	63	40
22. Middlesbrough	42	8	15	19	34	52	39

AWAY ATTENDANCES

	AGGREGATE ATTENDANCE	HIGHEST ATTENDANCE	LOWEST ATTENDANCE	AVERAGE ATTENDANCE
League:	460,839	51,496	9,677	21,944
League Cup:	60,274	31,192	14,330	20,091
All Competitions:	521,113	51,496	9,677	21,713

"ARE YOU WATCHING JIMMY GREAVES?"

DURING THE close season several players had left the City Ground. Jurgen Roeber - his family unable to settle in England - ended his short stay at the Club and signed for German side Leverkusen. John McGovern joined Second Division Bolton Wanderers as player-manager, resulting in Ian Bowyer assuming the role of Forest captain. In addition to this, Peter Shilton joined Southampton and David Needham went on a free transfer to North American Soccer League side Toronto Blizzard.

With veteran defender Colin Todd, the only summer signing worthy of note - he arrived from Birmingham at the ripe old age of 33 - some of the nation's more high profile soccer pundits were predicting a gloomy season ahead for the 'Reds'. ITV's very own 'expert' Jimmy Greaves, made himself extremely unpopular on Trentside with his pre-season prediction of a basement position by the turn of the year. "If Forest are out of the bottom six immediately after the Christmas programme, I'll pay £100 to the South Atlantic Fund," he promised in a tabloid newspaper.

The campaign kicked off in promising fashion, when goals from Walsh and Robertson (penalty) gave Forest a 2-1 victory over West Ham at Upton Park on Saturday, 28th August. Four days later, Manchester United visited the City Ground, and with the game finely balanced at 0-0, another promising result looked on the cards. Colin Todd's deliberate handball early on in the second half however, led to his sending off, an incident which completely changed the course of the game. United eventually ran out easy 3-0 winners.

The only consolation for the surprisingly low crowd of 23,956, was that prior to the game, Brian Clough and Garry Birtles were putting the finishing touches to a deal which would bring the striker home to the City Ground, after two years at Old Trafford. Although not at the top of his game during this spell at United, his form had certainly been better than that conveyed in the media. It was simply that he'd never really settled in the North. In fact, judging by the amount of time he'd spent in Nottingham - and particularly in the Cadland - during those two years, it was as if he'd never really been away. Garry is a Nottingham lad through and through and was absolutely delighted to be returning home to his beloved Chilwell.

More good news was on the horizon and just days later Dutch international goalkeeper Hans Van Breukelen arrived from Utrecht in a £165,000 deal. Both players made their debuts in the emphatic 4-0 home victory over Brighton the following Saturday. Unfortunately, Birtles aggravated an injury picked up in pre-season training and was substituted by youngster Steve Hodge. He then went on to miss the 4-3 defeat at Liverpool in midweek - a frustrating result considering Forest were leading 3-2 with only eight minutes to go - and the 4-1 defeat at Aston Villa on Saturday, 11th September. The attendances for these games at Anfield and Villa Park were 27,145 and 21,224 respectively.

All in all, Forest's home form over the first half of the season was excellent. Following the defeat by United, they went on to record eight victories and one draw in nine League matches at the City Ground before the turn of the year, not to mention three victories in the League Cup. One of these was the 6-1 demolition of Division One rivals West Brom and even more impressive, was the 7-3 annihilation of eventual Championship Runners-up Watford.

The visit of Arsenal on Saturday, 23rd October signalled the return of another former City Ground favourite, Tony Woodcock - their recent signing from Cologne. The yellow-shirted 'Gunners' were blasted apart by a rampant Forest - with Proctor, Birtles and Wallace all on target in an emphatic 3-0 victory. Unbeknown to many, there is a long-standing connection between the two clubs, stretching all the way back to when Arsenal were formed during the late nineteenth century. The original founder was former Forest goalkeeper F.W. Beardsley, who left Nottingham in 1887 after three years with the Club. Following his stint with the 'Reds', he went to South London to work at Woolwich Arsenal. There the 'Gunners' were formed, with Beardsley making the most of his Forest connections to obtain a set of red and white jerseys for his new club - hence Arsenal's traditional red and white strip. They later moved from their South London headquarters in Woolwich to their current home in Highbury, North London.

When Ipswich Town visited the City Ground two weeks after the Arsenal game, the 17,669 crowd included 160 Utrecht supporters - all members of the Hans Van Breukelen fan club back in Holland - who'd travelled over for the game. They struck up an instant rapport with local supporters and were rewarded with a fine performance from their hero and a 2-1 victory for the 'Reds'.

So far on their travels, Forest had won four, drawn one and lost six of their eleven games. Their 0-0 draw with Sunderland at home on Saturday, 1st January 1983, consolidated their SECOND position in the table behind leaders Liverpool and meant Jimmy Greaves had to dig deeply into his pocket to come up with a £100 donation to the Falklands Fund. Consequently, the City Ground reverberated to the sound of: *"Are ya watching, Are ya watching, Are ya watching Jimmy Greaves, Are ya watching Jimmy Greaves?"* throughout this goalless, but nevertheless exciting encounter with the bottom- of-the-table Wearsiders.

JUST how significant Forest's title challenge might have been, had it not been for a catalogue of injuries to key players throughout the season, we will never know. Suffice to say, the City Ground treatment room was a very busy place between the months of August '82 and May '83. Jan Einer Aas began the season desperately trying to recover from his ankle injury (although he finally gave up the fight in February '83 and retired from the game). Peter Davenport received torn ankle ligaments early on, which required surgery and kept him out for almost three months. Van Breukelen suffered a torn cartilage in the 'derby' game with Notts at Meadow Lane in December and was out for nearly four months - also after surgery. Robertson suffered a torn cartilage during the second half of the season, which kept him out for almost two months. And to cap it all, Anderson suffered a dislocated knee whilst on England duty in October, keeping him out for over four months.

Meanwhile experienced right back Kenny Swain was drafted in on loan from Aston Villa in October as cover for Anderson, with the deal eventually being made permanent. Then in January, talented midfielder Danny Wilson was signed from Third Division neighbours Chesterfield. Unfortunately for him though, he suffered a similar fate to many of Cloughie's signings. He joined the likes of Asa Hartford (and latterly Gary Megson, David Currie and John Sheridan) in playing only a handful of games for the Club before inexplicably being shown the door. To those of us who had immediately taken to his tough-tackling, no-nonsense style of play, this came as a big disappointment.

On Saturday, 8th January, Forest turned their attentions to the FA Cup and a visit to the Baseball Ground for a third round encounter with the 'Sheep'. A mediocre Second Division outfit, they were not expected to pose too many problems for the high-flying 'Reds'. However, the imagination of the East Midlands public had been stirred and a sell-out crowd of 28,494 - including 7,000 Forest supporters - filled the now decrepit 'Sheep-dip'.

As usual, the train seemed the most sensible option for this trip, although our pre-match refreshments would be consumed in the comfort and splendour of our own City Centre, rather than in the dull and dismal confines of downtown Derby. As the whole world knows, Derby is very much a poor relation to Nottingham - it's affluent neighbour and undisputed 'Queen of the Midlands'. What's more, I'm loathe personally to inject even so much as a penny of my hard-earned cash into the Derbyshire economy. And I'm not alone in these sentiments either.

A typical example of this, is the behaviour of fellow Forest supporter Eddie Edwards from Hucknall - an acquaintance of mine - who once sent his tearful wife all the way back to Toys 'R Us in Derby with strict instructions to return to the store every single Christmas present she'd just bought from there for the kids. Having discovered the illicit journey she'd made to 'Shitesville' with her mother for a bout of festive shopping, he went completely berserk with her. He insisted on a full and immediate refund, so he could buy exactly the same goods from the Nottingham branch of the store. What a sound chap!

On the day of the game, the very last watering hole we visited before catching a late service train, was the Bentinck, just yards from the station. Naturally, it was packed to the rafters with beer-swilling, singing supporters, every one of them on their way to the match. The whole place reverberated to the sound of:

'appy days are 'ere agen,
An' we're only 'ere for the beer agen,
An' the Popside's turned all queer agen,
'appy days are 'ere agen!

It was all fairly light-hearted stuff to be honest. That is, until a rather mean-looking gang of about thirty youths, congregated in the far corner of the pub, made their intentions crystal clear with the following rather sinister ditty:

All I want is a walking stick,
An 'and grenade and a building brick,
A Der-by fan to kick,
Oh wuddennit be luvv-erly!

Although not a football special, the train was packed solid with travelling Forest supporters. And by the looks of them, most had been on the pop for several hours. The walk to the ground from the station was relatively trouble-free, but this was hardly surprising really, considering the number of police on duty on the streets of Derby. Inside the ground, the travelling army from Nottingham was accommodated on the Popside terracing. The only thing keeping the two sets of supporters apart, were the iron railings running down the middle of the stand, plus the obligatory thin blue line of police. However, all around the ground small pockets of Forest supporters had infiltrated the home sections, having presumably obtained their tickets from the Baseball Ground. When the teams came out onto the pitch, the atmosphere was hostile and decidedly intimidating. What's more, there were skirmishes taking place all around the ground.

Although Forest were expected to achieve a comfortable passage through to the fourth round - on a quagmire of a pitch - nothing could have been further from the truth. They were out-fought and out-thought on every inch of the pitch by a Derby side who were clearly 'up for it' on the day. And, with Derby already 1-0 up, former Forest star Archie Gemmill - in his second spell with the 'Sheep' - curled a perfectly flighted free kick into the top corner of the net from twenty yards out, effectively killing the game at 2-0.

To make matters worse, when the referee's whistle brought the contest to an end, the pitch was invaded by thousands of celebrating 'Sheep-shaggers'. Just as their team had clearly been ready for a fight, so too were they. They swarmed straight towards the 'Forest' end, where a small pocket of seated supporters were the first to come under attack. And once the police had restored order in this part of the ground, they turned their attentions instead to the 6,000-plus who were crammed into the Visitors' Enclosure on the Popside.

At this particular point in the game's history - long before it was hijacked by middle-class wallies and their corporate hospitality suites - the majority of football stadiums were archaic and blessed with the obligatory perimeter fences. These were situated all around the ground and were meant to prevent pitch invasions - although they had clearly failed on this occasion. The long established terrace chant of: *"If it wasn't for the coppers you'd be dead,"* was never more appropriate than on this occasion. The Derby fans tried desperately to break through the line of police to get at the Forest fans. And on their part, the Forest fans were trying equally as hard to tear down the wrought-iron railings to get back at them. How those fences managed to withstand the sheer weight of numbers, God only knows - but withstand it they did - thank goodness.

What they couldn't prevent though, was the absolute barrage of coins and missiles which rained down on both sets of supporters. One Forest supporter from Beeston, John King - a well-known face around town at the time - had somehow managed to get onto the pitch and was mingling unmolested amongst the hordes of home supporters. He had one thing on his mind only: scooping up handfuls of coins as they piled up all around the edge of the pitch.

So volatile was the atmosphere at this game, I'm convinced had it not been for the sheer scale of the police operation - not to mention the sturdiness of those fences - deaths would have occurred inside the Baseball Ground that day. Without exception, I have never witnessed such hatred and loathing between rival supporters as was displayed on this occasion.

FOLLOWING their Derby debacle, Forest had only eleven days to prepare for what was undoubtedly their most important fixture of the season - Manchester United away in the quarter-final of the League Cup. I travelled by car to Old Trafford with John Farley, and having arrived at the stadium only minutes before kick off, was embarrassed to discover only around 1,000 supporters had bothered to make the trip north from Nottingham. As we stood shoulder-to-shoulder in the Scoreboard End - one whole pen full of us - I had never felt so ashamed in all my life. *"Come in a taxi, You must have come in a taxi,"* sang the United supporters, as they swayed up and down the terraces on either side of us.

For as long as I could remember, our away support had been something to be proud of. In fact, for a city the size of Nottingham, it had always been nothing short of immense: 14,000 to Newcastle in 1974; 25,000-plus to Munich in 1979; 12,000-plus to Madrid in 1980; not to mention the regular 3 to 5,000 who followed them all over during our bleak and lengthy stay in the old Second Division. And here we were, only three short years after being crowned Kings of Europe for the second time - with just a measly 1,000 having bothered to make the effort. And this was the quarter-final of a major domestic Cup competition for God's sake!

Perhaps the stay-away fans had had a premonition? Forest were completely inept and were swept aside by a rampant United. And as we trudged dejectedly out of the stadium, following a humiliating and totally one-sided 4-0 defeat, one thing was absolutely certain in my mind: there wasn't a cat in hell's chance of me coming back to Old Trafford in three days time for the scheduled League meeting between the two sides.

Having now slipped to fourth position in the table - ten points behind leaders Liverpool - and been dumped unceremoniously out of both Cup competitions within the space of only two weeks, Forest's only realistic objective now was a place in Europe. Unfortunately, their League form continued to diminish. They achieved just one solitary victory in their next twelve games up to the end of March, drawing five and losing six along the way.

By the time they took on Everton at the City Ground on Saturday, 2nd April, they'd plummeted to tenth position and were now 25 points behind Champions-elect Liverpool. Their 2-0 victory over the 'Toffeemen', courtesy of goals from Steve Hodge and Ian Bowyer, was their first in eleven competitive matches. However, this proved the turning point and they remained unbeaten from that point onwards. They won six and drew two of their eight remaining games.

The highlight of this impressive return to form - at least as far as I was concerned - was the 2-1 victory over neighbours Notts County, in front of a crowd of 25,554 - their highest of the season. Goals from Kenny Swain and Mark Proctor brought to an end the Magpies' impressive unbeaten run at the City Ground in the League which stretched all the way back to 1952. Since Forest's 5-0 victory in a Second Division encounter on 10th October that year, the 'Pies' had won seven and drawn one of their eight fixtures on the 'Red side of the Trent.' At least the Letters' Page of the Football Post would be free from gloating 'Magpies' for once.

DESPITE their appalling injury record, their strong finish to the season led to an impressive fifth position in the table after 42 games. Consequently, they had once again qualified for European competition and the 'Red Army' would be heading for the Continent the following season, after an absence of nearly three years.

The popularity of the 'beautiful game' however, was still very much at a low ebb - and not just in Nottingham. Although Forest's average home attendance in the League was a disappointing 17,851, with only five gates topping the 20,000 mark, they had also been playing at some sparsely populated venues on their travels. No less than nine of their away fixtures in the League - out of a total of twenty-one - had drawn crowds of less than 15,000. This included: 13,657 at West Brom; 14,716 at Sunderland; 12,987 at Birmingham; 10,880 at Stoke; and 9,760 at Coventry. Furthermore, only two attendances had topped the 30,000 mark: 30,662 at Tottenham and 38,615 at Old Trafford. And, when you deduct these two from the overall League average of only 18,917, the result is an average of just 17,262. Perhaps a good run in Europe next season would see some of the missing thousands returning?

FOOTBALL LEAGUE DIVISION ONE – FIXTURES

Date		Opposition	Venue	Competition	Score	Attendance
Aug	28	West Ham United	A	League	2-1	24,796
Sept	1	**Manchester United**	H	League	0-3	23,956
	4	**Brighton & Hove Albion**	H	League	4-0	13,709
	7	Liverpool	A	League	3-4	27,145
	11	Aston Villa	A	League	1-4	21,224
	18	**Watford**	H	League	2-0	16,550
	25	Tottenham Hotspur	A	League	1-4	30,662
Oct	2	**Stoke City**	H	League	1-0	17,222
	6	**West Bromwich Albion**	H	LC 2 - 1st Leg	6-1	11,969
	9	West Bromwich Albion	A	League	1-2	13,657
	16	**Birmingham City**	H	League	1-1	14,528
	23	**Arsenal**	H	League	3-0	17,248
	27	West Bromwich Albion	A	LC 2 - 2nd Leg	1-3	6,536
	30	Luton Town	A	League	2-0	12,648
Nov	6	**Ipswich Town**	H	League	2-1	17,669
	10	**Watford**	H	LC 3	7-3	14,973
	13	Southampton	A	League	1-1	18,178
	20	Sunderland	A	League	1-0	14,716
	27	**Manchester City**	H	League	3-0	18,845
Dec	1	**Brentford**	H	LC 4	2-0	16,479
	4	Notts County	A	League	2-3	23,552
	11	**Swansea City**	H	League	2-1	14,585
	18	Norwich City	A	League	1-0	13,334
	27	**Coventry City**	H	League	4-2	24,487
	28	Everton	A	League	1-3	25,160
Jan	1	**Sunderland**	H	League	0-0	20,382
	3	Brighton & Hove Albion	A	League	1-1	10,389
	8	Derby County	A	FA Cup 3	0-2	28,494
	15	**West Ham United**	H	League	1-0	17,031
	19	Manchester United	A	LC 5	0-4	44,413
	22	Manchester United	A	League	0-2	38,615
Feb	5	**Aston Villa**	H	League	1-2	16,352
	19	**West Bromwich Albion**	H	League	0-0	14,507
	26	Birmingham City	A	League	1-1	12,987
Mar	5	Arsenal	A	League	0-0	21,698
	12	**Luton Town**	H	League	0-1	14,387
	16	Stoke City	A	League	0-1	10,880
	19	Ipswich Town	A	League	0-2	17,530
	26	**Southampton**	H	League	1-2	13,461
Apr	2	**Everton**	H	League	2-0	14,815
	5	Coventry City	A	League	2-1	9,760
	9	**Tottenham Hotspur**	H	League	2-2	18,265
	16	Watford	A	League	3-1	17,537
	23	**Notts County**	H	League	2-1	25,554
	30	Manchester City	A	League	2-1	23,563
May	2	**Liverpool**	H	League	1-0	25,017
	7	**Norwich City**	H	League	2-2	16,308
	14	Swansea City	A	League	3-0	9,226

HOME ATTENDANCES

	AGGREGATE ATTENDANCE	HIGHEST ATTENDANCE	LOWEST ATTENDANCE	AVERAGE ATTENDANCE
League:	374,878	25,554	13,461	17,851
League Cup:	43,421	16,479	11,969	14,473
All Competitions:	418,299	25,554	11,969	17,429

FINAL LEAGUE TABLE - DIVISION ONE

Position	P	W	D	L	GF	GA	Pts
1. Liverpool	42	24	10	8	87	37	82
2. Watford	42	22	5	15	74	57	71
3. Manchester United	42	19	13	8	56	38	70
4. Tottenham Hotspur	42	20	9	13	65	50	69
5. Nottingham Forest	**42**	**20**	**9**	**13**	**62**	**50**	**69**
6. Aston Villa	42	21	5	16	62	50	68
7. Everton	42	18	10	14	66	48	64
8. West Ham United	42	20	4	18	68	62	64
9. Ipswich Town	42	15	13	14	64	50	58
10. Arsenal	42	16	10	16	58	56	58
11. West Bromwich Albion	42	15	12	15	51	49	57
12. Southampton	42	15	12	15	54	58	57
13. Stoke City	42	16	9	17	53	64	57
14. Norwich City	42	14	12	16	52	58	54
15. Notts County	42	15	7	21	55	71	52
16. Sunderland	42	12	14	16	48	61	50
17. Birmingham City	42	12	15	16	40	55	50
18. Luton Town	42	12	13	17	65	84	49
19. Coventry City	42	13	9	20	48	59	48
20. Manchester City	42	13	8	21	47	70	47
21. Swansea City	42	10	11	21	51	69	41
22. Brighton & Hove Albion	42	9	13	20	38	67	40

AWAY ATTENDANCES

	AGGREGATE ATTENDANCE	HIGHEST ATTENDANCE	LOWEST ATTENDANCE	AVERAGE ATTENDANCE
League:	397,257	38,615	9,226	18,917
League Cup:	50,949	44,413	6,536	25,474
FA Cup:	28,494	28,494	28,494	28,494
All Competitions:	476,700	44,413	6,536	19,862

"WHO'S YER FATHER, WHO'S YER FATHER, WHO'S YER FATHER - REFEREE?"

HAVING RETIRED from the game at the end of season 1981/82 due to poor health, Peter Taylor had rather surprisingly made a comeback as Derby's new manager during the summer of 1983. Cloughie, instrumental in negotiating a golden handshake for him upon his 'retirement', wasn't a happy man. What's more, his annoyance turned to downright indignation during the close season when Taylor was successful in luring John Robertson away from the City Ground - and all this whilst Cloughie was away on holiday in Majorca. And to add fuel to the fire, 'Robbo' made himself even more unpopular in Nottingham, when he publicly declared he'd joined the 'Sheep' because of their 'wonderful' supporters. He'd 'always admired them' apparently. (*Dun't it just mek ya want t' puke!*)

So incensed was Cloughie, he 'sent Taylor to Coventry' and virtually refused to acknowledge his existence. Furthermore, the release of his former partner's controversial book: "With Clough by Taylor" several years later only deepened the rift. So severe was this fall out, when Taylor died prematurely in 1990, they still hadn't settled their differences - in spite of Taylor holding out the olive branch on more than one occasion.

Although Forest had signed the experienced 30-year-old defender Paul Hart from Leeds before the start of the season, Mark Proctor, Stuart Gray and Willie Young had all departed, bringing to an end their relatively short careers at the City Ground.

The opening game of the season on Saturday, 27th August, brought Peter Shilton and his Southampton team-mates to Trentside. As I had done for the last eleven years, I took up my usual position at the back of the Bridgford End for this game. Having left the Civil Service at the beginning of 1981 for a career in Financial Services, I'd also lost touch with my one-time Forest cronies Chris Hooper, Kev Salmon, Ian Adkin et al, who used to stand with me on the Kop. Like many other 'ardent' supporters of the Championship/European Cup winning era, they'd long since disappeared from the scene.

By this time, my only remaining companion was brother-in-law Alan, who travelled with me to every home game. However, being in my eighteenth season of following the 'Reds', there were literally hundreds of faces familiar to me on the terraces of the City Ground. I would nod and exchange pleasantries with many of them, usually along the lines of: "Didja gaddarn last week?"... "Yeah - fuckin' crap weren't they!"... "Yeah, berra get ther finger owt this week...else thivadditt!"

Two individuals who always stood within yards of us on the Kop, were Pete Buxton ('Bucko') and Chris Humphries ('Tiff'). I'd been nodding and saying "Ey up" to both of them for a couple of years now, although we were yet to engage each other in conversation. However, prior to this game, Alan and I bumped into them in Wurlitzer's (now the Southbank Bar) on Trent Bridge and we struck up an instant rapport. Little did I know it at the time, but they would become good friends of mine. In fact, we ended up travelling all over the country together watching the 'Reds'.

A 1-0 defeat by Southampton, was followed by a Bank Holiday excursion to Old Trafford to take on Manchester United. I travelled to the game, as usual, with John Farley. And although he and I regularly travelled the length and breadth of the country following Forest - sometimes on the 'Bus from the Sal', sometimes by car - his appearances at the City Ground were at this time few and far between. Anyway, at least this trip to the 'Theatre of dreams' was more worthwhile than our previous one together, with Forest grabbing all three points in a 2-1 victory.

WHEN they entertained Notts at home on Sunday, 16th October, they were in a modest tenth position in the table, having accumulated thirteen points from eight games. After the victory at United, they'd gone on to register home victories over QPR and Luton Town, and picked up another three points at Norwich. They'd also shared the spoils in a four-goal encounter at Aston Villa and come away empty-handed from Anfield and White Hart Lane.

During the 3-2 victory over Norwich on Saturday, 3rd September, Colin Walsh picked up what at first seemed like a horrific injury, whilst diving to head home his third goal of the game. As he launched himself across the face of goal to convert Hodge's perfectly flighted cross; he was kicked in the head by a City defender. After lengthy treatment, he was stretchered from the pitch, with rumours already circulating he'd suffered a broken neck. Thankfully however, it turned out to be nothing more serious than heavy bruising and severe concussion, and remarkably, he was back in the side again for the next fixture against Luton seven days later.

It's one of football's great ironies, but whenever one of the game's 'firsts' is about to be registered, Nottingham Forest FC always seem to be involved. For example, the first team to play Manchester United in a League fixture after the Munich Air Disaster? - Forest! The first team to complete the equivalent of a whole season (42 matches) unbeaten? - Forest! The first team to retain the League Cup trophy? - Forest! The first team to be relegated from the English Premier League? - Forest! The list just goes on and on. And when the first-ever English League game was televised live from White Hart Lane on Sunday, 2nd October 1983, guess who provided Spurs with the opposition? - well Forest of course! Colin Walsh gave them the lead in this game, but they eventually lost 2-1, with Spurs scoring the winner in the last minute.

As mentioned earlier on in this book, the Forest v Notts fixture was also the first local 'derby' in the whole history of the game, world-wide. The first ever encounter took place on the Forest Recreation Ground on 22nd March 1866, with the return game on the Meadows Cricket Ground on 19th April, the same year. The result in both cases was 0-0. However, at the City Ground on Sunday, 16th October 1983, the result was 3-1 to Forest, with Wallace, Bowyer and Davenport grabbing the goals in front of a crowd of 26,657. Former Ipswich Town midfielder Frans Thijssen made his debut for the 'Reds' in this game, following his arrival on loan until the end of the season from North American Soccer League Side Vancouver Whitecaps.

At the time, the 'Pies' were managed by former Forest favourite Larry Lloyd, and included in their line-up ex-Forest men Justin Fashanu and Martin O'Neill. Fashanu had been kicked out of the City Ground by Cloughie at the end of season 1981/82 in a much-publicised incident involving the police, who were called in to remove him from the training ground. He'd since resumed his career at Meadow Lane following a £175,000 deal and was proving an influential figure in Notts' descent into the Second Division. Their desperate plight - they were third-from-bottom of the table - was not helped in any way when both he and David Hunt received their marching orders, leaving them to struggle on with only nine men for the final thirty minutes.

HAVING disposed of East Germans FC Vorwaerts by an aggregate score of 3-0 in the first round of the UEFA Cup in September, the 'Reds' were scheduled to take on PSV Eindhoven in Holland on 19th October in a second round, first leg tie. Having heard the draw, John and I both decided we were up for this one. We would be joined on our European adventure by mutual friend Steve Gilbert and two of John's mates from Mapperley, 'Cosmo' and 'Mickey the Fish', who incidentally are brothers. We made the rather brave decision to travel on the official Forest coaches, which as usual, were organised by Mel Cox. Unbelievably, the cost of this trip was a mere fifty pounds, plus the price of a match ticket. This included a cabin on the overnight ferry to Zeebrugge and a one-night stay in a pleasant and modern hotel in Eindhoven on the night of the match.

We departed from the City Ground on Tuesday at around 6.30-p.m. and headed for the East-Anglian port of Felixstowe. Although by no means illegal at the time, we were not allowed alcohol on the coach, much to our frustration. Consequently, we were more than ready for a drink or two by the time we boarded the ferry at around 11.00-p.m. Naturally, we headed straight for the bar and weren't surprised to find it already packed with Forest supporters. Once we'd pulled out of Felixstowe and were heading out into the North Sea, the bar opened up and the festivities began in earnest.

Although I'd only met Cosmo and Mick on a couple of occasions in the past, both John and Steve were great friends of mine. The five of us got on like a house on fire - assisted in no small way I feel, by the copious amounts of beer we were consuming - and it wasn't until late into the night we finally retired to our beds. As we made our way down to the cabins below, all we could hear coming from the Gents' toilets, was the sound of vomiting and retching youths. Still, it's a terrible thing you know, that 'sea-sickness'.

By early morning we'd docked at Zeebrugge, were out of bed, and raring to go. Eindhoven was only a hundred miles away, and our estimated time of arrival was around lunchtime. This would give us the whole afternoon to ourselves before departing for the stadium a couple of hours before the game.

Eindhoven turned out to be a very pleasant little town, with more than it's fair share of bars and cafés. Being in the middle of autumn, the weather was crisp and clear, and just about perfect for a cocktail of beer and football. Not surprisingly, the place was solid with Forest supporters, and soon we were hearing stories - many of them exaggerated no doubt - about confrontations between Nottingham's notorious 'Mad Squad' and Feyenoord fans in the streets of Rotterdam the night before. Ironically, while we were in Holland taking on Eindhoven, Feyenoord and their infamous supporters were in England taking on Spurs at White Hart Lane in the same competition.

When we arrived at the PSV Stadium prior to the game, following an afternoon filled with beer and laughter, we were very impressed with what we saw. The Radio, Television and Electronics giant Phillips, who own the club, had provided them with an ultra-modern, 26,000-capacity stadium. So 'state of the art' in fact, they'd even installed giant electric heaters in the roof of the stands to warm the crowd on cool evenings such as this. At first I thought it was the alcohol playing tricks on me, but once they were switched on, they didn't half take the chill out of the cold night air.

There were approximately 2,000 Forest supporters inside the comfortable, but compact stadium, and the noise they generated almost lifted the roof off. The travelling support from Nottingham was also bolstered by several hundred Utrecht supporters who'd made the relatively short journey across Holland to cheer on their adopted team - and of course their own local hero Hans Van Breukelen.

To round off a wonderful trip, Forest's performance was straight out of the top drawer. Peter Davenport scored one of the finest individual goals ever seen on the European stage. He picked up the ball deep in his own half, ran fully sixty yards - outpacing several PSV players along the way - and unleashed an unstoppable thirty-yard drive straight into the roof of the net. This sent the travelling 'Red & White Army' into a state of total frenzy. To add to the drama, Colin Walsh converted a last minute penalty to secure an excellent 2-1 victory for the 'Reds'.

Referring to the tremendous vocal support they'd received during the game, 'Walshy' commented the next day:

"Even before the game you could sense there was a buzz around the place. There was a great atmosphere for the game and our fans more than played their part in making it a great night."

Once the celebrations inside the stadium had died down, we made our way back into the town centre, comfortable in the knowledge we weren't leaving until after breakfast the following morning. There were still a few hundred Forest supporters in town, most of whom would be heading for home in the early hours of the morning.

Even after most of the bars had closed, we were still in the mood to celebrate our great victory. There was no way 'John Farley an' 'is boys' were goin' 'ome t' bed at this early hour! We set off in search of more action and wandered through the back streets of Eindhoven looking for a bar or a night-club which was still open. Within minutes, we found ourselves in the middle of the town's red-light district. We had to skirt round dozens of scantily clad women standing on street corners trying to catch the attention of passing motorists.

Having wandered the streets for what seemed an eternity, we finally came across a small bar at the bottom of a dimly-lit street. The blinds were pulled down across the windows at the front, but behind them a faint red light was visible. As we approached the entrance at the side, the door opened slowly from the inside and we were greeted very politely by a couple of burley doormen. "Can wi gerra drink in 'ere mate?" asked Steve loudly, to which one of them replied: "Yes of course gentlemen...come in," at the same time beckoning us inside.

One by one we trooped through the door and made our way hastily to the bar. "Five beers please," demanded Cosmo matter-of-factly, whilst the rest of us dug deeply into our pockets. Ice-cold beers duly arrived and we all sat down to enjoy. Within seconds though, half a dozen scantily dressed females appeared out of the darkness and sat down beside us. "You want business boys?" they asked as they sidled up, dangling their assets right under our noses. We looked at one another in absolute horror. "Shit...we're only in a fuckin' brothel," declared Mickey the Fish at the top of his voice, as the rest us fell about laughing. Never have I drunk a pint of lager so quickly. We were out of there in a flash - not that we were frightened mind you....just a bit skint - and we headed swiftly back towards the centre of town with our tails firmly between our legs. We decided unanimously a nightcap in the bar of the hotel would be a far safer and certainly less expensive bet.

Usually the journey home from any European Cup venue abroad is a long and mundane affair. However, this was certainly the exception. When we pulled into Zeebrugge the following afternoon, we joined a long queue of traffic waiting to board the ferry back to Felixstowe. Immediately in front of us were another couple of Forest coaches and two more carrying Dundee United supporters on their way home from a UEFA Cup tie in Belgium.

As we sat waiting for the long line of vehicles to roll up the ramp and onto the ferry, half a dozen police vans suddenly arrived from nowhere and within seconds, dozens of riot police were swarming all over the port. Now I know British (and in particular English) football supporters have a terrible reputation on the Continent, but this was completely over the top as far as we were concerned. Neither Forest supporters, nor Dundee United supporters to my knowledge, had ever been involved in any acts of hooliganism abroad in the past. It also seemed very unlikely there'd be anything worse than a bit of friendly banter once we were on board the ferry either.

However, the real reason behind this show of force soon became apparent, when approximately thirty minutes later, a large passenger ferry entered the port carrying a few hundred Feyenoord supporters. They were returning home from the game at White Hart Lane, and by all accounts, there had been a considerable amount of trouble on the streets of North London the previous evening, with rival supporters fighting running battles before and after the game. To make matters worse, this particular group of supporters had also caused considerable damage to the ferry on the way back across the North Sea, hence the reception committee waiting for them in Zeebrugge.

As the ferry pulled into the harbour, scores of chanting youths could be seen on the upper deck, bouncing up and down and waving their flags and banners around all over the place. It took the police ages to get them all off the ferry, through Customs and safely on their way home to Rotterdam.

Once the excitement was over, we were allowed to board our own ferry and continue the journey home. Within a few minutes we were all gathering in the bar, with both Forest and Dundee supporters mingling freely together. We chatted about our respective Cup exploits the previous evening and generally took the piss out of one another. The duration of this particular crossing is several hours long, and inevitably, by the time we were half-way across the North Sea, spirits were running very high indeed.

The final couple of hours were particularly enjoyable. We sang as many of our favourite Forest anthems as we could, with the United supporters returning the favour. Soon, we were all united in song and the atmosphere was absolutely fantastic. By the time we pulled into Felixstowe, we'd exchanged scarves and jerseys and the sound of ''FOREST AND UNITED'' was echoing all around the vessel.

This had been a fantastic evening and one I will certainly never forget. If only all football supporters could behave in this manner all of the time. The remainder of our journey home was low key in comparison, the coach filled as it was with drunken, snoring individuals. When I finally woke up several hours later, we were back in Nottingham and I had an almighty hangover. After waiting an eternity for a taxi home, I finally collapsed into bed in the early hours and slept until late the following day.

FOLLOWING their excellent victory in Holland, Forest were brought crashing down to earth by a comprehensive 4-1 defeat at Arsenal three days later. And as if that wasn't bad enough, four days after they could only manage a 1-1 draw at home to Third Division Wimbledon in the second leg of their second round League Cup tie. Having been beaten 2-1 in the first leg at Plough Lane, they made an early exit from a competition they'd dominated just a few short seasons before.

Lying in eleventh position in the table after accumulating 16 points from their first 10 games, they could only muster a 1-1 draw at home to Sunderland four days before the vital UEFA Cup return leg against PSV. However, a bright performance in an entertaining game against the Dutchmen led to Peter Davenport grabbing the only goal, to seal an aggregate 3-1 victory overall. And their reward was undoubtedly the tie of the next round, with Scottish giants Celtic providing the opposition. The first leg was scheduled to take place at the City Ground on Wednesday, 23rd November.

Fortunately, their form had improved considerably by the time the 'Green and White' hordes descended upon Nottingham. They won two out of three League games during this period, including a resounding 5-0 victory over Wolves at home. Celtic had been allocated 8,000 terrace and 3,000 seat tickets for this encounter and consequently would occupy the whole lower tier of the Executive Stand and approximately half the Bridgford End.

When the draw was originally made at the Atlantis Sheraton Hotel in Zurich, Forest Secretary Ken Smales asked Celtic's Jack McGinn: ''How many tickets will you want?'' ''What is your capacity?'' enquired McGinn. ''About 35,000,'' answered Smales. ''Can you let us have 32,000 please?'' responded McGinn audaciously! The thing is, given half the chance, Celtic would probably have sold the lot.

Although the game wasn't due to kick off until 7.30-p.m. on Wednesday, the fanatical Celtic hordes were pouring over the border and arriving in the East Midlands from as early on as Monday. Local hoteliers did a roaring trade for most of the week in fact. And amazingly, those who were unable to find accommodation, slept rough on the streets, despite the freezing cold temperatures.

On the day of the game, there were thousands of them in town and virtually every pub within a five-mile radius of the ground had been taken over. Unfortunately, despite the carnival-like atmosphere, there were skirmishes around the City Centre throughout the course of the day as rival gangs clashed. In fairness to the Celtic supporters, it appeared to be local youths who were the main perpitrators.

Despite these problems, it was good to see the City Ground packed to it's capacity again; something I hadn't seen for several seasons. Shortly after the kick off, there was a spillage of supporters onto the running track in the corner of the stadium where the bulk of the visiting supporters were housed. Newspaper reports the following day inaccurately suggested this disruption was caused by a barrier collapsing within the Visitors' Enclosure. In reality, the incident occurred only when a supporter who'd passed out in the middle of the terraces, was carried through the crowd to the waiting St.John's Ambulancemen at the front.

On the pitch, the freezing temperatures were mainly responsible for the poor standard of the game - it was questionable in fact whether the contest should have taken place at all. The Celtic supporters poured out at the end convinced a 0-0 draw would be enough for them to see off the 'Reds' in the second leg and therefore progress through to the quarter-final stage of the competition. And not for the first time, many of the game's pundits were also quick to write Forest off. Some people just never learn do they?

Much to my regret (even to this day), I was unable, due to work commitments, to join the small band of 2,000 supporters who headed north to Celtic Park for the second leg on Wednesday, 7th December. Fortunately, the highlights were on the telly later that evening and I was able to witness - albeit second hand - another night of European glory for the 'Reds'. Stunning goals by Steve Hodge and Colin Walsh were the highlights of a classic counter-attacking performance and were enough to give them a historic 2-1 victory, before a shell-shocked 66,938 crowd. And so, we were through to the quarter-final stages of this competition for the very first time.

NOW we could forget about Europe until March and concentrate instead on making some progress in the League. Three victories and one defeat in the next three games achieved exactly that, and by the time Forest entertained League leaders Liverpool on Saturday, 31st December, they'd moved up to a more promising sixth position, having amassed a total of 33 points from 19 games. A 1-0 defeat in this encounter in front of a sizeable crowd of 29,692, put a slight dent in their otherwise impressive record of late and tainted Nottingham's New Year's Eve celebrations.

Following a useful 3-2 victory over Luton at Kenilworth Road, it was time for Cup action once again, this time in the guise of an FA Cup third round tie against Southampton at the City Ground on Saturday, 17th January 1984. Unfortunately, for the third year in a row, the 'Reds' were bundled out of this competition at the first hurdle, losing 2-1 in front of a crowd of 19,271. They then went on to register four wins and two draws in their next six League games, elevating themselves to an impressive second position in the table, just three points behind Liverpool and with 14 games still to play. This impressive run included a thumping 5-0 victory over West Brom at the Hawthorns.

Successive 1-0 defeats by Arsenal at home on Saturday, 25th February and away at Wolves a week later, brought to an end their sequence of seven League matches unbeaten. However, they had no time to dwell on this sudden loss of form, with Austrians Sturm Graz due to arrive in Nottingham for a fourth round UEFA Cup tie. This took place at the City Ground on Wednesday, 7th March, where a solitary effort from Paul Hart gave them a slender 1-0 first-leg lead in front of a crowd of 19,459.

A harshly-conceded penalty before half-time in the second leg two weeks later, brought the aggregate score level and led to extra time being played. As he had done in Eindhoven though, Colin Walsh displayed nerves of steel when he slotted home Forest's winning goal - also from the penalty spot - to send them through to the semi-finals.

There, they were drawn against Belgians RSC Anderlecht, with the first leg due to take place in Nottingham on Wednesday, 11th April. And on the night, a Steve Hodge double rounded off an excellent performance - in front of a paltry 22,681 - in superb fashion, giving them a two-goal cushion to take with them to Brussels. They were now odds-on favourites to make it through to the Final, where an all-English encounter with Tottenham Hotspur was looking a distinct possibility.

ON Tuesday, 17th April, Forest lost 2-1 to Coventry City in a League game at Highfield Road, whilst at the same time, my wife was giving birth to our first child, Thomas Paul. As was the norm in those days, mother and baby were expected to spend several days in the QMC and would be allowed home on Saturday, 21st April - the day we were due to play Birmingham at the City Ground. As you can imagine, I was in a highly emotional state for the rest of that week - after all, it was almost seven years since I'd last missed a game at the City Ground!

As I paced up and down the living room at midday on Saturday praying for that telephone call saying: ''Come and get us,'' I couldn't help wondering what the City Ground would look like on a match-day without me inside. However, lady luck was on my side, and the long-awaited call finally came through half an hour later - fully two and a half hours before kick off. A mad dash along the A52 from Long Eaton to the hospital; was followed by another home with wife and baby in tow. And it was still only two o'clock when I kissed them both goodbye and set off for the match. With a bit of luck, I'd even manage a couple of pints in the Aviary at this rate.

A superb 5-1 victory over the 'Blues', with goals from Davenport (2), Walsh, Wallace and Bowyer, set Forest up perfectly for the semi-final second leg tie with Anderlecht the following Wednesday evening. And being the totally self-centred, chauvinistic git I am, I decided in spite of recent events on the domestic front, I'd also be making the journey to Brussels, convincing myself this would give mother and baby more time to bond. To be fair to the misses though, she went along with the whole thing without too much argument, even convincing the midwife I was out doing the shopping when she called in each day on her rounds. Apparently, she was full of praise for me, unlike some husbands she'd encountered in the past who ''just didn't seem to give a damn.''

At 2.00-p.m. on Tuesday, 24th April, I said goodbye to them both and set off to meet Steve Gilbert and Russ Thompson, the three of us having booked our tickets for the official Forest coaches. These were due to depart from the City Ground at around 6.00-p.m. Having been unhappy with the way we'd been treated by the Forest Officials on the trip to Eindhoven, John had decided instead to make his own way over. At £51 a time though, plus £6 for a match ticket, the three of us decided this excursion was such good value for money, we couldn't afford to miss it - despite the likelihood of being treated like 12-year-olds for the whole of the two days.

On top of the two coaches they were running, the Club had also chartered a 500-seater train (no thanks - done that one already!) priced £44 - including a match ticket - and 130 seats on a plane costing £200 plus match ticket. Although having originally been promised a total allocation of 2,000 tickets - comprising 1,000 for the terraces and another 1,000 for the seats - the Club were incensed to receive at first a total of only 750 of each. However, after a heated exchange, the missing 500 finally arrived.

In addition to the official trips arranged by the Club, there were scores of unofficial packages on offer through local Travel Agents in and around Nottingham. Forest's support within the 38,000-capacity Astrid Park Stadium was expected to be at least 4,000-strong.

Several days before the team was due to fly to Brussels; Cloughie made a very public statement saying he didn't trust foreign referees and was extremely concerned Spaniard Guruceta Muro would be officiating at this game. This deep mistrust stemmed from his European Cup days with the 'Sheep', when Italian giants Juventus had knocked them out at the semi-final stage. Prior to the first leg in Turin, their German international Helmut Haller - who'd played against England in the 1966 World Cup Final - had twice been spotted going into German referee Gerhard Schulenberg's dressing room before the match.

On hearing this news, Cloughie apparently went ballistic, accusing the Italians of offering him a bribe. Two harsh bookings during the game - which incidentally Derby lost 3-1 - ruled Roy McFarland and Archie Gemmill out of the second leg. A 0-0 draw at the Baseball Ground meant they'd gone out of Europe's most prestigious competition in very dubious circumstances.

The journey to Brussels, via the Dover-to-Ostend ferry, was a largely uneventful one. However, upon our arrival in the Belgian Capital, we were again highly impressed by the quality of our hotel. Having dumped our things and taken a quick shower, we were soon heading off into the centre of town looking for some action. We eventually ended up quite near the stadium, where we indulged in our customary pre-match refreshments. On our way across the city by tram, we'd spotted hundreds of Forest supporters wandering through the streets on their way to the game.

Several hours later, we made our way to the stadium to soak up some of the pre-match atmosphere. However, as we climbed the stairway leading to the back of the stand, it was obvious there were far too many supporters trying to gain entrance to this particular part of the stadium. We somehow managed to squeeze our way through the swaying crowd at the back, and clambered up onto a fence which ran down the middle and was keeping the two sets of supporters apart.

As it got nearer towards kick off, hundreds of supporters were trying to force their way into the stand. Those already inside got more and more agitated; fearing a potential disaster was looming. The stairway leading up to the back of the stand was seriously overcrowded with frustrated and angry supporters, all of them anxious not to miss the start of the game.

Suddenly, a number of supporters crammed inside the small enclosure began to clamber over the fence and into the Home Supporters' Section away to our left. Within minutes hundreds of others followed suit. This created just about enough space on the terraces for the overspill of fans outside to come pouring in.

By the time the game kicked off, there were probably 1,500 of us crammed tightly into the enclosure which, even at a squeeze, was meant to hold only about 1,000. And what's more, another 1,000 were now smack in the middle of the Anderlecht fans in the enclosure next to us - a recipe for disaster if ever I'd seen one. A further 1,000 travelling 'Reds' were seated in the stand directly opposite us on the other side of the stadium.

With a capacity crowd of 38,000 inside, there was a highly charged atmosphere right from the moment the game kicked off. And it was soon apparent Forest's two-goal lead from the first leg could easily be wrestled away from them. The quality of Anderlecht's football throughout the game was absolutely frightening. They stroked the ball around as if Forest weren't even out there on the pitch and made us look a very ordinary side indeed.

However, even more frightening, was the standard of the refereeing. The home side were getting the benefit of the doubt on every occasion. "Why couldn't Cloughie just have kept his big mouth shut?" I thought to myself, his outburst in the press uppermost in my mind as every decision went against us. And unfortunately - almost inevitably in fact - each controversial decision ignited serious outbreaks of trouble on the terraces away to our left.

Running battles took place, with several hundred Forest supporters on the rampage and hell-bent on battering anyone in the purple and white colours of Anderlecht. Each outbreak prompted scores of baton-wielding police to pour into the stands from their positions on the running track alongside the pitch. Then, on each occasion, having separated the warring factions, they returned rather foolishly to their positions around the perimeter of the pitch, leaving the troublemakers to vent their anger again minutes later.

All I could think about were the inevitable newspaper headlines the next day: *"FOREST THROWN OUT OF EUROPE AS FANS RUN AMOK IN BELGIAN CAPITAL."* And, as if that wasn't bad enough, Anderlecht - inspired by their brilliant young midfielder 'Enzo Scifo - continued to destroy us out there on the pitch. In spite of the appalling refereeing decisions coming thick and fast throughout the game - including a farcical penalty award following the most blatant dive I've ever seen on a football pitch - Anderlecht were so good, I was now fearing a hefty defeat.

However, it's goals that count in football and with two minutes left on the clock and the Belgians leading 3-0, Forest were still in with a shout when they won a corner out on the left. And when Paul Hart rose majestically at the far post to send an unstoppable header into the roof of the net, the 4,000-strong Forest army went absolutely berserk. Forest had surely made it through to the Final on the 'away goals' rule. Jubilation turned to despair within seconds however, when the 'adorable' Senior Muro disallowed the 'goal' for an infringement which no-one else in the stadium saw.

Upon the final whistle seconds later, thousands of jubilant Anderlecht supporters poured onto the pitch to celebrate their 'great' victory. Several hundred ran right across to our side of the ground and began taunting us from the other side of the perimeter fence. The Forest supporters caged in on the inside went crazy, scaling the six-foot high fence, standing between them and the baying Anderlecht supporters. However, whilst completely ignoring the home supporters, the police repeatedly baton-charged the Forest supporters, thus preventing them getting over onto the pitch.

Meanwhile those in the stand to our left just ran amok. Anyone in Anderlecht colours was fair game, and there were some ugly scenes indeed. And when we finally spilled out of the stadium ages after the game had finished, the brawling continued. We had to make our way through a tree-lined park in almost total darkness to get back to the coaches waiting to transport us back to the hotel. The night air was filled with the sound of violence, with youths screaming and shouting and the wail of police sirens. Altogether, a pretty frightening experience, although I was glad I wasn't an Anderlecht supporter.

We were all relieved to get back to the hotel, where we sat quietly drowning our sorrows. We weren't due to leave Brussels until early the next morning, but none of us was in the mood for a party. What's more, we were all very subdued during the journey home the following day and fearful of the consequences the Club would face after the disgraceful crowd scenes inside and outside the stadium. When we boarded the ferry, I bought several newspapers and sat down expecting to read all the gruesome details in graphic detail. What would the media's reaction be to the trouble and the controversial circumstances surrounding the game? I was amazed though, to find not the slightest mention, anywhere.

Now, had it been, for example, Chelsea or Leeds fans involved in this kind of trouble abroad, I'm convinced it would have been front-page news. However, as far as I'm aware, it didn't even get a mention on the local radio or television news. I was beginning to wonder if the whole thing had just been a bad dream or something, until speaking to other Forest supporters over the course of the next few games, who were equally as surprised by the lack of publicity surrounding the whole thing. Not that I was disappointed or anything; just totally baffled by the fact we appeared to have got off completely scot-free. The people of Brussels were not so keen to forget though, and when Tottenham visited the city for the first leg of the Final, there were some serious incidents involving locals and visiting supporters. One supporter from England was even shot dead in a bar prior to the game.

For many years after this controversial tie, those connected with the Club remained convinced the refereeing had been heavily stacked in the home team's favour. It had certainly been instrumental in the Belgians making it through to the Final and depriving Forest of yet more silverware. I was adamant Cloughie's comments prior to the game were to blame. How wrong I was?

The only consolation to the good people of Nottingham and Forest supporters everywhere, was that Spurs went on to beat Anderlecht over the two legs, albeit after a penalty shoot-out at the end of the second leg at White Hart Lane. However, as far as I was concerned, it was Forest who should have been lining up against Spurs. And with our record against the Londoners, I'm sure the UEFA Cup would now be sitting proudly in the Forest trophy cabinet - along with all the others.

It wasn't until 13 years later, following the death of referee Guruceta Muro, the truth finally emerged. In September 1997, former Anderlecht Chairman, Contsant Vanden Stock, admitted an amount of one million Belgian Francs (approximately £18,000) had been paid to the official on the day after the game. Despite his insistence this had been simply a loan, it was quite obviously a bribe - what else could it have been? What's more, the story had only now come out into the open because Mr. Vanden Stock was being blackmailed over the affair.

Despite lengthy investigations by the Belgian Police Authorities, the Belgian FA, and UEFA, to this day Anderlecht remain unpunished and Forest remain without compensation of any description. Just as we'd been cheated out of possible FA Cup glory by Newcastle supporters back in 1974, we had now been deprived of European glory a decade later. It could only happen to Nottingham Forest!

DESPITE the despair of their UEFA Cup exit, Forest's excellent form continued right up to the end of the season and they eventually finished in a creditable third position in the table - only six points behind Champions Liverpool. Their promising young side was rapidly maturing, with the likes of Steve Hodge, Colin Walsh, Peter Davenport and Steve Wigley coming on in leaps and bounds. Furthermore, a very promising 18-year-old defender by the name of Des Walker had also burst onto the scene in the 1-0 victory over Everton at the City Ground back in March. On a sad note, crowd favourite Hans Van Breukelen, having announced earlier on in the season he'd be returning to Holland to further his international career, joined PSV Eindhoven at the end of the season. He was carried shoulder high from the pitch by supporters following the 2-0 victory over Man U at the City Ground in the final game.

Although the average League attendance for the season was only 17,703 and the average in all competitions just slightly higher at 18,318, the City Ground had at least enjoyed a couple of impressive attendances during the course of the season. The highest of 34,084 for the visit of Celtic and the 29,692 for the game against Liverpool, provided some hope for the future, despite football's continuing lack of popularity. There was also a feeling amongst supporters that once again, the team were on the verge of something big. Only time would tell of course?

SEASON 1983/84 – STATISTICS

FOOTBALL LEAGUE DIVISION ONE – FIXTURES

Date		Opposition	Venue	Competition	Score	Attendance
Aug	27	**Southampton**	H	League	0-1	14,690
	29	Manchester United	A	League	2-1	43,005
Sept	3	Liverpool	A	League	0-1	31,376
	7	**Aston Villa**	H	League	2-2	16,379
	10	**Queens Park Rangers**	H	League	3-2	14,607
	14	**Vorwaerts**	H	UEFA Cup 1 - 1st Leg	2-0	14,994
	17	Norwich City	A	League	3-2	15,017
	24	**Luton Town**	H	League	1-0	16,296
	28	Vorwaerts	A	UEFA Cup 1 - 2nd Leg	1-0	18,000
Oct	2	Tottenham Hotspur	A	League	1-2	30,596
	4	Wimbledon	A	LC 2 - 1st Leg	0-2	7,554
	16	**Notts County**	H	League	3-1	26,657
	19	PSV Eindhoven	A	UEFA Cup 2 - 1st Leg	2-1	26,000
	22	Arsenal	A	League	1-4	22,874
	26	**Wimbledon**	H	LC 2 - 2nd Leg	1-1	13,718
	29	**Sunderland**	H	League	1-1	13,968
Nov	2	**PSV Eindhoven**	H	UEFA Cup 2 - 2nd Leg	1-0	16,934
	5	**Wolverhampton Wanderers**	H	League	5-0	13,855
	12	Everton	A	League	0-1	17,546
	19	**Ipswich Town**	H	League	2-1	14,979
	23	**Glasgow Celtic**	H	UEFA Cup 3 - 1st Leg	0-0	34,084
	26	Stoke City	A	League	1-1	11,655
Dec	4	**Leicester City**	H	League	3-2	23,247
	7	Glasgow Celtic	A	UEFA Cup 3 - 2nd Leg	2-1	66,938
	10	Watford	A	League	2-3	14,017
	17	**West Ham United**	H	League	3-0	14,544
	26	Birmingham City	A	League	2-1	14,482
	28	**Coventry City**	H	League	3-0	22,169
	31	**Liverpool**	H	League	0-1	29,692
Jan	2	Luton Town	A	League	3-2	12,126
	7	**Southampton**	H	FA Cup 3	1-2	19,271
	21	**Norwich City**	H	League	3-0	13,993
	23	Southampton	A	League	1-0	17,426
Feb	4	**Tottenham Hotspur**	H	League	2-2	21,428
	8	West Bromwich Albion	A	League	5-0	11,020
	11	Queens Park Rangers	A	League	1-0	16,692
	18	Sunderland	A	League	1-1	15,958
	25	**Arsenal**	H	League	0-1	20,045
Mar	3	Wolverhampton Wanderers	A	League	0-1	10,476
	7	**Raika Sturm Graz**	H	UEFA Cup 4 - 1st Leg	1-0	19,459
	14	**Everton**	H	League	1-0	13,647
	17	Aston Villa	A	League	0-1	16,270
	21	Raika Sturm Graz	A	UEFA Cup 4 - 2nd Leg	1-1	22,000
	31	Notts County	A	League	0-0	18,357
Apr	7	**West Bromwich Albion**	H	League	3-1	15,245
	11	**Anderlecht**	H	UEFA Cup SF - 1st Leg	2-0	22,681
	14	Ipswich Town	A	League	2-2	15,421
	17	Coventry City	A	League	1-2	9,818
	21	**Birmingham City**	H	League	5-1	15,323
	25	Anderlecht	A	UEFA Cup SF - 2nd Leg	0-3	38,000
	28	**Stoke City**	H	League	0-0	13,625
May	5	Leicester City	A	League	1-2	16,600
	7	**Watford**	H	League	5-1	13,732
	12	West Ham United	A	League	2-1	18,468
	16	**Manchester United**	H	League	2-0	23,651

HOME ATTENDANCES

	AGGREGATE ATTENDANCE	HIGHEST ATTENDANCE	LOWEST ATTENDANCE	AVERAGE ATTENDANCE
League:	371,772	29,692	13,625	17,703
League Cup:	13,718	13,718	13,718	13,718
FA Cup:	19,271	19,271	19,271	19,271
UEFA Cup:	108,152	34,084	14,994	21,630
All Competitions:	512,913	34,084	13,718	18,318

FINAL LEAGUE TABLE - DIVISION ONE

Position	P	W	D	L	GF	GA	Pts
1. Liverpool	42	22	14	6	73	32	80
2. Southampton	42	22	11	9	66	38	77
3. Nottingham Forest	**42**	**22**	**8**	**12**	**76**	**45**	**74**
4. Manchester United	42	20	14	8	71	41	74
5. Queens Park Rangers	42	22	7	13	67	37	73
6. Arsenal	42	19	9	15	74	60	63
7. Everton	42	16	14	12	44	42	62
8. Tottenham Hotspur	42	17	10	15	64	65	61
9. West Ham United	42	17	9	16	60	55	60
10. Aston Villa	42	17	9	16	59	61	60
11. Watford	42	16	9	17	68	77	57
12. Ipswich Town	42	15	8	19	55	57	53
13. Sunderland	42	13	13	16	42	53	52
14. Norwich City	42	12	15	15	48	49	51
15. Leicester City	42	13	12	17	65	68	51
16. Luton Town	42	14	9	19	53	66	51
17. West Bromwich Albion	42	14	9	19	48	62	51
18. Stoke City	42	13	11	18	44	63	50
19. Coventry City	42	13	11	18	57	77	50
20. Birmingham City	42	12	12	18	39	50	48
21. Notts County	42	10	11	21	50	72	41
22. Wolverhampton Wanderers	42	6	11	25	27	80	29

AWAY ATTENDANCES

	AGGREGATE ATTENDANCE	HIGHEST ATTENDANCE	LOWEST ATTENDANCE	AVERAGE ATTENDANCE
League:	379,200	43,005	9,818	18,057
League Cup:	7,554	7,554	7,554	7,554
UEFA Cup:	170,938	66,938	18,000	34,187
All Competitions:	557,692	66,938	7,554	20,655

"FOR EVER AND EVER, WE'LL FOLLOW OUR TEAM"

HAVING STOOD on the Bridgford End for the previous twelve seasons, I decided it was time for a change. So, along with Alan and my recently acquired friends Bucko and Tiff, I bought a seat ticket for the Main Stand during the summer. For several years now, we'd noticed from our vantage point high on the Kop, that the seats in the section nearest the corner flag - 'A' Block - were virtually always empty. This seemed an ideal place to head for, as we'd probably have the whole section to ourselves on match-days. Spoilt for choice, we eventually opted for the lower tier, Row H, Seat Numbers 16 to 19 inclusive.

The close season had brought with it a positive flurry of transfer activity. Having been carried shoulder high from the pitch by his adoring fans after the last game of the season, Hans Van Breukelen - as already mentioned - had joined Dutch side PSV Eindhoven, with young goalkeeper Hans Segers coming in the opposite direction as part of the deal.

Other comings and goings included: the purchase of Dutch midfielder Johnny Metgod from Real Madrid; centre-forward Trevor Christie from neighbours Notts County; right-back Jim McInally from Celtic; midfielder Gary Megson from Sheffield Wednesday; 17-year-old winger Franz Carr from Blackburn Rovers; and the departure of Viv Anderson to Arsenal and Ian Wallace to French club Stade Brestois.

The signing of Trevor Christie had become necessary not only due to Ian Wallace's move abroad, but also because of the likelihood of Forest being without Garry Birtles for half the season, following a spinal fusion operation. His skill and enthusiasm would be sorely missed in what promised to be another two-pronged assault on the domestic and European fronts. The 'Reds' had again qualified for the UEFA Cup, on the strength of their impressive third position in the table the previous season.

DURING the summer of 1984, the infamous Miner's· Strike had reached it's climax, culminating in hundreds of 'flying pickets' from the Yorkshire coal-fields converging on Nottinghamshire on a daily basis. They were unhappy with the majority of their colleagues in the East Midlands who'd carried on working throughout the dispute. There were ugly scenes all over the North of the County, as miner fought with miner, and the police were caught in the middle. Almost every violent confrontation was beamed live by television into our living rooms, morning, noon and night.

Armies of police officers were drafted into Nottingham each week from other forces across the country to help out with the situation. Having been run down quite considerably in recent years, the largely unused Army Barracks within Chilwell Garrison, was an ideal place to accommodate the scores of police - most of them 'hand-picked' for the picket lines - who arrived in the County every Sunday afternoon. Consequently, with wads of overtime money to spend and time to kill in the evenings, the pubs around Chilwell - particularly the Cadland - were packed solid.

Despite the initial novelty value and good-natured banter which existed early on between these visitors and locals, the boisterous - and at times loutish - behaviour of these so-called 'upholders of the law' soon became rather tedious. The large volume of alcohol they were consuming was having a detrimental affect on their behaviour and on a number of occasions, the local constabulary even had to be called in to prevent confrontations with fed up locals, from getting seriously out of hand. Suffice to say the population of Chilwell - with the exception of Ken, Landlord of the Cadland - breathed a collective sigh of relief when the dispute was finally brought to an end and we got rid of our unwelcome visitors once and for all. (Although I lived in Long Eaton at the time, I still did most of my socialising in Chilwell).

Having already witnessed the unacceptable behaviour of police at football matches during the course of the last two decades, my respect for them was now as low as it could possibly be. I'd seen many acts of provocation on their part over the years and observed their total contempt for virtually every football supporter under the age of forty - all hooligans in their eyes. I'd also witnessed so many instances of wrongful arrest; I'd completely lost count. And having now seen at first hand the behaviour of those brought in to handle the Miner's Dispute, my respect for them was non-existent.

CHAPTER 19

WELL it just had to happen, didn't it? The computer responsible for compiling the Football League's fixture lists, had - if you'll pardon the pun - 'pitted' Forest against South Yorkshire rivals Sheffield Wednesday - who'd just gained promotion from the Second Division - in the opening game of the season on Saturday, 25th August. And in view of the events which had taken place during the summer, a hostile reception for Forest's travelling supporters inside Hillsborough was absolutely guaranteed.

John and I travelled to the game on Beado's 'Bus from the Sal' and were amongst the 4,000 Forest supporters at the game. We were packed tightly into the small bank of terracing in the lower tier of the Leppings Lane End. There had been a distinct buzz around town prior to this game, and such was the interest, even ex-Townies like Mick Randall had 'come out of retirement'. He was running his own coach - also from the Sal - and had had tickets printed inviting all and sundry to attend the ''Randall's Vandals - Sheffield Reunion Party.''

The atmosphere inside the stadium was every bit as fierce as we'd expected. Large gangs of 'Sheffield Thugs' - or were they 'flying pickets'? - were in evidence amongst the sizeable crowd of 31,925. Constant chants of: *''SCABS! SCABS! SCABS! SCABS!''* from the Wednesday louts, were greeted with loud choruses of: *''Arthur Scargill - Worra Wanker, Worra Wanker!''* from the travelling 'Red Army'. The intimidation grew more and more intense as each one of Wednesday's three decisive 'strikes' hit the back of the Forest net. Peter Davenport's solitary reply added up to a surprising and embarrassing 3-1 defeat in a game we supporters really could have done without losing.

Four days later, Arsenal were in town for Forest's first game on home soil. We made our way down to our new seats just before kick off and were pleasantly surprised to find a number of our 'Stabbo' chums had also purchased tickets for this part of the ground. They were occupying the seats right next to us on Row H. Although the rest of 'A' Block was only sparsely populated - despite the reasonable crowd of 18,215 (reasonable for 1984/85 that is) - there were a number of 'older faces' from years gone by - mainly Bulwell lads - occupying the seats at the back of the stand. Although we weren't to know it at the time, Forest's infamous 'A' Block was already in it's embryonic stages.

A 2-0 victory over the 'Gunners', thanks to goals from new signing Johnny Metgod and the prolific Davenport, was followed by a 3-1 home victory over Sunderland the following Saturday, with Davenport this time grabbing an impressive hat-trick. This was followed by an incredible 5-0 victory away at Aston Villa four days later. Trevor Christie opened his Forest account in style, becoming the second player to bag a hat-trick, with the season only four games old. Ian Bowyer and Steve Hodge rounded off Forest's impressive tally in this emphatic victory.

Although they slipped up on QPR's plastic pitch the following Saturday - going down 3-1 - they were already sitting in an impressive third position in the table, with nine points from five games. This was boosted still further by a 3-1 victory over Luton at home on Sunday, 16th September. Their confidence was sky high going into the UEFA Cup first round, first leg tie against Belgians FC Brugge at the City Ground three days later. Unfortunately, they were unable to break down a resilient Brugge defence and the game ended 0-0 in front of a crowd of 18,307.

Although the Club were once again running coach trips to the return leg in Brugge, at a cost of £45 including match ticket, my experiences in Brussels only months earlier had made me reluctant to return to Belgium so soon. I decided to save my money instead for the next stage of the competition. However, a 1-0 defeat in the second leg put paid to my plans and I wouldn't after all be heading for the Continent again this season. Once again though, this defeat was not without controversy. Peter Davenport had what looked a perfectly executed 'goal' disallowed for offside with the score 0-0, and there was more than a hint of offside about Brugge's own winner. And all this after Gary Mills had seen his effort cancelled out for offside during the first leg in Nottingham.

IT was back to domestic action again the following Saturday and a single point in the 1-1 home draw with struggling Stoke City. Four days later, Second Division Portsmouth were in town for a League Cup second round, second leg encounter. Leading 1-0 from the first leg at Fratton Park two weeks earlier, Alan Ball's promotion-chasing side looked capable of causing an upset in Nottingham and consequently had the backing of a large following from the South Coast. As always when 'Pompey' are in town, there were some ugly scenes outside the ground before and after the game, as rival supporters clashed with one another, particularly on Trent Bridge. A commanding performance on the pitch however, gave Forest a comfortable 3-0 victory, with goals from Hodge, Wigley and Gunn in front of a crowd of 18,182.

A sudden and dramatic loss of form saw them lose four and draw one of their next five League games - including a 2-0 defeat at home to Liverpool in the first ever League game to be televised live from the City Ground. They also went out of the League Cup losing 1-0 in a third round replay against Sunderland at Roker Park. A 3-1 victory over Coventry on Saturday, 17th November, in front of a paltry Highfield Road crowd of just 9,895, stopped the rot; although by the time they took on neighbours Leicester City at home on Sunday, 25th November, they'd fallen from second position in the table at the end of October, to a far from impressive ninth.

Once again, the 2-1 victory over the 'Foxes' was marred by crowd trouble, with serious disturbances between rival supporters in the upper tier of the Executive Stand. On the pitch, Davenport was once again the Forest hero, grabbing both goals - one from the penalty spot - in front of a crowd of 21,463.

In spite of the game's continuing problems, it seemed the Club were at least trying to capture the hearts of Nottingham's younger population. By the end of October, membership of the 'Evening Post Junior Reds' had already climbed to an impressive 1,100 and would exceed the 1,500 mark by Christmas. These were encouraging signs for the future and an excellent example of Club and Local Newspaper working together for the good of the game.

Having lost their next Division One encounter 2-0 at Watford the following Saturday, the City Ground witnessed one of the most exciting League games for decades, when Manchester United came to town a week later. Having fallen behind to two early strikes from United's Gordon Strachan, goals from Steve Hodge and Gary Mills brought Forest right back into the game. They were now pushing forward in search of a winner.

Deep into injury time, the 'Reds' were awarded a free kick five yards outside the United box, bang in front of the Trent End. As Metgod shaped himself to take the kick, I looked up at the sky and said: "Please God - just this once - lerrim purrit in the net!" And for once, my prayers were answered in style, as the mercurial Dutchman curled a magnificent shot over the wall and into the roof of the net, sending myself and the majority of the 25,902 crowd absolutely wild.

A crushing 5-0 defeat at top-of-the-table Everton the following week - in which Gary Mills suffered a broken leg - brought us straight back down to earth again with a bump. But even the 'mighty' Everton, one of the so-called 'big five' and on their way to winning the Championship, could at the time only pull in a crowd of 22,487 for this game. This defeat was followed by a 2-0 victory at Sunderland on the Saturday prior to Christmas, when goals from Trevor Christie and Steve Wigley gave Forest the edge in front of a crowd of 21,235.

The 17,123 who were present to watch them beat Ipswich 2-0 at the City Ground on Boxing Day, were given a glimpse of what was to come in the future when - at the age of eighteen - Nigel Clough (son of Brian) was given his first team debut. Without making too much of an impression on the over-critical Forest faithful - who no doubt suspected a hint of nepotism - Clough Junior displayed a calmness on the ball which belied his tender years.

Another festive fixture at the City Ground on Saturday, 29th December again saw the visitors - Aston Villa - surge into an early two-goal lead. Whilst thoughts of Forest's dramatic comeback against United three weeks earlier were still fresh in my mind, it was beyond all reason to expect this could happen again, surely? But happen again, it most certainly did. First Davenport pulled one back before half-time, followed by another Metgod special, as he curled yet another stunning free kick into the back of the Villa net to level the scores. And remarkably, in the eighty-seventh minute, Davenport scored again - this time from the penalty spot - to secure another Forest victory. What a pity there were only 17,676 spectators present to witness this memorable game.

HAVING made only a handful of senior appearances for the 'Reds' in pre-season friendlies, Gary Megson - their expensive summer signing from Sheffield Wednesday - still hadn't figured in a single League or Cup game during his six months at the Club. This caused a considerable amount of frustration amongst supporters and must have been completely bewildering to the player himself - a tenacious, but stylish midfielder. Why Cloughie had to treat some of his signings in this manner, was always a big mystery to me, but Megson was not the first to receive such treatment, and he would certainly not be the last.

Newcastle United finally came to his rescue at the end of 1984 and ironically he was given an immediate opportunity to put one over on Cloughie, when the 'Magpies' were drawn against Forest at the City Ground in the third round of the FA Cup on Sunday, 6th January 1985. Quite often in those days, rather than buying my usual terrace, or more recently, seat ticket; when it came to Cup matches, I would indulge myself in some good old-fashioned nostalgia, and instead buy a ticket for the Trent End. The game against Newcastle was no exception and I made my way excitedly towards the middle section fully thirty minutes before kick off. I even left the rest of the lads in the pub, purely so I could soak up some of the pre-match atmosphere for a change.

By kick off, there were 23,582 spectators inside the ground - not a massive crowd by any means - but the Trent End itself was packed and the unique atmosphere generated by the FA Cup was very much in evidence. It brought memories of a bygone age flooding back to me, as I was pushed first one way and then the other, by a swaying mass of chanting, singing Trent Enders. The whole End swore their undying allegiance to the Club with their latest anthem:

For ever and ever,
We'll follow our team,
We're Nottingham For-est,
We rule supreme,

We'll never be mastered,
By you Geordie Bastards,
We'll keep the red flag,
Flyin' 'igh!

Whenever I hear this particular anthem - which incidentally is still going strong to this day, especially in the Main Stand 'A' Block - I can't help wondering just how many hundreds, possibly thousands, of people have declared their undying loyalty to the 'Reds' in this manner over the years, only to eventually end up pushing the proverbial shopping trolley around Sainsbury's on a Saturday afternoon. I can think of many apparently 'fanatical Reds' who have gone from on the one hand, never missing a game home or away for seasons on end, to suddenly and inexplicably, never setting foot inside a football stadium again!

It's no coincidence I feel that many of these 'disappearing' types share a number of common characteristics. For example: obesity; ugliness; lack of taste; probably never had a shag in their lives; and probably never even kissed a woman, despite being well into their twenties or even thirties. To many of these individuals, football is the perfect substitute for a woman and provides them with all the romance they need.

Take 'Bear' for example...When I was in my first year at Grammar School, there was a spotty-faced, greasy-haired, fourteen-stone 'caveman' in the fourth year, nicknamed 'Bear', owing to his uncanny resemblance to that particular species of mammal. He was a 'fanatical' Forest supporter and even at that time, hadn't missed a single game home or away for donkey's years. Whether it be Forest v Manchester United at home in a glamorous Cup tie, or Hartlepool United v Forest away on a wet Friday night in November for the 'Charlie Chiselwaite Testimonial', the Bear was sure to be there.

Many, many years later, long after I'd left school myself, I would still bump into him on my travels up and down the country watching the 'Reds'. Goodness knows how many consecutive matches he'd attended by this time, but it must have been hundreds. Then, all of a sudden, one day...it suddenly dawned on me: I hadn't seen him in ages. "Where the hell had he disappeared to all of a sudden?" I wondered. As far as I was concerned, a Forest match without Bear was like a City Ground meat pie without the obligatory four lumps of gristle! I was absolutely baffled.

"I know," I thought to myself, "I'll ask Big Glenn Caldow from Stabbo...he's bound to know." Glenn had been in my year at school and lived not far away from Bear in Stabbo - home of many a 'Forest Neanderthal' - and he sat on our row in the 'A' Block. At the next game, I sidled up to him and asked: "Ey up Glenn, eya seen 'ote o' Bear lately. Ayant seenim for yonks?" "Ooh 'im," replied Glenn, "Issonly gonnan gorrimsen a woman, ant 'e!"

Well, talk about knock me down with a feather. I couldn't believe it. One thing I did know for sure though, that'd be the last we'd ever see of the Bear. And sure enough, to this day, he hasn't set foot inside the City Ground, or any other ground for that matter, since. And on the rare occasion he's cropped up in conversation, those who still come into contact with him from time to time, tell me he has "no regrets whatsoever" his long affair with the 'Reds' ended so abruptly. If that really is the case - and I doubt it very much - he was never really that fanatical about Forest in the first place, was he? Maybe my theory about football in some cases being a substitute for women isn't really that far away from the truth after all? One thing I've never been able to fathom out though is this: why does anybody have to suddenly stop going to football matches, just 'cause a woman has come onto the scene? Surely, there's room in any man's life for both women and football?

One rather sad footnote to this story, is that 'Big Glenn' himself - having held out stubbornly until well past his 38th birthday - also eventually and rather tragically suffered a similar fate, and predictably, hasn't been seen within a five-mile radius of the City Ground since. The last I heard, wife, baby and shopping trolley were all doing well. As for Glenn himself, well he's had to take up a secondary occupation as a taxi driver, just to make ends meet - poor sod. Oh well, as they say: "Another one bites the dust"

THE game against the Geordies ended 1-1 with; yes you've guessed it, Gary Megson grabbing Newcastle's goal. An Ian Bowyer header earned Forest a replay at St.James' Park three days later, which they comfortably won 3-1. Goals from Davenport (penalty), Christie, and once again, that man Bowyer, gave them an impressive victory in front of a crowd of 25,166. Chris Waddle had earlier given Newcastle the lead following a corner, after goalkeeper Hans Segers had brilliantly turned aside Peter Beardsley's well-taken spot kick.

Forest's 'reward' for this excellent third round victory was another home tie, this time against Harry Bassett's Second Division newcomers Wimbledon. The 'Crazy Gang' once again proved more than a match for the 'Reds', and following a 0-0 draw at the City Ground on Saturday, 26th January, knocked us out of the competition, beating us 1-0 in the replay at Plough Lane four days later. For the second successive season therefore, the cultured brand of football for which Forest were renowned, had been steamrollered by the crudity and sheer brute force of the South London outfit.

In a month dominated almost entirely by the FA Cup, Cloughie celebrated his tenth anniversary in charge at the City Ground - the most eventful ten years in the history of our wonderful Club. During this period, NFFC had gone from struggling Second Division no-hopers - and virtual unknowns outside the UK - to Champions of Europe. What's more, they'd built a reputation for attractive, attacking football, which had made them a household name across the world. Thanks a million, Mr. Clough.

By the end of March, they were in eighth position in the table, having accumulated a total of 50 points from 32 games. With only ten games remaining, once more their only realistic objective was a place in Europe. However, five defeats, one draw, and only four victories up to the end of the season, left them in a disappointing ninth position after 42 games.

On a brighter note, at the end of May, Peter Davenport finally ended months of speculation about his future, when he signed a new three-year deal with the Club. With Birtles also nearing full fitness again, following his lengthy spell out through injury, the future was once again looking bright. And another very positive aspect of this campaign, had been the form of right-back Jim McInally. He'd made such an impact on the pitch, he'd deservedly been voted the 'Supporters' Player of the Year.'

UNFORTUNATELY, the popularity of the game remained at a low ebb. The dilapidated, crumbling stadia up and down the country were partly to blame - after all this was the 1980s - a time when the paying public were beginning to demand more for their money. But the lack of investment on the part of the Government, the FA, the Football League, and the Clubs themselves, was now threatening the very fabric of the game. It needed something drastic to shake it out of it's present state of apathy and decline.

An average League attendance at the City Ground of only 16,776 provided ample evidence all was not well. A total of eight League attendances below 15,000 couldn't, I'm afraid, simply be put down to the 'fickleness' of the Nottingham public. After all, the average League attendance for Forest's 21 away matches was just as uninspiring - only 19,922, despite their reputation for attractive football. Of these, no less than twelve were below 20,000, with the games at Coventry and Stoke drawing crowds of just 9,895 and 7,453 respectively.

SEASON 1984/85 – STATISTICS

FOOTBALL LEAGUE DIVISION ONE – FIXTURES

Date		Opposition	Venue	Competition	Score	Attendance
Aug	25	Sheffield Wednesday	A	League	1-3	31,925
	29	**Arsenal**	**H**	**League**	**2-0**	**18,215**
Sept	**1**	**Sunderland**	**H**	**League**	**3-1**	**15,760**
	5	Aston Villa	A	League	5-0	17,730
	8	Queens Park Rangers	A	League	0-3	13,507
	16	**Luton Town**	**H**	**League**	**3-1**	**18,605**
	19	**Club Brugge**	**H**	**UEFA Cup 1 - 1st Leg**	**0-0**	**18,307**
	22	West Ham United	A	League	0-0	17,434
	25	Portsmouth	A	LC 2 - 1st Leg	0-1	20,409
	29	**Norwich City**	**H**	**League**	**3-1**	**15,166**
Oct	3	Club Brugge	A	UEFA Cup 1 - 2nd Leg	0-1	24,983
	6	**Stoke City**	**H**	**League**	**1-1**	**14,129**
	10	**Portsmouth**	**H**	**LC 2 - 2nd Leg**	**3-0**	**18,182**
	13	West Bromwich Albion	A	League	1-4	13,056
	20	Newcastle United	A	League	1-1	28,252
	28	**Liverpool**	**H**	**League**	**0-2**	**19,838**
	31	**Sunderland**	**H**	**LC 3**	**1-1**	**14,291**
Nov	3	Southampton	A	League	0-1	17,818
	6	Sunderland	A	LC 3 -Replay	0-1	23,184
	10	**Tottenham Hotspur**	**H**	**League**	**1-2**	**21,306**
	17	Coventry City	A	League	3-1	9,895
	25	**Leicester City**	**H**	**League**	**2-1**	**21,463**
Dec	1	Watford	A	League	0-2	17,758
	8	**Manchester United**	**H**	**League**	**3-2**	**25,902**
	15	Everton	A	League	0-5	22,487
	22	Sunderland	A	League	2-0	21,235
	26	**Ipswich Town**	**H**	**League**	**2-0**	**17,123**
	29	**Aston Villa**	**H**	**League**	**3-2**	**17,676**
Jan	1	Chelsea	A	League	0-1	21,552
	6	**Newcastle United**	**H**	**FA Cup 3**	**1-1**	**23,582**
	9	Newcastle United	A	FA Cup 3 - Replay	3-1	25,166
	26	**Wimbledon**	**H**	**FA Cup 4**	**0-0**	**17,184**
	30	Wimbledon	A	FA Cup 4 - Replay	0-1	10,348
Feb	2	Norwich City	A	League	1-0	14,669
	9	**Queens Park Rangers**	**H**	**League**	**2-0**	**11,991**
	23	**Southampton**	**H**	**League**	**2-0**	**14,752**
Mar	2	Liverpool	A	League	0-1	35,696
	9	**Newcastle United**	**H**	**League**	**0-0**	**17,425**
	16	**West Bromwich Albion**	**H**	**League**	**1-2**	**12,663**
	20	**Sheffield Wednesday**	**H**	**League**	**0-0**	**17,648**
	23	Stoke City	A	League	4-1	7,453
	30	**West Ham United**	**H**	**League**	**1-2**	**13,560**
Apr	6	Ipswich Town	A	League	0-1	16,296
	10	**Chelsea**	**H**	**League**	**2-0**	**14,666**
	13	Arsenal	A	League	1-1	24,152
	20	**Coventry City**	**H**	**League**	**2-0**	**12,990**
	24	Luton Town	A	League	2-1	10,156
	27	Leicester City	A	League	0-1	13,886
May	**4**	**Watford**	**H**	**League**	**1-1**	**12,649**
	6	Manchester United	A	League	0-2	43,334
	11	**Everton**	**H**	**League**	**1-0**	**18,784**
	17	Tottenham Hotspur	A	League	0-1	20,075

HOME ATTENDANCES

	AGGREGATE ATTENDANCE	HIGHEST ATTENDANCE	LOWEST ATTENDANCE	AVERAGE ATTENDANCE
League:	352,311	25,902	11,991	16,776
League Cup:	32,473	18,182	14,291	16,236
FA Cup:	40,766	23,582	17,184	20,383
UEFA Cup:	18,307	18,307	18,307	18,307
All Competitions:	443,857	25,902	11,991	17,071

FINAL LEAGUE TABLE - DIVISION ONE

Position	P	W	D	L	GF	GA	Pts
1. Everton	42	28	6	8	88	43	90
2. Liverpool	42	22	11	9	68	35	77
3. Tottenham Hotspur	42	23	8	11	78	51	77
4. Manchester United	42	22	10	10	77	47	76
5. Southampton	42	19	11	12	56	47	68
6. Chelsea	42	18	12	12	63	48	66
7. Arsenal	42	19	9	14	61	49	66
8. Sheffield Wednesday	42	17	14	11	58	45	65
9. Nottingham Forest	**42**	**19**	**7**	**16**	**56**	**48**	**64**
10. Aston Villa	42	15	11	16	60	60	56
11. Watford	42	14	13	15	81	71	55
12. West Bromwich Albion	42	16	7	19	58	62	55
13. Luton Town	42	15	9	18	57	61	54
14. Newcastle United	42	13	13	16	55	70	52
15. Leicester City	42	15	6	21	65	73	51
16. West Ham United	42	13	12	17	51	68	51
17. Ipswich Town	42	13	11	18	46	57	50
18. Coventry City	42	15	5	22	47	64	50
19. Queens Park Rangers	42	13	11	18	53	72	50
20. Norwich City	42	13	10	19	46	64	49
21. Sunderland	42	10	10	22	40	62	40
22. Stoke City	42	3	8	31	24	91	17

AWAY ATTENDANCES

	AGGREGATE ATTENDANCE	HIGHEST ATTENDANCE	LOWEST ATTENDANCE	AVERAGE ATTENDANCE
League:	418,366	43,334	7,453	19,922
League Cup:	43,593	23,184	20,409	21,796
FA Cup:	35,514	25,166	10,348	17,757
UEFA Cup:	24,983	24,983	24,983	24,983
All Competitions:	522,456	43,334	7,453	20,094

"LETS ALL LAUGH AT DERBY, LET'S ALL LAUGH AT DERBY"

ONCE AGAIN, Cloughie had been busy during the summer, wheeling and dealing in the transfer market. Kenny Swain had gone to Second Division Plymouth Argyle, Paul Hart to First Division Sheffield Wednesday, and Trevor Christie to THIRD DIVISION Derby County. By the end of August, Steve Hodge would also join the exodus from the Club, with Cloughie finally agreeing to his transfer demands and allowing him to move across the Midlands to Aston Villa.

To balance things out, Stuart Pearce and Ian Butterworth arrived from Coventry City in a combined deal worth £400,000; the promising Neil Webb was snapped up from Portsmouth for £250,000; 33-year-old John Robertson returned on a 'free' after two miserable years down at the 'Sheep-dip'; and left-sided midfielder Brian Rice was purchased from Hibernian - the £175,000 fee ultimately being decided by a transfer tribunal.

Following minor surgery on his calves during the close season, the highly rated Chris Fairclough was expected to be out of action for only a short period of time. Unfortunately, this would be followed by a niggling groin injury, resulting in further surgery and a whole season on the sidelines.

The tragic loss of over forty lives in the 'Heysel Stadium Disaster' immediately before the European Cup Final in May 1985 had led to an indefinite ban on English clubs from competing in Europe. The blame for this appalling tragedy - which involved the supporters of Italian giants Juventus and those of Liverpool FC - had been laid fairly and squarely at the feet of Liverpool's travelling supporters. However, there is no doubt that other factors - such as the crumbling, dilapidated condition of the stadium in Brussels, a lack of crowd segregation, and no small amount of provocation on the part of a large number of Juve supporters - also contributed to the disaster.

NEIL Webb marked his League debut for the 'Reds' with a goal in the 1-1 draw against Luton at Kenilworth Road on the opening day of the season. Stuart Pearce and Ian Butterworth also made their League debuts in this game. This was followed by a 1-0 defeat at home to Sheffield Wednesday four days later, watched by a crowd of 18,367. Although the Main Stand 'A' Block had remained fairly sparsely populated throughout the previous season, it suddenly sprang to life with a vengeance during this game against the 'Owls'.

Just minutes after kick off, and with the usual last minute stragglers still making their way into the stand from the pub, a loud chorus of: *"We love you Wednesday, we do,"* rang out suddenly from the middle of the 'A' Block. Around thirty Wednesday supporters had infiltrated this section of the ground. However, they were immediately - and resoundingly - drowned out by two hundred snarling Forest supporters who rose to their feet all around them. The unwelcome guests were then subsequently rescued only by the prompt actions of the police and stewards, who shepherded them quickly out of the stand and around the edge of the pitch to the sanctuary of the Visitor's Enclosure.

From that moment on, it became 'Fortress 'A' Block', with visiting supporters entering only at their own peril. As time went by, the empty seats in this section were filled and the vociferousness of the supporters grew more and more intense. Their reputation also began to evolve. It remains to this day - on a good day that is - the most intimidating area of the City Ground. And in more recent years, the visiting supporters have been housed in the nearby lower tier of the Bridgford Stand, well within snarling distance of the 'A' Block.

The defeat by Wednesday was followed by a 2-1 victory over Southampton at the City Ground the following Saturday. This was followed by three consecutive defeats: 2-1 away to QPR, 3-1 at home to Man U, and 2-0 against Liverpool at Anfield. Thankfully, this depressing sequence of results was brought to an end in style, with a 3-0 victory over Leicester City at Filbert Street on Sunday, 8th September, thanks to goals from Webb, Rice and Davenport.

Forest's patchy form continued throughout September, but picked up dramatically again the following month. During October, they won no less than seven out of eight competitive games, including two in the League Cup. The first of these Cup games saw them complete a 7-0 aggregate victory over Bolton Wanderers, winning the second leg of their second round tie 3-0 at Burnden Park (having beaten them 4-0 in the first leg at the City Ground in September). The second saw them achieve a very satisfying 2-1 third round victory over the 'Sheep' at the Baseball Ground. Johnny Metgod and Franz Carr grabbed the goals in a dazzling Forest performance. And by the time West Brom visited Trentside on Sunday, 3rd November, the 'Reds' were sitting in eighth position in the First Division table with 22 points from 14 games played. Goals from Webb and Davenport gave them a 2-1 victory over the 'Baggies' in front of a better-than-average crowd of 19,610.

AS far back as October 1985, there had been speculation in the media concerning the formation of a new breakaway League in this country. Naturally, many clubs were anxious to tell the world why they should automatically be part of any new Super League and the list of around thirty included some very unlikely candidates indeed. For example: First Division Birmingham City - destined for relegation to Division Two at the time. Second Division Portsmouth and Sunderland - neither of whom were presently involved in the promotion race in that division. And, would you believe it - THIRD DIVISION Derby County? Secretary Stuart Webb claimed they should be the East Midlands' sole representatives...though God knows on what grounds?

With Forest undoubtedly the 'premier' football club in the Midlands - let alone the East Midlands - Webb's comments caused something of a stir amongst local supporters. His outlandish claims were quickly challenged in the Football Post. One letter from an individual called 'Butcher' of Stapleford - which was mainly 'tongue in cheek' - featured in the *YOU'RE TELLING US* section of the Post on Saturday, 2nd November. Not only did he strongly argue Forest's case for inclusion in the new 'Super League', but he also took a swipe or two at our 'woolly-backed' neighbours, declaring, amongst other things: "Derby are currently where they belong and would not get any more fans if they were in the First Division."

To say his comments stirred up a hornet's nest is an understatement. The following Saturday's Post was filled with letters of complaint from whining 'Sheep-shaggers', each one of them trying their hardest to justify Webb's ridiculous claims that the 'Rams' were superior to the 'Reds' in every respect. Here is a sample of their comments:

- *"He ('Butcher') is obviously one of many feeble fair-weather fans they (Forest) seem to attract."*
- *"If Derby returned to the Second Division - let alone the First - their gates would rise dramatically."*
- *"We do not need Man United, Liverpool or Spurs to make our gates look respectable."*
- *"Don't knock the support and pride of our wonderful club - something which Forest could never match."*
  Mansfield Ram

- *"If Derby County were back in Division One - where they belong - I'm sure they would have far better gates than Forest."*
  C.P. Kendall, Breaston

- *"There is no doubt in Derby supporters' minds that we will need a much larger capacity than 26,500 when we get back to the top."*
- *"Derby is a football town and ranks alongside clubs like Newcastle who will always be well supported. It is teams like these, which should be considered for a Super League."*
- *"Forest's claims for a place rest with Brian Clough and unlike Derby's support, he won't be around for ever."*
  Proud Rams' Fan, Ruddington

- *"Derby would not be out of place supporter-wise alongside Man United or Liverpool."*
- *"Derby were only in bad financial difficulties back in 1984 because of stupid spending. Their lifeline was their great support."*
  Stephen Hall, Wollaton

Well, I was flabbergasted. Not only were these letters full of inaccuracies - and born out of pure fantasy - but they were also plastered all over our very own Football Post. What planet were these people on? Talk about delusions of their own significance! I was livid - and determined to set the record straight. It has long been my view that many opinions - especially those of football supporters - are based largely on ignorance and bias, rather than on hard facts; and this has prompted me over the years to maintain meticulous records of my beloved NFFC. In addition, I have built up a complete collection of Forest programmes dating right back to season 1966/67 when I began actively supporting the Club. I also have virtually every book ever written about Forest and literally dozens of videos chronicling their exploits over the years. It was time for me to tell people the truth - so out came my pen and paper.

By the following Saturday, having just witnessed a depressing 2-0 defeat by Manchester City at the City Ground, I'd put the great 'Forest-Derby Supremacy' debate to the back of mind. As I settled down for an evening at home, I turned to my Football Post and began flicking through the pages. Suddenly, as I turned to the Letters' Page, I remembered my letter and the fact I'd posted it off several days earlier. And, to my surprise, there it was, under the very appropriate heading *"FACTS NOT MYTHS"* (their heading, not mine), my very own contribution to the great debate:

"I would like to educate those Derby County supporters who constantly see fit to criticise and compare Forest's support with that of their own.

I have compiled a summary of Forest's home attendances from 1966, when I began supporting the team, until the present date.

The highest average from their spell in Division one from 1966 until 1971/72 was by my reckoning 32,548 with the lowest of 21,433 in the relegation year.

In Division Two, the lowest average was 10,016 in their first season 72/73 to a best of 17,978 in 1977 when they were promoted.

The first season back in the top flight brought in 32,501 and not until 81/82 did the average fall below 20,000. Last season saw the lowest of 16,776.

It would be interesting to see if any of Derby's mythical '30,000' followers could provide the Rams' corresponding figures for the same period.

Furthermore, as I have missed only one home game since 69/70 - including testimonials and friendlies - and have followed Forest to 44 League grounds, Wembley (four times), Munich, Madrid, Amsterdam, Eindhoven and Brussels, and have been a season ticket holder for nine years, do I fall into the category of "one of many feeble fair-weather fans they seem to attract" as described by Mansfield Ram?

It's interesting to note how many Derby supporters find it necessary to read your excellent newspaper to keep up to date with the local football scene.

Are they missing out on something I wonder?"

Chris Broughton, Long Eaton

Editor's note: *"Modesty forbids us to imagine Derbyshire people flocking over the border to buy the FP. Let's just say there are quite a few Rams' fans who obviously live in Notts."*

Not surprisingly, having been presented with the facts, the debate suddenly died a death and we heard nothing more on this subject from the 'Sheep'. However, I feel it is necessary to elaborate just a little further so as to put this whole issue regarding attendances into it's true perspective. Yes, I will be the first to admit; Forest's gates at the time were abysmal. However, let's not forget that in general terms - as documented already in this book - the game of football was in serious decline. Whilst Forest struggled to pull in more than 17,000 in the League, virtually every other Club in the land was suffering a similar fate. Here are the attendance figures for a selection of Forest's away fixtures that season:

• 03-09-85 versus Liverpool at Anfield:	**27,135**
• 12-10-85 versus Aston Villa at Villa Park:	**15,315**
• 19-10-85 versus Newcastle United at St.James's Park:	**23,151**
• 26-12-85 versus Birmingham City at St.Andrews:	**10,378**
• 11-01-86 versus Tottenham Hotspur at White Hart Lane:	**19,043**

- 29-03-86 versus Coventry City at Highfield Road: **9,500**
- 05-04-86 versus West Bromwich Albion at the Hawthorns: **7,901**
- 08-04-86 versus Arsenal at Highbury: **15,098**
- 19-04-86 versus Manchester City at Maine Road: **19,715**

What's more, throughout the whole of season 85/86, no less than 11 of Forest's 21 League games away from home, drew crowds of less than 15,000. Only five topped the 20,000 mark and the average overall was a mere 17,210 - just 395 higher than Forest's own of 16,815.

Naturally, following this great debate over Derby's alleged 'supremacy' amongst Midlands clubs, and their 'massive' support, I waited with baited breath for their return to the top flight. There were several reasons why I was anxious to see them back in the First Division:

- Despite my loathing for them, the local 'derbies' between the two clubs were good for football in the East Midlands.
- We were assured of an easy six points a season!
- I was looking forward to witnessing at first hand the predicted 'stampede' of supporters heading towards the Baseball Ground - presumably in their tens of thousands?

And, having gained promotion in successive seasons, they returned to the top flight at the beginning of season 1987/88. Having watched the results on the opening day of the season - enjoying every minute of Forest's 2-1 win at Charlton Athletic - I waited eagerly for my Football Post to arrive, so I could check on the day's attendances - particularly the one at the Baseball Ground. Derby had entertained Luton Town that day in their first Division One fixture for nearly seven years. And, there it was, just as predicted, a breathtaking crowd of - wait for it - 17,204!

Just for the record, here are the 'Sheep's' first six attendances that season:

- 15-08-87 versus Luton Town: 17,204! - *"There is no doubt in Derby supporters' minds that we will need a much larger capacity than 26,500 when we get back to the top."* **(Proud Rams' Fan, Ruddington)**

- 29-08-87 versus Wimbledon: 15,165! - *"Derby would not be out of place supporter-wise alongside Man Utd or Liverpool."* **(Steven Hall, Wollaton)**

- 05-09-87 versus Portsmouth: 15,071! - *"Derby is a football town and ranks alongside Newcastle who will always be well supported."* **(Proud Rams' Fan, Ruddington)**

- 26-09-87 versus Oxford United: 15,711! - *"If Derby were back in Division One - where they belong - I'm sure they would have far better gates than Forest."* **(C.P.Kendall, Breaston)**

- 07-10-87 versus Southend United (League Cup): 12,118! - *"If Derby returned to the Second Division - let alone the First - their gates would rise dramatically."* **(Mansfield Ram)**

- 10-10-87 versus NOTTINGHAM FOREST: 22,394! - *"We don't need Man Utd, Liverpool or Spurs to make our average gates look respectable."* **(Mansfield Ram)**
  NO - JUST A VISIT FROM NOTTINGHAM FOREST FC!!!

I rest my case.

WITH the rapidly emerging talents of Franz Carr now dominating Forest's right wing position, winger Steve Wigley had completed a move to Second Division Sheffield United during October in the hope of gaining regular first team football once again. Following their victory over West Brom on 3rd November, Forest's form was patchy throughout that month, with them losing two and drawing one in the League. This was followed by a 3-1 defeat at QPR in the fourth round of the League Cup on Monday, 25th November.

On Monday, 9th December, I was admitted to the QMC for a third operation on a rather troublesome infection in my back. Having undergone surgery on the Tuesday afternoon, I had to endure an anxious few days waiting for the Consultant to let me know whether I'd be allowed home before the weekend. After all Forest were playing Luton on Saturday and I couldn't bear the thought of lying prostrate in a hospital bed, whilst the 'Reds' were in action at the City Ground.

As the weekend drew nearer, my chances of an early discharge seemed more and more remote. I was very frustrated by the time Saturday arrived and at 10.00-a.m. sat on my bed waiting for the Doctor to complete his rounds. By midday there was still no sign of him and my fingernails had by this time been bitten to the bone. He finally arrived at my bedside at around 1.00-p.m. and quickly gave me the once over. His verdict: I could get dressed and go home immediately. This was music to my ears; but I had absolutely no intention of going home. Having got out of my pyjamas and into my clothes in record time, I was on the phone to the misses with the strict instructions: ''Get yer arse down 'ere quick - and don't forget mi season ticket!''

By 2.00-p.m. I was sprawled across the back seat of the car being ferried to the City Ground. I went straight from my hospital bed to my seat in the Main Stand 'A' Block ('feeble fair-weather fans' indeed!). Forest's 2-0 victory, with goals from Neil Webb and Nigel Clough, gave me the perfect tonic, although I did my back no good at all when I leapt from my seat to celebrate Webby's opener.

The Christmas programme saw the 'Reds' pick up some useful points, thanks firstly to a 1-0 Boxing Day victory over Birmingham City at St.Andrews. This was followed by a 1-1 draw against second-placed Liverpool at the City Ground two days later. And a Neil Webb hat-trick in the 5-2 win over Coventry at home on New Year's Day brought his personal tally to five in just three games - not bad for a midfield player. Goals from Johnny Metgod and Peter Davenport completed the rout.

Not for the first time, the 'Reds' struggled against 'inferior' opposition in the third round of the FA Cup. They took on Second Division Blackburn Rovers at the City Ground on Saturday, 4th January 1986, where Birtles notched Forest's only goal in a 1-1 draw. He grabbed another in their 3-2 defeat at Ewood Park in the replay nine days later. Despite this setback, their form in the League was excellent during the early part of the year. A 3-0 victory over Spurs at White Hart Lane on 11th January, was followed by an impressive 3-2 victory over League leaders Manchester United at Old Trafford a week later. By the time they entertained QPR on Saturday, 1st February, they were sitting in eighth position in the table, with 43 points from 27 games. Two goals from Colin Walsh and one each from Franz Carr and Neill Webb gave them an easy 4-0 victory over the Londoners.

Not long after, there was another mini exodus from the Club, with first Jim McInally - the previous season's Supporters' Player of the Year - moving to Dundee United in February. He was followed by fourteen-goal hero Peter Davenport, who became the latest player tempted away from the City Ground by Manchester United, this time in a cut-price deal worth £600,000.

Things just seemed to fizzle out from that moment on and Forest ended the season in eighth position in the table with 68 points from 42 games. One pleasant aspect of the season though, was that Man U had surrendered a five-point lead at the top of the table at the half-way stage, to end up in fourth position. Liverpool landed the title with a total of 88 points - 2 ahead of Runners-up Everton.

Although as a young boy, I'd admired United from afar - after all, who could fail to be impressed by any side boasting the wonderful trio of Best, Law and Charlton - my respect for them had diminished rapidly over the years, mainly due to the arrogance of their supporters. This had built up finally into an intense disliking, a situation not helped by the fact they always seemed to be sniffing around our best players - and everyone else's for that matter. Ian Storey-Moore, Garry Birtles and Peter Davenport had all headed north to Old Trafford, and these would be followed in the future by Neil Webb and Roy Keane - although Keane is the only one to have flourished after making this particular 'step up' in his career.

THE average League attendance at the City Ground this season was a disappointing 16,815, with the highest being the 30,171 who witnessed the 0-0 draw with title-chasing Everton in the final home fixture of the season. The games against Manchester United and Liverpool also drew reasonable crowds of 26,274 and 27,141 respectively.

'*The Sheep-shagger!*'

SEASON 1985/86 – STATISTICS

FOOTBALL LEAGUE DIVISION ONE – FIXTURES

Date		Opposition	Venue	Competition	Score	Attendance
Aug	17	Luton Town	A	League	1-1	11,318
	21	**Sheffield Wednesday**	**H**	**League**	**0-1**	**18,367**
	24	**Southampton**	**H**	**League**	**2-1**	**12,643**
	27	Queens Park Rangers	A	League	1-2	10,748
	31	**Manchester United**	**H**	**League**	**1-3**	**26,274**
Sept	3	Liverpool	A	League	0-2	27,135
	8	Leicester City	A	League	3-0	14,247
	14	**Tottenham Hotspur**	**H**	**League**	**0-1**	**17,554**
	21	**Watford**	**H**	**League**	**3-2**	**12,921**
	25	**Bolton Wanderers**	**H**	**LC 2 - 1st Leg**	**4-0**	**10,530**
	28	West Ham United	A	League	2-4	14,540
Oct	**5**	**Ipswich Town**	**H**	**League**	**3-1**	**12,200**
	8	Bolton Wanderers	A	LC 2 - 2nd Leg	3-0	4,010
	12	Aston Villa	A	League	2-0	15,315
	19	Newcastle United	A	League	3-0	23,151
	26	**Arsenal**	**H**	**League**	**3-2**	**17,756**
	30	Derby County	A	LC 3	2-1	22,226
Nov	**3**	**West Bromwich Albion**	**H**	**League**	**2-1**	**19,610**
	9	Chelsea	A	League	2-4	17,743
	16	**Manchester City**	**H**	**League**	**0-2**	**15,140**
	23	Everton	A	League	1-1	27,860
	25	Queens Park Rangers	A	LC 4	1-3	13,052
Dec	**1**	**Oxford United**	**H**	**League**	**1-1**	**15,317**
	7	Sheffield Wednesday	A	League	1-2	22,496
	14	**Luton Town**	**H**	**League**	**2-0**	**12,078**
	20	Southampton	A	League	1-3	12,500
	26	Birmingham City	A	League	1-0	10,378
	28	**Liverpool**	**H**	**League**	**1-1**	**27,141**
Jan	**1**	**Coventry City**	**H**	**League**	**5-2**	**13,860**
	4	**Blackburn Rovers**	**H**	**FA Cup 3**	**1-1**	**15,772**
	11	Tottenham Hotspur	A	League	3-0	19,043
	13	Blackburn Rovers	A	FA Cup 3 - Replay	2-3	11,710
	18	Manchester United	A	League	3-2	46,717
Feb	**1**	**Queens Park Rangers**	**H**	**League**	**4-0**	**11,538**
	8	**Newcastle United**	**H**	**League**	**1-2**	**15,388**
Mar	8	Ipswich Town	A	League	0-1	12,658
	15	**Aston Villa**	**H**	**League**	**1-1**	**12,993**
	22	**Leicester City**	**H**	**League**	**4-3**	**14,484**
	29	Coventry City	A	League	0-0	9,500
	31	**Birmingham City**	**H**	**League**	**3-0**	**12,134**
Apr	**2**	**West Ham United**	**H**	**League**	**2-1**	**17,498**
	5	West Bromwich Albion	A	League	1-1	7,901
	8	Arsenal	A	League	1-1	15,098
	12	**Chelsea**	**H**	**League**	**0-0**	**18,055**
	19	Manchester City	A	League	2-1	19,715
	21	Watford	A	League	1-1	11,510
	26	**Everton**	**H**	**League**	**0-0**	**30,171**
May	3	Oxford United	A	League	2-1	11,845

HOME ATTENDANCES

	AGGREGATE ATTENDANCE	HIGHEST ATTENDANCE	LOWEST ATTENDANCE	AVERAGE ATTENDANCE
League:	353,122	30,171	11,538	16,815
League Cup:	10,530	10,530	10,530	10,530
FA Cup:	15,772	15,772	15,772	15,772
All Competitions:	379,424	30,171	10,530	16,496

FINAL LEAGUE TABLE - DIVISION ONE

Position	P	W	D	L	GF	GA	Pts
1. Liverpool	42	26	10	6	89	37	88
2. Everton	42	26	8	8	87	41	86
3. West Ham United	42	26	6	10	74	40	84
4. Manchester United	42	22	10	10	70	36	76
5. Sheffield Wednesday	42	21	10	11	63	54	73
6. Chelsea	42	20	11	11	57	56	71
7. Arsenal	42	20	9	13	49	47	69
8. Nottingham Forest	**42**	**19**	**11**	**12**	**69**	**53**	**68**
9. Luton Town	42	18	12	12	61	44	66
10. Tottenham Hotspur	42	19	8	15	74	52	65
11. Newcastle United	42	17	12	13	67	72	63
12. Watford	42	16	11	15	69	62	59
13. Queens Park Rangers	42	15	7	20	53	64	52
14. Southampton	42	12	10	20	51	62	46
15. Manchester City	42	11	12	19	43	57	45
16. Aston Villa	42	10	14	18	51	67	44
17. Coventry City	42	11	10	21	48	71	43
18. Oxford United	42	10	12	20	62	80	42
19. Leicester City	42	10	12	20	54	76	42
20. Ipswich Town	42	11	8	23	32	55	41
21. Birmingham City	42	8	5	29	30	73	29
22. West Bromwich Albion	42	4	12	26	35	89	24

AWAY ATTENDANCES

	AGGREGATE ATTENDANCE	HIGHEST ATTENDANCE	LOWEST ATTENDANCE	AVERAGE ATTENDANCE
League:	361,418	46,717	7,901	17,210
League Cup:	39,288	22,226	4,010	13,096
FA Cup:	11,710	11,710	11,710	11,710
All Competitions:	412,416	46,717	4,010	16,496

"FIVE HO, FIVE HO, IT'S BACK TO NOTTS WE GO"

A REMARKABLY quiet close season on the transfer front had seen only the departure of full-back Bryn Gunn to Peterborough United and the acquisition of central-defender Colin Foster from Orient and centre-forward Paul Wilkinson from Everton. There was promising news on the injury front, when it was announced that Chris Fairclough - missing for the whole of the previous campaign - was now on the mend and likely to be back in action shortly.

The season kicked off with a 2-0 defeat at Everton on Saturday, 23rd August, in front of a crowd of 35,198. Despite this setback, Forest more than played their part in a pulsating game, hitting the woodwork twice and being unfortunate not to come away with at least a point. This was followed by a resounding 4-0 victory over newly-promoted Charlton Athletic at the City Ground the following Wednesday. Neil Webb (2), Garry Birtles and Nigel Clough - the Supporters' Player of the Year for 1985/86 - were on target in front of a very disappointing crowd of 12,970.

To say they made a good start to the season is an understatement. By the end of September, they were on top of the First Division table, with no less than 19 points from 8 games played. Their six victories, one draw and a single defeat, had been achieved on the back of a goals tally which read: for - 23; against - 7. Following the comprehensive victory over Charlton, they'd gone on to draw 1-1 with Watford at home and had beaten West Ham 2-1 and Southampton 3-1 on their travels. This was followed by a 6-0 home demolition of Aston Villa, a 6-2 victory at Chelsea and another City Ground triumph over Arsenal - this time by a more modest 1-0. What's more, following his brace against Charlton, Neil Webb had grabbed another against the 'Hammers', two against the 'Saints', two against the 'Villains' and three more against the 'Pensioners' (a game in which Birtles also scored a hat-trick) - and all this from what was essentially a midfield player.

Surprisingly, during this surge to the top of the table, Colin Walsh had refused the offer of a new contract and moved south to Charlton Athletic. Forest were earning almost universal acclaim for the quality of their play both at home and away. And thankfully at last, their form was once again beginning to stir the imagination of the Nottingham public, who were slowly, but surely, returning to the City Ground in numbers.

A crowd of 25,371 saw the game against Arsenal, and when second-from-bottom Manchester United visited Trentside on Saturday, 4th October, the City Ground - for the first time in ages - was bursting at the seams. A crowd of 35,828 saw Birtles give Forest the lead, only for Bryan Robson to spoil the party by equalising for the visitors. Goal-keeper Chris Turner kept Forest at bay almost single-handedly for most of the game to earn United a desperately needed point.

A RESURGENT economy was playing it's part in encouraging the missing thousands back to English football stadiums. And in an attempt to spice things up a little further, the Football League introduced a 'play-off' system, which would come into effect at the end of the season. On 10th May 1987, the club in 5th position in Division Two would play the club in 19th position in Division One. The club in 4th position in Division Two would play the club in 3rd position in Division Two. The winners of each tie would then face one another in a two-legged play-off Final during week commencing 17th May. The winners would either gain or retain First Division status. The play-offs would supplement a two-up-three-down system which would apply for two seasons, and who's ultimate objective was to reduce the First Division from 22 to just 20 clubs by the beginning of season 1988/89.

Off the pitch as well as on, Cloughie was doing his utmost to woo the missing fans back to the City Ground. Anyone who was a regular at the time will recall that the Forest Ticket Office staff were to customer relations, what Saddam Hussein is to international peacekeeping. Possibly holding a gun to his head, the Forest manager had somehow encouraged the grumpiest of them all - Harry Willis - to have his picture taken for the Forest programme. His smiling face was featured in the Review for the Villa game, with the words 'Collector's Item' emblazoned across it.

On October 18th, Forest announced a profit of £473,000 for the year ending 31st May 1986. This was in contrast to a loss of £627,00 for the previous year. Naturally, the Club were delighted with this turnaround in their fortunes and very upbeat about the steady increase in attendances at the City Ground. After five games, the average stood at 21,184, compared to only 16,829 at the same stage the previous season. Membership of the Junior Reds was also heading rapidly towards the 2,000 mark, and would peak eventually at almost 3,000 before the season was out.

Forest's League form deteriorated slightly during October and November, but was almost compensated for by a good run in the League Cup. Having drawn 0-0 in the first leg, second round tie at Brighton at the end of September, they went on to finish off the 'Seagulls' 3-0 in the return leg in Nottingham on Wednesday, 8th October. Due to work commitments, I was stuck in Manchester and was unable - much to my frustration - to get back home for this game. Consequently, this ended my nine and a half year, 268-match, unbroken sequence of games at the City Ground. The last time I'd missed a match prior to this was on Wednesday, 27th April 1977 - and boy was I gutted!

Alas, I had to settle for the television highlights in the comfort of my hotel room later that evening. Franz Carr's 'Man of the Match' performance brought him two goals - the other was scored by Stuart Pearce from the penalty spot - and prompted a chorus of: *"Ooh-Ah-Franzie-Carr, Say Ooh-Ah-Franzie-Carr"* from the delighted Trent Enders. This particular chant was later adapted by Villa's Holte End to: *"Ooh-Ah-Paul McGrath,"* and subsequently of course by Manchester United's Stretford End to the more widely recognised: *"Ooh-Ah-Can-tona."*

Forest's next opponents in the competition were Crystal Palace, who were disposed of 1-0 in a third round replay at the City Ground on Bonfire Night, following a 2-2 draw at Selhurst Park the previous week. They were then drawn away to Bradford City in the fourth round, with the tie taking place at the Osdal Stadium on Wednesday, 19th November. This was at a time when Valley Parade was still being rebuilt after the devastating fire which had claimed over fifty lives at the end of season 1984/85.

There was a sizeable following from Nottingham amongst the crowd of 16,009 and they witnessed a blistering display from the 'Reds'. Goals from Carr, Metgod, Clough, Mills and Fairclough gave them a resounding 5-0 victory and saw them through to the quarter-final stages for the first time in four years. Several weeks later, an amusing letter from Forest supporter Ian Duckmanton of Kirkby-In-Ashfield appeared in the Forest Review for the game against Southampton, under the heading *"Fans of Snow White"*:

> *"All we seem to get in the Press is "football hooligans again." How refreshing to write about the other side of the story.*
> *I was lucky enough to visit a pub called "The Richardson Arms" just outside Bradford after Forest's Littlewoods Cup victory.*
> *It was obviously a very popular local and apart from myself and two friends and seven Forest fans who were playing darts with the regulars, everyone appeared to be from Bradford.*
> *When the band came on, everyone joined in the applause and a good time was had by all but the highlight of the evening was the very funny exit by the Forest lads.*
> *They marched through the pub on their knees singing "Five Ho, Five Ho, It's back to Notts we go." The final touch as the last one gave a cheery wave as the door swung shut behind them reduced the pub landlord to helpless mirth.*
> *Isn't this what being a football supporter is all about?"*

This humorous tale - so typical of the spontaneous wit of football supporters - reminds me of Sunday lunchtimes down at the Variety Club in Radford. I have a sneaking suspicion this particular establishment may well have provided Forest's 'Seven Dwarfs' with their inspiration. Sunday lunchtime is 'cabaret' time down at the Variety Club and consists of strippers, comedians, and the most hilarious slant on the game of Bingo you'll ever encounter anywhere.

Although the main attraction is undoubtedly the strippers - a fact borne out by the totally male-dominated audience - this is closely followed by the comedians - so blue they make even Chubby Brown seem inoffensive. However, the most bizarre aspect of the whole afternoon is unquestionably provided by the bingo. The owner of the club, who doubles as the compare, also calls the bingo. And his patter is unorthodox to say the least. A typical game goes something like this:

- *Right then...you miserable little bastards. It's eyes down an' don't forget wi playin' for the usual prize of five pounds for a full 'ouse. Yes...five complete English pounds.*
- *1 an' 1 - legs 11*
- *8 an' 8 - two fat ladies - 88*
- *1 an' 3 - unlucky fer some - 13*
- *2 an' 1 - key o' the door - 21*
- *4 an' 4 - all the fours - 44*
- *5 an' 0 - five ho - 50*
- *Five Ho! (The whole crowd joins in at this point)...Five Ho!...FIVE FUCKIN' HO!...FIVE HO, FIVE HO, FIVE HO, FIVE HO, FIVE HO...FIVE HO, FIVE HO, FIVE HO, FIVE HO, FIVE HO, FIVE HO!*
- *6 an' 6 - all the sixes - clickety-click - 66...and so on, and so on.*

The game then goes on as normal until a full house is called - with every number ending '0', such as 20, 30 etc., receiving the same treatment. Ultimately, the winner of the 'five whole English pounds' is ridiculed by the compare and the very drunken audience and the game ends as abruptly as it began. Although the whole thing is completely mad - and very repetitive - it's great fun, especially when you've had a skin-full. What's more, if Forest are playing at home straight after, it provides a perfect start to the day. You're always in the right frame of mind by the time you fall out of a taxi outside the City Ground just before kick off.

FOREST'S form during December continued to fluctuate and their 2-0 home victory over Man City on Saturday, 6th December, was followed by a 3-2 defeat at Newcastle the following Saturday and a 0-0 draw at home to struggling Southampton a week later. However, their blistering early season form ensured that despite another 2-1 defeat at Norwich on Boxing Day, they were still in a lofty second position in the table prior to the game against Luton Town at the City Ground on Sunday, 22nd November. Their 2-2 draw with the 'Hatters' saw them slip down two places to fourth, going into their New Year's Day encounter with Liverpool, also at home.

Once again it was refreshing to see the City Ground filled almost to it's capacity against the team who were just one point and one place above them in the table. Arsenal were in poll position at this stage with 45 points, followed by Everton on 41, with all four teams having played 22 games. Local boy Phil Starbuck - playing only his third senior game - scored Forest's goal in a hard fought 1-1 draw in front of a crowd of 32,854. Ian Rush - who else - scored a late equaliser for Liverpool.

Following a 0-0 draw at Aston Villa the following Saturday, it was time once again to switch our attentions to the FA Cup and a third round visit to Second Division Crystal Palace on Sunday, 11th January 1987. A heavy snowfall and freezing temperatures put this particular fixture in doubt right up until the last minute. Situated as it is in South London, Selhurst Park is an absolute pain in the arse to get to, so we decided to travel by train. We were delighted when the Club announced they were running a 'special'.

Although there were around 2,500 Forest supporters making the trip, only around three or four hundred did so by train. As we were led out of Selhurst Railway Station by a police escort numbering about two dozen, a small group of Palace supporters were immediately on our tail. They'd obviously been waiting for us to arrive, but no-one had paid much attention to them really. We did fall about laughing though when they chanted: *"Is this all you take away?"*

Now when it comes to away support, Palace are about in the same league as the QPRs, Blackburn Rovers and Charlton Athletics of this world. The words: *"Come in a taxi, You must have come in a taxi!"* definitely spring to mind. Although Forest aren't the best-supported club in the world by any means, our away support has always been immense - especially when compared to the likes of Crystal Palace.

As we made our way into the ground, the freezing cold temperatures almost took your breath away. In everyone's opinion this game should never have gone ahead. The pitch was frozen solid and looked more like a skating rink. Possibly the 11,618 supporters already inside Selhurst Park were the decisive factor in the end and the game went ahead as planned. But as soon as the teams took to the field, it was obvious that the Forest boys just didn't fancy it at all. The sight of Nigel Clough and several others prancing around in tights and gloves said everything to me. Even more worrying, was the fact not one of the Palace players was dressed in this manner.

Not surprisingly, ninety minutes later, we were trudging dejectedly out of the ground having once again succumbed to 'lesser opposition' at this very early stage of the competition. Having dealt with the conditions far more adeptly, Palace dominated the game from start to finish and the 1-0 score-line saw them comfortably through to the fourth round. And believe me, on an unbearably cold Sunday evening in January, after you've stood freezing your bollocks off for two hours watching your team skipping around like a bunch of fairies, it's a bloody long way home to Nottingham from South London. And this is made even worse by the thought you've got to go back to work again the next morning. "Never again," I decided - "Well, not 'til the next time anyway."

Thankfully the cold snap spared us another long trip back to Selhurst the following Saturday. The scheduled League meeting against Palace's ground-sharing neighbours Charlton Athletic was postponed. (Charlton have since of course returned to their traditional home at the Valley and it is now Wimbledon who have set up temporary home with the 'Eagles'). However, our next fixture - a League Cup quarter-final tie against Arsenal on Wednesday, 21st January - meant we were, after all, London-bound once again.

Our days of travelling to away games on the 'Bus from the Sal' long since over, our little gang - myself, Bucko, Tiff, Bodge, Big Lee and Tom Clough - had booked ourselves onto a bus from the Cricketers in Beeston. Bodge (Bucko's younger brother) and Big Lee (only recently out of the army) were the latest additions to our ever increasing gang and also season ticket holders with us in the 'A' Block. The bus was leaving the Cricks at 3.00-p.m. so we all booked the day off work and arranged to meet up in Beeston at 12.00-p.m. We'd decided to have a 'bit of a sesh' before departing for the Capital.

As you can imagine, we were all pretty 'happy' by the time we boarded the coach, and as we prepared to leave, spirits were running high. The sound of: *"We're on the march with Cloughie's Army, We're all goin' t' Wem-ber-ley,"* rang out as we set off. Not surprisingly, by the time we reached the M1, this had died down completely and everyone was already nodding off. It was only when we pulled onto London's North Circular Road two hours later, we all began to stir.

We reached Highbury at about 5.30-p.m. and with over two hours to go until kick off, rather predictably headed straight for the nearest boozer. Most of the bars around the ground had a mixture of Arsenal and Forest supporters inside, but it was pleasing and surprising to see the two sets of fans mixing freely together. I'm not too sure the Arsenal fans inside the last pub we dropped into before the game were overly impressed by our drunken antics though. We were a bit loud to say the least. And, with the benefit of hindsight, we were pushing our luck just a little.

When we finally spilled out onto the street, a large gang of around a hundred mean-looking youths was heading in our direction. As we stood motionless for a second or two, all manner of things raced through my mind - things like: "Oh shit - which way shall I run?" However, as they marched straight past us without even so much as a glance, it suddenly dawned upon me they were in fact Forest supporters. And, judging by the look on their faces, they were ready for battle. I was just glad they seemed to be heading away from the ground and in the opposite direction to us.

Surprisingly, although I'd visited most London grounds in the past - some of them many times - this was my first ever trip to Highbury. As we reached the turnstiles, I was intrigued by the fact that to gain access; we had to queue up outside a long row of old-fashioned terraced houses, behind which the Visitors' Enclosure in the Clock End was situated. Like most old grounds in this country, Highbury had been built smack in the middle of a residential area - one of the main reasons why they're now unable to re-develop the sight in line with their modern day requirements.

Although the game was an all-ticket affair, the volume of Forest's travelling support seemed to have taken the Metropolitan Police Force completely by surprise. They quickly had to re-define the area they'd cordoned off with ropes inside the Visitors' Enclosure, to cope with the surge of supporters trying to get into this part of the ground. There were around 6,000 who'd travelled down from the East Midlands, thousands of whom were packed into the Clock End. We were separated from the home fans by the customary six-foot high fence and a narrow strip of empty terracing.

Considering Arsenal are meant to be the footballing aristocrats of the South, I wasn't at all impressed by their stadium. The stands on either side were pre-historic in appearance, the Clock End simply an uncovered bank of terracing, not dissimilar to our own Bridgford End - although somewhat smaller - and the North Bank was, well, just another bank of terracing with a roof over the top. However, when the two teams took to the field, the atmosphere generated by the crowd of 38,617 was as good as any I'd experienced.

Amidst a loud chorus of: *"Nottingham, Nottingham, Nottingham,"* from the visiting hordes, I could hear quite distinctly away to my right, the sound of: *"Hello, Hello, Derbyshire Reds, Derbyshire Reds."* This prompted an even louder chorus of: *"Nottingham, Nottingham, Nottingham,"* from the majority of the travelling fans. I can only assume a large contingent from the Notts/Derbys border towns such as Ilkeston, Heanor, Ripley, Alfreton etc. had travelled down to London for this game and managed to congregate alongside one another on the terraces. There were certainly a couple of hundred of them and they kept us more than entertained throughout the game with their unique brand of humour. Still, I suppose they need a strong sense of humour, coming from Derbyshire!

By the end of a very disappointing night, Forest had deservedly lost 2-0, missed a second-half penalty, and gone out of the Cup without too much of a fight. I was now completely familiar with the 'Derbyshire Reds" full repertoire of songs though, each one proclaiming their allegiance to the Club. Their favourite, without a doubt, was:

> *When I was just a little boy,*
> *I asked my mother: What shall I be?*
> *Will I be Derby?*
> *Will I be Reds?*
> *Here's what she said to me:*
>
> *It's Forest-Forest,*
> *It's got to be Fo-o-rest,*
> *It's got to be Fo-o-rest,*
> *It's Forest, Forest!*

Just to round off a thoroughly miserable night; after the game there were some unsavoury incidents in the streets outside as rival Forest and Arsenal supporters clashed with one another. Apparently, the most serious incidents involved a 100-strong gang of supporters who'd travelled down from Nottingham on the service train - no doubt the same ugly looking mob we'd encountered before the game.

SO, we were now out of both domestic Cup competitions and had only a respectable League position to play for. When the 'Reds' lined up against Everton at the City Ground on Sunday, 25th January, for a live televised game, they were in fourth position in the table with 39 points from 24 games, 13 behind leaders Arsenal. Although a place in next season's UEFA Cup would, under normal circumstances, have been a realistic target, the blanket ban imposed on English clubs from competing in Europe still hadn't been lifted. A solitary Neil Webb effort against the 'Toffees' secured Forest three points in front of 17,009 people.

A total of six victories, six draws and six defeats in their final 18 games saw them eventually slip down to eighth position and once again finish the season empty-handed. The 1-0 defeat at home to Chelsea on Saturday, 28th February had also signalled the end of an unbeaten run of results at the City Ground stretching right back to 8th March 1986 and which included no less than 22 League and Cup games.

It was now seven years since we'd last lifted a trophy - the European Cup no less - although we'd threatened to do so on a number of occasions since. Despite this, some of the missing fans were slowly, but surely, returning to Trentside and to the game as a whole. At 19,090, the average home League attendance was 13.5% up on the previous season's 16,815. By the same token, at 19,839, the average League attendance on their travels was also 15.27% up on the previous season's 17,210. It had also been encouraging to see gates of 35,828 and 32,854 for the visits of Manchester United and Liverpool respectively. Perhaps the screening of live football on television - heavily criticised in some quarters - was actually taking the game to a wider audience and encouraging some of them back onto the terraces?

During the close season, Forest would be losing the services of Secretary Ken Smales, who'd announced his retirement after 29 years on the staff - 26 of them spent as Secretary. A former Yorkshire and Nottinghamshire County Cricketer, his experience in the job and dedication to the Club would be sorely missed. Clubs such as Forest would be unable to function effectively without the likes of Ken; his enthusiasm and loyalty an example to us all. Assistant Secretary, Paul White, had been pencilled in to succeed him - a very difficult task indeed.

SEASON 1986/87 – STATISTICS

FOOTBALL LEAGUE DIVISION ONE – FIXTURES

Date		Opposition	Venue	Competition	Score	Attendance
Aug	23	Everton	A	League	0-2	35,198
	27	**Charlton Athletic**	**H**	**League**	**4-0**	**12,970**
	30	**Watford**	**H**	**League**	**1-1**	**14,709**
Sept	2	West Ham United	A	League	2-1	21,305
	6	Southampton	A	League	3-1	14,604
	13	**Aston Villa**	**H**	**League**	**6-0**	**17,045**
	20	Chelsea	A	League	6-2	20,171
	24	Brighton & Hove Albion	A	LC 2 - 1st Leg	0-0	13,266
	27	**Arsenal**	**H**	**League**	**1-0**	**25,371**
Oct	**4**	**Manchester United**	**H**	**League**	**1-1**	**35,828**
	8	**Brighton & Hove Albion**	**H**	**LC 2 - 2nd Leg**	**3-0**	**16,036**
	11	Leicester City	A	League	1-3	18,402
	18	**Queens Park Rangers**	**H**	**League**	**1-0**	**17,199**
	25	Oxford United	A	League	1-2	10,219
	29	Crystal Palace	A	LC 3	2-2	12,020
Nov	**1**	**Sheffield Wednesday**	**H**	**League**	**3-2**	**23,303**
	5	**Crystal Palace**	**H**	**LC3 - Replay**	**1-0**	**13,029**
	8	Coventry City	A	League	0-1	16,089
	15	Luton Town	A	League	2-4	11,097
	19	Bradford City	A	LC 4	5-0	16,009
	22	**Wimbledon**	**H**	**League**	**3-2**	**15,575**
	29	Tottenham Hotspur	A	League	3-2	30,042
Dec	**6**	**Manchester City**	**H**	**League**	**2-0**	**19,129**
	13	Newcastle United	A	League	2-3	26,191
	20	**Southampton**	**H**	**League**	**0-0**	**15,394**
	26	Norwich City	A	League	1-2	22,131
	28	**Luton Town**	**H**	**League**	**2-2**	**20,273**
Jan	**1**	**Liverpool**	**H**	**League**	**1-1**	**32,854**
	3	Aston Villa	A	League	0-0	19,159
	11	Crystal Palace	A	FA Cup 3	0-1	11,618
	21	Arsenal	A	LC 5	0-2	38,617
	25	**Everton**	**H**	**League**	**1-0**	**17,009**
	31	Charlton Athletic	A	League	1-0	5,050
Feb	7	Watford	A	League	1-1	15,173
	14	**West Ham United**	**H**	**League**	**1-1**	**19,373**
	28	**Chelsea**	**H**	**League**	**0-1**	**18,317**
Mar	**7**	**Oxford United**	**H**	**League**	**2-0**	**12,298**
	14	Queens Park Rangers	A	League	1-3	11,896
	17	Arsenal	A	League	0-0	18,353
	22	**Leicester City**	**H**	**League**	**2-1**	**18,679**
	28	Manchester United	A	League	0-2	39,182
Apr	**4**	**Coventry City**	**H**	**League**	**0-0**	**13,507**
	14	Sheffield Wednesday	A	League	3-2	18,597
	18	Liverpool	A	League	0-3	37,359
	20	**Norwich City**	**H**	**League**	**1-1**	**14,446**
	25	Wimbledon	A	League	1-2	5,012
May	**2**	**Tottenham Hotspur**	**H**	**League**	**2-0**	**19,837**
	4	Manchester City	A	League	0-1	21,405
	9	**Newcastle United**	**H**	**League**	**2-1**	**17,788**

HOME ATTENDANCES

	AGGREGATE ATTENDANCE	HIGHEST ATTENDANCE	LOWEST ATTENDANCE	AVERAGE ATTENDANCE
League:	400,904	35,828	12,298	19,090
League Cup:	29,065	16,036	13,029	14,532
All Competitions:	429,969	35,828	12,298	18,694

FINAL LEAGUE TABLE - DIVISION ONE

Position	P	W	D	L	GF	GA	Pts
1. Everton	42	26	8	8	76	31	86
2. Liverpool	42	23	8	11	72	42	77
3. Tottenham Hotspur	42	21	8	13	68	43	71
4. Arsenal	42	20	10	12	58	35	70
5. Norwich City	42	17	17	8	53	51	68
6. Wimbledon	42	19	9	14	57	50	66
7. Luton Town	42	18	12	12	47	45	66
8. Nottingham Forest	**42**	**18**	**11**	**13**	**64**	**51**	**65**
9. Watford	42	18	9	15	67	54	63
10. Coventry City	42	17	12	13	50	45	63
11. Manchester United	42	14	14	14	52	45	56
12. Southampton	42	14	10	18	69	68	52
13. Sheffield Wednesday	42	13	13	16	58	59	52
14. Chelsea	42	13	13	16	53	64	52
15. West Ham United	42	14	10	18	52	67	52
16. Queens Park Rangers	42	13	11	18	48	64	50
17. Newcastle United	42	12	11	19	47	65	47
18. Oxford United	42	11	13	18	44	69	46
19. Charlton Athletic	42	11	11	20	45	55	44
20. Leicester City	42	11	9	22	54	76	42
21. Manchester City	42	8	15	19	36	57	39
22. Aston Villa	42	8	12	22	45	79	36

AWAY ATTENDANCES

	AGGREGATE ATTENDANCE	HIGHEST ATTENDANCE	LOWEST ATTENDANCE	AVERAGE ATTENDANCE
League:	416,635	39,182	5,012	19,839
League Cup:	79,912	38,617	12,020	19,978
FA Cup:	11,618	11,618	11,618	11,618
All Competitions:	508,165	39,182	5,012	19,544

"THERE'S A CIRCUS IN THE TOWN, IN THE TOWN"

DURING THE close season, Cloughie had given free transfers to two of the Club's most popular players, with Garry Birtles making the short trip across the River to join neighbours Notts County and Ian Bowyer becoming player-coach at Fourth Division Hereford United. Gary Mills also followed Birtles across the Trent and - rather disappointingly - Forest also lost the services of popular duo Johnny Metgod and Chris Fairclough, both of whom joined Tottenham Hotspur.

Rather than digging into the Club's ever expanding coffers to strengthen his now depleted numbers, Cloughie decided to rely mainly on his famous youth policy and promoted a cluster of promising youngsters into the first team set-up. Steve Chettle, Terry Wilson, Lee Glover and Phil Starbuck all joined Irish pair Garry Flemming and David Campbell, already firmly established in the first team squad. Twenty-four-year-old Tommy Gaynor was also purchased from Doncaster Rovers for a modest fee to bolster an attack now spearheaded by Nigel Clough and Paul Wilkinson.

Following the departure of Bowyer, Stuart Pearce had been appointed Club captain - a role he would fulfil with great distinction for many years. Cloughie's young pups would need all the encouragement and support Pearce's swashbuckling style could muster if they were to have any chance of surviving in the most demanding League in the world. However, if anyone was cut out to be a leader, it was 'Psycho' - already emerging as one of the most popular players of all time down at the City Ground.

THE 'Reds' began the season with a 2-1 victory away to Charlton Athletic on Saturday, 15th August. Cloughie's faith in his youngsters paid immediate dividends, with 17-year-old Glover scoring one of the goals on his League debut. The other came from Clough Junior who, at the ripe old age of 21, was almost a veteran. This was their first opening day victory since the 2-1 win at West Ham on 28th August 1982.

The first game at the City Ground on Wednesday, 19th August brought them a 1-0 victory over Watford and was followed by a 0-0 draw at home to Everton the following Saturday and a 1-0 victory over Newcastle at St.James's Park one week later. Their first defeat came in a seven-goal thriller at Chelsea on Saturday, 5th September, with Colin Foster, Neil Webb and Nigel Clough scoring Forest's goals. This was followed by their first home defeat of the season - 1-0 to Arsenal on Saturday, 12th September. During this game, they fielded their youngest ever team. When 18-year-old Terry Wilson came on as sub for David Campbell, the average age of the team was a mere 21 years and 364 days. And amazingly, when 18-year-old Steve Chettle came off the substitute's bench late on in the game to replace Lee Glover, the average age actually went back up again!

They bounced back immediately from these two setbacks by beating Coventry 3-0 at Highfield Road the following Saturday. Terry Wilson - making his full League debut - was amongst the scorers, with Franz Carr and Stuart Pearce (penalty) grabbing the others in front of a crowd of 17,519.

Ian Bowyer's Hereford United provided the opposition in the second round of the League Cup. And on the back of a 5-0 demolition in the first leg at the City Ground and a 1-1 draw in the second at Edgar Street, the 'Reds' progressed comfortably through to the third round, where they were drawn away to Manchester City. In the meantime, it was time for the 'Red Army' to renew some old acquaintances, with a long-awaited trip to the Baseball Ground to take on the recently-promoted 'Sheep'. This would be the first League meeting between the two clubs in almost eight years.

Although now living in Warrington, John Farley was still a regular on our away excursions and usually travelled down to Nottingham very early on a Saturday morning to meet up with us. Saturday, 10th October 1987 would be no exception and as usual, we'd made arrangements to meet in town early doors. A late train would transport us to the 'Sheep-dip'.

After a pint in most of our favourite haunts such as the Fountain, the Dog 'n Bear and the King John, we made our way down to the Bentinck Hotel just outside the station at around 12.30-p.m. Not surprisingly, it was packed to the rafters with lads, most of whom would also be making the short journey across the East Midlands by rail. All the same old 'we hate Derby' songs were pouring out and, as usual, everyone joined in with great enthusiasm. As ever, some 'clever dick' had come up with another, more topical anthem, bringing Nottingham's hatred of their neighbours right up to date. With reference to the 'Sheep's' current management, it went:

CHAPTER 22

There's a circus in the town,
IN-THE-TOWN,
Robert Maxwell is a clown,
IS-A-CLOWN;

An' Arthur Cox,
'as got the fuckin' pox,
An' Derby County's gooin' down,
GOOIN-DOWN!

We finally spilled out of the Bentinck at around 2.00-p.m. and soon we were heading for 'Sheep' territory. Although there'd been about a hundred or more inside the pub, there were at least three hundred travelling supporters on board our train. The small percentage of passengers who weren't going to the game and were just unfortunate enough to be on this train, appeared horrified by having to share their relatively short journey with scores of tanked up football supporters - and understandably so! However, as usual the majority of the 'Red & White Army' were loud, humorous, but most importantly, well-behaved.

As I gazed around the carriage, one thing in particular did occur to me - virtually every one of us was aged around thirty or over. I remember later speaking to one of the lads from Beeston, Pete Harrison, who unbeknown to me was also on this train and was amused when he remarked he'd travelled to Derby on the 'over 30s special'. Other than plenty of singing and chanting during the twenty-minute journey, the nearest thing to bad behaviour I observed, was when someone pulled the communications cord and the train screeched to a halt about two hundred yards short of Derby Station.

This led to a mass exodus from the carriages and confusion amongst the scores of police waiting on the station platform to escort us to the ground. As everyone poured through a side exit and out of the station, there was a wonderful sensation of 'getting one over' on the boys in blue - something which most essentially law-abiding football supporters of my generation will appreciate. We've had to endure decades of shoddy treatment at their hands, for no other reason than being young (well, once upon a time anyway), working-class, males who's only crime is that we prefer to spend our Saturday afternoons following our football team around the country, rather than being dragged around some God-forsaken shopping centre by the misses!

I find it ironic though, whilst travelling up and down the country by train in my suit and tie, going about my work, I've had absolutely no hassle whatsoever from aggressive police officers in railway stations. Not once has one of them come up to me, prodded me in the back and muttered those immortal words: ''Ere sonny, get over there and wait in line with the rest of the scum and if you give me any back-chat you're nicked!'' Not that the police could in any way be accused of stereotyping particular groups of people of course, especially young male football supporters.

Thankfully, there was very little trouble in Derby that day, although as usual, after ninety minutes of piss-taking we came away with maximum points, thanks to a Paul Wilkinson effort in front of no less than 22,394 people. (See Chapter 20: ''Let's all laugh at Derby!'') There was only one thing we could do of course after such an enjoyable and satisfying result - one which consolidated our fifth position in the First Division table compared with the 'Sheep's' thirteenth - and that was to get back to God's County as fast as possible and do some celebrating.

FOREST'S form throughout the months of October, November and December was excellent - apart from, a 3-0 League Cup defeat against Manchester City at Maine Road on 27th October. During this period, out of eleven games, they won eight, drew two and lost only one. They also scored no less than 29 goals, whilst conceding only seven. Some of their more notable victories within this impressive sequence of results were: 3-0 at home to both Sheffield Wednesday and Tottenham; 5-0 against Portsmouth and 4-0 against QPR - both also on Trentside; a 2-2 draw against Man U at Old Trafford; and a rare victory over Arsenal at Highbury on Boxing Day - this time by two-goals-to-nil.

The final game of 1987 resulted in an excellent 4-1 success over Coventry City in front of a City Ground crowd of 31,061 on Monday, 28th December. An own goal, two strikes from Tommy Gaynor and another from Terry Wilson, consolidated Forest's impressive third position in the table as they entered the New Year, having accumulated a total of 37 points from 18 games. However, with only one game in hand, they were a massive 10 points behind leaders Liverpool and three points behind second-placed Arsenal.

Surprisingly, the New Year didn't start too well. They lost 2-0 at home to Newcastle on New Year's Day in front of another sizeable City Ground crowd of 28,534, and then 1-0 to Everton at Goodison Park two days later. A third round FA Cup trip to Fourth Division Halifax Town gave the players the perfect chance to rediscover their winning ways and we supporters the opportunity of putting our relatively comfortable City Ground lives into their true perspective.

I was very fortunate to have got hold of one of the 1,380 tickets allocated to Forest for this trip to the Shay on Saturday, 9th January 1988. This allocation consisted of 1,000 terrace tickets and only 380 for the seats. As the Shay was on almost everyone's 'not yet visited' list, there was quite a scramble down at the ticket office once they went on sale. Bucko, Bodge, Big Lee, Tiff, John Farley and myself all managed to get there early enough however, and were soon making our arrangements for a day out in sunny Halifax.

The ground capacity at the time was a mere 4,000, and although by this time I'd already visited over 60 League grounds during my many years as a 'Red', this particular experience provided me with my biggest culture shock to date. Although quite a sizeable stadium, the majority of it - for safety reasons - was out of bounds to spectators. Apart from one moderately-sized stand on the far side of the ground where the majority of the seats were, there was a 'bus-shelter-come-stand' on the opposite side, and the 'terracing' at our end was nothing more than a steep grassy bank - and a very muddy one at that. The fact it was also a very cold, damp and grey winter's day, only added to the general misery and discomfort.

Whilst not wishing to denigrate the supporters of Halifax Town or indeed the good people of this pleasant West Yorkshire town, it really was like stepping back into the dark ages and made you realise just how lucky you were to have been born and bred in good old Nottingham and to have had the opportunity of following the 'Reds'. The comfortable 4-0 victory, courtesy of goals from Terry Wilson, Stuart Pearce, Calvin Plummer (back at the Club after a six-month loan spell with Finnish side Lahden Reipas) and Paul Wilkinson, not only put us through to the fourth round, but also put us back on the winning trail again.

Having already been drawn away to Man City in the League Cup, Halifax in the FA Cup and Reading in the Simod Cup, all in quick succession, we once again came out of the hat second when the draw for the fourth round of the FA Cup was made. This time we'd be heading to East London to take on Leyton Orient on Saturday, 30th January.

We'd long since lost touch with the 'Bus from the Sal' and had for some time been travelling to away matches under our own steam. Sometimes this would be by car; sometimes we'd hire a minibus; and quite often we'd simply jump on a service train. Forest's 6,000-ticket allocation for the tie at Brisbane Road had caused a groundswell of interest in Nottingham, even amongst the generally apathetic population of Chilwell and Beeston. Having got our heads together, Big Lee and I decided to take some positive action and organise our own coach for the game.

Lee was a good friend of Joe, who worked in the ticket office at Bartons in Chilwell and he managed to sort out a coach for us at a reasonable cost. Steve Jarman, another acquaintance of Lee's - and a sound lad - was a driver for Bartons and Joe also managed to wangle it for Steve to be our driver for the day. Basically, this meant we'd get away with anything we wanted.

Lee and I put the word about in the pubs around Beeston and Chilwell and very soon our respective phones were ringing like crazy and people we'd never even heard of were booking ''missen an' three o' mi mates'' onto the coach. By the end of the week, it was obvious things were getting a bit overcrowded, so Lee got back in touch with Joe and coach number two was put on standby. There'd also been a fair amount of interest amongst our friends in Stabbo, so we decided that following our first pick up at the Cricks in Beeston, we'd make another stop at the Man of Iron in Stabbo. Despite our prompting, they were a little vague as to how many seats they'd actually be requiring on the day.

The two coaches were due to depart at 9.00-a.m. on the morning of the game, and by 9.15, we'd already come to appreciate just what a frustrating and thankless task organising football coaches can be. With two 53-seaters to fill, there was an alarming number of people who it seemed just simply couldn't be bothered to get their fat, lazy arses out of bed. Consequently, there were only around 60 of us spread across the two coaches when we finally gave up waiting for any more last-minute stragglers and headed out of Beeston at 9.20-a.m. At best, we were anticipating around 15 to 20 getting on in Stabbo, so it was already looking like an expensive day out.

By 9.30, we were trundling through Stabbo heading towards the Man of Iron. As we pulled around the corner of Ilkeston Road onto Pasture Road, we were staggered to find an absolute mob of youths waiting for us outside the pub. Having already completed a headcount before our arrival, Big Glenn reliably informed us there were indeed 67 of them! This meant we'd got only 106 seats and a total of 127 passengers - many of these weighing in at 15 stone-plus. At six-foot two and around 15 stone, Big Glenn was no shrimp himself, not to mention his pal Marshy who weighed in at around 16 stone. However, the 20-odd stone Ba-Ba who'd belatedly decided to make a rare appearance at an away match, positively dwarfed these two.

Anyway, we managed somehow to cram everyone on board and were soon on the M1 heading south to London. This turned out to be a very lively journey with loads of banter flying around between the 'Stabbo Reds' and their Beeston and Chilwell counterparts. And of course, copious amounts of alcohol were being consumed. Up until this point in time, I'd always had this misguided notion that when it came to drinking, I was 'one of the lads'. I had of course never enjoyed the dubious distinction of an 'all-dayer' with 'the boys from Stabbo'. I realised from that moment on I really was only 'second division' by comparison.

Having demolished several crates of beer on the 120-mile trip south, they were itching to get into the pub, the second we pulled off the motorway. It was our intention though, to make our way towards the East End and indulge ourselves as near to Orient's Brisbane Road ground as possible. When we finally reached our destination, we found the place already teaming with travelling 'Reds'. Virtually every pub in the vicinity was packed to the rafters.

This turned out to be one of the best pre-match sessions I'd ever experienced. All the regular crew were there, including Big Lee, Bucko, Bodge, Tiff, Jacko, Andy Oakley etc., not to mention many other faces from both past and present. As on all such occasions, there was an abundance of pranksters and jokers amongst us. And in the form of Hoggy from Beeston, one of the 'Three Tenors'. Hoggy has always been a frustrated pop star, come cabaret artist, come opera singer, come comedian, come all-round entertainer. His party piece on many of our more high-profile away excursions was to serenade the whole pub - and anyone else within a five-mile radius - with his unique version of Pavarotti's Nessun Dorma.

He was in sparkling form on this occasion, treating everyone to his full repertoire of songs in each of the half-dozen pubs we visited. *"Hoggy, Hoggy, Give us a song, Hoggy, Give us a song!"* was the cry as soon as we converged on each pub - well as soon as we'd got the beers in anyway. And on each occasion, he immediately obliged with Nessun Dorma, followed by one of his many ballads, always directed towards the nearest unsuspecting and completely embarrassed young couple out trying to enjoy a lunchtime drink in their local. Egged on as he was by a loud chorus of: *"Hoggy! Hoggy! Hoggy!"* he'd stand on the nearest table and bellow out one song after another whilst we all fell about laughing - as did most of the locals.

As soon as we were ready to move onto the next pub, we'd drown him out with a chorus of: *"We're on the march with Cloughie's army,"* and head en-masse for the nearest exit. Unfortunately, he always managed to catch up with us somehow, despite trying our hardest to lose him.

It was around three minutes to kick off when we finally emerged, somewhat reluctantly, from the last pub (the game almost seems to get in the way on such occasions) and trooped off in the direction of the ground. The pub across the road emptied itself simultaneously and within seconds, there were around two hundred high-spirited youths marching briskly down the road. There wasn't a hint of trouble in the air though.

Perhaps fearing the worst, the Metropolitan Police Force were almost immediately upon us in numbers and we were quickly and aggressively shepherded to one side of the street. We found ourselves completely surrounded by dozens of police officers. Their attitude was extremely provocative, completely uncalled for, but sadly, very typical. What's more, anyone displaying the slightest hint of petulance or resistance towards their aggressive manner, was bundled into the back of a van and whisked away to spend the afternoon cooling off in a cell. It is on occasions such as these, when it isn't altogether impossible to imagine just what life in a 'Police State' would really be like. You also begin to question just why you bother going to football matches in the first place?

By the time we finally arrived at the ground, the game had already begun and our numbers had been severely depleted, thanks to the over-zealousness of the police. In addition to this, Kev Shakespeare had had the right sleeve of his expensive leather jacket half-severed by an out-of-control police dog, after remonstrating over the arrest of his younger brother Dave - for reasons known only to the two officers concerned. He was later charged with 'Speaking with an East Midlands accent', an offence which apparently carries a maximum of ten years in prison down in the South of England!

With a crowd of 19,212 packed tightly into Orient's neat little stadium, we managed to find our places at the back of the open terracing only after a great deal of pushing and shoving on our part. Such is the appeal of the FA Cup; the stand was packed from one end to the other with travelling supporters. What's more, whenever the 'Reds' are in London, their support is always bolstered by a large southern-based contingent. Whether these supporters are exiled 'Nottinghamians' or throwbacks to our Championship and European Cup winning era, or a combination of the two, I'm not sure. One thing is for certain; their support is both substantial and greatly appreciated.

A disappointing first-half performance from Forest, saw them struggling against a lively and determined Orient side, and for long periods of the game, another unlikely result looked on the cards - especially when the 'Os' took an unexpected lead. However, attacking the goal behind which the majority of their supporters were gathered, second- half efforts from Lee Glover and Calvin Plummer put the 'Reds' through to the fifth round - their late rally captured on Match of the Day. There's nothing more satisfying than knowing your team are about to be seen scoring two goals away from home by a large TV audience, with 6,000 ecstatic travelling fans going berserk in the background.

Having applauded our heroes from the pitch at the end, we poured out of the ground knowing we'd got a very important stop to make before leaving for home. We headed straight down the local 'nick' to pick up some of our absent friends. Although thankfully it has never happened to me during my lifetime, I can only imagine the sheer frustration of being arrested on some trumped-up charge by a less than honest copper, is only compounded by having to then make your way home alone from whatever God-forsaken town or city you're stranded in - and very often in the middle of the night. At least we managed to spare these poor souls this experience. It also gave Shakey an early opportunity to seek compensation for his mutilated jacket. He did beat a rather hasty retreat though, when the Duty Sergeant told him in no uncertain terms if he didn't ''piss off - and sharpish,'' he'd be joining the rest of his cronies in the cells for a couple of hours!

FOLLOWING their FA Cup victory in East London, Forest returned south three days later to take on Reading in the Simod Cup. And although Webby grabbed a goal against his former club, the 'Reds' were defeated by two-goals-to-one and were left to focus their attentions on an FA Cup fifth round tie against Birmingham City. Yet again they'd been drawn away, with the game scheduled for Saturday, 20th February.

For the time being, they were back in League action again - they were still in a healthy second position in the table - and duly disposed of Chelsea 3-2 at the City Ground on Saturday, 6th February. Goals from Colin Foster, Nigel Clough (penalty) and Gary Crosby - signed from Non-League Grantham Town in December on the recommendation of manager Martin O'Neill - earned them a vital three points in front of a crowd of 18,203. This was followed one week later by a 1-1 draw at Southampton, where Clough Junior was once again on the score-sheet.

So successful had our excursion to Orient been, we decided that 'Broughton & Hanna's Tours' would once again be on the road for the tie at Birmingham. Furthermore, our generous allocation of 12,000 tickets meant, with an abundance in circulation, we'd need not two, but three coaches this time around. We also came to the conclusion that due to the large number of supporters who'd be invading the pubs of Birmingham that day, we'd indulge ourselves in Beeston instead and arranged for the coaches to leave the Cricks at 1.30-p.m. This way, we were all guaranteed a drink before the game in what would be a trouble-free environment.

We arranged to meet in the Star on Middle Street at opening time and, not surprisingly, by 10.45-a.m., the place was almost bursting at the seams. Having enjoyed the first trip so much, the Stabbo boys had immediately pencilled themselves in for this one and by 11.00-a.m. were already in town. The hostelries of Beeston hadn't enjoyed a Saturday lunchtime like this in ages, as hordes of thirsty youths descended upon them like locusts.

By around midday, the majority of us were making our way to the Cricks, where we hoped to get another couple down us before setting off for Brum. By 12.30, I was becoming quite concerned by the sheer numbers converging on the pub, all of whom were obviously heading for the game. We had three 53-seaters waiting outside, but by this time, there were at least 200 youths packed inside. Having already been on the pop for the last two hours, spirits were riding high and the lounge resembled the middle pen of the Trent End. Every football anthem known to mankind was ringing out from the dancing, swaying choir. As usual, I was trying in vain to get everyone singing the first verse of 'Forest Ever Forest', but met with the usual sea of blank faces.

By 1.00-p.m. the local constabulary - obviously concerned Beeston's usual Saturday afternoon tranquillity was in danger of being seriously disrupted - decided to move in and send us on our way to the West Midlands. They ordered us to finish off our drinks and herded us onto the coaches. They seemed to care little about the serious overcrowding and gave us a motorcycle escort all the way down the A52 and out of Nottingham. This is probably the first time ever a group of football supporters have been thrown out of their own town by the police.

We'd no sooner got onto the A38 at Derby than the inevitable cries of: ''*Stop the bus, I want a wee-wee,*'' rang out from the back of the coach. Being a sympathetic soul, Steve Jarman willingly obliged and within seconds, 60 seriously tanked-up youths were lined up alongside the coach, unashamedly relieving themselves on the grass verge.

By the time we reached Burton upon Trent, we were making stop number two and once again the grass verge was under invasion. However, before we'd clambered back on board, a couple of outraged motorists - shocked and horrified by what they'd seen - had already reported us to the Staffordshire Police. A 'jam-sandwich' came roaring up behind us a couple of miles up the road; it's blue lights on and headlights flashing like crazy. Having read the riot act to Steve Jarman, they waved us on our way and we continued our eventful journey across the Midlands.

About three miles from St.Andrews we were met by more motorcycle police, who escorted us swiftly towards the stadium. We were led onto a huge coach park just outside where we parked up alongside scores of other coaches from Nottingham. There were thousands of Forest supporters making their way to the ground and soon we were hearing stories of all the skirmishes which had been taking place during the course of the day. I for one was relieved we'd stayed in Beeston and managed to avoid the trouble. There were however a number of minor scuffles as we made our way towards our end of the ground.

We'd been allocated the entire Tilton Road End - a massive bank of steep, covered terracing. Those with seat tickets however, had been given the upper tier of the Railway Stand at the opposite end and were surrounded by home supporters. From what I heard later, not only did they have to endure a torrent of abuse throughout the game, but they also had to run the gauntlet in the streets outside afterwards.

On the field, the game was by no means a classic, but a solid performance from the 'Reds' saw them through to the quarter-finals, thanks to a solitary first-half effort from 'Bing' Crosby. In a game where chances were few and far between, Nigel Clough nearly wrapped things up for Forest with a spectacular second-half volley which flew just inches over the bar. The travelling hordes were in buoyant mood as they spilled out of the ground, having applauded their heroes from the pitch. However, whilst we'd been celebrating inside the stadium, the streets outside had been filling up with Birmingham fans spoiling for a fight. Consequently, there were some ugly incidents on the way back to the coaches and the police really had their work cut out trying to keep the warring factions apart.

Eventually we arrived back at the coach park relatively unscathed and after what seemed an eternity, the police were ready to escort the seemingly endless convoy of coaches out of the city and back onto the A38. About half an hour later, as we hurtled along the dual carriageway at 80 miles per hour, John Smith - a Notts fan from Beeston - came bounding up to the front of the bus pleading with Steve Jarman to pull over as he was 'dying for a crap'. Although it was dark by this time and we would have been less conspicuous than we were on the way over to Birmingham earlier on in the day; following our little brush with the law, Steve was reluctant to pull over - despite Smithy's desperate pleas.

I was sitting right at the front of the bus chatting to Steve and jokingly suggested he should let the poor lad do his business out of the door. Amazingly, both of them seemed to think this was a cracking idea. Seconds later, Smithy was clinging tightly to the rail at the front of the bus with his clouts round his ankles and his bare arse sticking out of the door. I couldn't believe my eyes and just sat there open-mouthed. Everyone was falling about all over the place laughing hysterically. A perfect end to a perfect day...I suppose?

ALMOST inevitably, we came out of the hat second again when the draw for the quarter-finals was made. However, Arsenal at Highbury and a massive 14,000-ticket allocation, was a dream tie for us. Once again Big Lee was on the phone to Joe and this time we ordered four coaches. This was going to take some organising, but we had to get right on with it as the game was scheduled for Saturday, 12th March - just three short weeks away. We had absolutely no time to waste.

Despite the fact our allocation was quickly snapped up, there was an abundance of tickets in circulation around the pubs and clubs of Nottingham. In fact, anyone who wanted to get to the game badly enough, could lay their hands on one, or at least 'knew a man who could'. Consequently, almost everyone from Beeston and Chilwell who'd got the faintest interest in Forest wanted to travel on our coaches and within no time at all, we'd filled all four of them to capacity.

A 9.30-a.m. start at the Cricks would be followed by further pick-ups at the Charlton Arms in Chilwell and the Pavillion in Stabbo. All four coaches were chock-a-block by the time we left Nottingham at around 10.00-a.m. and joined the M1 Motorway. Because of the expected volume of traffic along the way, the plan was we'd head straight for London and then play it by ear.

As feared, the traffic was very heavy and very slow moving all the way. We were hitting one snarl-up after another. We'd only just reached Newport Pagnell by 11.30-a.m. and were still only half-way to London. The four coaches pulled up alongside one another at the Services and all four drivers buggered off for their free breakfast. We were soon back on the coaches, but had to wait an eternity whilst they sat in the restaurant leisurely stuffing their faces.

They seemed determined to make us wait and everyone was getting agitated, fearing we wouldn't even get to the Capital in time for a drink. For a laugh, one of the lads on the coach next to ours decided to take to the wheel himself and started mucking around with the controls. When he started the engine up, Mark Hemmingsley - or 'Ironhead' as he is otherwise known - just happened to be taking a walk along the roof of the coach, having clambered through an open skylight from inside.

Believing the driver had returned and that the coach was about to set off with him perched on top, he launched himself to the tarmac below. He hit the ground with an almighty thud and it was obvious he'd landed awkwardly. With his reputation at stake though, he simply jumped to his feet and clambered back on board, trying his best to convince everyone he was OK.

He'd been given his nickname by none other than Garry Birtles, during a Cadland Golf Society tournament at Ruddington Golf Course. Every year, a coach-load of regulars would head for Ruddington, half of them to play and the other half to act as caddies. At the end of the day, we'd all have a meal and a few drinks in the Clubhouse and then head back to the Cad for the rest of the evening.

On one particular occasion, Mark was acting as caddie and standing just yards away from Garry as he teed off at the first hole. As it was his first shot of the day, his aim was slightly askew and unfortunately he succeeded only in scoring a direct hit to the side of Mark's head. The ball ricocheted off him and flew into the rough about fifty yards away. Although you'd reasonably have expected him to be laid out unconscious by the sheer force of the blow, to the contrary, he never even batted an eye-lid. There and then, he was christened 'Ironhead' by Garry and the name has stayed with him ever since.

It was gone 12 o'clock by the time the drivers returned and not surprisingly they received a hail of abuse from their angry and frustrated passengers. However, we were soon back on the Motorway and back into the traffic jams. Not until after 1.00 o'clock did we get off the M1 and onto the North Circular. What we hadn't reckoned on though, was even worse congestion in North London. For some reason the Capital was almost at a standstill that day.

Consequently, we endured a further hour or more before we got within a couple of miles of Highbury. Wisely as it turned out, most of the Stabbo lads had jumped ship early on and headed for the nearest pub. The rest of us took a chance on getting a late drink nearer to the ground, although this was looking more and more unlikely as each minute ticked by. We were kept amused though by Ironhead, who was sitting right at the back of the coach in front of us, baring his enormous fat arse to the whole population of North London and generally acting like the complete head-case we know him to be. If indeed he had injured himself during his earlier fall from grace; he was certainly showing no signs of it at this point in the day.

Disappointingly, it was around 2.45-p.m. before we finally arrived at the stadium - five and a quarter hours after setting off. This was going to be the first time I'd seen a Forest match completely stone-cold sober for a long, long time. As we made our way towards the Clock End, we were confronted by the meanest looking bunch of youths I'd ever seen at a football match. Just as I was about to turn and walk the other way, I realised they were in fact Forest supporters. They looked as if they'd got things other than football on their minds and as they trooped by, I noticed the infamous Paul Scarrott amongst them, not to mention many old faces I recognised from Newark. I don't know what it is about Arsenal away, but it seems to attract the majority of Nottingham's hardcore hooligans.

Once inside the ground, I was overwhelmed by the sheer numbers who'd made the journey south from Nottingham. More than half the Clock End was occupied by Forest supporters, plus the whole lower tier of the West Stand. What's more, with a total of 51,570 inside the stadium, the atmosphere was fantastic. And it has to be said; Forest's travelling supporters were more than playing their part.

Despite a strong start from the 'Gunners', who came close to scoring on several occasions, it soon became apparent that Forest weren't there merely to make up the numbers. And when Paul Wilkinson thundered home an unstoppable twenty-five-yard pile-driver midway through the first half, the 14,000-strong army from Nottingham went barmy. As the game progressed, Forest's dominance grew and grew, and although we'd not reached the semi-final stages of this competition since those wonderful days back in the 66/67 season, it was beginning to look more than a distinct possibility.

During the half-time interval, I spotted the rather forlorn looking figure of Ironhead limping heavily along the running track at the side of the pitch. The steadying arm of a St.John's Ambulanceman was around his shoulder. Obviously in great pain, he was being led slowly and deliberately in the direction of the first-aid block.

When the game restarted, Forest were attacking the goal behind which we were gathered. Roared on by the massive following, they continued to dictate the pattern of play. When Brian Rice was put clean through, with only keeper Lukic to beat, an enormous roar of anticipation welled up from the middle of the terraces. Ricey kept his cool right up to the last second and although it looked for a moment as though his shot had been blocked, the ball looped up into the air and dropped agonisingly behind Lukic and into the back of the net.

We spent the rest of the game jumping up and down - apart from the last three minutes that is, after David Rocastle's late effort caused a few anxious moments - and, as we poured out of Highbury at the end, were ready to do some serious celebrating. We hadn't managed even a pint before the game, so our first port of call on the way home was gonna be the 'beer-off'. We were planning to invade the first one we came across once we were safely back on the North Circular Road.

Half an hour later, we were loading the coach up with as much beer as we could carry. We stood at the side of the road showing off our bounty to the endless stream of coaches and minibuses which passed us by. Having endured an alcohol-free day so far, we were all absolutely gagging and determined to make up for it in a big way - and were planning to carry on the party once we arrived back in Nottingham.

Once again, everyone agreed that 'Broughton & Hanna's Tours' had been a resounding success, and Lee and myself were already taking bookings for the semi-final. As for poor old Ironhead, following his trip to the QMC the following morning, his 'broken ankle' was put into plaster after surgery and he spent the next three months off work recuperating. He could definitely be counted out of the trip to Hillsborough on Saturday, 9th April, where we'd be taking on our old adversaries Liverpool.

FOR the time being, we had to turn our attentions to the League programme and the six games we'd got to negotiate prior to the semi-finals. Although our chances of winning the title were now non-existent - especially as we were twenty-odd points behind leaders Liverpool with only eleven games remaining - we were however still sitting in a creditable fourth position. We were six points behind second-placed Manchester United and due to play them at the City Ground on Saturday, 19th March. Ironically, we were also scheduled to play Liverpool at home on April 2nd - the Saturday before the semi-final.

Forest's impressive form continued and they won three and drew two of the aforementioned games. The victories all came at the City Ground and included a 2-1 success over the 'Sheep', a 1-0 victory over Portsmouth and a confidence boosting 2-1 win over - would you believe - Liverpool. All we needed now was a repeat performance a week later and we'd be on our way to the FA Cup Final for the first time in 29 years.

We were planning to take at least four coaches to Sheffield, but were flabbergasted to learn from Joe that suddenly Bartons weren't prepared to do business with us. Apparently, whilst we'd been loading up with alcohol on the North Circular on the way back from Arsenal - a strictly illegal activity by this time, thanks to Mrs Thatcher and her hatred of football supporters - some miserable Forest Official on a passing coach had clocked us spilling out of the off-licence with arms full of beer. He'd subsequently lodged a formal complaint with Bartons through the Club, throwing our travel arrangements into dissaray. What a thoroughly sad individual he must have been!

Oh well...Barton's loss was someone else's gain we decided, philosophically, and quickly turned our attentions to Skills Coaches. And they turned out to be most obliging. Four coaches laid on without the slightest hitch and all scheduled to pick up first at the Cricks and then onto the usual stopping off points at the Charlton Arms and the Pavilion.

Due to the significance of this game, we decided we'd get ourselves into Sheffield as early as possible on the day. We wanted to be within spitting distance of the ground when we spilled out of the pub just before kick off. Consequently, by 10.30 in the morning, we were already on the M1 heading north. Although Sheffield is only a short distance away from Nottingham, with around 27,000 supporters making this journey, we didn't expect to arrive much before midday.

Surprisingly, we'd been given more tickets than Liverpool and had been allocated the massive Spion Kop End of the stadium. This caused a furore on Merseyside and understandably so. With their more substantial support, it was difficult on the face of it, to argue with them. However, as they would be approaching Sheffield from a north-westerly direction and ourselves from a south-easterly one, accommodating them in the North Stand and the Leppings Lane End and us within the Kop and the South Stand, made geographic sense if nothing else. The two sets of supporters would at least be well segregated outside the stadium - a major consideration, it has to be said.

As expected, the motorway was chock-a-block with coaches, minibuses, transit vans and cars transporting the 'Red & White Army' northwards. There was a real buzz around Nottingham for this match, as indeed there had been throughout the whole of this exciting Cup run. There was a strong feeling that, at last, 'Old Big Ead' might be getting his hands on the one piece of silverware which had eluded him so far throughout his illustrious career.

Having endured a ninety-minute crawl up the motorway, we finally pulled off at junction 31 at around midday. Although we'd received a directive from the police in advance not to exit the M1 until junction 32, we completely ignored this - as did many others. This was in the vain hope we'd avoid the inevitable congestion on the way to the ground. As so many other travelling supporters were of the same mind, there was a substantial queue of vehicles on the slip road in front of us and this stretched all the way up to the traffic island at the top.

Directly in front of us, was a dirty white transit van, with Forest scarves hanging out of it's windows. There were no windows at all in the back - and probably no seats either for that matter - it was quite obviously not intended for carrying passengers at all. As it reached the roundabout, the driver appeared to be losing patience and began revving his engine frantically, whilst waiting for a gap to appear in the traffic. Having picked his moment, he let the clutch out and the vehicle screeched off like a Formula 1 racing car. As it did, it's rear doors flew open and half a dozen youths, each one clutching a can of beer, came spilling out of the back, ending up in a heap in the middle of the road. Fortunately, they managed to avoid injury and were immediately back on their feet and scrambling back into the van. They did so to loud cheers from everyone on the bus. And the best thing about it was that between them, they didn't even spill a drop!

An hour later, we arrived at the ground and were directed to our designated parking area by the police. There were thousands of fans in the vicinity and every pub within a two-mile radius was bursting at the seams. After walking a couple of miles, we finally managed to get a drink at the 'Liverpool' end. The pub was filled evenly with both Forest and Liverpool supporters. Thankfully, there wasn't the slightest hint of trouble and we enjoyed a very pleasant ninety minutes before setting off for the game around 2.30-p.m.

When we finally reached our end of the stadium, we joined the long, but orderly queue of fans trying to get in before the teams came out onto the pitch. Along with 22,000 others, we'd bought terrace tickets for the Kop which, when full to it's capacity with swaying, singing fans, was an awesome sight. The remaining 5,000 from Nottingham were seated in the South Stand, away to our left. Having made it through the turnstiles with only minutes to spare, we made our way briskly up the steps leading into the centre of the stand. The noise inside the stadium was incredible.

Such was the vastness of the crowd; we found it virtually impossible to fight our way onto the huge bank of terracing. The whole crowd was swaying in one direction, then the other, and it was only after a massive surge forward that we seized our moment and forced our way into the middle. We gradually made our way up to the very back of the terracing, although it took us at least ten minutes. In the meantime, the two teams were led out onto the field by referee George Courtney and his two linesmen to a crescendo of noise.

As we stood there right at the back of the stand, the sight in front of us was absolutely incredible. At the other end of the stadium - the Leppings Lane End - the Liverpool fans were packed tightly along the terraces from one side of the stand to the other. There were 51,627 people inside Hillsborough by the time the game kicked off. And Forest - who were in their changed strip of white shirts, black shorts and red socks - were kicking towards the Leppings Lane End and the massed ranks of Liverpool supporters.

The contest got off to a lively start, with both teams immediately on the offensive. It was apparent that Cloughie's young starlets weren't going to be overawed by the occasion or intimidated by their more illustrious opponents. However, despite their early promise, Forest suffered the agony of a thirteenth-minute penalty, confidently despatched into the back of the net by John Aldridge. Then, roared on by their passionate army of fans, Liverpool began to dominate the game, pinning Forest back in their own half and putting Steve Sutton's goal under siege. He made one brilliant save from Peter Beardsley, which effectively kept Forest's hopes alive. This seemed to raise their confidence a little and by the end of the first half, they were clawing their way back into the game.

Attacking the Kop End during the second half, the Forest players seemed visibly lifted by the noise coming from this end of the stadium. They were at last beginning to exert some pressure on the Liverpool goal. First Nigel Clough went close with a header, which looped just over the bar, and this was quickly followed by a powerful header from Colin Foster, saved by goalkeeper Bruce Grobbelaar.

However, on 52 minutes, and with Forest seemingly on top, Liverpool broke away down the left wing and John Barnes' perfectly flighted cross was met by Aldridge. He came steaming in at the near post to put the 'Scousers' 2-0 up with an absolutely breathtaking right-foot volley. This ripped the heart out of Forest and soon Steve Sutton was at full stretch to keep out a fierce shot from the tigerish Beardsley. Had this gone in, it would certainly have put the game beyond Forest, but instead, Sutton's heroics gave them renewed hope and they surged forward once again.

After 68 minutes, they finally got the reward their spirited efforts deserved, with Nigel Clough forcing the ball over the line. Gary Crosby's long throw-in from the right was headed on by Paul Wilkinson, and when Grobbelaar and defender Alan Hansen got into a tangle trying to clear their lines, young Cloughie was there on the edge of the six-yard box to pounce. Roared on, they went in search of an equaliser - just as their predecessors had done on the same ground against Tottenham in 1967. Sadly however, just as in this game, time was against them and their late rally was all to no avail.

As I'd been too young to attend the Spurs game, I hadn't previously experienced the heartache of losing an FA Cup semi-final. It was without doubt, my saddest day as a Forest supporter and one I found difficult to come to terms with. As we trudged dejectedly out of Hillsborough, I was hoping like mad that we'd never suffer this fate again. There would be no partying in the pubs and clubs around Nottingham on this occasion.

SUCH are the ironies of football, when Forest turned their attentions back to the League the following Wednesday, their opposition was none other than Liverpool of course. And, whilst the semi-final had been a fairly close run contest, it wasn't the case this time around. Liverpool ran out easy 5-0 winners in front of an Anfield crowd of 39,535. With the exception of our halcyon days in the late 1970s, when we'd enjoyed some famous victories over them, we've always - at least during my lifetime anyway - been little more than whipping boys for the mighty Anfield machine. This emphatic score-line is by no means untypical in the long history of Liverpool versus Forest encounters.

When we lined up for the last game of the season against Luton Town at home on Sunday, 15th May, we were still in an incredible third position in the First Division table. Only Liverpool and Man U - undoubtedly the two biggest clubs in the land - had stood between us and another League Championship title. This was some achievement for a club the size of Forest and another example of the genius of manager Brian Clough. The biggest frustration to me though, is that in terms of population etc., Nottingham is simply unable to compete with the likes of Liverpool and Manchester and will never have the same pulling power as their respective clubs.

A 1-1 draw against the 'Hatters' confirmed Forest's final position of third. They'd won 20, drawn 13 and lost only 7 of their 40 League encounters. And, with a total of 67 goals scored - and only 39 conceded - they were also the third highest scorers, behind the two aforementioned clubs. Cloughie's exploits this season, had led to him being offered the Welsh National Team Manager's job - albeit on a part-time basis - but he was denied this opportunity by the Forest Board. This was probably the one and only time during his long reign at the Club that they actually stood up to him in any way, shape or form. It was the right decision however, as far as the Club were concerned.

Although we'd now gone exactly eight years without lifting a major trophy, we had won the G Mex Six-a-side Tournament in Manchester, and the Mercantile Credit Football League Centenary Event at Wembley during the course of the season. I couldn't help casting my mind back to the last time we'd won some apparently insignificant silverware - the Anglo-Scottish Cup back in season 1976/77 - and just what we had gone on to achieve immediately afterwards. What's more, Cloughie had also added strength to the squad this time around. Before the season was over, he signed midfielder Garry Parker from Hull City in a £250,000 deal. As far as I was concerned, the prospects for the future were once again looking pretty good.

The average home attendance in the League had also climbed a little this season to 19,264, with the highest being the 31,061 who'd turned out for the visit of Coventry City. However, promising as this may have been, I longed for the days once more, when crowds of 30,000-plus were the norm down at the City Ground.

SEASON 1987/88 – STATISTICS

FOOTBALL LEAGUE DIVISION ONE – FIXTURES

Date		Opposition	Venue	Competition	Score	Attendance
Aug	15	Charlton Athletic	A	League	2-1	6,021
	19	**Watford**	**H**	**League**	**1-0**	**14,527**
	22	**Everton**	**H**	**League**	**0-0**	**20,445**
	29	Newcastle United	A	League	1-0	20,111
Sept	2	**Southampton**	**H**	**League**	**3-3**	**14,173**
	5	Chelsea	A	League	3-4	18,414
	12	**Arsenal**	**H**	**League**	**0-1**	**18,490**
	19	Coventry City	A	League	3-0	17,519
	23	**Hereford United**	**H**	**LC 2 - 1st Leg**	**5-0**	**11,617**
	26	Norwich City	A	League	2-0	13,755
Oct	7	Hereford United	A	LC 2 - 2nd Leg	1-1	3,905
	10	Derby County	A	League	1-0	22,394
	17	**Sheffield Wednesday**	**H**	**League**	**3-0**	**17,685**
	24	**Tottenham Hotspur**	**H**	**League**	**3-0**	**23,543**
	27	Manchester City	A	LC 3	0-3	15,168
	31	Manchester United	A	League	2-2	44,669
Nov	14	**Portsmouth**	**H**	**League**	**5-0**	**15,851**
	21	West Ham United	A	League	2-3	17,216
Dec	5	Wimbledon	A	League	1-1	5,170
	13	**Queens Park Rangers**	**H**	**League**	**4-0**	**18,130**
	19	Oxford United	A	League	2-0	7,891
	26	Arsenal	A	League	2-0	31,211
	28	**Coventry City**	**H**	**League**	**4-1**	**31,061**
Jan	1	**Newcastle United**	**H**	**League**	**0-2**	**28,534**
	3	Everton	A	League	0-1	21,680
	9	Halifax Town	A	FA Cup 3	4-0	4,013
	16	**Charlton Athletic**	**H**	**League**	**2-2**	**15,363**
	23	Watford	A	League	0-0	13,158
	30	Leyton Orient	A	FA Cup 4	2-1	19,212
Feb	3	Reading	A	Simod Cup	1-2	9,096
	6	**Chelsea**	**H**	**League**	**3-2**	**18,203**
	13	Southampton	A	League	1-1	13,314
	20	Birmingham City	A	FA Cup 5	1-0	34,494
Mar	5	Sheffield Wednesday	A	League	1-0	19,509
	12	Arsenal	A	FA Cup 6	2-1	51,570
	16	Queens Park Rangers	A	League	1-2	8,316
	19	**Manchester United**	**H**	**League**	**0-0**	**27,598**
	26	Tottenham Hotspur	A	League	1-1	25,306
	30	**Derby County**	**H**	**League**	**2-1**	**25,017**
Apr	2	**Liverpool**	**H**	**League**	**2-1**	**29,188**
	4	Portsmouth	A	League	1-0	17,528
	9	Liverpool	N	FA Cup SF	1-2	51,627
		(Played at Hillsborough, Sheffield)				
	13	Liverpool	A	League	0-5	39,535
	20	**West Ham United**	**H**	**League**	**0-0**	**15,775**
	30	**Wimbledon**	**H**	**League**	**0-0**	**14,314**
May	4	**Norwich City**	**H**	**League**	**2-0**	**11,610**
	7	**Oxford United**	**H**	**League**	**5-3**	**12,762**
	13	Luton Town	A	League	1-1	9,018
	15	**Luton Town**	**H**	**League**	**1-1**	**13,016**

HOME ATTENDANCES

	AGGREGATE ATTENDANCE	HIGHEST ATTENDANCE	LOWEST ATTENDANCE	AVERAGE ATTENDANCE
League:	385,285	31,061	11,610	19,264
League Cup:	11,617	11,617	11,617	11,617
All Competitions:	396,902	31,061	11,610	18,900

FINAL LEAGUE TABLE - DIVISION ONE

Position	P	W	D	L	GF	GA	Pts
1. Liverpool	40	26	12	2	87	24	90
2. Manchester United	40	23	12	5	71	38	81
3. Nottingham Forest	**40**	**20**	**13**	**7**	**67**	**39**	**73**
4. Everton	40	19	13	8	53	27	70
5. Queens Park Rangers	40	19	10	11	48	38	67
6. Arsenal	40	18	12	10	58	39	66
7. Wimbledon	40	14	15	11	58	47	57
8. Newcastle United	40	14	14	12	55	53	56
9. Luton Town	40	14	11	15	57	58	53
10. Coventry City	40	13	14	13	46	53	53
11. Sheffield Wednesday	40	15	8	17	52	66	53
12. Southampton	40	12	14	14	49	53	50
13. Tottenham Hotspur	40	12	11	17	38	48	47
14. Norwich City	40	12	9	19	40	52	45
15. Derby County	40	10	13	17	35	45	43
16. West Ham United	40	9	15	16	40	52	42
17. Charlton Athletic	40	9	15	16	38	52	42
18. Chelsea	40	9	15	16	50	68	42
19. Portsmouth	40	7	14	19	36	66	35
20. Watford	40	7	11	22	27	51	32
21. Oxford United	40	6	13	21	44	80	31

AWAY ATTENDANCES

	AGGREGATE ATTENDANCE	HIGHEST ATTENDANCE	LOWEST ATTENDANCE	AVERAGE ATTENDANCE
League:	371,735	44,669	5,170	18,586
League Cup:	19,073	15,168	3,905	9,536
FA Cup:	160,916	51,627	4,013	32,183
Simod Cup:	9,096	9,096	9,096	9,096
All Competitions:	560,820	51,627	3,905	20,029

"AND NOW YER GONNA BELIEVE US, WE'RE GONNA WIN THE LOT!"

FOREST'S ACHIEVEMENTS during the previous campaign had led to a thirty per cent increase in season ticket sales during the close season. Meanwhile, the squad had been further strengthened by the acquisition of former City Ground favourite Steve Hodge from Spurs in a £550,000 deal, and the £120,000 signing of full-back Brian Laws from Middlesbrough. Surplus to requirements, Paul Wilkinson had been sold to Watford for a fee of £300,000 and popular goalkeeper Hans Segers had moved onto Wimbledon.

The season began in less than convincing fashion with a 2-1 defeat away to Norwich on Saturday, 27th August. This was followed two days later by a 4-1 Merseyside thrashing at the hands of Liverpool in the Mercantile Credit Trophy. And incredibly, the next four League games all ended 1-1. These were the home fixtures against Sheffield Wednesday and Derby County, and the away games at Everton and Aston Villa. Not a very auspicious start to the season overall.

A visit to Nottingham by Third Division Chester City in the first leg of the League Cup second round on Wednesday, 28th September gave them the chance to get their shooting boots on. And this they did in style, as goals from Pearce, Clough (2), Webb, Hodge and Gaynor gave them an overwhelming 6-0 victory. If only they'd saved one for the following Saturday's 0-0 stalemate with Luton at the City Ground?

Their first League victory came one week later with a 2-1 success over QPR at Loftus Road. A Nigel Clough penalty and a Colin Foster thunderbolt helped them plunder all three points. An emphatic 4-0 victory then followed at Chester in midweek, where a Gary Crosby strike and a Tommy Gaynor hat-trick, saw them through to the next round - the aggregate score being a whopping 10-0.

Cloughie had already made up his mind the attack needed strengthening and moved to bring in striker Lee Chapman from French First Division side Niort for a fee of £290,000. The 28-year-old ex-Stoke City, Arsenal, Sunderland and Sheffield Wednesday striker had been the subject of a close season bid, but opted for a 'more lucrative' move into French football. However, after Niort's financial promises failed to materialise, he was itching to return to England and delighted to be joining Forest, ahead of a whole host of clubs vying for his signature.

Meanwhile, the Club's return to prominence of late hadn't gone un-noticed by England manager Bobby Robson, who drafted no less than four Forest players into his squad for the game against Denmark at Wembley in September. Steve Hodge, Neil Webb, Stuart Pearce and Des Walker all figured in this game. This was beginning to look like the old days once again. All we needed now was some silverware just to confirm we really were back in the big time.

Chapman made his debut in the 2-2 draw at Millwall on Saturday, 22nd October. Despite building up a comfortable 2-0 lead, thanks to goals from 'Harry' Hodge, the 'Reds' let things slip from their grasp and ended up conceding a late equaliser to Teddy Sheringham. Four days later, a City Ground crowd of 29,755 was treated to a 2-1 victory over Liverpool and saw 19-year-old Mark Crossley making his debut in goal. Brian Rice's second-half effort was cancelled out by Ian Rush, only for Forest to storm up-field from the kick off and regain the lead straight away with a Neil Webb pile-driver from the edge of the box. What's more, had keeper Mike Hooper not turned Nigel Clough's 71st minute penalty onto a post, the victory would have been even more emphatic.

Lee Chapman scored his first goal for the Club during the 1-0 victory over Newcastle at St.James's Park on Saturday, 29th October. This win moved them up to fifth position in the table, having accumulated 15 points from 10 games. Four days later, Coventry visited the City Ground for a third round League Cup encounter - a game which saw Gary Charles making his senior debut at the tender age of 18. Goals from Foster, Hodge and Clough gave Forest the edge in a five-goal thriller in front of 21,301 people.

The forthcoming home League fixture against second-placed Arsenal was switched to Sunday, 6th November, to accommodate the television cameras. The switch did nothing for Forest's rhythm and they suffered the indignation of a 4-1 hammering in front of a watching audience of millions. Despite gaining an early first-half lead, thanks to Nigel Clough's alertness in the box, the 'Gunners' went on to rip them apart with a powerful display of counter-attacking football, reminiscent of Cloughie's own Championship winning team of the 1977/78 season.

Following a 3-3 draw at West Ham, a 0-0 draw at home to Coventry and a 1-0 victory at

Charlton Athletic - all in the League - the month of November ended with a trip across the East Midlands to take on Second Division neighbours Leicester City in the fourth round of the League Cup. A sizeable following from Nottingham was amongst the crowd of 26,704, which packed Filbert Street for this eagerly awaited 'derby'. And despite the 0-0 score-line, the game was fast and entertaining and took place amidst an extremely hostile atmosphere. Chances were created at both ends but keepers Steve Sutton and Paul Cooper were both at their best, pulling off a string of fine saves to keep the respective forward lines at bay. Forest's best efforts came late on in the game, despite being without the services of skipper Stuart Pearce, who'd been given his marching orders in the 46th minute, following a scything challenge on a Leicester forward. First winger Franz Carr smashed a thunderous drive straight at the City keeper, and then Clough sent a last-minute free kick crashing against the bar. Not surprisingly, the intimidating atmosphere inside the ground was just as evident on the streets outside, and not for the first time in my life, I endured an uncomfortable walk back to Leicester Station after the game.

Goals from Chapman and Clough gave Forest a 2-1 victory in the replay two weeks later, watched by a City Ground crowd of 26,676. They were now through to the quarter-finals of the competition, where they were drawn at home to First Division QPR. With the tie some five weeks away, they could switch their attentions back to the League campaign for the time being.

Following two draws and a defeat during the final month of the year, the 'Reds' - backed by a substantial following - travelled to Old Trafford on Boxing Day to take on Manchester United. By this time Neil Webb was making overtures about a move to a bigger club and rumours of a big-money deal with United were gathering momentum in both Nottingham and Manchester. Webby's performance that day, led to cries of "Yer bloody welcome to 'im" from many of the travelling Forest supporters who trooped out of the stadium at the end having witnessed a comfortable 2-0 victory by United. Frustratingly, with the score at 1-0, Webby somehow conspired to launch an early second-half effort over the United crossbar from only two feet out. This would have put Forest right back in the game, but succeeded only in raising a few eyebrows in the United Directors' Box.

Such are the ups and downs of football, having travelled to Sheffield Wednesday on New Year's Eve, half expecting a repeat performance; we were in for a pleasant surprise, as the 'Reds' were back to their clinical best. Goals from Tommy Gaynor, Webby himself and Harry Hodge, rounded off a blistering performance and caused the large following to jig out of Hillsborough in buoyant mood at the end, celebrating an emphatic 3-0 victory. What a way to round off the year!

THE New Year began with a 2-0 victory over Everton at the City Ground on Monday, 2nd January, in front of a crowd of 26,008. Midfielder Garry Parker scored his first goal for the Club and striker Tommy Gaynor added a second to give Forest only their second home win of the season in the League. This victory brought to an end their worst spell on Trentside for thirteen years.

The following Saturday they overcame Ipswich Town at home in a third round FA Cup tie. An own goal from Frank Yallop set them on their way, with Gaynor and Chapman also on target in a 3-0 success. Following on from their third round League Cup encounter with Coventry City earlier on in the season, this was only the second time they'd been drawn at home in any Cup competition since 4th January, 1986. And with another home tie against Queens Park Rangers in the quarter-final of the League Cup looming, it seemed that at last their luck was beginning to change.

In the meantime they travelled to Stamford Bridge on Tuesday, 10th January, to take on Chelsea in the first round of the Simod Cup. With the scores level at 1-1 after ninety minutes, the tie went into extra time. But Forest went on to score another three times and cruised through to the next round. Chapman, Gaynor, Pearce (penalty) and Parker were all on target. Five days later, they were back in the Capital again and once more came away with a victory. On this occasion Spurs were the victims, with Garry Parker and Nigel Clough grabbing the goals in a 2-1 victory. This game was televised live and a crowd of only 16,903 turned up at White Hart Lane to watch.

On Wednesday, 18th January, a crowd of 24,065 was inside the City Ground for the League Cup quarter-final tie against QPR. And the 'Reds' turned in a memorable performance with striker Lee Chapman the star of the show. First he gave them an early lead with a looping header, only for Mark Stein to pull one back for the visitors. He then restored the advantage with a side-footer past keeper David Seaman, before Nigel Clough added a third. The first half drama wasn't over yet and the tall striker blasted his way to a hat-trick before the interval with a powerful right foot shot into the bottom corner of the net.

Amazingly he went on to add a fourth in the second half, following an incisive left wing cross from Stuart Pearce. And although Wayne Fereday pulled one back for Rangers, the 5-2 score-line at the end saw the City Ground erupt in celebration. Unfortunately the whole occasion was then marred by an ugly confrontation involving none other than Forest manager Brian Clough.

As hundreds of fans swarmed onto the pitch at the end, Cloughie decided to take the law into his own hands. Rather than making his way down the tunnel to the dressing room with his players, he stood on the running track outside his dugout and threw punches at several young fans as they ran by.

Not surprisingly the whole incident was relayed in graphic detail to a watching television audience later that evening, with opinion divided as to whether his actions were justified. The debate raged on in the press for several days, with many applauding his one-man stand and many others, like me, feeling he'd overstepped the mark on this occasion.

Cloughie himself seemed full of remorse and invited four of his victims down to the City Ground so they could all kiss and make up under the glare of the local news cameras. Whether this was a genuine attempt to say sorry or just a clever publicity stunt, we will never know, but I for one wasn't convinced. What's more I considered his subsequent fine of £5,000 and token touch-line ban very lenient. Other managers seem to take little notice of supporters encroaching onto the pitch to celebrate an important victory, so I couldn't fathom why Cloughie had reacted in this manner?

FOLLOWING the drama of this quarter-final encounter, the 'Reds' were drawn against Third Division Bristol City in a two-legged semi-final scheduled for the following month. Having not appeared in a Wembley Final since that unfortunate League Cup defeat by Wolves back in 1980, most supporters were optimistic the lowly 'Robins' would pose few problems and we'd be heading for the 'Twin Towers' once again.

In the meantime, it was back to League action and a Midlands 'derby' against Aston Villa at home on Saturday, 21st January. This is a fixture I've always looked forward to for a number of reasons. Firstly, with the two cities only a matter of fifty miles apart, there's always a typical 'derby' atmosphere. Secondly, there is always a sizeable following from the West Midlands. And finally, with both clubs traditionally playing a passing game of football, there is rarely a dull encounter between the two. Fortunately this game proved to be no exception, and goals from Hodge, Pearce, Parker and Laws, earned Forest an emphatic 4-0 victory, watched by a crowd of 22,662.

After this game, they then went on to play in three different competitions in the space of just eleven days. The first of these was a Simod Cup tie against Ipswich at Portman Road, where goals from Hodge, Pearce and Crosby gave them a 3-1 victory and a passage through to the semi-finals. Next on the agenda, was a fourth round FA Cup tie at home to Leeds United - a game watched by a crowd of 28,017. On this occasion, goals from Chapman and Parker saw them safely through to the fifth round. The Forest supporters' faith in the team was now rapidly growing and cries of: *"An' now yer gonna believe us, We're gonna win the lot!"* rang out around the City Ground.

Their main strength as a team was undoubtedly the goal-scoring acumen of the midfield trio of Neil Webb, Steve Hodge and Garry Parker. So far during the season they had between them weighed in with a total of eighteen goals. 'Webby' and 'Nosy' had notched five apiece, whilst 'Harry' had bagged himself an impressive tally of eight. Even captain Stuart Pearce had scored three times - an excellent contribution from left-back. The darting runs into the penalty area from deep, which were the trademark of both Hodge and Webb, made Forest a very potent force going forward, especially on the counter. Parker's guile and skill on the ball added the final ingredients to a perfectly blended midfield.

It was back to League action once again on Saturday, 4th February and a visit to Kenilworth Road, home of Luton Town. At the time, Luton had made their stadium a 'no-go' area for visiting supporters - a move which had not endeared them to the rest of their Division One counterparts. Playing exclusively in front of their own supporters gave them a distinct advantage - as did their despised plastic pitch. Consequently, only a privileged few from Nottingham - in other words, those who'd managed to obtain tickets illicitly - were there to witness Forest's 3-2 win, thanks to goals from Parker and Clough (2). Incredibly, this was their tenth consecutive victory in all competitions.

Following a 0-0 draw at home to QPR the following Saturday, Forest supporters geared themselves for the first leg of the semi-final encounter with Bristol City. This was scheduled to take place at the City Ground on Wednesday, 15th February and the 'Reds' were odd-on favourites to progress through to the Final. Despite their status as underdogs, City brought with them a sizeable and boisterous following from the West Country.

It turned out to be anything but a romp for the 'Reds' though, against a very determined and workmanlike outfit. What's more, when the visitors took an unexpected lead through Paul Mardon, a major upset looked on the cards. Fortunately for Forest and the majority of the 30,016 crowd, a late own goal from City's John Pender saved their blushes on the night and at the same time, threw them a lifeline for the second leg at Ashton Gate eleven days later.

Their busy Cup schedule meant they first had to negotiate a tricky fifth round FA Cup tie against Second Division Watford on Sunday, 19th February, followed by a Simod Cup semi-final against Crystal Palace - also from Division Two - at the City Ground three days later. In essence, the next eleven days would make or break Forest's season.

'Broughton & Hanna's Tours' were once again back in business for the trip to Vicarage Road, although with the game being televised live by the BBC, there was only sufficient demand for one 53-seater coach on this occasion. Following our rather successful dealings with Skills during the previous season's Cup run, I made a trip down to their Radford headquarters to make the necessary arrangements and of course hand over the required deposit. We'd decided to stop off at St.Albans on the way, after departing from the Cricks at around 9.30-a.m.

By this time, we'd established a regular crew of lads for these away excursions and every trip was proving to be a laugh-a-minute experience. Other than Big Lee and myself, some of the other ever-presents were Bucko, Bodge, Tiff, Jacko, Andy Oakley, Garry Mason, Chris Don, Hoggy, Mark Hurst, Colin Norton and Simmo - not to mention Steve 'Cooperman' Cooper, Russ Jolley and the one and only John Farley. Other regulars included Tom Clough, Steve Adcock, Mart Northfield, Kev and Dave Shakespeare - all from the Chilwell-Beetson area - and from Stabbo, Mick Holmes and brothers Gary and Steve McGrath. Even 'our Graham' came out of his self-imposed exile on occasions just to sample the fun.

The only drawback with hiring our coaches from Skills was that we never seemed to get the same driver more than once. Consequently, it was almost impossible to establish any kind of rapport with them. During this trip to Watford though, all this was about to change - and without question, an extra dimension was about to be added to our already pleasurable days out.

On the face of it, the silver-haired, sixty-something 'Paddy' with a strong Southern-Irish accent, who turned up at the Cricks that Sunday morning to pick us up, seemed a bit of a grumpy old bugger, to be honest. First of all he was having a moan about having to do a detour to St.Albans on the way as this 'wasn't on his pre-determined route map' or something. Then he was whinging on about the amount of alcohol we were consuming on the journey south. And, to cap it all, he was stamping his feet when we all arrived back at the coach late after an extended lunchtime session and was even threatening to bugger off without some of the lads if they ''weren't back within the next few minutes.'' We just couldn't understand his attitude. After all, we'd left him a whole fifteen minutes to get us to the game!

Anyway, get there we eventually did, albeit several minutes after kick off. And somewhat out of breath following a mad dash from the coach park, we took up our places on the terraces alongside 3,000 travelling 'Reds' and settled down to watch a very entertaining game. At that time, there was a bizarre craze amongst football supporters up and down the country, for bringing with them to away matches inflatable objects which were in some way representative of their club or hometown. For example, Grimsby Town supporters had been recently featured on Match of the Day with thousands of inflatable fish. Quick as a flash, most football clubs - NFFC included - had seized upon the opportunity and their respective commercial outlets were churning the damn things out by the thousand. Predictably, ours were mainly inflatable trees, with the words ''Forest - Wembley 1989'' emblazoned across them.

Bored with this, the 'Red & White Army' had taken things a stage further, and notwithstanding the scores of 'Forest' trees on display inside Vicarage Road, there were a whole host of others. Everything in fact from giant cigarettes, fried eggs and beer bottles, to an assortment of blow-up dolls and, would you believe, even a few airbeds! It certainly added some colour to the proceedings and, though it may have been the norm at the time, it doesn't half look odd when you look back at video footage of games played during this era.

Out on the pitch, the 'Reds' were on fire that day and strolled to a comfortable 3-0 victory. Neil Webb opened the scoring with a long-range effort in the first half and a Lee Chapman header from Franz Carr's right wing cross put us two-up early in the second half. A blistering right foot shot from Brian Laws wrapped things up late on. The 'Red & White' contingent amongst the watching crowd of 18,044 went home very happy indeed.

By the time we'd made it back to our coach, queued for an eternity to get out of the coach park and eventually reached the M1, time was already running away from us and there was a distinct possibility of us not getting back home in time for a decent drink. But, having earlier established that the grumpy Irishman's name was Michael 'something-or-other', Cooperman decided to amend this slightly and henceforth, he would be known simply as 'Michel'. When he announced it to all and sundry, it even brought a smile to 'Michel's' face.

"Whip-round for Michel," declared Cooperman, as he wandered up and down the coach bullying everyone into parting with "at least a nugget." As we were still a hundred miles from Nottingham at this point, this was indeed puzzling behaviour on his part - particularly as this activity would normally have taken place right at the end of the journey. Once his baseball cap had been filled to overflowing, Cooperman's motives became abundantly clear. He made his way to the front of the coach and announced to 'Michel' at the very top of his voice: "Get us back to Beeston before 9 o'clock and it's yours."

Well, talk about 'light the blue touch paper and watch him go!' Within seconds, 'Michel' had turned into the 'Demon Coach Driver from Hell' and nothing but nothing on this earth was going to stop him claiming his bounty. Any motorists unfortunate enough to get in his way, immediately incurred his wrath: "Get out o' der way, ya fuckin' ijjit" he bellowed at them, followed by a two-minute spell of main beam and a coach full of cheering and applauding passengers.

Every time someone refused to move over to let us past, there were shouts of: "Gi 'im some fuckin' bright eyes, Michel," from the back of the bus. And he would immediately respond, earning himself another round of applause. The question of whether we'd get back before the 9 o'clock deadline soon became a formality. And when Cooperman handed over the sixty-odd quid to him at the end of the journey, we had gained a friend for life. Everyone thanked him profusely as they disembarked from the coach outside the Cricks and his parting words were: "Make sure yer ask for me again next toime lads." And funnily enough, that's exactly what we had in mind already.

THE next seven days would determine whether the glory days were about to return to the City Ground. Although the Simod Cup wasn't exactly the most prestigious competition in the world, victory over Crystal Palace in the semi-final in Nottingham on Wednesday, 22nd February, would at least put the 'Reds' through to a Wembley Final and give them a taste, and more importantly, an appetite for success once again.

The fact that a crowd of 20,374 turned out for the game was indicative the supporters at least were interested in this apparently 'meaningless' competition. It has to be said though, there was a decent following from South London on the night. Thankfully, Forest proved too strong for their Second Division opponents and goals from Neil Webb (2) and Stuart Pearce gave them a comfortable 3-1 victory. *"Wembley, Wembley, Here we come, Wembley - Here we come!"*

As we set off for Bristol four days later, we all wondered if it would be a case of: *"Tell mi mam - mi mam, To put the champagne on ice, We're goin' t' Wembley twice, Tell mi mam - mi mam?"* Whatever happened, by 5.30 that evening, we'd have the answer?

The game was televised live, which was good news for Forest supporters, as the Club had received an allocation of only 5,000 tickets. Despite the shortage, we had once again managed to fill our coach and once again 'Michel' would be our driver and guide for the day. In view of it's close proximity to Bristol, the ancient City of Bath was pencilled in for our pre-match stopover. We arrived just minutes before opening time.

There aren't many more pleasant places to enjoy a lunchtime session with your mates and as usual we had an excellent two and a half hours. As is the norm on such occasions, much of this time was spent reminiscing about days gone by and whether or not the good times were about to return. The short journey to Ashton Gate which followed gave us an opportunity to loosen our vocal chords and ensure we'd be in fine voice once inside the ground.

When we arrived, we had only a short walk to our end of the stadium. This was a large uncovered area of terracing, which housed visiting supporters on one side and home supporters on the other. As usual only a large fence and a thin blue line of police separated us. It was absolutely freezing that day and to make matters worse, the heavens opened and it began to pour with rain. This was no shower though - it was ice-cold and torrential and made even worse by a strong, swirling wind. What's more, in my wisdom I'd put on my brand new leather jacket for this trip and by the end of the day it would be shrivelled up and just about ruined.

The game wasn't the best contest in the world by any means, but it was a semi-final and the atmosphere was electric, despite the severe weather conditions. There was plenty of battling out there on the pitch, but very little in the way of goal-mouth incident. As away goals don't count double in this competition, a 0-0 score-line after 90 minutes would put the tie into extra time. It was getting colder and colder by the minute, and with the driving rain lashing into our faces, I can honestly say this is the most uncomfortable I've ever been in my life at a football match.

As I looked around, all I could see was a sea of shivering, blue faces. What we badly needed was a goal to warm us, but with only a minute to go, it was City who very nearly took the lead, as a scrambled effort bounced back into play off of an upright. Despite the rain, we were somewhat relieved when the referee blew his whistle, indicating the game would go into extra time.

It wasn't until the second period we finally got what we'd all been praying for, when a cross from the right by Neil Webb was thumped into the roof of the net by Garry Parker from twelve yards out. Fittingly, it was scored at our end of the ground and this sent the travelling 'Red & White Army' into raptures. All of a sudden, the freezing rain didn't matter and thousands of us were bouncing up and down singing: *"We're on the march with Cloughie's Army, We're all goin' t' Wem-ber-ley."*

When the referee blew his whistle to finally bring this contest to an end, the players swarmed across the pitch towards us and joined in the celebrations. It had been a long time since our last meaningful visit to Wembley, but at this precise moment in time, it seemed well worth the wait. When we spilled out of the ground, hundreds of City supporters were lying in wait and there were some ugly skirmishes on the way back to the coach park. It was such a relief to get back to the warmth of our coach, where 'Michel' was waiting with the engine running and the heaters on full blast. What a sound chap!

ON Saturday, 11th March, Forest travelled to Highbury to take on Arsenal in a League clash. Following their hugely embarrassing 4-1 defeat against the 'Gunners' earlier on in the season, the avenging 3-1 victory was very satisfying indeed. Nigel Clough, Franz Carr and Stuart Pearce grabbed the goals in front of a 39,639 crowd. The fact that Arsenal were riding high at the top of the First Division table at the time, made it all the more enjoyable.

Clough was on the score-sheet again in midweek during the 1-1 draw with Newcastle at the City Ground. Considering Forest's rich vein of form, this result against the relegation-doomed Geordies was surprising to say the least. However, with an FA Cup quarter-final tie against Man U at Old Trafford looming, this hiccup was soon forgotten.

The interest in this game was immense - and not just in Manchester. Forest's 12,000 allocation had soon been snapped up and United manager Alex Ferguson commented that, such was the demand for tickets, the tie could easily have been sold out twice over in Manchester alone. And with such demand in our part of the world, we quickly put in an order for two coaches. Not surprisingly, we were fully booked within a matter of days.

We decided we'd make an early start and that Warrington would be blessed with our presence this lunchtime. All the usual faces turned out for this one and spirits were running high as we pulled into this pleasant Cheshire town at around 11.00-a.m. As John Farley had lived there for a number of years, he would act as our guide for the day and quickly led us to the first watering hole.

You can imagine the look of horror on the landlord's face as a hundred thirsty youths came bursting through his front door, each one demanding instant service from his beleaguered bar-staff. Still, it was also obvious we were only 'here for the beer' and he had absolutely nothing whatsoever to fear. In fact, the only thing he and all the other landlords in the area would have to worry about, was whether they'd have enough beer in their cellars to last until closing time.

We had a fantastic three hours with loads of banter, plenty of singing and a humungous amount of alcohol. As ever, there wasn't a hint of trouble. By the time we returned to our coaches, we were all steaming drunk - not surprising really, considering the large amounts of beer which had also been consumed on the way up from Nottingham earlier on in the day.

The singing continued all the way to Manchester and by the time we arrived at the ground only minutes before the game, we were hyped up and ready for the contest. The atmosphere inside Old Trafford was unbelievable - by far the best I've ever experienced at a football match, even to this day. There was a capacity crowd of 55,052, with every one it seemed joining in the singing and chanting. On such occasions, there's no place quite like Old Trafford - truly the 'Mecca' of English football.

We were seated in the upper tier of the Scoreboard End, with the remainder of the travelling support packed tightly into the terraces below us. Inevitably, the BBC's Match of the Day cameras were there and this would enable the rest of the population to sample the atmosphere later on that evening. With the United fans in the Stretford End giving us a blast of: *"Glory, Glory, Man United..."* we responded magnificently with our own latest anthem:

For the first twenty minutes the noise was incessant, with both sets of fans trying their utmost to out-sing each other. Undoubtedly the 12,000-strong Forest Army were more than holding their own. The game itself was fast and furious and this only fuelled the passion amongst the massive crowd. As the game unfolded, it became clear Forest were relying on the counter-attacking style which had served them so well over the years.

Although United were on the offensive most of the time, the Forest defence remained firm. What's more, whenever they countered, with the pace of Carr down the right and the vision of Clough and Webb in midfield, they always looked capable of conjuring something up. And much to the delight of the travelling hordes, following a darting run down the right by Carr, Forest took a 43rd minute lead.

Having danced his way past United's stand-in left-back Lee Sharpe, his low right wing cross was turned into the empty net by Garry Parker running in at the far post. With the United fans stunned into silence, the Scoreboard End went into a state of frenzy. We spent the rest of the first half taunting them and the two teams left the pitch at half-time to a standing ovation.

It was backs-to-the-wall stuff for Forest after the break. As United piled on the pressure, the noise increased almost to fever pitch and they went agonisingly close on several occasions. A dramatic goal-line clearance from Steve Hodge following a corner, led to the United players swarming all over referee Brian Hill. They were adamant McGrath's powerful header - flicked on by McClair - had crossed the line. Then in the dying seconds, a low Steve Bruce effort brushed the outside of a post, causing him to fall to his knees in despair.

As United surged forward in search of an equaliser, they played right into Forest's hands and the 'Reds' weren't without their own scoring opportunities late on. In fact, Chapman should have increased their lead, but somehow failed to connect with Carr's pinpoint cross, following another brilliant run down the right.

When the referee finally signalled the end of the game, we began to celebrate, while the United fans poured dejectedly out of the ground. Although it was commonplace at this time to keep visiting supporters inside after the game, I noticed the gates had been opened up straight away at our end of the ground and many Forest supporters were beginning to stream out. This was a recipe for disaster if ever I'd seen one. And sure enough, as we made our way out onto the steps at the back of the stand, we walked straight into an almighty punch-up, which was already raging between hundreds of rival supporters in the street below. About 300 Forest supporters were completely surrounded by an army of United thugs and despite the intervention of the police - many of them on horseback - they were kicking the living daylights out of each other.

Not fancying a trip home in the back of an ambulance, I stayed right where I was - as did most Forest supporters - and we watched the goings on from the top of the steps. By this time the exits were awash with police officers and stewards, frantically trying to push everyone back inside the ground. Once the situation had been brought under control, we were shepherded out of the stadium and escorted back to our coaches, vans and trains by an army of police.

By the time we arrived home several hours later, our earlier excesses had well and truly caught up with some individuals. As I made my way into the Charlton for a 'swift one', I couldn't help laughing at the unconscious Martyn Northfield who was being bundled into the back of a taxi. He and Tom Clough had been drinking Jack Daniel's from a hip flask all day, as well as putting away about a gallon of ale in Warrington. Fair play to Tom though, who despite being completely arse-holed himself, was at least still standing - well just about anyway. I was even more amused about thirty minutes later when we nipped across to the Cadland for one, only to find Northfield's misses in there all togged up and waiting for him - they were supposed to be going out for a meal together that evening! When she discovered he'd been sent home unconscious in a taxi, she went ballistic. I wouldn't like to have been in his shoes the next morning.

FOLLOWING a midweek defeat by Spurs at the City Ground, we were facing another exciting trip the following Saturday. This time we would be descending in our thousands upon our 'nearest and dearest' of neighbours, Derby County. The 2-1 defeat by Spurs - during which Forest had taken the lead through Parker, only for David Howells to equalise and Vinny Samways to snatch a last-minute winner - had brought to an end an impressive unbeaten run of eighteen games. Consequently, we were anxious to return to winning ways in this eagerly awaited local 'derby'.

Quite incredibly, this wasn't an all-ticket affair and would therefore be a case of 'first come first served' on the day. We knew there was enormous interest in this fixture in Nottingham, and managed to get our hands on some seat tickets, despite Forest's meagre allocation of only 1,000. At least we were guaranteed to get in on the day. The cost of admission onto the terraces of the Osmaston Stand was only £5 and this was also sure to swell Forest's travelling support.

Not surprisingly, following the fantastic result at Old Trafford the previous weekend, not to mention their exceptional form away from home throughout the season, thousands made the short journey across the East Midlands. Shortly before kick off, it was absolute bedlam in the streets outside the Baseball Ground. Even with our tickets for the seats, it was almost impossible to fight our way through the throng of supporters desperately trying to force their way through the turnstiles. Things were getting well and truly out of hand and this was due in no small way to the over-aggressive tactics of the police. Somehow we managed to reach the turnstiles and gain entrance to the upper tier of the stand.

When we reached our seats, we were staggered to find the terraces below us already packed to overflowing. There wasn't a cat in hell's chance of getting any more supporters into this section of the ground. And, having just witnessed for ourselves how many Forest fans were outside, we were starting to fear the worst. As it got nearer to kick off and the last few seats in our section filled up, there was only one topic of conversation, and that was the complete and utter chaos going on outside the turnstiles.

Minutes after kick off, scores of police officers began to line up around the edge of the pitch immediately in front of the Osmaston Stand. Seconds later, several hundred supporters who appeared from behind the stand, were led along the running track and shepherded into the empty section of terracing between the Visitors' Enclosure and the Popside away to our left. As they trooped by, they were roundly applauded by the swaying mass of fans in front of us and jeered loudly by the home supporters - although in truth I don't think anyone could believe what they were seeing. It emerged later that things had gotten so out of hand outside, the police decided it would make more sense to open up this empty section of terracing and let them all in for nothing, rather than face the possibility of them rampaging through the streets of Derby looking for blood. A sensible course of action if you ask me?

With the exception of my first ever visit to the Baseball Ground as an eleven-year-old way back in 1969, this was undoubtedly the biggest following we'd ever taken to the 'Sheep-dip'. And not only did we have the upper-hand on the terraces, out there on the pitch the 'Reds' were also in dominant mood. A Steve Hodge pile-driver from the edge of the box put them in front in the first half - much to the delight of the travelling hordes - and when Mark Wright fell over the ball attempting a back-pass late on in the game, Lee Chapman gratefully despatched it into the back of the net to wrap things up. We spent the last ten minutes taunting the 'Sheep' as they sneaked out of the ground in their thousands. It just doesn't come any better than this - two Wembley Finals already in the bag; an FA Cup semi-final against Liverpool coming up in three weeks' time; plus victory against the enemy - and on their turf!

FOREST warmed up for their League Cup Final encounter against Luton with three League games in the space of just nine days. The first of these brought them a 2-0 victory over Manchester United at the City Ground, with Stuart Pearce and Lee Chapman grabbing the goals in front of a crowd of 30,092 - their highest of the season. The second saw them crash to a demoralising 4-1 defeat against Wimbledon at Plough Lane. And the third saw them redeem themselves with a comfortable 2-0 home victory over Norwich City.

With only two defeats in their last 23 competitive games, Forest were odds-on favourites to lift their first major trophy in nine seasons. Our official ticket allocation of 30,000 was soon snapped up and many thousands were also obtained on the black market. Seats were priced at £32, £26, £20 and £12, whilst terrace tickets were available at £9 apiece. We opted for the £26 seats in the upper tier of the 'Tunnel End'.

As usual the Final would take place on a Sunday - 9th April being the designated date - and consequently many fans headed for London on the Saturday. Our single coach - once again hired through Skills and of course driven by 'Michel' - would instead make an early start on the morning of the game. We were fortunate in that for many years, a few of the lads from Chilwell who worked in the Building Trade, had lived and worked down in London from Monday to Friday and returned home to Nottingham only at the weekends. They always stayed in Paddington and were well known by most of the pub landlords in this area. Their main haunt was 'Murphy's Bar', owned by a very friendly and hospitable Irishman known simply as 'Murphy'.

When we left Chilwell at 8 o'clock that morning, our immediate destination was Paddington, South-West London. Arrangements had been made for us to slip in through the back door of Murphy's at 10.00-a.m. - two hours before opening time. 'Michel' put his foot down and made sure we arrived in good time, therefore guaranteeing us some quality drinking time prior to the game. Also working down there on a regular basis, were a gang of lads from Clifton and we'd made arrangements to meet up with them in Paddington. They'd organised their own coach from the Clifton Bridge Inn at Silverdale - otherwise known as the 'Ponderosa'.

When we arrived, 'Michel' parked up just fifty yards from the bar, so as to ensure a swift getaway when we left at around 2 o'clock. This would get us to the stadium in good time for the game. As we filed in through the back door, it was pleasing to see the place already packed solid - the Clifton lads having already arrived several minutes earlier. Once we were all inside, the relatively small bar was bursting at the seams - not bad for 10 o'clock on a Sunday morning.

There were extra bar-staff on duty just to cope with the rush and bags of food available for the hungry hordes. There was a wonderful atmosphere, and within no time at all, I was on my sixth pint of Murphy's - and I'd never even tasted the stuff before. When the bar officially opened at 12.00-p.m., it became so overcrowded, a few of us decided to have a wander down the road to find somewhere a bit more comfortable in which to drink. And it was obvious we weren't the only ones privy to Paddington's unique Licensing Hours - there were Forest supporters everywhere.

We returned to Murphy's about an hour later. By this time most of the lads had spilled onto the street outside and were lapping up the warm spring sunshine. We spent the next forty minutes treating the local residents to our full repertoire of songs and taking the mickey out of anyone unfortunate enough to walk by. Almost reluctantly, as 2 o'clock approached, we made our way slowly back to the coach and headed off for Wembley.

Despite the heavy London traffic, 'Michel' got us to the stadium well before kick off. We had time to sample the unique atmosphere along Wembley Way - and Tom Clough even had time to sort out a big-mouthed Luton supporter who was at the front of a gang of thugs squaring up to some Forest supporters - before going inside and making our way to our seats. Although I'd now been to Wembley on many occasions, often to watch England, it was wonderful to be back again with the 'Reds'. As the teams were led out onto the field by Brian Clough and Ray Harford, the noise inside the stadium was incredible.

The teams lined up as follows:

FOREST:		LUTON TOWN:	
1	Steve Sutton	Les Sealey	1
2	Brian Laws	Tim Breaker	2
3	Stuart Pearce (Captn.)	Ashley Grimes	3
4	Des Walker	David Preece	4
5	Terry Wilson	Steve Foster (Captn.)	5
6	Steve Hodge	David Beaumont	6
7	Tommy Gaynor	Danny Wilson	7
8	Neil Webb	Roy Wegerle	8
9	Nigel Clough	Mick Harford	9
10	Lee Chapman	Ricky Hill	10
11	Garry Parker	Kingsley Black	11

Subs: Steve Chettle	Subs: Darren McDonough
Lee Glover	Raphael Meade

Once the formalities were over and the game got under way, it was obvious Luton were going to provide the 'Reds' with much stiffer opposition than had been predicted. Although Lee Chapman had a 'goal' ruled out for offside in the fifteenth minute, Forest weren't having things all their own way. In fact, but for the agility of Steve Sutton, the 'Hatters' would have gone into the lead when Ashley Grimes hit what looked an unstoppable twenty-five-yard drive towards the top right hand corner of the net. With his back arched, 'Sooty' somehow managed to fingertip the ball over the bar and out for a corner.

However, in the thirty-fifth minute, Luton deservedly took the lead, when a right wing cross from Danny Wilson was headed firmly into the back of the net by Mick Harford, despite Sutton getting a hand to the ball before it crossed the line. Although Forest managed to rally themselves late on in the half, the score remained 1-0 when referee Roger Milford blew the half-time whistle.

As they had done against Southampton in 1979, the 'Reds' came out for the second half needing to overturn a one-goal deficit, and kicking towards their near 40,000 army of fans at the 'Tunnel End' of the stadium. And, just as it had been all those years before, the noise generated by the travelling hordes was almost deafening. What's more, within nine minutes of the re-start, the team had risen to the challenge and the scores were level. A magnificent through ball by Webb put Hodge clean through on goal. As he rounded keeper Les Sealy, he was brought crashing to the ground, earning Forest a penalty. The ice-cool figure of Nigel Clough stepped up and despatched a low shot into the right hand corner of the net.

The Trent End choir got right behind the team and soon Luton were well and truly on the rack. In the sixty-eighth minute, Tommy Gaynor broke down the right wing and sent over a deep, inch-perfect cross for the on-rushing Webb. He'd beaten the off-side trap and was bearing down on goal on the far side of the penalty area. He controlled the ball superbly on his instep, and in one movement, despatched it into the back of the net, lifting the roof off the stadium. The noise with which this effort was greeted was incredible. It seemed in an instant, almost a decade of frustration had been lifted from within our souls.

When Cloughie added a third on seventy-six minutes, sweeping the ball into the net following another cross from Gaynor, the contest was almost over. For the remainder of the game, the 'Tunnel End' reverberated to the sound of: *"And it's Nott-ing-ham-For-est, Nottingham Forest FC, We're by far the greatest team, The world has ever seen!"* The final whistle was greeted with rapturous applause.

When Psycho held the trophy aloft, the sound of: *"Hello, Hello, Forest are back, Forest are back,"* rang out all over North-West London. At last, after all these years, we really were back in the big time. Not that Cloughie seemed overwhelmed by the occasion. He made a quick exit down the tunnel, stopping only to bow to his adoring fans, before leaving the players and supporters to enjoy the occasion together. This had been another wonderful day out at Wembley and, we hoped, the first of many in the future. We were of course already due to return in three weeks' time to take on Everton in the Simod Cup Final. And preparations for this trip were already well under way.

A MIDWEEK League game against Southampton at the City Ground was sandwiched between this Wembley triumph and a second successive FA Cup semi-final against Liverpool at Hillsborough. The 'Saints' were soundly beaten by three-goals-to-nil, with Clough (penalty), Pearce and Gaynor all on target. The players were left with just three days to prepare themselves for another massive game. Were they to overcome the might of Liverpool - second in the table behind Arsenal and chasing a League and Cup double - then they would qualify for a record third Wembley Final in one season.

We had two coaches running to this one and just as for the previous encounter, we arrived in Sheffield well in advance of the 3 o'clock kick off. We enjoyed a few beers in a pub near to the stadium and left at around 2.30-p.m. We were full of optimism and confident that after a gap of thirty years, we would once again be appearing in an FA Cup Final. When all is said and done, all the other Cup competitions are just poor relations.

Once again, we'd received the lion's share of tickets and been allocated the Spion Kop End of the stadium. Having made our way through the turnstiles, we climbed to the back of the terraces and got ourselves settled for the game. The pre-match atmosphere was, as usual, something to behold, with both sets of supporters making their presence felt. One thing which did strike me as odd though, as I gazed around the stadium, was that the two end sections of terracing in the Leppings Lane End opposite, seemed to be very sparsely populated. In contrast, the middle section was full almost to overflowing.

As we neared kick off, I was very puzzled by the small number of Liverpool fans making their way into that part of the stadium. I even began to wonder if there'd been some kind of boycott by their supporters in protest over their inferior ticket allocation. Their displeasure with the ticket arrangements had been well documented prior to the game. Their main complaint was that the size of their support compared to that of our own, warranted a larger share of the tickets. And to be fair, it was difficult to argue with them.

By the time the teams had been led out onto the field and were preparing for kick off, the situation at the other end of the stadium seemed much as it had been fifteen minutes earlier, except the middle section of the stand was now even more overcrowded. Strangely, the sections at either side remained virtually empty.

Having stood at the Leppings Lane End on many occasions in the past watching the 'Reds', I was very familiar with the layout of the stand. The main turnstiles were situated about twenty yards from the back, and once inside, there was a fairly large concourse where the toilets and refreshments were situated. If seated in the upper tier of the stand, from here you would simply make your way up the appropriate staircase.

However, if you had a terrace ticket, you had a choice of three entrances into the stand. You could either head for the tunnel directly in front of you, which led straight into the middle section, or you could go the long way round to one of the far entrances, which took you into either of the two end sections. Large dividing fences split the lower tier into three distinct sections of terracing and right along the wall at the front stood a six-foot high fence, the top of which was bent back over into the stand at an angle. This made it almost impossible for anyone to climb over and get onto the pitch.

Common sense alone would tell you, that once the middle section was full, it was a fairly simple task to close the entrance to the tunnel. If necessary, a simple cordon of police officers across the entrance would suffice. Anyone arriving after this could simply be directed towards the two end sections of terracing. In any case, your natural reaction when coming through the turnstiles and being confronted with a line of police like this, would be to head straight for one of the two side entrances. Unfortunately, such a simple strategy was obviously beyond the imagination of the South Yorkshire Police.

Unbeknown to the majority of those inside the stadium, a large number of Liverpool fans with tickets for the Leppings Lane End had arrived late. There had been major traffic jams on the way into Sheffield from the North-West and - as is quite normal before any football match - many supporters had been enjoying a drink prior to the game. They'd left it as late as possible before making their way to the ground. The result was, many thousands were still outside queuing as the game was about to start. Although alarming in itself, this is by no means an unusual occurrence at a major sporting event in this day and age. It is certainly a situation which any competent and experienced police force should have been able to deal with quite routinely.

With effective communication between those on duty outside the stadium and those inside, various simple measures could have been taken in order to avert panic. Firstly, the kick off could have been delayed indefinitely - something which could easily have been relayed to those outside, via the public address system and by using loud hailers. Assurances could have been given that under no circumstances would the game commence until everyone was inside. Secondly, as mentioned earlier, the middle section of terracing could have been closed off without too much difficulty. Finally, with all the technology such as video equipment and two-way radios at their fingertips, effective crowd surveillance both inside and outside the stadium could have ensured a proactive approach towards any potential problem areas.

Not only did the South Yorkshire Police fall woefully short on this occasion, I would even go as far as to say, that they were mainly responsible for the chaos which unfolded. How on this earth they came to the conclusion that opening up the main gates to the Leppings Lane End would alleviate the situation just beggars belief?

As a result of their actions, an uncontrollable stampede ensued, with hundreds of supporters heading straight for the middle section of the stand, which of course was already dangerously overcrowded. With hundreds of people bearing down upon them from behind, those at the front of the terraces just never stood a chance. What those poor souls must have endured is beyond comprehension?

As all of this unfolded, it appeared at first from our end, to be some sort of crowd disturbance. The police on duty inside the stadium could be seen clearly pushing supporters who'd managed to scale the fence at the front of the Leppings Lane End, back down onto the terraces. The Forest supporters initially voiced their displeasure at what they perceived to be an act of hooliganism on the part of the Liverpool supporters. However, as the minutes ticked by and the game was brought to a dramatic halt by the referee, it became obvious that this wasn't the case and that a serious situation was beginning to develop. Scores of supporters were being dragged into the seats above by a sea of hands stretching down from the upper tier.

Very soon, the goal-mouth at that end was awash with people, many lying prostrate on the ground. Supporters, policemen and St.John's ambulancemen were rushing around everywhere, a look of despair etched into their faces. The players had long since departed from the pitch and all we could do was stand there looking on, unable to offer any assistance. Hundreds of people were trying desperately to unravel the mass of tangled bodies piling up at the front of the terracing.

Dozens of Forest supporters climbed out of the stand to our left and made their way across the pitch to help. Many of them were ripping down advertising hoardings which they used as makeshift stretchers. They carried many of the injured to our end of the pitch, where they were laid out in the goal-mouth. Some of them were lying completely motionless and friends and relatives - perhaps even complete strangers - were kneeling beside them apparently trying to comfort them.

A number of people around us were carrying transistor radios and listening to running commentaries of the drama as it unfolded before our very eyes. Rumours began to filter through the crowd that there'd even been a number of fatalities. "Nonsense," we thought, unable to accept something of this magnitude could be occurring inside one of our most prestigious of football stadiums.

To my absolute horror, I saw a St.John's ambulanceman place a coat over the face of a man who'd been lying motionless on the pitch right in front of us for about fifteen minutes. Only then did it begin to sink in - some of these poor souls weren't just injured - they were dead. The whole situation was surreal. We'd left home that morning expecting to see a game of football, but instead were witnessing the most appalling tragedy ever to occur at a sporting venue in this country. And we could do absolutely nothing but just stand and watch.

Eventually, an announcement came over the public address system that the game had been abandoned and we were to make our way calmly out of the stadium. Everyone inside Hillsborough that day - and there were over 50,000 of us - was in a state of complete and utter despair. "Could this really be happening?" we asked ourselves. As we filed out through the gates and made our way slowly back to the coaches, no-one uttered a word. By the time we reached ours, the sheer scale of the tragedy was already beginning to unfold. As we sat listening to the radio, we were devastated by the news there'd been a dozen fatalities. This rose sharply to twenty, then thirty, then fifty, then seventy, and so on. By the time we pulled out of the coach park, the final figure was more than ninety.

Following a quiet and subdued journey back to Nottingham, the coach dropped us off outside the Charlton. Most of us trudged quietly into the pub and headed straight for the bar. If ever I'd needed a drink, it was now. There was only one topic of conversation from that point on, as we went over every terrible moment in graphic detail. It's history now that ninety-six supporters lost their lives in this tragedy and the City of Liverpool was left reeling. However, the events of that day had a profound affect on everyone who was there, not just those from Liverpool. There were over 25,000 Forest supporters inside Hillsborough and many vowed they would never set foot inside a football stadium again.

Later the following week, I made arrangements to meet up with Shakey and Chris Norrish at 7 o'clock on the Sunday morning. We were determined to drive up to Liverpool and pay our respects to those who had lost their lives, by laying a wreath on the pitch at Anfield. We took with us an array of Forest scarves and emblems, which we would also leave at the stadium.

We arrived in Liverpool at around 9 o'clock and once we'd parked up on Stanley Park, joined the massive queue of people winding it's way through the streets around the stadium. Although still relatively early in the morning, it was already several miles long.

There was a sombre mood about the place, with most people still in shock and clearly struggling to come to terms with the whole thing. We were moving at a snail's pace all morning and consequently it was four hours before we came within sight of the famous Shankley Gates. The scenes which greeted us were incredible. There were flags, banners and replica shirts from virtually every club in Britain - and from all over Europe - draped across the gates. Hundreds of wreaths and floral tributes lay on the ground in front of the entrance accompanied by messages of sympathy and many bearing the names of those who'd perished. I'd never experienced anything so poignant in my life and, after the scenes I'd witnessed the weekend before; it was almost too much to bear.

When we eventually made our way into the stadium, we were staggered by what we saw. The Kop was a sea of colour. Tens of thousands of flags and scarves were draped over the barriers and laid out across the terraces. The goalposts and crossbar and a large area of the pitch in front of the stand were plastered with tributes. Right up to the half-way line, there was a thick carpet of flowers and wreaths.

As we made our way along the running track at the edge of the pitch we were befriended by a smart young 'Scouser' with a strong Liverpool accent. He asked us if he could lay his wreath alongside ours. He'd noticed our Forest scarves and was overwhelmed by the fact we'd travelled all the way up from Nottingham to pay our respects. He introduced himself as John Murray and began introducing us to a group of his friends also amongst the crowd.

When we climbed over the wall and onto the Kop End, he followed us and was adamant he wanted to hang his scarf next to ours. We made our way to the back of the stand searching for a suitable place for them, but by this time, there was little room available. Eventually, having found a suitable spot, we secured them in place, then sat down on the terraces and stared out onto the pitch. We were completely overwhelmed by the whole experience.

After a few minutes, we made our way back down onto the pitch to lay our wreath on the half-way line. John placed his next to ours. It was time for us to leave, so we made our way towards the exit at the far end of the stadium. ''Would you come for a drink with us lads, before you go home to Nottingham?'' asked John, completely out of the blue. ''Thanks for the offer, but we really have to be getting on our way - it's been a long day and we've got a hell of a journey in front of us...and besides, I'm driving,'' I replied politely. ''Please lads, we'd really appreciate it if you'd come back to our Social Club with us, just for a quick one,'' he pleaded.

Somewhat reluctantly we agreed and John travelled back with us in our car so he could direct us all the way to the Huyton Labour Club. When we arrived, his mates were waiting for us in the car park outside. Within seconds we were signed in and John was at the bar getting them in. ''Come over 'ere and meet some of the lads,'' he said, as he handed out the drinks. He marched across to the far side of the Club, where a large group of his pals were sitting. It was handshakes all around, and once John had informed them we were Forest supporters who'd travelled up to lay a wreath inside Anfield, the drinks were flowing thick and fast. ''Ere we go lads, get deese down yer necks,'' said one chap, then another, and then another. Very soon, they'd bought us so many, there was no room left on the table. The only trouble was, I was driving and therefore unable to indulge. As you can imagine, Shakey and Chris were in their element. Suddenly, the music was lowered and the landlord of the Club stood on a chair in the middle of the room and announced to all and sundry who we were and what we were doing there. And, as the three of us squirmed with embarrassment, the whole place erupted into spontaneous applause - followed by yet more drinks. People were queuing up just to shake our hands and to say how much they appreciated our gesture. This was all too much for Shakey and he sat there in the corner blubbering.

As closing time approached, I was anxious to get going. Not surprisingly, with a belly full of ale now inside them, the other two just didn't give a damn. ''Ave you eaten today lads?'' asked a middle-aged man sitting at our table. ''No, not really,'' Shakey replied. ''Right den, you're not goin' anywerr, until you've been back to our place for some grub,'' he declared. Little did we know that 'back at his place' there was only a Christening going on and the house was packed full of friends and relatives. I was very embarrassed and felt we were just intruding. My concerns were completely misplaced though and everyone was friendly beyond belief. In fact, they made us feel as if we were part of the family.

They crammed as many sandwiches, sausage rolls and chicken legs as they could into a couple of carrier bags, before the whole street - including John and his mates - waved us off outside. By the time we pulled onto the M62, Shakey and Chris were both fast asleep, and 'muggins 'ere' was left with the task of getting us all safely back to Nottingham. (In view of Forest's impending League fixture against Liverpool at Anfield on Wednesday, 10th May - just three days after the re-arranged semi-final tie - John had invited us all back up and we were toying with the idea of running a coach from the Charlton and dropping into the Huyton Labour Club again before and after this game.)

The next evening, Shakey rang me to see if I'd read the Evening Post. Having been overwhelmed by the hospitality we'd received that day, he'd contacted the Post and they ran the following story on Monday, 24th April:

FOREST FANS 'TREATED LIKE KINGS'

A Nottingham Forest fan broke down in tears at the depth of affection shown to him by the people of Liverpool.

Kevin Shakespeare and his friends, Chris Broughton and Chris Norrish, were given a standing ovation at the Huyton Labour Social Club when they visited Liverpool as it reeled from the shock of the Hillsborough tragedy.

They were invited to join celebrations at the home of a Liverpool family to toast the christening of a godson.

Kevin, 26, took a wreath to Anfield to mark his respect for the fans who lost their lives.

When Liverpool fan John Murray realised Kevin and his friends were from Nottingham, he asked them if he could place his wreath next to theirs.

It was then that the overwhelming warmth of the Liverpool people took over.

Kevin said: "It was unreal. We were treated like kings. They said one of their friends was taking Hillsborough very badly and could we go back to the pub and cheer him up.

"The next thing we knew, the landlord was on a chair announcing us. We couldn't drink all the drinks they bought us."

Kevin and his friends were so moved that they are now trying to organise an under-13 football match between their Attenborough team and the local team from Liverpool.

ON the same weekend we went to Anfield, Forest were back in action again on the Saturday and headed north to take on Middlesbrough at Ayresome Park. Following a perfectly observed minute's silence, they went on to claim all three points in an entertaining 4-3 victory. Neil Webb, Lee Chapman (2) and Garry Parker grabbed the goals.

The following week - Sunday 30th April - we were embarking on another trip to Wembley, this time for the Final of the Simod Cup against Everton. The ticket prices for this game were: seats -£16, £14, £12 and £9; and standing - £6. Despite the awful goings on at Hillsborough, Forest quickly managed to dispose of their entire allocation of 30,000. However, despite their status as one of the so-called 'Big Five' clubs, Everton were unable to sell even half of theirs.

'Broughton & Hanna's Tours' were once again on the road, and by 8 o'clock that morning, had already left Nottingham bound for Paddington. Although the M1 was, as usual, awash with red and white, there was scarcely a blue and white emblem to be seen - even after we'd merged with the M6 just south of Leicester. 'Michel' got us there nice and early once more and by this time 'good old Murphy' had already opened up the back door for us again.

Although no-one could claim the Simod Cup is anything more than a 'Mickey Mouse' affair, it was still a Wembley Final and we Forest supporters were treating it as such. And it wasn't as if we'd been devoid of such occasions over the years. This was my sixth Wembley trip in only eleven years - not to mention two European Cup Finals. What a pity the Everton supporters were so unenthusiastic about it all. And let's face it, it's not as if they win the FA or League Cup every other year is it? The apathy of the blue half of Merseyside - and the subsequent wide-open spaces at their end of the stadium - were the only things that marred an otherwise splendid occasion.

Although there were only 46,608 spectators inside the famous old stadium - predominantly Forest supporters - the teams were given a rousing reception when managers Brian Clough and Colin Harvey led them out onto the field.

The line-ups that day were as follows:

	FOREST:	EVERTON:	
1	Steve Sutton	Neville Southall	1
2	Brian Laws	Neil McDonald	2
3	Stuart Pearce (Captn.)	Pat Van Den Hauwe	3
4	Des Walker	Kevin Ratcliffe (Captn.)	4
5	Terry Wilson	Dave Watson	5
6	Steve Hodge	Paul Bracewell	6
7	Tommy Gaynor	Pat Nevin	7
8	Neil Webb	Trevor Steven	8
9	Nigel Clough	Graeme Sharp	9
10	Lee Chapman	Tony Cottee	10
11	Garry Parker	Kevin Sheedy	11
	Subs: Steve Chettle	Subs: Wayne Clarke	
	Franz Carr	Stuart McCall	

Once the pre-match formalities were over and referee Allan Gunn got the game under way, it was immediately apparent that this was going to be an exciting contest. With the Simod Cup not exactly the most important competition in the world, the players seemed relaxed, whilst at the same time adopting a competitive approach.

With only eight minutes on the clock, Everton - attacking the 'Tunnel End' occupied by the Forest hordes - went into the lead. Tony Cottee latched onto a defence splitting pass from Trevor Steven, beat two Forest defenders to the ball, and coolly slotted it under the advancing Steve Sutton.

On thirty-three minutes Forest were level. A Tommy Gaynor corner from the right was headed on by Chapman and swept home from ten yards out by Parker. The scores remained all-square at half-time and the teams left the field to a standing ovation.

Dramatically, within five minutes of the re-start, Everton were back in front. A superb through ball from the impressive Kevin Sheedy, picked out Graeme Sharp bursting through the centre of the Forest defence. He beat two defenders to the ball and sent a looping volley over the advancing Sutton and into the back of the net.

This was followed by goalmouth incident at both ends of the field, culminating in Parker scoring one of the finest individual efforts Wembley has ever seen. It was midway through the second half when an Everton corner from the right was scrambled clear by Walker. He played the ball to Clough who was just on the edge of the Forest area. He played a reverse pass straight into the path of the on-rushing Parker, who by this time had sprinted from his defensive position in the middle of his own box. He took the ball in his stride and, pursued by a posse of Everton players, ran the full length of the pitch. As he approached the Everton box, two defenders were bearing down on his shoulder. He took the ball wide to the right and, seeing keeper Neville Southall racing out towards him, slotted it underneath him and into the bottom left hand corner of the net. This sent the Forest supporters at that end of the stadium wild with delight.

After ninety minutes of non-stop, end-to-end action, the scores remained level at full-time and the contest moved into extra time. Cloughie prepared his players for the extra period in his own unique manner - by remaining firmly on the bench for the whole of the three-minute break!

Just two minutes into extra-time, with the 'Reds' once again attacking the 'Tunnel End', Chapman made it 3-2 with a firmly struck shot from the right hand edge of the penalty area. Forest were in front for the first time in the game. The drama continued, and with just three minutes of the first period remaining, Everton were level when Pat Nevin's right wing cross was headed powerfully home by the unmarked Cottee.

Remarkably, there was even more drama to come during the second period. Firstly, Sutton somehow managed to turn Sharp's powerful shot up into the air and onto the underside of the crossbar. What's more, as it dropped down towards the goal-line, he was able to smother it just a split second before the on-rushing Cottee arrived. Thankfully, he managed to clutch it firmly to his chest, keeping Forest in the game.

Finally, just to cap it all, with only two minutes left on the clock, Nigel Clough put substitute Franz Carr away down the right. He narrowly beat the off-side trap, took the ball to the by-line, and slotted an inch-perfect cross into the path of the on-rushing Chapman, who toe-poked it into the back of the net. Game, set and match to Forest!

The unpredictable Mr. Clough then led his victorious team up the steps to personally accept the Cup from FA Secretary Ted Croker. He was cheered every inch of the way by the travelling 'Red & White Army'. When he held the trophy aloft, all 30,000 rose to acclaim him. This had been a breath-taking game, a wonderful occasion, and a great day out for everyone concerned. After recent events, it was exactly what the doctor ordered.

THREE days later, and sitting in fourth position in the table, Forest easily disposed of mid-table Millwall 4-1 at the City Ground to claim another three vital League points. Goals from Gaynor, Hodge and Parker, plus an own goal from Steve Wood, gave them their twenty-third victory in twenty-nine competitive games. It was also ideal preparation for their re-arranged semi-final encounter against Liverpool at Old Trafford, scheduled for the following Sunday.

Although Old Trafford's capacity at the time was 55,000, both Forest and Liverpool had been unable to sell their entire allocation of tickets for the game. Naturally, both sets of supporters had been deeply affected by the events of Hillsborough just three short weeks before. Forest sold slightly fewer than 18,000, with Liverpool selling around 20,000. In total, the two clubs had returned 12,000 tickets, with a crowd of around 38,000 expected on the day.

With many Forest supporters giving this game a miss, we organised just one coach.

However, with many regular passengers to call upon, we didn't have too much difficulty filling it. That aside, it was a very subdued trip up to Manchester, and with kick off scheduled for 12.30-p.m., a fairly sober one too.

When we arrived at the coach park at Old Trafford Cricket Ground, the number of supporters heading towards the stadium pleasantly surprised me. Understandably, the atmosphere was very quiet and thankfully, there wasn't the slightest hint of trouble in the air. Once inside the stadium, you could immediately sense a feeling of warmth and friendliness between the two sets of supporters. A strip of red and white tape hundreds of yards long was unfurled by a group of Forest supporters in the upper tier of the Scoreboard End. It was passed over a sea of heads until it stretched all the way around the ground. It appeared to unite the two sets of supporters and culminated in the whole crowd joining together in a loud rendition of Liverpool's famous anthem: *"You'll never walk alone."*

Due to traffic congestion outside, the kick off was sensibly delayed until 1.15-p.m. (Why couldn't they have done this at Hillsborough?). Those of us already inside the stadium had to twiddle our thumbs waiting for the rest of the fans to arrive, whilst the millions watching at home on television were treated to recorded highlights of the previous season's FA Cup encounter between the two clubs - a game which of course had ended in victory for the Merseysiders.

Eventually, referee Ray Lewis - who'd officiated at the ill-fated tie at Hillsborough - led the teams out onto the field. Much to our amazement - and for reasons known only to themselves - just seconds before the game kicked off, the Liverpool supporters suddenly launched into a full-blooded rendition of: *"Altogether now...We hate Nott-ing-ham-For-est!"* This caused consternation at our end of the stadium - especially as many Forest supporters had spent much of the last three weeks busily raising money for the victims of the tragedy. Within seconds, the atmosphere inside the stadium was transformed into one of open hostility.

There was an intense feeling in the Forest camp that most of the population outside Nottingham were willing Liverpool on to victory in this game. And with Everton having already reached Wembley, this would ensure an all-Merseyside Final on 20th May - a fitting tribute to those who'd perished. There's no doubt in my mind that a Forest victory would have been a very unpopular one. Even some Forest supporters had mixed feelings about the whole thing. On the one hand, we were of course hoping for a Forest victory, whilst on the other, there was definitely an air of just wanting to get the whole thing over and done with.

With only four minutes gone, Liverpool took the lead. A fierce shot by John Barnes was brilliantly parried by Steve Sutton; only for John Aldridge - the scourge of Forest over the years - to head the rebound up into the air, over the stranded keeper and into the net. Disappointingly, Barnes' effort owed as much to the defensive shortcomings of Brian Laws and Tommy Gaynor - as they challenged one another for the ball in the air - as it did to the striker's own quick thinking.

Although they spent the first thirty minutes pegged back almost entirely in their own half, Forest did venture far enough forward in the thirty-third minute for Neil Webb to blast an equaliser with a low shot from twenty yards out. Goalkeeper Bruce Grobbelar got a hand to the ball, but just failed to stop it crossing the line. Aldridge then slammed a header against the Forest bar just minutes later, following brilliant work out on the right by Barnes - but the scores remained level at half-time.

Sadly for us, thirteen minutes after the re-start, following a short corner from the right by Houghton, Aldridge - who else - rose unmarked in the six-yard box to head the ball into the roof of the net, restoring Liverpool's lead. And as far as Forest were concerned, it was downhill all the way from there. On seventy-two minutes, with Old Trafford still reverberating to the sound of: *"We're on the march with Kenny's army,"* Liverpool increased their lead to 3-1; and on this occasion with more than a little help from the Forest defence. Under pressure from Barnes, Laws managed to side-foot Beardsley's right wing cross straight into his own net. And, as if this wasn't bad enough, Aldridge incensed the Forest camp by trotting over to the distraught full-back and giving him a congratulatory pat on his head. What a complete tosser!

That's how the scores remained and with the Liverpool supporters - and most of the country no doubt - celebrating their 'wonderful' victory, we made our way quietly out of Old Trafford. After arriving outside the Oak in Beeston at around 5.30 that evening - an hour and a half before opening time - we slipped quietly round the back, where the landlord was waiting to let us in. And there we sat drowning our sorrows for the next few hours. Personally, I was just glad the whole thing was now behind us and at last, things could return to normal.

AS mentioned earlier, only three days later, the two teams were due to meet again, this time in a

League match at Anfield. By this time, we'd organised our coach to the game and a stopover at the Huyton Labour Club was very much on the agenda. Whilst for us, this was a fairly meaningless game - and a midweek one at that - we were extremely pleased with the turnout of around thirty-five people.

When we pulled into the car park outside the Huyton Labour Club (situated incidentally in one of the roughest areas of Liverpool) at around 6.00-p.m., John and his posse were there to greet us. There were quite a few people inside the Club, but only about a dozen were actually going to the game. They'd laid on a feast of food, which we gratefully tucked into over the course of the next sixty minutes. In the meantime, we handed over the £200 we'd collected for the Hillsborough fund and a Forest shirt which Garry Birtles had kindly managed to get signed by all the players. John was going to raffle this off in the Club with the proceeds also going towards the fund. Although the drinks were flowing, by 7.00-p.m., we were preparing to leave for the ground. John and his mates Mick, 'Tan-Tan', 'Slasher' (can't imagine how he got that nickname?) and a few others, came with us on the coach. They also stood with us in the Visitors' Enclosure inside Anfield, and after Liverpool's 1-0 victory, escorted us back to the Club for even more food and drinks.

We were totally 'pie-eyed' by the end of the evening. And, as we left the Club at around midnight, we thanked John and his friends profusely for their wonderful hospitality and invited them all down to Nottingham for a weekend after the football season was over. *(Half a dozen of them took us up on this offer during the summer and we had a fantastic two days trawling round the pubs and clubs in town. They thought Nottingham was fantastic and John even came back down again for Shakey's wedding later on that year. And although we did make a return trip to the Huyton Labour Club on our next visit to Anfield, we eventually lost touch with them all - as you do. The last I heard of John, he'd left Liverpool and was living and working down in London).*

Forest finished off their season with a 4-0 home victory over Charlton Athletic, a 2-2 draw against Coventry City at Highfield Road, and a 2-1 defeat at the hands of West Ham at the City Ground. They ended up in a creditable third position in the First Division table.

As for Liverpool, having beaten Everton 3-2 in the Final, they went on to have the League title - and consequently the double - snatched from their grasp during the very last game of the season by Arsenal. They travelled up to Anfield needing a 2-0 victory to take the Championship themselves and, having taken the lead through Alan Smith, grabbed a second in the last minute of the game through Michael Thomas to secure a famous victory. Although not really wishing to see Liverpool fall at the very last hurdle, the sight of John Aldridge sitting in the middle of the pitch breaking his heart after the final whistle, brought back memories of his little gesture to Brian Laws' after his own goal in the semi-final at Old Trafford. "Serves you right, scumbag," I thought to myself.

Apart from the truly awful tragedy of Hillsborough and all that went with it, this had been a wonderful season for Forest. Two more trophies to polish, third in the First Division table, and a rapidly expanding army of admirers up and down the country. The average League attendance at the City Ground was 20,796, with the highest being the 30,092 who turned up for the visit of Man U. At 21,417, the average in all competitions was slightly more impressive - but not a lot!

SEASON 1988/89 – STATISTICS

FOOTBALL LEAGUE DIVISION ONE – FIXTURES

Date		Opposition	Venue	Competition	Score	Attendance
Aug	27	Norwich City	A	League	1-2	13,488
	29	Liverpool	A	Mercantile Credit	1-4	20,100
Sept	3	**Sheffield Wednesday**	H	**League**	**1-1**	**18,963**
	10	Everton	A	League	1-1	30,003
	17	**Derby County**	H	**League**	**1-1**	**24,818**
	24	Aston Villa	A	League	1-1	23,039
	28	**Chester City**	H	**LC 2 - 1st Leg**	**6-0**	**11,958**
Oct	1	**Luton Town**	H	**League**	**0-0**	**15,340**
	8	Queens Park Rangers	A	League	2-1	11,295
	12	Chester City	A	LC 2 - 2nd Leg	4-0	4,747
	22	Millwall	A	League	2-2	16,074
	26	**Liverpool**	H	**League**	**2-1**	**29,755**
	29	Newcastle United	A	League	1-0	24,765
Nov	2	**Coventry City**	H	**LC 3**	**3-2**	**21,301**
	6	**Arsenal**	H	**League**	**1-4**	**19,038**
	12	West Ham United	A	League	3-3	21,682
	19	**Coventry City**	H	**League**	**0-0**	**17,250**
	26	Charlton Athletic	A	League	1-0	6,411
	30	Leicester City	A	LC 4	0-0	26,704
Dec	3	**Middlesbrough**	H	**League**	**2-2**	**17,742**
	10	Southampton	A	League	1-1	15,259
	14	**Leicester City**	H	**LC 4 - Replay**	**2-1**	**26,676**
	18	**Wimbledon**	H	**League**	**0-1**	**16,427**
	26	Manchester United	A	League	0-2	39,582
	31	Sheffield Wednesday	A	League	3-0	20,470
Jan	2	**Everton**	H	**League**	**2-0**	**26,008**
	7	**Ipswich Town**	H	**FA Cup 3**	**3-0**	**20,743**
	10	Chelsea	A	Simod Cup	4-1	8,457
	15	Tottenham Hotspur	A	League	2-1	16,903
	18	**Queens Park Rangers**	H	**LC 5**	**5-2**	**24,065**
	21	**Aston Villa**	H	**League**	**4-0**	**22,662**
	24	Ipswich Town	A	Simod Cup	3-1	16,498
	28	**Leeds United**	H	**FA Cup 4**	**2-0**	**28,017**
Feb	4	Luton Town	A	League	3-2	10,465
	11	**Queens Park Rangers**	H	**League**	**0-0**	**19,690**
	15	**Bristol City**	H	**LCSF - 1st Leg**	**1-1**	**30,016**
	19	Watford	A	FA Cup 5	3-0	18,044
	22	**Crystal Palace**	H	**Simod Cup**	**3-1**	**20,374**
	26	Bristol City	A	LCSF - 2nd Leg	1-0	28,084
Mar	11	Arsenal	A	League	3-1	39,639
	15	**Newcastle United**	H	**League**	**1-1**	**20,800**
	18	Manchester United	A	FA Cup 6	1-0	55,052
	22	**Tottenham Hotspur**	H	**League**	**1-2**	**23,098**
	25	Derby County	A	League	2-0	25,174
	27	**Manchester United**	H	**League**	**2-0**	**30,092**
Apr	1	Wimbledon	A	League	1-4	7,687
	5	**Norwich City**	H	**League**	**2-0**	**19,872**
	9	Luton Town (At Wembley Stadium)		LC Final	3-1	76,130
	12	**Southampton**	H	**League**	**3-0**	**18,948**
	15	Liverpool (At Hillsborough, Sheffield)		FA Cup SF	(Abandoned)	
	22	Middlesbrough	A	League	4-3	20,778
	30	Everton (At Wembley Stadium)		Simod Cup Final	4-3	46,608
May	3	**Millwall**	H	**League**	**4-1**	**15,982**
	7	Liverpool (At Old Trafford, Manchester)		FA Cup SF	1-3	38,000
	10	Liverpool	A	League	0-1	39,793
	13	**Charlton Athletic**	H	**League**	**4-0**	**17,637**
	15	Coventry City	A	League	2-2	14,003
	18	**West Ham United**	H	**League**	**1-2**	**21,003**

HOME ATTENDANCES

	AGGREGATE ATTENDANCE	HIGHEST ATTENDANCE	LOWEST ATTENDANCE	AVERAGE ATTENDANCE
League:	395,125	30,092	15,340	20,796
League Cup:	114,016	30,016	11,958	22,803
FA Cup:	48,760	28,017	20,743	24,380
Simod Cup:	20,374	20,374	20,374	20,374
All Competitions:	578,275	30,092	11,958	21,417

FINAL LEAGUE TABLE - DIVISION ONE

Position	P	W	D	L	GF	GA	Pts
1. Arsenal	38	22	10	6	73	36	76
2. Liverpool	38	22	10	6	65	28	76
3. Nottingham Forest	**38**	**17**	**13**	**8**	**64**	**43**	**64**
4. Norwich City	38	17	11	10	48	45	62
5. Derby County	38	17	7	14	40	38	58
6. Tottenham Hotspur	38	15	12	11	60	46	57
7. Coventry City	38	14	13	11	47	42	55
8. Everton	38	14	12	12	50	45	54
9. Queens Park Rangers	38	14	11	13	43	37	53
10. Millwall	38	14	11	13	47	52	53
11. Manchester United	38	13	12	13	45	35	51
12. Wimbledon	38	14	9	15	50	46	51
13. Southampton	38	10	15	13	52	66	45
14. Charlton Athletic	38	10	12	16	44	58	42
15. Sheffield Wednesday	38	10	12	16	34	51	42
16. Luton Town	38	10	11	17	42	52	41
17. Aston Villa	38	9	13	16	45	56	40
18. Middlesbrough	38	9	12	17	44	61	39
19. West Ham United	38	10	8	20	37	62	38
20. Newcastle United	38	7	10	21	32	63	31

AWAY ATTENDANCES

	AGGREGATE ATTENDANCE	HIGHEST ATTENDANCE	LOWEST ATTENDANCE	AVERAGE ATTENDANCE
League:	396,510	39,793	6,411	20,868
League Cup:	135,665	76,130	4,747	33,916
FA Cup:	111,096	55,052	18,044	37,032
Simod Cup:	71,563	46,608	8,457	23,854
Mercantile Credit:	20,100	20,100	20,100	20,100
All Competitions:	734,934	76,130	4,747	24,497

"TOTTENHAM - WE ALWAYS BEAT TOTTENHAM"

THE MAIN transfer activity down at the City Ground during the summer, was the departure of midfielder Neil Webb, who'd finally secured his long awaited move to Manchester United. Like many before him and many since, he'd decided it was time to make his name on the bigger stage. Throughout the whole of the previous season, he'd been stalling over a new contract and had kept everyone guessing as to whether or not he'd be staying at the Club.

To make matters worse, once his contract finally expired and he confirmed his intention to leave, United tried to get him on the cheap. With the two clubs at loggerheads, a tribunal finally settled the fee and United had to cough up £1.5 million. The day he signed for them, he became a very unpopular figure in Nottingham and was quickly given the nickname 'Fat Wallet' by disgruntled Forest supporters.

Following his departure, Cloughie immediately drafted in Leeds midfielder John Sheridan as his replacement - the fee £650,000. This went some way towards appeasing the supporters, with over 10,000 investing in season tickets and at the same time generating revenue in excess of £1 million.

Although summer transfer activity had been fairly muted, there was plenty to come during the early months of the season. Full-back Gary Fleming joined Man City in August, defender Colin Foster went south to West Ham a month later, and Lee Chapman moved onto Second Division Leeds United in December. On the other hand, before Christmas Icelandic midfielder Toddy Orlygsson was signed from KA Akureyri and striker Nigel Jemson arrived from Preston North End, both in deals worth £150,000. And they were followed in January by the arrival of striker David Currie from Second Division Barnsley in a £700,000 deal.

Forest's season began on Saturday, 19th August with a 1-1 draw against Aston Villa at the City Ground, watched by a crowd of 26,766. This was followed by a similar result against Norwich City at Carrow Road four days later. And in fact, the first half of the season proved pretty unremarkable overall, with the 'Reds' winning 7, drawing 5, and losing 7, and sitting in a modest tenth position in the table at this stage. During this period, they'd scored only 24 goals, whilst conceding a total of 18.

The high spots to date had been the 2-1 thrashing of the 'Sheep' at the City Ground in August; the 3-0 success over Man City at Maine Road in November; and the 3-2 victory over Spurs at White Hart Lane at the end of December - incidentally Cloughie's 1,000th League game in charge. In addition to this, they'd also made good progress in the League Cup, making it through to the quarter-final stages, where they'd been drawn at home to Spurs on Wednesday, 17th January. Along the way, they'd disposed of Third Division Huddersfield Town in a two-legged second round tie, drawing 1-1 at home and 3-3 in the second leg at Leeds Road, to go through on the 'away goals' rule. In the third round, having drawn 0-0 against First Division Crystal Palace at Selhurst Park, they went on to win the replay 5-0 at the City Ground. Another all-First Division clash in round four saw them dispose of Everton down on Trentside, with Lee Chapman grabbing the only goal of the game.

HAVING been formed in 1865, New Year's Day, 1990 heralded the start of the Club's 125th year. And what better way to start such an auspicious year, than with a live televised League fixture against top-of-the-table Liverpool at the City Ground.

With the unusual kick off time of 5.05-p.m., we were left with over two hours to kill after being kicked out of Wurlitzer's at closing time. And to make matters worse, it was freezing cold and absolutely tipping it down with rain. When the game did finally kick off, the wet and muddy conditions weren't conducive to Forest's normal passing game and they quickly fell behind to two goals from Ian Rush.

Whilst in his playing days, George Best had been undoubtedly one of the world's greatest footballers, during his career as an ITV soccer pundit, he never quite reached the same dizzy heights. His half-time prediction that the game was "as good as dead" and that "there was no way back for Forest in the second half," proved about as reliable as a Michael Fish weather report. A rousing second-half performance from the 'Reds' saw them salvage a point in dramatic style.

CHAPTER 24

First a superb header from Steve Hodge and then a penalty from the ice-cool Clough brought the scores level, sending the bedraggled holiday crowd of 24,581 home happy and leaving old 'Georgie Boy' wiping the egg off his face.

The following Sunday, it was the BBC's turn to invade the City Ground - on this occasion for a third round FA Cup tie against Manchester United. And whilst Cloughie was celebrating fifteen years in charge at Forest, Alex Ferguson's future in charge of Britain's biggest club was, on the other hand, beginning to look rather perilous. He'd achieved very little since his appointment in November 1986.

Despite spending millions on the likes of Mike Phelan from Norwich, Gary Pallister from Middlesbrough, Danny Wallace from Southampton, Paul Ince from West Ham, and of course old 'Fat Wallet' himself from Forest, United still found themselves sitting in a rather uncomfortable 15th position in the First Division Table. They'd also recently suffered the humiliation of a 5-1 thrashing at the hands of neighbours Manchester City at Maine Road.

However, it was one of their home grown stars, Mark Robins, who saved the day for Fergie, when he grabbed the only goal of the game to give United a 1-0 victory in front of a crowd of only 23,068. Not that United were short of support though, having sold their entire allocation of 8,000 tickets. It's history now they went on to lift the Cup, giving Fergie his first taste of success south of the border. There is a widely-held view within the game, that this victory over Forest on Saturday, 7th January 1990, saved his bacon and heralded the beginning of the most successful period in United's history.

And whilst this game may have been 'make or break' for Fergie, Forest's forthcoming League Cup quarter-final tie against Spurs ten days later, was certainly their most important of the season. If we could just make it past them, we'd be through to the last four again, with a damned good chance of making it through to Wembley for the second year in a row. And although the 'Reds' built up a comfortable two-goal lead in this game, with goals from Crosby and Parker - one in each half - Spurs were in no mood to capitulate. They battled right through to the bitter end and goals from Gary Lineker and Steve Sedgley dramatically brought the scores level, earning them a replay at White Hart Lane. Incidentally, the crowd of 30,044 was Forest's biggest of the season.

HAVING made his debut in the 1-1 draw at Luton on Boxing Day, Nigel Jemson achieved hero status amongst Forest supporters when he scored his first goal for the Club in the 2-0 victory over the 'Sheep' at the 'BBG' on Saturday, 20th January. Steve Hodge opened the scoring early on with a thumping twenty-yard drive that whizzed past the outstretched arms of Peter Shilton, before 'Jemmo' followed suit minutes before the break. His low shot followed a mazey run, which saw him leave several hapless defenders in his wake. He'd been an ever-present in the side since Christmas and his overall performance against the 'Rams' more or less guaranteed him his place for the trip to Spurs.

Forest were assured of a sizeable following for this all-ticket affair in North London and we decided to travel down on the special train. As expected, it was packed out and carried with it, the usual quota of 'dick-heads'. You know, the sort that get drunk before you've even reached Leicester and sing loudly all the way down there - much to everyone's annoyance - and then never so much as open their mouths once inside the ground where it really matters. Consequently, having arrived at our destination, our small group of about half a dozen, hung back for a minute or two to allow the main group of supporters out of the station. As they disappeared up the road, surrounded by an army of police officers, they could be heard in the distance chanting and singing like a group of schoolchildren on their way to the zoo.

Conveniently, just outside the station was a smashing little pub, and whilst the others were being marched briskly towards the alcohol-free stadium, we were enjoying a much-needed pint or two. Unfortunately, one or two of the 'dick-heads' had also sidestepped the police escort and found themselves inside the pub. They were soon beginning to seriously test the nerves of the locals, so we took it upon ourselves to have a quiet word and made it abundantly clear just how to behave when on someone's else's territory. And with the likes of Tom Clough and Mart Northfield amongst us, they soon got the message. From that point on their behaviour was nothing short of impeccable. Fortunately, by the time we left about twenty minutes before kick off, they'd long since departed and we were comfortable in the knowledge that with them out of the way, we'd have a fairly trouble-free stroll to the ground...or, so we thought.

The distance from the railway station is probably no more than a mile, but along the way, you have to pass a couple of pubs which are frequented by some of the 'main' Tottenham boys. In our midst that evening was a fella called Paul Keeling - a thoroughly decent chap - who was unfortunately naïve enough to believe you can walk through the streets of North London shaking hands with the opposition, declaring yourself to be a 'True Red' and coming out with the likes of: ''And may the best team win!''

Despite numerous warnings that he should just keep a low profile like the rest of us, he persisted with his one-man public relations exercise. The locals were bemused to say the least by his behaviour and we were becoming more and more anxious by the minute. Without warning, about twenty-yards after the aforementioned public houses, the inevitable happened and he was left groping around on the floor with a bloody nose and a couple of teeth missing. His assailants had pounced suddenly and then quickly slipped back into the darkness before we could come to his rescue. And, unbeknown to us, the incident hadn't gone un-noticed either by a twenty-strong gang of youths who'd spilled out of the pub just behind us.

Suddenly, I heard the sound of: ''Get the Norfern Barstards'' and turned to see three designer-clad youths getting stuck into Mart Northfield, who was about three paces behind Cloughie and about ten yards behind the rest of us. Before we had time to react, Cloughie was straight into the thick of the action and sent one of them stumbling backwards with a cracking right hook. Seconds later, assailant number two was also writhing in agony - and counting his vitals - following a sharply aimed kick from Cloughie's right boot. What's more, by this time, Martyn had completely lost it and was angrily pursuing assailant number three, who immediately sought refuge in the middle of his twenty-strong gang of associates. For some reason, they didn't seem too enthusiastic about joining in.

If ever there were two individuals you should avoid having a confrontation with outside a football ground - or anywhere else for that matter - then it has to be Messrs Tom Clough and Mart Northfield. Not only are the two of them very tasty when it comes to a bit of 'unarmed combat' - only when provoked of course - but they both share an intense dislike of anyone who hails from south of Long Eaton. For Tom especially, a Cockney accent is like a red rag to a bull. Many times in the past, he's described to me in graphic detail his recurring dream, where a coach-load of Cockneys on their way home from a football match drop into the Cadland for a drink and start getting a bit too lairey for their own good. Led by Tom, all the locals band together to send them fleeing back to their coach like frightened rabbits!

Anyway, on this particular occasion, our would-be attackers had very quickly realised they weren't just dealing with any 'Tom, Dick or Harry' and that they'd probably bitten off more than they could chew. They couldn't make up their minds whether to risk life and limb by having a go, or just back off altogether. In the end they did neither and consequently a game of cat and mouse ensued all the way down the high road. Tom and Mart were completely surrounded, with the rest of us simply observing from a safe distance. Both of them repeatedly threatened to tear their pursuers apart limb from limb if they dared come within another yard. And although in the end it became almost comical to watch, I for one was relieved when we finally made it to the turnstiles and the whole thing just petered out.

We were soon inside the ground and soaking up the atmosphere. There were around 5,000 Forest supporters amongst the crowd of 32,357 and this helped to generate the unique kind of atmosphere associated only with an important Cup tie such as this. This was stoked up even further when the game got off to a flying start and Nayim put Spurs ahead in the first minute. In those days though, the 'Reds' were made of pretty stern stuff and always capable of fighting their way back, be it early on in the game, or in the final stages.

Fortunately, this would be no exception and following Steve Hodge's equaliser, Nigel Jemson put them 2-1 up with a stunning right foot drive past keeper Eric Thorsvedt. Paul Walsh nearly spoilt the party for the travelling 'Red & White Army' when he came off the substitute's bench to equalise for the home side. But 'Harry' Hodge was having none of it and waltzed through a static Spurs defence to slot a low angled shot into the far corner of the net. We were through to the 'semis' again and a showdown with Midlands rivals Coventry City.

Amazingly, this was our fifth win in our last six visits to White Hart Lane and as we spilled jubilantly out onto the streets at the end of the game, a famous chant was born. The sound of: *''Tott'nam, We always beat Tott'nam, We always beat Tott'nam, We always beat Tott'nam,''* rang out around North London.

AWAY from the Cup, our somewhat mediocre position of tenth in the League table at the half-way stage of the season had now improved, and we were sitting in a more familiar fourth position. We had accumulated a total of 36 points from 23 games played. Despite the changes in personnel earlier on in the season, Cloughie had once again got the players firing on all four cylinders. There was however one particularly frustrating aspect of his team selection and that was his refusal to pick new signing John Sheridan - the man brought in at such great cost to replace Neil Webb.

Since his arrival at the Club in the summer, he'd made just one senior appearance, and even that was a second round League Cup tie against lowly Huddersfield Town way back in September. Exactly what he'd done to upset the great man will probably always remain a mystery, although one of the many rumours circulating was that he'd been the ringleader of a drunken furore in a hotel bar during the Club's pre-season tour of France which involved mainly young apprentices.

This whole situation surrounding Sheridan was almost a carbon copy of the 'Asa Hartford' and 'Gary Megson' sagas, both of which had occurred during Cloughie's reign at the Club. Another victim was the unfortunate David Currie who, following his expensive arrival from Barnsley, hardly figured and never managed to establish himself on the first team stage. Apart from four appearances as a substitute, he went on to make only four full senior appearances before the end of the season.

In February 1990, the findings of the Taylor Report - set up to investigate the Hillsborough Disaster - were published. Amongst it's many far-reaching proposals, the most radical was the recommendation for compulsory all-seater stadiums for First and Second Division clubs by no later than August 1994. This report was set to change the face of football, as we knew it - effectively dragging it kicking and screaming into the twenty-first century.

At this particular moment in time, Forest supporters were pre-occupied with their impending League Cup semi-final first leg tie against the 'Sky Blues' at the City Ground. This was scheduled for Sunday, 11th February and was to be televised live by ITV.

As it had been the previous season when we'd taken on Bristol City at the same stage of the competition, the weather was absolutely appalling on the day of the game. Possibly this was the reason for the surprisingly low crowd of only 26,153. Although those standing on the uncovered terraces of the Bridgford End - mostly Coventry supporters thankfully - were getting the soaking of their lives, those of us in the relative luxury of the Main Stand, Executive Stand and Trent End, were shielded from the downpour.

As you would expect, there was a tremendous atmosphere inside the stadium as the teams came out onto the field. The large following from Coventry made their presence felt and this helped the visitors settle into their stride. Despite a perennial struggle to retain their First Division status since promotion to the top flight in 1967, at this moment in time the 'Sky Blues' were enjoying life in mid-table. They were more than capable of giving the high-flying 'Reds' a run for their money.

Nevertheless, the ever-reliable Nigel Clough gave Forest a first-half lead from the penalty spot and in doing so, reduced the fervour of the 'Sky Blue Army'. And, despite an incident-packed forty-five minutes, the score remained at 1-0 when referee Paul Harrison brought the first half to an end. After the break though, the impressive Steve Livingstone brought Coventry right back into the game with an early equaliser. With only ten minutes left on the clock, the scores were still level and it looked as if Forest would be left with an uphill task in the second leg two weeks later.

That is of course until inspirational skipper Stuart Pearce stepped up to hammer home a thunderous twenty-five-yard free kick from the right hand edge of the box on eighty minutes. The City Ground erupted to the sound of: *"Psy-cho-o! Psy-cho-o! Psy-cho-o!"* from the jubilant Forest supporters, happy that the 'Reds' would be taking with them to the second leg, a big 'Psycho-logical' advantage. That's how it stayed until the final whistle when the wet, but happy hordes left the stadium with a smile on their faces.

With an allocation of 5,000 tickets for the second leg at Highfield Road, it goes without saying that 'Broughton & Hanna's Tours' took to the road once again. A big disappointment though, was that during the summer, we'd lost the services of 'Michel', who'd received his marching orders, apparently for fiddling his expenses. This meant we'd quickly have to 'educate' his replacement, so as to ensure the same high standards of service would be maintained. In other words, plenty of booze allowed on the coach, a natural break whenever we wanted one, total contempt for all other road users, a three-hour piss up in the destination of our choice en-route, and right foot down to the floorboards all the way home. It would be necessary to cross his palm with silver, but only after he'd delivered the goods of course.

We left Nottingham bright and early on the morning of the game - Sunday, 25th February. As was customary on these occasions, prior to setting off, Big Lee had informed us all that our - or rather his - chosen destination for our pre-match beverages, would be Bedworth in Warwickshire. The only problem of course, was that when we arrived at 11.30-a.m., it was closed!

Having invaded en-masse the cash-point machines in the middle of the town's deserted shopping precinct - where all fifty of us indulged in some friendly banter with a couple of very nervous looking youths wearing Coventry shirts - we wandered off down the main street looking for a pub which might just be open early doors. Eventually we stumbled across a Social Club of some description, where they were busy letting locals in through the back door, despite the fact that it was still twenty minutes before opening time. ''We'll 'ave some o' this,'' we decided and in we trundled behind them, much to the astonishment of the landlord and his bar-staff. They were probably expecting nothing more exciting than a normal Sunday lunchtime session, but the thirsty hordes kept them more than amused for the next three hours.

And by the time we called it a day, not only had they been completely run off their feet, but they'd also had to endure every Trent End anthem from *"I was born under a Trent End goal"* to *"With a bow-legged chicken an' a knock-kneed hen."* Even the locals were joining in by the end of the session.

With just over thirty minutes to go before the scheduled 3.30-p.m. kick off, we were once again cutting it fine by the time the coach pulled out of the car park. Our spirits were naturally very high and we were confidently expecting another victory and another trip to the 'Twin Towers' at the end of April.

Our happy mood came to an abrupt end when we pulled up outside Highfield Road ten minutes before kick off. As we disembarked in an orderly fashion, we were immediately pounced upon by a battalion of police officers. They obviously considered us to be hooligans of some description - let's face it, we were football supporters after all - and as such, had quickly decided we were fair game. There were obviously some serious brownie points up for grabs as far as they were concerned. Never mind about the rapists, muggers and armed robbers out there on the streets, when you've got some innocent football supporters to have a go at!

They converged on us from all directions, several on horseback, and at least half a dozen with snarling Alsations at their feet. What's more, we were also pursued very closely by two large vans, packed with reinforcements. In modern times, most of us have become accustomed to the term 'Zero Tolerance', but the West Midlands Police Force - proven many times over to be the most corrupt in the land - had already adopted this policy way back in February, 1990.

They pushed and shoved us around; not to mention verbally abused us, all the way from the coach park to the stadium. Every twenty-five yards or so, they'd bring everyone to an abrupt halt, and bundle several of our group into the back of a police van. I'd witnessed some miscarriages of justice in my time - particularly in and around the football stadiums of the West Midlands - but never had I seen such a flagrant abuse of power in my life. At least a dozen from our coach had been carted off, only to miss the game as a result. And, had it not been for the intervention of an elderly Forest supporter who just happened to be following behind and who witnessed the whole incident, who knows where it may have ended? He made it quite clear he was jotting down the numbers of the main perpetrators and told them in no uncertain terms he'd be reporting them to their superiors immediately after the game.

When we finally made it to the 'sanctuary' of the stadium, where the behaviour of the officers on duty inside was almost on a par, the players were already out there on the pitch. I'd no sooner parked my bum on my seat, than my trusty bladder had let me down once again and I had to disturb everyone around me by fighting my way back to the toilets underneath the stand (they don't call me 'Sparrow Bladder' for nothing!). Suitably relieved, I dashed back up the steps and into the stand, only to disturb the very same people yet again. ''I'm gerrin' bleedin' sick o' this mate,'' remarked one rather unhappy looking fella, as I squeezed past him on the way back to my seat. ''Bollocks,'' I responded, diplomatically. ''Yeah, an' I'm gerrin' fed up wi' it an' all,'' added a middle-aged bloke sitting just three seats away to my left. ''Well you can bollocks an' all, y'old fart!'' I added.

Thinking nothing more of it, I settled down into my seat and turned my attentions to the game, which by this time was in full flow. However, the unrest away to my left continued: ''Ya shunt 'ave a drink before the game if ya can't tek yer ale,'' declared the middle-aged bloke at the top of his voice. "Folks like you are nothin' burra bloody nuisance," he whinged on, sounding not unlike Victor Meldrew. "Why don't you just stop yer moaning an' watch the bloody game," I retorted, as I leaned across Jacko and his brother Pete who were occupying the two seats in between us, looking him straight in the eye as I did so.

The bickering continued for several minutes, with insults flying first one way and then the other. I was beginning to enjoy myself by this time and began nudging Jacko every time I let fly with another sarcastic remark. Jacko never uttered a word and just sat there watching the game, completely uninterested in what was going on either side of him. Thankfully, the whole incident petered out and I was able to get on with cheering the lads on.

Forest defended resolutely throughout - as they had a habit of doing when required - and at the end of the contest, it was the large contingent from Nottingham who left the stadium in celebratory mood. We were Wembley bound once again, and no sooner had we got back on the coach, than we were plotting our long weekend in the Capital some two months down the line.

ONE week after their semi-final victory over the 'Sky Blues', Forest entertained Man City in a League fixture down at the City Ground. This game is memorable only for the bizarre and controversial manner in which Gary Crosby's solitary goal gave the fourth-placed 'Reds' a 1-0 victory, plunging City deep into the relegation mire.

Following a raid on the City goal during the second half, the ball eventually ended up 'safely' in the hands of keeper Andy Dibble. As he stood in the middle of his six-yard box, the ball resting in the palm of his right hand, he was blissfully unaware that winger Gary Crosby had run off the pitch behind his goal. With most of the players jogging off up the pitch towards the half-way line, their backs towards goal, the ghost-like figure of Crosby, tip-toed his way back onto the pitch immediately behind him.

My seat in the 'A' Block was directly in line with the edge of the six-yard box, so I had a bird's-eye view of the action - as did everyone else around me. We quickly sussed out what was about to happen, as did the City fans opposite us in the lower tier of the Executive Stand. "Look behind you," they appeared to be shouting in true pantomime fashion, as we all sat there praying he wouldn't. However, their cries were in vain as Dibble remained completely oblivious to what was going on. Suddenly, Crosby emerged at his side, crouched down almost to waist height, and cheekily headed the ball out of his hands. Then, quick as a flash, and before the bemused keeper could react; he despatched the ball into the empty net - much to the delight of everyone in the 'A' Block.

Not surprisingly, all hell broke loose, particularly as a couple of Forest players who'd witnessed the whole thing, joined him in a celebratory jig to the half-way line. The now very irate keeper, along with all of his team-mates, swarmed all over referee Roger Gifford. They were adamant the 'goal' shouldn't be allowed to stand. But poor old Mr. Gifford, along with the majority of the players and most of the crowd, hadn't even seen the incident. He ran over to consult his linesman and an anxious thirty seconds ensued. We weren't sure whether to carry on cheering or fall out of our seats laughing. On the other side of the stadium, the City fans were going berserk. Surely, the 'goal' had to be disallowed?

Finally, after what seemed an eternity, he made his decision - the goal would stand. The next day the papers were full of it. Some agreed with the ref's decision, whilst others criticised him severely. The fact that it was the only goal of the game made it all the more controversial. Even as a die-hard Forest supporter, I have to admit it should never have been allowed to stand. Still, as they say: "Swings and roundabouts!"

Before all this drama unfolded, I'd been sitting enjoying my usual pre-match pint with Jacko in Wurlitzer's, when conversation turned to the previous weekend at Highfield Road and in particular my little altercation with the 'old fart' who'd been sitting next to him and Pete. It hadn't escaped my attention that from time to time during the game, the three of them had engaged each other in conversation, and it had crossed my mind that they may have even been acquainted in some way. "Who was that miserable old git" I enquired? After a short pause, Jacko sat back in his seat, looked me straight in the eye and calmly responded: "Well actually...it was George - my old man!"

Now if ever in my life I've wanted the ground to open up and swallow me, then it was at this precise moment in time. Never have I been so embarrassed. "Why didn't you tell me it was your Dad?" I asked him. He just shrugged his shoulders and laughed. "Serves him right anyway," he added, "he's an argumentative old sod at the best of times!"

FOREST'S League form took a bit of a nosedive between then and the League Cup Final encounter with Second Division Oldham Athletic on Sunday, 29th April. The 'Latics' had taken a number of impressive First Division scalps en-route to Wembley and consequently, the 'Reds' were expecting a tough game. A month before the Final, Cloughie bolstered the squad with the signing of 22-year-old Ian Woan from Vauxhall Conference side Runcorn for a fee of £80,000. Everyone was hoping the cultured left winger would give Forest the kind of balance down the left they'd lacked since the days of John Robertson.

The controversial victory over Man City had been followed by a 3-0 defeat at Arsenal four days later. Coventry then arrived at the City Ground the following Saturday hoping to exact revenge for their semi-final defeat just two weeks earlier. David Currie scored his first senior goal for the 'Reds' that day, but unfortunately this wasn't enough to save them from going down 4-2 to the rampant visitors.

After picking up a point in a 1-1 draw at Charlton Athletic a week later, they went on to lose four games on the trot. A 2-0 setback at QPR, was followed by a 1-0 defeat at home to Wimbledon, a 4-0 trouncing at Everton, and a 3-1 defeat at home to Spurs ("*We always beat Tottenham*" indeed!). By this time, we'd dropped to ninth position in the table, having accumulated 44 points from our 32 games to date.

Still, it wasn't all doom and gloom down on Trentside. After all, we were busily finalising our plans for the eagerly awaited trip to the 'Twin Towers'. With the stadium now strictly all-seater, Forest had been allocated 30,000 tickets. Seats were priced £35, £28, £25, £15 and £10. As usual, we opted for a prime spot in the upper tier of the 'Tunnel End' which would once again accommodate the travelling hordes from Nottingham.

With the game scheduled for Sunday, we'd decided to make a weekend of it and a coach-load of us set off for the Capital at around 10.00-a.m. on the Saturday morning. We were travelling down on speck and decided that Kings Cross would be the most likely place to find cheap and available accommodation for the night.

Within an hour of our midday arrival, every one of us had managed to find some digs. Very soon we were enjoying our first pint in a nearby pub and having the crack with about a dozen Oldham fans who'd also arrived in town early. We had a fantastic afternoon chatting and swapping football stories with them. It was particularly pleasing to learn they hated Man U just as much as the rest of us, especially as they are near neighbours. They loved Cooperman to bits, despite boring us all to death with his entire repertoire of jokes and anecdotes. Mind you, he was on great form that afternoon and had everyone falling about with laughter. It's amazing how hilarious even the shitiest of jokes can be when you're on your sixth pint of beer!

We'd arranged to meet Big Lee, Garry Mason and Cob outside the Punch and Judy in Covent Garden later that evening. They'd travelled down together on the Friday night and were dossing down in a friend's flat somewhere in the middle of London. Although we'd arranged to meet up with them at 7.30-p.m., at 6.30-p.m. we were still sitting in the boozer in Kings Cross enjoying a laugh with Cooperman and our new found friends from Lancashire. Somehow, we managed to drag ourselves back to the digs for a quick shower and a change of clothes, and following a mad dash across West London by tube, met up with them as planned.

It was rumoured that most of the 'Townies' were meeting up in Covent Garden that evening and we were looking forward to a right good knees up down in the West End. Sadly though, the local doormen seemed to have got wind of this and had decided the party simply wasn't going to get off the ground. "Couples only," we were politely told at the entrance to the Punch and Judy. It was exactly the same story at the next pub...and the next one...and the next.

Almost an hour had passed by and still we hadn't sampled our first pint of the evening. "Enough was enough" we decided and eventually jumped back on a tube and headed for our favourite old haunts in Paddington. There we were assured of a warm welcome and a drink after hours if we wished. Besides, it would give us an opportunity to find out if Murphy was opening up for us first thing in the morning as he had done in the past. After all, we had to have breakfast somewhere.

We had a very enjoyable evening in the end and made it back to Kings Cross just after midnight. As you do on such occasions, we rounded things off with enough junk food to last a lifetime, before heading back to the digs in the early hours.

We were up bright and early the next morning and by 9.00-a.m. were back in Paddington getting stuck into a lager breakfast. This was followed by a two-hour singsong in the street outside the bar. You could tell the locals were really warming to us by now, as they were constantly up at their windows waving and gesturing that we were going to win by "two nil" or something!

When we finally made our way to the stadium with about half an hour to spare before kick off, it was no surprise to find the two sets of supporters mixing freely together. There wasn't a hint of trouble in the air. And had it not been for the fact I'd have been wearing the wrong colours, I'd have definitely swapped shirts with an Oldham supporter outside the stadium. Not only is blue my favourite colour, but the 'Latics" shirt for this Final was the most stylish I'd ever seen.

The line-ups for the big game were:

FOREST:		OLDHAM:	
1	Steve Sutton	Andy Rhodes	1
2	Brian Laws	Dennis Irwin	2
3	Stuart Pearce (Captn.)	Andy Barlow	3
4	Des Walker	Nicky Henry	4
5	Steve Chettle	Earl Barrett	5
6	Steve Hodge	Paul Warhurst	6
7	Gary Crosby	Neil Adams	7
8	Garry Parker	Andy Ritchie	8
9	Nigel Clough	Frankie Bunn	9
10	Nigel Jemson	Mike Milligan (Captn.)	10
11	Franz Carr	Rick Holden	11
Subs: Terry Wilson		Subs: Roger Palmer	
Tommy Gaynor		Gary Williams	

As usual, it was a scorching day and the temperature inside the sun-drenched stadium must have been difficult for the players to contend with. Despite this, once all the pre-match formalities were over and referee John Martin of Hampshire got the game under way, there were no signs that the attitude or the commitment level of the two teams would be affected in any way.

Forest went into this Final having won just one of their last ten competitive games, and it wasn't surprising that Oldham - despite being underdogs - had the better of the early exchanges. Attacking the 'Tunnel End', the 'Latics' had the bulk of the possession, although in terms of goal-scoring opportunities, honours were just about even. In the fifth minute of the game Franz Carr's header from a right wing corner was brilliantly saved by Andy Rhodes, the Oldham keeper, who threw himself to his right to turn the winger's powerful effort round a post.

Steve Sutton then pulled off a superb save at the other end, turning Andy Ritchie's powerful fifteen-yard shot over the bar. Although the action wasn't exactly 'end to end' chances were being created by both sides, and once again Andy Rhodes showed his agility when saving Parker's excellent shot. Minutes later Carr went close again, when his deflected shot passed just inches wide of the post. This was the last significant action of the half and the teams left the pitch at half-time with the scores still level at 0-0.

Within three minutes of the re-start, Forest were in front. Nigel Jemson headed Steve Sutton's long goal-kick into the path of Nigel Clough. He took the ball on a couple of strides before slotting an inch-perfect pass through the heart of the Oldham defence and straight into the path of the onrushing Jemson. Although the advancing keeper managed to save his first effort, the ball fell very kindly for 'Jemmo' and he was able to side-foot the rebound into an empty net. It was his fifth and most significant goal of the season.

This took the wind right out of Oldham's sails, and for a while they were pinned back by the rampant Forest forward line. When Garry Parker went clean through on goal, Rhodes raced out of his area to handle the ball and this gave Forest a free kick smack in the middle of Stuart Pearce territory. His thunderous effort cannoned off the head of the unfortunate Earl Barrett, knocking him out cold. Fortunately, he was back on his feet once again following lengthy treatment from the Oldham Physio. The 'Reds' were really flying now and the sound of: "Aye-Oh, Aye-Oh, We are the Forest boys," rang out all around them.

Gradually, Oldham regained their composure and their competitive spirit brought them right back into the game. A header from substitute Roger Palmer led to a spectacular fingertip save from Sutton. The atmosphere inside Wembley was beginning to reach fever pitch. Commentator Brain Moore even described it as a "throwback to the old days."

Having left themselves somewhat exposed at the back; there was always the danger that Forest's counter-attacking style may catch Oldham out on the break. Another ferocious free kick from Stuart Pearce brought about another fine save from the impressive Rhodes to keep Oldham in the game (no sign of Earl Barrett in the wall on this occasion strangely?). Fortunately, the score remained 1-0 when the referee's whistle brought the contest to an end, and once again the League Cup was on it's way back to Nottingham and the City Ground trophy cabinet.

Des Walker was given the 'Man of the Match' award and was presented with the Alan Hardaker Trophy. As he made his way up the famous old steps to pick up his Winners' Medal, the sound of: *"You'll never beat Des Walker,"* rang out from the 'Forest' end of the stadium.

Although this hadn't been a vintage Forest performance, we poured out of Wembley happy in the knowledge that for the second year in succession, we'd claimed one of the domestic game's big three prizes. Slowly but surely, it seemed we were re-emerging as one of the major forces within the English game.

BUOYED by their Wembley triumph, Forest ended their League campaign in a fairly impressive fashion. Three days after this League Cup Final victory, they entertained Manchester United at the City Ground. This gave the Forest faithful an opportunity to welcome old 'Fat Wallet' back home to Nottingham for the first time since his much-criticised move to Old Trafford the previous summer.

Remarkably, goals from Parker, Pearce, Clough and Chettle, put Forest 4-0 up inside the first twenty-five minutes, and that's how it stayed right up until the end. Not surprisingly, Webby endured a 90-minute onslaught from the unforgiving Trent Enders. It must have been sheer purgatory, made worse by the fact United were about to end the season thirteenth in the table, four places behind Forest. So much for leaving the City Ground to 'further his career'!

On the very last day of the season, we travelled up to Hillsborough to see the 'Reds' take on Sheffield Wednesday. This was a crucial relegation decider for the South Yorkshire outfit. If Luton failed to win their final game against Derby at the Baseball Ground, or the 'Owls' managed to pick up at least a point against Forest, then they would stay up and the 'Hatters' would be relegated to Division Two.

A crowd of 29,762 witnessed a stylish Forest performance, and two goals from captain Stuart Pearce and one from the in-form Jemson, gave them an impressive 3-0 victory. With only minutes left on the clock, news filtered through to the home supporters that the final score at Derby was 2-2 and they all began to celebrate their First Division 'survival'.

However, they'd been badly informed and no sooner had the game ended, than news of Luton's last-gasp winner came over the public address system. The Wednesday supporters were absolutely distraught and tears were flowing all around - not least from their flamboyant manager Ron Atkinson. A minority amongst the large travelling contingent from Nottingham taunted them with chants of: *"Goin' down, Goin' down, Goin' down."* The majority though, like myself, were a little more dignified. There are many teams you'd happily wish to see relegated from the top flight, but Wednesday aren't one of them. In fact, I'd go as far as to say, I'd have given them the points on the day, meaningless as they were to us. You could argue that there's no room for sentiment in football, but I have to say, there was absolutely no pleasure whatsoever in sending Wednesday down into the Second Division.

All around, this had been another successful season for the 'Reds'. Ninth position in the First Division table and yet another triumph in the League Cup. The average League attendance at the City Ground was 20,609, with the highest being the 26,766 who turned up for the game against Aston Villa on the opening day of the season. We weren't that far away from being an excellent side. Just another couple of additions to the playing staff during the summer and we'd surely be competing for honours again the following season?

Date	Opposition	Venue	Competition	Score	Attendance
Aug 19	**Aston Villa**	H	**League**	**1-1**	**26,766**
23	Norwich City	A	League	1-1	18,267
26	Millwall	A	League	0-1	12,140
30	**Derby County**	H	**League**	**2-1**	**24,061**
Sept 9	Chelsea	A	League	2-2	21,523
16	**Arsenal**	H	**League**	**1-2**	**22,216**
20	**Huddersfield Town**	H	**LC 2 - 1st Leg**	**1-1**	**18,976**
23	Crystal Palace	A	League	0-1	12,899
30	**Charlton Athletic**	H	**League**	**2-0**	**18,189**
Oct 3	Huddersfield Town	A	LC 2 - 2nd Leg	3-3	13,262
14	Coventry City	A	League	2-0	15,792
21	Wimbledon	A	League	3-1	5,184
24	Crystal Palace	A	LC 3	0-0	14,250
28	**Queens Park Rangers**	H	**League**	**2-2**	**19,442**
Nov 1	**Crystal Palace**	H	**LC 3 - Replay**	**5-0**	**18,625**
4	**Sheffield Wednesday**	H	**League**	**0-1**	**21,864**
12	Manchester United	A	League	0-1	34,182
18	Manchester City	A	League	3-0	16,238
22	**Everton**	H	**LC 4**	**1-0**	**21,324**
25	**Everton**	H	**League**	**1-0**	**20,709**
29	**Manchester City**	H	**Zenith Cup 2**	**3-2**	**9,275**
Dec 2	Aston Villa	A	League	1-2	25,575
9	**Norwich City**	H	**League**	**0-1**	**18,939**
17	**Southampton**	H	**League**	**2-0**	**16,437**
22	Aston Villa	A	Zenith Cup 3	1-2	6,531
26	Luton Town	A	League	1-1	10,754
30	Tottenham Hotspur	A	League	3-2	33,401
Jan 1	**Liverpool**	H	**League**	**2-2**	**24,581**
7	**Manchester United**	H	**FA Cup 3**	**0-1**	**23,068**
13	**Millwall**	H	**League**	**3-1**	**18,065**
17	**Tottenham Hotspur**	H	**LC 5**	**2-2**	**30,044**
20	Derby County	A	League	2-0	24,176
24	Tottenham Hotspur	A	LC 5 - Replay	3-2	32,357
Feb 3	**Crystal Palace**	H	**League**	**3-1**	**19,739**
11	**Coventry City**	H	**LCSF - 1st Leg**	**2-1**	**26,153**
17	**Chelsea**	H	**League**	**1-1**	**22,500**
25	Coventry City	A	LCSF - 2nd Leg	0-0	25,900
Mar 3	**Manchester City**	H	**League**	**1-0**	**22,644**
7	Arsenal	A	League	0-3	31,879
10	**Coventry City**	H	**League**	**2-4**	**18,750**
17	Charlton Athletic	A	League	1-1	6,690
24	Queens Park Rangers	A	League	0-2	14,653
31	**Wimbledon**	H	**League**	**0-1**	**16,821**
Apr 4	Everton	A	League	0-4	17,795
7	**Tottenham Hotspur**	H	**League**	**1-3**	**21,668**
14	Liverpool	A	League	2-2	37,265
16	**Luton Town**	H	**League**	**3-0**	**17,001**
21	Southampton	A	League	0-2	17,006
29	Oldham Athletic (At Wembley Stadium)		LC Final	1-0	74,343
May 2	**Manchester United**	H	**League**	**4-0**	**21,186**
5	Sheffield Wednesday	A	League	3-0	29,762

HOME ATTENDANCES

	AGGREGATE ATTENDANCE	HIGHEST ATTENDANCE	LOWEST ATTENDANCE	AVERAGE ATTENDANCE
League:	391,578	26,766	16,437	20,609
League Cup:	115,122	30,044	18,625	23,024
FA Cup:	23,068	23,068	23,068	23,068
Zenith Cup:	9,275	9,275	9,275	9,275
All Competitions:	539,043	30,044	9,275	20,732

FINAL LEAGUE TABLE - DIVISION ONE

Position	P	W	D	L	GF	GA	Pts
1. Liverpool	38	23	10	5	78	37	79
2. Aston Villa	38	21	7	10	57	38	70
3. Tottenham Hotspur	38	19	6	13	59	47	63
4. Arsenal	38	18	8	12	54	38	62
5. Chelsea	38	16	12	10	58	50	60
6. Everton	38	17	8	13	57	46	59
7. Southampton	38	15	10	13	71	63	55
8. Wimbledon	38	13	16	9	47	40	55
9. Nottingham Forest	**38**	**15**	**9**	**14**	**55**	**47**	**54**
10. Norwich City	38	13	14	11	44	42	53
11. Queens Park Rangers	38	13	11	14	45	44	50
12. Coventry City	38	14	7	17	39	59	49
13. Manchester United	38	13	9	16	46	47	48
14. Manchester City	38	12	12	14	43	52	48
15. Crystal Palace	38	13	9	16	42	66	48
16. Derby County	38	13	7	18	43	40	46
17. Luton Town	38	10	13	15	43	57	43
18. Sheffield Wednesday	38	11	10	17	35	51	43
19. Charlton Athletic	38	7	9	22	31	57	30
20. Millwall	38	5	11	22	39	65	26

AWAY ATTENDANCES

	AGGREGATE ATTENDANCE	HIGHEST ATTENDANCE	LOWEST ATTENDANCE	AVERAGE ATTENDANCE
League:	385,181	37,265	5,184	20,272
League Cup:	160,112	74,343	13,262	32,022
Zenith Cup:	6,531	6,531	6,531	6,531
All Competitions:	551,824	74,343	5,184	22,072

"WE ALL AGREE, WALKER IS WORTH MORE THAN DERBY"

ALTHOUGH THINGS had been quiet on the transfer front during the close season, it had by no means been an uneventful summer. Stuart Pearce, Des Walker and Steve Hodge had all been members of Bobby Robson's England squad contesting the World Cup Finals in Italy. A thigh injury had reduced the unfortunate Hodge to the role of spectator throughout the tournament, but Walker and Pearce had both played key roles.

It's history now that England suffered a semi-final defeat at the hands of Germany, but the manner in which we were beaten still leaves a sour taste in my mouth, even after all these years. Having taken a rather fortunate lead thanks to a deflected free kick, the Germans were on the rack for most of the game. And when Gary Lineker notched England's equaliser in the second half, it seemed there would be only one outcome to the game.

Throughout the tournament, World Cup fever had gripped the nation. Pubs and clubs all over the country were showing the action live on the big screen and were packed solid for every game. I'd watched all England's games in the Charlton Arms and the atmosphere was incredible. With the amount of chanting and singing that was going on, we might just as well have been in the middle pen of the Trent End. Each victory was greeted like we'd won the Final itself, with the ensuing parties lasting well into the night.

There were about a hundred of us packed into the bar for the semi-final encounter, and when Lineker's low shot from six yards out hit the back of the net, the place erupted. People were dancing on the tables and beer was spilling around all over. The sound of: *"Eng-er-land, Eng-er-land, Eng-er-land,"* rang out around the whole pub.

When the game went into extra time, the tension became almost intolerable. When Chris Waddle's low twenty-five-yard drive cannoned off a post with only seconds remaining, the Germans had once again managed to avoid defeat. The penalty shoot-out was unbearable to watch, and when Stuart Pearce's powerful effort was saved, the writing was on the wall for England. Chris Waddle blasted the final effort six feet over the bar to seal England's fate and leave us all shaking our heads in disbelief. Several tears were shed that night, but on reflection, the team had done the nation proud. The fact that 70,000 fans gave them a hero's welcome when they returned to Luton Airport, is testimony to the quality of their performances overall. The abuse that Pearce would receive at the hands of supporters up and down the country however, as a result of his crucial penalty miss, could hardly have been imagined at the time.

On the local scene, speculation had been rife during the summer that Des Walker was on his way to Italian giants Juventus. Forest issued one denial after another and insisted they weren't about to part with their most valuable asset. At the beginning of August, we were finally put out of our misery, with the 'Reds' turning down Juve's massive £5 million bid for the classy defender. Had Walker been allowed to leave, the fee would have been a world record for a defender.

Away from the football field, Cloughie had received an honorary degree for his services to the City of Nottingham. He was awarded a Master of Arts at Nottingham University in July. During his long reign at the Club, not only had he made Nottingham Forest FC a household name the world over, but he'd also raised the profile of the City, thereby bolstering the local economy.

In order to comply with the recommendations of the Taylor Report, Mike Holford, the recently retired Chief Superintendent of the Nottinghamshire Constabulary, had also been appointed to the role of Ground Safety and Security Consultant down at the City Ground.

To the relief of all football supporters up and down the country, UEFA had also finally lifted the ban on English clubs from competing in Europe - with the exception of Liverpool, that is, who's supporters had been responsible for our long exile in the first place. Manchester United would be our representatives in the Cup Winners' Cup, with Aston Villa competing in the European Cup. They'd been Runners-up to League Champions Liverpool at the end of the previous season.

A WEEK before the season began; David Currie's brief and unsuccessful spell at the Club was brought to an end, when he joined Oldham Athletic for an undisclosed sum. In the season's opening fixture against QPR at the City Ground, Nigel Jemson continued where he'd left off the previous season, scoring Forest's solitary goal in a hard fought 1-1 draw, watched by a crowd of 21,619.

Three days later we were off to Anfield to see the 'Reds' take on Liverpool. Owing to a number of injuries to key players, 19-year-old Roy Keane - signed from League of Ireland side Cobh Ramblers the previous May for just £15,000 - was drafted into the squad. It was only an hour before kick off when Cloughie informed the youngster he'd be making his senior debut for the Club.

Despite their disappointing 2-0 defeat, Keane's performance on the right hand side of midfield was so impressive; he soon became an ever-present in the side. Once again, Cloughie's refreshing attitude to youth had paid big dividends. Even at this early stage of his career, it was obvious the Irishman had a big future in the game.

Forest made reasonable progress over the first two months of the season and by the time they entertained Tottenham at the City Ground on Saturday, 27th October, they were sitting in sixth position in the table, having accumulated thirteen points from a total of nine games. They'd won three, drawn four and lost two, scoring twelve goals and conceding eleven along the way. Their victories consisted of a 3-1 home success over Southampton, a 1-0 win over Manchester United at Old Trafford, and a 3-1 victory over Everton at the City Ground. Stuart Pearce scored a glorious thirty-yard free kick in the game at United - poetic justice really considering the barrage of abuse he'd received throughout the game. *"Who lost the World Cup? Stuart Pearce, Stuart Pearce,"* chanted the Stretford Enders over and over again.

It's ironic, how upset these same supporters became more recently when David Beckham received similar treatment following his disgraceful antics in the 1998 World Cup in France. How does it go again lads? *"You can shove yer fuckin' England up yer arse!"* Funny...I don't remember you singing that one back in 1990.

In the early months of the season, the 'Reds' made steady progress in the League Cup, disposing of Fourth Division Barnsley 5-1 on aggregate in round two, and then defeating Plymouth Argyle 2-1 at Home Park in the third round.

Sadly, on 5th October, the death of former assistant manager Peter Taylor was announced to the world. He'd died suddenly whilst on holiday in Majorca. Nottingham born and bred, Taylor was considered by many to have been the brains behind the most famous partnership in football, and was held in extremely high regard by Forest supporters. When we filed into the City Ground for the home game against Everton on 7th October, we did so expecting to pay our last respects to the great man. Inexplicably though - and to everyone's disgust - there were no tributes to him, even over the public address system, and incredibly no minute's silence either, prior to the game. The only public acknowledgement by the Club came three weeks later in the form of a one-page tribute by Chairman Maurice Roworth in the Forest Review for the game against Spurs. Yet another public relations disaster on the part of the Club I feel.

On November 24th, the 'Reds' travelled to Derby to take on the relegation-threatened 'Sheep'. By this time, the lower tier of the Osmaston End - the Visiting Supporters' Enclosure - had been made all-seater. This had the effect of dampening the normally volatile 'local derby' atmosphere. As usual though, the travelling Forest contingent taunted their 'sheep-shearing' cousins for most of the game, particularly the 'hard nuts' in the 'C' Stand away to our right. The best chant of the afternoon came after Des Walker had once again thwarted a promising Derby attack: *"We all agree, Walker is worth more than Derby,"* sang the 'Red & White Army.'

Unfortunately, despite the heroics of Walker, for once the 'Sheep' got the better of us and stole a rare 2-1 victory. Still, they needed the points more than we did, owing to the fact they were plummeting rapidly towards Division Two and several more years of obscurity. What a shame!

Four days later, it was off to Highfield Road to take on Coventry in the fourth round of the League Cup - a game I missed due to work commitments. Having switched on my car radio some thirty-five minutes into the game, you can imagine my horror when I learned we were already 4-0 down. A Kevin Gallagher hat-trick and another from Steve Livingstone had given the 'Sky Blues' an apparently 'unassailable' lead. It seemed we were on our way out of the competition we'd totally dominated for the last two seasons. I switched off the radio in disgust and concentrated on getting to my next appointment. However, as half-time approached, I just couldn't resist another up-date and on it went again. And boy, oh boy, was I in for a surprise? Amazingly, by this time, a Nigel Clough hat-trick had brought the 'Reds' right back into the game. And when Garry Parker made it all-square just eight minutes after the break, it seemed we were about to pull off one of the most amazing fight-backs in the Club's history. Disappointingly though, this wasn't to be, as Steve Livingstone popped up to score a decisive fifth for the 'Sky Blues' in the sixty-fifth minute. This brought to an end Forest's incredible 22-match unbeaten run in the competition.

In the 2-1 victory over QPR at Loftus Road on December 15th, Nigel Clough became only the seventh player in Forest's entire history to score one hundred senior goals for the Club. He joined the following elite band:

- Granville Morris: **220 goals**
- Wally Ardron: **124 goals**
- Johnny Dent: **123 goals**
- Ian Storey-Moore: **120 goals**
- Enoch 'Knocker' West: **104 goals**
- John Robertson: **100 goals**
- Nigel Clough: **100 goals**
   ('Our Nige' subsequently went on to score many more for the Club of course.)

One week later, and backed by a sizeable contingent from Nottingham, Forest travelled to Bramall Lane to take on Sheffield United. The 'Blades' were languishing at the foot of the table, having failed to win a League game all season, and having accumulated just four points. Roared on by their large following, Forest soon raced into a 2-0 lead with goals from Roy Keane and Stuart Pearce. However, rather inexplicably, they let the home side right back into the game and allowed them to earn a decisive 3-2 victory. What's more, this proved the turning point in their season and they went on to finish well above the relegation zone, thus enhancing manager Dave Bassett's growing reputation as a 'Harry Houdini' character.

An eventful year ended with a 2-1 Boxing Day victory over Wimbledon at the City Ground, watched by a dismal crowd of only 16,221. Stuart Pearce and Roy Keane were on target for the 'Reds' against possibly the most unattractive side in the top division at that time. The following Saturday, Manchester City gained some revenge for the controversial defeat at the City Ground during the previous campaign, when they left Trentside with a well-earned 3-1 victory. Giant Scottish defender Colin Hendry produced one of the most accomplished rearguard performances I'd ever seen, prompting me to wish he'd been of English origin instead.

FOREST began the New Year in style, romping to a 6-2 victory over Norwich at Carrow Road on 2nd January. Goals from Keane (2), Clough, Wilson, Crosby and an own goal from Polston gave them a comprehensive win against a team two places above them in the League table.

The following Sunday, we were off on the FA Cup trail once again, with a trip to South West London in order to take on Crystal Palace at Selhurst Park. 'Broughton & Hanna's Tours' hit the road again and, back in favour with Joe down at Bartons by this time, we'd now dispensed with the services of Skills Coaches. Besides, things had never been quite the same since they'd sacked 'Michel'.

A trip to the Capital was always a popular one - Sunday Roast or no Sunday Roast - and consequently, a full coach-load indulged in another very enjoyable lunchtime session down in the 'Smoke'. The game was screened live on television and the watching audience saw the 'Reds' scrape out a hard-fought 0-0 draw, in front of just 15,396 people. A decent 3-0 home victory over Coventry in the League the following Saturday, followed by a 1-1 draw at Southampton a week later, precluded the replay against Palace. This eventually took place on Monday, 21st January. Having been originally scheduled for Wednesday, 9th January, it had been postponed due to a waterlogged pitch, re-scheduled for the following Wednesday, only to be postponed yet again at the eleventh hour, this time because of a frozen pitch.

The drama surrounding this tie continued right up to the last moment. Ian Wright gave the 'Eagles' a fifty-sixth minute lead, only for Terry Wilson to level in the seventy-third. That's how it stayed until seven minutes into extra time, when Stuart Pearce broke forward in typically cavalier fashion to hammer the 'Reds' into the lead. Then, with only seconds remaining, keeper

Mark Crossley raced out of his goal to clear a poorly-hit back pass from Roy Keane upfield, but unfortunately it landed at the feet of Palace winger John Salako. With the keeper still out of his goal, he sent an audacious forty-five-yard chip sailing over his head and into the back of the net to earn the visitors a second replay.

On the toss of a coin, the venue was once again the City Ground, and unbelievably, the tie was once again postponed, this time due to fog. When it finally got under way on Monday, 28th January, two goals from Garry Parker and another from Gary Crosby gave Forest a comfortable 3-0 victory. This earned them a fourth round trip to St.James's Park to take on Newcastle United. Prior to this, we had a home League fixture to deal with the following Saturday against, erh...Crystal Palace!

Having lost this latest contest against the 'Eagles' 1-0, the 'Reds' duly travelled to the North-East for their delayed Cup tie on Wednesday, 13th February. Although the rest of the gang - Big Lee, Garry Mason (a Geordie himself but a mad Forest supporter), Andy Oakley, Bucko, Bodge, Jacko etc. - all intended to make the trip (despite the sub-zero temperatures which prevailed), none of these individuals are old enough to remember with any clarity, exactly what had taken place when we travelled to St.James's Park for that infamous FA Cup tie, way back in 1974.

Well I could remember it, and vividly. I also remember the vow I made at the time, that I would never set foot inside that stadium again in my life. And, despite their cajoling, I had no intention whatsoever of going back on this. My stubbornness meant I missed an excellent Cup tie however. Having been 2-0 down after only twelve minutes, the 'Reds' fought back magnificently with goals from skipper Stuart Pearce and Nigel Clough, to force a replay at the City Ground the following Monday.

Forest's biggest crowd of the season - 28,962 - saw goals from Steve Hodge, Nigel Clough and Stuart Pearce, earn them a comfortable 3-0 victory in this replay, and consequently, a place in the fifth round. Ever since that quarter-final 'farce' back in '74, I've always considered any victory against the Geordies - and fortunately there have been many - to be just that little bit special. And this was no exception.

Our opponents in round five were Southampton, and surprise-surprise, once again it was Forest who had to travel. The game took place at the Dell on Monday, 25th February, and a goal from Steve Hodge earned them a share of the spoils and a replay back at the City Ground a week later. And, despite going behind in this game to a fourteenth-minute strike from the diminutive Rod Wallace, a superb hat-trick from England Under-21 centre-forward Nigel Jemson gave the 'Reds' a well-earned victory and sent the majority of the 26,633 crowd home happy. We were now through to the quarter-finals, but incredibly, were drawn away once again, this time to Norwich City the following Saturday.

On this occasion, a replay wasn't necessary. A solitary effort from Roy Keane in front of a 24,018 crowd gave them a rock-solid 1-0 victory and a third semi-final appearance in only four years. Fortunately, our opponents were Second Division high-flyers West Ham United. With all due respect to them, they provided - on paper at least - a far less daunting task than we'd faced in our two most recent semi-final encounters. What's more, this also left North-London giants Tottenham and Arsenal to fight it out between themselves for the other Cup Final place. Due to the anticipated demand for tickets, this tie would take place at Wembley Stadium.

Both games were scheduled for Sunday, 14th April, with the all-London affair kicking off at 12.00-p.m., and the Forest-West Ham tie at Villa Park three and a half hours later. For the time being though, it was back to League action for the twelfth-placed 'Reds', who hadn't won a League game since the 3-0 victory over Coventry two months earlier.

On Saturday, 16th March, a Terry Wilson effort earned them a share of the spoils against Manchester United at the City Ground in the first of three consecutive draws. The others were 1-1 against Arsenal at Highbury and a 0-0 stalemate at Everton. These were followed by a now familiar defeat at the hands of Wimbledon at Plough Lane - this time by three-goals-to-one.

We did manage to exact revenge on Sheffield United at the City Ground on April Fool's Day, achieving a 2-0 victory thanks to a brace from Tommy Gaynor. This was our first League victory in ten games. At the time of our defeat against them at Bramall Lane back in December, they'd been bottom of the table with no victories in sixteen games and had accumulated only four points. As previously mentioned, their 3-2 success was effectively the turning point of their season. Since then they'd gone on to win a further nine matches and accumulated a total of 35 points from 30 games played. Incredibly, they were now just one place behind us in the table.

A 3-1 defeat against Manchester City at Maine Road the following Saturday, was then followed by a 1-0 success over the relegation-doomed 'Sheep' at the City Ground on Wednesday, 10th April, four days before the scheduled semi-final at Villa Park. I was working away in Manchester that week and therefore missed out on another gratifying victory over our 'nearest and dearest'. I had to admire from afar our part in their eventual relegation to the Second Division. It was also the first home game I'd missed since the second round League Cup tie against Brighton on 8th October 1986, and the first home League game since way back on 27th April 1977, against Oldham Athletic. And, to add insult to injury, it was the first encounter of any description I'd missed between the two sides, since the 'Sheep's' promotion to the First Division back in 1969. Still, as people are always quick to point out...we Forest supporters are just so bloomin' fickle!

OUR 20,000 allocation for Villa Park, consisted of 10,000 terrace tickets for the Holte End, around 7,000 seats for the impressive North Stand, and the remainder for the not-so-impressive Whitton Lane Stand (since transformed into the very impressive Doug Ellis Stand). West Ham had been allocated a similar number, with around 12,000 in the other half of the Holte End and the remainder for the all-seated Trinity Stand on one side of the ground.

Not surprisingly, Big Lee and I had been busily making arrangements and with no trouble whatsoever; we'd quickly filled two coaches for this game. One of Steve Howarth's mates from Long Eaton, Kev West, who'd been travelling on our coaches for several seasons now and who was a complete nutter, had also arranged for us to drop into a smashing pub on the outskirts of 'Brum' on our way to the game. He worked as some sort of rep in the brewing industry and had many connections up and down the country. Somehow he'd persuaded the landlord to reserve the pub almost exclusively for our own use, virtually from opening time to kicking out time. They'd also laid on an abundance of food and snacks and installed a couple of televisions, so we could keep watch on the other semi-final at Wembley. This was being screened live on BBC1, as was our tie against the 'Hammers' later on. Mind you, with around 120 extremely hungry and thirsty souls packed into his pub for almost three hours, the landlord was absolutely raking it in.

Whilst drowning ourselves in booze, gorging ourselves silly, and singing ourselves hoarse, we also managed to catch most of Tottenham's excellent 3-1 victory over the 'Gunners'. Gazza was at his inspirational best, scoring a spectacular thirty-yard free kick and generally running the show from midfield. The Final was destined to be an entertaining contest; especially if Forest were to provide the opposition on the day.

Following another fantastic lunchtime session, we made our usual last-minute dash to the game, arriving at Villa Park with only minutes to spare. The stadium was bathed in sunshine as the teams took to the field and, as you might expect for an FA Cup semi-final, the atmosphere was electric. Many of the West Ham fans had arrived in fancy dress - with Viking Warriors the order of the day - and this gave the whole thing a carnival-like atmosphere.

The young Forest side included 21-year-old Gary Charles who, despite making his senior debut for the Club in a League Cup tie against Coventry City two years earlier, had only recently established himself as a first team regular. Furthermore, on the left hand side of midfield, Ian Woan was playing in only his fourth senior game since his arrival from Non-League Runcorn - and this was the semi-final of the FA Cup no less. The West Ham line-up included former Forest star Colin Foster at the heart of it's defence.

The opening ten minutes of the game were relatively quiet, with both teams sizing one another up. In fact, the only real excitement early on, was when a low shot from Garry Parker went just inches wide of a post following a quick counter-attack from Forest in the seventh minute.

The game came to life quite dramatically in the twenty-sixth minute, when Gary Crosby broke away from West Ham defender Tony Gale, only to be hauled down just outside the box. It seemed to most of the watching 40,041 crowd, to be little more than a clumsy challenge, worthy of at most a booking. But, as is so often the case, referee Keith Hackett of Sheffield saw it differently and gave the unfortunate defender his marching orders, much to the dismay of the 20,000 'Hammers' fans, who went absolutely berserk. Whilst in my opinion it was definitely a foul, never in a million years was it a sending off offence.

This incident seemed to rouse West Ham, who came at Forest with a vengeance. Following a corner from the right, a Colin Foster shot from close range was blocked by the Forest defence. George Parris then crashed the rebound against an upright from eighteen yards out - a lucky escape for the 'Reds'. Despite this, the scores remained level at half-time and, as the two teams left the pitch for a well-earned break, the topic of conversation was the controversial dismissal of Gale and what likely impact this would have on the outcome of the game.

When the second half got under way, Forest were kicking towards the massive Holte End, housing 10,000 of their travelling supporters, myself included. The view from the back of this enormous bank of terracing was absolutely fantastic, although when play was up the other end of the field, the players looked more like 'Subutteo' figures. I'd stood on this end once before, when we took on Bristol Rovers in a third round, second replay back in January 1977 - a game which we'd won 6-0 (see Chapter 11 - ''Brian Clough and Peter Taylor''). I was praying for a similar result against the 'Hammers.'

To our delight, we didn't have to wait long for our one-man advantage to pay dividends. In the fiftieth minute, following a neat link up between Clough and Keane, the Irishman slotted a defence-splitting pass into the path of Gary Crosby, who went on to despatch a low, right-foot shot into the bottom corner of the net.

West Ham weren't finished yet though, and minutes later responded with a Stuart Slater shot from twenty-yards out, which cannoned back into play off Mark Crossley's right hand post. Forest still had a game on their hands, but once more they began to pile on the pressure. A blistering twenty-yard effort from Keane zipped inches over the crossbar, bringing about a loud chorus of: *"You've lost that loving feeling"* from the Forest supporters. (Incidentally, I haven't a clue what the relevance of this song is to Forest, or why it came to prominence on the banks of the River Trent in the first place?)

In the sixtieth minute, the relentless Forest pressure finally took it's toll on the weary West Ham defenders. Roy Keane played a neat one-two with Glover on the edge of the box before slamming them into a decisive 2-0 lead. Minutes later, a brilliant curling effort from Parker was turned over the bar by the agile Micklosko in the 'Hammers'' goal.

In the seventieth minute, defender Colin Foster completely misjudged a long throw-in from the right from Crosby and the ball deflected off Nigel Clough straight into the path of the on-rushing Pearce. He slammed a firm right-foot shot into the back of the net from only six yards out, claiming his twelfth goal of the season. (Considering none of these had come from the penalty spot, this was an excellent tally for a left-back.)

As we ran up a chorus of: *"Brian Clough's a football genius,"* the West Ham fans responded immediately with chants of: *"Billy Bonds' Claret 'n' Blue Army."* And, much to their credit, they continued non-stop for the final twenty minutes of the game, even though their battered and bruised team were taking a severe 'hammering'.

Following a neat one-two with Glover, Gary Charles' eighty-first minute effort from twelve yards out, made it 4-0 to the 'Reds', although this did nothing to dampen the enthusiasm of the West Ham supporters. They turned up the volume even more, almost raising the roof off the stadium. They showed just what fantastically loyal supporters they are, even in the face of such adversity.

Brian Clough - his objective for the day seemingly achieved - left the arena with one minute left on the clock. As he made his way down the tunnel, he received rapturous applause from the 'red and white' half of Villa Park. The final whistle ended West Ham's misery and 20,000 'Travelling Trickies' began to celebrate the Club's first FA Cup Final qualification since 1959. This was also the signal for John Farley to rush from his seat in the Whitton Lane Stand away to our right and onto the pitch. He did a celebratory jig in the centre circle for the watching TV audience of millions - including his very own Managing Director. Even from my position right at the back of the Holte End, I couldn't miss him. He was wearing a bright maroon and rust coloured jumper - hardly the most inconspicuous of garments, to say the least. Not surprisingly, he had some explaining to do the next morning when he returned to work!

BUOYED no doubt by this comprehensive semi-final success, Forest went on the rampage during the final five League games of the season. They won four and drew one of these fixtures, scoring no less than twenty goals along the way, whilst conceding only five.

A 7-0 (yes - seven-nil!) victory over Chelsea at the City Ground on Saturday, 20th April, was followed by a 5-0 demolition of Norwich City - also on Trentside - four days later. Then, in a dress rehearsal for the Cup Final, they took on Spurs at White Hart Lane on Saturday, 4th May, where the honours were even in a 1-1 draw. It was back to the City Ground two days later, where they defeated Liverpool 2-1 in a game televised live and which attracted a crowd of 26,181. Five days later, on the final Saturday of the League programme, Leeds United provided the opposition in a 4-3 thriller at the City Ground, watched by a crowd of 25,067.

Over this three-week period, they'd elevated themselves from fourteenth position in the First Division table, to a very creditable eighth. Their final tally of 54 points from 38 games consisted of fourteen victories, twelve draws and twelve defeats. In total, they'd scored 65 goals and conceded 50.

During the run-in to the end of the season, we'd been preparing ourselves for FA Cup Final Day on Saturday, 18th May. Despite Wembley's 80,000 capacity, both clubs received a meagre allocation of only 21,500 tickets. Both could have sold double this amount easily. The fact that 37,000 tickets would be distributed to the rest of the world and his dog, speaks volumes for the state of the game nowadays.

Although some of these are distributed amongst the grass-roots element, the majority end up as 'freebies' for the parasites and hangers-on who seem to appear at all major sporting events in this country. Whilst the 'Forest-mad' factory worker with a wife and three kids to support, who can't afford a season ticket, but goes to matches whenever he can, finds it impossible to lay his hands on a ticket; the 'corporate hospitality' machine is dishing them out like confetti to every 'Tom, Dick and Harry', irrespective of whether they've ever been to a game or not. Needless to say, thousands of these tickets end up on the black market and in the hands of unscrupulous touts. The result is that legitimate supporters have to virtually re-mortgage their homes, just to fulfil a lifelong ambition of seeing their team play in an FA Cup Final at Wembley.

As I was still working away in Manchester during the week, Big Lee was left with the task of arranging this trip all on his own. He booked two coaches, one of which would travel down to London on the Friday, with the other leaving first thing on Saturday morning. As there was no chance of me getting back from Manchester in time for Friday's excursion, I was delegated the responsibility of ensuring things went according to plan on Saturday.

We set off bright and early, having arranged to meet up with the 'Friday crew' down in Murphy's Bar later that morning. Prior to leaving, I'd spoken to Lee by phone, only to be informed that he'd had his wallet stolen the night before whilst out on the town. Not only had it contained all his spending money for the weekend, but crucially, it also contained his match ticket. He was inconsolable.

By the time we met up with the others in Paddington, we'd had a whip-round for him on the way down. The first thing we did was to present him with a wad of cash, for which he was extremely grateful. Although this wasn't necessarily going to get him into the stadium, he would at least be able to drown his sorrows in style, whilst the rest of us enjoyed the game. Besides, Big Russ Jolly hadn't got a ticket either - although he never seemed to go anywhere with one, but always managed to get into see the action somehow - so he would at least have a drinking partner to help wile away the afternoon. It would also give him a fighting chance of buying a ticket on the black market, should one be available at the right price.

We stayed in Paddington for the full lunchtime session - although we did send the two empty coaches on their way to the stadium early on, just so they could park up in a reasonable spot. We later made our way across London by tube. When around fifty of us piled onto the train at Paddington, we found ourselves completely surrounded by scores of boisterous Spurs fans also on their way to the game. Although things were fairly tense all the way through to Wembley Park tube station, apart from a bit of 'friendly' banter between the two rival groups and a fair amount of chanting and singing, there was no real sign of any trouble.

It was a long walk down Wembley Way, but it was great to see there were plenty of Forest supporters around. On the face of it, we didn't appear to be too outnumbered by our North London opponents. By this time, Big Lee had almost given up hope of finding a ticket. He'd decided instead to find himself a friendly looking policeman - no mean feat in itself - and explain what had happened, in the slim hope he'd be allowed into the stadium anyway. "Ya've got no bloody chance youth!" was the general consensus of opinion, as we bade him farewell outside and headed for the turnstiles.

Once inside, we established where our seats were, before grabbing one last beer from the refreshments at the back of the stand. Eventually we made our way down to the seats and began to watch the pre-match formalities. As the view was so crap from this part of the stadium, we all stood on our seats and joined in with a loud chorus of: *"We're on the march with Cloughie's Ar-my, We're all goin' to Wem-ber-ley."* This echoed all around the 'Tunnel End' of the stadium.

We'd already decided that anyone caught sitting in Big Lee's seat would be carted off towards the nearest policeman and asked to do some serious explaining. However, the chances were, it would only have been poor old 'Mr Factory Worker', who'd just forked out his last two hundred quid to some Cockney Spiv outside the stadium! The 'seats' turned out to be nothing more than long wooden benches anyway, therefore it was impossible to determine exactly who was sitting - or in our case standing - where. About five minutes after we'd arrived, who should come bounding down the steps, but Big Lee himself, flanked by a couple of serious looking police officers. And who was following just two steps behind them? Well, none other than a beaming Russ Jolly of course. He'd only gone and done it again hadn't he...the jammy so and so!

As the pre-match atmosphere began to build, it emerged there were considerably more Spurs fans inside Wembley than Forest. I would even go as far as to say we were outnumbered by about two to one. The bulk of the black market tickets had obviously been circulating around London and been snapped up by local supporters. Although this was hard to swallow, we were determined not to let them out-sing us on Cup Final Day.

When Brian Clough and Terry Venables led the teams out, they received a rapturous reception from the 80,000 crowd, who between them had paid out well in excess of £2 million in gate receipts. Having lined up in front of the Royal Box, the players then stood to attention whilst the crowd joined in the traditional singing of 'Abide with me', followed immediately by the National Anthem. Being every inch as patriotic as our North London counterparts, we stuck out our chests and joined in with great enthusiasm. What a pity the supporters of Liverpool and Everton hadn't done the same three years earlier when they'd met in the famous all-Merseyside encounter. They'd jeered and whistled loudly right throughout, whilst the band had struggled to make themselves heard. Damned heathens!

The teams were then presented to Prince Charles and Princess Diana, followed by the Duke and Duchess of Kent, who's job it would be to hand over the trophy at the end of the game. *(In view of her tragic death six years later, I'm glad I managed to see Diana in the flesh at least once during her lifetime).* Once the formalities were over, the players ran over to their respective ends of the stadium to warm up and were greeted by rapturous applause from their supporters.

The line-ups that day were as follows:

	FOREST:	SPURS:	
1	Mark Crossley	Eric Thorstvedt	1
2	Gary Charles	Justin Edinburgh	2
3	Stuart Pearce (Captn.)	Pat Van Den Hauwe	3
4	Des Walker	Steve Sedgley	4
5	Steve Chettle	David Howells	5
6	Roy Keane	Gary Mabbutt (Captn.)	6
7	Gary Crosby	Paul Stewart	7
8	Garry Parker	Paul Gascoigne	8
9	Nigel Clough	Vinny Samways	9
10	Lee Glover	Gary Lineker	10
11	Ian Woan	Paul Allen	11
	Subs: Brian Laws	**Subs:** Paul Walsh	
	Steve Hodge	Nayim	

The average age of the Forest side was only 23. Cloughie had put his faith in youngsters Lee Glover and Gary Charles, rather than opting for the experience of Brian Laws and 'Harry'

Hodge who, much to their disappointment, had been consigned to a place on the bench.

Referee Roger Milford got the game under way, with Forest kicking away from the 'Tunnel End' during the first period. With less than a minute on the clock, Gascoigne made his intentions clear with a chest-high challenge on Garry Parker, which went completely unpunished, much to the dismay of the Forest supporters. The sound of: *"You-Fat-Bastard!"* rang out from our end of the stadium.

The first few minutes were very tentative, with little in the way of goal-mouth incident. A number of heavy tackles were flying in from both sides though. Then, in the sixteenth minute, Gascoigne scythed down Gary Charles just outside the Tottenham penalty area, badly injuring himself in the process. It was a terrible challenge. However, following extensive treatment from the Spurs Physio, Roger Milford again chose to be lenient.

Stuart Pearce stepped up to slam the resulting twenty-yard free kick high into the roof of the net, putting the 'Reds' 1-0 up, and sending the whole of Nottingham into a frenzy (well the red majority of it anyway). This was effectively the first real shot of the game. Before Spurs kicked off again, Gascoigne slumped to the floor and began writhing around in agony. Eventually he was stretchered off with what turned out to be a career-threatening knee injury and which would keep him out of the game for many months. As he'd committed two appalling fouls leading up to this injury, he should have undoubtedly been sent from the field, rather than carried from it. The fact he wasn't, was extremely baffling, but significantly it meant he could be replaced by substitute Nayim, who would go on to play a crucial part in the game.

As they began to press forward in search of an equaliser, Gary Lineker latched onto Paul Allen's low cross from the right to sweep the ball past keeper Mark Crossley and into the back of the net. Fortunately for Forest, the linesman had raised his flag and the 'goal' was ruled out for offside. Television replays showed the striker was quite clearly in an on-side position when the ball was played and consequently Forest had had a very lucky escape.

Although chances were few and far between for Forest, Gary Crosby could and should have increased their lead when he was put clean through on goal by Ian Woan's clever pass on twenty minutes. However, keeper Eric Thorstvedt came out to smother the winger's rather tamely-struck effort and keep Spurs in the game.

The Londoners continued to dominate and Paul Allen went close with a diving header, which was well caught by Crossley. Then, on thirty-two minutes, Paul Stewart sent Lineker clean through on goal, only for Crossley to send him sprawling inside the area. Roger Milford had no hesitation in awarding the spot kick, but amazingly chose not to even book Crossley, who in reality was lucky to stay on the field. Lineker stepped up to smash his penalty hard and low to 'Big Norm's' left, but he acrobatically turned it around the post, to the delight of the travelling hordes from Nottingham. Somehow it was beginning to look like Forest's name was on the Cup and, as they trooped from the pitch at half-time still a goal to the good, it was difficult to envisage them not winning this game.

Forest had more of the play in the early stages of the second half, and although they weren't playing particularly well, they did create one or two half-chances. Roy Keane almost went clean through but was checked at the last minute by David Howells, before Garry Parker went close with a twenty-yard effort minutes later. It was now pretty much end-to-end stuff, but in the fifty-fifth minute, Spurs pulled level. The hard-working Allen, following a sweeping cross-field pass from Nayim, put Paul Stewart clean through and he slammed the ball home from twelve yards out. It was nothing more than Spurs deserved, having dominated for long periods of the game.

From this moment on, the Londoners really began to pile on the pressure, with Vinny Samways and Nayim totally dictating the play. Steve Hodge replaced the tired looking Woan in a last ditch attempt to nullify the threat from midfield. The 'Reds' were playing quite well, but seemed unable to create any chances. The fans responded with chants of: *"Come on you Reds"* and *"Brian Clough's Red and White Army,"* but still the chances were few and far between.

With ten minutes left, Spurs sent on Paul Walsh in place of Samways, which meant they were now playing with three up front - a very bold move indeed by manager Terry Venables. However, on eighty-three minutes, it was Forest who were presented with the perfect opportunity of grabbing the winner. Nigel Clough was bowled over on the edge of the box, giving them a free kick right in the middle of 'Psycho' territory. As Pearce lined up to have a crack at goal, Garry Parker stole in on the blind side to float in an innocuous effort which bounced off the Tottenham wall and over the bar for a corner. Had Pearce taken it, then I'm sure the keeper would have at least been tested.

In stoppage time, Howells went close for Spurs, but his header from Nayim's right wing cross was well saved by Crossley. This was the final piece of action before the referee's whistle signalled the end of normal time. The players trooped over to their respective benches for a rub down and a few inspirational words from their managers. However, for reasons known only to Cloughie, he chose to spend the entire five minute break chatting casually to a couple of policemen standing in the tunnel underneath the Royal Box. Given the youthfulness and general inexperience of the Forest side, it is inconceivable that a few words of encouragement from the great man wouldn't have proved beneficial at such a crucial moment in time.

When the contest got under way again, Forest were kicking away from the 'Tunnel End' of the stadium. It was immediately apparent that Venables had lifted his players during the break and Spurs poured forward in search of a winner. In the fourth minute of extra-time, Walsh cracked a looping header from Nayim's cross against the Forest crossbar, with Pearce putting the rebound out for a corner. From the resulting cross, Stewart headed the ball across the face of goal, where the unfortunate Des Walker - attempting to clear his lines - managed only to send his diving header high into the roof of his own net. Poor old 'Dessie' was distraught, and as the Spurs supporters went wild, we just stood with head in hands, unable to believe what had happened.

Minutes later, Forest earned themselves a free kick in virtually the same position they'd scored from earlier on in the game. However, on this occasion, Psycho's firmly-struck shot cannoned off the Spurs' defensive wall. This was their only serious effort of the first half.

During the second period, Spurs continued to dominate, with Forest finding it almost impossible to make any impact. Brian Laws replaced the unimpressive Glover with ten minutes left on the clock and at last they began to press forward in search of an equaliser. Gary Charles' volley then whizzed past a post following a corner from the right and it was now Tottenham's turn to defend, which they did resolutely right through to the bitter end.

The travelling 'Red & White Army' got behind them throughout, despite the fact that for the last two minutes at least, Forest were unable to get even a touch of the ball. The whole thing was very painful to watch, but referee Roger Milford finally put us out of our misery and the Forest players sank to their knees.

On reflection, Spurs thoroughly deserved their eighth Cup Final victory, having undoubtedly been the better side on the day. There had been a couple of decent individual performances from Forest players, such as Roy Keane and Gary Charles, but the likes of Crosby and in particular Glover, had looked well out of their depth. Perhaps if 'Harry' Hodge had been on from the start, and Cloughie had given his boys a pep talk before extra time, then things may well have been different? Unfortunately, we will never know.

This was the eighth major Cup Final I'd had the privilege of watching Forest in during my twenty-five years as a supporter. It was only the second time I'd tasted defeat. For any supporter, seeing your team lose on such a special occasion, is without doubt the worst experience you can have. You certainly wouldn't want to make a habit of it anyway.

DESPITE this Cup Final defeat, it had been another memorable season for the 'Reds' and their appreciative army of supporters. Eighth position in the First Division table; the 'Sheep' finishing bottom and relegated to Division Two again; average home League attendances up by almost 2,000 to 22,138; not to mention another trip to Wembley.

The Club had also announced ambitious plans for the redevelopment of the City Ground in the very near future. Effectively, in addition to being one of the country's premier clubs out there on the pitch, this would ensure we also had the off-field facilities to match. These were exciting times in the history of our much-loved Club.

Date		Opposition	Venue	Competition	Score	Attendance
Aug	25	**Queens Park Rangers**	H	League	1-1	21,619
	28	Liverpool	A	League	0-2	33,363
Sept	1	Coventry City	A	League	2-2	12,630
	8	**Southampton**	H	League	3-1	18,559
	15	Crystal Palace	A	League	2-2	20,545
	22	**Arsenal**	H	League	0-2	26,013
	26	**Burnley**	H	LC 2 - 1st Leg	4-1	17,987
	29	Manchester United	A	League	1-0	46,766
Oct	7	**Everton**	H	League	3-1	25,790
	10	Burnley	A	LC 2 - 2nd Leg	1-0	11,415
	20	Chelsea	A	League	0-0	22,403
	27	**Tottenham Hotspur**	H	League	1-2	27,347
	30	Plymouth Argyle	A	LC 3	2-1	17,467
Nov	3	Leeds United	A	League	1-3	30,409
	10	Aston Villa	A	League	1-1	25,797
	17	**Sunderland**	H	League	2-0	22,757
	21	**Newcastle United**	H	Zenith Cup 1	2-1	9,567
	24	Derby County	A	League	1-2	21,729
	28	Coventry City	A	LC 4	4-5	16,304
Dec	1	**Luton Town**	H	League	2-2	16,498
	15	Queens Park Rangers	A	League	2-1	10,156
	22	Sheffield United	A	League	2-3	20,394
	26	**Wimbledon**	H	League	2-1	16,221
	31	**Manchester City**	H	League	1-3	24,937
Jan	2	Norwich City	A	League	6-2	17,043
	6	Crystal Palace	A	FA Cup 3	0-0	15,396
	12	**Coventry City**	H	League	3-0	18,344
	19	Southampton	A	League	1-1	16,044
	21	**Crystal Palace**	H	FA Cup 3 - Replay	2-2	23,201
	28	**Crystal Palace**	H	FA Cup 3 - 2nd Replay	3-0	22,164
	30	Barnsley	A	Zenith Cup 2	1-2	6,692
Feb	2	**Crystal Palace**	H	League	0-1	17,045
	13	Newcastle United	A	FA Cup 4	2-2	29,231
	16	Sunderland	A	League	0-1	20,394
	18	**Newcastle United**	H	FA Cup 4 - Replay	3-0	28,962
	23	**Aston Villa**	H	League	2-2	22,036
	25	Southampton	A	FA Cup 5	1-1	18,512
Mar	2	Luton Town	A	League	0-1	9,577
	4	**Southampton**	H	FA Cup 5 - Replay	3-1	26,633
	9	Norwich City	A	FA Cup 6	1-0	24,018
	16	**Manchester United**	H	League	1-1	23,859
	20	Arsenal	A	League	1-1	34,152
	23	Everton	A	League	0-0	23,078
	30	Wimbledon	A	League	1-3	6,392
Apr	1	**Sheffield United**	H	League	2-0	25,308
	6	Manchester City	A	League	1-3	25,169
	10	**Derby County**	H	League	1-0	25,109
	14	West Ham United (At Villa Park, Birmingham)		FA Cup SF	4-0	40,041
	20	**Chelsea**	H	League	7-0	20,305
	24	**Norwich City**	H	League	5-0	17,641
May	4	Tottenham Hotspur	A	League	1-1	30,891
	6	**Liverpool**	H	League	2-1	26,181
	11	**Leeds United**	H	League	4-3	25,067
	18	Tottenham Hotspur (At Wembley Stadium)		FA Cup Final	1-2	80,000

HOME ATTENDANCES

	AGGREGATE ATTENDANCE	HIGHEST ATTENDANCE	LOWEST ATTENDANCE	AVERAGE ATTENDANCE
League:	420,636	27,347	16,221	22,138
League Cup:	17,987	17,987	17,987	17,987
FA Cup:	100,960	28,962	22,164	25,240
Zenith Cup:	9,567	9,567	9,567	9,567
All Competitions:	549,150	28,962	9,567	21,966

FINAL LEAGUE TABLE - DIVISION ONE

Position	P	W	D	L	GF	GA	Pts
1. Arsenal	38	24	13	1	74	18	83 *
2. Liverpool	38	23	7	8	77	40	76
3. Crystal Palace	38	20	9	9	50	41	69
4. Leeds United	38	19	7	12	65	47	64
5. Manchester City	38	17	11	10	64	53	62
6. Manchester United	38	16	12	10	58	45	59 **
7. Wimbledon	38	14	14	10	53	46	56
8. Nottingham Forest	**38**	**14**	**12**	**12**	**65**	**50**	**54**
9. Everton	38	13	12	13	50	46	51
10. Tottenham Hotspur	38	11	16	11	51	50	49
11. Chelsea	38	13	10	15	58	69	49
12. Queens Park Rangers	38	12	10	16	44	53	46
13. Sheffield United	38	13	7	18	36	55	46
14. Southampton	38	12	9	17	58	69	45
15. Norwich City	38	13	6	19	41	64	45
16. Coventry City	38	11	11	16	42	49	44
17. Aston Villa	38	9	14	15	46	58	41
18. Luton Town	38	10	7	21	42	61	37
19. Sunderland	38	8	10	20	38	60	34
20. Derby County	38	5	9	24	37	75	24

* Arsenal had two points deducted for disciplinary reasons
** Manchester United had one point deducted for disciplinary reasons

AWAY ATTENDANCES

	AGGREGATE ATTENDANCE	HIGHEST ATTENDANCE	LOWEST ATTENDANCE	AVERAGE ATTENDANCE
League:	426,932	46,766	6,392	22,470
League Cup:	45,186	17,467	11,415	15,062
FA Cup:	207,198	80,000	15,396	34,533
Zenith Cup:	6,692	6,692	6,692	6,692
All Competitions:	686,008	80,000	6,392	23,655

"WE'RE THE PRIDE OF NOTTINGHAM"

AS USUAL the close season was over in a flash. One minute we were welcoming home our defeated Wembley warriors in the Old Market Square and listening to poor old 'Dessie' making his heartfelt apologies for scoring Tottenham's winning goal. And the next we were sitting outside the Aviary on a sunny August afternoon, hoping for an opening-day victory over visitors Everton.

It had been a very busy summer, with many Forest supporters making a second journey to Wembley at the end of May to cheer on our neighbours Notts County in the Second Division Play-Off Final against Brighton. The 'Pies' won this game 2-0, thus securing their promotion to the top flight once again. There had also been plenty of activity on the transfer front, with players coming and going in droves. And, having been awarded an OBE in the New Year's Honours List; Cloughie had also enjoyed a trip to the Palace to meet the Queen.

Steve Hodge had joined Leeds United, bringing to an end his second successful spell at the City Ground. Brian Rice had joined Scottish club Falkirk after six fairly uninspiring seasons with the 'Reds'. And Franz Carr had joined Second Division Newcastle United in a £250,000 deal. Promising young defender Carl Tiler had been drafted in from Second Division Barnsley for a fee of £1.5 million, and prolific striker Teddy Sheringham had arrived from Millwall in a £2 million deal. He'd scored no less than 38 goals for the South London outfit during the previous season alone.

The fact the Club had showed a willingness to delve into the transfer market had inspired a total of 14,000 supporters to purchase season tickets during the summer. This transfer activity continued throughout the month of August, with 22-year-old striker Phil Starbuck joining Third Division Huddersfield Town on a free transfer, and Northern Ireland international Kingsley Black - the subject of constant transfer speculation for months - finally joining the 'Reds' from Luton Town in a £1.5 million deal.

Forest had also been well represented on the international front, with no less than five players joining Graham Taylor's England squad for a mid-summer tour 'Down Under'. Regular England quartet Des Walker, Stuart Pearce, Nigel Clough and Steve Hodge, had been joined by their young Forest colleague Gary Charles who, given both his youthfulness and his relative lack of experience, had been given a surprising call-up by the England supremo. The fact he actually played in the games against New Zealand and Malaysia confirmed he hadn't been taken along simply for the ride.

The size of the First Division had been increased once again - and surprisingly so, given the already heavy demands of the domestic season - from twenty to twenty-two clubs. This added another four games to an already overcrowded fixture list. The overwhelming call from within the game for a breakaway 'Premier League' was now also gathering momentum.

For the first time in four years, the 'Reds' began the season with a victory, when they defeated the 'Toffee-men' 2-1 in front of a City Ground crowd of 24,422. Despite going behind to a goal from Polish star Robert Warycha, the two Nigels - Clough and Jemson - turned the game on it's head. Firstly, 'Cloughie' fired in a vital equaliser and then, with only three minutes remaining, 'Jemmo' smashed home the winner past goalkeeper Neville Southall.

Three days later, they went down 1-0 to Leeds United at Elland Road, and on the following Saturday made the very short journey across Trent Bridge to take on the newly-promoted 'Magpies' - a fixture I always look forward to almost as much as those against our real enemy the 'Sheep'.

The rivalry between the two Nottingham clubs is a very peculiar one indeed. Historically, Forest supporters have always been very sympathetic towards Notts, cheering loudly when the City Ground scoreboard tells us they're '1-0 up at Doncaster Rovers', and even venturing down to Meadow Lane on occasions in order to cheer them on when the 'Reds' haven't got a game. Many of us have even gone to the trouble of following them down to Wembley on a couple of occasions - as previously mentioned - to lend our much-needed support to their promotion quest via the play-offs. Personally, having been born and bred in Nottingham, I feel a certain affinity to all the local clubs, including Mansfield Town, and feel I have as much right as anyone to cheer them on, should I so wish.

On the other hand however, the majority of County supporters (and Stags fans for that

SEASON 1991/92

CHAPTER 26

261

matter) seem to hate Forest and Forest supporters with a vengeance. What's more, they seem to hate us even more, because we simply refuse to hate them. What a hypocritical bunch they are though? One minute they're begging us to follow them down to Wembley just to swell their numbers; the next they're hurling insults at us and coming out with junk such as: *"Always shit on the red side of the Trent."*

Over the years, I've somehow managed to ignore their rather pathetic attitude towards us...that is, until more recent times anyway. Lately, my tolerance has snapped, to the point where I now treat them with the contempt they deserve. I've come to the conclusion that there are all kinds of people who, like myself, are in love with the game of football. There are the intelligent and articulate types, the loyal and passionate types, the humorous and witty types, the fair-minded and reasonable types, and of course...there are Notts County supporters!

This reminds me in fact of a letter I once read in the 'Agony Aunt' column of a certain daily newspaper. It went something like this:

Dear Marj,

I'm a 22-year-old male who enjoys cross-dressing, am into bondage and sado-masochism, and until recently used to spend most of my time cruising through the red-light area of Nottingham looking for under-age rent boys.

Since my release from Lincoln Prison three months ago, having served out my three-year jail term for armed robbery, I've found it almost impossible to get myself a proper job and have therefore been unable to find a legitimate method of funding my serious crack and cocaine habit.

My father is too busy running his money-laundering business to bother himself with my plight and my mother has never been the same since Dad left her for a woman half his age when I was just three-years-old and she had to go on the game just to make ends meet. Since my three older sisters teamed up with her a couple of years ago to open what is now Nottingham's premier massage parlour, they also seem to have little or no time for me either.

About a month ago, just as my life was at it's lowest ebb and I was even contemplating suicide, I met the most fantastic, gorgeous, beautiful young woman I'd ever seen and fell head over heels in love with her, and she with me. We are now in the middle of an intense and passionate affair and are already discussing the possibility of marriage and children. She's already taken me home to meet her parents and I struck up an instant rapport with her father who is a vicar at the local church.

I'm absolutely madly in love with her and am determined that nothing whatsoever should come between us. My dilemma though is this...should I be completely honest with her and tell her that my 28-year-old brother Melvyn is a Notts County supporter?

I suppose to most Forest supporters, a victory over Notts is a little bit like eating your Christmas dinner really - it's not exactly something you look forward to all year round, but when it does come, you tend to savour every moment of it. And on this particular occasion, there was plenty to savour from our red-shirted heroes, as they walloped our black and white neighbours 4-0.

It was a boiling hot August afternoon and a crowd of 21,044 packed into what was then a very old and crumbling Meadow Lane. As usual, the County supporters were considerably outnumbered by their red and white counterparts from across the River, a substantial number of whom were packed tightly onto the large open Kop End of the ground. The remainder had to be content with the rather ramshackle conditions which prevailed within the old County Road Stand, which stood (and only just!) to the left of the Kop.

Despite a closely fought, goalless first half, the 'Reds' came out with all guns blazing in the second as they attacked the Kop End of the stadium. Gary Crosby broke the deadlock with a glancing header from Roy Keane's cross after fifty-five minutes, with full-back Gary Charles adding a second nine minutes later. Then in the sixty-ninth minute, Roy Keane rather unselfishly squared the ball to the unmarked Sheringham who, from only three yards out, gratefully tapped it into an empty net to score his first goal for the Club (he quickly earned himself the nickname 'Tap-in Teddy' amongst Forest supporters). And finally, in the seventy-fourth minute, Keane got on the score-sheet himself when he carefully slotted the ball home from sixteen yards out, thereby completing the rout. The drinks certainly flowed in town that night, although strangely enough, there didn't seem to be too many Notts supporters about.

BY the beginning of November, Forest's unremarkable start to the season - they'd won only five and drawn two of their fourteen League games to date - saw them sitting in a disappointing seventeenth position in the table, having accumulated just 17 points. However, on the Cup front, they'd disposed of Third Division Bolton Wanderers 9-2 on aggregate in the second round of the League Cup, and had progressed through to the third round of the Zenith Data Systems Cup (formerly the Simod Cup), courtesy of an impressive 3-1 win against Leeds at Elland Road. This had been followed by a third round League Cup victory over Second Division Bristol Rovers, a game in which the young Scott Gemmill scored one of the goals in a 2-0 victory - his first for the Club since making his debut in the 3-1 defeat at Wimbledon the previous season.

Off the pitch, Nigel Jemson had joined Sheffield Wednesday in an £800,000 deal; all 22 First Division clubs had tendered their resignations from the Football League in favour of the new FA Premier League which was due to commence at the beginning of season 1992/93; and Forest had announced their latest plans for the redevelopment of the City Ground.

Although they'd originally planned to rebuild the Trent End first of all, followed by the Bridgford End, a row with the City Council had caused a rethink. It was subsequently decided that work on the new Bridgford Stand would take priority. The Council were holding out for more than ten times the going rate for renting a small strip of extra land along the Trent Embankment which the Club would need to utilise when constructing the impressive new stand. At the end of the season, the builders would move in and demolish the 'Kop End', replacing it with a two-tiered, all-seater stand. It was hoped this would be completed during the early part of the following season. This was exciting news for Forest supporters who'd been demanding these improvements for many years now.

November and December proved slightly more promising on the League front, with three victories and one draw in a total of six games. This propelled the 'Reds' up the table to a more creditable eleventh position. By this time, Cloughie had decided midfielder Garry Parker was surplus to requirements and had sold him to Aston Villa for a modest £650,00 at the end of November.

Bottom-placed Luton Town visited the City Ground on Wednesday, 1st January 1992, and despite their lowly position, gave Forest a scare. Had it not been for Des Walker's late equaliser - his first ever goal for the Club and one which sparked amazing scenes of celebrations on the City Ground terraces - the 'Hatters' would have stolen all three points.

A good percentage of the 23,809 crowd had already left the ground when Des went on a long, mazey run through the heart of the visitors' defence. This ended with him smashing the ball past goalkeeper Steve Sutton (ironically on loan from the 'Reds' at the time) and high into the roof of the net. It was the kind of moment in football you can wait your whole life for and when it eventually comes along you are completely unable to contain yourself. Poor old Des had never scored before during his entire professional career (except famously at the wrong end of course!) and I'm almost certain he hasn't managed to conjure up another one since. I'm just glad I was one of the few thousand who'd hung around long enough to witness this 'once in a lifetime' occurrence.

The following Saturday, attentions once again turned towards the FA Cup, with Second Division Wolves arriving at the City Ground for a third round tie. A total of 27,068 fans turned out to see the 'Reds' progress through to the fourth round with a 1-0 victory, thanks to a lone effort from Nigel Clough. Their reward was another home tie in the fourth round against Fourth Division Hereford United, scheduled to take place on Sunday, 26th January.

In the meantime, Forest's busy schedule included a trip to Crystal Palace on Wednesday, 8th January, for a League Cup quarter-final fixture. Once again, the prolific Clough was on target in a 1-1 draw, earning them a replay back on Trentside. The following Saturday, Notts County made the short trip across Trent Bridge for the return League fixture between the two sides. For the first time since the League Cup quarter-final tie against Spurs two years earlier, the 'full-up' signs were on display above the turnstiles, with 30,168 supporters crammed inside the ground long before kick off. Thousands of disappointed fans were turned away - as they had been for the aforementioned fixture - and a sack-full of complaints flooded into the City Ground the following week. Although Kingsley Black gave them the lead in the third minute of the game, there would be no repeat of the early season massacre at Meadow Lane. Having missed a hat-full of chances, they allowed the 'Pies' back into the game, and a fifty-second-minute equaliser from Richard Dryden gave them a share of the spoils.

BY this time, my son Thomas was almost eight-years-old and, not surprisingly, absolutely Forest-mad. Although I'd taken him to many minor games, such as pre-season friendlies and County Cup matches, being a completely selfish git who enjoyed his pre-match pint with the lads, I'd so far managed to leave him at home for the more important games. However, this was becoming more and more difficult by the week and, quite frankly, I was now running out of excuses. Besides, I was also feeling extremely guilty about the whole situation.

Since the first day he could stand, all he ever wanted to do was kick a football around. And when he wasn't re-enacting Forest's League Cup / Simod Cup / FA Cup exploits on the back lawn, he was sitting cross-legged on the living room floor watching videos of these very same encounters. He'd watched them so many times in fact; he could recite every single match commentary word for word. Most Saturday and Sunday mornings, I'd wake to the sound of Brian Moore or John Motson - accompanied by Thomas of course - describing in graphic detail one Cup Final goal or another. In the background, the sound of: *"You Reds! You Reds! You Reds!"* could be heard echoing around the living room. And when you've been out on the beer the night before, that's the last thing you need at 7 o'clock in the morning!

Anyway, unable to contend with the guilt any longer, I'd reached a compromise with him: from now on, provided he stayed off my case with regards to League games, I'd take him to all the League Cup and FA Cup games in the future. I'd never sat in the Executive Stand before - apart from when we'd played Tampa Bay Rowdies in a friendly many seasons before - so I bought two upper tier seats for the forthcoming FA Cup fourth round tie against Hereford United. I reckoned at the tender age of eight, he wasn't quite ready for the excitement and rigours of the 'A' Block.

It was a strange feeling on the day, sitting high up there in the stand, looking down on the rest of the stadium. It was like it wasn't the City Ground at all, but some far away stadium elsewhere. There were thousands of Hereford fans amongst the 24,259 crowd, but after all, it was their 'Cup Final' (hark at me - I sound just like a Man City fan!). They were packed tightly across the wide-open spaces of the Bridgford End, away to our left. Despite there being no roof over this end of the ground, they were very noisy indeed, and it was obvious they were going to enjoy every minute of it - apart from the result that is, which was 2-0 to Forest. The goals came from skipper Stuart Pearce and striker Teddy Sheringham - the latter being a stunning half-volley in the final minute of the game. As I made my way back to the car after the final whistle, with a happy and excited son in tow, I felt very satisfied with myself indeed. At last, I'd put my responsibilities as a father before anything else, and for once I was going home with a clear conscience.

The following Saturday, we were really on the receiving end, when Harry Bassett's Sheffield United came to town. The whole ninety minutes were quite surreal really, as the 'Blades' - fourth-from-bottom of the table - hammered us 5-2. Now this kind of thing just didn't happen to Forest - well, not at home anyway, and certainly not during Cloughie's reign. Looking back though, maybe this was an early sign of things to come - but at the time, we were completely oblivious to that and merely treated it as a freak result.

All was forgotten, just four days later, when Crystal Palace visited the City Ground for the League Cup quarter-final replay. A superb hat trick from striker Teddy Sheringham and a typical effort from Stuart Pearce gave Forest a 4-2 victory, and once again we were on the Wembley trail. All that stood in the way, was a two-legged semi-final tie against Spurs - and as they say: *"Tottenham - we always beat Tottenham!"*

The first leg took place at the City Ground on Sunday, 9th February and was shown live on ITV. This undoubtedly had some affect on the attendance, which was a woefully short 21,402. The game itself was no showpiece either, with Teddy Sheringham grabbing Forest's only goal in a dour 1-1 draw. This did however, set things up nicely for the second leg at White Hart Lane, scheduled for Sunday, 1st March.

Before this second leg, Forest had a few other important fixtures to negotiate, starting with a ZDS Cup Northern Area Final, first leg tie against Leicester at Filbert Street the following Wednesday. The winners of this two-legged affair would go through to the Final at Wembley on Sunday, 29th March. Although this game hardly warranted a mention outside of the East Midlands, another trip to Wembley wasn't to be sniffed at. Cloughie was adamant his players should treat this encounter with our Second Division neighbours with total respect.

A crowd of 19,537 - including around 3,000 from Nottingham - squeezed into Filbert Street that evening to watch a closely fought encounter. We had the 'pleasure' of sitting in the 'bus shelter' that passes for a stand on the East Side of the ground opposite to where the impressive new Main Stand now sits. It really was like stepping back into the dark ages, although we did have great fun taunting the home supporters with chants of: *"Worra dump, Worra dump, Worra dump,"* throughout the game.

Although Forest v Leicester matches are considered to be 'local derbies', the rivalry between the two sets of supporters is - as with Forest and Notts - a little one-sided. Generally, most Forest supporters couldn't give a toss one way or another about Leicester. On the other hand, they hate us intensely. With the two cities only 30 miles apart, it's easy to understand why. What's more, given the amount of success Forest have enjoyed over the years, compared to Leicester's sustained periods of mediocrity and failure, there's bound to be a little bit of envy on their part. However, I think it's fair to say, that Forest supporters are just far too busy hating the 'Sheep' to care one iota about the likes of Leicester, or Notts for that matter.

Owing to injury, Forest were without inspirational skipper Stuart Pearce for this game and were given a tough test in this first-leg tie. They endured a tremendous amount of pressure from the Second Division outfit, but hit back by taking a seventy-third minute lead through Scott Gemmill, who clipped a close range effort past City keeper Kevin Poole - much to the delight of the 'Travelling Trickies'. In the eightieth minute though, City levelled the tie, when Colin Gordon headed home from close range. A draw was a fair result at the end of the day, and it set Forest up nicely for the second leg two weeks later.

With two trips to Wembley already on the cards, Forest were determined to make it three, as they lined up at the City Ground the following Saturday to take on Second Division Bristol City in the fifth round of the FA Cup. And in front of 24,615 people, they proved too strong for the West Country outfit, running out easy 4-1 winners. Goals from Pearce, Clough, Sheringham (penalty) and an own goal from Andy Llewellyn sealed their victory. This earned them a quarter-final trip to Second Division Portsmouth on Saturday, 7th March.

Following a 1-1 home draw against Chelsea in the League the following Saturday, Leicester were next on the agenda four days later. A crowd of 21,562 confirmed that the East Midlands public at least, were taking the ZDS competition seriously. Not surprisingly, the 'Reds' held the upper hand throughout this game, and goals from Crosby and defender Darren Wassall - his first for the Club since making his debut against Southampton on 13th February 1988 - gave them a comfortable 2-0 victory and another trip to the 'Twin Towers'.

Once the celebrations had died down, Forest had the opportunity of making it two in four days, when they travelled south to London for the League Cup semi-final second leg against Spurs. With an allocation of 6,000 tickets for this tie, we had no problem at all filling a coach and 'Broughton & Hannas Tours' were back in business once again.

With the kick off scheduled for 3.00-p.m., we decided to head straight for North London and have a few drinks within walking distance of the ground. By the time we arrived, there were hundreds of Forest supporters already in town. We immediately found ourselves inside an enormous pub, filled with faces we knew from Nottingham. The landlord had rather kindly laid on a disco for our entertainment and the beer began to flow. During the course of the afternoon, the singing grew louder and louder and the atmosphere got better and better and, just as we were about to polish off our last few drinks and begin making our way to the stadium, the DJ suddenly announced that, due to a bomb scare, the kick off had been delayed for an hour. Not only that, but the bar would remain open for our benefit. So loudly did everyone cheer following this announcement; you would have been forgiven for thinking that Forest had been given a bye through to the Final.

When we did finally crawl through the door an hour later, we were well-oiled. The torrential rain went some way towards sobering us up on the long walk to the ground, but it has to be said, the majority of Forest supporters inside White Hart Lane that afternoon, were well and truly pissed. This probably accounts for the fantastic atmosphere they generated throughout the game.

Forest hadn't lost at Spurs during their last seven visits, so confidence was high amongst the travelling 'Red & White Army'. When the game finally kicked off, the rain had turned the pitch into a virtual mud-bath. Still, both teams were renowned for their attractive, passing style of football, and there was nothing to suggest this game would be anything other than entertaining.

It was fast and furious stuff right from the first whistle and both sides were looking to grasp the initiative early on. After only ten minutes, the 'Reds' were in front, following good work from Gemmill on the edge of the Spurs' box. As the ball ran loose to Glover, he hammered a low left foot shot past keeper Eric Thorstvedt from sixteen yards out. The large band of Forest supporters behind the Tottenham goal went absolutely berserk. Forest were soon on fire and the chances started coming thick and fast. Despite this, Spurs dragged themselves back into the game on fifteen minutes, when Lineker rose majestically to head home Gordon Durie's cross from the left. This was turning into a classic Cup tie and the crowd of 28,216 were generating an atmosphere to match.

Just before the break, Forest had Mark Crossley to thank for keeping the scores level. Paul Stewart's crisp shot on the turn was whistling towards the bottom corner of the net, when he flung himself to his right and turned it onto the post. This had been an action packed half, full of end-to-end football and consequently, the players left the field to a standing ovation upon the half-time whistle. I'm certain the millions watching at home on television must have been just as impressed.

The game continued in a similar vein during the early part of the second half. The Forest supporters responded with a loud chorus of: *"Brian Clough's Red 'n White Army,"* which they kept going for fully twenty minutes. It grew louder and louder every time the 'Reds' went close and eventually began to drive the Spurs fans wild. They tried their hardest to drown it out with chants of: *"We are Tottenham, We are Tottenham, Super Tottenham, From the Lane."* But as soon as this began to fade away, the sound of: *"Brian Clough's Red 'n White Army,"* re-emerged from the background and just grew louder and louder and louder.

On the pitch, the 'Reds' were turning on the style, despite the mud and slush - not to mention the continuing rain. A tremendous thirty-yard effort from defender Darren Wassall was tipped over the bar by 'Eric the Viking' on sixty minutes, and this was followed by an excellent twenty-five-yard free kick from Nigel Clough, which was also turned around the post. Determined not to be outdone, Crossley then saved well from the dangerous looking Paul Stewart - the man all Forest supporters loved to hate.

Although Forest pressed forward and looked dangerous throughout, their quest for a winner came to nothing. The battle-weary players had to steal themselves for an extra thirty minutes of combat and the wet and bedraggled supporters did their level best to lift their spirits once again.

During the first half of extra time, Forest, who were kicking towards their travelling army of fans, went on the offensive once again. In the 101st minute of the game, they took the lead once more and this time in dramatic style. An out-swinging, right wing corner from Gary Crosby, was met full on by the on-rushing Roy Keane, who's bullet-like header crashed into the roof of the net from ten yards out. We went absolutely bananas behind Thorstvedt's goal. The sound of: *"You've lost that lovin' feeling,"* rang out around White Hart Lane. Then, though I say it myself, we surpassed even our own very high standards, with a loud chorus of: *"Blue moon, You started singin' too soon, An' now your dreams 'ave all gone, Cos Roy Keane's made it two-one!"*

Our red-shirted heroes held out gallantly until the end and, once again, we were on our way to Wembley. Our opponents in the Final on Sunday, 12th April, would be either Middlesbrough or Manchester United, who would contest the other semi-final three days later.

THE following Saturday, we were on the Cup trail yet again, with 5,000 Forest supporters heading to the South-Coast to watch the 'Reds' take on Portsmouth in the quarter-final of the FA Cup. As usual, we were making a day of it and had planned to have a night out in Southsea after the game. However, in view of the rather fearsome reputation of the 'Pompey' supporters, some of us had serious reservations about a night of drinking in Portsmouth.

As expected, the atmosphere inside Fratton Park was intimidating, to say the least. It seemed as if every thug within a fifty-mile radius had turned out for this one and were amongst the crowd of 25,402. We'd been allocated the Milton End - a large bank of uncovered terracing which comfortably held 5,000 standing supporters. Hundreds of 'Pompey' yobs in the stands either side of us seemed concerned only with hurling insults at us throughout the entire ninety minutes of the game. They seemed to care little about what was taking place out there on the pitch itself.

To make matters worse, Forest were absolutely abysmal on the day and fortunate to escape with only a 1-0 defeat. Quite frankly, the Second Division outfit played us off the park, and when Mark Crossley dropped what should have been a simple catch at the feet of Alan McLaughlin, the striker was left with the simple task of slotting the ball into an empty net from just two yards out. The Fratton Park faithful went berserk and the more they turned up the volume, the less the Forest players seemed to be up for it.

One amusing incident, which had occurred at half-time though, did give the travelling supporters something to cheer about at least. Immediately behind the Milton End, stands a long row of old-fashioned terraced houses and visiting supporters can look down upon them from the back of the stand. As I made my way to the refreshment area behind the stand during the interval, I noticed that scores of Forest supporters were hanging over the fence at the back. They were taunting a rather embarrassed looking chap who was perched high up on his roof carrying out some sort of renovation or maintenance work on his property.

Having finished the job in hand, he clambered onto the top rung of his ladder, which was leaning up against the guttering, and started his descent from the roof. Just as he'd got to about the third rung down, the guttering gave way under his weight and the ladder disappeared from underneath him. Fortunately, just at the last second, he managed to grab hold of the chimney-stack right in front of him and ended up dangling precariously from the rooftop. Somehow, he gradually managed to drag himself back up onto the roof, where he sat red-faced behind his chimney stack, whilst two hundred Forest supporters taunted him with a loud chorus of: *"Where's yer lad-der gone? Where's yer ladder gone?"* This little incident was worth the entrance fee all on it's own - which is a lot more than can be said for Forest's performance!

Upon the final whistle, the 'Pompey' supporters poured onto the pitch in their hundreds and began to celebrate their unexpected - but nevertheless well deserved - victory. Within minutes, their attention had turned to other things...namely us! They swarmed across the pitch towards us and it was only the swift action of the police that prevented a full-scale riot from taking place. Although Forest have more than their own fair share of 'nutters', it has to be said that the travelling contingent from Nottingham were very restrained indeed. In fact, I would go as far as to say, their behaviour was impeccable, given the amount of provocation.

The police kept us all inside the ground until the crowds had dispersed and eventually we were escorted back to the safety of the coach park. When a dozen police despatch riders eventually began to escort the cavalcade of coaches out of the city about twenty minutes later, we peeled off and headed in the direction of Southsea, as planned. As we trundled through the streets of Portsmouth, the prospect of spending an evening in the town became less and less appealing. There were 'Pompey' supporters everywhere, especially outside the pubs, and we had a few scary moments along the way. Sensibly, we decided to give Southsea a miss and carried on instead to Chichester, some ten miles away. There, we expected the atmosphere to be a little less intimidating.

Having arrived about twenty minutes later, we parked up and arranged for everyone to meet up back at the coach at midnight. The majority of us then sprinted across the road and piled into a pub called the Globe, situated about fifty yards from the coach park. As we queued up at the bar, we could hear singing coming from one of the other bars within the pub. One of the bar-staff informed us that the room at the back was packed solid with 'Pompey' fans out on the town celebrating their team's great victory. On the evidence of what we'd encountered earlier, we decided to keep a low profile and consequently our mood for the first hour of the evening was a largely subdued one. Having already seen our team humiliated out there on the pitch, the last thing we needed now was a mass punch up just to round the day off.

Eventually the singing petered out as the 'Pompey' fans drifted away and at last we were able to relax. Once we'd had a few beers, our spirits were lifted and we were ready for a good night out on the town. It was dark when we left the Globe and headed off down South Street, the main thoroughfare through the town. After a couple of minutes we came across another pub called the Hogshead, which had both it's front windows wide open. As we got nearer and nearer, the distinctive sound of the 'Pompey Chimes' could be heard drifting through the windows and out into the cool night air. As we sidled slowly past, we could see a large group of youths dancing around inside the bar, having a right good knees-up.

Our curiosity got the better of us, and we decided to go inside and investigate. As we poured in through the door, the whole place fell silent. It was like a 'wild west' saloon and for a few anxious moments you could have heard a pin drop. Everyone just stood there looking at each other. There were about twenty-five of us and probably the same number of them. Suddenly Big Lee piped up with: "Well done lads, your lot deserved the win today." Thankfully those few carefully chosen words did the trick and the ice was immediately broken. As some of the lads queued up for the beers, the rest of us mingled, and within a couple of minutes everyone was having a laugh and a joke together and exchanging pleasantries.

Within half an hour, we were all the best of friends and our hosts were offering to take us on a pub-crawl around the town. And that was an offer we couldn't refuse. We went on to visit just about every pub in Chichester and were well impressed with both the nightlife and the friendliness of the locals. There was loads of banter exchanged throughout the evening and not the remotest hint of any trouble. In fact, after closing time, we all staggered back towards the coach park together, even stopping off for fish and chips along the way. And, as we set off for home, our newly acquired friends stood at the side of the road waving us off. This had turned out to be a fantastic night out and almost made up for the team's disappointing display earlier on in the day.

THIS unexpected exit from the Cup at the hands of Portsmouth was followed by four League victories on the trot. A 2-0 success over Coventry at Highfield Road, was followed by a further three at home. These came against Norwich City (2-0), title-chasing Manchester United - confirmed as our opponents in the forthcoming League Cup Final - (1-0) and Manchester City (2-0). Consequently, as we prepared for the ZDS Cup Final against Southampton at Wembley on Sunday, 29th March, we were in very good shape indeed.

I'd promised to take Thomas to this game - his first ever trip to Wembley - and naturally he was extremely excited about the whole affair. He'd been begging me to take him to Wembley ever since we'd played Everton in the Simod Cup Final several years earlier when he was five-years-old. He'd pleaded with me to take him to that game, but I was having none of it. I was going off on the piss with the lads and that was that. What a selfish bastard I was! I vividly remember leaving the house early that morning and seeing his sobbing face pressed up against the front window, begging me to come back for him. I'd been haunted by the memory ever since and was determined to put things right on this occasion.

As usual, we'd arranged a coach for the game and naturally, we were heading for Paddington first of all. It was a bright spring day and when we eventually arrived, we all sat outside Murphy's Bar enjoying a few pre-match drinks. We'd arranged to be back on the coach at around 2.00-p.m., so we could get to the stadium well before kick off. Sometimes though, these things just don't go according to plan and, for one reason or another, it was about ten past when we arrived back at where the coach should have been waiting for us...but amazingly, wasn't.

Apparently, a few people had arrived back on time and the driver, despite their protests, took it upon himself to leave the rest of us behind at exactly five minutes past. Consequently, we were stranded miles away from Wembley, with less than fifty minutes to go before kick off. We headed immediately for the nearest tube station and, not really having the faintest idea where we were going, jumped on the first train that pulled in. About fifteen minutes later, someone decided we were within walking distance of the stadium and we piled off at the very next stop. In actual fact, we were still a fair distance away and consequently had to trek through the streets for miles - our chances of getting there before kick off diminishing rapidly.

Poor old Tom was struggling to keep up with us and I virtually had to drag him along behind me. When we finally made it to the stadium, the game was already well under way and Tom's 'special day out' was in serious danger of being ruined. The only thing that could make up for it now, would be a brilliant performance by the team...and they weren't about to disappoint.

Kingsley Black and Scott Gemmill gave them a commanding 2-0 lead in a fast and furious display of incisive attacking football. Unfortunately though, the 'Saints' came right back into the game, scoring twice themselves and taking the contest into extra time. Undeterred, Forest pressed forward in search of the winner, and once again took the lead through Gemmill. Despite late pressure from Southampton, they managed to hold out until the end and ultimately claim another piece of silverware to add to their already impressive collection. The appreciative 67,688 crowd gave the two teams a standing ovation at the end and skipper Stuart Pearce - having had to leave the pitch during the game because of injury - hobbled up the steps to collect the trophy.

When we returned to the coach after the celebrations were over, those of us who'd been left behind in Paddington gave the driver a piece of our mind. ''This trip had been organised privately,'' we reminded him, and therefore ''we could leave for the game at whatever time we wished.'' Needless to say, he never drove one of our coaches again.

Two days later, the 'Reds' were back in London, this time to take on Arsenal in a League fixture. And although they took a 3-1 lead in this game, with goals from Keane, Clough and Woan; for the second time in two days, they allowed the opposition to pull back the deficit and on this occasion had to make do with a point.

With Mark Crossley and young Andrew Marriott now vying for the goalkeeper's jersey, long-serving Steve Sutton - a very popular figure amongst Forest supporters - decided it was time to move on. Consequently, after fifteen loyal years at the City Ground, he moved to his hometown club, Derby County, on a free transfer.

Seemingly unable to avoid the Capital at this point in the season, Forest then travelled down to Wimbledon two days later, where they were on the receiving end of a 3-0 thumping in front of an abysmal crowd of just 3,542. This was followed two days later by a 2-0 defeat at home to high-flying Sheffield Wednesday - who at the time were third in the table behind Manchester United and Leeds United respectively. This was worrying form indeed as they prepared to take on the Old Trafford giants in the League Cup Final the following weekend. Their confidence received a timely boost in midweek though, with a 1-0 victory over Southampton at the Dell - their fifth game in the space of only ten days and their second victory over the South-Coast club during this period.

TICKETS for the Final were priced at £14, £19, £24, £29, £34, £40, and a whopping £75 or £78 in the Olympic Gallery. The two clubs had been allocated around 30,000 each. And, having treated Thomas to a trip to the 'Twin Towers' two weeks previously, my selfish tendencies had once again re-surfaced for this one. In any case, owing to the significance of the occasion, we were definitely heading down to London for the whole weekend. Our coach set off from Beeston at 10.00-a.m. on the Saturday morning and it was our intention to stop off for a drink on the way down. Paddington was our ultimate destination, where we were hoping to find some digs for the Saturday evening.

We travelled south along the M40 as this would take us more or less straight into Paddington, thereby enabling us to miss the Saturday afternoon traffic chaos which normally prevails on London's North Circular Road. Once we reached Oxford, we pulled off the motorway and in no time at all found ourselves outside a picturesque little pub in the middle of a country lane. It was a perfect spring day and we sat on the grass verge outside for about two hours, enjoying a few beers in the warm midday sunshine. At that precise moment in time, I couldn't think of anything else I'd rather be doing.

Fed and watered, we continued on our way, arriving in Paddington late on in the afternoon. We had no problem whatsoever getting digs and I ended up having to share with John Farley and Tiff. Bucko, Bodge and Jacko were sharing the room next door, whilst the rest of the clan were scattered around in various other bed and breakfast establishments within spitting distance of our own. By six o'clock, every one of us was showered, suited and booted, and out on the town.

Throughout the years, every single one of our previous trips to Wembley had been entirely trouble-free affairs, with rival supporters mixing freely together and even sharing the odd joke or two along the way. However, on this occasion, Manchester United were our opponents and, whenever they're in town, there's guaranteed to be trouble. They are without doubt, the most arrogant, obnoxious, innately aggressive group of football supporters walking this planet. Consequently, the general atmosphere around the Capital that evening, was one of confrontation and intimidation. So much so in fact, that by around 9.30-p.m., most of us had drifted back into Paddington, in the vain hope of at least enjoying a couple of hours of peace. The trouble is...United fans are a bit like dog-shit - they get everywhere! They were crawling all over London, and consequently, even in Paddington - our second home - we were unable to escape their attentions.

Having rounded off the evening as usual with a midnight feast of junk food, we arrived back at the digs in the early hours of the morning. There we found Jacko sound asleep on the floor outside his room. Throughout the course of the evening we'd gradually got split up into smaller groups, with some ending up in Indian or Chinese restaurants. It's amazing how wonderful a Chicken Vindaloo tastes when you've got a gallon of ale inside you! Every one of us came home with a similar tale to tell - that of a night filled with one uncomfortable encounter after another with large groups of aggressive, snarling 'Mancs'.

After some much-needed kip, we were up bright and early the next morning and on our way back to the pub. By 9.30-a.m., there were around fifty of us hanging about outside Murphy's, basking in the early morning sunshine. Some fifty yards up the road was another bar, which we'd also frequented many times in the past. Obviously sensing an opportunity to rake in some extra cash on a Sunday morning, the owner suddenly appeared in the street outside and beckoned us inside. As there'd been no sign of Murphy's opening at this point, we were off up the street like a shot - after all, there's no room for sentiment when it comes to such important matters.

Within half an hour, at least another hundred or so - all mainly from the Chilwell-Beeston area - had also arrived at the bar. Like us, they'd turned up expecting to find Murphy's open, but had soon sussed out what was going on just yards up the road. By mid-morning, we'd already sunk a tidy few and our early morning hangovers were now history. What's more, there was a tremendous atmosphere building up inside the bar and we were now really beginning to get into the swing of things. Having always indulged ourselves exclusively in Paddington during previous visits to Wembley, we'd decided for once, to have a change of scenery. Our plan was that once we reached opening time, we'd shoot off to Kilburn on the underground and have a few more drinks before heading off for the stadium.

Around thirty of us left the bar just before midday and set off in the direction of the railway station. It was a relatively short journey across London and, having arrived at Kilburn tube station, we headed straight for the nearest pub - a small Irish bar called the Coalpitz, situated about two hundred yards down Kilburn High Road. As we made our way down the street, we could see in the distance, large groups of people drinking outside the various pubs and bars along the way.

When we entered the pub, it was already fairly well populated with Forest supporters, who were quietly enjoying their pre-match pints. There was also a small group of around twenty to thirty United supporters - some of them even had Manchester accents - but everyone was mingling together freely and getting along just fine. While John Farley was getting the drinks in, I nipped across the road to a phone box in order to give Sue a ring, just to let her know I was still alive and having a good time.

Although as a rule I don't wear Club colours, on occasions such as these, almost everyone dons a Forest shirt and consequently I was determined not to be the odd one out. Having chatted away to Sue for a couple of minutes, I suddenly became alarmed by the sight of a large gang of youths who'd just emerged from the railway station and were heading down the road in my direction. There were about a hundred of them and I said to Sue: 'I 'ope this lot are Forest supporters, cos if they're not and they clock my Forest shirt, I might just be in for a spot of bother.''

As they got nearer, I recognised a few of them and was able to breathe a sigh of relief. Although I didn't particularly know any of them, when you've been going to matches as long as I have, you just get to know the faces. ''It looks to me as if there's about to be some trouble,'' I remarked to Sue, ''I think I'll get back across the road a bit sharpish and back into the safety of the pub.''

When I got back, a few of the lads inside had noticed the mob drifting past the front window of the pub and had spilled out onto the pavement, craning their necks to see what was going on. As I'd come back across the road, I'd had a quick glance down the street in the general direction of the mob and was very concerned by what I'd seen. There were literally hundreds of youths - obviously United supporters - charging up the street to confront this relatively small gang of Forest supporters

The odds were overwhelmingly stacked in favour of the United supporters and, not surprisingly, within seconds, the mob from Nottingham was on the retreat. This was only after a hail of bottles and bricks had been exchanged between the two warring factions. Inside the bar, we all began to back away from the door, as scores of terrified youths came racing by, seemingly fleeing for their lives. Unfortunately for us though, the last few stragglers, unable to escape their pursuers, came flying into the bar in an attempt to seek refuge.

Through the open doorway, all we could see was a baying mob of youths several hundred strong. They seemed hell-bent on spilling blood. Although they outnumbered us by around ten-to-one, they wouldn't have all been able to get through the door at the same time. Therefore just a handful of brave souls at the front of the bar nearest the door (I wasn't one of them incidentally) were managing to hold them at bay.

Unable to storm the pub, they vented their anger with a hail of missiles. Everything under the sun - bricks, bottles, lumps of wood and concrete - were raining down on us through the door and what was left of the window. I was stuck in a small alcove about ten feet away from the front entrance, completely unable to move, with bricks, stones and bottles whizzing past my ears and shattering all over the wall behind me.

Within minutes, the front of the bar was completely wrecked. Through the huge hole in the wall - where only minutes earlier there had been a large frosted-glass window - the baying mob were clearly visible. I just couldn't believe the sheer number of youths involved and couldn't fathom why the police hadn't yet arrived on the scene?

In an attempt to protect themselves, many of the supporters inside the bar were returning the missiles as best they could. What's more, some even began to dismantle chairs and tables and throw them out of the window also. This was just a desperate attempt to keep their attackers at bay. All around us, women were hiding under tables screaming. Very soon, there wasn't a single beer glass, bottle, or ashtray left on the premises. Even all the optics from behind the bar had been demolished.

By the time the police finally arrived on the scene and began to disperse the mob, the inside of the Coalpitz resembled a war-zone. When at last it was safe enough for us to make our escape onto the streets outside, we had to trudge through a pile of debris strewn about all over the floor. The landlord was absolutely beside himself and just stood there sobbing. There was virtually nothing left of his pub. It was like a bomb had gone off in there.

Personally, I've never experienced anything so frightening in my life. One minute we'd been enjoying a quiet drink in a warm and friendly environment; the next, we were in danger of losing our lives. I actually thought I was going to die in that bar right there and then, such was the viciousness of the mob and the ferocity of their attack. The whole thing seemed to last for an eternity, but in reality was probably over in only a matter of minutes. Whatever, we were all in a state of severe shock and not surprisingly, had sobered up very quickly.

Apart from the fact my hair was filled with splinters of glass, I'd come out of it all relatively unscathed. Others hadn't been so lucky however, and everywhere I looked, there were people with head-wounds, bleeding profusely. The irony of it all was that some of the walking wounded were United supporters who'd been drinking alongside us in the bar before the 'Battle of Kilburn' commenced. In a nutshell, this rampaging mob of half-wits were actually responsible for attacking their fellow supporters.

As we made our way out into the street, we asked a couple of police officers why it had taken them so long to bring the situation under control. They informed us it was due to the sheer size of the mob, which they estimated had been 500-strong!

We were absolutely shell-shocked by the whole experience and decided it was time to cut short our pre-match 'festivities' and head for the sanctuary of the stadium. We made a bee-line for the railway station and jumped on the first Wembley-bound train. The fifteen-minute journey was a very subdued one, with little or no conversation taking place. The whole occasion had been completely ruined by this terrifying incident - easily the worst I'd encountered in over a quarter of a century watching football. The fact we were about to see our team take part in another major domestic Cup Final, seemed almost irrelevant at this moment in time.

The following week, we found out on the grapevine that the whole thing had been pre-arranged between the respective hooligan elements of both clubs. From what we could gather, the majority of the Forest 'boot boys' - apparently content that they'd gained the upper-hand during the previous evening's clashes around the Capital - had decided to remain in Stanmore, where they'd gathered prior to the game, and give this one a miss. Consequently, hopelessly outnumbered, the relatively small band of youths that had turned up as arranged, were, quite simply, on a hiding to nothing.

Before 2.00-p.m., we were inside Wembley and calming our nerves with a few stiff drinks down in the refreshment area which runs all the way around the underneath of the stadium. This was a unique experience for most of us - being inside a football ground fully an hour before kick off. We were still very subdued at this point - almost unable to comprehend what had just happened.

As the stadium gradually filled up, we made our way towards our seats and began to soak up the pre-match atmosphere. The usual half-hearted chants of: *''We're on the march with Cloughie's Army,''* rang out from the 'Tunnel End' of the stadium. Irritatingly for us, it was soon apparent that a large number of United supporters had somehow managed to get tickets for our end of the stadium and were already beginning to make themselves heard.

When the two teams came out onto the pitch, we became incensed by the fact that a whole block of maybe 2,000 seats - situated right in the middle of the Forest section - were occupied by United followers. Sporadic fighting broke out almost immediately between the two sets of supporters. Very soon, punch-ups were taking place all around us. The atmosphere was very intimidating - most unusual for a Wembley Cup Final. But then again...Manchester United and their 'wonderful' supporters were in town, weren't they?

The line-ups for this game were:

One notable absentee from the Forest line up was skipper Stuart Pearce, who'd suff-ered an injury two week's earlier in the ZDS Final against Southampton. This meant that Des Walker - the subject of intense specu-lation concerning a

	FOREST:	UNITED:	
1	Andrew Marriott	Peter Smeichel	1
2	Gary Charles	Paul Parker	2
3	Bret Williams	Denis Irwin	3
4	Des Walker (Captn.)	Steve Bruce (Captn.)	4
5	Darren Wassell	Mike Phelan	5
6	Roy Keane	Gary Pallister	6
7	Gary Crosby	Andre Kanchelskis	7
8	Scott Gemmill	Paul Ince	8
9	Nigel Clough	Brian McClair	9
10	Teddy Sheringham	Mark Hughes	10
11	Kingsley Black	Ryan Giggs	11
	Subs: Brian Laws	Subs: Neil Webb	
	Lee Glover	Lee Sharpe	

summer move to Italy - had assumed the role of captain.

When referee George Courtney got the game under way, Forest - who were playing in their usual red and white strip - were kicking away from the 'Tunnel End.' Although they struggled to find any rhythm in the first few minutes, a superb breakaway early on saw Roy Keane making a surging run through the heart of the United defence. This ended with Smeichel comfortably saving his low shot from twenty yards out. Shortly afterwards, a Brian McClair effort was disallowed at the other end, after Hughes had pulled back Darren Wassell before crossing from the right.

However in the fifteenth minute, McClair once again had the ball in the back of the Forest net, and on this occasion, quite legitimately. Having played a neat one-two with Ryan Giggs just outside the box, he ran on to slot the ball home from ten yards out. That was the signal for yet more confrontation at our end of the stadium, as the celebrating United supporters were set upon by disgruntled Forest supporters.

After twenty-four minutes, Brian Laws replaced Gary Charles, who was clearly struggling, having only just returned from injury. As the 'Reds' began to press forward in search of an equaliser, Laws sent a scorching twenty-five-yard drive well wide of Smeichel's goal. Despite United's early dominance, Forest were gradually coming into the game and were beginning to go forward in numbers. Chants of: *"Come on you 'Reds',"* echoed around Wembley from the unusually subdued Forest contingent.

Shortly before the break, a neat Forest move ended with Teddy Sheringham flashing a header from Laws' right wing cross, just inches over the bar. However, the score remained 1-0 to United as Mr. Courtney brought the first half to an end. Roy Keane's penetrative runs through the middle of the park had been the highlight of a less than convincing first half performance.

As we made our way down to the refreshment area at half-time, it soon became clear that the situation between the two sets of supporters was about to turn nasty once more. The Forest supporters were incensed by the presence of United supporters at our end of the stadium and were going absolutely berserk under the stand. It seemed that anyone wearing United colours was fair game, as hundreds of youths ran amok. As I emerged from the Gents' toilets, I encountered numerous battered and bloodied youths wearing blue and white United shirts, cowering behind the scores of police officers who were now on hand, trying to break up the trouble.

Never, during my previous nine visits to Wembley to see Forest had I encountered anything other than minor incidents as far as trouble is concerned. Yet on this occasion, virtually the whole weekend had been filled with aggression and confrontation. Not only had we spent most of the Saturday evening avoiding gangs of drunken 'Mancs' - every one of them spoiling for a fight - but we'd also had to endure a near-death experience in Kilburn two hours before the game. And now, to cap it all, here inside the stadium itself we were witnessing running battles between gangs of snarling youths. I for one just wanted the whole damn thing to come to an end right there and then.

Almost reluctantly, I returned to my seat for the second half. The first ten minutes were pretty much end-to-end, with half-chances being carved out by both teams. Paul Ince rattled a twenty-yard effort just wide of the Forest goal, before Wassell's last ditch challenge on the same player denied United again. Forest's response came in the form of a crisp drive from Kingsley Black from the edge of the box, which was well held by Smeichel. Laws then dramatically cleared a McClair effort off the line after Marriott had spilled the ball to Hughes, who squared it across the face of the empty goal and straight into the path of the on-rushing striker.

In search of an equaliser, Forest then mounted a series of attacks on the United goal; this was a period in which they twice went close, following in-swinging corners from the left. Following a foul on the edge of the box, Nigel Clough then sent a superb curling twenty-yard free kick, inches wide of the angle. Agonisingly, the ball just failed to curve enough and ended up crashing into the side netting. At the other end, Giggs then sent an excellent left foot shot wide, after an incisive run down the right wing.

With only seconds left on the clock, Gary Crosby's right wing cross led to thirty seconds of havoc in the United box, with the ball ricocheting about all over the place as shots rained in from every direction. Sadly for us though, this was all in vein and the referee's whistle brought the contest to an end. This meant that United had captured the League Cup trophy for the first time in their history.

Immediately after our sad and forlorn-looking players had been up to collect their Runners-up medals, we were out of the stadium like a shot and heading back to our coaches. Hillsborough apart, this had been the worst trip I'd ever been on during twenty-six years of watching my beloved 'Reds'. Unfortunately, for all the wrong reasons, it is a weekend I will never forget, for as long as I live.

OF their six remaining League fixtures, the most interesting was the forthcoming trip to Old Trafford on Easter Monday - 20th April. Fighting it out with Leeds at the top of the table, this was a game Man U simply had to win, were they to stand any chance of capturing their first League Championship trophy since season 1966/67.

I was on my way to Scotland that day, where I would be working during the week, and was unable to get to the game. However, as I headed up the M6, I was just miles from Manchester as the game was in full flow. With the match commentary blaring out from my radio, and the game taking place only a matter of miles away, I felt I was there in spirit at least.

A crowd of 47,576 packed into Old Trafford and it was perhaps poetic justice that Forest secured an impressive 2-1 victory, with goals from Scott Gemmill and Ian Woan. Effectively, this put paid to United's title hopes and the Championship ended up at Elland Road. I've no doubt Forest were a popular toast in Leeds that day. I for one was delighted to see them miss out, but would have gladly swapped this result for the one at Wembley a week earlier, even though this would have gifted United the League Championship. Still, whichever way you look at it, it was sweet revenge for all the injustices we'd endured during that miserable weekend.

The season ended with Forest in a reasonable eighth position in the table and two more Cup Final appearances behind them. Attendances at the City Ground had also been on the increase, with an average in the League of 23,720. Furthermore, only one League attendance had failed to hit the 20,000 mark and not surprisingly, this had been for the visit of Wimbledon. This fixture drew a crowd of 19,707, though who knows, if they'd brought with them more than a taxi full, then this may also have topped the 20,000 mark?

It was now time to forget about football for a few months and concentrate on other things. Apart from, that is, the odd trip or two down to the banks of the River Trent during the summer to see just how the builders were getting on with the new Bridgford Stand. Yes...that's how sad we football supporters really are!

SEASON 1991/92 – STATISTICS

FOOTBALL LEAGUE DIVISION ONE – FIXTURES

Date		Opposition	Venue	Competition	Score	Attendance
Aug	17	**Everton**	H	**League**	**2-1**	**24,422**
	20	Leeds United	A	League	0-1	29,457
	24	Notts County	A	League	4-0	21,044
	28	**Tottenham Hotspur**	H	**League**	**1-3**	**24,018**
	31	**Oldham Athletic**	H	**League**	**3-1**	**23,244**
Sept	4	Manchester City	A	League	1-2	29,146
	7	Sheffield Wednesday	A	League	1-2	31,289
	14	**Wimbledon**	H	**League**	**4-2**	**19,707**
	21	Aston Villa	A	League	1-3	28,506
	25	**Bolton Wanderers**	H	**LC 2 - 1st Leg**	**4-0**	**19,936**
	28	**West Ham United**	H	**League**	**2-2**	**25,613**
Oct	5	Queens Park Rangers	A	League	2-0	13,508
	8	Bolton Wanderers	A	LC 2 - 2nd Leg	5-2	5,469
	19	Sheffield United	A	League	2-4	23,080
	22	Leeds United	A	Zenith Data Cup 2	3-1	6,145
	26	**Southampton**	H	**League**	**1-3**	**20,026**
	30	**Bristol Rovers**	H	**LC 3**	**2-0**	**17,529**
Nov	2	Norwich City	A	League	0-0	13,014
	16	**Coventry City**	H	**League**	**1-0**	**21,154**
	19	Aston Villa	A	Zenith Data Cup 3	2-0	7,859
	23	**Crystal Palace**	H	**League**	**5-1**	**22,387**
	30	Chelsea	A	League	0-1	19,420
Dec	**4**	**Southampton**	H	**LC 4**	**0-0**	**17,939**
	8	**Arsenal**	H	**League**	**3-2**	**22,095**
	10	Tranmere Rovers	A	Zenith Data Cup 4	2-0	8,034
	14	Liverpool	A	League	0-2	35,285
	17	Southampton	A	LC 4 - Replay	1-0	10,861
	22	**Leeds United**	H	**League**	**0-0**	**27,170**
	26	Tottenham Hotspur	A	League	2-1	31,079
	28	Oldham Athletic	A	League	1-2	16,496
Jan	**1**	**Luton Town**	H	**League**	**1-1**	**23,809**
	4	**Wolverhampton Wanderers**	H	**FA Cup 3**	**1-0**	**27,068**
	8	Crystal Palace	A	LC 5	1-1	14,941
	11	**Notts County**	H	**League**	**1-1**	**30,168**
	19	Everton	A	League	1-1	17,717
	26	**Hereford United**	H	**FA Cup 4**	**2-0**	**24,259**
Feb	**1**	**Sheffield United**	H	**League**	**2-5**	**22,412**
	5	**Crystal Palace**	H	**LC 5 - Replay**	**4-2**	**18,918**
	9	**Tottenham Hotspur**	H	**LCSF - 1st Leg**	**1-1**	**21,402**
	12	Leicester City	A	ZDS Cup NA Final - 1st Leg	1-1	19,537
	15	**Bristol City**	H	**FA Cup 5**	**4-1**	**24,615**
	22	**Chelsea**	H	**League**	**1-1**	**24,094**
	26	**Leicester City**	H	**ZDS Cup NA Final - 2nd Leg**	**2-0**	**21,562**
Mar	1	Tottenham Hotspur	A	LCSF - 2nd Leg	2-1	28,216
	3	Crystal Palace	A	League	0-0	12,608
	7	Portsmouth	A	FA Cup 6	0-1	25,402
	11	Coventry City	A	League	2-0	11,158
	14	**Norwich City**	H	**League**	**2-0**	**20,721**
	18	**Manchester United**	H	**League**	**1-0**	**28,062**
	21	**Manchester City**	H	**League**	**2-0**	**24,115**
	29	Southampton (At Wembley Stadium)		ZDS Cup Final	3-2	67,688
	31	Arsenal	A	League	3-3	27,036
Apr	2	Wimbledon	A	League	0-3	3,542
	4	**Sheffield Wednesday**	H	**League**	**0-2**	**26,105**
	8	Southampton	A	League	1-0	14,905
	12	Manchester United (At Wembley Stadium)		LC Final	0-1	76,810
	14	Luton Town	A	League	1-2	8,014
	18	**Aston Villa**	H	**League**	**2-0**	**22,800**
	20	Manchester United	A	League	2-1	47,576
	22	**Liverpool**	H	**League**	**1-1**	**23,787**
	25	**Queens Park Rangers**	H	**League**	**1-1**	**22,228**
May	2	West Ham United	A	League	0-3	20,629

HOME ATTENDANCES

	AGGREGATE ATTENDANCE	HIGHEST ATTENDANCE	LOWEST ATTENDANCE	AVERAGE ATTENDANCE
League:	498,137	30,168	19,707	23,720
League Cup:	95,724	21,402	17,529	19,144
FA Cup:	75,942	27,068	24,259	25,314
ZDS Cup:	21,562	21,562	21,562	21,562
All Competitions:	691,365	30,168	17,529	23,045

FINAL LEAGUE TABLE - DIVISION ONE

Position	P	W	D	L	GF	GA	Pts
1. Leeds United	42	22	16	4	74	37	82
2. Manchester United	42	21	15	6	63	33	78
3. Sheffield Wednesday	42	21	12	9	62	49	75
4. Arsenal	42	19	15	8	81	46	72
5. Manchester City	42	20	10	12	61	48	70
6. Liverpool	42	16	16	10	47	40	64
7. Aston Villa	42	17	9	16	48	44	60
8. Nottingham Forest	**42**	**16**	**11**	**15**	**60**	**58**	**59**
9. Sheffield United	42	16	9	17	65	63	57
10. Crystal Palace	42	14	15	13	53	61	57
11. Queens Park Rangers	42	12	18	12	48	47	54
12. Everton	42	13	14	15	52	51	53
13. Wimbledon	42	13	14	15	53	53	53
14. Chelsea	42	13	14	15	50	60	53
15. Tottenham Hotspur	42	15	7	20	58	63	52
16. Southampton	42	14	10	18	39	55	52
17. Oldham Athletic	42	14	9	19	63	67	51
18. Norwich City	42	11	12	19	47	63	45
19. Coventry City	42	11	11	20	35	44	44
20. Luton Town	42	10	12	20	38	71	42
21. Notts County	42	10	10	22	40	62	40
22. West Ham United	42	9	11	22	37	59	38

AWAY ATTENDANCES

	AGGREGATE ATTENDANCE	HIGHEST ATTENDANCE	LOWEST ATTENDANCE	AVERAGE ATTENDANCE
League:	454,509	47,576	3,542	21,643
League Cup:	132,297	76,810	5,469	27,259
FA Cup:	25,402	25,402	25,402	25,402
ZDS Cup:	109,263	67,688	6,145	21,852
All Competitions:	721,471	76,810	3,542	22,545

"GOODBYE ALL, GOODBYE ALL, WE'RE SAYING GOODBYE TO IT ALL"

THE CITY of Nottingham had been awash with rumours during the summer months regarding the 'goings on behind closed doors' down at the City Ground. Firstly, how had Manchester United supporters managed to get their hands on a whole block of two thousand-plus tickets for the 'Forest End' of Wembley back in April? Surely, someone on the inside of the Club must have been responsible? Everyone from Chairman Fred Reacher, down to the office tea boy, seemed to have come under suspicion at one point or another. Even the great Cloughie himself had had the odd finger or two pointed in his general direction. (One sacked member of the ticket office staff, Andrew Plumb, later went on national television and accused him outright of selling off the tickets for his own personal gain - although this was never substantiated of course.)

The other controversial topic concerning the 'Reds', had been the sale of central- defender Des Walker - probably the most accomplished centre-half ever to wear the famous Garibaldi - to Italian Club Sampdoria at the end of the previous season. Whilst the transfer itself wasn't entirely unexpected, the size of the fee - just £1.5 million - was nothing short of staggering. Wasn't this the same Des Walker who, less than two years ago, had been the subject of a massive £5 million bid from Juventus? Or the same Des Walker who was still only 26-years-old and an ever-present in the England side? "What about the other £4 million?" was the question on most people's lips. The whole thing just didn't seem to add up. Why would the Club almost give away their most prized asset? It wasn't as if he was even out of contract or anything.

As usual however, the vast majority of Forest supporters - too laid back for their own good at times - had simply accepted it and got on with the task of renewing their season tickets. Although myself and the usual mob - Big Lee, Bodge, Andy Oakley, Garry Mason, Cob, and Jacko - had renewed our tickets for the 'A' Block, we'd decided however, that as soon as the new Bridgford Stand was completed, we'd be transferring over at the very first opportunity. Work on the impressive 7,515-seater stand was well under way as the new season approached, and it was expected to be fully completed in time for the game against Ipswich Town at the end of October.

Yet another controversial incident, which had allegedly taken place during pre-season training, had led to the unexpected departure of Darren Wassall to Derby County in June, in a deal worth £550,000. Widely tipped to assume the already-departed Walker's defensive responsibilities, the highly-rated defender had apparently been involved in an unsavoury training ground incident with manager Brian Clough. At least one national newspaper suggested Cloughie had spat on Wassall's injured hand, causing him to storm off in a huff, vowing never to kick a ball in anger again for the 'Reds'. This was indeed a great pity, as he was rapidly emerging as a player of great quality. Once again however, this story was entirely unsubstantiated.

The climax of Forest's pre-season preparations, was their participation in the four-club Makita Tournament, which was due to take place at Elland Road on the first weekend in August. The other clubs taking part were: Leeds United; Italy's Sampdoria (including Des Walker); and Germany's Stuttgart. Opposition of such quality were sure to provide the 'Reds' with ideal preparation for the new campaign - the inaugural season of the FA Premier League.

Not wishing to miss out on the opportunity of a whole weekend away on the piss, we decided to obtain tickets for both days of the tournament. We also decided that Scarborough would be our destination for the Saturday evening stopover. Forest and Sampdoria were due to get the tournament under way on the Saturday afternoon, followed shortly after by Leeds versus Stuttgart. The winners of each game would contest the Final the following day, whilst the other two teams would scrap it out for third and fourth spot.

There was a reasonable turn out from Nottingham on the first day, with around two thousand making the 70-mile journey north. However, such was the ineptitude of Forest's performance against the classy-looking Italians, most of them left Elland Road afterwards vowing not to return on the Sunday. In fact, having witnessed a very depressing 2-0 defeat - during which the Leeds fans had taunted us with chants of: *"You'll never beat Des Walker"* - we even discussed the possibility ourselves of giving the next day a miss and going on an 'all-dayer' in Scarborough instead.

We hadn't booked any digs in advance, therefore upon our early-evening arrival in the busy East Yorkshire resort, following a fairly substantial journey from Leeds, we decided that splitting up into pairs would represent our best chance of finding a room each for the night. Whilst Big

Lee and Andy headed off in one direction, Bucko and Bodge scurried off in another, and Garry and Jacko in yet another. As John Farley and I watched them all from a distance, being turned away from one B&B after another, it soon became apparent that finding a bed for the night wasn't going to be at all easy. Still, John and I had a cunning plan...Whilst the rest of them concentrated their efforts on the over-crowded establishments situated in the busiest area of the town, we decided instead 'to head for the hills'. This turned out to be a wise choice indeed. No sooner had we made it to the top of the hill overlooking the resort, than we stumbled across an excellent little hotel, where we managed to obtain a room with a view of the bay, for the very modest price of £25 between us. Having arranged to meet up with the rest of the gang later on in a pub aptly named 'The Nottingham'; we were absolutely convinced they'd be green with envy when we told them all about our rather 'palatial' accommodation.

Pleasingly, the pub was packed full of Forest supporters when we eventually met up as arranged at around 7.30-p.m. There was a big crowd in from Cotgrave, including Ady Cooper - brother of Steve 'Cooperman' Cooper of Chilwell. Ady and his cronies had often travelled with us in the past on 'Broughton & Hanna's Tours'; consequently there was a fair bit of banter flying around the pub for the first hour or so. What's more, earlier on, I'd made the fatal mistake of telling Sue in the middle of an argument we were having on the phone that: "I'd got to go...'cause I've got to meet the lads in a pub called 'the Nottingham' in two minutes time." Our relationship was still in it's embryonic stages at the time, following my recent divorce, and she was still a little on the insecure side; not really all that comfortable with my weekend excursions away with the lads (after all, we were bound to be on the 'pull' all weekend, weren't we?).

Anyway, just as things were starting to get really lively, the landlord of the pub bellowed at the top of his voice: "Is there a Chris Broughton in 'ere...cos I've got 'is misses on the phone?" As you can imagine, there was instant uproar as fifty lads taunted me mercilessly while I stood at the bar trying to reason with the now very unreasonable Sue, who wanted me to tell her how much I loved her and that I wasn't about to run off with the first tart I encountered that evening. Being the romantic fool that I am, I just put the receiver down and ran!

Eventually we all began to go our separate ways and the evening gradually fizzled out into a fairly quiet affair. We had a great deal of difficulty getting into the pubs situated along the popular sea-front area of the town - the bouncers must have been aware of the mini invasion from Nottingham, despite the fact that as usual, no-one was wearing any colours - so we eventually drifted back into the outskirts of the resort, where we were able to enjoy a quiet drink and a chat in the less crowded back-street establishments.

Almost reluctantly, we headed back to Leeds the next morning to see the 'Reds' take on Stuttgart. Unfortunately, another woeful performance - and another defeat, this time 1-0 - left us holding the wooden spoon, and wishing we'd all stayed at home in Nottingham for the weekend. We left Elland Road shortly after this game, and to this day even, I have no idea who the eventual winners of the tournament were. Host club Leeds took on Sampdoria in the Final, but we were already back home in 'God's County' by the time this particular contest was over. One thing which had dawned on me though, was the fact that, unless something dramatic happened on the transfer front - and quickly - we were surely destined to struggle this season.

The only new talent of any significance however, which had arrived at the City Ground during the summer, was that of midfielder Ray McKinnon, purchased from Scottish club Dundee United for a fee of £750,000. And to most people south of the border, he was an unknown quantity.

FOREST launched their Premiership campaign with a home fixture against Liverpool at the City Ground on Sunday, 16th August. The game was televised live by Sky Sport - their first ever live Premiership fixture. Considering that Forest hold virtually every other 'first' in the whole history of the game in this country, it's hardly surprising that they should also feature in Sky Sport's Premiership debut.

A restricted crowd of 20,038 crammed into the rapidly changing stadium to witness an impressive 1-0 victory by Forest, courtesy of Teddy Sheringham's excellent 28th-minute strike. This was then followed by a 2-0 midweek defeat at the hands of Sheffield Wednesday at Hillsborough, and a shocking 5-3 defeat by Oldham Athletic at Boundary Park the following Saturday.

We'd travelled up to Lancashire confident of an easy Forest victory, only to find ourselves 5-0 down to the 'Latics' before we'd even drawn breath. Only at this point, did we start to play, pulling a goal back eventually through Stuart Pearce and a brace from substitute Gary Bannister

- on a month's trial at the Club following a free transfer from West Brom - and thereby giving the score-line a more respectable look about it.

Unfortunately for us, this defeat at Oldham turned out to be Sheringham's last game for the 'Reds'. At first, it seemed his surprise £2.1 million transfer to Tottenham Hotspur had been called off by Forest, but within twenty-four hours the deal was back on again and he was winging his way down to the Capital to sign on the dotted line. This particular transfer deal later triggered the infamous 'bung' scandal, in which it was alleged that certain members of the Forest management team received the sum of £50,000 in used notes, stuffed into a brown paper bag, handed over to them at a service station somewhere on the M1 motorway.

This matter has still not been fully resolved even to this day, although if there is the remotest shred of truth in these allegations, then it is a very sad indictment of the Club's hierarchy at that time. It is also an enormous slap in the face to the many thousands who put their hard-earned cash into the Club season after season. Surely those involved in the game at this level earn more than their fair share, without having to manipulate illicit transfer dealings in order to line their pockets still further? I'm sure the grass-roots supporters will never learn the real truth of the matter but, what with the League Cup Final ticket scandal of the previous season, the 'missing' millions from the sale of Des Walker to Sampdoria, the Darren Wassall incident, and now this, something was definitely amiss down at the City Ground at this particular moment in time?

To cap it all, during the course of the following six weeks, things just went from bad to worse. By the time we entertained Arsenal at home on Saturday, 17th October, we were already firmly rooted to the bottom of the Premier League table, having won just one and drawn three of our first ten games. Our tally of only ten goals scored, compared to twenty-one conceded, had left us with a measly six points to show for our efforts to date. There was a clear message springing out from the Premiership basement to the Club's seemingly complacent management: ''Buy a striker now...or face the distinct possibility of relegation at the end of the season!''

The only response so far, had been the offer of a one-year contract to the now very-ordinary looking Bannister who, quite frankly, was looking well past his sell-by date. Meanwhile, following it's completion a full two weeks ahead of schedule, the impressive new Bridgford Stand came into use for the very first time for the visit of the 'Gunners'. The total cost of construction had amounted to £4.28 million, towards which the Football Trust had provided a re-development grant totalling £1.9 million.

In their wisdom, the Club had rather surprisingly decided to designate the whole of the 4,700-capacity lower tier - by far the most impressive section of the entire stadium - to visiting supporters. Only the Forest Board could make such a decision, but as usual, they put forward the fickle excuse - and one incidentally which the present Board still maintain to this day - that this was on the advice of the Nottinghamshire Constabulary, and was a decision based entirely in the interests of crowd segregation and safety. In my own rather humble opinion however - and seemingly that of every other Forest supporter I speak to on the subject - this argument is absolute bollocks! It would be just as easy to house visiting supporters in the lower tier of the Executive Stand, just as they had done for many seasons before this. No, the simple truth of the matter, is that it boils down to one thing, and one thing alone: MONEY. With such a large capacity in this section of the ground, and with the tendency of most visiting clubs to bring with them a sizeable following to the easily accessible City of Nottingham, there's more money to be had by keeping things this way.

Whilst on the subject of the Bridgford Stand, why is it, that no-one at the Club has ever come forward to explain to us properly, it's rather strange design? For some inexplicable reason, we've ended up with just half a stand - at least as far as the upper tier is concerned anyway. And apart from all the rumours about the local residents objecting, and problems with daylight in the immediate vicinity, as far as I'm aware, there has never been any official statement from the Club on this matter.

A crowd of 24,862 was inside the revamped stadium for the visit of Arsenal to witness yet another defeat - this time by one-goal-to-nil. This was Forest's seventh of the season so far, leaving them firmly anchored to the foot of the table.

Four days later they managed to record only their second League victory of the season, when they overcame Middlesbrough by one-goal-to-nil at the City Ground, thanks to an opportunist effort from winger Kingsley Black, in front of a crowd of only 16,897. Although this rare success provided some glimmer of hope to the City Ground faithful, it was followed by a 0-0 draw at Sheffield United the following Saturday, and successive 1-0 home defeats against Ipswich Town and Everton over the following two weekends. A 1-1 draw away to Crystal Palace in their next fixture was followed by yet another home defeat a week later, this time at the hands of Southampton. This defeat - in which 29-year-old Neil Webb made his comeback for the 'Reds' following his £800,000 transfer from Old Trafford - typified the kind of luck they were getting at the time. They threw everything bar the kitchen sink at the 'Saints' for virtually the whole ninety minutes of the game, and still ended up losing 2-1. Despite their lowly position, the players were at least displaying the kind of fighting spirit necessary if they were to stand any chance of avoiding the drop.

On a brighter note, good progress had been made in the League Cup, with victories over Stockport County and Crewe Alexandra putting them through to the fourth round of the competition, where they were due to meet Spurs at the City Ground on Wednesday, 2nd December. Two blistering goals - one from Ian Woan in the first half and another from Roy Keane in the second - gave them an impressive 2-0 victory on the night, in front of an ecstatic crowd of 22,312. Then, obviously buoyed by this performance, they travelled to Elland Road three days later and simply destroyed Leeds United by four-goals-to-one. Despite being only mid-table at the time, it should be remembered that they were in fact reigning League Champions, so the significance of Forest's victory should not be underestimated. Leeds had no answer on the day to the powerful running of Roy Keane from midfield, added to the guile and skill of Neil Webb and Nigel Clough. Keane bagged a couple of goals, with Cloughie and substitute Kingsley Black completing the rout.

When we set off on the train for Birmingham the following Saturday to see them take on Aston Villa, we were beginning to think that just maybe, there was some light at the end of the tunnel. Although their away support was still substantial, Forest's generally fickle support in and around the Chilwell and Beeston area, had led to the mothballing of 'Broughton & Hanna's Tours' for the time being. The dozen of us, who were still regulars away from home, had turned our attentions to the train instead. For most Saturday away matches, we'd catch the earliest available service train from Nottingham which would ensure we always arrived before opening time. We'd then spend the best part of four hours drinking in the town centre, before jumping into taxis and arriving at the ground usually several minutes after kick off. Immediately after the game, we'd make our way back into the town centre by whatever mode of transport available and go straight back on the piss. Eventually, we'd stagger back to the railway station to catch the last train home to Nottingham - and you can imagine what state we were usually in by then.

As it was only a couple of weeks before Christmas, we were in festive mood as we took to the streets of downtown Birmingham. Big Lee had even got hold of half a dozen Santa hats, which we'd daubed with slogans such as: ''Sack the board'', and ''Reacher out.'' We were going to wear these inside the stadium.

We had a wonderful session around 'Brum' that lunchtime before setting off for the game in our taxis with only minutes to spare before kick off. As we made our way to our seats along the front row of the Visiting Supporters' Section in the North Stand, we must have looked like the seven dwarfs (well...six of them at least) with our little red Santa hats bobbing around all over the place. As usual, the West Midlands Police were in hospitable mood - ejecting from the ground, or carting away, anyone who dared to step out of line during the game - for example, anyone going to the toilet without putting their hand up first!

Roy Keane put us into the lead early on in the game with a looping shot from almost thirty yards out. The large following from Nottingham went berserk (leading to another surge of ejections from the over-zealous police and stewards) and for a while it seemed that Forest really had turned the corner. However, shortly before half-time, a weak back-header from centre-half Carl Tiler, gifted Villa a goal, and from that moment on, the game slipped from our grasp. The final score was 2-1 to the home side and, as we slipped out of the ground seconds after the final whistle, we were convinced more than ever before that the Gods were conspiring against us. Despite the widely held view amongst the game's pundits that Forest were simply 'too good to go down', this was now looking more and more likely with the passing of each game. Boy did we drown our sorrows that night before catching the last train home to Nottingham.

THE Christmas programme came and went, bringing with it just one more point - courtesy of a 1-1 draw at home to Wimbledon - leaving Forest five points adrift at the bottom of the table. A live televised FA Cup third round tie at home to Southampton on Sunday, 3rd January, was our first fixture of the New Year and drew a paltry crowd of only 13,592. Perhaps these were the kind of crowds we could look forward to the following season, were we - as seemed likely - to end up playing First Division football? However for a change, the dwindling band of supporters did have something to cheer about, as goals from Roy Keane and Neil Webb in the space of two minutes just before half-time, gave Forest a hard-earned 2-1 victory after they'd fallen behind to an early strike from Matt Le Tissier.

This was followed one week later by a rare victory in the League as the 'Reds' came back from Coventry with a 1-0 success under their belts. Ian Woan scored the only goal of the game, giving their morale a timely boost just three days before the League Cup quarter-final tie against Arsenal at Highbury. Unfortunately, the 'Gunners' turned out to be too strong for us, dashing our hopes of yet another Wembley appearance with a 2-0 victory, in front of a restricted crowd of only 25,568.

Remarkably, just four days after this disappointing League Cup exit, mid-table Chelsea visited the City Ground and were soundly beaten by three-goals-to-nil. Gary Bannister was the Forest hero with two goals - one in each half - with Toddi Orlygsson grabbing the other, and thereby sending the majority of the 23,249 crowd home with a smile on their faces. Despite the worryingly small crowd which had turned out for the FA Cup tie against the 'Saints', the Nottingham public had been turning up in force all season for Forest's League fixtures. Considering they had occupied bottom place all season and, that until the opening of the new Bridgford Stand two months into the season, the capacity had been restricted to just over 20,000, the average League attendance at the City Ground after eleven games was a fairly healthy 20,306. In addition to this, the away support had been immense. This tremendous support had not gone un-noticed by the Forest manager either. Having often been critical of the Nottingham public during his time at the Club, Cloughie at last acknowledged the Forest faithful: *"We've had our problems this season but I've taken a lot of strength from other areas - like the superb support we have continued to get from you. The level of support we have had at away games is nothing short of staggering and I can't thank those people enough for the backing they have given us,"* were just some of his comments.

Forest's fight for Premiership survival received a huge blow during the month of January when inspirational skipper Stuart Pearce was injured whilst on international duty. During a training session at the England camp, he received a serious groin injury, which eventually required surgery and ultimately kept him out of the side for the remainder of the season. On a brighter note, their 2-0 victory over fellow strugglers Oldham Athletic at the City Ground on 30th January, lifted them off the bottom of the table for the first time in twenty-two weeks. Furthermore, having drawn 1-1 at home to Middlesbrough in the fourth round of the FA Cup one week earlier, they travelled to Ayresome Park on Wednesday, 3rd February for the replay and progressed through to the fifth round of the competition with a convincing 3-0 victory. Bannister, Clough and Woan were the goal-scoring heroes on this occasion.

Uncertain whether we'd be enjoying the luxury of Premiership football the following season, we were making the most of every away trip at this time, and in particular the likes of Old Trafford and Anfield. When Forest visited Liverpool the following Saturday, we set off on the 8.30-a.m. service train from Midlands Station determined to indulge in another of our all day drinking binges. There were a large number of travelling 'Reds' on board, although there were only twelve of us in our particular group. Once again the plan was to catch the last available service train back to Nottingham that evening, which was scheduled to leave Liverpool at 9.30-p.m.

We arrived at Lime Street station at around 11.00-a.m. and spent the first two hours drinking quietly in the city centre, before jumping into taxis which ferried us to 'The Arkle' - a pub situated only a hundred yards from the ground. Conveniently, it's just a short walk from the turnstiles at the Anfield Road End - the Visiting Supporters' end of the ground. It was packed full of singing and chanting Forest supporters - a situation which would have been unheard of ten years before.

At five minutes to three, we were still sat in the Arkle drinking. At two minutes to three, we were in our seats in the Anfield Road End waiting for the game to kick off. There was a superb following from Nottingham, and we simply sang our hearts out for the whole of the game, which ended 0-0. At ten minutes to five, we were back in the Arkle and back on the beer. At 6.30-p.m., we were being ferried once again by taxis back into the city centre. By 8.00-p.m., I was almost unconscious and being told to 'pull myself together' by Big Lee. It was easy for him to talk - he could sink a couple of gallons without batting an eye-lid. But then again, at six foot four inches tall and weighing in at eighteen stones, he does have a distinct advantage over the rest us. That aside, when it comes to drinking, most of us are only in the 'Nationwide Conference' compared to Lee, who undoubtedly enjoys 'Champions' League' status.

Having somehow managed to compose myself, I got my second wind, and was soon back amongst the throng. We hopped from one boozer to another, mainly in the famous 'Cavern Club' area of the city. Liverpool is a place I had worked in on many occasions in the past; therefore I was more than familiar with it's lively atmosphere. We cared not a jot about the time, even though we were now well past the time of our last train home to Nottingham. Somehow, when you've had a belly full of ale, trivial little things like being stranded 130 miles from home on a cold winter's evening in February, just don't seem that important.

It wasn't until around 10.00-p.m. that we finally decided to make a move. Sadly, the drink had obscured our thinking and we were deluding ourselves that the train may have been miraculously delayed, or that another unscheduled one would conveniently come trundling into the station just as we arrived. We were completely wrong of course and the best suggestion that any of the seemingly uncaring ticket office staff could come up with, was that we ''hop on a train to Manchester - in fact that one over there waiting on platform three - 'cause you might just be lucky and manage to catch a late connection back to the East Midlands from there.'' It was only when we arrived at Manchester's Victoria Station at around midnight - just as the shutters were going down on the whole place - that we realised this rather 'helpful' suggestion had probably had more to do with moving a dozen unwanted drunken football supporters off their patch and onto someone else's, than with helping us to solve our own transportation problems. Still, you can hardly blame them can you?

So, there we were, cold and hungry, stranded in the early hours of Sunday morning in the middle of Victoria Station. As far as we could reason, we had only a limited number of options open to us: It was either freeze to death on the station all night and get the first train home in the morning; go and search for some cheap digs for the night; or find an alternative mode of transport. We quickly decided that freezing on the station all night just wasn't an option. Almost spontaneously, we climbed over a perimeter wall and dropped down onto the pavement outside the station. Fortunately for us, we immediately found that the answer we were looking for was right there in front of us - yes, a late night taxi rank.

Four of us clambered into the first taxi, four into the next, and finally, four into another. ''Err...Nottingham please,'' declared John Farley, who'd climbed into the front seat, the rest of us already wedged firmly into the back. ''Nottingham?'' exclaimed the startled Pakistani driver, almost unable to comprehend what he'd just been asked. ''Yes please,'' confirmed John. ''And how much will that be, by the way?'' he added nonchalantly, as if he'd just jumped into a black cab in 'Slab Square' and asked to be taken to Beeston. ''Errm...£80.00,'' came the slightly hesitant reply, as if hoping that this would put us off and we'd immediately jump out of his cab. ''That'll do nicely thanks,'' we all replied, having given each other a nod and a wink.

Just two short hours later we were back home in good old Nottingham, with John directing our weary and worried looking driver to a cash-point machine in Long Eaton Town Centre, where he was to withdraw his share of the fare. As I climbed into my lovely, comfortable bed, not ten minutes later, and snuggled up to Sue's warm and welcoming arse, I just marvelled at what good value for money my own twenty pound share of the fare had been. And to think, I could still have been freezing my bollocks off on Manchester's Victoria Railway Station.

HAVING no desire to repeat our little escapade of the previous weekend, our trip down to Highbury on Saturday, 13th February, for Forest's important FA Cup quarter-final tie against the 'Gunners', was by bus - in fact the 'Bus from the Sal'. This particular excursion had been resurrected again several years earlier and ran to almost every away game, whether it be for an important Cup tie such as this one, or indeed for any 'run of the mill' League game. Because Big Lee and Bucko knew virtually everyone in town at the time, we never had too much difficulty getting ourselves booked onto this bus, although it did tend to be a bit of a free-for-all whenever it pulled up outside the Maid Marion Café. We always seemed to end up leaving dozens of disappointed and frustrated youths behind.

There was a good following from Nottingham, although as the new North Bank was still under construction, there was a restricted attendance and therefore a restricted number of tickets available to Forest supporters. Big Lee had obtained our tickets direct from Highbury, therefore - apart from a scattering of infiltrators from Nottingham - we were seated almost exclusively amongst Arsenal fans in the lower tier of the ancient and decrepit-looking West Stand, about three rows from the back. Because the lower tier dips right under the upper tier, whenever the ball goes above head height, it disappears completely out of view. I couldn't help remarking to the lads, how frustrating it must be sitting in these seats when Arsenal are playing Wimbledon at home. This drew a smile or two from the Forest fans a few rows in front of us and more than a few scowls from the Arsenal fans around us.

As in most encounters with Arsenal, Forest were absolutely awful, going down 2-0, thanks to a double strike from the prolific ''Ian Wright-Wright-Wright''. Not only that, the unfortunate Neil Webb badly injured his Achilles tendon and, following surgery, would be out for the rest of the season. As you can imagine, there were no celebrations down in London that night. No, it was straight back on the bus and straight back home to Nottingham for a change.

A week later, the 'Reds' picked up another useful League win against Middlesbrough at Ayresome Park, where the young Steve Stone (complete with hair) scored one of the goals in a 2-1 victory, with Nigel Clough grabbing the other. Then, four days later, a Gary Crosby effort against Queens Park Rangers at the City Ground gave them a 1-0 victory and another three vital points. At this stage we were third-from-bottom and beginning to look at least capable of avoiding the drop.

Sadly, a 2-0 defeat at home to Manchester City the following Saturday, put the mockers on things again and this was followed by a 1-1 draw - also at the City Ground - against Crystal Palace in midweek. As we travelled up to Goodison Park on Saturday, 13th March, we did so requiring another victory if we were to stand any chance of pulling away from the relegation zone. John Farley and I decided to break with tradition on this occasion and were taking our women with us to the game. Having stayed in the Adelphi Hotel on a regular basis whilst working up in Liverpool, I'd managed to book the four of us in for the Saturday evening using the cheap corporate rates I always used whilst up there on business. We intended to have a night out on the town after the game and John had booked us a table at a pleasant little Italian restaurant called 'Est Est' down in Albert Dock for around 7.30 that evening. How romantic?

We drove up to Liverpool early that morning, booked into the hotel around mid-day and set off into town for a few drinks. When we arrived at the ground shortly before kick off, we bumped into Big Lee and the rest of the crowd (who incidentally, were absolutely appalled we'd shunned them and brought the women with us) just as we were making our way through the turnstiles. As usual, there was a large and enthusiastic following from Nottingham and everyone was getting behind the team right from the start.

There'd been a change in the rules of the game prior to this season with goalkeepers no longer able to pick up the ball from a deliberate back-pass, other than from a chest-down or a header. Unfortunately some referees were applying this rule far too rigidly and, with Forest already 1-0 down in the first half from a Tony Cottee strike, Everton were awarded an indirect free kick only four yards from goal after the ball had ricocheted off a defender and into keeper Mark Crossley's hands. This is just typical of the sort of luck you encounter when you are near the bottom of the table and desperately in need of points. The ball was subsequently rolled inches to the left, where it was despatched with great ferocity by Cottee into the roof of the net, to put Everton 2-0 up. To make matters worse for the travelling fans, Forest really were playing abysmally at this time and not surprisingly, the diminutive striker soon grabbed his third goal of the game, leaving the 'Reds' with an absolute mountain to climb.

Big Lee was out of the ground and back in the pub up the road by half-time - as were a few others - but the majority of us stayed in our seats and decided to spend the rest of the game cheering the lads on. With relegation now beginning to look almost inevitable, a loud chorus of: *"Goodbye all, Goodbye all, We're saying goodbye to it all, And as we are saying goodbye to it all, We're saying goodbye to it all,"* rang out from the somewhat philosophical Forest faithful. Although the team rallied quite significantly during the second half, the score remained 3-0 to the 'Toffee-men' at the end. However, the 'Travelling Trickies' had sung themselves hoarse throughout the whole of the second half and were able to leave Goodison with their heads held high.

The striker we'd been crying out for all season had finally arrived just prior to the Everton game in the form of Robert Rosario from Coventry City. However, he had a two-match suspension hanging over him when he arrived at the City Ground, causing him to miss the defeat on Merseyside and the subsequent 3-0 defeat which the 'Reds' also suffered against Norwich City at home just four days later. He finally made his debut in the 1-1 draw at home to Leeds on Sunday, 21st March, but it was evident right from the start, that in no way was he going to be the answer to our prayers in front of goal. He'd hardly been a prolific scorer at Coventry, or indeed during his time with previous club Norwich City. In fact, Coventry had been using him in a midfield role during the tale-end of his career with them. Had Cloughie not 'bottled it' earlier on in the season and pulled out of the proposed £1.5 million purchase of Southend's Stan Collymore, we would probably have found ourselves somewhere in the top half of the table by now. For reasons known only to the great man himself, he'd got cold feet right at the last moment and instead we'd now ended up with someone whose credentials hardly matched up to the size of the task which lay ahead of him.

A victory finally came our way at the end of the month when goals from Keane and Clough gave us a vital 2-1 win at Southampton. Keane had only just signed a new three and a half year contract, although as it later transpired, this particular transaction seemed to have more to do with increasing his value on the transfer market, than with any long term commitment to the Club on his part. That aside, his important contribution for the time being had left Forest in twentieth position, just one point behind Sheffield United who were outside the relegation zone. With eight games left to play, there was perhaps still a glimmer of hope.

Off the pitch, Cloughie had been honoured for his services to the game locally, by being awarded the Freedom of the City of Nottingham. He became only the 31st Freeman of our City and it was as if the whole of Nottingham was saying to him: "We might be in a bit of a pickle right at this moment in time...but we'll certainly never forget what you've done for us over the last eighteen years." It also seemed to be a bit of a two-fingered gesture towards those in the press who'd suggested Cloughie had a drink problem and that this was the cause of all Forest's current woes. Little did they know that the same rumours had been sweeping Nottingham for several years by this time, although it hadn't stopped him getting us to Wembley half a dozen times in the last five seasons. The fact was that he could do little or no wrong in the eyes of the Nottingham public - and rightly so.

Due to their current plight, the Club announced that the redevelopment of the Trent End would be put on ice for a period of twelve months. Work would now commence on the proposed 7,000-seater stand at the end of season 1993/94. Were we to end up being relegated, the first priority would certainly be to restore Premiership football to the City, and although the ambitious plans to develop the stadium still further were to be applauded, it would be no good having a 'state of the art' City Ground, if the team were only good enough to half fill it every time they were at home. The installation of the much-needed under-soil heating however, would still go ahead during the close season as planned.

THE month of April began very badly on the pitch with successive home defeats, firstly at the hands of Aston Villa, and then Blackburn Rovers, who left the City Ground with 1-0 and 3-1 victories respectively. John and I decided to take our young sons, Thomas and Dean, down to London on Saturday, 10th April, to see them take on Queens Park Rangers in what was now virtually a 'do or die' game for the 'Reds'. Once again, there was a massive following from Nottingham amongst the crowd of only 15,815. And what a game we witnessed, with goals raining in from every direction throughout the ninety minutes. Rangers ran out eventual winners by four-goals-to-three. Two goals from Kingsley Black and another from Gary Bannister had put Forest 3-2 up with only minutes of the game left. However, to our bitter disappointment, the prolific Les Ferdinand popped up to claim his third and fourth goals of the game and send us home empty-handed once again. How we failed to get something out of this game, God only knows, but then this had been a familiar story all season? We were absolutely shattered as we left Loftus Road and climbed back into the car for the two-hour journey home. Having listened to the results on the radio, we were even more disturbed to find we were once again propping up the rest of the division. Yes, with only six games to go, we were four points away from the safety zone.

We were still in with a mathematical chance of staying up, and a 2-1 victory over Spurs (who else!) at the City Ground two days later gave us renewed hope. Kingsley Black and Robert Rosario - with his first goal for the Club - were on target, sending the crowd of 25,682 jigging home across Trent Bridge afterwards. Unfortunately, successive trips to the Capital to take on Wimbledon and then Arsenal yielded only one point and left us standing fairly and squarely on the relegation trap door. Worse still, came the shattering news that Cloughie had decided to retire at the end of the season, whether or not we were relegated. For many supporters, the thought of Forest playing First Division football next season without Cloughie at the helm was almost too much to bear.

When Sheffield United visited the City Ground on Saturday, 1st May, nothing less than an emphatic victory would keep our beloved 'Reds' in the Premiership. Sadly, an emotional crowd of 26,752 saw Forest defeated by two-goals-to-nil and therefore, after fifteen long seasons in the top flight, we were relegated. In spite of this, Cloughie was given a standing ovation by both sets of supporters at the end of the game. There was hardly a dry eye in the house as the great man took his final bow and left the City Ground arena for the very last time.

When you think that teams like Coventry City and Southampton had been flirting with relegation for many, many years at this point, Forest - without even so much as a hint in the last decade and a half - had managed it at the first attempt. No last-minute escapes for us I'm afraid, with the writing having been on the wall for seemingly the whole of the season. Once more, we had unwittingly claimed another first: the first club to be relegated from the new English Premier League.

Being Forest supporters though, we decided we were going to bow out of the top flight in style. Ipswich Town away the following Saturday was to be our last Premiership game and the travelling 'Red Army' were planning to descend on East Anglia in their thousands to indulge in a giant relegation party. We were definitely having some of that and, like hundreds of others, were planning to spend the rest of the weekend in Great Yarmouth. Big Lee got the luxury coach ordered and Andy Oakley booked twenty-five of us into a bed and breakfast for the Saturday night. If this was to be our last taste of top-class football for a while, then we were certainly determined to make the most of it.

WE arrived in Ipswich at around 11.30 in the morning. By this time virtually the whole of the town was awash with red and white. There were literally hundreds of Forest supporters thronging the streets, beer glasses in hand, making the most of the warm spring sunshine. Many had turned up in fancy dress and this made for a carnival-like atmosphere. As usual, there were plenty of high spirits, but little or no trouble. In circumstances such as these, Forest supporters are undoubtedly some of the most well-behaved and humorous on this planet. However, when severely provoked, they can be as bad as any other.

As time wore on and the beer flowed more and more freely, the rapidly growing crowd of travelling supporters were getting more and more boisterous. The Saturday afternoon shoppers were treated to the Trent End's full repertoire of songs and anthems: *"We'll be back, We'll be back, We'll be back as Cham-pi-ons! We'll be back as Champions,"* declared the mob, over and over again. And the thing was, we really meant it. We were absolutely convinced Forest's stay in the First Division would be a short one. Indeed, there were already plenty of T-shirts on display emblazoned with the slogan: *"NFFC - ON LOAN TO DIVISION ONE."*

As it got near to kick off, the crowds gradually began to disperse, drifting off in twos and threes towards Portman Road. Forest's official allocation of tickets for the game was only around five thousand, but there were easily seven thousand inside the stadium. Apart from filling the Visiting Supporters' Section of the Cobbold Stand, which held several thousand, there were large pockets of travelling fans in most parts of the ground, especially the Churchman's Stand which was predominantly filled with Garibaldi shirts. Although Cloughie had said his City Ground farewells one week earlier, he was still in charge for this game and most Forest supporters who'd made the journey, had done so in order to pay homage to the great man for one last time. And although you never want to see your team lose on any occasion, the result of this game or indeed the quality of the performance would be completely inconsequential.

As it turned out, Forest's performance was absolutely abysmal and they were swept aside - in the first half at least - losing the game eventually by two-goals-to-one. To their credit, the Forest supporters got right behind them throughout the whole dreadful ninety minutes. And, when the referee's final whistle brought the curtain down over our long and miserable season, we swarmed like ants onto the playing surface from all four corners of the stadium. The Ipswich fans joined in the festivities, the two sets of fans dancing around together all over the pitch. *"We want Cloughie! We Want Cloughie!"* chanted the mob, as we gathered at the edge of the pitch, adjacent to the players' tunnel. To our bitter disappointment, we didn't get him, and we can only assume he was too overcome with emotion to take yet another 'final' bow.

After what seemed like an eternity, we took the hint and began to make our way out of the ground and back onto our coaches outside. We had about a sixty-minute journey to Yarmouth in front of us, and as the convoy of coaches going back to Nottingham sped off in one direction, we peeled off and headed in the other. I was absolutely wrecked following our marathon lunchtime drinking spree and, as there were a few spare seats on our fifty-three seater coach, I grabbed a couple for myself and got my head down. The next thing I knew we'd arrived in Yarmouth and were pulling up outside our 'pleasant' little guesthouse. Although Andy had managed to book half of us into this particular establishment for the evening, the rest of the crew had to set off in search of some digs of their own. We'd all arranged to meet up in a bar around the corner at 7.30-p.m., although the way I was feeling, all I wanted to do was go straight to bed.

No sooner had we pulled up outside the guesthouse than the front door had swung open to reveal - in all her glory - 'mine host' for the evening - a 'Hilda Ogden' look-alike, arms folded defensively, hair in curlers, and wearing one of those all-in-one aprons that 'yer grandma' used to wear when she was doing her spring cleaning. "You won't find a single flea in any of my beds," she boasted, as one-by-one she snatched our twenty pound notes from us the second we walked through the door. And she was right...they were all married with families!

I had the great misfortune that evening of sharing a room with Cooperman. "How on earth was I gonna get any sleep tonight?" I thought to myself, knowing full well that I'd once more have to listen to his full repertoire of jokes long into the early hours of the morning - the same ones I'd now heard him tell a thousand times before. Still, at least he didn't produce any women's underwear from his bag on this occasion, as he had done when he'd shared a room with little Baz Cunningham a few years earlier down in London for one of the League Cup Finals.

Knowing full-well he'd be sharing with Baz on that particular occasion, he'd slipped one of his wife's basques into his bag before leaving home, and calmly took it out before hanging it on the wardrobe door as he and his startled - and extremely worried - room-mate were getting settled into their room. Baz's face was an absolute picture when he came down to meet the rest of us in the bar shortly after checking in and he couldn't wait to tell us what he'd just witnessed. Cooperman refused to be drawn on the subject all evening and as the night wore on, you could tell that Baz wasn't sure whether he was joking with him or whether he was displaying some bizarre and kinky side that no-one knew about. It all turned out to be a joke of course, but Cooperman neither denied nor confirmed Baz's story, simply grinning to himself every time the subject was mentioned and winking or blowing a kiss across the room at his apprehensive looking companion. The funniest thing though, was actually trying to imagine what he'd have looked like prancing about in this saucy little number, especially when you consider he's six foot tall, eighteen stone-plus, and has his hair cropped down to the bone. (Unless the plan was that Baz should slip into it instead). The mind boggles!

Very soon we were on the town and, as expected, the place was absolutely crawling with Forest supporters. It seemed that several hundred had decided to make a weekend of it and had descended upon the resort, turning it into a kind of 'Nottingham-By-The-Sea'. Despite having tried to freshen myself up in the shower before setting out on the town, I was still feeling decidedly the worse for wear. It was pretty obvious to me even at this early stage of the evening, that I wasn't going to last the course. In fact, I was feeling absolutely dreadful.

By about 10.00-p.m., having forced three or four pints down me, I'd simply had enough. I said my goodbyes to the rest of the gang and, despite much piss-taking, headed back towards the hotel. It was one of those 'three steps forward and two steps sideways' routines all the way back, but somehow I managed to find my way. (You always do though don't you? It's as if you've got some kind of homing device built into your system somewhere.) "Next time that bloody bed comes around, I'm gonna gerrin it," I said to myself as I stood there swaying in the middle of my room, my clothes in a tangled heap on the floor beside me. By the time my head hit the pillow, I was fast asleep. In fact, it would be fair to say I immediately slipped into a coma.

Several hours later, as I lay there blissfully snoring away, some of the others were beginning to arrive back at the hotel and decided to have some fun at my expense. Tony Wright from Stabbo (or 'Toby Jug' as he's more commonly referred to, due to the fact he's an absolute slap-head with enormous sticking out ears!) and Kelvin Willetts from Bulwell decided that between them, they'd give me another shower. Not the usual kind though...but one which would get me into a real lather. Fastened to the wall, just a few feet along the corridor from my room, was a large, red fire extinguisher. Whilst Kel carefully removed it from it's bracket and got it ready for 'firing', Tony quietly opened the bedroom door so he could accurately pinpoint my position to his grinning companion. God knows exactly what I was dreaming about at the precise second it went off, but all of a sudden I was completely overwhelmed by this incredible drowning sensation. As my mouth, ears and nose filled to the brim with foam - which incidentally was coming at me with incredible force - I spluttered into semi-consciousness. There in the doorway was the silhouetted figure of my SAS-style assailant, with what looked like some sort of liquid-filled bazooka pointing straight at me through the darkness. The force of the foam had me completely pinned to the bed. The best I could manage, was to wriggle around frantically for what seemed like an eternity, like some demented soul trying desperately to escape from a straitjacket.

By the time the contents of the offending vessel had been emptied, I was just beginning to come to my senses and, despite being severely stunned by this whole rather surreal incident, realised that this was by no means just a dream. My assailants though, were long since gone, and as I jumped out of my completely saturated bed and squelched across the sodden carpet towards the light-switch, the sound of laughter could be heard coming from the corridor outside. As I switched on the light, I was absolutely amazed by the scenes of devastation within that room. The walls, the ceiling, not to mention the beds, the wardrobe and the dressing table, were all completely saturated and dripping with foam. As I stood there soaking wet in nothing but my underpants, I thought to myself: "Ow the bloody 'ell, am I gonna sleep in 'ere for the rest of the night?"

Just as I was beginning to despair, in walked Cooperman - like a night in shining armour - his arms full of clean, dry bed linen, which he'd just 'half-inched' from someone else's room. In no time at all, the beds were changed and I was settling down for the night once again - or trying to at least, in between listening to a dozen of his worst jokes. As he'd rescued me from a very uncomfortable night, I felt obliged to humour him and laughed sympathetically at all of them. Although he denied any involvement in the incident with the fire extinguisher, I was certain he knew who the culprits were, and I was determined to seek them out first thing in the morning.

I awoke at about 7.00-a.m. to the sound of Cooperman shouting obscenities out of the bedroom window to some poor youth passing by in the street below. He was probably only going to the newsagents to get his early morning paper and must have been quite startled by the sight of this shaven-headed beast hanging out of the second-floor window telling him to: "Get yer nob out!" I looked around the room and in the daylight; the evidence of last night's commando raid was all around us. "How the hell are we going to hide this lot from 'Hilda'?" I thought to myself as I got dressed and made my way down for breakfast - which turned out to be one rasher of bacon, a runny egg, one slice of toast and a cup of tea which looked like it'd only been 'shown' a teabag. "Bollocks to her," I thought, "the stingy old cow. She's had twenty quid each off twenty-five of us - that's five hundred quid in all - an' all she can come up with is 'ten bob's worth' of bacon between us. Serves 'er bleedin' right!"

Once I'd finished this 'hearty' meal, smoked a couple of fags and read the Sunday papers, it suddenly dawned on me that I was now feeling alright and had completely recovered from my mystery illness of the previous evening. In fact, as we were planning not to leave Yarmouth until later on in the afternoon, I was even quite looking forward to a few drinks that lunchtime. 'Hilda' had kindly allowed us to leave our bags in the hotel after we'd checked out and we'd arranged to return for them later. When we finally went out at opening time, I was amazed to find that virtually every pub we went in was filled with Forest supporters. "Haven't they got homes to go to?" I wondered.

Following a very pleasant three hours, it was time to go and we made our way back to the hotel for our things. As we piled onto the waiting coach outside, a stern-faced 'Hilda' collared Big Lee in the doorway, just as he was about to join the rest of us on the coach. "One of your lot's gone and wet the bed!" she declared angrily. "Whoever it is, owes me some money for dry-cleaning," she added. (God only knows how she'd failed to notice the rest of the devastation in that room?) "Alright, let me go an' 'ave a word wi the lads," replied Lee. "I'll see if wi can a' a whip-round for ya, mi-duck," he re-assured her. By this time, the rest of us were up at the windows, craning our necks to see what was going on. We'd soon sussed that she wasn't very happy.

With that, Lee walked purposefully towards the coach, showing no signs of emotion whatsoever on his face. "Drive on," he demanded at the top of his voice as he clambered aboard. The driver duly responded and, as the coach pulled off, every one of us, including Lee, was up against the window waving to her as we passed by her front doorstep. 'Hilda's' face was an absolute picture. She stood there with her arms folded and her mouth open wide, as fifty of us fell about laughing all over the bus. She just couldn't believe what we'd done to her. "Bloody football hooligans!" she probably thought to herself.

DESPITE our relegation blues, we'd ended the season with a right good laugh and were already confidently predicting our speedy return to the top flight. The Nottingham public were still firmly behind the 'Reds', partly due to the fighting spirit which the team had shown throughout the season and partly due to the prolonged period of success they'd enjoyed during Cloughie's reign. Even though we'd been propping up the division for the whole of the season, the average League gate was still a creditable 21,866. And this had been achieved despite a two-month period of restricted attendances due to ground improvements. All the Club needed now, was a new manager - Martin O'Neill and Frank Clark were high on the list of candidates - and a surge in season ticket sales. One thing was for certain: It would be a very busy close season!

SEASON 1992/93 – STATISTICS

FA PREMIER LEAGUE – FIXTURES

Date		Opposition	Venue	Competition	Score	Attendance
Aug	16	**Liverpool**	H	**League**	**1-0**	**20,038**
	19	Sheffield Wednesday	A	League	0-2	29,623
	22	Oldham Athletic	A	League	3-5	11,632
	29	**Manchester United**	H	**League**	**0-2**	**19,694**
	31	Norwich City	A	League	1-3	14,104
Sept	5	Blackburn Rovers	A	League	1-4	16,180
	12	**Sheffield Wednesday**	H	**League**	**1-2**	**19,420**
	21	**Coventry City**	H	**League**	**1-1**	**17,553**
	23	Stockport County	A	LC 2 - 1st Leg	3-2	7,968
	26	Chelsea	A	League	0-0	19,760
Oct	3	Manchester City	A	League	2-2	22,571
	7	**Stockport County**	H	**LC 2 - 2nd Leg**	**2-1**	**15,573**
	17	**Arsenal**	H	**League**	**0-1**	**24,862**
	21	**Middlesbrough**	H	**League**	**1-0**	**16,897**
	24	Sheffield United	A	League	0-0	19,152
	28	Crewe Alexandra	A	LC 3	1-0	7,042
	31	**Ipswich Town**	H	**League**	**0-1**	**21,411**
Nov	7	**Everton**	H	**League**	**0-1**	**20,941**
	21	Crystal Palace	A	League	1-1	15,330
	28	**Southampton**	H	**League**	**1-2**	**19,942**
Dec	2	**Tottenham Hotspur**	H	**LC 4**	**2-0**	**22,312**
	5	Leeds United	A	League	4-1	29,364
	12	Aston Villa	A	League	1-2	29,015
	20	**Wimbledon**	H	**League**	**1-1**	**19,362**
	28	Tottenham Hotspur	A	League	1-2	32,018
Jan	3	**Southampton**	H	**FA Cup 3**	**2-1**	**13,592**
	9	Coventry City	A	League	1-0	15,264
	12	Arsenal	A	LC 5	0-2	25,568
	16	**Chelsea**	H	**League**	**3-0**	**23,249**
	23	**Middlesbrough**	H	**FA Cup 4**	**1-1**	**22,296**
	27	Manchester United	A	League	0-2	36,085
	30	**Oldham Athletic**	H	**League**	**2-0**	**21,240**
Feb	3	Middlesbrough	A	FA Cup 4 - Replay	3-0	20,514
	6	Liverpool	A	League	0-0	40,453
	13	Arsenal	A	FA Cup 5	0-2	27,591
	20	Middlesbrough	A	League	2-1	15,639
	24	**Queens Park Rangers**	H	**League**	**1-0**	**22,436**
	27	**Manchester City**	H	**League**	**0-2**	**25,956**
Mar	3	**Crystal Palace**	H	**League**	**1-1**	**20,603**
	13	Everton	A	League	0-3	21,271
	17	**Norwich City**	H	**League**	**0-3**	**20,799**
	21	**Leeds United**	H	**League**	**1-1**	**25,148**
	24	Southampton	A	League	2-1	18,005
Apr	4	**Aston Villa**	H	**League**	**0-1**	**26,742**
	7	**Blackburn Rovers**	H	**League**	**1-3**	**20,467**
	10	Queens Park Rangers	A	League	3-4	15,815
	12	**Tottenham Hotspur**	H	**League**	**2-1**	**25,682**
	17	Wimbledon	A	League	0-1	9,358
	21	Arsenal	A	League	1-1	19,024
May	1	**Sheffield United**	H	**League**	**0-2**	**26,752**
	8	Ipswich Town	A	League	1-2	22,093

HOME ATTENDANCES

	AGGREGATE ATTENDANCE	HIGHEST ATTENDANCE	LOWEST ATTENDANCE	AVERAGE ATTENDANCE
League:	459,194	26,752	16,897	21,866
League Cup:	37,885	22,312	15,573	18,942
FA Cup:	35,888	22,296	13,592	17,944
All Competitions:	532,967	26,752	13,592	21,318

FINAL LEAGUE TABLE - FA PREMIER

Position	P	W	D	L	GF	GA	Pts
1. Manchester United	42	24	12	6	67	31	84
2. Aston Villa	42	21	11	10	57	40	74
3. Norwich City	42	21	9	12	61	65	72
4. Blackburn Rovers	42	20	11	11	68	46	71
5. Queens Park Rangers	42	17	12	13	63	55	63
6. Liverpool	42	16	11	15	62	55	59
7. Sheffield Wednesday	42	15	14	13	55	51	59
8. Tottenham Hotspur	42	16	11	15	60	66	59
9. Manchester City	42	15	12	15	56	51	57
10. Arsenal	42	15	11	16	40	38	56
11. Chelsea	42	14	14	14	51	54	56
12. Wimbledon	42	14	12	16	56	55	54
13. Everton	42	15	8	19	53	55	53
14. Sheffield United	42	14	10	18	54	53	52
15. Coventry City	42	13	13	16	52	57	52
16. Ipswich Town	42	12	16	14	50	55	52
17. Leeds United	42	12	15	15	57	62	51
18. Southampton	42	13	11	18	54	61	50
19. Oldham Athletic	42	13	10	19	63	74	49
20. Crystal Palace	42	11	16	15	48	61	49
21. Middlesbrough	42	11	11	20	54	75	44
22. Nottingham Forest	**42**	**10**	**10**	**22**	**41**	**62**	**40**

AWAY ATTENDANCES

	AGGREGATE ATTENDANCE	HIGHEST ATTENDANCE	LOWEST ATTENDANCE	AVERAGE ATTENDANCE
League:	451,756	40,453	9,358	21,512
League Cup:	40,578	25,568	7,042	13,526
FA Cup:	48,105	27,591	20,514	24,052
All Competitions:	590,439	40,453	7,042	22,709

"WHEN HE GETS THE BALL, HE SCORES A GOAL, GARY-GARY CHARLES"

HAVING BEEN turned down by Martin O'Neill, their first choice to succeed Brian Clough as manager, the Forest Board turned their attentions to former left-back Frank Clark, who was now General Manager of Leyton Orient. He quickly relinquished his position with the Third Division outfit and was installed as the new City Ground supremo on 12th May 1993, just four days after the last game of the season at Ipswich. Rumour had it that O'Neill, the then manager of Wycombe Wanderers, turned the job down when the Forest Board refused him permission to bring in his own backroom staff, insisting instead that those partly responsible for the Club's recent demise should remain on board.

The month of June had seen a flurry of transfer activity; with firstly Nigel Clough departing from the City Ground, following his anger at allegations made in the tabloid newspapers by Director Chris Wootten concerning his father's drinking habits. The £2.275 million fee which Liverpool eventually had to pay for his services following a transfer tribunal, was scant compensation for the loss of such a talented player, who was simply "Forest - through and through." Clark wasted no time however in bringing new blood into the Club, spending £1.5 million on central-defender Colin Cooper from Millwall and £2 million on striker Stan Collymore from Southend United. Ironically, both of these players had been on Cloughie's shopping list in recent times. Perhaps his most significant piece of business during the summer though, was the signing of skipper Stuart Pearce on an extended four-year contract. Not surprisingly, this led to an immediate surge in season ticket sales.

On the other hand, it was inevitable that Roy Keane would be on his way out of the Club at the first opportunity - despite his shirt-kissing antics throughout the course of the relegation campaign and his constant assurances that: "Nottingham was now well and truly his 'adopted' home." And the favourites as ever for his signature, were Manchester United. Why is it that, whenever we have a really top-class player in our ranks at the City Ground, the vultures of Manchester begin to hover in the skies around West Bridgford? Ian Storey-Moore, Garry Birtles, Peter Davenport and Neil Webb, for example - all England internationals and all supporters' favourites - had been lured away to the bright lights of Old Trafford in the past. And, whilst the Forest Board were considering United's £3.75 million offer, full-back Gary Charles - himself an England international - slipped quietly out of Nottingham and joined the 'Sheep' for a fee of £750,000. How about that for a backward career move?

On 19th July Keane signed for United, but even the most die-hard Forest supporter couldn't deny that he'd given his all for the 'Reds' during his relatively short career on Trentside and that he would certainly go on to achieve the highest honours the game has to offer, something he was unlikely to do had he stayed in Nottingham. Other less high-profile deals had seen striker Gary Bull - cousin of Wolves' Steve Bull - arrive at the Club on a free transfer after Barnet were unable to fulfil their contractual obligations to him and a number of other players, and Des Lyttle drafted in from Swansea City for a fee of £375,000. On the other hand, both Gary Bannister and Toddi Orlygsson had joined First Division rivals Stoke City on free transfers.

The supporters' response to all this, was that no less than 13,500 season tickets were renewed during the course of the summer - a figure which had risen to an impressive 15,000 by the time Forest entertained the 'Sheep' in their first City Ground fixture. Not a bad response following relegation and the loss of star players from a supposedly fickle Nottingham public. There weren't many clubs around at the time that could have boasted such overwhelming support given the circumstances. What's more, the City Ground had seen a crowd of 23,381 turn up on 25th July to see England beat Turkey 1-0 in the Final of the European Youth Championships. Here, the kick off had been delayed by no less than twenty-five minutes to cope with the incoming crowds.

THE season kicked off with a seaside trip to Southend on Sunday, 15th August, the game being put back a day to accommodate ITV's 'Central Match Live.' Although most of the gang had travelled down on the Saturday - as had many hundreds more from Nottingham incidentally - I was still on my way home from holiday in Crete at the time and was therefore unable to make the journey until the morning of the game. John Farley and I had arranged to go down to the

South Coast on a minibus from Beeston, and when it finally arrived to pick us up outside the Charlton Arms at 9.30-a.m., we were already an hour behind schedule. It turned out also to be no more than a tatty old transit van with bench seats running down either side at the back, which we had to share with around fifteen other youths. And the driver; well he was something else? Now I don't like flying much, but I'd have happily got back on that aeroplane and endured another four and a half hour flight to Crete rather than risk the return journey back to Nottingham after the game in that 'jalopy' and with 'Reginald Molehusband' driving.

Anyway, as it turned out, we actually managed to arrive in Southend in one piece at around lunchtime. In contrast to the pouring rain which we'd left behind in Nottingham some three hours earlier, the sun was shining brightly on the South Coast and not surprisingly, outside every pub in the vicinity of the ground were scores of beer-swilling Forest supporters. We soon caught up with Big Lee, Andy, Garry and the rest of the lads, who immediately brought us up to speed with the goings on of the previous day. By all accounts, in scenes reminiscent of the 'Mods and Rockers' era of the early-1960s, there had been running battles all over the seafront throughout the course of the afternoon and evening as rival gangs of Forest and Millwall fans had slugged it out with one another. (Southend is apparently a popular weekend haunt for South Londoners during the summer months). From what I can gather, there had already been some bad blood between the two in the recent past and this particular encounter was only the latest in a feud which would continue throughout the course of the season.

The majority of the travelling army from Nottingham were - thankfully - boisterous, but generally very well behaved. Consequently, it turned out to be a most enjoyable lunchtime session with copious amounts of ale, plenty of singing and of course the usual amount of banter. As we finally made our way towards the ground shortly before kick off, it became clear just how many fans had made the long journey south to see the 'Reds' make their debut in the First Division. It was also at this point that we received by far the most disappointing news of the whole weekend: star striker Stan Collymore - the man we'd all been dying to see make his League debut - had come down with a mystery illness and wouldn't be playing. (Little did we know it, but this would be just the first of many similar disappointments concerning the man that Forest supporters had quickly nicknamed 'Stan the man').

Inside the ground, a large proportion of the travelling 'Red Army' were packed like sardines into an uncovered section of terracing at the South End (no pun intended) of Roots Hall. There were also several thousand seated in the East Stand away to our right. To say that the facilities were 'basic' is an understatement and, in the absence of any toilets in this area, many supporters - their bladders filled to bursting - were simply peeing up the wall at the back of the stand.

Within seconds of the game getting under way, the 'Reds' were behind following a horrendous injury to keeper Mark Crossley, who was left unconscious in the six-yard box following a goal-mouth scramble. As the ball ricocheted off the unfortunate Crossley, it bounced into the empty net off striker Brett Angell with the keeper lying prostrate on the ground. Following lengthy treatment - during which he was bandaged up like a mummy - he was able to continue, although clearly suffering from concussion. Fortunately, our beloved skipper Stuart Pearce came to the rescue before half-time, confidently dispatching a penalty into the back of the net following a foul on Lee Glover. 1-1 is how it stayed until the final whistle and as we poured out of the ground at the end, we weren't at all impressed with life in the First Division. If early impressions were anything to go by, this season was going to be an ordeal at best. It goes without saying, that John and I cadged a lift home with Lee and the gang in their minibus afterwards and despite it being a bit of a tight squeeze, at least it wasn't a life-threatening experience.

The Football League had at least been kind to us and presented us with the perfect opening fixture at the City Ground some three days later: yes, as mentioned earlier, against none other than our old 'woolly-backed' friends from just down the A52. Even if the game itself didn't turn out to be too exciting, at least we'd enjoy ninety minutes of fun taking the piss out of our 'country cousins'. The one thing that always amazes me about a Forest versus Derby fixture in Nottingham though, is the fact that the travelling 'Sheep' always arrive at the City Ground disguised as human beings - only to reveal their sickly Puma tops once inside the sanctuary of the Visitors' Enclosure. They then vanish into thin air once again, immediately after sneaking out of the ground at full-time. They're either extremely concerned by the thought of a trip to this wonderful City of ours, or they just don't like to be seen in public dressed in sheep's clothing - what you might call 'Closet Sheepshaggers' I suppose. You can almost imagine them sneaking down to the local meeting of the 'S.A.' ('Sheepshaggers Anonymous') and nervously confessing their sins to groups of other equally sad individuals: ''Err...my name's Melvyn...and I watch Derby County.''

A crowd of 26,684 squeezed into the City Ground for what was Forest's first home League fixture outside the top flight for almost sixteen years. Unfortunately, as is often the case with local 'derbies', the game was hardly a classic. Michael Forsyth eventually broke the deadlock early in the second half when his shot from fifteen yards out gave the 'Rams' the lead. However, Ian Woan came to Forest's rescue, smashing home a superb equaliser from twenty yards out, much to the relief of the City Ground faithful. Then Big Bob Rosario almost became the most popular man in Nottingham just before the end of the game when he turned brilliantly in the area only to smash a thunderous shot inches wide of the post. On reflection, 1-1 was a fair result on the night and Forest were left with just two points on the board after two games. The next day, Frank got his chequebook out once again, splashing out £600,000 on experienced Norwich City midfielder David Phillips. An extremely versatile player, Phillips could operate in almost any position and would prove to be an extremely valuable member of the squad.

Three days later the 'Reds' picked up their first win of the season in an amazing game against Grimsby Town at the City Ground, which ended 5-3. Kingsley Black gave Forest the lead early on in the first half and this was quickly followed by a bizarre own goal by Paul Futcher. His back-pass to goalkeeper Paul Crichton, although firmly struck, looked harmless enough. However, the keeper swung his boot wildly at the ball, missing it completely, and it rolled agonisingly over the line and into the back of the net right in front of a very amused Trent End. Clive Mendonca pulled one back for the 'Mariners' before half-time, but an early second-half strike by Lee Glover increased the lead to two goals once again. Jim Dobbin then made it 3-2, Ian Woan made it 4-2, Mendonca pulled another one back, and finally a diving header from Bob Rosario made it 5-3. What a cracker!

'Stan the man' made his much-awaited debut in the following game away to one of his former clubs Crystal Palace in midweek. Unfortunately, despite his presence, the 'Eagles' ran out easy 2-0 winners. Although I was unable to make the journey down to Selhurst Park, I was determined to get to as many away matches as possible this season - after all, being in the First Division seemed quite a novelty to most Forest fans; and let's face it, we'd be back up in the Premier League again next season, wouldn't we? So it was off to Kenilworth Road on Saturday, 28th August, to take on Luton Town. A young John Hartson ran the Forest defence ragged all afternoon, but it was the 'Reds' who eventually ran out winners, with Ian Woan scoring a fine individual effort in the second half, making the final score 2-1. Having fallen behind to a Hartson strike early on in the first half, Kingsley Black had been on hand only minutes later to sweep in the equaliser against his former club.

The next League action came two weeks later with yet another away excursion, this time to Oakwell to take on Barnsley. An estimated 6,500 fans made the relatively short journey up the M1 from Nottingham on what was a beautifully sunny day. As usual, we enjoyed an excellent three-hour lunchtime session in the centre of the small, but pleasant South Yorkshire town. Almost every pub it seemed was packed full of visiting supporters and reportedly, there were some fairly ugly skirmishes going on around the town as rival fans clashed with one another. Although we didn't witness any trouble, we did however see a very large and ugly looking mob of youths from Nottingham come wandering by one of the pubs we were drinking in. And by the looks of them, they weren't there merely on a shopping expedition.

If this game stands out for anything in particular, then it has to be Forest's abysmal performance on the day. In fact, without a doubt, it turned out to be their most inept of the season. They were extremely lucky to come away with only a 1-0 defeat, and they left the field at the end of the game to a chorus of boos from the Spion Kop End of the ground, where the majority of the travelling 'Red Army' were housed. In fact, so poor was the performance that Frank Clark went out of his way to apologise to the travelling supporters in the press the day after the game.

Despite their uninspiring start to the season, they were still considered 'box office viewing' as far as Central Television were concerned, with their next two League fixtures pencilled in for live coverage. The first of these was at home to Stoke City the following Saturday and as ever, the club from the Potteries would bring with them a substantial following, many of whom would look and behave like 'Neanderthals'. Per head of population, Stoke-on-Trent must have by far the largest percentage of hooligans than any other city in the land. Without exception, whenever they are in town, there is trouble. One thing I will say in their favour though, they don't half make some noise, particularly with their famous rendition of Tom Jones' 'Delilah.' They sound like they've all had singing lessons. Perhaps it's their close proximity to Wales that does it?

New signing David Phillips made his senior debut for the 'Reds', but this wasn't enough to prevent them going 3-0 down against the rampant visitors. David Regis and Mark Stein (from the penalty spot) gave them a 2-0 half-time lead, and when Stein added a third with a glorious twenty-yard volley early on in the second half, Forest looked dead and buried and the 4,000 Tom Jones sound-alikes were in full voice. However, within minutes David Phillips had pulled a goal back for Forest and when Psycho blasted in a thunderous free kick from the edge of the box midway through the second half, it looked odds on they'd eventually claw their way back into the game. It was certainly compelling stuff for the watching crowd of 20,843 and for the millions of viewers at home, but sadly, despite the 'Reds' piling on the pressure, the score remained 3-2 to the visitors at full-time. Apart from the excitement of the game itself, my abiding memory of that afternoon, is the sight of hundreds of rampaging red and white striped 'cavemen' marauding across Trent Bridge only minutes after the final whistle. I'm not suggesting for one minute that all Forest supporters are angels or anything, and I don't doubt that the 'Nutters from Notts' were also out in force, but the sight of Stoke fans on the rampage in a 'foreign' town is by no means an unusual one.

Although Collymore had now made three League appearances in the famous Garibaldi, he had yet to open his League account. However, when Forest travelled over to North Wales on Tuesday, 21st September, to take on Second Division Wrexham in a League Cup second round tie, he gave the relatively-small travelling band of Forest supporters a glimpse of what was to come in the future. I was still working up in Manchester at the time and made the sixty-mile trip to the Racecourse Ground with a Wrexham fan who lived in Manchester. Imagine that - born and bred in Manchester and, due to a family connection in Wales, a die-hard 'Robins' fan? Deserves a medal if you ask me. Anyway, as I sat next to him in the stands, surrounded by xenophobic Welshmen, I purred with delight as I watched 'Stan the man' turn on the style big time. During the course of that ninety minutes, he showed he had everything you could wish for in a footballer, let alone a striker: the ability to pass or cross a ball with precision - I saw him strike several fifty-yard passes from one side of the pitch to the other - pace, power, balance and control; and above all, a predatory instinct for scoring goals.

Firstly a powerful header, then a simple tap-in from six yards out from the tall, but muscular striker, gave Forest a 2-0 lead early on. A Gary Bennett penalty then brought Wrexham back into the game shortly before half-time, but once again the big man restored the two-goal lead, and chalked up his first hat-trick for the Club, with a fantastic individual effort following a fifty-yard run with the ball at his feet. And despite the fact that the home side eventually fought their way back into the game with goals from John Paskin and the dangerous-looking Bennett, I left the ground having witnessed probably the most complete performance I'd ever seen from a centre-forward, albeit against not the most auspicious of opposition. It was obvious to me, that in Collymore, Forest had acquired themselves a striker of supreme quality. ''Watch out Division One - Stan's coming to get ya!'' I thought to myself, as we made our way back to Manchester after the game.

Despite the erratic nature of their performances to date, the 'Reds' were certainly playing their part in some high-scoring and extremely entertaining games. And their next League game away to Bolton Wanderers - screened live on television the following Sunday - was no exception. Clark's latest signing, goalkeeper Tommy Wright - a Northern Ireland international - snapped up from Newcastle United, was drafted into the team for this trip to the North-West to replace the out-of-form Crossley. However, despite Forest going 2-0 up early on in the first half, with goals from Collymore and David Phillips - a wonderful 30-yarder - injuries to Bob Rosario and Ian Woan - who were replaced by youngsters Harvey and Howe - turned the game on it's head. David Lee pulled one back before half-time and Alan Thompson added a second shortly after the break. And although 'Stan the man' put the 'Reds' back in front once more, David Lee scored his second of the game to level the scores at 3-3, and Mark Patterson popped up in the box to stroke in Bolton's winner late on in the game. As far as ITV's watching audience at home were concerned, it was 'ten out of ten' for thrills and entertainment value. But for the thousands of watching Forest supporters, it was yet another three points lost. To be quite honest, our hopes of a quick return to the Premier were looking a trifle optimistic at this point, to say the least.

To make matters worse, the following evening, dramatic allegations were broadcast on ITV's World in Action programme relating to fraudulent goings on at the Club during the reign of Brian Clough and his assistant Ron Fenton. Former ticket office employee Andrew Plumb made a series of allegations regarding the distribution of League Cup Final tickets for the infamous tie against Manchester United at Wembley in 1992. He accused the managerial duo of selling bundles of tickets on the black market for their own personal gain whilst the then Chairman Fred Reacher, apparently aware of what was taking place right under his nose, simply turned a blind eye.

Although the Club itself called in the Fraud Squad to investigate these allegations, not surprisingly, nothing was ever proven. I for one simply cannot believe that such highly-paid and highly-respected individuals as these would stoop to these depths just to line their already bulging pockets still further. One thing is for certain though, someone was responsible for putting a block of two thousand tickets for the 'Forest end' of Wembley into the hands of United supporters, leading to mayhem in the stadium both during and after the game. As I watched the programme, I was amazed to see graphic newsreel footage of some of the violence which had taken place that day. This included the attack on the Coalpitz in Kilburn which we'd quite innocently become caught up in. The whole thing sent a shudder down my spine as the memories of that awful afternoon came flooding back to me. (See Chapter 26: "We're the pride of Nottingham").

DESPITE a 3-1 win over Wrexham in the second leg of their second round League Cup tie at the City Ground and a very promising 2-1 win over Premiership West Ham in the third round - also at home - by the time they entertained neighbours Notts County in the League on Saturday, 30th October, Forest were sitting in a very disturbing 20th position in the First Division table. Their tally of only 13 points from 12 games made for very depressing reading. Three consecutive home games had seen them draw 1-1 with Portsmouth, beat Tranmere Rovers 2-1, and draw 0-0 with Oxford United. Their only away excursion in the space of five weeks had seen them defeated 1-0 by near neighbours Leicester City on Sunday, 24th October, in yet another televised contest. Whilst the game itself was crap, one particularly amusing incident which took place at half-time, still brings a smile to my face even to this day. The Visiting Supporters' Enclosure at Filbert Street in those days was housed in one side of the South Stand - or Spion Kop as it was more commonly known - with a large wrought-iron 'cage' separating visitors from the Leicester supporters, who occupied around two-thirds of the same stretch of terracing. During the half-time interval, I made my way slowly down to the bottom of the stand to buy the Leicester City Review from a programme seller on the other side of the perimeter fence.

As I stood browsing through my programme only yards away from the pitch, my attention was drawn to a rather vivacious young lady who was parading around the edge of the playing area in a skimpy outfit, holding aloft a board depicting the time of the 'Golden Goal' - City were already 1-0 up, thanks to a rather fluky David Speedie header. Quite predictably, as she strutted her stuff along the edge of the pitch immediately in front of the Forest supporters, a spontaneous chorus of: *"Get yer tits ourt, Get yer tits ourt, Get yer tits ourt for the lads,"* rang out from the travelling 'Red Army.' Expecting her to be a little embarrassed by such loutish behaviour, you can imagine my surprise and amusement when she suddenly stopped dead in her tracks, gestured towards the Leicester supporters on the other side of the fence and mouthed: "For them - yes...for you lot - NEVER!" One-nil to the Foxy Lady methinks.

A fine second-half header from 'Big Stan' - his forehead bandaged up following an earlier clash of heads - gave Forest a much-needed 1-0 victory in the above mentioned game against County, securing them a vital three points. And, considering Notts were only two places above Forest in the table at the time, a crowd of 26,721 was quite impressive, to say the least. Three days later, the 'Reds' suffered a humiliating 3-1 defeat at home to a rampant Millwall side and left the pitch to a chorus of boos from the disgruntled crowd of 17,584. Supporters were rapidly losing patience with the lack of spirit being shown by a number of players.

So bad had been their recent run of form, even we were contemplating not making the short journey to St.Andrews the following Saturday to see them take on Birmingham City - a trip that under normal circumstances we'd have undertaken without hesitation. The deciding factor though, was the news that Frank Clark's latest signing, Norwegian international Lars Bohinen - signed from Lillestroem for £450,000 - would make his debut for the 'Reds', provided he recovered from a stomach upset. We agreed it was worth taking a chance on this one - a decision which, as it turned out, we most certainly did not regret. Such had been the lack of interest prior to this game, only a handful of us made the journey to 'Brum' in a couple of cars. Following a 'drink or two' outside the city, we arrived at St.Andrews at around ten to three and parked up in the car park just across the road from the Visitors' Enclosure in the Tilton Road End. Thinking we'd be part of only a small following from the East Midlands, we were quite surprised to hear the coach park attendant remark that: "Judging by the number of cars and vans that had arrived, it seemed half the population of Nottingham had made the journey."

Once inside the ground, this was obviously a slight exaggeration, but nevertheless there were a good 2,500 at least. Having recovered in time, Bohinen was fit enough to take his place in the side and it was soon apparent he wasn't short on ability. His presence seemed to lift the whole team and within thirteen minutes the 'Reds' were in front, courtesy of a speculative twenty-yard shot from Collymore, which somehow managed to find it's way past the City keeper. In the second half Lee Glover added a superb second, firing in from the edge of the penalty area after beating two players, and then grabbed himself another from close range in the 75th minute - 3-0 to the 'Mighty Reds!' Little did we know it at the time, but this result, and more importantly the performance, would be the turning point of the whole season.

The game at Birmingham was the first of four consecutive away matches in the League during November. 'Stan the man' scored a brilliant equaliser in the 1-1 draw against Wolves at Molyneux four days later and, after the scheduled fixture at home against Peterborough the following Saturday had been called off, we were heading back to the West Midlands for the third game on the trot on Sunday, 21st November, to do battle with West Brom. Once again our Sunday lunches had been disrupted by ITV's 'Central Match Live', although this didn't deter around 3,000 supporters from making the fifty-mile journey to the 'Black Country' on a freezing cold day. Once again 'Big Stan' came up trumps, scoring a couple of 'butes' in Forest's convincing 2-0 victory. Rather ominously as far as the rest of Division One was concerned, he'd now scored fourteen goals in his last fourteen games. Furthermore, when he bagged yet another two - one of them an absolutely stunning individual effort - in the 3-2 victory against Sunderland at Roker Park the following Saturday, he showed that his goalscoring exploits for the season were by no means over.

After what had seemed like an eternity since their last home fixture, Forest finally made an appearance at the City Ground again on Wednesday, 1st December, to take on Premiership Manchester City in a fourth round League Cup tie. A 0-0 draw in this game, meant that at least as far as I was concerned, the replay at Maine Road two weeks later, would be a 'home' game of sorts. Moss Side is only a few short miles from the Castlefield Hotel where I'd been staying every Monday to Friday for the past twelve months. In between these two fixtures, Forest captured another vital three points with a rather fortuitous 1-0 home victory over Birmingham City, with 'Blues'' central-defender Chris White scoring an unfortunate own goal, following an excellent cross from the right by Collymore.

Although Man City themselves were going through a rough patch at the time, they were however a Premiership side with a reputation for having a large and loyal band of supporters. Imagine my surprise therefore when there were only 14,117 people inside Maine Road for this fourth round replay, at least two thousand of which were Forest supporters. What's more, having bought my ticket from the main office immediately prior to the game, I found myself sitting amongst the home fans and was absolutely staggered to hear the level of abuse they were aiming towards their own players for virtually the whole of the ninety minutes. They were even moaning and whinging to one another half an hour before the game had started, much to my amusement. It just goes to show that reputations aren't always as well earned as they might be.

The only respite the beleaguered City players got during the whole of the game, was a brief period following Michel Vonk's opening goal - a thunderous header from a cleverly-worked free kick out on the right - which put the home side 1-0 up. However, after substitute Neil Webb equalised for the 'Reds' in the second half, the volume of abuse almost reached fever pitch. Surrounded by some pretty mean looking City supporters, when Colin Cooper fired in the winner in the 87th minute, following a brilliant one-two with Webb, I could hardly contain myself. But contain myself I did, despite watching the Forest supporters in the next section to me going absolutely berserk. It is my decided opinion, that visiting supporters who, for whatever reason, find themselves sitting amongst the home fans, should show a little respect and keep their mouths firmly shut, therefore not antagonising their hosts. On the other hand, if as you should be, you are seated in the Visitors' Enclosure, then serious piss-taking is completely acceptable and part and parcel of the great 'footballing experience.'

I got up especially early the next morning, bought every newspaper I could lay my hands on, and cut out all the back-page headlines relating to the game. I arrived at work well before most of my colleagues, dragged a six-foot high flip-chart stand into the middle of the large open plan office and plastered the newspaper cuttings all over it. Smack in the middle of it I wrote in big letters: *"Blue Moon, You started singing too soon, And now your dreams have all gone, Cos Forest beat you two-one!"* Needless to say, I wasn't the most popular person in Manchester that day.

THREE days before the League Cup tie at Maine Road, the 'Reds' had been due to tackle the 'Sheep' down at the 'BBG.' Big Lee, Andy, Garry, Bucko, Bodge and myself had all managed to get our hands on tickets, despite Forest's pitiful allocation of only 1800; although, with the game scheduled to be live on ITV, the whole of the Nottingham public would be able to witness Forest's inevitable humiliation of the 'Rams.'

On the morning of the game, it was absolutely belting it down with rain. So much so, that we had to shelter in a pub in Long Eaton for almost two hours before setting off by train from the station on Tamworth Road. The only downside of using this mode of transport to get to the 'Cesspit', is that there are actually one or two 'Sheepshaggers' who live in L.E. and surrounding district - well after all, it is in Derbyshire you know - and therefore you have to put up with their presence - and the smell - for the whole of the fifteen minute journey. Still the amount of piss-taking which you're able to cram into such a short journey, more than makes up for the awful stench. It amazes me though how the poor little souls just seem to take it on the chin, without even a hint of retaliation. I suppose they're just resigned to the fact that they're inferior to us in every sense.

Having arrived in 'Shitesville', we made our way out of the station and headed off in the general direction of the ground, the rain still lashing down. Strangely, there didn't seem to be too many people around. Within five minutes of arriving however, we bumped into a couple of Forest supporters walking in the opposition direction, who quickly solved the mystery of the deserted streets for us - the bloody game had been postponed due to a waterlogged pitch. What a bitch! Do you know, we had to go all the way back to Long Eaton and dry off for another three hours in the Royal Oak? Three cheers for the new Sunday opening hours.

We consoled ourselves in the knowledge that, following our trip to Man City, the festive period would be upon us, followed almost immediately in January by a trip to Hillsborough to take on Premiership Sheffield Wednesday in the third round of the FA Cup. Don't you just love this time of the year? And, just to get the festivities under way, Southend visited the City Ground on Sunday, 19th December, where, watched by a crowd of 21,641, Forest put on probably their most polished display of the season. Although the final score was only 2-0, with Cooper and Black grabbing the goals, the performance oozed class from start to finish. And when you consider you could quite comfortably have squeezed Southend's away following into a telephone kiosk - and the fact that the 'Reds' were still only eleventh in the table prior to this game - the size of the crowd was pretty impressive in my book. Nor did it go unnoticed by Chairman Fred Reacher either, who remarked prior to the following fixture at home to Middlesbrough on December 27th - which incidentally drew a crowd of 26,901:

> *"Our Support this season has been absolutely magnificent and I must pay tribute to the superb gate of 21,641 for the Southend match on the weekend before Christmas. The level of our attendances has been a source of inspiration to us all this season. We are the envy of everyone in the First Division - thanks to you!"*

The game against 'Boro' ended in a 1-1 draw, Stan Collymore grabbing the equaliser in the 69th minute. Whilst this may have been slightly disappointing, Forest would more than make up for it the following day at Bristol City, a game which we travelled to on Jack's 'Bus from the Sal.' We had a great time, due in no small part to Forest's convincing 4-1 victory, and the fact that there were plenty of old faces on Jack's bus and consequently a great deal of reminiscing in the pubs around Bristol after the game. Despite a goalless first half, 'Stan the man' put us 1-0 up on 57 minutes, only for Rob Edwards to equalise one minute later. Webby then added Forest's second, and Collymore scored an excellent third, before Ian Woan grabbed a fourth to seal a superb victory for the rampant 'Reds.' We stayed in Bristol until midnight, drank the place dry, and then slept blissfully all the way back home to Nottingham. This was turning out to be a wonderful Christmas, especially as we were now up to eighth position in the table, a mere ten points behind leaders Crystal Palace.

Yet another home game on New Year's Day, this time against promotion hopefuls Charlton Athletic, brought yet another bumper City Ground crowd - 26,543 to be precise. There was also more acknowledgement prior to this game of Forest's excellent support during the season to date, this time from Supporters Club spokesman Tim Gough who commented:

"It's probably unprecedented that a club enjoys record season ticket sales in the summer following relegation. It is certainly unprecedented that a Nottingham Forest Chairman should stand and applaud when the City Ground attendance is announced. Yet this was the case against Southend United when almost 22,000 fans turned up on a bitterly cold Sunday with the Trent End gates being shut ten minutes before the kick off. Mr. Reacher's acknowledgement of the fans' support was singularly the most overt gesture of appreciation by a member of the Forest Board and did not go unnoticed either by the media or the fans...cheers Mr. Chairman! Much has rightly been written of Forest's 22,000 average crowd being the highest in Division One and higher than all but ten in the Premiership. A look at other clubs' home gates reveals that Forest's magnificent travelling support has enabled no less than six clubs so far to record their highest attendance of the season."

The game against Charlton was disappointing for two reasons. Firstly, the fact that a Gary Nelson equaliser earned the Londoners a share of the spoils; and secondly, that Des Lyttle was booked by the referee for celebrating his first goal for the 'Reds.' Whatever is this game of ours coming to, when you can't get excited about scoring a goal - the very thing the game is all about? Once again, Forest's excellent away form - five victories and one draw in their last six games - more than made up for it, when they travelled to Vicarage Road two days later to take on Watford. Despite falling behind to a Colin Cooper own goal in the 29th minute, they gave their massive travelling support plenty to cheer about when second-half goals from Cooper - this time in the right net - and Scott Gemmill, gave them a 2-1 victory. Having quickly sold out of their official allocation of 4,800 tickets for this game, many more travelled down from Nottingham on speck on the day, boosting Forest's support amongst the crowd of 14,539 quite substantially. There were even five coach-loads of Plymouth Argyle supporters crammed in amongst the travelling army from Nottingham, following the late postponement of their own away fixture due to the weather.

For the third round FA Cup tie at Hillsborough, we'd been allocated no less than 7,000 tickets - every one of them snapped up in no time at all. We decided that 'Broughton & Hanna's Tours' should be on the road again, with Chesterfield designated as the lunchtime bingeing venue. Needless to say, we were in town early, and as ever, a wonderful time was had by all - except the local inhabitants of this 'town with the crooked spire.' It was worryingly near to kick off time before we got anywhere near to Hillsborough. In fact it was so late when we finally arrived, the coach driver had to drop us off right outside our end of the ground - the Leppings Lane End. By the time we eventually made it into our seats in the upper tier, the game was fully five minutes old. For many years now, it has been an ambition of mine to actually arrive at an away game on time, following a pre-match drinking session with Big Lee. He has to be almost prised out of the pub and dragged kicking and screaming onto the coach. Now I know some of Forest's away performances leave a lot to be desired, but they're not that bad!

The atmosphere inside the stadium was absolutely incredible. The magic of the FA Cup just seems to bring the best out in football supporters and both sets of fans played their part in raising the roof off of Hillsborough. The large following from Nottingham swelled the crowd to a sizeable 32,488 - not bad at all for what was only a third round tie. The seats in the upper tier are made entirely of wood and it soon became apparent to the travelling 'Red Army' that the volume of noise could be enhanced quite considerably by banging them up and down on their substantial metal frames. It would begin as a quiet rumble from the back of the stand and gradually gather momentum row by row until it reached the front. By this time it resembled the sound of thunder to those in the lower tier, who could be seen craning their necks as they looked up to see where the din was coming from?

It was a typical cut and thrust Cup tie, with both teams playing their part. When Wednesday took a ninth-minute lead, courtesy of a Mark Bright header following Nigel Worthington's free kick, this didn't deter either the Forest players or the fans. Although the game was fairly even, at times you'd have thought Forest were the home side, such was the noise coming from the Leppings Lane End. I suppose it was a combination of things which inspired the 'Travelling Trickies' to such great heights of passion: the magic of the FA Cup; the fact that no precious promotion points were at stake; the number of fans who'd made the forty-mile journey; and the fact that most of them were as pissed as farts! Whatever, it was a sensational afternoon - one of those which you never forget - and made even better by Colin Cooper's last-gasp equaliser for the 'Reds' which ensured a replay back at the City Ground. It was no more than the players or the magnificent supporters deserved.

Without wishing to 'flog a dead horse', Chairman Fred Reacher's comments a week later, are once more worthy of repetition:

> ''You had to be at Sheffield last Saturday to appreciate the contribution our fans made to the side deservedly coming back from a goal down to earn a replay.
>
> It's a long time since I have heard Forest supporters make so much noise and I was as delighted for them as I was for the manager and his players when Colin Cooper headed the equaliser.
>
> It gave me a great boost to hear the volume turned up at Hillsborough and I know the same went for the players who just could not fail to be lifted by the atmosphere generated by the 7,000 supporters who made the journey up to Yorkshire.
>
> When you think of that size of following allied to the tremendous gates we have had at the City Ground this season, I think we have removed once and for all the belief in certain quarters that we are not a big club.
>
> I think it's also time to kill that equally cheap jibe that our supporters are ''fickle''.
>
> For many years it was thought - outside Nottingham, I hasten to add - that they would only follow a successful side. But that's proved to be total hogwash.
>
> The fact that we have sold so many season tickets in a year in which we were relegated from the top flight underlines the fact that we have as loyal support as there is around.
>
> I wonder how many other clubs in the country would sell around 15,000 season tickets before a ball was kicked in a season that followed relegation?
>
> We've continued to sell season tickets, too - the current figure stands at about 16,500 after people have taken up the option to take advantage of the ''half season ticket'' offer - and it's been marvellous to see that kind of backing rewarded.''

Now I know Mr. Reacher had his fair share of critics whilst he was Chairman of the Club, but no-one can deny he was 'Forest - through and through' (and probably still is for that matter). I went to school with his son Mick during the early-seventies, at a time when Fred was Landlord of the Carlton Hotel. Both he and Mick were Forest mad even then and I'm absolutely convinced every decision he made during his Chairmanship was made with the best interests of both the Club and it's supporters at heart.

ON Sunday, 16th January, we travelled up to Birkenhead to see the 'Reds' take on Tranmere Rovers at Prenton Park in, would you believe, yet another game televised live by ITV. Once again, there was an excellent turn out from Nottingham on what was a bitterly cold day. In the 29th minute of the game, Crossley sent Pat Nevin sprawling in the penalty area and, whilst giving away a penalty, was extremely fortunate, given the present climate, to stay on the pitch. Not surprisingly, Aldridge slotted home the spot kick for Rovers and a gloomy outcome looked on the cards for the strangely under-par 'Reds'.

It wasn't until late into the second half that they began to make a real fight of it, and when Cooper made it 1-1 in the 80th minute, most of the frost-bitten Forest supporters inside the ramshackle little stadium, would have probably settled for a draw right there and then. Not our red-shirted warriors though, who poured forward in search of the winner. And much to everyone's surprise, up popped Gemmill in the 84th minute of the game to tap the ball home from two yards out, following excellent work on the right from Glover. When we left the ground after the game, I remarked to the rest of the lads: ''Wi a bit o' luck, that's the last time we'll ever 'aff t' come back to this God-forsaken place!'' Oh, how wrong I was.

Three days later, we entertained Sheffield Wednesday in the third round FA Cup replay at the City Ground where, in front of a crowd of 25,268, we were out-fought, out-played, out-sung by the Wednesday supporters, and quite frankly, out-classed. A tidy 2-0 victory for the 'Owls' meant that with the exception of the League Cup, we could concentrate our minds on the small matter of achieving promotion back to the Premiership at the first attempt. And guess what we were doing the following Sunday afternoon? Well of course, we were entertaining Wolves at the City Ground in ITV's 'Central Soccer Match Live' - there's a surprise for you. By this time, with 43 points on the board from 25 games, we were already up to a very respectable sixth position in the table, only three points behind the leaders. Some two places behind us in the table, Wolves proved very stubborn opposition and held out throughout the ninety minutes for a well-earned 0-0 draw. *"Nowhere, Forest are goin' no-where!"* the travelling Wolves fans taunted us with throughout the game, perhaps sensing our frustration.

Prior to the Wolves game, the Club unveiled their plans for the construction of the new £5.1 million, 7,300-seater Trent End, with work scheduled to commence immediately the last ball of the season had been kicked. Also during the close season, the long-awaited installation of under-soil heating - postponed during the previous summer due to the hosting of the European Youth Cup Final - would also take place. As a consequence of these improvements, the City Ground capacity during the early stages of the following season would be restricted to just 22,000. However, once completed, the overall capacity would be back up to a more realistic 31,000. Impressed by the high standard of facilities now on offer, UEFA had also designated the City Ground as one of the venues for the forthcoming Euro '96 Competition.

Also off the field, the purchase of Norwegian international Alf Inge Haaland - a deal originally set up by Cloughie - had at last been finalised after he managed to obtain the necessary work permit. The versatile young player, who could operate either in defence or in midfield, had been picked up for a modest £250,000 from Byrne F.K. In addition to this, second string goalkeeper Andy Marriott had joined Second Division Wrexham in a £200,000 deal.

On Wednesday, 26th January, Forest entertained Tranmere Rovers in the quarter- final of the League Cup. Unfortunately, a 1-1 draw meant that the unthinkable had happened: Yes, just thirteen days after vowing never to return to Prenton Park again, here we all were trundling back up the M6 motorway to do just that. And it was even worse this time; not only did the pitch resemble a ploughed field, but also the 'Reds' were completely out-classed by Merseyside's least glamorous club. A first-half header from the diminutive Pat Nevin and a late second-half effort from Tony Thomas made the final score 2-0 to Rovers and left us all wondering just what we were destined to scrape out of this topsy-turvy season of ours.

The following weekend, Leicester City were the Sunday visitors to Nottingham for what promised to be a pulsating East Midlands 'derby.' With the 'Reds' still in sixth position in the table, some two points and two places behind the 'Foxes', the game attracted a crowd of 26,616, despite the fact that it was also screened live by ITV. And what a game it turned out to be. The opening stages - played in pouring rain on a soggy pitch - were fairly even. Then, City goalkeeper Kevin Poole raced out of his goal-mouth and sent a misplaced clearance straight into the path of the on-rushing Gemmill who, despite being 35 yards out, sent a swerving half-volley soaring past the rapidly retreating keeper and into the roof of the net. On the stroke of half-time, Gemmill was on hand again, sweeping home a second from twelve yards out after getting the better of two defenders on the edge of the box. In the second half, Lee Glover added a third after turning brilliantly in the box, before Ian Woan majestically swept home the fourth from twenty yards out to complete the humiliation. With ten minutes still left on the clock, only a handful of Leicester's 4,000-strong travelling support remained in the ground. This was one of those completely unexpected results, but the standard of Forest's performance left me absolutely glowing with pride.

The big games were now coming thick and fast and the following Saturday, we made the very short journey over Trent Bridge to take on our 'nearest and dearest' of neighbours Notts County. It was my first visit to the recently refurbished Meadow Lane and, although they'd rebuilt virtually the whole of the stadium for less than the cost of a half-decent striker, I have to say I was very impressed with the general standard of facilities. Certainly more impressed than with the result of the game, which ended 2-1 to the 'Magpies.' And definitely far more impressed than with the moronic attitude of a large percentage of their supporters, who's sheer unadulterated hatred of anything in red was abundantly clear throughout the whole ninety minutes. Gary McSwegan broke the deadlock in the second half, drilling home a low shot from twelve yards out to put the 'Pies' 1-0 up, only for David Phillips to level in the 84th minute. Exactly one minute later however, following a left wing corner, Charlie Palmer's thunderous header restored County's lead. Up until this particular point in my life, I'd always considered myself to be something of a 'closet' County supporter, always happy to see them doing well, albeit from the 'Red side of the River'. But the attitude of their fans that day brought a swift and decisive end to any affinity I may have had for the club in the past. In fact, as far as I was concerned, from that moment on, they could all just fall into the River Trent and drown for all I cared!

This setback was followed by two more: a 1-1 draw at home to Crystal Palace the following week; and a 1-0 defeat away to Oxford United the week after. This left us in ninth position in the table, eleven points behind leaders Palace and seven points behind Charlton who occupied the other automatic promotion spot. And the thought of ending up in the play-offs just left me cold. Still, the one good thing was, with 16 games left to play, there were still 48 points up for grabs. And what a difference 17 days can make, especially when you win five games on the trot, picking up 15 priceless points along the way, and in the bargain, elevating yourself to second position in the table.

Consecutive 2-0 home victories over Peterborough United and Luton Town were followed by a 1-0 victory at Stoke - and yes there were running battles in the streets outside between rival supporters yet again - and two more decisive home successes. Following a 1-0 midweek victory over Barnsley, a City Ground crowd of 23,846, witnessed an astonishing game against mid-table Bolton on Saturday, 19th March. Although Phil Brown put the visitors 1-0 up on 23 minutes, Steve Chettle made it 1-1 and Stuart Pearce was on hand to put the 'Reds' 2-1 up before half-time. Then in the second half, Collymore, who'd been missing through injury for the last fifteen games, came off the bench to score with his first touch of the ball. The atmosphere inside the City Ground when he appeared at the side of the pitch waiting to come on, was such that it's almost impossible to describe. The feeling of expectation amongst the crowd - fully justified when he ran straight onto a long clearance from Mark Crossley and slotted the ball under the advancing keeper - was so intense it sent a tingle right down my spine. And when the ball hit the back of that net - well I swear the Bridgford End roof up above me was lifted twenty feet into the air.

And then, just to add to the drama, within minutes he was making his exit from the pitch, having delivered a forearm smash to the face of a Bolton defender and receiving his marching orders from the referee. A late effort from Scott Green then made the score 3-2 and we had to endure a very uncomfortable last few minutes waiting for the referee to blow his final whistle, before pouring out of the City Ground and heading straight for a few celebratory drinks on the way home. And there was plenty of drama still left to come before the season was out.

Shortly before the transfer deadline in March, Frank Clark had invested £200,000 in Southend striker Jason Lee, bought as cover for the injured Collymore. Although he was by no means another 'Stan the man', his never say die approach - always popular on Trentside - quickly established him as a bit of a cult figure amongst the fans. He made his debut in the game against Luton at the City Ground on 5th March and went on to figure in the next four games including the aforementioned game against Bolton. Although 'Big Stan' was now back in action, he would shortly be serving a three-match ban following his fisticuffs in that particular game, therefore the tall, gangly striker would shortly be experiencing first team football once again.

Collymore was used as a lone striker for the next game away to Portsmouth, where once again Forest's form dipped dramatically and they were lucky to come away with only a 2-1 defeat. Despite this setback, they remained in second position in the table; three points clear of Leicester in third place, as they went into the home game against Watford on Wednesday, 30th March. Lee partnered Collymore up front for this game, although it was the midfield duo of Neil Webb and Steve Stone who scored Forest's goals in a vital 2-1 victory. With Collymore suspended, Bob Rosario then partnered Lee for the next three matches, the first of which was away to Middlesbrough the following Saturday. The partnership was an instant success with Lee scoring his first goal for the Club and 'Big Bad Bob' grabbing the other in a 2-2 draw.

Two days later on Easter Monday, Forest entertained Bristol City at the City Ground where, despite their best efforts in front of a sizeable Bank Holiday crowd of 24,162, they could only manage a 0-0 draw. Rosario missed the sitter of a lifetime in this game, somehow managing to blast the ball over the bar from only two yards out. We were now faced with two consecutive trips to South London, the first of these to the Valley on Saturday, 9th March, to take on Charlton Athletic who, despite their early season promise, were now almost out of the promotion picture themselves. John Farley and I finally succumbed to the nagging of our respective sons Dean and Tom and agreed to take them with us to London for this game. No piss-up on this occasion then! Still, we were left with something to celebrate as Jason Lee's 28th minute strike gave us a priceless 1-0 victory and another three precious promotion points.

With that rather pleasant trip behind us, we now faced one of an entirely different nature: Millwall away at the New Den. Despite my 28 years as a Forest supporter, and the fact I'd travelled the length and breadth of the country watching them over the years, I'd never been to Millwall before and believe me; I wasn't looking forward to doing so on this occasion. I could always remember the time when Forest played them away in a third round FA Cup tie way back in January 1972. No-one outside of London was even aware of their reputation at the time, not least the several hundred Forest supporters who naively waived goodbye to the Evening Post photographers at Midland Station before clambering aboard the 'Forest special' which had been chartered to take them to the game. I distinctly remember the front-page picture of them in that Saturday's Post, all proudly displaying their red and white scarves and flags before setting off. And this was at a time when Forest supporters themselves carried with them a quite fearsome reputation. Well, not only did the 'Reds' lose 3-1 to the Second Division outfit on that occasion, but the travelling supporters were given a day they would certainly remember, as they got chased about all over the place before, during and after the game by hordes of rampaging South London Dockers.

Anyway, in spite of this, and many more chilling stories I'd heard since, many from supporters with first-hand experience, I decided it was now time for me to venture down to the 'Lion's Den', in order to sample the atmosphere for myself. In any case, at 36 years-of-age now, who was going to pick on an old man like me? As the day of the game drew nearer - Sunday, 17th April to be precise - it became more and more tempting to just stay at home and watch it on Central Match Live. I'd even been advised by a colleague of mine at work - a Birmingham City supporter who'd travelled down there himself earlier on in the season to watch the 'Blues' - that if I wanted to risk the journey, I should travel down by coach. This was because the coach park is directly outside the Visitors' Enclosure and only a thirty-yard walk from the turnstiles. Oh how I wished later I'd taken heed of these wise words.

There were eight of us who set off from Beeston that morning in two cars: Bucko, myself, our Pete, and Nigel Guthrie in one car; and Big Lee, Garry Mason, Bodge, and Lee's sister's boyfriend Darren in the other. Rather than venturing all the way into South London for a drink, we pulled up at the very first pub we came to after crossing Tower Bridge. Well at least we were 'Sarf of the River.'

It was considerably close to kick off however, by the time we arrived at the New Den, by which time the two drivers - Nigel and Darren - had managed to lose each other completely. It was soon obvious that we were close to the ground, as there were hundreds of people thronging the streets. We came across a huge industrial estate, where we managed to park the car on a large, but surprisingly secluded car park. As we walked in the general direction of the stadium, we made a point of remembering the name of the road on which the car park was situated: 'Juno Way.'

There wasn't a Forest supporter in sight as we came within striking distance of the stadium and I could sense, even then, we were getting one or two funny looks from inquisitive Millwall fans as we wandered aimlessly through the adjoining streets. One particular gang of around a dozen youths - well blokes really, several of them well into their forties - looked decidedly unsavoury, as they walked slowly along swigging bottles of beer and being generally obnoxious. What's more, it was very unnerving to discover, when we finally arrived at the stadium gates, that the Visiting Supporters' Enclosure was situated at the opposite end of the stadium to the one we'd parked our car in. We were somewhat relieved when we finally reached the safety of the North Stand turnstiles, having walked all the way along the wide-open concourse, which surrounds the stadium.

Our seats were in the upper tier of the stand, although, much to our surprise, the 4,000-strong following from Nottingham easily filled the whole of this section and most of the lower tier also. Ask any Millwall fan and I'm sure he'll tell you the same story: there are very few visiting teams who bring support of this volume with them to the New Den. Even when the game got under way, my mind was still on how we were going to get back to the car unscathed after the match. I had the kind of sinking feeling in the pit of my stomach that had been part and parcel of going to away games in the late-sixties/early-seventies, when violent confrontation between rival gangs of supporters was common-place. I hadn't experienced this feeling for many years now. The fact that Forest had also brought with them their own very gruesome-looking mob, and the stories we were hearing of major pre-match skirmishes, only added to my concerns.

As the game progressed I couldn't believe the sheer hostility of the Millwall supporters inside the ground. Old men, little boys, middle-aged women, you name it, they were all at it. Whenever the ball went out of play for a Forest throw-in, you could see them all surging forward to spit on and hurl abuse at the Forest players. I just couldn't believe my eyes. And when Millwall went 1-0 up through Jamie Moralee, it became even more volatile. A large gang of youths - including the unpleasant-looking mob we'd seen outside before the game - suddenly appeared in the seats in the lower tier of the East Stand and congregated in the corner just yards from the Forest supporters in the section below us. I was hating every minute of this.

Following the half-time interval, the 'Nutters from Notts' made their way down to the lower tier and there was a war of attrition developing between the two ugly-looking mobs. The police presence inside the ground became decidedly high profile, although as is often the case with the Metropolitan Police Force, they seemed unable - or simply uninterested - in removing the main antagonists from the stadium. Perhaps they reckoned that by keeping them within the confines of the ground, they were more able to keep the two rival factions apart. When 'Stan the man' - back from suspension - equalised early on in the second half, whilst inevitably being pleased by such an important Forest goal, I just thought to myself: ''OH SHIT!''

When Dave Mitchell restored the home side's lead late on in the game, I was almost beginning to breath a sigh of relief; only for Steve Stone to equalise yet again with a rare diving header with only minutes left on the clock. The majority of Forest supporters were in raptures by this time - but they were undoubtedly the lucky bastards who only had a thirty-yard walk back to their coaches after the game. We were going to have to go through hell and back just to get back to our car. I remember looking at my watch at exactly a quarter to five and feeling physically sick. And when the final whistle eventually sounded, my legs turned to jelly. The others weren't saying a lot either. Mind you, there was no need really, we were all thinking exactly the same thing: ''I'm gonna die and I want mi mummy!''

We poured out of the ground and watched in envy as the bulk of the travelling supporters clambered happily back onto their buses. ''Bastards'', I thought to myself. We nervously gestured to one another that we had to go right at this point. The only thing was; two large twenty-foot wrought iron gates had suddenly appeared outside the stadium and had been pulled shut, rendering it impossible to get back round to the other side of the ground. In addition to this, about two hundred rival Forest and Millwall fans were by this time stoning each other through the gaps in the railings. They were surging backwards and forwards at one another, occasionally managing to get in the odd kick or punch through the fence.

We got out of there quick and headed back towards where the coaches were parked. We were tempted to clamber aboard one of them and worry about the car later, but thought better of it in the end. To our right, there was a large railway arch, through which the vast majority of Forest supporters who hadn't travelled down by coach seemed to be heading. We followed them through, but as we got to the other side, they all seemed to be turning left into the street in front of us, but it was quite obvious that we needed to go right. The only trouble with this idea, was that the streets were filled with literally hundreds of Millwall supporters, all hanging around like vultures and quite obviously wishing to spill some blood. There was a line of policemen and women keeping the two sets of supporters apart. ''Which way to Juno Way Car Park?'' I nervously asked a policewoman who was standing nearby, hoping she'd point to the left, but knowing full well she'd point to the right. ''Oh thank you'', I replied, pretending to be grateful after she'd pointed to where all the Millwall fans were standing and uttered the words: ''You need to go straight down there, through the railway arches, round past the back of the stadium, down the main road, and it's on your right,'' as if deliberately trying to frighten the life out of us.

''Right then lads, we've got to go this way,'' I declared nervously, gesturing towards the street full of Millwall fans to our right. ''Yeah, you've gotta go this way laads,'' retorted a Millwall fan standing about two yards away on the other side of the 'thin blue line' of police. He was grinning from one side of his face to the other and rubbing his hands together in anticipation. Panic-stricken, we looked at one another, looked again in the direction of the hordes of bloodthirsty youths that were hanging around like vultures, and just stood there shaking our heads. ''Bollocks to this for a game o' soldiers,'' I said after deliberating for a second or two, ''There's no chance on this bleedin' earth that we're goin' in that direction. They've got our cards well and truly marked! Come on, let's get back through this railway arch and just jump on a bus home to Nottingham.''

With that, we were heading back sharpishly in the direction of the coach park. As we approached the archway, we noticed two or three 'Townies' hanging around furtively, trying to weigh up the situation. It was almost as if they were on a reconnaissance mission or something. They were definitely Nottingham lads as we all recognised their faces. Suddenly, one of them turned around, whistled loudly and began gesturing frantically with his right hand. Within seconds about a hundred and fifty youths emerged from under the railway arch and came marching briskly, but silently towards us. They were all dressed in designer gear, such as 'Stone Island' jackets and baseball caps, and many of them had scarves (not Forest scarves) covering their faces. As they flashed past us, one or two of them gave us a little look as if to say: ''Are these Millwall or what,'' but they had no time to stop and find out as they were quite obviously on a more important mission.

Almost directly opposite the railway arch, was a side-street, and this was where the majority of the Millwall fans - several hundred of them - were lying in wait like hungry-looking wolves. The mob from Nottingham simply poured out from under the railway arch and swept across the road straight into the middle of them. An enormous roar went up and very soon the sound of fist connecting with head and boot connecting with thigh could be heard coming from the middle of the crowd. The Millwall fans were immediately on the back foot - as if they'd been taken completely by surprise - and were retreating rapidly down the street. Effectively, in one fell swoop, the 'Nutters from Notts' had cleared the street to our right - our only escape route - completely, and we didn't hesitate, we were off like a shot. As we went past the street opposite, all we could see in the distance were hundreds of battling youths running around all over the place. But by this time the Millwall fans had retreated so far back down the road, it was impossible to make out exactly what was happening. The residents of the high-rise flats which ran the from one end of the street to the other, were all out on their balconies watching the confrontation and many of them were cheering loudly and applauding, as if they were watching an episode of 'Gladiators.' We were absolutely gob-smacked over what had just taken place. And in fact, had we not witnessed it with our very own eyes, there is no way we'd have ever believed it in a million years. I for one, was fully expecting to see the heavily-outnumbered Forest fans come streaming back up the road any minute, hotly pursued by their angry opponents.

Fortunately for us however, this never happened and we were able to make our way towards the other end of the stadium relatively unhindered. I have always wondered just what happened down that street. Did the police eventually arrive and break up the fight? Or did the mob just carry on brawling all the way to North London? As much as I am appalled by violence of this nature, I cannot help feeling that we owed this unruly mob from Nottingham an enormous debt of gratitude for getting us out of a right pickle. They were of course completely oblivious to this fact...but thanks anyway lads! Little did we know it at the time however, but this would turn out to be nothing more than a temporary respite.

As we got to the end of the street and were approaching another set of railway arches, which would take us back through onto the perimeter of the stadium, we came across - to our absolute horror - one poor unfortunate Forest supporter who'd been so badly beaten, he was lying motionless in the gutter, his face completely covered in blood. A young girl was kneeling down beside him cradling his head in her lap and two other young girls were standing anxiously by, waiting for medical help to arrive. There was absolutely nothing we could do to help, so we carried on under the railway arches. (I remember reading a letter in the following Saturday's Football Post from a group of Forest supporters describing the same incident, and stating that they'd been so concerned by the state of the poor lad, they'd stopped at a police station in London on the way home to find out whether or not he was still alive?)

As we made our way along the secluded path under the railway arch, there were small pockets of Millwall fans lurking in every corner. Amazingly, we made it through to the other side unchallenged. We were now on the footpath that ran alongside the stadium, and it was difficult to tell just who was friend and who was foe. We hadn't seen Lee or the rest of them since losing them prior to the game and hadn't a clue where they'd parked their car or indeed whether they'd even made it to the game or not. As we reached the other end of the stadium, we came to the main road which led up to the industrial estate where we'd parked the car. As we came to the end of the path, we veered off to the left and down a small incline, at the bottom of which stood a hot-dog stand. Gathered around this stand, was a large gang of Millwall fans, in the middle of which stood our 'friends' from earlier on in the day.

All of a sudden, they'd sussed out a couple of Forest supporters from amongst the passing crowds and set about them. They were kicking them around all over the place and, to my amazement, even the hot-dog seller was joining in. He could clearly be seen in his white grease-stained apron, in the thick of the action, putting the boot in on one of these poor unfortunate sods. As our Pete, Bucko and Nigel headed off down the slope in front of me; I carried straight on and ended up walking across a footbridge which ran straight over the main road - why, I haven't a clue? I don't know whether I just panicked, or something inside me was telling me we'd be better off splitting up. As I got to the other side of the bridge though, I suddenly realised it went straight into the middle of a housing estate and that there was no path down to the main road. I immediately turned tail, walked briskly back across the bridge, turned left, went down a grassy slope, jumped over the wall at the bottom, and found myself in the middle of the main road. I was smack in the middle of around two hundred Millwall fans and they were after blood. Fortunately not mine.

I decided just to act cool. I pulled the collar on my leather jacket right up, tightened my checked blue scarf around my face, and strutted along in the middle of the road amongst them. If I just acted normal, no-one would even give me a second glance, or at least, that's what I hoped. If someone as much as tried to make casual conversation with me though, my Nottingham accent would mean I was a dead man. By this time I could see our Pete and the others about a hundred yards up the road, also completely surrounded by Millwall fans, but trying equally as hard as me just to blend in. Every now and then, the baying mob would pick out another lonesome Forest supporter and the pursuit would begin. One poor lad was chased like a frightened rabbit for about two hundred yards until he was caught and kicked to the floor like an animal. As he curled up in a ball to protect himself, there were around a dozen youths kicking him about like a football. One particularly nasty youth with distinctive red hair was kicking him viciously over and over again in the head. It made my stomach turn but there was just nothing I could do to help the poor lad. Suddenly a police van came screaming round the corner, screeched to a halt, and about six policemen jumped out and bolted across the road to his rescue. The mob scattered, but old 'Gingernut' just couldn't resist one last swipe at him before he made off. Fortunately, this gave the first copper just enough time to make a dive forward and bring him crashing to the ground with one of the best rugby tackles I've ever seen. Within seconds, he was being dragged across the road and bundled into the back of the police van. "Serves you right, you vicious little bastard," I thought to myself as the doors slammed shut behind him.

I'd just about caught up with the others as we approached 'Juno Way', the road on which we'd parked the car. There were hostile-looking youths lurking on both sides of the street, but the little incident with 'Gingernut' had created the perfect diversion and we were able to slip unnoticed onto the industrial estate and in the direction of the car park. There was still another five or six hundred yards to go however and, with the place almost completely deserted, if some eagle-eyed bastard spotted us now, we just wouldn't stand a chance. We never uttered a word to one another as we made our way up the road. When we finally arrived at the car, we jumped in, started the engine, and made our way slowly out of the car park and down towards the main road, which was still filled with hundreds of youths. We kept a low profile while we were crawling along in the South London traffic, as we still ran the risk of being spotted and having to run the gauntlet of angry youths. It was another ten minutes before we were completely out of harms way and able to breathe a sigh of relief. We relived the nightmare amongst ourselves all the way home to Nottingham and none of us could believe that we'd managed to get out of there alive. One thing which we were all agreed on though was this: there was no chance on this earth that any of us would ever, under any circumstances, be going back to the New Den to watch Forest take on Millwall again. Not even if both clubs were fighting it out for the Premiership title, it was the last match of the season, and whoever won was crowned League Champions. No, I for one would be sitting at home with a can of lager in my hand, watching it on the telly!

THE following Saturday, Forest took another step closer to promotion with a 2-1 victory over West Brom at the City Ground. Steve Stone and Colin Cooper put them 2-0 up, before Bob Taylor pulled one back for the 'Baggies' on 85 minutes to leave the vast majority of the 24,018 crowd chewing their fingernails for the final five minutes of the game. We now had just four games to go, the first three of which were away from home and the last of which was at home against Sunderland.

The first of these four fixtures was the re-arranged clash against the 'Sheep' at the 'BBG.' Although I was one of the fortunate 1800 who still had a ticket for this game, I was still working away in Manchester from Monday to Friday and was unfortunately unable to make it back in time. Such was the significance of this game, in addition to the 19,300 who were 'packed' into the 'Sheep-dip', there were another 8,000 watching it on the big screen down at the City Ground. I had to make do with intermittent score flashes on the car radio in the hotel car park in Manchester. Anyone passing by, must have thought I was demented or something, as I jumped up and down in celebration at the news of Colin Cooper's first-half strike from a free kick twenty-five yards out, which gave the 'Reds' a precious 1-0 lead. Despite this, they were by no means having things all their own way and Mark Crossley had to make a string of first-half saves to keep them in front.

In the second half, the game remained fairly even until a bizarre own goal from former Forest star Gary Charles in the closing minutes. His completely unnecessary back-pass from an acute angle, clipped off Steve Stone's legs and into the back of the net, to the delight of both the Forest players and the 1800 fans were who packed into the Visitors' Enclosure on the Pop-side. *"Gary Charles, Gary Charles, Gary-Gary Charles, When 'e gets the ball, 'e Scores a goal, Gary-Gary Charles,"* sang the travelling 'Red Army' gleefully. We were almost there now; all we needed was a victory away to Peterborough three days later and promotion back to the Premiership was assured. And this was a game I wasn't going to miss at any price.

We all met up at Midlands Station early on the Saturday morning to catch the 10.30-a.m. service train to Peterborough - about a fifty-minute journey from Nottingham. Needless to say, with over 10,000 'Travelling Trickies' expected to make the journey, the train was absolutely packed to the rafters. I sat next to Garry Mason, with John Farley and Big Lee sitting opposite. Bucko, Bodge and Andy Oakley sat to our left. As the train stood on the station waiting to pull out, conversation inevitably centred on today's game and our impending promotion. Behind Big Lee and John, sat what can only be described as a 'bit of an anorak' who took it upon himself to join in our conversation at frequent intervals. About 45 to 50 years-of-age, dressed like a complete nerd, and of course completely on his lonesome, he was determined to give us all the up-to-the-minute team news, and his opinions on which players would have the biggest influence on the game etc. We just kept glancing at one another and winking and doing our utmost to humour the poor soul.

About fifteen minutes after pulling out of Nottingham, Garry - completely ignoring the 'NO SMOKING' signs, adorning every window of the carriage - lit up a cigarette. Although it was over a year now since I'd packed up, I wasn't in the least bit offended. However, completely out of the blue came the sound of: ''Put that cigarette out,'' from the direction of old 'Mr. Lonely' sitting behind John and Lee. Naturally, Garry just completely ignored him and got on with enjoying his fag whilst reading the back page of his newspaper. ''If you don't put that cigarette out, I'm going to report you to the guard,'' declared 'Mr. Lonely' a couple of minutes later. ''Well fuck off and report me to the guard then, you sad little bastard,'' replied Garry, at which point 'Mr. Lonely' got up and dashed off towards the back of the train to do exactly that. We all just fell about laughing.

About five minutes after Garry had finished his fag, 'Mr. Lonely' re-appeared at the back of the carriage with the ticket collector and stood there pointing in the direction of where Garry and I were sitting. Over marched this scruffy-looking guy, who stuck his face about two inches away from mine and said: ''This is a 'no smoking' train and if you light up again, you'll be thrown off at the next station!'' Now talk about 'red rag to a bull.' I sat bolt upright, put my face right into his and replied: ''Why don't you get your bad breath out of my face, 'Baldrick', and just go away and get your facts straight - I don't even bleedin' well smoke!''

At this, he became all flustered and confused and retreated off down the carriage, repeating his threats to throw us all off the train and leaving 'Mr. Lonely' to return to his seat. Needless to say, for the remainder of the journey, the sad little git had to endure a torrent of abuse from almost everyone in the carriage. ''I can't think why you've got no friends?'' and ''Here's ten pence pal - go an' ring all yer mates,'' being just a couple of the jibes thrown in his direction. At least it made the rest of the journey interesting if nothing else.

As we piled off the train at Peterborough Station, about a hundred youths descended from another on the opposite platform, which had just pulled in from Newark. *''Newark Town, Newark Town, Newark Town,''* they chanted as they poured out of the station just in front of us. I'd always liked the Newark crowd and had got to know quite a few of them over the years; they're a complete bunch of nutters, but nice with it. We followed them out of the station and headed straight towards the town centre. It was still only 11.30 in the morning, but the whole place was already full of Forest supporters. Every single pub we came across was packed, but the local landlords were absolutely brilliant, welcoming us all in with open arms. The atmosphere around Peterborough that lunchtime was fantastic; almost akin to the streets around Wembley on Cup Final Day, with supporters drinking, dancing and singing all over the place. There were also lots of old faces around, many of whom I hadn't seen for a long, long time.

When we finally made our way to the stadium several hours later, there was a sea of red and white from one end to the other. I would estimate around seventy-five per cent of the 14,010-strong crowd were Forest supporters, the majority of whom were young males between the ages of twenty and thirty-five. Our tickets were for the Chris Turner Stand - an uncovered bank of terracing along one side of the ground. This was so packed with swaying youths, that we climbed onto the top of the wall at the back - along with dozens of others - in order to get a grandstand view of the game. To our right, the bulk of the travelling supporters were packed tightly into the Moys End of London Road - a reasonably large bank of covered terracing not unlike (although somewhat smaller) than our very own Trent End at the time. There were also several thousand 'Travelling Trickies' in the Main Stand seats on the opposite side of the ground. We were all ready for a feast of football from the 'Reds' and a subsequent promotion carnival - unfortunately though, the Peterborough players had failed to read the script beforehand.

Incredibly, with only seven minutes on the clock, the 'Posh' were 2-0 in front and the 'Red Hordes' stood there silent and bewildered. Brian McGorry opened the scoring with virtually their first attack of the game, with the prolific Ken Charlery adding a second just minutes later. As far as we were concerned, the unthinkable had happened. Here we were flying high in the table and we were being trounced by a team who were bottom of the League, having won just eight games all season. The whole thing was just surreal. Any minute now, I was going to wake up and find it was all just a bad dream.

Things began to get better from that point on though and the 'Reds' began to take a grip of the game. And when 'Big Stan' burst through the 'Posh' defence to make it 2-1 just before half-time, a 'Roy of the Rovers' outcome to the game seemed a distinct possibility. Roared on by their huge following, Forest really set about the opposition in the second half. When Stuart Pearce's diving header from a right wing corner brought the scores level, this signalled a celebratory pitch invasion by hundreds of youths who seemed to emerge from all four corners of the ground. The atmosphere inside London Road was now just unbelievable and the players couldn't fail to be uplifted by it. And when 'Big Stan' once again burst through the Peterborough defence in the closing minutes to blast the ball high into the roof of the net, the scenes of celebration inside the stadium had to be seen to be believed. Once again hundreds swarmed onto the pitch to mob the players, and those who remained on the terraces were jumping around like demented Chimpanzees.

Seconds before the referee blew his final whistle; he gestured to the players to make a run for the tunnel. As he did so, literally thousands of fans poured onto the pitch, myself included. You'd have thought we'd won the World Cup, so much did it mean to the supporters of Nottingham Forest FC to have made it back to the Premier League, and at the first attempt. I was so happy; I scrounged one of Garry's cigarettes, laid down in the middle of the pitch and enjoyed the best smoke I'd had in years. So much for packing in a year ago then!

I smoked a few more that night as well as we celebrated promotion in Nottingham City Centre along with a few thousand others. As it turned out, we would have still been promoted that day; even without 'Big Stan's' 23rd and 24th goals of the season, such were the other First Division results. Somehow though, the drama of the game entirely befitted the occasion and provided all of us with yet another wonderful memory to add to our already-substantial list. Be it good or bad, there is never a dull moment when you are a supporter of Nottingham Forest.

All we had to do now, was get the final away fixture of the season at Grimsby out of the way three nights later and we could welcome our newly-promoted heroes back to the City Ground the following Sunday in style. Having grabbed a point in the 0-0 draw at Blundell Park, the team emerged to a crescendo of noise from the capacity crowd of 27,010 who turned out for the final fixture against Sunderland. The Nottinghamshire Constabulary had warned us in the previous night's Evening Post to watch out for trouble, which was expected to occur between rival supporters at this game. Apparently, a notorious gang of Sunderland 'supporters' known as the 'Seaburn Casuals' were coming down to Nottingham for a showdown with their 'infamous' Forest counterparts 'the Naughty Forty,' following trouble at Roker Park earlier on in the season. Now this was a new one on me. We'd had 'Bernie's Boot Boys' back in the late-sixties/early-seventies, 'Randall's Vandals' in the late-seventies, the 'Mad Squad' and the 'Executive Crew' in the early-eighties, but I'd never heard of the 'Naughty Forty.' Perhaps this was the very same crew who had unwittingly come to our rescue at the Millwall game - although if that was the case, the 'Naughty One-Hundred-And-Forty' would have been a more fitting description.

Unfortunately, the predicted trouble did materialise, with an otherwise good natured and friendly occasion being marred by running battles in the streets around the ground both before and after the game. Forest raced into a 2-0 lead in this game, with goals from captain Stuart Pearce (pen) and 'Stan the man' - his twenty-fifth of the season - seemingly rounding of their season in style. However, a brave fight-back from the visitors resulted in Don Goodman reducing the deficit on 82 minutes and Craig Russell equalising with only four minutes left on the clock. Still, it didn't really matter anyway, and on the final whistle, thousands of fans swarmed onto the playing surface like ants to carry the players shoulder-high from the pitch. Frank Clark's pre-match appeal for supporters to stay off the pitch at the end of the game so the team could indulge in a celebratory lap of honour, had fallen on deaf ears and instead they had to remain firmly locked in their dressing room until the crowds dispersed. The supporters eventually made their way across the pitch to the lower tier of the Bridgford Stand, where amazingly, they shook hands with and applauded the visiting two thousand supporters who'd made the journey down from the North-East (or from Cotgrave) - a sight which was very pleasing to see. What a pity this spirit didn't prevail outside the ground only minutes later, when the police had to act swiftly to prevent a full-scale confrontation taking place on Radcliffe Road.

THIS had turned out to be yet another eventful season in the history of Nottingham Forest FC. Having been relegated the previous season, Clarky's revamped side had bounced back to the Premiership at the very first attempt. What's more, the Forest supporters had at last, well and truly shaken off their undeserved reputation for being fickle. Having stood by the team throughout the relegation season, over 16,500 had bought season tickets for this First Division promotion campaign. The average League attendance at the City Ground was also a very healthy 23,050 - something a number of Premier Clubs would have been more than happy to achieve. Twenty out of the twenty-three home fixtures attracted crowds in excess of 20,000 and no less than six attracted crowds of over 26,000. The highest of the season was the 27,010 who turned out for the final game at home to Sunderland, with the lowest being the 17,584 who attended the Millwall game. All we needed now was for Clarky to spend wisely during the summer and we would surely go from strength to strength again next season? One thing was for sure; we were back in the big time again and hopefully to stay.

SEASON 1993/94 – STATISTICS

FOOTBALL LEAGUE DIVISION ONE – FIXTURES

Date		Opposition	Venue	Competition	Score	Attendance
Aug	15	Southend United	A	League	1-1	8,609
	18	**Derby County**	**H**	**League**	**1-1**	**26,684**
	21	**Grimsby Town**	**H**	**League**	**5-3**	**23,225**
	24	Crystal Palace	A	League	0-2	15,048
	28	Luton Town	A	League	2-1	9,788
Sept	8	Derby County	A	Anglo/Italian Cup	2-3	6,654
	11	Barnsley	A	League	0-1	13,280
	15	**Notts County**	**H**	**Anglo/Italian Cup**	**1-1**	**7,347**
	19	**Stoke City**	**H**	**League**	**2-3**	**20,843**
	21	Wrexham	A	LC 2 - 1st Leg	3-3	7,860
	26	Bolton Wanderers	A	League	3-4	10,578
Oct	**2**	**Portsmouth**	**H**	**League**	**1-1**	**20,727**
	6	**Wrexham**	**H**	**LC 2 - 2nd Leg**	**3-1**	**11,619**
	16	**Tranmere Rovers**	**H**	**League**	**2-1**	**20,771**
	20	**Oxford United**	**H**	**League**	**0-0**	**18,462**
	24	Leicester City	A	League	0-1	17,624
	27	**West Ham United**	**H**	**LC 3**	**2-1**	**17,857**
	30	**Notts County**	**H**	**League**	**1-0**	**26,721**
Nov	**3**	**Millwall**	**H**	**League**	**1-3**	**17,584**
	6	Birmingham City	A	League	3-0	16,966
	10	Wolverhampton Wanderers	A	League	1-1	21,621
	21	West Bromwich Albion	A	League	2-0	15,581
	27	Sunderland	A	League	3-2	16,968
Dec	**1**	**Manchester City**	**H**	**LC 4**	**0-0**	**22,195**
	4	**Birmingham City**	**H**	**League**	**1-0**	**22,061**
	15	Manchester City	A	LC 4 - Replay	2-1	14,117
	19	**Southend United**	**H**	**League**	**2-0**	**21,641**
	27	**Middlesbrough**	**H**	**League**	**1-1**	**26,901**
	28	Bristol City	A	League	4-1	20,725
Jan	**1**	**Charlton Athletic**	**H**	**League**	**1-1**	**26,543**
	3	Watford	A	League	2-1	14,539
	8	Sheffield Wednesday	A	FA Cup 3	1-1	32,488
	16	Tranmere Rovers	A	League	2-1	8,500
	19	**Sheffield Wednesday**	**H**	**FA Cup 3 - Replay**	**0-2**	**25,268**
	23	**Wolverhampton Wanderers**	**H**	**League**	**0-0**	**23,008**
	26	**Tranmere Rovers**	**H**	**LC 5**	**1-1**	**20,066**
	29	Tranmere Rovers	A	LC 5 - Replay	0-2	12,578
Feb	**6**	**Leicester City**	**H**	**League**	**4-0**	**26,616**
	12	Notts County	A	League	1-2	18,655
	19	**Crystal Palace**	**H**	**League**	**1-1**	**24,232**
	26	Oxford United	A	League	0-1	9,346
Mar	**2**	**Peterborough United**	**H**	**League**	**2-0**	**19,329**
	5	**Luton Town**	**H**	**League**	**2-0**	**22,249**
	12	Stoke City	A	League	1-0	20,550
	16	**Barnsley**	**H**	**League**	**2-1**	**20,491**
	19	**Bolton Wanderers**	**H**	**League**	**3-2**	**23,846**
	26	Portsmouth	A	League	1-2	12,578
	30	**Watford**	**H**	**League**	**2-1**	**23,044**
Apr	2	Middlesbrough	A	League	2-2	17,056
	4	**Bristol City**	**H**	**League**	**0-0**	**24,162**
	9	Charlton Athletic	A	League	1-0	12,330
	17	Millwall	A	League	2-2	12,543
	24	**West Bromwich Albion**	**H**	**League**	**2-1**	**24,018**
	27	Derby County	A	League	2-0	19,300
	30	Peterborough United	A	League	3-2	14,010
May	3	Grimsby Town	A	League	0-0	11,930
	8	**Sunderland**	**H**	**League**	**2-2**	**27,010**

HOME ATTENDANCES

	AGGREGATE ATTENDANCE	HIGHEST ATTENDANCE	LOWEST ATTENDANCE	AVERAGE ATTENDANCE
League:	530,168	27,010	17,584	23,050
League Cup:	71,737	22,195	11,619	17,934
FA Cup:	25,268	25,268	25,268	25,268
Anglo/Italian Cup:	7,347	7,347	7,347	7,347
All Competitions:	634,520	27,010	7,347	21,880

FINAL LEAGUE TABLE - DIVISION ONE

Position	P	W	D	L	GF	GA	Pts
1. Crystal Palace	46	27	9	10	73	46	90
2. **Nottingham Forest**	**46**	**23**	**14**	**9**	**74**	**49**	**83**
3. Millwall	46	19	17	10	58	49	74
4. Leicester City	46	19	16	11	72	59	73 *
5. Tranmere Rovers	46	21	9	16	69	53	72
6. Derby County	46	20	11	15	73	68	71
7. Notts County	46	20	8	18	65	69	68
8. Wolverhampton Wanderers	46	17	17	12	60	47	68
9. Middlesbrough	46	18	13	15	66	54	67
10. Stoke City	46	18	13	15	57	59	67
11. Charlton Athletic	46	19	8	19	61	58	65
12. Sunderland	46	19	8	19	54	57	65
13. Bristol City	46	16	16	14	47	50	64
14. Bolton Wanderers	46	15	14	17	63	64	59
15. Southend United	46	17	8	21	63	67	59
16. Grimsby Town	46	13	20	13	52	47	59
17. Portsmouth	46	15	13	18	52	58	58
18. Barnsley	46	16	7	23	55	67	55
19. Watford	46	15	9	22	66	80	54
20. Luton Town	46	14	11	21	56	60	53
21. West Bromwich Albion	46	13	12	21	60	69	51
22. Birmingham City	46	13	12	21	52	69	51
23. Oxford United	46	13	10	23	54	75	49
24. Peterborough United	46	8	13	25	48	76	37

* Promoted via the play-offs

AWAY ATTENDANCES

	AGGREGATE ATTENDANCE	HIGHEST ATTENDANCE	LOWEST ATTENDANCE	AVERAGE ATTENDANCE
League:	338,125	21,621	8,500	14,701
League Cup:	34,555	14,117	7,860	11,518
FA Cup:	32,488	32,488	32,488	32,488
Anglo/Italian Cup:	6,654	6,654	6,654	6,654
All Competitions:	411,822	32,488	6,654	14,707

"HE'S GOTTA PINEAPPLE ON 'IS 'EAD"

FOLLOWING THEIR successful promotion campaign, manager Frank Clark's only summer signing had been that of Dutch international striker Bryan Roy. Fresh from World Cup duty in the U.S.A., twenty-four-year-old Roy was purchased from Italian side Foggia for a fee of £2.5 million. With the likes of Collymore, Cooper and Bohinen having been brought in the previous season, Clark was of the opinion his current squad of players were good enough to hold their own in the Premier League. The Nottingham public also seemed to share this belief, with over 20,000 investing in season tickets.

The only significant outgoing transfers of the summer had been the £225,000 sale of Lee Glover to First Division Port Vale and the departure of full-back Brett Williams on a free transfer. I had never particularly rated either of them myself and was quite relieved to see the Club at last parting with players of this standard. Off the field, the impressive new Trend End had been taking shape and it's substantial framework was now beginning to dominate the skyline along the Trent Embankment. Work was expected to be completed by February 1995, increasing the City Ground capacity to a more realistic 30,500. In the meantime, visiting supporters would be restricted to just 800 seats in the lower tier of the Executive Stand. The majority of those who'd stood for years on the terraces of the old Trend End, would, for the time being, occupy the 4,700 seats in the lower tier of the Bridgford Stand.

Tickets for Forest's first match of the season at Ipswich - where ironically they had played their last Premiership fixture - were at a premium. I was one of the lucky 3,000 who'd managed to lay their hands on one and travelled down to Portman Road to see Bryan Roy make his League debut. It was quite apparent that many more Forest supporters had bought tickets directly from Ipswich, as large pockets of travelling supporters were evident in several other parts of the stadium - not least the Churchman's Stand away to our left. And Roy didn't disappoint us either, firing home a superb twenty-yard strike to give Forest a deserved 1-0 victory and sending the large Nottingham contingent home happy.

We couldn't have asked for a more fitting City Ground curtain raiser, than the visit of Manchester United some two days later - a match which was televised live by Sky. The atmosphere inside the City Ground generated by the restricted crowd of 22,072 was absolutely incredible. Having had to put up with visiting supporters sitting in the stand below us for two seasons now, it was fantastic to have over 7,000 Forest supporters occupying the whole of the Bridgford End and getting right behind the 'Reds' from the first whistle. The packed Main Stand 'A' Block away to our left only intensified the noise. And, not surprisingly, Roy Keane received a very hot reception indeed; he was jeered and whistled everytime he got the ball. Chants of: *"Judas! Judas!"* rang out throughout the game.

A stunning first-half volley from United's Andrei Kanchelskis, temporarily silenced the volatile crowd, but with players of the calibre of Collymore and Roy in the side, Forest were always in with a chance against the Premier League Champions. And before half-time, the 'Reds' were level after Collymore broke through the United defence to smash home an unstoppable shot, and in the process, almost lift the roof off the City Ground - well three sides of it at least.

This had been an excellent start for Forest and from that point on; things just got better and better. A 1-0 home victory over East Midlands rivals Leicester City - promoted with Forest via the play-offs - the following Saturday, was followed by a 2-1 midweek victory over Everton at Goodison Park. When they took on Sheffield Wednesday at the City Ground some ten days later, they were already sitting in third position in the table, having accumulated ten points from their first four games. When the fixture list first came out in the summer, Saturday, 10th September was the only fixture I was interested in, as John Farley had announced he was getting married on that day and had asked me to be his best man. I was praying for Wimbledon away - or anyone away for that matter - but I was beside myself when I saw that my heroes were at home to the 'Owls.' Whether I liked it or not, I was going to miss a home game for the first time in ages and I just couldn't understand John's thinking: how on earth could he plan his wedding day in the middle of the football season? Some people just have no consideration for others whatsoever!

On the day of the wedding, there were transistor radios galore outside the church, every one of the lads desperate to know how Forest were getting on. Between the church and the reception, I managed to listen to at least twenty minutes of second-half commentary on my car radio and was both ecstatic at the news of their fantastic performance and thoroughly pissed off that I wasn't there to witness it. Steve Stone's first-half shot had been deflected into the net by Kingsley Black to give

Forest the lead, and in the second half, Bohinen's thunderous volley from fifteen yards out had increased this lead. And despite Graham Hyde pulling one back for Wednesday, the 'Reds' continued to dominate the game. I waited with baited breath as Stuart Pearce stepped up to hammer home their third from the penalty spot after Simon Coleman had handled in the box, and was positively ecstatic when Bryan Roy raced through and rounded the keeper to slot the ball home from a tight angle, following Bohinen's defence-splitting pass.

I was absolutely pissed as a fart by the time I stood up to make my speech at the reception, but there was no way Mr. Farley was going to escape without some serious piss-taking - especially having made me miss a Forest match at the City Ground. Having later sneaked out of the evening reception to watch the 'Rampant Reds' on Match of the Day in the bar next door, I returned to the party just in time to join in with the rest of the lads in a chorus of: *"We've got the whole world in our hands,"* after DJ 'Filthy Phil' had finally succumbed to our requests and agreed to play it especially for the Groom. It was just like being in the Trent End again as we jumped around all over the dance floor singing Forest songs for the next half an hour, much to the bewilderment of the remainder of John and Susannah's guests.

OFF the field, winger Gary Crosby had joined Second Division Huddersfield Town on a free transfer and striker Gary Bull had teamed up with his former manager Barry Fry on a month's loan at Birmingham City. On the field, Forest continued to impress. A 1-1 draw at Southampton was followed by a 2-1 victory over Third Division Hereford United in the first leg of the League Cup second round. This was followed on Saturday, 24th September, by a victory of exceptional quality against Tottenham at White Hart Lane. Steve Stone's strike from just three yards out gave the 'Reds' an early lead, following good work down the right by Collymore. And despite Tottenham's equaliser before half-time from Ilie Dumitrescu, they laid siege to the Tottenham goal in the second half. A right wing cross from Stone led to Roy restoring the lead with a brave diving header, and minutes later the same two players combined again to give the 'Reds' a 3-1 lead. Bohinen then added a superb fourth - chipping the ball over the keeper from twenty-five yards out and even earning applause from the home fans - to round off what had been a brilliant performance.

The footballing world was now beginning to take notice of Clark's rapidly emerging side, with Sky TV pencilling in Forest's next two home fixtures - against Queens Park Rangers and Wimbledon - for live coverage. The first of these produced five second-half goals, with Stan Collymore's last-gasp winner giving Forest all three points. This was followed by a 0-0 draw at Hereford in the second leg of their League Cup tie in midweek, and a pulsating 3-3 draw away to Man City the following week, where Ian Woan scored another last-minute effort to earn the 'Reds' a share of the spoils. And the game against the 'Dons' also provided the watching public with a feast of football. Bohinen gave Forest a 1-0 first-half lead, slamming the ball into the roof of the net, following a classic counter-attacking move. In the second half, Collymore picked the ball up on the half-way line, beat no less than three defenders, before slamming an unstoppable thirty-yard shot past keeper Hans Segers in the Wimbledon goal. Ian Woan then added a third before Marcus Gayle's late consolation for the visitors.

We were up to our old tricks again the following week when we travelled to the West Midlands for the game against Aston Villa. Having finally managed to prise Big Lee out of the pub only minutes before the game, we were still walking down Witton Lane on our way to the ground when Bryan Roy was pulled down in the box in the first minute to earn Forest a penalty. Before we'd managed to make our way through the turnstiles, Stuart Pearce had slammed home the resulting penalty to give us the lead. We then had to wait until the second half to see some goal action for ourselves, with Steve Stone firing home a bobbling shot from eighteen yards out, following a half-cleared right wing corner from Ian Woan - 2-0 to the 'Super Reds'.

We were now unbeaten in thirteen games so far this season, and a trip to First Division Wolves in midweek for a third round League Cup tie gave us a chance to make it fourteen. Although Wolves fought back in this game from 2-0 down to level the scores, Stuart Pearce then settled the issue with a late thirty-yard free kick which took a deflection on it's way into the net making the final score 3-2 to the 'Reds'. The visit of Blackburn Rovers to the City Ground the following Saturday however, brought this impressive sequence of results to an abrupt end. They simply had no answer to the strike-power of Sutton and Shearer (otherwise known as 'S.A.S') with Sutton grabbing two excellent goals in a 2-0 victory for the visitors. Ironically, born and raised in Nottingham, Sutton was a Forest supporter as a boy and used to drool over the likes of Trevor Francis from the City Ground terraces. Having then moved to East Anglia with his family as a teenager, he was snapped up by local club Norwich City. What a pity he hadn't stayed in Nottingham and been snapped up by his 'hometown' Club.

This defeat against Rovers seemed to have a detrimental effect on the confidence of the whole team, leading to a run of seven games without a victory. This sequence of games also included defeats against Liverpool, Chelsea, Leeds United and Second Division Millwall (2-0 at home in the fourth round of the League Cup), and draws against Newcastle United and Arsenal. This barren run was finally brought to an end, with a crushing 4-1 victory over Ipswich Town at home on Saturday, 10th December, with all five goals coming in a pulsating first forty-five minutes. Prior to this fixture, Forest had dropped to fifth position in the table with 29 points from 17 games played. They were ten points behind the leaders, who ironically were Blackburn Rovers, the team responsible for starting the rot.

The following week, they faced without doubt, their toughest challenge of the season to date, with a visit to the 'Theatre of Dreams' to take on Champions Manchester United who, rather dauntingly, had so far failed to concede a single goal at Old Trafford all season. With Stan Collymore already beginning to make noises in the National Press - via his agent Paul Stretford - about being unhappy at the City Ground, he was out to impress United boss Alex Ferguson, who he was convinced was about to make him his next signing. Whilst his eagerness to impress in this game may have proved beneficial to Forest and their supporters in the short term, in the long term, a good performance from the big striker, may well have led to his departure sooner rather than later. It has to be said, that at this particular stage of his career, he was beginning to enjoy a less-than-harmonious relationship with some of his team-mates and quite a number of the Club's supporters, particularly those in the 'A' Block.

Fortunately, the whole of the Forest team - including Stan - rose to the occasion and gave United a lesson in football that day. Having already had what looked like an excellent effort disallowed due to offside, 'Big Stan' struck a beautiful curling thirty-yard effort into the roof of the net to put the 'Reds' 1-0 up in the first half. This was followed up by a Stuart Pearce shot from the edge of the box in the second half which found it's way into the net via a deflection off United's Mark Hughes, and at 2-0, Forest were cruising. And in spite of a late headed goal from Frenchman Eric Cantona, they came away from Old Trafford with all three points and their collective confidence well and truly restored. Unfortunately, Manchester United became 'Moanchester United' the next morning in the National Press, with Alex Ferguson accusing Forest of 'kicking them off the park' and Paul Ince insisting that Stuart Pearce - his England colleague - had made racist remarks to him during the game. How dare anyone have the audacity to come to Old Trafford, play better than United, and return home with a victory under their belts? It should never be allowed!

Following a 0-0 draw away to Coventry City on Boxing Day - the worst game of the season to my recollection - the players had to quickly dash back to Nottingham to prepare for the next day's City Ground fixture against Norwich City. Prior to this game, the Club announced that the 4,200 seats in the upper tier of the new Trent End Stand would be available for the very first time for the visit of Second Division Plymouth Argyle in the third round of the FA Cup on Saturday, 7th January. Lars Bohinen secured all three points against the 'Canaries' when he scored directly from a corner out on the left (who cares...they all count you know!). The 'Reds' then played appallingly in their disappointing 3-1 defeat at West Ham the following Saturday, the only bright spot being the fact that young Paul McGregor scored his first senior goal for the Club, albeit a late consolation.

Speculation concerning Collymore's apparent unhappiness at the Club grew stronger and stronger over the festive period, culminating in his non-appearance for the game against Crystal Palace at the City Ground on Monday, 2nd January. His mystery illnesses and injuries were now becoming a regular thing; a situation which was causing considerable unrest amongst Forest supporters. There's nothing worse than when some highly-paid prima donna - probably earning more in a week, than the average supporter earns in a whole year - doesn't really want to play for his club anymore. And the fact the club have invested hugely in order to secure his services in the first place, only compounds the issue. No individual is bigger than the club. The fans are what the club is all about. Players come and go, managers come and go, directors come and go, but in the main, supporters are around forever. I know literally hundreds of faces down at the City Ground; faces I've bumped into a thousand times before over the decades - as far away from Nottingham as Munich and Madrid, everyone of them deeply passionate and totally committed to the Forest cause. Anyone who isn't proud to pull on that Garibaldi shirt - whether he's earning peanuts or whether he's on twenty grand a week - should quite simply piss off!

Collymore's deputy for the Palace game, Gary Bull - back at the City Ground after his loan spell with Birmingham - scored his first senior goal for the Club, and in doing so, secured all three points for the 'Reds' in a 1-0 victory. Prior to the game, when Collymore's name was mentioned over the Tannoy system, there had been a significant amount of booing emanating from various parts of the stadium. When Collymore returned to the side the following week against Plymouth, he had a chip on his shoulder the size of 'Slab Square' and his attitude throughout the game was like that of a spoilt child. What's more, when he latched onto Steve Stone's brilliant through ball and rounded the advancing keeper, before coolly slotting the ball into the empty net to give Forest a first-half lead, he immediately strutted over to the Main Stand 'A' Block, made arrogant gestures towards them, and then trotted back to the half-way line, completely ignoring the rest of his team-mates in the process. What a prick!

Scott Gemmill added another to give Forest a 2-0 victory and send them through to a fourth round encounter against Crystal Palace at the City Ground, three weeks later. The Club also announced prior to the Plymouth game, that all 4,300 Bridgford lower tier season ticket holders were being moved into the upper tier of the Trent End (capacity 4,200!) in time for the next home game against Aston Villa on Saturday, 21st January. Before this though, we had the small matter of a trip to Ewood Park the following Saturday to take on League leaders Blackburn Rovers. There was an incredible turn out from Nottingham for this game - including a guest appearance from the almost defunct 'Broughton & Hanna's Tours' - with the 'Travelling Trickies' entirely filling the lower tier of the Darwen End, which has a capacity of 6,500. What a pity then that this volume of support failed to inspire the Forest players, who quite frankly, were played off the park for the whole of the ninety minutes. Goals from Paul Warhurst, Jason Wilcox, and an own goal from Steve Chettle gave the classy-looking Blackburn outfit an easy 3-0 victory and made the likes of Collymore look nothing more than second-rate. One thing I was impressed with though, was the transformation which had taken place at Ewood Park during the 'Jack Walker' era. The last time I'd been there in the early-eighties, the place looked like it had been condemned!

When Villa arrived at the City Ground the following Saturday, they brought with them sufficient supporters to entirely fill the lower tier of the Bridgford Stand, which by now had been vacated by the Forest supporters. They'd gone back to their 'ancestral' home in the Trent End. Given the large number of visiting supporters inside the stadium, the overall attendance of 24,598 was somewhat disappointing, and very difficult to explain. After all, Forest were still riding high in the Premiership table in fourth place and were well on course for a place in Europe the following season. The Villa fans, all too aware of the current unrest surrounding Stan Collymore - a self-confessed Villa fan - taunted us throughout the game with chants of: *"Collymore - sez you're all Wankers!"* and *"Collymore - is a Villa fan!"* although they didn't like it much when he equalised for Forest in the second half. John Fashanu had given Villa a first-half lead, sweeping home an excellent left wing cross from Steve Staunton, but in the second half Forest were awarded a penalty after Ugo Ehiogu brought down Bryan Roy in the box, right in front of the Villa fans. With Stuart Pearce out of the side through injury, Collymore held his nerve, despite an absolute barrage of abuse from the 'Claret and Blue Hordes', to slam the ball past goalkeeper Nigel Spink and into the roof of the net. He then set off on one of his crazy celebratory jigs right along the running track in front of them, as they piled forward into the cordon of stewards, who successfully prevented them from getting their hands on him. What a pity! The last laugh was on them however, when Dean Saunders headed home a late winner for Villa, following another brilliant cross from the elegant-looking Staunton.

The most frustrating thing about Collymore, was the fact that, despite being an absolute 'dick-head', he was a player of exceptional quality; someone who could turn a certain 0-0 draw into a 1-0 victory with just one flash of brilliance. And it has to be said he'd won many games for Forest almost single-handedly during his time with the Club. Undoubtedly, without his brilliance in front of goal, Forest would still have been languishing in the First Division and certainly not in the enviable position of a top-six place in the Premiership, chasing a coveted place in Europe. He underlined this fact just four days after the Villa game, when he grabbed both Forest's goals in a creditable 2-0 victory over Chelsea at Stamford Bridge. And, judging by the rather paltry crowd of only 17,890, this was long before being a Chelsea supporter, had become a fashion statement in and around the Home Counties of London.

FOR the FA Cup tie against Palace the following Saturday - my curiosity having got the better of me - I traded in my usual seat in the Bridgford Stand and instead bought tickets for myself and Tom in the upper tier of the Trent End. At this point in time, although I only took him to the occasional League game, the arrangement where I took him to every single Cup game at the City Ground remained firmly in tact. This meant I could still go on the piss with the lads before the vast majority of games; a ritual I had indulged in for many years now, but one which I knew I would eventually have to give up for his sake. And to be honest, he was absolutely bonkers about Forest, had been virtually since the day he was born, and still is to this day - in fact he just gets worse and worse as he gets older. Can't think where he gets it from?

I was really impressed with the facilities in the new stand: the refreshment area overlooking the Trent Embankment; the view out across the City (a sight I could happily look out over for hours); the incredible view of the pitch and the rest of the stadium; and the fact there wasn't an away fan within two-hundred yards of me. Just my cup of tea really. Unfortunately, the only thing that spoilt the whole occasion, was the result. Palace took the lead in the first half when Chris

Armstrong's looping far post header dropped over the head of Mark Crossley and into the back of the net. And, despite the fact Lars Bohinen did one of his: "I'll just pop this into the back of the net then from this corner" routines, to make it 1-1 before half-time, a blistering header from Iain Dowie in the second half settled the game. Things could have been so different, had either Steve Stone or Brian Roy's first-half efforts not cannoned back into play off an upright.

It was back to my normal seat the following week for the visit of Liverpool and back on the piss with the lads before the game. Waking up on a Saturday morning after a hard week's graft and a night out on the tiles on Friday, to the prospect of Liverpool at home, is what being a football supporter is all about. A nice soak in the bath, a 'cholesterol special' for breakfast, followed by a brisk walk round the corner to the bus-stop at 11.30 for the journey into town. Rendezvous with the lads in the Tavern In The Town (sadly no more) or Yates's Wine Lodge, followed by one in the King John, and then another in the Queens. Then a walk into the Meadows for one in the Riverway, and eventually finish up in Wurlitzer's (now the Southbank Bar) for the last couple. Watch an excellent game, played in front of a large crowd, with a cracking atmosphere inside a pleasant, modern stadium. See Forest take the lead - Collymore sliding the ball home at the far post after great work down the left from Bryan Roy. Laugh at Phil Babb getting sent off for Liverpool, enjoy end-to-end football as usual, with the only blot on the landscape coming in the form of a last-minute equaliser from Robbie Fowler - well it is Liverpool, what do you expect? A quick pint in town after the game, before jumping on the 6 o'clock bus back to Chilwell. Dinner on the table when you get home at 6.30, Football Post tucked safely under your arm. Gulp down your dinner like you haven't eaten in days. Sneak off to the bedroom and lay on the bed for a quick read of your paper. Get woken up by the misses an hour later. Wash and freshen up, then put your 'glad rags' on. Negotiate the two-mile walk into Beeston with the wife on your arm (completely sobered up by the time you get there of course). Talk football to all your friends and acquaintances all night in the Wine Bar, whilst plying the misses with drinks. Call in at the takeaway on the way home at midnight for a large kebab with lashings of chilli sauce. Almost sober up again by the time you've walked all the way home. Smoke your last fag of the day (probably your thirtieth on a day like today), washing it down with a large cup of coffee and a dose of late night television. Crawl into bed...and, if you're really, really lucky...now am I dreaming, or have I just died and gone to heaven?

Unfortunately for me, this would be the last time I'd be indulging in this all-day Saturday ritual, as I was due to leave Nottingham three weeks later and move - with my job - across the Midlands to Birmingham. From now on - with a 120-mile round trip by car to every single home game - my Saturday afternoon excursions, would be almost entirely alcohol-free affairs; just a couple of pints in Wurlitzer's before each game in fact. Still, my number one passion is and always has been Forest, as opposed to alcohol, although as the saying goes: "You don't have to be pissed to watch Forest...but it certainly helps!"

Three away games on the trot after the Liverpool game - against Newcastle, Arsenal and QPR - and only one point gained from all three fixtures, meant the 'Reds' were sitting in fifth position in the table going into the home game against Spurs on Saturday, 4th March. The lower tier of the Trent End was now completed and the stand was officially opened prior to the game by Kenneth Clarke, QC, MP, Chancellor of the Exchequer, himself a life-long Forest supporter. (I was really hoping he'd win the Tory Party leadership battle after the resignation of John Major in 1997 and eventually become Prime Minister, just so we could get the chant: "The P.M. is a Forest fan," going at away matches). Mr. Clarke was accompanied by Peter Lee, the Chief Executive of the Football Trust, who kindly handed over a cheque for £2.13 million to Chairman Fred Reacher, towards the cost of the development. With the £150,000 that had also been spent on the pitch during the close season for the installation of new drains and under-soil heating, the facilities on offer down at the City Ground were now second-to-none. The stadium would indeed be a fitting venue for the 'Euro '96 Competition' due to be staged fifteen months later.

A crowd of 28,711 were inside the revamped stadium that day, and were rewarded with an excellent game - but then Forest versus Spurs encounters are rarely anything less. After a goalless first half, Teddy Sheringham gave Spurs the lead early on in the second. As Forest pressed forward in search of an equaliser, the Trent End rose to applaud the arrival of 'Super Sub' Jason Lee, who replaced Bryan Roy up front. His 'never say die' attitude had turned him into a bit of a cult figure on Trentside, although most supporters would agree that a place on the substitute's bench was about the best he could have hoped for when both Collymore and Roy were fit and available for selection. He seemed to have an immediate impact on the game, his aerial ability causing a considerable amount of panic amongst the Spurs defenders. Lars Bohinen struck a fantastic thirty-yard equaliser soon after Lee's arrival, the ball simply screaming into the roof of the net. It was one of those goals that you wait all season for and one that lives on in your memory long afterwards. Then Big Jason himself decided to get in on the act as he latched onto the end of a lofted ball from

Woan, as keeper Ian Walker hesitated on the edge of his box. After winning the initial challenge, the ball fell kindly for him and he was able to prod it into an empty net as two Spurs defenders bore down on him. 2-1 to Forest and the crowd were going wild. However, the drama was not yet over and Colin Calderwood sent the large travelling 'Yid Army' home happy, when he equalised from close range in the dying minutes.

A midweek 2-1 victory over Everton at the City Ground, was then followed by a thumping 4-2 victory over Leicester at Filbert Street the following Saturday. With a place in Europe still well and truly on the cards, Forest's form was on the up-and-up as they approached the latter stages of the season. A 3-0 victory over Southampton at home on Saturday, 18th March, was then followed by an excellent 3-0 demolition of European rivals Leeds at the City Ground four days later. This performance was their most clinical of the season, with two Bryan Roy efforts and another from strike-partner Collymore effectively killing the game off before half-time.

On April Fool's Day, I turned out to be the biggest fool in the Midlands, when I decided to stay at home in Birmingham instead of driving over to Nottingham and travelling with the rest of the lads up to Hillsborough to see Forest take on Sheffield Wednesday. That afternoon, Forest turned in probably their most complete performance ever - well certainly during my three decades of watching them anyway. A Stuart Pearce free kick put them 1-0 up early on, followed by Ian Woan's twenty-yard strike which made it 2-0. Before half-time, Bryan Roy increased the lead to 3-0, having been put clean through by the cultured left foot of Bohinen. A Mark Bright penalty early in the second half, following a foul by Little on Sinton, gave the 'Owls' a glimmer of hope, but unfortunately for them, this was only short-lived. Bryan Roy made it 4-1 to the 'Reds', before a Collymore 25-yarder made it 5-1. 'Big Stan' was there again minutes later to make it 6-1, before an audacious chip from the outside of Bohinen's right boot rounded it off at 7-1. Not only did the travelling 'Red Army' rise to their feet to applaud, but so too did the rest of the 30,060 crowd, who'd witnessed an absolutely sensational display of attacking and counter-attacking football from Forest for virtually the whole of the ninety minutes. And there was I, stuck in Birmingham, only able to keep up with it all via my transistor radio and commentary by the 'Radio Five Live' sports team.

The crowd of 28,361 who turned up at the City Ground the following Saturday for the visit of West Ham, were obviously hoping for more of the same. Typically though, it turned out to be a case of "After the Lord Mayor's show" for the 'Reds', as they could only manage to scrape a 1-1 draw with the relegation-threatened 'Hammers'. Julian Dicks gave the visitors the lead with a stunning thirty-yard free kick, but after a late rally from Forest, Collymore smashed home the equaliser from close range, following a cross from the left by Roy. The most amusing aspect of this game, came when Jason Lee made a late appearance as substitute, to a chorus of: *"He's gotta Pineapple on 'is 'ead, He's gotta Pineapple on 'is 'ead,"* from the travelling West Ham fans. Although Lee subsequently became the butt of frequent Mickey-taking from comedians Frank Skinner and Dave Baddiel on their 'Fantasy Football' television show, it was most definitely the West Ham fans who first started this chant, much to the amusement of the large City Ground crowd.

Four more victories - over Norwich City, Coventry City, Crystal Palace and Manchester City - and one draw in their last five games, gave Forest an impressive third place in the table at the end of the campaign. No less than 22 victories and 72 goals had given them a tally of 77 points and a place in the following season's UEFA Cup Competition. The last two Saturdays of the season brought with them two consecutive pitch invasions from jubilant Forest supporters, the first of these after the 1-0 victory over Manchester City at the City Ground, and the second after the 2-2 draw against Wimbledon at Selhurst Park. The game against City brought in Forest's biggest crowd of the season - 28,822 - whilst many thousands also made the trip down to London for the season's finale against the 'Dons.'

Despite the restricted capacity for two thirds of the season, the average League attendance at the City Ground was a creditable 23,625. Not one League game had attracted a crowd of less than 20,000, with the lowest of the season not surprisingly being the 20,187 who turned out for the Wimbledon game - a fixture which was also screened live on the television. With European football to look forward to once again in Nottingham the following season, we could now say with some justification, that this wonderful Football Club of ours was well and truly: "BACK IN BUSINESS!"

FA PREMIER LEAGUE – FIXTURES

Date	Opposition	Venue	Competition	Score	Attendance
Aug 20	Ipswich Town	A	League	1-0	18,882
22	**Manchester United**	**H**	**League**	**1-1**	**22,072**
27	**Leicester City**	**H**	**League**	**1-0**	**21,601**
30	Everton	A	League	2-1	26,689
Sept 10	**Sheffield Wednesday**	**H**	**League**	**4-1**	**22,022**
17	Southampton	A	League	1-1	14,185
21	**Hereford United**	**H**	**LC 2 – 1st Leg**	**2-1**	**10,076**
24	Tottenham Hotspur	A	League	4-1	24,558
Oct 2	**Queens Park Rangers**	**H**	**League**	**3-2**	**21,449**
4	Hereford United	A	LC 2 – 2nd Leg	0-0	8,965
8	Manchester City	A	League	3-3	23,150
17	**Wimbledon**	**H**	**League**	**3-1**	**20,187**
22	Aston Villa	A	League	2-0	29,217
26	Wolverhampton Wanderers	A	LC 3	3-2	28,369
29	**Blackburn Rovers**	**H**	**League**	**0-2**	**22,131**
Nov 5	Liverpool	A	League	0-1	33,329
7	**Newcastle United**	**H**	**League**	**0-0**	**22,102**
19	**Chelsea**	**H**	**League**	**0-1**	**22,092**
26	Leeds United	A	League	0-1	38,191
30	**Millwall**	**H**	**LC 4**	**0-2**	**12,393**
Dec 3	**Arsenal**	**H**	**League**	**2-2**	**21,662**
10	**Ipswich Town**	**H**	**League**	**4-1**	**21,340**
17	Manchester United	A	League	2-1	43,744
26	Coventry City	A	League	0-0	19,224
27	**Norwich City**	**H**	**League**	**1-0**	**21,010**
31	West Ham United	A	League	1-3	20,644
Jan 2	**Crystal Palace**	**H**	**League**	**1-0**	**21,326**
7	**Plymouth Argyle**	**H**	**FA Cup 3**	**2-0**	**19,821**
14	Blackburn Rovers	A	League	0-3	27,510
21	**Aston Villa**	**H**	**League**	**1-2**	**24,598**
25	Chelsea	A	League	2-0	17,890
28	**Crystal Palace**	**H**	**FA Cup 4**	**1-2**	**16,790**
Feb 4	**Liverpool**	**H**	**League**	**1-1**	**25,418**
11	Newcastle United	A	League	1-2	34,471
21	Arsenal	A	League	0-1	35,441
26	Queens Park Rangers	A	League	1-1	13,363
Mar 4	**Tottenham Hotspur**	**H**	**League**	**2-2**	**28,711**
8	**Everton**	**H**	**League**	**2-1**	**24,526**
11	Leicester City	A	League	4-2	20,423
18	**Southampton**	**H**	**League**	**3-0**	**24,146**
22	**Leeds United**	**H**	**League**	**3-0**	**26,299**
Apr 1	Sheffield Wednesday	A	League	7-1	30,060
8	**West Ham United**	**H**	**League**	**1-1**	**28,361**
12	Norwich City	A	League	1-0	19,005
17	**Coventry City**	**H**	**League**	**2-0**	**26,253**
29	Crystal Palace	A	League	2-1	15,886
May 6	**Manchester City**	**H**	**League**	**1-0**	**28,822**
13	Wimbledon	A	League	2-2	15,341

HOME ATTENDANCES

	AGGREGATE ATTENDANCE	HIGHEST ATTENDANCE	LOWEST ATTENDANCE	AVERAGE ATTENDANCE
League:	496,128	28,822	20,187	23,625
League Cup:	22,469	12,393	10,076	11,234
FA Cup:	36,611	19,821	16,790	18,305
All Competitions:	555,208	28,822	10,076	22,208

FINAL LEAGUE TABLE - FA PREMIER

Position	P	W	D	L	GF	GA	Pts
1. Blackburn Rovers	42	27	8	7	80	39	89
2. Manchester United	42	26	10	6	77	28	88
3. Nottingham Forest	**42**	**22**	**11**	**9**	**72**	**43**	**77**
4. Liverpool	42	21	11	10	65	37	74
5. Leeds United	42	20	13	9	59	38	73
6. Newcastle United	42	20	12	10	67	47	72
7. Tottenham Hotspur	42	16	14	12	66	58	62
8. Queens Park Rangers	42	17	9	16	61	59	60
9. Wimbledon	42	15	11	16	48	65	56
10. Southampton	42	12	18	12	61	63	54
11. Chelsea	42	13	15	14	50	55	54
12. Arsenal	42	13	12	17	52	49	51
13. Sheffield Wednesday	42	13	12	17	49	57	51
14. West Ham United	42	13	11	18	44	48	50
15. Everton	42	11	17	14	44	51	50
16. Coventry City	42	12	14	16	44	62	50
17. Manchester City	42	12	13	17	53	64	49
18. Aston Villa	42	11	15	16	51	56	48
19. Crystal Palace	42	11	12	19	34	49	45
20. Norwich City	42	10	13	19	37	54	43
21. Leicester City	42	6	11	25	45	80	29
22. Ipswich Town	42	7	6	29	36	93	27

AWAY ATTENDANCES

	AGGREGATE ATTENDANCE	HIGHEST ATTENDANCE	LOWEST ATTENDANCE	AVERAGE ATTENDANCE
League:	521,203	43,744	13,363	24,819
League Cup:	37,334	28,369	8,965	18,667
All Competitions:	558,537	43,744	8,965	24,284

"ONE TEAM IN EUROPE, THERE'S ONLY ONE TEAM IN EUROPE"

CHAPTER 30

THE MOST predictable transfer activity of the close season had been the £8.5 million sale of want-away striker Stan Collymore to Liverpool. Despite repeatedly stating his desire to leave Forest throughout the course of the previous season - something which he had rather cunningly done via his agent Paul Stretford - he then had the audacity to ask for a half a million pound cut of the transfer fee on the grounds he hadn't actually asked for a transfer himself. Wot a wanker! Needless to say, the Forest Board told him where to get off and despite pursuing the matter through the FA, and then subsequently through the courts, to this day - as far as I'm aware - he's never received a penny from this transfer deal. In the eyes of the fans, leaving the Club was bad enough itself, but wanting a share of the transfer spoils was just taking the piss. Not surprisingly therefore, the name 'Collymore' is not a particularly popular one in and around Nottingham these days.

At the time, the £8.5 million was a record fee for a player in this country and, spent wisely, should have allowed Forest to continue their development as a Premiership outfit. Frank Clark certainly wasted no time in splashing out £2.5 million on Arsenal's unsettled striker Kevin Campbell, £2 million on midfielder Chris Bart-Williams from Sheffield Wednesday, and a further £1.8 million on unknown Italian striker Andrea Silenzi from Torino. Despite the loss of Collymore, this flurry of transfer activity encouraged no less than 17,500 supporters to renew their season tickets.

Although the Club remained fairly tight-lipped about the whole Collymore affair, the fans didn't. He was vilified in the Letters' Page of the Football Post and absolutely crucified in the Forest fanzine 'The Tricky Tree.' The wonderful thing about 'fanzines' - which emerged in the late 1980's - is that they are written by the fans, for the fans. Consequently, there is no pussyfooting around when it comes to such matters. Where the official Forest Review magazine has to retain a certain amount of dignity at times like this, the fanzines simply tell it as it is. Neil Webb had received similar treatment several years earlier from the 'Brian' fanzine - the first of many Forest fanzines which have emerged over the years - following his transfer to Man U, as had Roy Keane several years later when he decided to up and leave following our relegation season in 1992/93.

I've always been an avid fan of all the Forest fanzines; eagerly awaiting publication of every issue and then reading them from cover to cover once I get home from the match. It's so refreshing to know that other people are every bit as passionate about Forest as you are and most of the articles and letters therein are well-written, interesting and on the whole, extremely amusing. The 'Brian' fanzine first came onto the scene in 1988, followed by 'The Tricky Tree' and 'The Garibaldi.' After a run of many seasons, and consequently, many issues, 'Brian' rather sadly and suddenly disappeared, as did 'The Garibaldi.' These were subsequently replaced by 'Forest Forever' and more recently by 'Everywhere We Go' and 'Red Raw'. It must take up a monumental amount of someone's time to write, produce, print, and then circulate these publications and it isn't therefore surprising that they have a fairly limited shelf life. There must be very little profit to be had for those who do produce these magazines and it can only therefore be the individual or group of individuals' love of the Club which drives them on. Considering that they're written and produced by mainly ordinary people, the quality of some of the articles and letters is of the highest standard. Take for example the following brilliant piece of poetry written in Notts dialect by a chap named Tom Perry, which featured in the Tricky Tree in 1996 and which was sent in by his son. Entitled "The Queen Goes to the Match," it's an absolutely wonderful example of the Notts accent:

It were Sunday night down at th' palace,
And th' queen 'ad gone early to bed,
She sat up looking through th' Football Post,
Wi 'er crown stuck on th' back of 'er 'ead;

She was checkin' up on 'er Littlewoods,
To see if she'd gorrowt to cum,
When she 'appened to notice that Forest,
'Ad walloped the Villa ten none;

By Cow Phil worrabout that then?
This Forest side's pretty 'ot stuff,
Ah know Liz replied 'Is Sir Dukeship,
It's all down to that Brian Clough;

Wot y'on about ya gret stupid wally,
Yo must a bin livin' in th' dark,
Cloughie's bin gone a year or two now,
They run wi a chap called Frank Clark;

Anyroad they must be worth watchin',
They a team that ah wud like to see,
Worrabout us goin' next Satday,
We cud nip up there, just yo an' me?

His Dukeship 'ed a look in his diary,
Ah'll check that we've nowt else to do,
Yeh, that should be rate enuf Liz duck,
Ah'll try an' get tickits for two;

So straight off the very next mornin',
Sekertery rings up City Ground,
Two tickets please, for their majesties,
Just let me know how many pound;

It were Clarky issen warrud ansud,
An' at fust 'e thow it were a joke,
But wot finally convinced 'im,
Was the very posh way the chap spoke;

Now please don't go telling the papers,
Just keep this between you and hus,
For the Queen and her noble Prince Consort,
No pressmen, no cameras, no fuss;

Just make sure of a space for the Rolls,
And perhaps my good man you'll play host,
A couple of seats hin the Trent End,
And we'll put you a cheque in the post;

Well, when it got round to the Satday,
Rolls nosed it's way out palace gate,
City Ground, cum on don't spare the 'orses,
Get cracking, ah don't want to be late;

They were there 'alf-an-'our 'fore th' kick-off,
Everything was so very discrete,
It were Clarky an' th' Chairman that met 'em,
An' took 'em along to their seat;

They were several Forest fans near 'em,
Who started wen 'er Queenship sat down,
It cudn't be?, cud it?, no corse not,
If it was she'd be warin a crown;

The game it were brilliant, excitin',
An' they joined in the Robin 'ood roar,
They were 'ollerin' an' shoutin' an' stampin',
Wen a Forest man went through to score;

It seemed no time before it were 'arf time,
The Reds 'ad done so much to please,
An' a lass came round wi sum bottles o' brown,
An' two bags o' pie, chips, an' peas;

The second arf went by so quickly,
When the end came Liz 'eaved a great sigh,
Well ah mus say ah really enjoyed that,
Ah'll remember it 'till day that ah die;

Then Clarky an th' Chairman took 'em away,
To gerem a drink at th' bar,
Now that's nice on yu squire said 'is Dukeship,
Ah just felt like some crisps an' a jar;

Ah gerra bit like that mesen said the boss,
Ah really do know wot yo mean,
Now if yo can spare just a minit or two,
Wud yo like to meet sum of the team?

Wen 'e sed this the eyes of 'er Queenship,
Shone bright like a glowin' fag end,
Oh, ah wud that, she sed, cud we really?
No prob, replied Clarky, ah'll send;

There were Pearcy, an' Crossley, an' Chettle,
An' others of that 'appy band,
Is Dukeship were quite overcome,
As he shook every man by the 'and;

But we all know that very old sayin',
All good things mus' cum to an end,
Wesul 'av to be going said th' Queenship,
Ahv affairs of the state to attend;

When the Rolls went out the back entrance,
The lads gave 'em three 'earty cheers,
An' all were quite moved, cos were plain to see,
Her Queenship were very nigh tears;

She leaned out o' th' winder an' blew 'em a kiss,
Ahm over the moon we came up,
If yo lads can mek it to Wembley this year,
I'll be there to present yo wi' th' cup;

She sat there in the back seat and thinkin',
As the Rolls it purred South through the dark,
If ah weren't the Queen of all England,
Ah'd like to be Missus Frank Clark!

I personally adore the East Midlands accent, from the broadness of the North Nottinghamshire and Derbyshire drawl to the street slang of inner-city St.Anns and Hyson Green. However, despite it's many famous characters and personalities, within the high-profile world of entertainment and sport, no-one outside the East Midlands, seems to have the slightest idea what the native dialect is. I remember several years ago, watching GMTV one morning when Sue Pollard of Hi-De-Hi fame was a guest on the programme. Sue hails from Bulwell and has a pronounced Nottingham accent. Presenter Lorraine Kelly turned to her and asked: "Come on then Sue...just what accent is that you've got anyway?" to which Ms Pollard replied: "Well it's East Midlands intit." The bemused looking Ms Kelly then paused for a few seconds before declaring: "East Midlands...I thought that was an airport - *giggle, giggle, giggle.*" Ignorant cow!

Now everyone knows what a Scouse, a Geordie, a Mancunian, or a Cockney accent sounds like; in fact it almost seems compulsory nowadays if you want to be a television or radio personality to speak in at least one of the above tongues. Well, I'd like to see some recognition of the Nottingham accent on the television. I'd love to turn on the telly at half past seven one of these nights and hear the sound of: "Ey up mi ducks. It's Fridi night, an' it's Top o' the Pops, intit!"

Even the famous film Saturday Night, Sunday Morning based on Nottingham author Alan Sillitoe's best-selling novel of the same name, got the accent completely wrong. The 1960 motion picture, depicting life in working-class Nottingham in the late 1950's, starred Albert Finney as Arthur Seaton, a young hard-working, hard-living lad from the Meadows and Hilda Baker as his over-bearing mother. Young Arthur would sweat his guts out all week in the Raleigh Cycle factory and then hit the town hard on a Saturday night. Sadly, despite this being a much-acclaimed film at the time, whoever was responsible for giving the cast elocution lessons, seemed to believe the Nottingham accent was nothing more than the usual 'bog standard' Northern accent - a cross between a Lancashire and a Yorkshire accent. Consequently, young Arthur sounded more like a character from Emmerdale Farm than he did a streetwise Nottingham lad; more's the pity. The only person I've ever heard successfully imitating an East Midlands' accent is comedian and impressionist Alistair McGowan when he's taking off Gary Lineker, who of course was born and bred in Leicester. Next time we have a television series or film based on Nottingham, I'd like to see strictly local actors involved, and then we might just see some authenticity creeping in and the profile of the Nottingham accent - which is as distinct and colourful as any other regional accent - being raised across the rest of the country.

HAVING remained unbeaten in their last thirteen matches of the previous season, Forest began the new campaign in similar style. An exciting 4-3 victory away to Southampton on the opening day of the season was followed by a 0-0 draw at home to Chelsea four days later. The atmosphere generated by the City Ground crowd of 27,007 was typical of a midweek encounter at the beginning of a season, but thoroughly impressed my son Thomas. Having in the past only really sampled the rather subdued atmosphere of City Ground League Cup ties against lowly opposition, Forest's 'newest' season ticket holder could hardly catch his breath after sampling the genuine article for the very first time.

West Ham were the next visitors to Trentside the following Saturday when, as in the previous season's encounter, the two sides fought out a 1-1 draw. In addition to this, the West Ham fans took great delight in taunting substitute Jason Lee with their now famous 'Pineapple' chant when he came off the bench late on in the game. One very welcome visitor that day was sixties' hero Joe Baker, back in town for a special benefit weekend held in his honour. So popular is Joe with Forest supporters even to this day, when news of the two heart attacks he'd recently suffered reached Nottingham, members of the Cotgrave Branch of the Supporters Club quickly got together to organise a benefit weekend on his behalf. This consisted of a dinner/speakers' night on Friday, 25th August, at the Trent Bridge Inn, followed by a disco at the JFK Club with Joe as the guest of honour. The pub-crawl which then ensued after the West Ham game the following day, which was attended by many of Joe's former team-mates (the game that is, not the piss-up!) culminated in hundreds of Forest fans besieging the QE in town, which subsequently reverberated to the sound of: *"Zigger-Zagger, Zigger-Zagger, Joe-Ba-ker!"* long into the night.

A 1-1 draw away to Arsenal in midweek, during which Kevin Campbell opened his account for the 'Reds' to cancel out David Platt's stunning first-half volley, was then followed by a similar result against Coventry at Highfield Road the following Saturday. So, as the players flew out to Sweden a couple of days later to take on Malmoe in the first round of the UEFA Cup, they did so on the back of an unbeaten run in the League which now stretched back over an impressive eighteen matches. However, despite taking the lead in this game through Ian Woan, a stirring second-half performance by the Swedes gave them a 2-1 first-leg lead - although the precious away goal gave Forest more than a glimmer of hope for the second leg in Nottingham a fortnight later.

It was back to winning ways the following weekend, with an action-packed 3-2 victory over Everton at the City Ground in Sky TV's 'Sunday afternoon special.' And, despite a 3-2 setback away to Bradford City in the second round of the League Cup on Tuesday, 19th September, they picked up another League point at Aston Villa the following Saturday, when Des Lyttle's diving header in the last minute cancelled out Andy Townsend's opening goal at the other end.

The atmosphere inside the City Ground for the second leg of the UEFA Cup tie against Malmoe on Tuesday, 26th September - despite the attendance being a rather modest 23,817 - was absolutely incredible. Although the outcome of the game was balanced on a knife-edge throughout, the vociferous Forest crowd roared them onto victory. It took a brilliant second-half strike from Dutchman Bryan Roy to seal the victory, but the players were unanimous in praising the tremendous support they'd received throughout the ninety minutes. *"In my ten years at the City Ground, I don't think I've heard so much noise coming down onto the pitch. It was that good I wish I had been in the 'A' Block myself!"* commented skipper Stuart Pearce after the game.

FOR the next couple of months, Forest's season went pretty much according to plan. Without exactly sparkling, they continued to carve out some decent results in the League, whilst making further progress in the UEFA Cup. They did however, suffer a further setback in the League Cup at the hands of Second Division Bradford City in the second leg of their second round tie. Although Stuart Pearce put the 'Reds' 1-0 up in the 18th minute of the game and Andrea Silenzi restored the lead in the second half following Paul Showler's equaliser, the lanky figure of Ian Ormondroyd popped up in the 89th minute to plant a firm header into the back of the Forest net and put the 'Bantams' through on aggregate. The travelling army of around 4,500 from West Yorkshire went absolutely berserk upon the final whistle and I could still hear them celebrating inside the ground when I got back to my car on County Hall about ten minutes later.

Progress in the UEFA Cup came about at the hands of French side Auxerre who were, to say the least, a very talented outfit. A Steve Stone lob in the first leg in France gave Forest a vital 1-0 lead to bring back with them to Nottingham where, despite a ninety-minute onslaught by the impressive Frenchmen, the two sides fought out a 0-0 draw in front of 28,064 appreciative supporters. Stoney's goal proved decisive over the two legs, with Forest's reward being another trip to France, this time to take on Olympique Lyonnais during the month of November. The first leg was scheduled to take place at the City Ground on Tuesday, 21st November.

League successes continued in the form of three consecutive home victories over Manchester City, Bolton Wanderers and Wimbledon, and an away victory over Tottenham at White Hart Lane. A further point was also earned on their travels when they drew 1-1 at Queens Park Rangers. Amazingly, by the time they travelled to Blackburn Rovers on Saturday, 18th October, they were not only riding high in the table, but had also set a Premiership record of 25 matches unbeaten. This has since been beaten of course by Manchester United, but their 42-match unbeaten record in the old First Division during the 1977/78 and 1978/79 seasons still remains in tact.

Trust Forest to bring this excellent unbeaten run to an end in such dramatic style though, allowing Blackburn to run up a score-line more befitting a rugby match. An Alan Shearer hat-trick, plus two from the traitor himself Lars Bohinen - Rovers' £750,000 signing from Forest who'd recently exercised a cleverly-written get-out clause in his contract - and one each from Mike Newell and Graeme Le Saux, added up to an embarrassing 7-0 thrashing. It was one of those Saturday evenings when you don't exactly rush down to your local for a pint - especially when you live in Birmingham - just in case someone brings up the subject of football. In fact, you feel like putting a bag over your head for a few days for fear of being recognised in the street!

By the following Tuesday evening, both players and supporters had finally come out of hiding and were ready to face the Frenchmen of Lyon, who were in town and hoping to make progress in the UEFA Cup at Forest's expense. Anyone who'd expected the weekend walloping to have had an adverse affect on the players' confidence though, was simply underestimating the resolve of Frank Clark's squad. Without being the most gifted collection of players in the world, the one thing they did have in their armoury, was the ability to carve out a result, and sometimes against the toughest of opposition.

As with most French sides, Lyon played skilful, attractive football, without ever really threatening the Forest goal. As the game progressed, another stalemate looked on the cards. That is, until Clarky took a gamble on youth by throwing youngsters Paul McGregor and Bobby Howe into the fray with less than half an hour of the game remaining. The speed and energy of these two appeared to immediately unsettle the previously unflappable Lyon defenders and consequently, sensing a positive result might just be on the cards after all, the City Ground crowd began to respond. The sound of: *"Cum on 'u Reds,"* echoed all around the stadium. When the French keeper foolishly came out to the edge of his penalty area to challenge for the ball, the lively looking Howe was able to pounce on his feeble clearance and send a crisp volley hurtling towards the roof of the net. Just as he was about to celebrate what would have been a famous goal, defender Florent Laville stuck out an arm to deflect the ball wide of the post. Not only did the referee immediately award Forest a penalty, but he also instantly gave the unfortunate defender his marching orders. Inevitably, the ever-dependable 'Captain Marvel' stepped up to thunder the ball low to the keeper's left, only for him to pull off an excellent save at the foot of the post. All was not lost however, as the on-rushing McGregor was first to the rebound to crash the ball low into the far corner of the net from only three yards out. There were only seven minutes left on the clock and the Forest faithful were ecstatic. The sound of: *"One team in Europe, There's only one team in Europe,"* rang out to the watching television audience. 1-0 may not have been the best result in the world, but it was certainly one the resilient 'Reds' were capable of hanging onto during the second leg in France.

Just six days later, the sprightly McGregor was on hand once again to put Forest 1-0 up against visiting Champions Manchester United, once again in front of a watching Sky audience of millions. However, that cheating 'Frog' - Eric Cantona - managed to con the referee into awarding a second-half penalty to United by falling over completely unchallenged in the box, much to the consternation of the sizeable 29,263 crowd (except of course the genuine United supporters in the lower tier of the Bridgford Stand and the several hundred 'once-a-season-wonders' sporting United shirts and distinctive East Midlands accents who had, as usual, infiltrated most other parts of the ground - sad little gits!). Cantona himself stepped up to stroke the ball home to make it 1-1, thereby giving the visitors a share of the spoils.

A 1-1 draw at Bolton the following Saturday was followed by a solid performance in Lyon three days later. Despite everything the classy Frenchman could throw at them, the 'Reds' held firm throughout the ninety minutes of this tie to remain England's sole representatives in Europe this season. Although this performance had 'Frank Clark' (slightly boring, though extremely effective) written all over it, as I sat at home watching it on the telly, I was beginning to get itchy feet. My appetite for trekking across Europe again was certainly beginning to grow. All it needed was a decent tie in the next round - the quarter-final stages scheduled for the following March - and I would almost certainly be packing my overnight bag and heading south for the Continent.

Christmas was now looming and Forest continued their run of 1-1 draws in the League, firstly at home to Aston Villa and then away to Manchester City at Maine Road on Monday, 18th December - on Sky yet again. This sequence of four draws was then broken by a 3-1 defeat at high-flying Newcastle on the Saturday before Christmas, and followed by festive victories over Sheffield Wednesday and Middlesbrough - both 1-0 and both at the City Ground. As I made my way home to Birmingham along the M42 on New Year's Day, following my New Year's Eve celebrations in Nottingham with Mr. Farley and friends, I was jumping up and down like a madman when the Radio 5 Live team announced firstly, that an early Steve Stone effort had given Forest the lead against Liverpool at Anfield, and latterly that Ian Woan had increased this lead to 2-0. Forest were apparently running riot against 'Big Stan' and Co., a fact which was borne out later that evening on Match of the Day. Unfortunately the treacherous striker had to choose this particular day to turn in his best performance so far in a Liverpool shirt, setting up Robbie Fowler for the first goal with a brilliant run and cross from the left and then repeating the trick only seconds before half-time for the same player to score again. He then went one better in the second half, smashing Liverpool into the lead and subsequently causing Colin Cooper to turn his dangerous cross into his own net to secure a 4-2 victory. Although I obviously didn't go to this game, many Forest fans that did, were appalled by Collymore's behaviour; a number of two-fingered gestures towards the Visiting Supporters' Enclosure and his usual inane celebrations immediately in front of them after scoring his goal. That boy deserves a damn good slappin' if you ask me!

A late Stuart Pearce equaliser at First Division Stoke City the following Saturday earned the 'Reds' a third round FA Cup replay at the City Ground and at the same time saved them from another embarrassing defeat. It also set them off on a run which would see them progress all the way through to the quarter-final stages of the competition. They dealt rather easily with the men from the Potteries in the replay on Wednesday, 17th January, before appearing to falter once again this time at home to Second Division Oxford United in the fourth round. However, despite only managing to scrape a 0-0 draw in this game, they ran out comfortable 3-0 winners in the replay at the Manor Ground, with Kevin Campbell, Ian Woan (penalty) and Andrea Silenzi grabbing the goals.

Tottenham Hotspur came out of the hat to provide Forest with their fifth round opposition, a tie scheduled to take place at the City Ground on Monday, 19th February. As I drove over from Birmingham late that afternoon, there wasn't even the slightest hint in the air of what would come our way no more than three hours later. Understandably for mid-February it was a bitterly cold evening when the game kicked off at 8.00-p.m. and the odd snowflake or two were just beginning to fall. This subsequently turned into quite a heavy downfall, but with all the activity taking place on the pitch, it didn't seem to have too much chance of settling. However, within minutes, what had started out as a shower, then developed into a blizzard and not only was the pitch beginning to disappear under the deluge, so were the players themselves.

Within fifteen minutes of the kick off, the conditions had changed from being almost perfect to absolutely impossible. From where I was sitting in the upper tier of the Bridgford, I could see no further than the edge of the penalty area in front of me and only a handful of players were visible. The referee had no alternative but to abandon the game and the frost-bitten crowd of only 17,000 were told to leave the ground. Now I've encountered some pretty severe driving conditions in my time, but I have never been so alarmed as I was that evening as I tried to make my way home. In fact as I travelled along the A453 from Clifton towards junction 24 of the M1, I was convinced my car would become buried in snow and that my frozen remains would be dug out several days later. I was a very relieved man indeed when I finally reached the motorway island some two hours after leaving the City Ground - a distance of no more than twelve miles.

There were vehicles skidding around all over the place on the M1 and I was pretty pleased to be turning straight off onto the M42 where, despite the conditions being equally as bad, the volume of traffic was considerably lighter. As I got further and further away from Nottingham, the conditions gradually became better and better until amazingly, by the time I reached Tamworth, there wasn't an ounce of snow or ice anywhere in sight. If I hadn't seen the 'highlights' on television later on that evening, I'd have been convinced the whole experience was a dream. The Evening Post the next day carried stories of all the Spurs fans who'd ended up being stranded in Nottingham, with scores of them having to seek refuge for the night in local drinking hostelries - poor souls!

The game was hastily re-arranged for Wednesday, 28th February, but the drama of this tie was still far from over. Two goals apiece from Tottenham's Chris Armstrong and Forest's Ian Woan - both superb free kicks in the absence of skipper Stuart Pearce - meant that a replay at White Hart Lane was necessary. Before this game could be played, the 'Reds' had the small matter of a UEFA Cup quarter-final first leg tie to deal with. Ironically, they'd been drawn against Bayern Munich in this stage of the competition, with the first leg scheduled to be played in Germany on Tuesday, 5th March. Having travelled to the Bavarian Capital all those years before to see them lift the European Cup for the first time, this was a trip I just couldn't miss.

BEING an acquaintance of 'Wishy' Whitehead of Cotgrave - the guy who'd been mainly responsible for the Joe Baker benefit weekend earlier on in the season - John Farley had managed to book the two of us onto the coach he was running to Munich from the Crown on Arkwright Street. It was due to leave the pub late on Sunday night after a 'UEFA Cup party night' which had been organised to give the 'troops' a damn good send off - or that's how it seemed to me at least.

John and I were in town early to get a few beers down us in some of our favourite haunts such as Foremans, the Coach & Horses, Yates's and the King John, before making our way down to the Crown at around 9.00-p.m. There were quite a few familiar faces around town; many of whom were carrying rucksacks or sports bags, so it was apparent they were also Munich bound - possibly on Wishy's bus. I've never really been much of a 'Townee' myself, unlike John, therefore although I know many of the 'faces' around town, having seen them many times before down at the match, I know very few of them to talk to. Quite the opposite to John however, who seems to know everybody in Nottingham. In fact, when you're out with him it's almost impossible to indulge him in conversation for more than a couple of minutes, before he's off reminiscing with this person or that person about the 'good old days.'

When we arrived at the Crown the party was already in full swing, with a disco taking place in the lounge at the front and food being dished out in the bar at the back. There were Union Jacks and flags of St.George hanging all over the walls and every other person it seemed was wearing a red Garibaldi shirt. By 10.00-p.m., people were dancing all over the place and standing on chairs and tables singing Forest songs to each carefully selected record. The women were out in force to wave their men goodbye before they set off on their European adventure. There were some really rough and ready looking people around and it seemed to me that we would be amongst some of Nottingham's most serious thugs during our five-day trip across the Continent.

We were slightly pissed, to say the least, by the time we clambered aboard the large double-decker coach, which was waiting outside the pub at closing time. Although thankfully there was a toilet on board, I made sure I'd emptied my sparrow-like bladder about fifty times before leaving the pub. John and I went upstairs and took our seats right at the front. By the time we pulled off - with about thirty people standing outside waving us off - about half a dozen of the Cotgrave lads had taken up the seats next to and immediately behind us. Three of them - all Scottish lads - had apparently come out that night just for the piss up, with no intention whatsoever of even going to the game. They'd decided to go only at the very last minute, consequently, they had no passports, no change of clothes, or of course any German currency. Still, not one of them seemed at all concerned. We had a long journey in front of us, so I decided it was time to get some shut-eye.

We were planning to make our way across to France via the Channel Tunnel and within a few hours we'd arrived in Folkestone. The duty-free shop did a roaring trade for the hour or so we were waiting to get on board 'Le Shuttle.' I'm not one for drinking on the bus - my bladder has never allowed me to be - so I gave away my duty-free vouchers to Trevor Brown who was gathering together as many as he could. One way or another, he was determined to ensure his trip to Munich and back would be financed by the sale of as much contraband as possible. When the driver finally manoeuvred the coach carefully onto the train, the sheer length of it amazed me; it seemed to go on forever. When we finally came to a halt several hundred yards inside, large metal shutters were drawn across the carriage in front of us and behind us, enclosing us inside our very own compartment.

Within half an hour, we'd arrived in France and were whizzing unhindered through Customs. Such is the uncomplicated nature of travel around Europe these days, I don't think I got my passport out of my jacket pocket once during the whole of the journey. Consequently our companions from Cotgrave had nothing to fear - not that they seemed to be worrying too much about anything other than getting as much alcohol down their necks as they could.

Our first stop for refreshments was at a motorway service station in Belgium in the early hours of Monday morning. John and I had a quick wander around the place to stretch our legs and grab a can of pop and several bars of chocolate. As we queued to pay for these in the crowded shop, all we could see around us, were youths from our bus helping themselves to as much alcohol and food as they could manage to stuff up their jumpers or down their trousers. Now, if people want to nick things from motorway service stations on the Continent, then that's their business. However, if by any chance someone had happened to notice what they were up to - and they must have been absolutely blind not to - then there was a very good chance that every last one of us on board that bus would have been dragged off down to the nearest police station and charged with shoplifting - guilty or not guilty.

Having paid for our goods, John and I returned hastily to the bus and got stuck into our goodies. We could still see people helping themselves to things as we gazed out of the window of the bus, which was parked only about twenty yards from the shop. Gradually one or two of them started to make their way back and the first to arrive were a couple of the Scottish lads from Cotgrave. ''Are ya no drinkin' anythin' lads?'' said one of them as he stood in front of John and I with a freshly nicked bottle of vodka in his hands. ''No, not at the moment thanks,'' John replied hesitantly. ''What di yi want then boys? Whiskey, vodka, brandy?'' ''No, we're fine thanks mate, no problem,'' I insisted. ''No, I'll go an' get yi a bottle o' somethin.' Brandy? Yeah, brandy,'' he declared, before getting back off the bus, going back into the shop, and nicking yet another bottle of spirits, albeit this time on our behalf. I looked at John and said: ''What the fuckin' hell are we doing here on this bus? We're gonna end up in some Belgian nick staring at four walls after being charged with shopliftin', when we should be in Munich 'avin a good time and watching the 'Reds'.'' ''Yeah, an' 'ow the bleedin' 'ell are we gonna explain that to our bosses when we get back 'ome to England?'' added John.

To our absolute relief, the bus pulled out of the service station completely unchallenged and in the absence of any flashing blue lights behind us within the next couple of hours, John and I were able to breathe a sigh of relief and even settle down for a few hours sleep. By daylight, we were well on our way across Belgium and were heading for the German City of Cologne where we would spend the rest of the day. By this time, the inside of the bus resembled a refuse tip; there were empty sandwich and chocolate wrappers all over the place and literally hundreds of empty beer cans and bottles rolling around on the floor. Every time we went round a corner, they would roll from one side of the bus to the other, making an almighty din. Every so often, the bus would screech to a halt and the very angry looking driver would come rushing up the stairs to protest at the noise. ''Will you lot put those bloody things into these plastic bags please and give us all some peace down here,'' he pleaded as he threw a pile of black bin liners to the front of the bus. Everyone just completely ignored him and the debris just grew more and more substantial and the noise louder and louder as the journey progressed. I can only assume the driver grew accustomed to the noise, as he seemed eventually to give up the fight. Either that or he just realised how futile his protests were. One thing I do know though: it became so irritating as the journey wore on, I was desperate to get off that bleedin' bus by the time we finally arrived in Cologne at around lunchtime.

We weren't leaving Cologne until midnight, so we had around eleven hours of drinking and 'sightseeing' in front of us as we all headed off up the street towards the nearest bar. Once inside, John and I teamed up with a lad called Stuart Shepherd - one of about five youths I know from Sandiacre who used to go to the match together - who'd been sitting downstairs on the bus, being wonderfully entertained by big Dave Heron from Clifton who'd been telling jokes and larking about from the moment we set off. All you could hear upstairs was the muffled sound of his gruff, gravel-like voice bellowing out almost continuously, followed by howls of laughter from the twenty or so passengers who were seated downstairs. It must have been worth the fare alone, just to be down there listening to him. An ex-Para, he's about six foot four, with long mousey coloured hair, a big thick moustache, and is built like a brick shithouse. Definitely not someone you'd want to mess with, but one of the funniest blokes around. Stuart told us how no-one had managed to get a wink of sleep downstairs, due to his antics.

Although most of the passengers on our bus - around sixty to seventy people I would estimate - were crowded into that first bar, gradually small groups began to drift off and go their own separate ways. The three of us decided to do likewise and very soon we were heading off towards the centre of the city. Cologne is a very large city with a population of around a million people and the one thing it is not short of is bars and restaurants. Having walked for several hundred yards, we came across a very quiet looking bar situated about twenty yards down a small side-street. Quiet that is, until we made our way through the entrance, and came across the very familiar sound of Dave Heron, who was propping up the bar entertaining half a dozen bemused locals.

The afternoon whizzed by and very soon the city was beginning to come to life; and, considering it was only a Monday night, it was very lively indeed. Everywhere we went, we seemed to bump into people from our bus who, despite having been on the razzle now for more than twenty-four hours, were remarkably well-behaved. For several days, we'd been hearing stories on the local and national news of trouble in Munich and the fact that dozens of youths from Nottingham had already been arrested for a variety of offences, ranging from being drunk and disorderly to causing grievous bodily harm. This had been my only reservation about the trip - especially as we were going on the bus from the Crown - but so far all we'd encountered was a bit of petty thieving and a great deal of good-natured banter.

We spoke to quite a few of the local inhabitants during the course of the evening and we found them to be very friendly and hospitable. One young lad in his mid-twenties told us he'd moved to Cologne from his home town of Munich because of it's fantastic night-life, which he insisted was the same every night of the week. Judging by what we'd seen so far, it was difficult not to believe him. He also claimed there were over 2,500 bars and night-clubs in and around the city and that you were able to party twenty-four hours a day if you wanted.

At around 11.00-p.m., we stumbled across a pleasant little bar, where a couple in their forties insisted on buying the three of us drinks. They were fascinated by the fact we were on our way to Munich to watch Forest and, as they were 1.F.C. Cologne supporters could vividly remember Forest's famous European Cup semi-final victory against them in 1979, and their subsequent victory over Malmoe in the Final. We were absolutely amazed when they described their arch-rivals from Munich as 'Sheep-shaggers' and they were equally amazed when we enlightened them about our very own 'woolly-backed' neighbours from 'Shitesville' back home in the East Midlands. There are at least two Cologne supporters who are reminded of Derby County now every time the word 'Sheep-shagger' is mentioned in conversation. It makes you feel good to know you've helped in some way to spread the word around Europe as well as back home in England.

We got back to the coach with only minutes to spare before the twelve o'clock deadline. However, at least three others weren't so lucky and were left behind to fend for themselves - poor sods. Now it's bad enough missing your last train home from Liverpool on a Saturday night after a game, but imagine being left behind in a foreign country many hundreds of miles away? I never did find out what became of these unfortunate souls, but I'm certain they didn't catch up with us in Munich and they definitely weren't on the coach on the way home. Perhaps they're still out there now enjoying themselves, who knows?

We were scheduled to arrive in Munich nice and early on Tuesday - the day of the game - and our first port of call would be the Olympic Stadium so we could buy some tickets. No-one on the bus had any as the Club would only let you buy one if you travelled with them on their officially arranged trips. Having sampled the 'delights' of European travel with Forest in the early-eighties and been treated like a twelve-year-old, there wasn't a cat in hell's chance of me ever going on an official Club tour again. I was more than happy to take a chance on getting one in Germany, even from a tout if necessary.

As the night wore on, the temperature dropped by the minute. The last time Forest had been in Munich, we'd been basking in ninety-degree temperatures and jumping around in the fountains in the Marianplatz area of the city. It must have been twenty degrees below on this occasion and consequently, a half-inch thick layer of ice had formed on the inside of the coach windows. It was so cold in fact, that although I was full to the brim with ale, it was almost impossible to get any sleep. Just as I was beginning to doze off though, everyone on the upstairs of the bus was brought well and truly to their senses as someone decided to race to the top of the stairs and let off a CS gas canister. Fortunately for us, the bus had just come to a halt, so we were able to quickly disembark and breathe in some much-needed air on the pavement outside. It was the weirdest sensation I'd ever experienced and I was left coughing, spluttering and gasping for breath for fully five minutes, whilst at the same time frantically rubbing my eyes in a desperate attempt to regain my vision. And this was someone's idea of a practical joke! Yeah...what a side-splitter.

We finally arrived in Munich at around 8 o'clock in the morning and the bus headed straight for the stadium. We then had to hang around for about two hours until one of the many ticket offices dotted around the complex finally opened up. The game was by no means sold out and we were easily able to buy tickets for the Visiting Supporters' Enclosure, as were many other Forest supporters who'd travelled independently and were queuing up at the ground alongside us. With this rather important task having been fulfilled, we set off for the centre of Munich to find some digs for our proposed twenty-four hour stay in the city. Amazingly, this we were able to do with ease. We pulled the bus up outside a pleasant hotel on the perimeter of the city, whilst one of the lads nipped inside and asked: "Have you got room for seventy for the night?" and within minutes Mr. Farley and I were checking into our very pleasant twin room, complete with en-suite bathroom, satellite television and tea and coffee-making facilities.

Boy did I enjoy jumping into that shower and freshening up. There's nothing worse than being stuck in a beer-drenched, fag-stenched bus for almost two days with a bunch of farting, belching football supporters. I felt positively rejuvenated when we walked back out of the hotel to meet Stuart, having had my first wash and change of clothes in two days. I was now raring to go. We had around nine hours to kill before the game and there was only one place I was heading for: the Hofbrauhaus Bier Keller, which is situated in the aforementioned Marianplatz area of the city. With memories of 1979 still etched in my mind, I was absolutely convinced it would be packed to the rafters with Forest supporters, especially as around four thousand were expected to make the trip. Many hundreds had apparently been arriving in the city throughout the previous few days.

It was a long walk into the centre of Munich and by the time we arrived at our destination - having popped into McDonalds for a feast along the way - we were gagging for a beer. I was a little surprised and disappointed that we'd encountered virtually no other Forest supporters during our three-mile hike and I was almost beginning to think my nostalgic trip back to the Bavarian Capital, might just turn out to be a bit of an anti-climax. In view of the weather, I wasn't at all surprised to find absolutely no-one dancing around in the fountains in the Marianplatz, but I was expecting to at least come across a few hearty souls drinking in the streets outside the various bars and bier kellers in that area of the city - but we didn't encounter a soul.

After a couple of beers in a nearby bar, we finally arrived at the doors of the Hofbrauhaus Bier Keller, where we were surprised to encounter several rather gruesome-looking doormen. Fortunately, without hesitation, they let us inside. As we made our way across to some empty seats in the middle, I was once again disappointed to find there were only a couple of hundred Forest supporters inside, although the place was just about full to it's two thousand capacity. Still, within minutes we'd ordered an enormous glass of Bavarian beer each and found ourselves sitting amongst a gang of young lads from Nottingham. They told us the place had been packed with Forest supporters the previous night, but due to a fairly serious disturbance at the end of the evening, the police were strictly monitoring the situation today, hence the burley minders on the door. Apparently, they were being quite cagey about who they let in, which to my mind, probably counted out the majority of Forest's travelling supporters.

Having downed the first beer with consummate ease, we ordered a second, and a third, and so on. I'd been looking forward to getting my face into one of these glasses since the moment we left Nottingham, and they were so big, you could almost climb inside them and swim in your beer whilst drinking it. It was pure nectar, but very strong indeed and very soon we were all in a 'happy' frame of mind. What's more, the place was now rapidly filling up with Forest supporters, as wave after wave arrived every ten to fifteen minutes. We could only assume that as each plane or coach-load arrived in the city, they headed straight for this famous landmark. The Um-pa Band was now also getting into full swing, with many of the tunes being familiar ones, such as *'Roll out the barrel.'* This, as every Forest fan knows, sits very comfortably with the words: *"Shit on the Derby, Shit on the Derby tonight."* The atmosphere was really beginning to warm up and it was still only mid-afternoon - with more than five hours left before kick off. By this time only a handful of locals remained and there must have been close on 2,000 Forest supporters inside the place. By all accounts, there were long queues forming outside and some supporters were resorting to desperate measures to get in and join the party. At one stage, one of the window frames on the opposite side of the room was removed by a gang of youths standing on the tables nearby and about twenty of their mates poured in from outside.

The place was in uproar when the Central Television cameras turned up to interview a Forest supporter who'd travelled to Munich for the European Cup Final in 1979, got himself arrested and banged up for a few days, and stayed out there ever since. Right throughout the interview, the sound of: *"We are the best team in the land, This no-one can deny, We will follow the Forest,"* bellowed out all around, followed by the sound of: *"Rule Britannia, Britannia rules the waves, Britons never-never-never, Shall be slaves."* This was turning out to be everything I'd wanted it to be and I was in my element.

The party lasted for most of the afternoon, but by around 5.00-p.m. small groups of fans had begun to drift off, making their way towards the Olympic Stadium, which was situated several miles outside the city centre. We finally called it a day at around 5.30-p.m. and staggered outside into the fresh air. We were determined at first to walk all the way to the stadium. However, this changed within a matter of minutes and very soon we were clambering into the back of a taxi. Consequently, we arrived at the impressive Olympic Village within a matter of minutes and found ourselves with a couple of hours left to kill before kick off. There were thousands of people already within the complex and with numerous beer tents, fast food bars and restaurants within the vicinity; we certainly weren't short of things to do. The only problem was the sheer cold; there was snow and ice everywhere and, with a bitterly cold wind, the temperature was several degrees below zero.

In contrast to the vast army of Forest supporters we'd encountered in the Marianplatz, there seemed to be very few milling around outside the ground. Although with a near 40,000 crowd expected for this game, the travelling 'Red Army' had probably just been swallowed up within the sheer mass of people. We left it as late as possible before making our way to the turnstiles and into the Visitors' Enclosure. Once inside, we were quite pleased - and relieved - to see there were at least 4,000 'Travelling Trickies' amongst the crowd. However, with a capacity of around 80,000, the actual crowd of 38,000 gave the stadium a half-empty look about it. As ever, there were some amusing sights to behold amongst the travelling Forest contingent. Ashley White, who I believe originates from Clifton, but spends most of his time abroad selling timeshare apartments, was there in fancy dress as usual. Over the years I've spotted him at most major games Forest have been involved in - for example, League Cup Finals at Wembley - dressed in various guises, but he'd certainly surpassed himself on this occasion. As I stood with John and Stuart right at the back of the stand, standing proudly in the middle of the Forest supporters, was a Russian Army Officer in all his regalia, saluting the Bayern fans seated all around us. Not exactly the sort of thing you'd expect to see in the middle of a football crowd, but nonetheless a very amusing sight.

Once the game got under way, with Forest kicking towards the same end of the stadium Trevor Francis had famously headed the winning goal in during the European Cup Final seventeen years earlier - the Bayern crowd immediately began to get behind their players. Although German football supporters are extremely enthusiastic and make an awful lot of noise, they are about twenty-five years behind us in the way they dress and act at football matches. They were all dressed up like Christmas trees, with scarves hanging from their waistbands, tied to their wrists and around their heads, cut off denim jackets with badges and pennants sewn all over them and generally acting like buffoons. It reminded me very much of being at school in the early-seventies - all that long hair and flares and stuff - without a doubt, the most 'un-cool' decade of the twentieth century!

Roared on by their decidedly unfashionable hordes, Bayern soon took a grip of the game, and it was no surprise when they went into the lead on sixteen minutes through Jurgen Klinsmann - still an excellent player despite being in his twilight years - who powerfully headed home a cross from the right. As if this wasn't bad enough, we then had to endure the sound of an organ blasting out across the stadium in celebration - an experience more in keeping with an ice hockey match than a football match. Much to everyone's surprise - especially the Bayern fans who were still celebrating deliriously - Forest then went straight down to the other end and equalised through a Steve Chettle header at the far post, sending 4,000 'nutters from Notts' into raptures at 'our' end of the stadium.

With intense pressure exerted on the Forest defence throughout the remainder of the half, it seemed almost inevitable that Bayern would score a second, and this they did through Mehmet Scholl just one minute before the break. But in spite of almost constant second-half pressure from the classy-looking German outfit, the 'Reds' hung on valiantly until the end, leaving the tie well balanced for the return leg in Nottingham a fortnight later; and with what could turn out to be a valuable away goal under our belts.

As we poured out of the stadium, it was pleasing to see the two sets of supporters were mingling freely together without so much as a hint of trouble. Although we'd been hearing horror stories prior to the game concerning the behaviour of a large number of Forest supporters who'd been in the city for the last few days, we'd witnessed nothing more than high spirits since our arrival earlier on in the day. As we were staying in Munich for the night, John and I had arranged to meet up with Big Lee after the game, who had himself been over there for several days already. We had a couple of drinks with him and his pal in a bar near to the stadium, before heading back to the centre of the city and eventually back to our hotel. One thing we did find, much to our surprise, was that in sharp contrast to Cologne, Munich is a pretty duff place to be after ten o'clock on a Tuesday night. Consequently, the evening was something of an anti-climax. I left John drinking downstairs in the hotel bar with several dozen others off our bus at around 1.00-a.m. and went off to bed.

When I gradually began to emerge from my coma at around 7.30-a.m., I was somewhat startled to find John sitting slumped on a chair on the far side of the room. He was still fully-clothed, clutching a half-empty bottle of wine, with his face down on the dressing table about three inches away from the television, which was still switched on. As his bed hadn't been slept in, I can only assume he'd been there since staggering up to bed at God knows what time in the morning. What a waste of the 75 Deutsche Marks he'd parted with for his share of the room? As the bus was due to leave at 8.30-a.m., I tried quickly to rouse him, before jumping into the shower, hastily dressing and heading downstairs for breakfast. To my surprise, when I got down there, everyone else was already finishing off theirs and about to climb on board the bus, which in fact was leaving at 8.00-a.m. - ten minutes later. I ran back upstairs, kicked John all over the room trying to wake him and told him to get his finger out or he'd be spending another day in Munich. This seemed to have the desired effect and he was dressed and down within a matter of minutes, by which time I'd managed to stuff a couple of cold pieces of toast and a cup of lukewarm coffee down my throat. No such luck for John though as the coach was all ready to leave by the time he arrived in reception. Needless to say, I had no sympathy with him whatsoever - the drunken bum.

The journey home to Nottingham was a long and tiring one, with most of us trying to catch up on some much-needed sleep. On the Wednesday morning, I left John sleeping like a baby and went and sat next to Simmo, spending several hours reminiscing about the old days when he was running his buses from the Sal back in the early-seventies. Although I'd seen him on many occasions since those days, I'd never actually had a conversation with him. I was itching to find out just what had happened to all the old faces over the years, many of whom had seemingly vanished off the face of the earth. He still knew the whereabouts of most of them, and what they were up to nowadays; although a few had just done a disappearing act altogether. I brought him up to date with what our Graham, Wags, Ollie and Mick Coll were doing, and the fact Swinie and Tom Clough were still the best of pals even after all these years (although I'm not sure whether he actually remembered any of them). I was somewhat surprised to find he still indulges in the odd bit of rough 'n tumble at games when it takes his fancy, despite his less than tender years.

By the time the bus dropped us off outside the Crown at around mid-day on Thursday - 84 hours after setting off - I was more than ready for some serious kip. As I trudged off home to Birmingham, I was happy in the knowledge that once the sheer drudgery of this near-1500 mile round trip had begun to fade; I'd be left with some great memories of yet another European adventure. "Who knows," I thought to myself, "I might even get round to writing that book about it all one of these days?"

JUST four days later, it was back to FA Cup action and a journey to White Hart Lane to take on Spurs in the delayed fifth round replay. I was far too knackered to make the journey south to London and instead kept abreast of developments via the commentary on Radio 5 Live. Although Brian Roy put Forest 1-0 up, a Teddy Sheringham free kick put the tie firstly into extra time and eventually into a penalty shoot-out. Mark Crossley - undoubtedly one of the foremost penalty stoppers in the game - put the 'Reds' through to the quarter-final stages of the competition by saving from Clive Wilson, Ronny Rosenthal, and that man Sheringham. Big Norm set off like a rabbit after the crucial match-winning save from Teddy, hotly pursued by the rest of his team-mates who, much to their shame, struggled to catch him. He ran the entire length of the pitch to celebrate in front of the delirious travelling hordes from Nottingham who were packed into the opposite end of the stadium. I enjoyed every single minute of it on Match of the Day as I got stuck into my sixth can of Carling Premier, but I just couldn't help wishing I'd gotten off my big, fat, lazy arse and gone down to 'the Lane' to watch the whole thing live.

Aston Villa were waiting patiently in the wings to take on Forest in the sixth round at the City Ground just four days later. I had the dubious pleasure of being caught up in the middle of the travelling Villa hordes as I made my way back to my spiritual home along the M42 late on the Wednesday afternoon. Now I don't know whether Forest's sixteen previous Cup ties already this season had made the good folk of Nottingham just a little bit blasé about the FA Cup, or whether the aforementioned fixtures had caused a serious drain on the old pocket; but considering Villa's 4,000-plus following, the crowd of only 21,067 was extremely disappointing. There was a time in the not-too-distant past when a third round tie even against mediocre Second Division opposition would have seen 30,000 or more flocking to the City Ground in anticipation; but for an FA Cup quarter-final, you'd have had to queue all night long just to stand any chance of getting a ticket. Oh how times have changed?

For what it's worth, I bought a ticket for the 'A' Block for this game - just like the old days - and stood amongst Forest's most notorious and vociferous supporters, hoping to soak up the real atmosphere of an important Cup tie once again. Unfortunately, Forest produced one of their most inept performances of the season and were sent crashing out of the competition by one of their former stars Franz Carr, who just happened to be on loan to Villa at the time. He sent an excellent twenty-yard shot crashing into the roof of the net after ghosting past several defenders in a manner reminiscent of his days down at the City Ground several years earlier.

Although now out of the FA Cup, we were of course still in Europe and very much looking forward to the visit of Bayern Munich in the second leg of the UEFA Cup quarter-final on Tuesday, 19th March. Despite the game being televised live, there was still a healthy 28,844 people inside the City Ground for this one. To say the Germans demolished the 'Reds' though, wouldn't do their performance any justice whatsoever - they were absolutely awesome. Watching Jurgen Klinsmann and Co. in the visitors' attack, made me realise just what a 'powder-puff' strike-force we really had here on Trentside at the time with the likes of Bryan Roy and Kevin Campbell up front.

Campbell - brought in at great expense to replace Collymore - was rapidly becoming the flop of the century. Christian Ziege and Thomas Strunz gave Bayern a 2-0 half-time lead, before Klinsmann began to wreak havoc in the second half, grabbing two goals himself in the process. Sandwiched between his two efforts, was another from Jean-Pierre Papin. It was real 'men against boys' action out there on the famous City Ground turf, and when Steve Stone finally grabbed a late consolation for the 'Reds', half the crowd had already long-since retired to the pub. Whilst having to admire the Germans - not for the first time - it was totally embarrassing to be a Forest supporter that evening, especially as the whole nation had witnessed the humiliation live on the telly. The 'Sheep-shaggers' must have been killing themselves with laughter at this one!

Despite this humiliation a crowd of 29,058 returned to the City Ground just four days later to cheer the 'Reds' on against Liverpool. This game heralded the return of the prodigal son himself - Stan Collymore - and if he thought he was going to have an easy time of it, he was wrong. He suffered constant barracking throughout the whole game - well until he was substituted late on and disappeared down the tunnel in a characteristic show of arrogance, kissing the badge on his Liverpool shirt. Up to that point he'd been booed vociferously every time he went anywhere near the ball. For most of the first half, the sound of: *"No-one likes you, No-one likes you, No-one likes you - Collymore! Greedy Bastard, Greedy Bastard, Greedy Bastard - Collymore!"* had echoed around the ground with at least 20,000-plus joining in. This was followed by constant chants of: *"One Greedy Bastard - There's only one Greedy Bastard!"* And he hated every single minute of it - I've never seen a player so rattled and uncomfortable out there on a football pitch. He was non-existent right up to the point manager Roy Evans took pity on him and brought his nightmare to an end. The fact that a Steve Stone effort gave Forest a well-earned three points made it all the more sweet and I left the ground determined to celebrate that evening, especially as I was staying over in Nottingham for the night. What you might describe as a perfect day all round really.

Despite this victory against the 'Scousers', and the fact they went on to record another couple of decent results against Spurs at home (2-1) and Leeds away (3-1), Forest suffered another two worrying defeats before the end of the season. The first of these was a 5-1 mauling at the City Ground, this time at the hands of mid-table Blackburn Rovers, and the second, a 5-0 whitewash against Champions-elect Manchester United at Old Trafford. Now I know you could argue that finishing ninth in the Premier League and progressing through to the quarter-final stages of both the FA Cup and the UEFA Cup doesn't exactly add up to a disastrous season - an achievement which many clubs could only dream about - but I was getting seriously concerned about the Club's future under the guidance of Frank Clark. Never before had I seen them suffer so many substantial defeats during the course of one season - 7-0 at Blackburn, 4-2 at Liverpool, 5-1 at home to Bayern, plus these latest heavy defeats at home to Blackburn and at Man U. What's more, many of their victories this season had been unconvincing ones and the style of play under Clarky was dull to say the least. He'd also wasted millions on what at the time, looked very ordinary players - the likes of Campbell, Bart-Williams (later to blossom into one of our best players) and Silenzi had hardly set the City Ground alight and all seemed lacking at this level of the game.

The support they'd received from the Nottingham public throughout the season was impressive. The average League gate was a creditable 25,915 - the highest for sixteen years - with every single fixture attracting a 20,000-plus crowd. The highest of these was the 29,263 for the visit of Manchester United, closely followed by the 29,058 for the visit of Liverpool. And when you include the fixtures against Auxerre and Bayern Munich, no less than fifteen attendances were in excess of 25,000, ten of which were over 27,000. The lowest League crowd of the campaign - not surprisingly - was the 20,810 who turned out for the less-than-attractive visit of Wimbledon back in November.

Relegated Queens Park Rangers provided Forest with their final serious opposition of the season, a game which the 'Reds' won easily by three-goals-to-nil. Quite a sizeable following came up from North-West London for their 'relegation party' and they amused us all with chants of: *"Port Vale on a Tuesday night, Port Vale on a Tuesday night,"* which they sang over and over again throughout the ninety minutes. There was the customary pitch invasion at the end of the game with supporters converging like ants from all four corners of the ground to carry the players shoulder high from the field. But the curtain had not quite come down yet over Forest's season; there was still the small matter of Stuart Pearce's testimonial game against Newcastle United on Wednesday, 8th May. Without doubt, the most popular player ever to pull on the famous Garibaldi shirt, borne out by the fact that over 23,000 fans - unprecedented for a City Ground testimonial - turned up to pay homage to the great man. They gave him the most rapturous reception ever afforded a Forest player, and even the five hundred or so Newcastle fans who'd made the journey south, rose to applaud him onto the pitch before the start of the game, which his Forest XI eventually won by six-goals-to-five. Although testimonials are usually drab, boring affairs, this was a pretty special and emotional occasion for everyone connected with the Club and I think Stuart was left in absolutely no doubt just what the Nottingham public think of him: he is without doubt the greatest hero in these parts since Robin Hood and I'm sure he'll be remembered with great affection for many decades to come.

During the summer, the City Ground would be playing host to the European Championships, with Portugal, Croatia and Turkey all due to play their group matches on Trentside. This was testimony to just how far the ground had been developed in recent years and the fact it was now one of the most modern and attractive venues in the country. Such a setting deserves to be hosting top-class football; and with Euro '96, followed by another season of Premiership action to come, this was exactly the case!

SEASON 1995/96 – STATISTICS

FA PREMIER LEAGUE – FIXTURES

Date		Opposition	Venue	Competition	Score	Attendance
Aug	19	Southampton	A	League	4-3	15,164
	23	**Chelsea**	**H**	**League**	**0-0**	**27,007**
	26	**West Ham United**	**H**	**League**	**1-1**	**26,641**
	29	Arsenal	A	League	1-1	38,248
Sept	9	Coventry City	A	League	1-1	17,219
	12	Malmoe	A	UEFA Cup 1 - 1st Leg	1-2	12,486
	17	**Everton**	**H**	**League**	**3-2**	**24,786**
	19	Bradford City	A	LC 2 - 1st Leg	2-3	9,288
	23	Aston Villa	A	League	1-1	33,972
	26	**Malmoe**	**H**	**UEFA Cup 1 - 2nd Leg**	**1-0**	**23,817**
	30	**Manchester City**	**H**	**League**	**3-0**	**25,620**
Oct	4	**Bradford City**	**H**	**LC 2 - 2nd Leg**	**2-2**	**15,321**
	14	Tottenham Hotspur	A	League	1-0	32,876
	17	Auxerre	A	UEFA Cup 2 - 1st Leg	1-0	20,000
	21	**Bolton Wanderers**	**H**	**League**	**3-2**	**25,426**
	28	Queens Park Rangers	A	League	1-1	17,549
	31	**Auxerre**	**H**	**UEFA Cup 2 - 2nd Leg**	**0-0**	**28,064**
Nov	6	**Wimbledon**	**H**	**League**	**4-1**	**20,810**
	18	Blackburn Rovers	A	League	0-7	27,660
	21	**Lyon**	**H**	**UEFA Cup 3 - 1st Leg**	**1-0**	**22,141**
	27	**Manchester United**	**H**	**League**	**1-1**	**29,263**
Dec	2	Bolton Wanderers	A	League	1-1	17,342
	5	Lyon	A	UEFA Cup 3 - 2nd Leg	0-0	35,000
	10	**Aston Villa**	**H**	**League**	**1-1**	**25,790**
	18	Manchester City	A	League	1-1	25,660
	23	Newcastle United	A	League	1-3	36,531
	26	**Sheffield Wednesday**	**H**	**League**	**1-0**	**27,810**
	30	**Middlesbrough**	**H**	**League**	**1-0**	**27,027**
Jan	1	Liverpool	A	League	2-4	39,206
	6	Stoke City	A	FA Cup 3	1-1	18,000
	13	**Southampton**	**H**	**League**	**1-0**	**23,321**
	17	**Stoke City**	**H**	**FA Cup 3 - Replay**	**2-0**	**17,372**
	20	Chelsea	A	League	0-1	24,482
	31	**Leeds United**	**H**	**League**	**2-1**	**24,465**
Feb	3	West Ham United	A	League	0-1	21,257
	7	**Oxford United**	**H**	**FA Cup 4**	**1-1**	**15,050**
	10	**Arsenal**	**H**	**League**	**0-1**	**27,222**
	13	Oxford United	A	FA Cup 4 - Replay	3-0	8,022
	19	**Tottenham Hotspur**	**H**	**FA Cup 5**		**17,000**
		(Abandoned - snow blizzard)				
	24	Everton	A	League	0-3	33,163
	28	**Tottenham Hotspur**	**H**	**FA Cup 5**	**2-2**	**18,600**
Mar	2	Sheffield Wednesday	A	League	3-1	21,930
	5	Bayern Munich	A	UEFA Cup QF - 1st Leg	1-2	38,000
	9	Tottenham Hotspur	A	FA Cup 5 - Replay	1-1	31,055
		(Forest won 3-1 on penalties after extra time)				
	13	**Aston Villa**	**H**	**FA Cup 6**	**0-1**	**21,067**
	16	Middlesbrough	A	League	1-1	29,392
	19	**Bayern Munich**	**H**	**UEFA Cup QF - 2nd Leg**	**1-5**	**28,844**
	23	**Liverpool**	**H**	**League**	**1-0**	**29,058**
	30	Wimbledon	A	League	0-1	9,807
Apr	6	**Tottenham Hotspur**	**H**	**League**	**2-1**	**27,053**
	8	Leeds United	A	League	3-1	29,220
	13	**Blackburn Rovers**	**H**	**League**	**1-5**	**25,273**
	17	**Coventry City**	**H**	**League**	**0-0**	**24,629**
	28	Manchester United	A	League	0-5	53,926
May	2	**Newcastle United**	**H**	**League**	**1-1**	**28,280**
	5	**Queens Park Rangers**	**H**	**League**	**3-0**	**22,910**

HOME ATTENDANCES

	AGGREGATE ATTENDANCE	HIGHEST ATTENDANCE	LOWEST ATTENDANCE	AVERAGE ATTENDANCE
League:	492,391	29,263	20,810	25,915
League Cup:	15,321	15,321	15,321	15,321
FA Cup:	89,089	21,067	15,050	17,817
UEFA Cup:	102,866	28,844	22,141	25,716
All Competitions:	699,667	29,263	15,050	24,126

FINAL LEAGUE TABLE - FA PREMIER

Position	P	W	D	L	GF	GA	Pts
1. Manchester United	38	25	7	6	73	35	82
2. Newcastle United	38	24	6	8	66	37	78
3. Liverpool	38	20	11	7	70	34	71
4. Aston Villa	38	18	9	11	52	35	63
5. Arsenal	38	17	12	9	49	32	63
6. Everton	38	17	10	11	64	44	61
7. Blackburn Rovers	38	18	7	13	61	47	61
8. Tottenham Hotspur	38	16	13	9	50	38	61
9. Nottingham Forest	**38**	**15**	**13**	**10**	**50**	**54**	**58**
10. West Ham United	38	14	9	15	43	52	51
11. Chelsea	38	12	14	12	46	44	50
12. Middlesbrough	38	11	10	17	35	50	43
13. Leeds United	38	12	7	19	40	57	43
14. Wimbledon	38	10	11	17	55	70	41
15. Sheffield Wednesday	38	10	10	18	48	61	40
16. Coventry City	38	8	14	16	42	60	38
17. Southampton	38	9	11	18	34	52	38
18. Manchester City	38	9	11	18	33	58	38
19. Queens Park Rangers	38	9	6	23	38	57	33
20. Bolton Wanderers	38	8	5	25	39	71	29

AWAY ATTENDANCES

	AGGREGATE ATTENDANCE	HIGHEST ATTENDANCE	LOWEST ATTENDANCE	AVERAGE ATTENDANCE
League:	524,604	53,926	9,807	27,610
League Cup:	9,288	9,288	9,288	9,288
FA Cup:	57,077	31,055	8,022	19,025
UEFA Cup:	105,486	38,000	12,486	26,371
All Competitions:	696,455	53,926	8,022	25,794

"OH SANDY-SANDY, SANDY-SANDY-SANDY-SANDY AN-DER-SON"

EXILED HERE in Birmingham, information about my beloved Forest is hard to come by. Consequently, I'd spent the summer months frantically scouring the pages of Ceefax and Teletext looking for news of any impending transfer activity. At this moment in time, the only occasions I did manage to obtain concrete news about the 'Reds' was when I visited Nottingham at the weekends (most weekends of course) and bought either Saturday's Evening Post or, during the football season, the Football Post. Any friends or family who visited me in Birmingham also knew they had to stop and pick a Post up for me on the way over or there'd be hell to pay. Alas, I also have to admit that my son Thomas, who still lives in Nottingham with his mother, also regularly videos the Sports News on Central Television (I have to put up with loads of crap about the 'Blues' and the Villa on Central West Midlands) and then plays the soundtrack to me over the phone at seven o'clock each evening. He also reads the back page of the Post to me most nights as well. Now is that sad or what?

Being so concerned about the lack of quality in the Forest squad during the previous campaign; I was convinced that without some decent summer signings, we'd be destined for a long, hard season. I was slightly pleased therefore when the services of Dean Saunders were acquired for the sum of £1.5 million from Turkish side Galatasary. Although now reaching the climax of his career, he had a prolific goal-scoring record with previous clubs Oxford United, Liverpool, Aston Villa, 'Sheep-dip County', and the previously mentioned Turks. I was confident he still had a couple of decent years left in him and might just solve one or two of our problems up front. In addition to this, on the back of a few decent performances for Croatia during Euro '96 - a couple of which were at the City Ground - Clarky had seen fit to splash out another £1 million on central-defender Nikola Jerkan from Real Oviedo of Spain. (The season's first issue of the Tricky Tree had a picture of Nikola on the front cover with Frank standing behind him, hands on top of his shoulders. The caption above read: *"DO YOU THINK I CAN DO IT FRANK?"* To which Clarky's response was: *"WELL IF ANYONE CAN, JERKAN!"*).

Other less significant transactions had seen Oxford United winger Chris Allen arrive on a permanent basis for a fee of £400,000, following his reasonably successful loan spell during the previous campaign, and Kingsley Black ending his five-year spell at the Club with a move to First Division Grimsby Town for a nominal fee. What's more, 'Big Bad Bob' Rosario had also announced his retirement from the game after a two-year battle against a serious knee injury. Pleasingly, keeper Mark Crossley had also turned down a big money move to Leeds and instead pledged his future to Forest by agreeing to sign a new four-year contract.

Speaking of Euro '96, those jammy Krauts were at it again, weren't they - going through undeservedly to the Final following their penalty shoot-out victory over our lads in the semis? What do we have to do to put one over on them, eh? I really thought our name was on that Cup, especially after our somewhat fortuitous victory over Spain (what about Psycho's reaction after his penalty success?), the superb 2-0 victory over the 'Jocks' and the wonderful 4-1 demolition of the Dutch (now that's what I call total football!). I'm almost as proud of being English as I am of being from Nottingham, so I was pretty distraught when we went out that night, as was the rest of the country. I watched most of England's games in local pubs around Birmingham and the atmosphere was fantastic. The Brummies are so patriotic it's unbelievable. When that second goal went in against the Scots, they went absolutely berserk in the pub I was in: two hundred youths wearing England shirts jumping around all over the place as if we'd won the World Cup. God only knows what the reaction would have been if we'd actually won the competition? I think there'd have been a week-long street party in South Birmingham where I live. Still, I'm sure it would have been pretty much the same in Nottingham, and the rest of the country for that matter.

We had an early chance to judge for ourselves what might lay in store for Forest this season, when the City Ground hosted the four-team Umbro tournament on Saturday, 3rd and Sunday, 4th August. League Champions Manchester United, Chelsea, Forest and Ajax Amsterdam were the teams involved. And what a mouth-watering prospect this was?

I decided to make a weekend of it and bought tickets for both days, as did the rest of the gang. As far as I was concerned it was the perfect opportunity to have a night out in Nottingham on the Saturday, as well as indulging myself in a feast of football for two days. It also meant I could take Jacko up on his offer of cheap accommodation at his hotel - the Balmoral on Loughborough

Road, West Bridgford - just a three hundred yard walk from the City Ground and only a couple of miles out of town. I arrived in Nottingham nice and early on the Saturday morning to meet up with John Farley for a few beers before the game. Sue and John's new misses, Elizabeth, were planning on spending the afternoon shopping in town whilst John and I were at the game. Later that evening, we'd arranged to meet up with Andy, Garry and Lee, plus their respective partners, plus Sue's best friend Debbie and her husband Mel - a Derby supporter. And God was he in for some stick, being a lone 'Sheep-shagger' amongst a gang of Forest fans!

The competition kicked off with United versus Ajax early on in the afternoon - a game which ended 2-1 to the Dutchmen (ha-ha!) - and this was followed by Forest versus Chelsea almost immediately after. There were no less than 27,000 spectators inside the stadium to watch the first day's proceedings, but unfortunately this second fixture was pretty dull and ended goalless. Ruud Gullit's side did however win the ensuing penalty shoot-out by four-goals-to-three. There were several thousand United and Chelsea fans amongst the crowd: the United fans occupying the whole of the Bridgford Stand and the Cheslea fans the lower tier of the Executive Stand. The rest of the ground was predominantly made up of Forest supporters, apart from a very small group of Ajax fans in the upper tier of the Executive. Amongst these were the famous Teletoeters Band, who follow the Dutch national side all over the world. They created a carnival-like atmosphere throughout the whole of the tournament and were extremely well-received by the large crowd.

We had a great night on the town after the first day's proceedings had ended and sure enough Mel was on the receiving end of a monumental amount of abuse. Although I hate to admit it, two of the nicest blokes I know in the whole world both happen to be Derby supporters - Mel and a lad called Gary Radford from Beeston. And do you know what? Both of them were born and bred in Nottingham and have their respective fathers to blame for poisoning their minds at a young and tender age, which incidentally, just happened to be when Derby were winning the League Championship under a certain Mr. Clough in the early nineteen-seventies. Otherwise known as 'jumping on the bandwagon', I believe?

It was Forest versus United for the wooden spoon first thing on the Sunday afternoon and, not surprisingly, with fewer United fans inside the ground, at just over 21,000, the crowd was somewhat smaller than for the previous day. The Chelsea fans already in the ground for this game, were overwhelmingly on Forest's side. And when Kevin Campbell finally broke the deadlock with only nine minutes left, they were jumping up and down nearly as much as the Forest supporters were. Unfortunately, United decided to step things up a little and promptly despatched three late goals past 'Big Norm' to earn a comprehensive 3-1 victory. Whilst the defeat itself was bad enough, it was made all the worse by the most obnoxious United fan you could ever wish to encounter anywhere. He had a strong Irish accent and was seated about five rows in front of us in the upper tier of the Trent End. He was bellowing and yawping all the way through the game and making the sort of arrogant remarks you'd only associate with a United 'supporter' - and especially one who doesn't even come from Manchester. With a half-empty West Bridgford Stand at the opposite end of the stadium, what the hell was he doing smack in the middle of the Trent End in the first place? And they wonder why nobody likes them? The chap he was sat next to - who was obviously with him - had a local accent and was clearly a Forest supporter. However, rather than just telling him to 'shut the fuck up,' he sat there like a prick letting him wind everyone in the stand up to breaking point. If that had been me sitting next to him, I swear I'd have launched him over the wall and into the bottom tier of the Trent End.

Anyway, in view of the support afforded us by the Chelsea fans during this game, it was only natural we should return the compliment when they took on Ajax in the Final later on. Mind you, it wasn't difficult to admire the flair and attacking style of the Londoners as they ran the famous Dutch outfit ragged throughout most of the game. They ran out fairly comfortable 2-0 winners to lift the trophy and send the vast majority of the crowd home reasonably happy. This had been an excellent curtain-raiser for the new season, but it had also confirmed the fears of many Forest supporters that this was indeed going to be a long and arduous season.

IT was Coventry City away on the first day of the season - a game I had to miss as I'd been invited to Mick Bench's fortieth birthday party, which was due to kick off in the Cadland at lunchtime. In any case, on the last couple of occasions I'd been to Highfield Road, the game had turned out to be absolutely crap and I'd spent most of the ninety minutes seething at the activities of the West Midlands Police Force. As usual, they were arresting one supporter after another for doing absolutely nothing wrong! An old school-mate of mine from Stabbo - Andy Ibbett - who's a joiner and works with a gang of lads from Coventry on jobs up and down the country, took his young son Matthew with him to this game and sat amongst the travelling Forest supporters in the Visitors'

Enclosure in the Mitchell and Butler Stand. With Forest amazingly romping home to a 3-0 victory - thanks to a brilliant Kevin Campbell hat-trick - Andy was taunting his Coventry City mates in the nearby West Stand, when he was promptly dragged off by the boys in blue and thrown into the cells. He was later charged under the new: ''Not allowed to enjoy yourself at a football match Act, 1996,'' an offence for which he later received a substantial fine. As they carted him off to the cells, they weren't interested in the fact he'd been merely exchanging banter with his work-mates, and didn't give a toss that his thirteen-year-old son had been left unaccompanied in the ground as a result of their unreasonable actions. Young Matt would have to fend for himself after the game. Fortunately, he was able to scrounge a lift home with some lads he bumped into from Stabbo.

Anyway, while Andy - and no doubt numerous other innocent Forest supporters - were ruing the fact they'd made the journey to the West Midlands that day, I was back 'home' in Nottingham enjoying Benchy's all-day bash outside the Cad. As is always the case, the first Saturday of the football season proved to be another glorious and sunny affair, so shorts and T-shirts were the order of the day. This gave me the perfect opportunity to show off my recently acquired 'Forest' tattoo which I'd had done in a top studio called Midland Tattoo in Cannock in the West Midlands. It had been a lifelong ambition of mine to have the old Forest badge - the Nottingham Coat of Arms with the letters 'NFFC' above - tattooed onto my upper-arm, but I'd refrained from doing so for a number of reasons. Firstly, I'd seen so many 'bodge' jobs over the years, there was no way on this earth I was going to let just anyone near my arm with a needle full of ink, unless I was absolutely sure about their artistic ability. Secondly, I'd always naively believed that as I grew older and wiser, I'd live to regret having a tattoo of any description, let alone a Forest one. However, I was now 38-years-old, had a responsible and well-paid job, but still I longed for one.

The crunch finally came when I was away on a course, staying in Bath with a number of my colleagues from around the U.K. I was sitting having a late night drink in the hotel bar with one of them - a Wolves fan - when he showed me a tattoo he'd recently had done to cover up one of those 'do it yourself' jobs from his early teens. It was on his lower arm and depicted a Wolf's head. I was absolutely stunned by how life-like it was; so detailed in fact, it looked like a photograph. That was it - I made my mind up there and then: I was off to Cannock to get my Forest badge done at the very first opportunity.

The following Saturday, when I nipped over to Nottingham to pick up the kids for the weekend, I called in to see Swinie to give him an old Forest shirt of mine. He's a graphic designer and had agreed to design a badge for me which I could take with me to Cannock. The tattooist would then copy this onto my arm.

Swinie's design was brilliant and I duly booked my appointment to see the tattooist - and you could only get into see this man by booking weeks in advance. And when the big day finally came around, I certainly wasn't disappointed. As far as I was concerned, the finished article was 'the dog's bollocks' and had been well worth the long wait. All the lads back home in Chilwell seemed to agree as well, judging by the admiring glances at Benchy's party. In fact, I'm sure if this particular tattooist had been based in Nottingham; he'd have had a queue of Forest supporters outside his shop the very next day!

Naturally, Forest's excellent 3-0 victory against the 'Sky Blues' was the toast of the evening and consequently, when I returned to Nottingham once again four days later to see them take on newly-promoted Sunderland at the City Ground, I was confident that another three points were virtually in the bag. How wrong I was though, as Sunderland absolutely wiped the floor with us, running out convincing 4-1 winners in front of a crowd of 22,874. ''That bleedin' Niall Quinn,'' I thought to myself after the game, ''he should be playing basketball, not football, the lanky git!'' Sour grapes of course, after he'd wreaked havoc in the Forest defence all night, helping himself to two of the goals and making the other two along the way.

The doubts that had been nagging me all summer regarding the quality of Forest's squad, returned with a vengeance from that moment on, and the season slowly but surely developed into a nightmare. Having drawn 1-1 at home to Middlesbrough the following Saturday, they then let a two-goal lead slip away in their 2-2 draw at Southampton four days later. And, as if that wasn't bad enough, good old Garry Mason only went and arranged his wedding day for Saturday, 7th September, meaning the whole gang had to miss the 'derby' game against Leicester at home the following week. To make matters worse, he was tying the knot at St.Giles' Church in West

Bridgford - literally a stone's throw from the City Ground - and at 3.00 o'clock that afternoon - the inconsiderate bastard!

We all piled into The Manor for a drink before the ceremony - and as best man, Big Lee stuck out like a sore thumb in his top hat and tails. And the place was packed full of red-shirted Forest supporters going to the game - lucky gits. I was just glad to get out of there, as it was indeed a painful experience knowing I was going to be stuck inside some stuffy old church when I should have been sat in my seat at my true place of worship. ''Why had Garry done this to me?'' I lamented. ''What's wrong with getting married in June or July like real football supporters?'' Still, what can you expect from a Geordie anyway?

Now just to rub salt into the wounds, as we stood around outside the church waiting for the beautiful bride, Donna, to arrive, the roar of the City Ground crowd could clearly be heard drifting across West Bridgford and into the churchyard. For me, this was proving to be a really painful experience. It's hard to describe really, but Forest playing at home without me present, is a bit like fish 'n chips without the fish. At least once inside the church, the noise of the crowd would be drowned out by the sound of the choir - or at least that's what I'd hoped?

By 3.45-p.m. - half-time - the boring bit was over and we were dashing off to the reception. Now I don't know whether Garry was just taking the piss or what, but he'd only gone and booked his reception at Trent Bridge Cricket Ground. Consequently, whilst waiting 'anxiously' for the happy couple to arrive, not only could we now quite clearly hear the roar of the crowd as we formed an orderly queue at the bar; but we could actually see out of the window across the cricket pitch and straight into the City Ground. We had to endure another forty-five minutes watching the upper tier of the Trent End jumping up an down like jack-in-the-boxes every time Forest were on the attack. And the suspense was killing me.

In reality, it hadn't been nearly as exciting as it had seemed from where we were standing. The 0-0 score-line was announced to all and sundry over the microphone at 5.00-p.m. Apparently, the most exciting incident of the whole ninety minutes, was Steve Stone being stretchered off with a serious knee injury; one which would unfortunately keep him out of action for the rest of the season. We were determined to make up for missing the game though, and Garry and Donna's wedding day ended just as the last couple (including my own in July '95) had done - with about twenty of us taking over the dance floor for the last half an hour to leap around all over the place whilst singing along to: *''Hi-Ho-We-Hate-Der-by!''* and *''We've got the whole world in our hands,''* much to the amusement of the other guests.

The following Saturday, a fourth-minute strike from Alfie Haaland against Man U at Old Trafford gave Forest's travelling support something to cheer about. However, their joy was short-lived and United went on to score four without further reply. The alarm bells were certainly ringing by this time. The players seemed totally lacking in confidence and Frank Clark seemed incapable of inspiring them in any way, shape or form. In a game that was now totally dominated by money, the financial incentives for remaining in the Premier League were extremely high and clubs such as Forest simply couldn't afford to drop down a division. Sky Television - very much the dominant force in English football - had pledged that clubs staying in the Premier League at the end of the season could look forward to a windfall of between £8 and £10 million. The way the team were now performing, this didn't seem to be much of an issue down on Trentside.

Sadly, in September, former Forest coach Jimmy Gordon died at the age of 80. Clough and Taylor had famously brought him back into football during the halcyon days of the late-seventies and he'd been a very popular figure amongst supporters. He had of course also served them well during their days at Derby County. He'll certainly go down in history as an integral member of the most famous management team ever to grace the corridors of the City Ground.

On Saturday, 21st September, West Ham United visited the City Ground and gave us the run around for the whole of the ninety minutes. In the end, we were very fortunate to escape with only a 2-0 defeat. (A 47-year-old Peter Shilton was in the 'Hammers'' squad that day incidentally). And things didn't get any better after this game, with a string of draws and defeats sending us dangerously close to the foot of the table by mid-October. There was a great deal of unrest amongst the supporters by this time and speculation about a possible take-over of the Club had been gathering momentum for some time. The News of the World announced that multi-millionaire Grant Bovey, owner of Watershed Videos and a lifelong Forest supporter, was about to put in a bid for the Club. (He later hit the headlines for his very public romance with TV presenter Anthea Turner). Other consortiums were also beginning to show an interest in the Club and all the various proposals would be discussed at the Annual General Meeting, scheduled to take place on 31st October.

As a result of this meeting, Chairman Fred Reacher was, somewhat surprisingly, replaced by Irving Korn and Director Chris Wootten replaced by Jamie Mellors. This of course had little to do with what was taking place out there on the pitch and the 'Reds' continued their descent to the very foot of the table. By the time they took on Blackburn Rovers at the City ground on Monday, 25th November - in the second of three consecutive home games to be screened live by Sky - the sorry statistics were: played 13; won 1; drawn 5; lost 7; goals for 10; goals against 22; points 8; position 20th.

Off the pitch, youngster Paul McGregor - still only 21 and yet to fulfil his obvious potential - was also beginning to emerge as a possible pop star of the future. He was lead singer of a local Indie-band called 'Merc', which had been receiving rave reviews, both locally and nationally. It was common knowledge that a number of leading music company executives were closely monitoring the band's progress, including Alan McGee, the man credited with discovering 'Oasis.' When McGregor and his band played a gig at Nottingham's Rock City, the packed audience consisted not only of hundreds of Forest supporters - who gave several loud renditions of: *"We 'ate Der-by, And we 'ate Der-by"* - but also several players. With Nottingham's thriving night-life and apparently thriving music scene, the fact there have been so few famous bands from this City over the years, has always been a big mystery to me. I for one was hoping McGregor's career both on and off the pitch would flourish in a big way and that this would encourage more local bands to strike out for the big time.

DURING the month of December, details were emerging of just who the main contenders for a take-over of the Club really were. The strongest of these - and certainly the supporters' favourite - was a Nottinghamshire consortium led by millionaire Sandy Anderson - himself a supporter and season ticket holder. His strongest rivals it seemed, were a consortium made up of Phil Soar - author and lifelong Forest supporter - Monte Carlo based businessman Laurie Lewis and former Tottenham Hotspur Chairman Irving Scholar. Although the Board of Directors were initially in favour of the Nottinghamshire consortium, the destiny of the Club wouldn't be decided before Christmas, and not before final proposals from both consortiums had been submitted and considered. An Extraordinary General Meeting of the Club had been called for 6th January, at which point it was hoped this long drawn out affair would be brought to a conclusion.

On 19th December, and with only one win under his belt in 17 games - this coming way back on the first day of the season at Coventry - Frank Clark finally decided to do the decent thing and resign. Although he'd guided the 'Reds' back to the Premiership at the first time of asking and subsequently taken them back into Europe, he seemed to have completely and utterly run out of ideas. No matter what he tried, Forest's record-breaking sequence of League games without a victory, just went on and on. As patient as the Forest faithful are, they were now calling for his head and he had to go. It was time for a few fresh ideas down at the City Ground and there was only one man the supporters were clamouring for: and that was Stuart Pearce.

To their credit, the Forest Board listened and offered Pearce the position of Caretaker Boss until the end of the season. Having asked for twenty-four hours to think things over, he was duly installed as player manager in time for the game at home to Arsenal on Saturday, 21st December. There was a buzz of excitement around the whole City prior to this game, particularly as he'd brought in Nigel Clough - one of the most popular players of all time on Trentside - on loan from Manchester City and drafted him straight into the squad.

Prior to the Arsenal game, the findings of an FA Premier League Fan Survey were published and the following facts about supporter life at the City Ground emerged:

- Only two thirds of Forest season ticket holders were born within 20 miles of the City Ground - the third lowest figure in the Premier League. (Oh no...not a 'mini Man U' surely?)
- More than six out of ten Forest season ticket holders always take their school age children to football.
- One quarter of Forest fans saw their first Forest home game when aged 20 years or older.
- 23 per cent of Forest fans have already supported another club before Forest. (Sacrilege!)
- 28 per cent of Forest season ticket holders said that 'the way the club played' was a factor in determining their support.
- Only 17.4 per cent of Forest season ticket holders think police/stewards are too strict with some behaviour at football - the second lowest figure in the Premier League. (Obviously the survey wasn't commissioned in the 'A' Block!)
- 55.3 per cent of Forest season ticket holders would like the game to experiment with video aids.
- 34.8 per cent of Forest fans think the increased use of red and yellow cards is protecting 'flair' players - the second highest total in the Premier League.
- 74 per cent of season ticket holders travel to matches in their own car - the third highest total in the Premier League.

Psycho's first game in charge turned out to be a passionate and full-blooded affair in front of a sizeable City Ground crowd of 27,384. Such was the interest in this game, the BBC's Match of the Day cameras were present and it would be the main feature of the programme. Alfie Haaland turned out to be the Forest hero, scoring both goals in a 2-1 victory - their first since August 17th. The fact his second goal secured a last-minute win for the battling 'Reds' made the whole occasion even more thrilling for the long-suffering home supporters. You'd have thought we'd won the Cup when the final whistle went, such was the atmosphere inside the stadium. What a start to Psycho's managerial career!

However, just five days later on Boxing Day, Champions Manchester United were in town and determined to spoil the party. They ripped the 'Reds' apart from start to finish and ran out easy 4-0 winners. *"Stuart Pearce, Stuart Pearce, What a difference you have made,"* chanted the United supporters as the game drew to a close. Smug bastards! I wonder what some of their so-called 'supporters' would do if they'd had to experience a couple of relegation seasons in the space of only four years. At least we were still turning up in numbers at the City Ground, despite the fact we'd been down at the wrong end of the table all season. Our average home League attendance thus far was a creditable 24,240 - and up until the Arsenal game just five days before, the 'Reds' hadn't even recorded a single home victory.

Undeterred by this 4-0 drubbing, Forest went to Filbert Street two days later and carved out a creditable 2-2 draw against Martin O'Neill's battling Leicester side, with Colin Cooper and Nigel Clough grabbing the goals. A Kevin Campbell effort then earned them all three points at West Ham United on New Year's Day and they were now off the bottom of the League at long last, replaced by fellow strugglers Southampton. As the take-over battle raged on in the background, they prepared to take on First Division Ipswich Town at home in the third round of the FA Cup on Saturday, 4th January. As I sat waiting to meet the rest of the lads in the King John before the game, I read with great interest, the Evening Post's two-page article setting out Sandy Anderson's plans for the future of the Club, should his bid be accepted by the shareholders at the forthcoming EGM. During the game, the majority of the rather sparse crowd of only 14,681 made their own feelings known with continuous chants of: *"Oh Sandy-Sandy, Sandy-Sandy-Sandy-Sandy-An-der-son!"* This particular game also highlighted the gulf between the Premier and the First Division as Forest ran out easy 3-0 winners, with Chris Allen and Dean Saunders (2) grabbing the goals.

With the Club almost £12 million in debt, it was fast reaching the point where the take-over saga had to be resolved. At this point in time, it seemed the Nottingham Consortium led by Anderson were clear favourites to acquire the 75 per cent of the votes needed at the EGM. The three members of this local consortium were: Anderson himself - boss of the Derby-based Porterbrook Group, which made millions from rail leasing at the time of privatisation; Nottingham venture capitalist and Forest season ticket holder Nigel Doughty; and Charlie Scott - Chief Executive of the Cordiant (previously Saatchi) Advertising Group.

Up until the middle of December, the three members of the Bridgford Consortium were: Phil Soar - author and Chief Executive of Blenheim Exhibitions and a lifelong Forest supporter; Lawrie Lewis - Monaco-based businessman with a personal fortune of £55 million; and his near neighbour and fellow tax exile Irving Scholar - the former Chairman of Tottenham Hotspur. Both these consortiums had held meetings with the Forest Board, who were rumoured to favour the Anderson-led group.

On 10th December, Scholar and chums were actively canvassing Forest shareholders for their support. They knew they only required just over 25 per cent of the votes to scupper the Nottingham Consortium's bid. To bring about a change to the Club's Articles of Association or indeed any change to the Club's constitution, there had to be a 75 per cent majority amongst the Club's 203 shareholders. These consisted of the seven unpaid members of the Board, some former directors, one or two former players, and a wide selection of Nottingham citizens who shared a passion for Forest. Originally 209 shares had been issued at £1 each, although with six shareholders having died and the shares not having been re-issued; the number was now down to the aforementioned 203. Shares were not transferable and could neither be sold nor inherited. There was also a considerable waiting list to become a member of the Club and therefore a shareholder.

On 18th December - one day before their official offer document to shareholders - Lewis pulled out of the Bridgford Consortium's £10 million bid. It seemed therefore that Anderson would go to the EGM on January 6th unopposed. However, at the last minute, they secured the support of property tycoon and Saracens Rugby Club owner Nigel Wray and respected businessman Julian Markham. Soar, Scholar and Wray were able to address the shareholders at the EGM in an attempt to vote down the Anderson bid. To the absolute despair of the vast majority of Forest supporters, Anderson managed to gain only 111 votes - 40 short of the necessary 75 per cent. He was now out of the running.

So, what had gone wrong? Well the crux of the matter was of course, money. Crucially, the Anderson Consortium were not offering the shareholders any financial incentives up front - you know, those same shareholders who'd invested the massive sum of £1 each into the Club to become members in the first place - this would only come in the future, as and when the Club was successfully floated. The Bridgford Consortium on the other hand were offering them an immediate financial incentive. So the tens of thousands of Forest supporters who just weren't privileged enough to have a say in the matter, were sold down the river by the 92 shareholders who refused to vote for the Anderson Consortium. What a bunch of self-centred, greedy bastards those particular individuals are.

The next day, assistant manager Alan Hill - a shareholder himself - resigned so he could link up again with Frank Clark who'd been appointed as manager of First Division Manchester City. The Club were hoping to call another EGM in early-to-mid-February in order to finally resolve the take-over.

Back on the field of play, the 'Reds' continued their mini-revival under the leadership of Stuart Pearce. The visit of Ruud Gullit's cosmopolitan Chelsea - Gianluca Vialli, Gianfranco Zola et-al - drew a crowd of 28,355 to the City Ground on Saturday, 11th January. And, just for a moment or two, you might have been forgiven for thinking that Forest were top of the table, as opposed to second-from-bottom, such was the quality of their performance. For the first time all season, they actually had a game-plan and looked by far the better of the two teams throughout the whole of the ninety minutes. Pearce himself scored the first goal - slamming home a first-half free kick from the edge of the box - with Bart-Williams adding a stunning second late on to secure an excellent 2-0 victory and prompt chants of: *"We're stayin' up, We're stayin' up, We're stay-in', Forest's stay-in' up!"* from the delighted majority amongst the crowd. Des Lyttle was employed throughout the game as a man-to-man marker on the diminutive Zola. And so effective was he, the Italian international never even got within sight of goal; 'Bruno' simply followed him across every inch of the pitch, cutting off his supply line and rendering him completely ineffective.

We'd now reached the dizzy heights of third-from-bottom and I don't know about anyone else, but I was suffering from vertigo! And things could only get better - 'cause next weekend we were due to meet Spurs at home - and as everyone knows: *"Tottenham, We always beat Tottenham!"* And guess what?...That's exactly what we did, with the recalled Bryan Roy grabbing both goals in a 2-1 victory in front of another sizeable crowd of 27,303. And as if that wasn't enough, we only then travelled to St.James's Park one week later and sent high-flying Newcastle United crashing out of the FA Cup. Two goals from Ian Woan - the second an absolutely superb twenty-five yard volley - gave us a 2-1 fourth round victory and sent 36,000-plus Geordies home in stunned silence. So, having won just one League game out of the first eighteen of the season under Frank Clark, Psycho's record to date - including two FA Cup ties - read:

PLAYED 8; WON 6; DRAWN 1; LOST 1; GOALS FOR 14; GOALS AGAINST 9

What a transformation there had been since he'd taken over the reigns just 36 days earlier. All we needed now, to secure our Premiership future, was for the take-over saga to be resolved - and quickly. Unfortunately - unlike most other clubs - Nottingham Forest FC, seems to have it's very own self-destruct button. Consequently, the whole affair just dragged on and on, with one Consortium after another coming in, and then out of the reckoning. And just to make matters worse, the rumour mill which exists in Nottingham was working overtime, to the extent it became almost impossible to separate fact from fiction. It was rapidly turning into a soap opera, with more twists and turns, and more cloak-and-dagger wheeling and dealing, than the boardroom of the Ewing Oil Company. As usual, it was the supporters - the silent majority - who suffered the most. The uncertainty off the pitch gradually began to have an affect once again on the pitch, with consecutive defeats in the League at home to fellow-strugglers Coventry and away to Everton, and a disastrous and confidence-sapping 1-0 defeat at Second Division Chesterfield in the fifth round of the FA Cup.

With affairs off the pitch now destined to be resolved at the EGM on Monday, 24th February, the rumours continued to sweep through the City. Firstly, we were told that Grant Bovey had re-emerged on the scene, this time with a £25 million backer - none other than Monaco-based Lawrie Lewis, the man who'd suddenly got cold feet at the last minute way back in December, effectively scuppering the Bridgford Consortium's initial bid. And then it was rumoured that the Anderson Consortium were set to come back into the frame with an improved offer for the Club and one which would possibly satisfy the greed of the shareholders. (It emerged later that the Bovey/Lewis partnership had indeed been genuine, with Lewis once again backing out at the eleventh hour!). And finally, American Pulitzer Prize-winning journalist Albert Scardino - husband of Pearson's new Chief Executive Marjorie Scardino - was in the running with a serious offer. He'd teamed up with Jonathon Barnett, agent to cricket star Brian Lara, and Sir David White, Chairman of the Area Health Authority and a Forest shareholder.

However, as they say: "Cometh the hour - Cometh the man," and by the time the big day arrived, only the Bridgford Consortium were still left in the frame, the other contenders having finally dropped out of the bidding with two days still to go. Consequently, with the shareholders having voted 189 to 7 in favour of the Bridgford Consortium, Messrs. Soar, Scholar and Wray emerged from the meeting with broad smiles lighting up their faces. The shareholders themselves, no doubt scurried off to the pub together to celebrate their new-found wealth. Aside from winning the Lottery, this would undoubtedly turn out to be the best £1 they'd ever invested in their lives. But at what long-term benefit, or cost, to the Club and it's genuine supporters, only time would tell?

Within days, the new regime had appointed Crystal Palace manager Dave Bassett as the Club's General Manager. Officially his function was to oversee the general running of the Club - transfers in, transfers out etc. - whilst playing only a peripheral role alongside Pearce when it came to such matters as team selection and tactics. Unofficially however, it was rumoured that the two of them didn't see eye-to-eye and that Pearce was somewhat annoyed by the whole situation. Initially, the players responded in a positive manner, and, having achieved a 0-0 draw at home to fifth-placed Aston Villa two days before the long-awaited take-over, they went down to White Hart Lane the following weekend and stole all three points in a 1-0 victory, thanks to a goal from Dean Saunders. What - a win - at Tottenham? Now there's a surprise for you.

With just eleven games to go, they were just outside the bottom three, having accumulated a total of 27 points to date - 17 of these in the last ten games since Pearce had taken to the helm. Immediately below them were West Ham with 25 points from 27 games; Southampton with 24 points from 26 games; and at the very foot of the table, Middlesbrough, with just 19 points from 26 games. The next opposition were Sheffield Wednesday, who came to the City Ground in sixth position and full of confidence on Wednesday, 5th March. Unfortunately, a series of defensive blunders by Forest gifted the Yorkshiremen the game and they left Trentside with an easy 3-0 victory under their belts. And when your confidence has taken that kind of knock, the last place you'd wish to visit immediately afterwards is Highbury to take on Championship-chasing Arsenal. Although we had claimed a famous victory against them in Psycho's first game in charge way back on 21st December, there would be no repeat on this occasion and Forest left North London having suffered a convincing 2-0 defeat.

Having acquired the Club for the princely sum of around £17 million, once the £12 million worth of debt had been eradicated, Messrs. Scholar and Co. made the balance of cash available to Bassett and Pearce to inject some new blood into the team. The only question on everyone's lips though was: "Had it all come just a little too late?" Having found himself in dispute with Scottish Premier giants Celtic, Dutch striker Pierre Van Hooijdonk was the first to arrive on 10th March, for an initial outlay of £3.5 million. He signed a five-year contract and the deal could eventually cost the 'Reds' £4.5 million, depending on appearances and goals scored. Upon his arrival, the six foot five inch striker declared:

"I want to make it clear to everyone that keeping Forest in the Premier League is the most important thing - not the personal success of Pierre Van Hooijdonk.

"I'm just delighted to be playing in the Premier League with Forest. I think it's the strongest League in Europe at the moment and getting the chance to play for a club like Forest is a big honour.

"They are still a big name in Europe from the success they had in winning the European Cup and I'm really looking forward to helping them enjoy more success in the future.

"Of course, it's a concern that Forest are near the bottom of the Premier League table but the club have shown faith in me and I hope I can repay them.

"I have a five year contract and I won't leave if Forest go down. I wouldn't have signed for them if I intended to do that

"I'm an ambitious player and I've come to the right place to fulfil those ambitions."

It was so refreshing to hear these 'sincerely spoken' words in times of great selfishness and greed within the game. Here, we truly had a player who would bust a gut for our great Club and who would always put the interests of the team and the supporters before those of his own. If only there were more Pierre Van Hooijdonks in this world - what a truly wonderful place it would be?

Promising young striker Ian Moore was also drafted in from Tranmere Rovers at a cost of £1 million and stylish midfielder Brian O'Neill arrived from Celtic on loan. Van Hooijdonk made his debut in the 1-1 draw at Blackburn Rovers on 11th March and his home debut in the 1-1 draw at home to Liverpool the following Saturday. With Forest now back in the bottom three once again, a crowd of 29,181 - the biggest of the season - turned up at the City Ground for this game. Ian Woan grabbed the equalising goal for Forest after Robbie Fowler had put the 'Scousers' ahead early on. Pierre looked reasonable, but not brilliant, and the large crowd left the ground slightly frustrated to say the least.

This was followed by further 1-1 draws away to Sunderland on Saturday, 22nd March, and Middlesbrough, two days later - the fourth such result on the trot. And with Forest still only one point away from the safety-zone, bottom-of-the-table Southampton visited the City Ground on Saturday, 5th April, for a relegation clash which had 'SIX-POINTER' stamped all over it. Unfortunately, the 25,134 crowd were treated to an absolutely gutless performance by the 'Reds' and the 'Saints' ran out worthy 3-1 winners. It was now obvious to all and sundry that Forest just weren't up for it, although we had to wait an agonising two weeks for our next fixture against Leeds United, also at the City Ground.

We were now rock bottom of the table, three points away from safety, and with just four games to go. It was reaching the point where we were relying on our closest rivals - Middlesbrough, Sunderland, West Ham, and Southampton - to drop points. In other words, our destiny was no longer in our own hands. What's more, a 1-1 draw against Leeds just wasn't enough to have any positive impact on the relegation issue. The only bright spot was that Pierre bagged his first goal in a Garibaldi shirt to give the 25,565 crowd some semblance of hope for the future. A defeat against the 'Sheep' at 'Shitesville' the following Wednesday would put the issue beyond doubt. But thankfully, we were spared this particular embarrassment, thanks to a battling 0-0 draw. I think even the players realised just how much that meant to us supporters.

When we lined up for the penultimate game of the season - at home against Wimbledon - we were still not mathematically relegated. However, it was all over bar the shouting. A tame 1-1 draw finally consigned us to the First Division once again. We now had just one fixture to come on the final Sunday of the Premiership campaign, and that was away at Newcastle. And, unlike Ipswich away on the final day of the 1992/93 season, there would be no 'relegation party' this time around.

Despite another abysmal season down at the City Ground, the supporters of NFFC had once again emerged with a lot of credit. With only one win in their first seventeen games and only three at home all season, the average League attendance was still an impressive 24,586. The highest of these was the aforementioned 29,181 for the visit of Liverpool, with the lowest being the 17,525 for the live televised visit of Blackburn Rovers in November. Amidst all the glory I had enjoyed in my 31 years of watching them, I had now endured the absolute pain and despair of seeing Forest relegated on no less than three occasions. I was hoping beyond all hope this would be the very last time I'd have to go through such a demoralising and desperate experience.

SEASON 1996/97 – STATISTICS

FA PREMIER LEAGUE – FIXTURES

Date		Opposition	Venue	Competition	Score	Attendance
Aug	17	Coventry City	A	League	3-0	19,468
	21	**Sunderland**	**H**	**League**	**1-4**	**22,874**
	24	**Middlesbrough**	**H**	**League**	**1-1**	**24,705**
Sept	4	Southampton	A	League	2-2	14,450
	7	**Leicester City**	**H**	**League**	**0-0**	**24,105**
	14	Manchester United	A	League	1-4	54,984
	18	**Wycombe Wanderers**	**H**	**LC 2 - 1st Leg**	**1-0**	**6,482**
	21	**West Ham United**	**H**	**League**	**0-2**	**23,352**
	24	Wycombe Wanderers	A	LC 2 - 2nd Leg	1-1	6,310
	28	Chelsea	A	League	1-1	27,673
Oct	12	Leeds United	A	League	0-2	29,225
	19	**Derby County**	**H**	**League**	**1-1**	**27,771**
	23	West Ham United	A	LC 3	1-4	19,402
	28	**Everton**	**H**	**League**	**0-1**	**19,892**
Nov	2	Aston Villa	A	League	0-2	35,110
	18	Sheffield Wednesday	A	League	0-2	16,390
	25	**Blackburn Rovers**	**H**	**League**	**2-2**	**17,525**
	30	Wimbledon	A	League	0-1	12,608
Dec	**9**	**Newcastle United**	**H**	**League**	**0-0**	**25,762**
	17	Liverpool	A	League	2-4	36,126
	21	**Arsenal**	**H**	**League**	**2-1**	**27,384**
	26	**Manchester United**	**H**	**League**	**0-4**	**29,032**
	28	Leicester City	A	League	2-2	20,833
Jan	1	West Ham United	A	League	1-0	22,358
	4	**Ipswich Town**	**H**	**FA Cup 3**	**3-0**	**14,681**
	11	**Chelsea**	**H**	**League**	**2-0**	**28,355**
	19	**Tottenham Hotspur**	**H**	**League**	**2-1**	**27,303**
	26	Newcastle United	A	FA Cup 4	2-1	36,434
	29	**Coventry City**	**H**	**League**	**0-1**	**22,619**
Feb	1	Everton	A	League	0-2	32,567
	15	Chesterfield	A	FA Cup 5	0-1	8,890
	22	**Aston Villa**	**H**	**League**	**0-0**	**25,239**
Mar	1	Tottenham Hotspur	A	League	1-0	32,805
	5	**Sheffield Wednesday**	**H**	**League**	**0-3**	**21,485**
	8	Arsenal	A	League	0-2	38,206
	11	Blackburn Rovers	A	League	1-1	20,485
	15	**Liverpool**	**H**	**League**	**1-1**	**29,181**
	22	Sunderland	A	League	1-1	22,120
	24	Middlesbrough	A	League	1-1	29,888
Apr	**5**	**Southampton**	**H**	**League**	**1-3**	**25,134**
	19	**Leeds United**	**H**	**League**	**1-1**	**25,565**
	23	Derby County	A	League	0-0	18,087
May	**3**	**Wimbledon**	**H**	**League**	**1-1**	**19,865**
	11	Newcastle United	A	League	0-5	36,554

HOME ATTENDANCES

	AGGREGATE ATTENDANCE	HIGHEST ATTENDANCE	LOWEST ATTENDANCE	AVERAGE ATTENDANCE
League:	467,148	29,181	17,525	24,586
League Cup:	6,482	6,482	6,482	6,482
FA Cup:	14,681	14,681	14,681	14,681
All Competitions:	488,311	29,181	6,482	23,252

FINAL LEAGUE TABLE - FA PREMIER

Position	P	W	D	L	GF	GA	Pts
1. Manchester United	38	21	12	5	76	44	75
2. Newcastle United	38	19	11	8	73	40	68
3. Arsenal	38	19	11	8	62	32	68
4. Liverpool	38	19	11	8	62	37	68
5. Aston Villa	38	17	10	11	47	34	61
6. Chelsea	38	16	11	11	58	55	59
7. Sheffield Wednesday	38	14	15	9	50	51	57
8. Wimbledon	38	15	11	12	49	46	56
9. Leicester City	38	12	11	15	46	54	47
10. Tottenham Hotspur	38	13	7	18	44	51	46
11. Leeds United	38	11	13	14	28	38	46
12. Derby County	38	11	13	14	45	48	46
13. Blackburn Rovers	38	9	15	14	42	43	42
14. West Ham United	38	10	12	16	39	48	42
15. Everton	38	10	12	16	44	57	42
16. Southampton	38	10	11	17	50	56	41
17. Coventry City	38	9	14	15	38	54	41
18. Sunderland	38	10	10	18	35	53	40
19. Middlesbrough	38	10	12	16	51	60	39 *
20. Nottingham Forest	**38**	**6**	**16**	**16**	**31**	**59**	**34**

* Middlesbrough had 3 points deducted for failing to fulfil a fixture at Blackburn Rovers

AWAY ATTENDANCES

	AGGREGATE ATTENDANCE	HIGHEST ATTENDANCE	LOWEST ATTENDANCE	AVERAGE ATTENDANCE
League:	519,937	54,984	12,608	27,365
League Cup:	25,712	19,402	6,310	12,856
FA Cup:	45,324	36,434	8,890	22,662
All Competitions:	590,973	54,984	6,310	25,694

"WELL I NEVER FELT MORE LIKE SINGING THE BLUES"

NOT SURPRISINGLY, Stuart Pearce's brief managerial career at the City Ground had come to an end immediately after Forest's failed relegation battle. Perhaps more surprising, was his decision to leave the Club altogether, rather than stay on and lead the 'Reds' back into the Premiership. He joined Newcastle United on a free transfer, claiming this provided him with his only realistic chance of playing for his country again. If truth were known, the fact the new Forest Board had installed Dave Bassett alongside him as General Manager, had probably been the catalyst for his departure. As expected, Bassett immediately assumed the manager's role and quickly recruited former Malmoe manager Bobby Houghton as his assistant.

Alfie Haaland had also decided the First Division was no place for him to ply his trade and quickly legged it to Premiership Leeds United. With the two clubs at loggerheads over the transfer fee, a figure of £1.6 million was eventually set by a tribunal, thereby giving Forest a healthy profit on a player who never really caught the imagination of the Nottingham public. Another high-profile departure was that of Brian Roy, who brought his own personal nightmare to an end by joining German Bundesliga side Hertha Berlin in a £1 million deal. Having been a popular figure in his early days at the Club, he had eventually fallen from grace badly following some pretty feeble and inept displays during the cut and thrust of the relegation battle. Put him in a side challenging for honours and he would undoubtedly be an asset - but when the chips are down and it's time to roll up your sleeves and get stuck in, he is nowhere to be seen. Consequently, he left the City Ground under a cloud, and in contrast to all the pleasant things he'd had to say about the City upon his arrival in the summer of 1994, he left proclaiming to the world: "The only thing Nottingham has got going for it is Robin Hood - and he's dead!" Why players like him can't just depart with a bit of dignity and humility, goodness only knows? It seems some people just have to blame everyone and everything around them for their own shortcomings.

The new management team also decided Jason Lee's 'talents' would be better served away from the City Ground, and he was sold to Watford for a fee of £250,000. Not the most gifted player by any stretch of the imagination, he'd certainly endeared himself to the Forest faithful with his blood and guts performances in the red Garibaldi. Forest supporters have always appreciated a player who gets stuck in and he wasn't without his admirers by any means. This was indeed a player who was proud to wear a Forest shirt and wanted to play for the Club. The Collymores, the Roys, and latterly the Van Hooijdonks of this world, would do well to take a leaf out of his book.

Despite this mini exodus from the Club, 'Harry' Bassett had wasted little time in bringing in replacements. French utility man Thierry Bonalair arrived on a free transfer from Swiss side Neuchatel Xamax; midfielder Andy Johnson was prised away from Norwich City for a fee of £2.2 million; full-back Alan Rogers was brought in from Tranmere Rovers for £1.7 million; ex-England midfielder Geoff Thomas was captured on a free from Wolves; Swiss national goalkeeper Marco Pascola was lured from Italian side Cagliari for £750,000; and finally, central-defender Jon Olav Hjelde was brought in from Norway's top club Rosenborg for a bargain £600,000.

In their 'wisdom' the new City Ground hierarchy had dramatically increased season ticket prices and were charging £20 at the turnstiles for those who'd chosen instead to pay on the day. The 'justification' for this enormous hike in costs was: "Forest were essentially still a Premier Club, and if you want to fly first-class, you don't pay economy-class prices." Now somehow, when you're waking up on a cold and damp Saturday morning in November and you've got Crewe Alexandra at home to look forward to, those words just don't seem to ring true. Despite an increase of some 38 per cent in the cost of renewing our season tickets (mine and Thomas's that is), I decided once again to cough up without much of an argument. I did however send my written comments on the matter to new Chief Executive Phil Soar, although, not surprisingly, I never received the courtesy of a reply. (He was no doubt too busy counting his money). Whether the Nottingham public in general would be prepared to pay considerably more to watch First Division football than to see the likes of Manchester United, Chelsea and Arsenal on the Premier League stage, remained to be seen however.

THE opening fixture of the season was the kind you dream about all summer long - Port Vale away! Big Lee had managed to get half a dozen of us booked onto the 'Bus from the Sal' - now being organised by 'Hippo' from Clifton. It was going straight from town up to Ripley to pick up 'Slim' and all the other Derbyshire boys - or rather to meet up with them in a pub in the town centre at 9.30-a.m. Naturally, it was an hour before we left Ripley and headed off for our next port of call, Uttoxeter in Staffordshire. The coach was absolutely packed full and unfortunately it was such a crate, it was struggling like mad to make it up and down those rolling Derbyshire hills. Mind you, when looking around at some of the passengers, it was hardly surprising really. Big Lee, Slim and Hippo alone must have a combined weight of sixty stones!

Anyway, it finally crawled into Uttoxeter at around 11.30-a.m., and within no time at all, Andy, Bucko, Bodge, Big Lee and myself were sitting together in a pub putting the world to rights and reminiscing about the same old things we always reminisced about. Boy was it good to be back again, Port Vale or no Port Vale? It goes without saying, being the first day of the football season, it was an absolute scorcher, with temperatures easily up into the eighties. It also goes without saying it was very late when we left Uttoxeter some half a dozen pints later and headed for the ground. In fact, when we arrived at Vale Park, ours was the last of many coaches to be carefully manoeuvred into the visitors' parking enclosure just thirty yards outside the ground. There were hundreds of 'Travelling Trickies' queuing to get into the Hamil Road Stand, and they were bemused to see a bus load of drunken old farts singing loudly and banging on the windows like a bunch of retards.

The Visitors' Enclosure at Vale Park holds a total of 4,550 supporters - and in some comfort I might add - and it was absolutely full to it's capacity. You'd have hardly believed we'd just been relegated - and in such humiliating circumstances - and for the second time in just five seasons. The large following got behind the lads right from the start and, despite a less-than-convincing performance, 'Super Kevin Campbell' popped up to score the only goal of the game seconds before half-time. The pick of the new boys was undoubtedly Jon Olav Hjelde, but it was also good to see Steve Stone back in a red jersey and giving the side the sort of balance down the right, which had been so sadly lacking throughout the previous campaign. I wasn't the only one who was impressed with Hjelde's performance either, as an un-named Italian Serie A side reportedly tabled a £3 million bid for him within days of this game. Had the Forest Board accepted it, then the £2.4 million profit would surely have represented one of the 'deals of the decade.' Thankfully, with a speedy return to the Premiership being the Club's primary objective, the Italians received a polite: ''Thanks - but no thanks.''

This victory was followed by a thumping 8-0 triumph over Third Division Doncaster Rovers at Belle Vue in the first round of the League Cup two days later. Pierre Van Hooijdonk, Dean Saunders and that man Hjelde grabbed two goals apiece, with Geoff Thomas and Chris Allen completing the rout. This was followed by an impressive 4-1 hammering of Norwich City at the City Ground the following Friday evening in front of the Sky TV cameras. The new and very unpopular £20 entrance fee and the live television coverage, conspired to keep the crowd down to a modest 17,178, but those who did bother to turn up, went home mightily impressed, especially with Geoff Thomas, who scored a couple of cracking goals. Van Hooijdonk and Kevin Campbell grabbed the others.

On Saturday, 23rd August, Forest were due to play Oxford United at the Manor Ground. As Hoggy from Beeston was getting married the following week, Big Lee, in his capacity as 'Best Man,' decided his stag party should consist of a coach trip down to the game, followed by a night out somewhere on the way back up to Nottingham. On the strength of this, I arranged to stay over in Nottingham and made an early morning dash over to Chilwell to meet up with Andy outside the Blue Bell Inn. Having picked up the other 'fifty-odd' lads at various points around Beeston, the coach was due to pick us up last at around 9.30-a.m. Consequently, when it had failed to arrive by 10.00-a.m., Andy and I suspected something had gone decidedly wrong.

It was around fifteen minutes later when it finally turned up - a plush fifty-three seater carrying Big Lee, Hoggy...and eight other embarrassed souls. With just a dozen of us having bothered to turn up - obviously a popular lad, Hoggy - Lee had no choice but to cancel the whole thing there and then, losing his fifty pound deposit in the process. Mind you, we were still determined to make a day of it, with the first item on the agenda, a trip south to Oxford. We asked the coach driver to nip us into town in the vain hope someone would be running a bus from the Sal. As we piled off outside the Maid Marion Café, there was no-one around. As we stood there for a few seconds debating whether just to abandon the whole idea and go on an 'all-dayer' around town, a tatty old blue transit van suddenly screeched to a halt ten yards away and a youth stuck his head out of the window and yelled: ''Gooin' t' the match lads?'' And without a moment's hesitation, we were all nodding and piling on board. ''Jus' gorra nip up Hyson Green an' pick up mi mate, who's gooin' 'knocking' down in Oxford while we're at the match,'' explained another youth sitting in the front passenger seat of this excessively over-laden heap of scrap metal. ''OK mate," Lee responded, whilst the rest of us were thinking: "How the fuckin' ell are we gonna squeeze another bugger in 'ere, let alone one wi a bag full o' clobber 'e's teckin wi 'im to flog?"

'Knocking' is a word used to describe the activity of selling cheap, shoddy goods door-to-door to vulnerable housewives and pensioners at extortionate prices, on the pretence that you are a poor, hard-done-by individual who is out of work and just simply trying to scratch out a meagre living for yourself, your wife and your six kids. It originated in Nottingham, has been going on for a number of years now, and not surprisingly, has received a great deal of adverse publicity in both the local and national press. Several vanloads of door-to-door 'salesmen' pour out of Nottingham almost on a daily basis, heading for various parts of the country. There, they saturate carefully-selected housing estates with their low quality goods and are half-way home to Nottingham with pockets full of cash, before their unsuspecting victims have even had the chance to get this rubbish out of it's wrapper.

Within minutes we were pulling up outside the Acorn Club on Gregory Boulevard and were invited in by our newly-acquired 'friends' for a couple of 'swift 'arfs' before we set off for Oxford. So, there we were sitting in some grotty little Club in Hyson Green at 11 o'clock on a Saturday morning, boozing with a load of down-and-outs, whilst waiting for some youth we'd never even met who wanted to go 'knocking,' when we should have been enjoying Hoggy's stag party somewhere in Oxfordshire. And the irony is that when our 'knocking' friend did finally turn up, he took one look at us and decided to take this particular Saturday off. So it was around 11.30-a.m. when we actually left Hyson Green and another twenty minutes before we were on the motorway. Consequently, the plan was we'd drive straight down to Oxford and have a drink somewhere in the vicinity of the ground.

When we arrived outside the Manor Ground around two hours later and parked up, we were surprised to find the streets filled with travelling Forest supporters who were surrounded by dozens of Thames Valley police officers. "What's goin' on 'ere then?" we asked a small group of disgruntled youths who were arguing and jostling with a couple of stewards. "The Visitors' Enclosure's full up already and they've gone 'n shut the turnstiles," came the reply. This came as a complete shock to us, as the game wasn't even all-ticket and we'd been assured by the Forest ticket office that we'd be able to pay on the gate. The truth of the matter was, that Oxford had offered an allocation of terrace tickets to Forest, but - for reasons known only to themselves - they'd declined. Consequently, with the Visitors' End of the ground full, and no further seat tickets available for visiting supporters, an estimated 1,500 supporters had made a wasted 100-mile journey south. Thanks a million Forest.

Hoggy's big day was rapidly turning into a disaster and on top of this, hundreds of supporters were locked out and determined to make their feelings known. The result was that the Thames Valley police reacted in the only way they know how: by going on the offensive. Firstly, they brought in the horses, followed by the dog-handlers, and suddenly, what had been nothing more than a low-key protest, was in serious danger of turning into a full-scale confrontation. As far as we were concerned, if we weren't going to get into the game, we were at the very least going to enjoy a drink or two in the vicinity of the ground. We left the bulk of the protesters arguing the toss with the police and scuttled off to a bar down at the bottom of the street. There were dozens of Forest supporters inside enjoying a drink and generally trying to make the most of a bad job. However, this so-called 'free society' we're all living in, doesn't in fact extend itself to mere football supporters. So within minutes, 'Mr. Plod and Co.' arrived on the scene and ordered the landlord to stop serving immediately.

Once again, tempers were beginning to fray, and once again, we left the two sides arguing it out and marched briskly down the road to the next pub about half a mile away. Incidentally, this was also full of Forest supporters. As it was a glorious day, we got the beers in and sat outside with around fifty others. We heard the faint roar of the crowd in the distance, which confirmed the game had now kicked off. It was so frustrating sitting there knowing the lads were in action just a few hundred yards away and we couldn't get in to see them. However, our frustration diminished more and more as each pint went down. In fact, after about three or four, we were all feeling pretty happy sitting there in the warm afternoon sunshine, having a laugh, a bit of a sing-song, and generally bothering nobody - especially the landlord, who was coining it in.

It was too good to last though and sure enough by about 3.30-p.m., the boys in blue had arrived on the scene once again, only this time they decided to observe from a distance. They formed a cordon all the way around the front of the car park, allowing no-one to enter or leave. Whilst we all sat enjoying a beer, they stood in line staring at us as if we were a bunch of low-lifes, about to erupt at any moment into an orgy of violence and anarchy. They had cameras trained on us the whole time, van-loads of reinforcements waiting around the corner ready to pounce if necessary, and their approach was wholly confrontational. Their body language suggested we were the absolute scum of the earth and they just couldn't wait to get stuck into us. The hilarious thing about it all, was the fact there wasn't a hooligan amongst us. When you've been going to Forest as long as I have, you know who the hooligans are - you've seen their faces and observed their activities often enough from a distance. And you'd think, with all the intelligence the police have at their fingertips these days, they'd know the difference between a gang of hardened thugs and a group of law-abiding citizens out enjoying a day at the match. As far as I was concerned, the whole exercise was just a complete waste of taxpayers' money. I bet the real criminals around Oxford and the rest of the Thames Valley area were having a field day. I wonder how many little old ladies were mugged on the way back from the shops that day, while this bunch of shirkers were standing around in the sunshine doing absolutely bugger all but spoiling for a fight?

Anyway, I for one hadn't come all this way not to see some football. So, about fifteen minutes from full-time, I slipped off through the crowd with Bodge and jogged slowly back up the road towards the ground. We made our way up the alleyway which leads to the Visitors' Enclosure and as soon as the gates opened to let a couple of supporters out, we slipped in un-noticed and onto the terraces. Chris Bart-Williams had earlier put Forest 1-0 up, and they were hanging on grimly with ten minutes to go. Goalkeeper Dave Beasant, who Bassett had just signed on loan from Southampton, was playing a blinder and protecting our slender lead almost single-handedly. When the final whistle blew it was a big relief and as we poured out of the ground with the rest of the crowd, it was satisfying to know we'd at least managed to see some of the game, albeit just a few minutes.

Within minutes we were back at the pub with the rest of the gang and almost immediately, the boys in blue decided it was time to close the pub and send us all on our way. We'd had enough of Oxford anyway and it's over-aggressive police force, so we all jumped back in the van and headed for home. We stopped off for a couple in Northampton on the way home and still got back to Nottingham in time to have a few more in Beeston - after all, we were on a stag party! All in all, for a day which had started out so badly, Hoggy's piss up had turned into a memorable one after all. Not only had we enjoyed a pleasant afternoon in the sunshine; we'd also returned home with three points in the bag, and were sitting comfortably at the top of the First Division with maximum points from our first three games.

Given the behaviour of the police down in Oxford, it was somewhat ironic that the following Saturday when we entertained Queens Park Rangers at the City Ground, the Forest Review carried a feature congratulating the Club's supporters on their impeccable behaviour during the disastrous relegation campaign of the previous season. Voted the Club with the best-behaved supporters in the Premier League by a team of independent observers, Club chairman Irving Korn had recently been presented with a cheque for £20,000 from Geoff Thompson, Vice Chairman of the Football Association and Chairman of the Fair Play Committee. I felt like sending a copy of this article to the Chief Constable of Thames Valley Police and telling him to stick his fifteen hours of wasted video footage right up his arse - sideways!

A 4-0 victory over QPR maintained Forest's position at the top of the table, although when Frank Clark returned to the City Ground four days later with his struggling Manchester City side, they brought us right back down to earth with a bump, leaving Nottingham with a convincing 3-1 victory. When we could only manage a 0-0 draw away to Swindon the following Sunday and then lose again by one-goal-to-nil at Sheffield United a week later, suddenly everything in the garden wasn't looking quite so rosy. We were now down to fifth place in the table with thirteen points from seven games and things began to look even worse when Second Division Walsall came away from Nottingham with a 1-0 victory in the first leg of a League Cup second round tie. Although some pride was subsequently restored with a 1-0 home League victory over Portsmouth on Saturday, 20th September, this was short-lived and a 2-2 draw at Walsall's Bescott Lane Stadium on Wednesday, 24th September, sent us crashing out of our favourite Cup competition.

One thing which we were beginning to learn however, was that a side managed by 'Harry' Bassett was never on the floor for long and the victory over Portsmouth had put the 'Reds' back on top of the table, a position which was consolidated with a further 1-0 victory, this time over Stoke City, and also at the City Ground. During the month of September, the Forest Board announced the Club was to be floated on the Alternative Investment Market of the London Stock Exchange. Whilst this had always been the intention of the new owners, it just didn't seem the right time to me. Surely the ideal time to embark on a venture of this nature, would be immediately following a return to the Premiership, when the popularity of the team in and around the City of Nottingham would be at it's very peak. Despite my own reservations, I was however determined to fulfil a life-long ambition and duly applied for my 500 shares.

Amidst a great deal of hype from the Board, the flotation took place on Friday, 10th October

SEASON 1997/98

1997 - a significant day in the Club's illustrious history. Unfortunately, although the Club had now acquired a further 4,500 'legitimate' shareholders, a disappointing total of only £1.9 million had been raised. Having acquired the Club for a paltry £16 million in the first place, Messrs. Wray and Scholar were already showing their true colours to the Nottingham public - they were nothing more than hard-nosed businessmen, in it purely to make a fast buck. Not only had they made Forest the most expensive football team to watch outside the Premier League - and by an absolute mile at that - but they'd now embarked on an ill-timed flotation exercise at a time when a disastrous relegation campaign was still fresh in the minds of all Forest supporters.

As I've said before, there is never a dull moment in the fortunes of this Football Club of ours and during the run up to the flotation exercise, revelations were beginning to emerge from the Continent that Belgian club Anderlecht had indeed bribed the referee prior to Forest's ill-fated UEFA Cup semi-final defeat in Brussels back in 1984. As explained earlier on in this book, following alleged blackmail attempts by an intermediary apparently involved in the affair, Belgian police had been called in by Anderlecht to investigate the matter in February 1997. It transpired that former chairman Constant Vanden Stock was now admitting the sum of one million francs (£18,000) had been paid to the Spanish referee Guruceta Muro the day after the game. Vanden Stock's son Roger - the current Chairman of the club - confirmed this in a radio interview although he was trying to justify the whole affair by claiming the payment had been merely a loan.

Ask any Forest supporter who was in Brussels on 26th April 1984, and they will tell you the same story: quite simply, on the night, we were robbed right, left and centre. An outrageously dodgy penalty decision and a sensationally disallowed Paul Hart 'goal' in the final minute of the game, were just two of many mind-blowing decisions which went against us on the night. Anderlecht's subsequent 3-0 victory, gave them a 3-2 aggregate victory overall and put them through to the Final where they lost to Spurs on penalties. Paul Hart's powerful header would have put Forest through on the 'away goals' rule and why the referee was never put on the spot and asked to justify his inexplicable decisions, no-one will ever know. It's certainly a night that I, and at least 4,000 other travelling Forest supporters, will never, ever forget. (See Chapter 18: "Who's yer father, Who's yer father, Who's yer father - referee?"). Sadly though, even to this day, and despite promises of a full investigation by UEFA, Forest have received no compensation of any description.

Whilst the Board were involved in both the flotation of the Club and negotiations with UEFA over the bribery affair, 'Harry' Bassett caused consternation amongst the fans by accepting a £2.5 million offer from West Ham for Club captain Colin Cooper - arguably one of Forest's most accomplished defenders since the days of Kenny Burns and Larry Lloyd. Fortunately, due to his great love of the Club and the City, it was Cooper who scuppered the deal. He decided to stay on and help in the fight for promotion. What on earth Bassett was thinking, accepting a bid for one of our most influential players, only he will ever know, but Forest supporters breathed a collective sigh of relief when he announced he was staying. More good news came our way in October when Steve Stone signed a new four and a half year contract, said to be worth a staggering £17,000 a week. Now, as good a player as he was, that's an awful lot of money for someone who couldn't hit a barn door from two yards. For an attacking midfielder, his goals-per-game ratio was appalling, with most of his efforts ending up in either the upper tier of the Trent End or the Bridgford Stand. For that amount of money, if I'd been the manager, I'd have had him back in for extra training every afternoon and made him concentrate on his shooting, until he got it absolutely right. Peter Shilton used to come back in every day for extra training during his days at the Club - entirely of his own volition - and he was the best goalkeeper in the world at the time, by a long chalk.

WITHOUT ever looking the class act we'd been during the 'Clough' era, 'Bassett's Reds' continued to play effective, if not always attractive, football. And in fairness to him, although he'd brought with him to the City Ground a reputation for playing the long-ball game, he never really employed these tactics whilst Forest manager. Under his guidance, the 'Reds' remained in the top two of the First Division right throughout the months of October, November and December. By the time they entertained Swindon Town on Boxing Day, watched by a crowd of 26,500, they'd accumulated a total of 45 points from 23 games and were sitting in second position in the table, with only 'goals scored' separating them from leaders Middlesbrough. They'd won 13, drawn 6, and lost only 4, scoring a total of 37 goals and conceding only 21 along the way. What's more, with a total of 28 goals between them in all competitions, Kevin Campbell and Pierre Van Hooijdonk had both re-discovered their scoring touch in impressive fashion. Being the dead-ball specialist within the team, the lanky Dutch striker had scored the lion's share of the goals with a personal tally of 18. Nevertheless, 'Super Kev' was quite definitely in blistering form and was at last beginning to win over the previously unimpressed Nottingham public in a big way.

During the months of November and December, several players had also found themselves surplus to requirements at the City Ground. David Philips had joined Huddersfield Town on a free transfer; Andrea Silenzi - never given a fair chance on Trentside in my opinion - had left the Club and returned to Italy by mutual consent; and Dean Saunders had, rather surprisingly, joined Sheffield United on a free transfer. Earlier on in the season, Bassett had turned down a £400,000 bid for him from Premiership club Everton, insisting he was worth far more and giving the impression he was insulted by the offer. Considering we now had businessmen and entrepreneurs running the Club, I just couldn't come to terms with that one?

Forest's first-half performance against Swindon was clinical and efficient, and at 3-0, the game was effectively over as a contest by the half-time interval. Two excellent strikes from Campbell and another from the hugely popular Andy Johnson had put us in an unassailable position. During the half-time interval, the entertainment was almost as good. Since the very first game of the season, a small, but extremely enthusiastic band of supporters in Section T of the Executive lower tier, had been waging a battle with the stewards - and sometimes the police - because of their wish to remain standing during the game. Now for some obscure reason, in today's all-seater stadiums, this is simply not allowed. Apparently it contravenes Paragraph 7, Sub-section 3, of the previously mentioned ''Not allowed to enjoy yourself at a football match Act, 1996''.

Consequently, minutes into every match, the same old game of cat and mouse would begin. Firstly the stewards would move in to tell the two hundred-strong gang to be seated or else. The offending individuals would politely tell them to ''bollocks'' and remain standing. They'd scuttle off dejectedly, their authority having been well and truly undermined, only to return with their supervisors minutes later and threaten the 'ringleaders' with fifty lashes and seven days' solitary confinement. At this point some of them would concede some ground and perch themselves on top of their seats. Then things would get really, really heavy and the 'blue meanies' would move in, making a couple of arrests. The rest of the lads would then think to themselves: ''Fuck it - what's the point?'' and just sit down and sulk. Anyway, in order to avoid a big fine under the above-mentioned regulations, the Club's hierarchy had written to all season ticket holders in this section of the ground prior to this game, telling them to ''comply with the regulations or else.''

Now I just can't for the life of me see what harm they were doing? Alongside the Main Stand 'A' Block and the Trent End, they were always there right behind the team, helping to generate a half-decent atmosphere, even if it was a dull and boring game. Surely the type of supporters who are the life and soul of any football club? Well apparently not it would seem - at least to those faceless men in grey suits who, in their infinite wisdom, decide what is and what is not acceptable for us in this life of ours. Unfortunately, these are the same anonymous people who make it their duty to blight every aspect of our daily lives. The same boring anoraks who get paid a king's ransom to come up with one pointless new idea and associated set of rules after another. You know, like the genius who sat in his office one day and came up with the 'brilliant' one to stop calling linesmen 'linesmen' and instead, refer to them as 'referee's assistants.' What a fucking useful idea that was! Now we can't sit through a game of football on the telly, without hearing the commentator mutter those immortal words: ''I thought the linesman was wrong to give off-side there - whoops sorry, I mean the referee's assistant. Sorry, I just can't get used to calling him that.'' No - 'cause that's the whole idea - you're not ever meant to get used to it, cause the whole thing about these people, is that they exist for no other reason than to make everyone's life even more complicated than it already is! (There - got that one off my chest.)

Anyway, back to the story and back to those particular individuals in Block T. Their determination to stand up for their rights was so intense, I was really beginning to admire them from my vantage point in the Upper Bridgford. Some 'smart Alec' amongst them, obviously figuring to himself: ''Well if you can't beat 'em, join 'em,'' had brought to the game about fifty florescent green vests and had dished them out to all the lads during the half-time interval. Just as the second half was about to get under way, they all came trooping back to their seats and stood there pretending to be stewards. Those of us in the Bridgford Stand who'd been watching this miniature soap opera unfold during the course of the season, just fell about laughing and, it has to be said, so did the did the genuine stewards. I swear I even saw a policemen break into a smile.

It turned out to be a very productive festive period, and the 'Reds' followed up their eventual 3-0 victory over Swindon with a 3-2 win at Frank Clark's relegation-threatened Manchester City. It seemed that, having played a significant part in Forest's relegation from the Premiership the previous season, Clarky was now on the verge of going one better and taking City into the Second Division. Now, for a club that size and with their resources, this was nothing short of scandalous.

Our attentions were then drawn to the FA Cup once again and a trip south to Charlton

Athletic - a team we had beaten so comprehensively at home in the League back in November. After Forest's fifth goal had gone in during that particular game, the 'A' Block had taunted the surprisingly large following from South London with chants of: *"Twenty quid - and you're 5-2 down, Twenty quid - and you're 5-2 down!"* and: *"What a waste of twenty quid!"*

But this time around, it was Charlton and their fans who had the last laugh, as the men from the Valley ripped Forest apart, running out 4-1 winners and sending us crashing out of the Cup at the first hurdle. So convincing was their victory, the score actually flattered Forest. It was back to Nottingham with our tails well and truly between our legs after this game, believe me.

Although the New Year had begun with a heavy defeat, the 'Reds' did exactly what they'd been doing all season and bounced back immediately the following week with a 2-1 victory at home to Port Vale. This kept them in second place in the table and still on target for one of the two automatic promotion places. As exciting as the play-offs are from a neutral's point of view, they must be absolute hell on earth to the genuine supporters of the clubs involved. Give me the 'humdrum' of a Runners-up position any day! The first month of 1998 also saw another two departures from the Club, with assistant manager Bobby Houghton leaving to become coach of the Chinese national side and young Bobby Howe joining Swindon Town in a £30,000 deal.

Having lost 1-0 against Norwich at Carrow Road on Saturday, 17th January, Forest then made amends the following Saturday when a strike by Colin Cooper earned them all three points in a 1-0 victory in North-West London against QPR. When lowly Oxford United - complete with ex-Forest striker Nigel Jemson - visited the City Ground the following weekend, the vast majority of the 18,392 crowd were expecting an easy three points for the 'Reds.' However, a superlative performance by winger Joey Beauchamp - which included two excellent individual strikes - led to a shock 3-1 victory for the visitors and once again reminded supporters there was a long way to go before promotion was assured. Although they had gone into this game at the top of the table, and with a five-point lead over second-placed Middlesbrough, the North-East club had a game in hand and were still hot on their heels. Once again, they bounced back the following week with a precious 1-0 victory over Portsmouth at Fratton Park.

On Thursday, 12th February, the Club's brand new 2,000 square foot Superstore was officially opened for business, although the majority of supporters had to wait until the home game against Huddersfield Town the following Tuesday evening to have a look around for themselves. I have to say, following all the hype; my own initial reaction was one of disappointment, although as time has gone by I've grown to like it more and more. In fact, I'd now go as far as to say it is well in keeping with a club of Forest's stature. There is a good range of merchandise, which is of decent quality, despite being a little pricey. However, as it's all in a good cause, the average supporter like myself doesn't mind paying a bit over the odds.

A 3-0 victory over Huddersfield - in which Van Hooijdonk scored an incredible thirty-yarder from out on the left - enabled us once again to leapfrog over new leaders Middlesbrough and back to the top of the table. Although Forest and Boro' were taking it in turns to head the Division, Sunderland were now also emerging as automatic promotion contenders. With only fifteen games left, manager Dave Bassett decided to strengthen his squad by drafting in on-loan winger Damien Johnson from Premiership Blackburn Rovers, and paying Swansea City £175,000 for the services of central-defender Christian Edwards. The tension was really beginning to mount and, as Forest could only manage to draw their next two games away to Stoke City and Tranmere Rovers, they once more allowed Boro' to return to the top of the table. However, it was now time for the showdown of the season, as the two 'giants' of the First Division prepared to slug it out at the City Ground on Sunday, 1st March - kick off 1.00-p.m. - in front of the Sky Television cameras.

Having played a total of 16 League fixtures at the City Ground so far this season, Forest's average home attendance stood at 19,020. Now considering the appalling relegation battle of the previous campaign, the massive hike in season ticket prices, the twenty quid entrance fee on match-days, the 'quality' of some of the opposition, and the fact not one visiting club had taken up their full allocation of tickets all season, I don't think this was at all bad. Not wonderful by any means - but not bad, in my opinion. On the other hand of course, Middlesbrough, with their brand new Cellnet Riverside Stadium (a virtual carbon copy of Derby's 'Shite Park' incidentally), had suddenly, out of nowhere, attracted a thirty-thousand-plus following and had been packing them in all season, despite having also dropped out of the Premiership with Forest less than twelve months before. Now I can remember only a few short years earlier, when they were struggling to attract gates of 8,000 for their home fixtures, and their old stomping ground, Ayresome Park, was never full to it's 20,000-ish capacity. In fact, had AC Milan or Barcelona been visitors to Teesside, I doubt if they'd have filled the ground.

Now fair play to the club's ambitious owners, who'd had the foresight to make a significant £16 million investment in their new stadium; spent heavily on bringing top quality foreign players such as Emerson, Juhnino and Ravenelli into the squad; and managed to tap in to football's recent and meteoric rise in popularity in a big, big way. But to suggest Middlesbrough supporters were the finest and staunchest in the land, would have been somewhat exaggerated, I feel. However, in keeping with their other neighbours in the North-East, they also seem to believe the hype that in order to support your football club with a passion and an undying loyalty, you just have to be a Geordie or a Mackem or whatever they call themselves on Teesside. Well this quite simply isn't the case. There are a million and one factors to take into consideration when determining such things and the loyalty of any club's support should be judged over decades, not just over a couple of seasons.

Anyway, not surprisingly, the 2,500 Boro' fans amongst the 25,286 crowd were feeling very sure of themselves on this occasion with all the usual predictable chants early on in the game such as: *"Shit Ground - No Fans,"* and *"Sell all your tickets - You couldn't sell all your tickets."* The fact they were top of the table coming into this game and had failed miserably themselves to sell their full allocation of tickets was of course entirely lost on them. But it wasn't long before they were sinking down into their seats and hiding their heads in shame, as Forest produced undoubtedly their finest performance of the season. They walloped them 4-0 and once again knocked them off top spot. Colin Cooper, Pierre Van Hooijdonk (2) and Kevin Campbell were the goal-scoring heroes, but the whole team contributed to a totally one-sided affair, which led to hundreds of the previously cocksure visitors scurrying off to the exits long before the end with chants of: *"Cheerio, Cheerio, Cheerio,"* from the delighted home contingent ringing in their ears. And I loved every minute of it!

Just three days after this excellent performance against Boro', their North-East neighbours Sunderland, third in the table, arrived at the City Ground to do battle with the new Division One leaders. Such was the interest in this game, a crowd of 29,009 turned out, with at least 5,000 having travelled down from Wearside (and Cotgrave). Despite Forest being full of confidence prior to this encounter, Sunderland took the game by the scruff of the neck and absolutely blitzed their way to a comprehensive 3-0 victory. They battled for every loose ball as if their lives depended on it and it really did seem like men against boys out there for the whole of the ninety minutes. How Sunderland weren't at the top of the table, I just couldn't fathom, having watched them simply destroy Forest?

In true Bassett style however, the 'Reds' bounced back impressively the following Saturday, running out easy 4-1 winners over Crewe Alexandra at Gresty Road. With Van Hooijdonk injured, the versatile Chris Bart-Williams played up front alongside Kevin Campbell and scored one of the goals himself. The impressive Campbell helped himself to a hat-trick, and in doing so increased his personal tally for the season to 16. This was followed up with another valuable three points a week later, courtesy of a 3-0 home victory over Bury. Prior to this game the top of the table had looked like this:

Position		P	W	D	L	GF	GA	Pts
1.	Middlesbrough	36	21	8	7	61	36	71
2.	**Forest**	**36**	**21**	**8**	**7**	**60**	**33**	**71**
3.	Sunderland	36	20	9	7	67	38	69
4.	Charlton	36	18	8	10	63	46	62

So with 10 games to play, it was looking almost certain the two automatic promotion places would be claimed by two of the current top three teams. But there was still a lot of nail-biting to do in the East Midlands and the North-East of England. And with the likes of Birmingham City, Charlton, Sheffield United, Ipswich and Wolves still to play, Forest were assured of a difficult run-in to the end of the season.

The game against Birmingham at St.Andrews on Saturday, 21st March, provided me with my first 'home' game in ages and for once it was me who could relax on a Saturday morning whilst waiting for Lee, Andy, Gaz and Bucko to arrive. As they were stopping over at my house for the evening, we were assured of a full day's drinking, and sure enough, we were sat in my local - the Journey's End in Acocks Green - by 11.30-a.m. As St.Andrews is only around three miles from where I live, we stayed in the Journey's until around 2.30-p.m. and then jumped into taxis, which dropped us off outside the ground about ten minutes before kick off. Forest's performance was by no means a classic, and when they went 1-0 down late on in the second half from a dubious looking penalty, the large following from Nottingham feared the worst. However, Van Hooijdonk had other ideas, crashing a twenty-yard free kick low into the corner of the net with less then ten minutes to go, and then majestically curling in a twenty-five-yard strike in the dying seconds. We left the ground accepting we'd been extremely lucky to steal all three points, but agreeing that playing badly and still winning is how Championships are won. We certainly enjoyed our night out in Birmingham on the strength of it anyway.

The following Saturday, Forest were not so lucky and for the second time this season were on the receiving end of a four-goal blast from Charlton at the Valley, although two goals from Campbell gave the final score an air of respectability. The three encounters between these two teams - including the third round FA Cup tie - had yielded no less than 18 goals. But, all credit to the players; they bounced back immediately with an emphatic 3-0 victory over Sheffield United at the City Ground on Wednesday, April 1st. This was followed by a 2-1 home victory the following Sunday against play-off hopefuls Ipswich Town, a convincing 3-0 victory at Bradford City one week later, and an excellent 3-0 home victory over Wolves on Easter Monday in front of the Sky Television cameras. With just three games left, the 'Reds' were four points clear at the top of the Division, and were almost home and dry.

When they travelled to Stockport County on Saturday, 18th April, I was on my way down to Luton to attend our Graham's wedding. We all had to settle for score flashes on the radio during the afternoon reception, although the 2-2 result was hardly what we had hoped for, especially as other results had gone against us. However, a victory over Reading the following weekend would assure us of promotion, and once more the Sky Television cameras would be there to follow the action. To add to the tension, a defeat for Reading would consign them to the Second Division the following season.

In view of the significance of this game, I decided I'd stay over for the night in Nottingham. I needed a few stiff drinks just to get me through this fixture, and assuming we achieved promotion, there was no way on this earth I was going to miss out on the celebrations. Just to be on the safe side, I also booked a day off work on the Monday. The pubs around the ground were packed solid before the game, although with a 1.00-p.m. kick off, there wasn't much chance of having a skin-full. Still there was a tremendous atmosphere around the place, and despite the fact the game was live on TV, there was an excellent crowd of 29,302. Unfortunately, the players looked as if the pressure was too much to bear and put in a below-par performance for most of the ninety minutes. However, just as the game seemed to be petering out into a disappointing 0-0 draw, up popped Chris Bart-Williams in the middle of the penalty area. He latched onto a Colin Cooper free kick, skinned his marker, and despatched the ball firmly into the far corner of the net. The whole place just erupted, with 28,000-plus Forest supporters going absolutely ballistic. European Cups, League Championships, League Cups, I've seen the lot - but never have I been so ecstatic in all my life. We were going back to the Premier once again. And this time, with an ambitious new Board in charge, that's where we were bound to stay.

When the final whistle blew, the celebrations began in earnest. Inevitably, thousands of fans swarmed onto the pitch from every part of the stadium. My son Tom and his mate Scott, had swapped their Bridgford Upper tickets for seats in the lower tier of the Executive for this game, just so they could join in the traditional end of season pitch invasion. I watched them running across the pitch with their flags in their hands and saw them disappear into the heaving mass of fans who'd gathered outside the players' tunnel. When the celebrations were over, we headed for Wurlitzer's where the partying had already begun. After a quick one in there, we dashed across the Bridge to the Aviary, where Derby versus Leicester from 'Shite Park' was just kicking off on the big screen. There were quite a few Reading fans in there also; drowning their sorrows following their descent into Division Two. I must admit that despite my sheer elation at Forest's promotion, I did feel very sorry for them and a little guilty that it should have been Forest who finally pushed them through the relegation trapdoor.

Now although both Leicester and Derby are our staunchest East Midlands rivals, when it comes to sheer unadulterated hatred and contempt amongst Forest supporters, there really is no contest whatsoever. When Leicester took a first-minute lead in this game, the whole pub just erupted with joy. People were jumping up and down as if Kevin Campbell himself had just bagged another for the 'Reds'. When they went 2-0 up, then 3-0 up, and then 4-0 up - all within the first twenty minutes or so - I was really beginning to think I'd died and gone to heaven. The 'Super Reds' promoted to the Premiership not ninety minutes earlier, a night of celebration in the finest city on the planet ahead of me, and the 'Sheep-shaggers' 4-0 down at home in front of a live television audience of millions. Now this was just too damn good to be true!

Once we'd finished laughing at our 'woolly-backed' neighbours, we headed off into town and got down to some serious partying. Although town is always pretty full on a Sunday night, it's not unbearably so. When we piled into Yates' at around 8.00-p.m., it was predominantly full of Forest supporters and very soon everyone was jumping around and singing, much to the annoyance of the resident DJ - you know, that really good-looking bloke - who was turning up the volume as loud as he could and looking all miserable because nobody wanted to listen to his stupid bloody music. All we wanted to do was celebrate and so the singing just got louder and louder and he just got more and more annoyed. All the old favourites were coming out and when Slim and his gang from Ripley got going, the whole place was in full swing. Without a doubt, the favourite song of the night was: *"Well I never felt more like singing the blues, When Forest win and Derby lose, Oh ba-by, You've got me singing the blues, Sing! Sing! Sing!"* which seemed to go on and on for most of the night. The celebrations went on long after closing time and a mob several hundred strong hung around on the pavement outside Yates' singing loudly and refusing to go home until the early hours of the morning. Boy was I glad I'd booked the next day off work. When I finally woke up around lunchtime I felt like I'd just gone ten rounds with Mike Tyson. Still, it's not every day of the week your team wins promotion back to the Premier League is it?

With a total of 93 points in the bag, we were not only promoted, but also Champions of the First Division. Consequently, half the population of Nottingham wanted tickets for West Brom away - the final game of the season on Sunday, 3rd May. As I was once again staying over in Nottingham for the Sunday evening celebrations, I drove across the M42 at seven o'clock in the morning to meet the lads, as we were going to West Brom on a coach from the City Ground which was due to leave at around 9.30-a.m. So, within an hour of arriving in Nottingham from Birmingham, I was trundling back across the M42 to West Brom. The things you do for love?

There were six or seven thousand 'Travelling Trickies' inside the Hawthorns for this one, including several hundred who nearly caused a riot by jumping up and down in the Birmingham Road End when Steve Stone gave Forest a first-half lead. Many fans who'd been unable to get hold of tickets in Nottingham, had simply taken a midweek trip to 'Brum' and bought tickets for the home sections of the ground. Fortunately, the police reacted quickly to prevent a full-scale incident and led the uninvited guests around the edge of the pitch and into the packed Visitors' Enclosure in the Smethick End of the stadium. The game ended one apiece and the players were given a standing ovation when they came back out onto the pitch after the final whistle. Even the West Brom fans who remained inside the stadium sportingly joined in the ovation.

This had been an excellent promotion campaign. Harry Bassett had achieved the objective he'd been set when brought into the City Ground - an immediate return to the Premier League. This had been his eighth promotion campaign during his career. And although Forest hadn't always appeared convincing, they hadn't lost two games in succession throughout the entire season. After each of their eight defeats in the League, they'd bounced straight back the following game with either a draw or a victory. They'd also ended the season with a tally of 94 points from 46 games and scored a total of 82 goals along the way. Strikers Van Hooijdonk and Campbell had also enjoyed a prolific partnership up front, scoring an incredible 57 goals between them in all competitions. Van Hooijdonk's total of 34 for the season, was the highest by a Forest player since the days of Wally Ardron.

And despite paying the highest admission charges in the whole of the Nationwide League, Forest supporters had also once again turned up in numbers. An average League attendance at the City Ground of 20,583 is not to be sniffed at, especially as the Visiting Supporters' Section was more often than not, virtually empty. The highest attendance of the season had been the 29,302 for the visit of Reading, with the lowest being the 16,701 for the visit of Stockport County. Although we didn't quite look like a Premiership outfit, a summer spending spree of around £10 million on three quality players would do the trick. All we had to do now was wait for Messrs. Soar, Wray and Scholar to live up to their promises, that once Premiership status had been restored, they would be investing heavily to ensure the Club's long term future in the top flight.

SEASON 1997/98 – STATISTICS

FOOTBALL LEAGUE DIVISION ONE – FIXTURES

Date		Opposition	Venue	Competition	Score	Attendance
Aug	9	Port Vale	A	League	1-0	12,533
	11	Doncaster Rovers	A	LC 1 - 1st Leg	8-0	4,547
	15	**Norwich City**	**H**	**League**	**4-1**	**17,178**
	23	Oxford United	A	League	1-0	9,486
	27	**Doncaster Rovers**	**H**	**LC 1 - 2nd Leg**	**2-1**	**9,908**
	30	**Queens Park Rangers**	**H**	**League**	**4-0**	**19,169**
Sept	**3**	**Manchester City**	**H**	**League**	**1-3**	**23,552**
	7	Swindon Town	A	League	0-0	13,051
	13	Sheffield United	A	League	0-1	24,536
	17	**Walsall**	**H**	**LC 2 - 1st Leg**	**0-1**	**7,841**
	20	**Portsmouth**	**H**	**League**	**1-0**	**17,292**
	24	Walsall	A	LC 2 - 2nd Leg	2-2	6,037
	27	**Stoke City**	**H**	**League**	**1-0**	**19,061**
Oct	3	Huddersfield Town	A	League	2-0	11,258
	18	**Tranmere Rovers**	**H**	**League**	**2-2**	**17,009**
	21	**West Bromwich Albion**	**H**	**League**	**1-0**	**19,243**
	24	Reading	A	League	3-3	12,610
Nov	**1**	**Crewe Alexandra**	**H**	**League**	**3-1**	**18,268**
	4	Bury	A	League	0-2	6,137
	8	Sunderland	A	League	1-1	33,160
	15	**Birmingham City**	**H**	**League**	**1-0**	**19,610**
	22	**Charlton Athletic**	**H**	**League**	**5-2**	**18,532**
	26	Middlesbrough	A	League	0-0	30,143
	29	Ipswich Town	A	League	1-0	17,580
Dec	**6**	**Bradford City**	**H**	**League**	**2-2**	**17,943**
	14	Wolverhampton Wanderers	A	League	1-2	24,635
	20	**Stockport County**	**H**	**League**	**2-1**	**16,701**
	26	**Swindon Town**	**H**	**League**	**3-0**	**26,500**
	28	Manchester City	A	League	3-2	31,839
Jan	3	Charlton Athletic	A	FA Cup 3	1-4	13,827
	10	**Port Vale**	**H**	**League**	**2-1**	**17,639**
	17	Norwich City	A	League	0-1	17,059
	24	Queens Park Rangers	A	League	1-0	13,220
	31	**Oxford United**	**H**	**League**	**1-3**	**18,392**
Feb	7	Portsmouth	A	League	1-0	15,033
	17	**Huddersfield Town**	**H**	**League**	**3-0**	**18,231**
	21	Stoke City	A	League	1-1	16,899
	24	Tranmere Rovers	A	League	0-0	7,377
Mar	**1**	**Middlesbrough**	**H**	**League**	**4-0**	**25,286**
	4	**Sunderland**	**H**	**League**	**0-3**	**29,009**
	7	Crewe Alexandra	A	League	4-1	5,759
	14	**Bury**	**H**	**League**	**3-0**	**18,846**
	21	Birmingham City	A	League	2-1	24,663
	28	Charlton Athletic	A	League	2-4	15,815
Apr	**1**	**Sheffield United**	**H**	**League**	**3-0**	**21,512**
	5	**Ipswich Town**	**H**	**League**	**2-1**	**22,292**
	11	Bradford City	A	League	3-0	17,248
	13	**Wolverhampton Wanderers**	**H**	**League**	**3-0**	**22,863**
	18	Stockport County	A	League	2-2	9,892
	25	**Reading**	**H**	**League**	**1-0**	**29,302**
May	3	West Bromwich Albion	A	League	1-1	23,012

HOME ATTENDANCES

	AGGREGATE ATTENDANCE	HIGHEST ATTENDANCE	LOWEST ATTENDANCE	AVERAGE ATTENDANCE
League:	473,430	29,302	16,701	20,583
League Cup:	17,749	9,908	7,841	8,874
All Competitions:	491,179	29,302	7,841	19,647

FINAL LEAGUE TABLE - DIVISION ONE

Position	P	W	D	L	GF	GA	Pts
1. **Nottingham Forest**	**46**	**28**	**10**	**8**	**82**	**42**	**94**
2. Middlesbrough	46	27	10	9	77	41	91
3. Sunderland	46	26	12	8	86	50	90
4. Charlton Athletic	46	26	10	10	80	49	88 *
5. Ipswich Town	46	23	14	9	77	43	83
6. Sheffield United	46	19	17	10	69	54	74
7. Birmingham City	46	19	17	10	60	35	74
8. Stockport County	46	19	8	19	71	69	65
9. Wolverhampton Wanderers	46	18	11	17	57	53	65
10. West Bromwich Albion	46	16	13	17	50	56	61
11. Crewe Alexandra	46	18	5	23	58	65	59
12. Oxford United	46	16	10	20	60	64	58
13. Bradford City	46	14	15	17	46	59	57
14. Tranmere Rovers	46	14	14	18	54	57	56
15. Norwich City	46	14	13	19	52	69	55
16. Huddersfield Town	46	14	11	21	50	72	53
17. Bury	46	11	19	16	42	58	52
18. Swindon Town	46	14	10	22	42	73	52
19. Port Vale	46	13	10	23	56	66	49
20. Portsmouth	46	13	10	23	51	63	49
21. Queens Park Rangers	46	10	19	17	51	63	49
22. Manchester City	46	12	12	22	56	57	48
23. Stoke City	46	11	13	22	44	74	46
24. Reading	46	11	9	26	39	78	42

* Promoted via the play-offs

AWAY ATTENDANCES

	AGGREGATE ATTENDANCE	HIGHEST ATTENDANCE	LOWEST ATTENDANCE	AVERAGE ATTENDANCE
League:	392,945	33,160	5,759	17,084
League Cup:	10,584	6,037	4,547	5,292
FA Cup:	13,827	13,827	13,827	13,827
All Competitions:	417,356	33,160	4,547	16,052

"BIG FAT RON'S RED AND WHITE ARMY!"

1998 WAS a year in which the football season just seemed to go on and on. Typically, England had experienced their usual mixture of poor form and misfortune during France '98, losing out eventually in the knock out stages to old adversaries Argentina. A dubious first-minute penalty and a harshly awarded free kick just outside the box in the first half had led to both of the Argentinian's goals. An Alan Shearer penalty and a Michael Owen wonder goal had seen England first equalise and then take a deserved lead, with the Argies looking well and truly rattled for most of the first pulsating forty-five minutes. Then of course, early in the second half, disaster struck when that cheating slime-ball Simeonie went down as if he'd been blasted by a shotgun. David Beckham brushed his leg feebly with the instep of his boot, as he lay pole-axed on the floor following a scything tackle by the Argentine midfielder. It's history now that Beckham received his marching orders and England had to battle on with only ten men for the rest of the game. It's also history that we were denied a dramatic last-minute winner when the referee inexplicably disallowed Sol Campbell's powerful header into the roof of the net following a corner.

Despite battling all the way through extra time like men possessed, the ten-man England team then had to experience the misfortune once again of going out of the biggest tournament in the world by way of a penalty shoot-out. On this occasion David Batty was the player unfortunate enough to miss the vital spot kick and go down in history as the man responsible for our exit from the competition. With football being essentially a team game, the fact such important matches are decided on this basis, is a complete and utter injustice in my book. Give me extra time followed by the 'golden goal' rule any day. Still, as much as I hate the 'Frogs', it was good to see them go on and win the competition on their home soil with some of the most attractive football ever seen.

Whilst all this was going on, Nottingham's footballing public - well the red and white ninety per cent at least - were waiting with baited breath for Messrs. Scholar, Wray and Soar to come up with the kind of Premiership transfer kitty which they'd earlier promised would materialise once promotion back to the Premier League had been secured. And when the announcement came, it was without doubt the biggest anti-climax of the decade. The total sum made available to Harry Bassett for his assault on the biggest league in the world? - £3 million. What an insult to the good folk of Nottingham! After all the bullshit we'd been given twelve months earlier when the 'gang of three' were trying to justify their extortionate ticket prices to the thousands of disappointed and angry supporters who'd just seen their team relegated and were now being forced to pay Premiership prices to watch Nationwide League matches - this was almost too much to take. And just add insult to injury, what else had they got on their agenda for us? Well of course, yet another massive hike in season ticket prices.

But as the summer months unfolded, the goings on down at the City Ground just went from the sublime to the ridiculous. Like a bolt out of the blue, striker Kevin Campbell was sold off to Turkish club Trabzonspor for a fee of £3 million and contract rebel Scott Gemmill was placed on the transfer list (I wasn't too unhappy about the latter personally). And all this while Dave Bassett was away on holiday. Having gone away thinking he'd secured the futures of both players, he came home to find his pre-season preparations in tatters. Just what were this Forest Board of Directors up to? Amidst all this, striker Ian Moore was also hived off to Stockport County for £800,000 and the squad was now looking seriously depleted. And, as if this wasn't bad enough, frustrated by the Club's unwillingness to invest £2 million in his Dutch International team-mate Wim Jonk, who'd decided to leave PSV Eindhoven, Pierre Van Hooijdonk announced to the world he'd played his last game for the 'Reds' and wouldn't be returning to the City Ground at any price. Now wasn't this the same player we'd paid £3.5 million for in 1997 and who'd signed a four and a half year contract? And what's more, exactly where in his contract did it state he'd be responsible for deciding which players the Club would purchase?

The whole thing was now becoming a farce and it was quite apparent just where all the decisions regarding the buying and selling of players were being made - the boardroom and not the manager's office. And if we needed any further evidence that Scholar and his cronies were attempting to secure Premiership survival on the cheap, then we had to look no further than the list of players who had been brought into the Club. These included:

- Unknown striker Jean-Claude Darcheville on a season's loan from French side Rennes.
- Similarly unknown French full-back Matthieu Louis-Jean from Le Havre, also on loan.
- Thirty-five-year-old midfielder Glyn Hodges on a further three-month contract following his free transfer from Hull City the previous March.
- Striker Dougie Freedman from First Division Wolves for £900,000.
- Winger Andy Gray (son of Frank) from Leeds United for £200,000.
- Midfielder Nigel Quashie from First Division QPR for £2.5 million.

CHAPTER 33

In addition to this, former Fulham and Brentford manager Mickey Adams had also been drafted in as assistant manager. And the final straw came when Club captain and supporters' favourite Colin Cooper was allowed to move back to his hometown club Middlesbrough in a £2.5 million deal, with the season only days old. Now forgive me if my mathematics are wrong, but by my calculations this little lot added up to £6.3 million in players sold and £3.4 million in players bought - a profit to the Club of £2.9 million. So, not only had the Board of Directors failed to come up with the Premiership transfer package promised when acquiring the Club on the cheap, but they'd also now reneged on their meagre offering of £3 million as well. The whole thing was a shambles and an insult to the many thousands of supporters who'd stood by the team through thick and thin and put their hard-earned money into the Club, year after year, after year. It was blatantly obvious from the word go, this was going to be yet another long and difficult season for Forest's long-suffering fans.

WITH Forest's opening fixture of the season being a Monday evening 'Sky Special' against Champions Arsenal at Highbury, we had to sit out the opening Saturday of the new campaign. And although most Forest supporters feared the worst, the 2-1 defeat which the 'Gunners' inflicted upon us, turned out to be a surprisingly close encounter. When Geoff Thomas struck an excellent equaliser in the 76th minute, following a perfect one-two on the edge of the box, it looked for all intents and purposes as if the 'Reds' were about to secure an unlikely point. Unfortunately though, Marc Overmars rounded off a fine individual performance on the night, by grabbing the winner just three minutes later. Forest emerged with a lot of credit from the game though, with the breathtaking speed of Frenchman Jean-Claude Darchville in particular catching the eye.

The following Saturday, Midlands rivals Coventry City were in town for the season's City Ground curtain-raiser and on this occasion a well struck effort from Steve Stone six minutes into the second half, earned Forest all three points. Much to everyone's delight, this was followed up a week later by an excellent 2-1 victory against Southampton at the Dell, with second-half goals from Darchville and Stone. So, with the 'Reds' sitting pretty in third place in the table with six points from three games, the pre-season doom and gloom was now beginning to look just a little bit misplaced. In fact, as we prepared to take on Everton at home on Tuesday, 19th September, we did so in the knowledge that a victory would send us to the top of the table.

Unfortunately for us, our new found optimism proved somewhat premature, as second-from-bottom Everton took complete control of the contest, and ran out easy winners with two clinically-taken goals from the impressive Duncan Ferguson. Judging by the unusually large contingent of Everton fans amongst the crowd of 25,610, they must have had an inkling before this game that a surprise was on the cards. One thing which did annoy me though - other than the result - was the fact that when the attendance figure for the game was flashed across the electronic scoreboard during the second half, the travelling Everton fans responded with chants of: "*Shitty Ground, Shitty Ground, Shitty Ground,*" as if to say: "Is that the best that you can do?"

Well all I can say in response is this: It's alright when your team's enjoyed an unbroken 44-year run in the top flight of English football, which stretches right back to the 1954/55 season - but when you've suffered two relegation seasons in only the last six years, your fan base is bound to have been eroded just a little. In fact, it's fair to say, it can take a number of years to woo the missing thousands back into the fold. And considering Everton are meant to be one of the so-called 'Big Five' of English football, I could only ever remember them once bringing anything like a decent following to Nottingham, and that was way back in season 1985/86 when they were neck and neck with Merseyside neighbours Liverpool for the League Championship, going into the last couple of games. That's not to say their support at home is unimpressive though, with crowds of over thirty thousand being the norm these days. But you only have to look back to the early part of Howard Kendall's very successful reign as manager in the eighties, to see this hasn't always been the case. During this particular period in time, Goodison Park attendances of around 13,000 were not unusual.

The game against Everton was when the tide really began to turn for Forest. As everyone knows, there really is only one club around when it comes to setting records, and that's NFFC. The longest unbeaten record in the old First Division (42 games); the longest unbeaten record in the Premier League (25 games) - to name but two. But our red-shirted 'warriors' were now about to accomplish the kind of record you wouldn't wish upon your worst enemy:

- September passed by without another victory - in fact a 0-0 draw and two defeats added up to one measly point out of a possible twelve;
- October brought one draw and two defeats out of three and saw us plummet into the bottom three, despite investing £1.5 million in Crystal Palace striker Neil Shipperley and Van Hooijdonk finally calling a halt to his one-man strike;
- November brought with it three draws and two defeats:
- And just to round the year off nicely, December saw us scrape another two draws and suffer another three defeats.

Not surprisingly, we ended the year in what had now become very familiar Premiership territory for the Club: anchored firmly to the bottom of the table. And although manager Harry Bassett - just like Cloughie and Frank Clark before him - seemed to have completely lost the plot, it wasn't as if the team had enjoyed one ounce of good fortune all season. For example, three successive home games - starting with the 'Sheep' at home on Monday, 16th November - had all ended 2-2, after Forest had looked certain to capture all three points. Having gone behind against Derby, goals in quick succession from Dougie Freedman and Van Hooijdonk gave us the lead, only for us to throw it away at the death. And when the lads trooped off at half-time to a standing ovation and with a 2-0 lead under their belts against Aston Villa in our very next City Ground encounter, we looked as if we were a team of world-beaters. How we managed to throw this one away - and almost lose it in the dying seconds - God only knows? But throw it away we did. And finally, just to cap it all, having once again secured a seemingly unassailable 2-0 lead against fellow strugglers Blackburn Rovers in our very next home game, we committed 'hara-kiri' yet again, allowing new signing Nathan Blake to score his first two goals for the Lancashire outfit - his second deep into injury time - to bring the scores level and send the 22,013 crowd home in despair.

By this time, being a Forest supporter was becoming a very difficult thing to live with; the humiliation of one disaster after another - both on and off the pitch - was almost unbearable. Not only had we seen the Board dismantle last season's Championship-winning team before a ball had even been kicked in anger, but we'd now gone a total of seventeen League games without a victory, thereby equalling the existing Premiership record which we had also set two seasons before. On top of this, everyone associated with this once-proud Club of ours, had had to endure the indignation of seeing rebel Dutchman Pierre Van Hooijdonk walk back into the City Ground and, worst of all, back into the first team - that's how desperate we were. If truth be known, had the team been riding high in the table, the overwhelming majority of supporters would have happily pushed the sulking, mardy-arsed twat off the top of Trent Bridge, rather than allow this self-opinionated, arrogant git to come sauntering back into Nottingham without so much as an apologetic bone in his lanky body? Unfortunately, beggars can't be choosers, and we needed him badly in our side. Besides which, we could always kick the scumbag bag into touch once he'd helped us rescue our Premiership status.

Following the 1-1 draw at home to fellow-strugglers Southampton on Monday, 28th December - the final game of 1998 - a crowd of several hundred disgruntled and angry supporters converged on the Main Stand car park and began to demonstrate against the Board outside the main entrance to the ground. Although there were half-hearted chants of: *"We want Bassett out,"* the main thrust of the supporters rage was undoubtedly aimed at 'Cockney Spivs', Scholar and Wray, who between them were rapidly turning our Club into the laughing stock of football. Not surprisingly, no-one from the Club was available for comment, and the crowd eventually began to disperse having made their point, and having gained a little publicity.

I think deep down most supporters felt extremely sorry for Dave Bassett and angry at the way the Club's hierarchy had treated him. They'd originally brought him in with the objective of achieving an instant return to the Premiership, a task he'd achieved with distinction. All he'd asked of them in return, was a realistic sum of money to invest in the kind of quality players capable of keeping Forest in the top flight. On that score, they had failed him badly. What's more, the Club's overall transfer policy seemed to be entirely outside the manager's jurisdiction, with players being sold against his will and on at least a couple of occasions, after he had seemingly secured their long term futures with the Club, albeit only verbally.

Given the situation with Van Hooijdonk, any honourable and reasonable Board of Directors, would have let him rot in Holland for the remaining three years of his contract, by which time he'd have been well past his prime and neither use nor ornament to anyone. But no - there was too much of their precious money tied up in him for that wasn't there? So what did they do? Much to the obvious consternation and even embarrassment of Bassett, they went cap in hand to him whilst he was skulking away in his native Holland and almost begged him to come back to England and straight back into the team. In fairness to Bassett - a man of integrity - he just about managed to contain his thoughts and opinions on the matter, although on the inside he must have been absolutely seething - and justifiably so. The Forest supporters deserve some credit too. Many other supporters up and down the country would have run him out of town; either that or a lynch mob would have been waiting to string him up from the nearest lamp-post. But without exactly welcoming him home, the contempt in which he was held by the majority, was suppressed for the good of the team.

Having been dumped out of the League Cup by Manchester United's reserve team back in October, we now faced the prospect of a further Cup embarrassment when we were drawn out of the hat against First Division strugglers Portsmouth in the FA Cup third round. A true measure of just how pissed off a club's supporters are with the fortunes of their team, can always be made by how many bother to turn up when they are unable to use their season tickets to get in and have to buy a ticket in advance or on the day of the game. Well, on Saturday, 2nd January, 1999, the Forest supporters gave an overwhelming indication of just how they felt at that precise moment in time, when a crowd of only 10,092 turned up to watch this tie - and at least 2,500 of these were 'Pompey' supporters!

Mind you, as I sat there watching probably the most inept, lacklustre display I'd ever witnessed by a Forest team, I couldn't help wishing I'd stayed at home also. They were absolutely diabolical and didn't seem to have a clue. Either that, or they just didn't care - it was one or the other? Consequently, they were played off the park by a supposedly inferior team and ended up suffering yet another demoralising 1-0 defeat. No-one really cared that we'd been dumped out of the Cup again, but anyone who cared about NFFC who was there that day, couldn't help but feel anger at what we had now been reduced to: we were in a worse position now, in terms of quality and attitude on the field of play, than we'd been two years previously when Messrs. Scholar, Wray and Soar came onto the scene carrying glossy pamphlets full of empty promises.

The scenes in the Main Stand car park after the game said it all. This time the mob wanted blood and on this occasion the police seemed to sense the crowd meant business, as they threw a cordon around the main entrance. The mob was angry and wanted some action now, before it was too late. Once again, Scholar and Wray were the main targets of abuse, but it has to be said, they were also calling for managerial heads to roll. Rumours soon spread around the car park that Bassett had quit. Chants of: *"Stuart Pearce's Red and White Army,"* began to ring out. When the police made a half-hearted attempt to disperse the crowd, everyone sat down on the floor and refused to budge. This was our Club, and we weren't going to sit around peacefully any longer while a bunch of 'Cockney Wideboys' hammered nails into our coffin. *"Oh Sandy-Sandy, Sandy-Sandy-Sandy-Sandy-And-er-son,"* chanted the mob over and over again, more in anger than in hope. And this time, no-one was going anywhere until the people responsible for our plight had heard what we had to say. Whether it made any difference no-one really knows, but within a couple of days, the Forest Board had reacted in the only way they knew how: by making Dave Bassett the scapegoat and dismissing him. And just to be consistent, they didn't even have the guts or the decency to tell him to his face - they announced it in a tabloid newspaper on Monday, 4th January. What a bunch of low-lifes we had running our Club!

IN a last ditch attempt to rescue the Club's Premiership status, the Forest Board immediately set out to obtain the services of football's very own 'Red Adair', Mr. Ron Atkinson. Having worked similar minor miracles in the past at both Coventry City and latterly Sheffield Wednesday, they were convinced he was the man who could steer the 'Reds' out of trouble without having to spend millions of pounds in the transfer market in the process. True to form though, just when we needed someone with his charisma and presence to come breezing into the Club without delay, Big Ron was away topping up his suntan in the Caribbean. Whilst it was a fairly safe bet a man of his calibre and reputation would find it almost impossible to resist the challenge of rescuing a Club like Forest - and you kind of got the impression he'd always held the 'Reds' in fairly high regard - it was quite clear he wanted to finish off his holiday first, at the very least.

In the meantime, whilst Atkinson was thinking over their offer - and no doubt making a few very important phone-calls - Scholar and his cronies put assistant manager Micky Adams in temporary charge for the next vital League game away to Coventry City. Apparently held in high esteem by the players, at least a couple of them had gone on record as saying that Adams was the ideal man for the job. Judging by the quality of the performance at Highfield Road however; you wouldn't by any means have got the impression they were trying to put him in the frame for the job. They were absolutely abysmal, and worst of all, allowed City's Nottingham-born striker Darren Huckerby to plunder a superb hat-trick in a 4-0 defeat.

As we sat there anchored firmly to the foot of the table, I couldn't help lamenting the number of Nottingham-born players who were - much to my immense frustration - currently plying their trade in the Premier League, but alas at other clubs. In fact when you analysed things further, three of the top ten strikers around at the time were all born and bred in the City. Firstly, there was Huckerby himself - a former Clifton All-White and, as a youngster, well known in local football; then there was Chris Sutton - then of Blackburn Rovers - born and raised a Forest supporter, but destined to move from his Nottingham home to East Anglia as a young teenager; and not forgetting of course, Andy 'Honest guv - I'm a Cockney really' Cole, a former star of Nottinghamshire schools football, despite having rather mysteriously developed a 'Landen' accent as an adult. (Now come on Andy - there's no shame in being a Nottingham lad from Lenton Abbey - you don't have to pretend to be a Cockney for people to think you're a 'cool dude'. After all, since you left these parts, we've even acquired running water and electricity, and rumour has it, there's now even a boutique, two wine bars, a restaurant and one night-club in the City Centre!)

Now I just couldn't help despairing at the depths our once great Club had sunk to, when local players of this calibre were being allowed to slip through the net as youngsters. Can you imagine them even wanting to play for anyone else during the heady days of the Clough/Taylor era, when winning both domestic and European honours was the norm down on Trentside. Without wishing to sound like a crusty old fart or anything, can you imagine if Forest had missed out on Nottingham-born players such as Tony Woodcock, Viv Anderson, Garry Birtles, Stevie Hodge and Chris Fairclough

- all players who'd not only served their hometown Club with great pride and distinction, but had also gone on to do the same for their country. It's enough to make Robin Hood turn in his grave.

Whilst on this subject - assuming they were all of the same generation - how do you think this squad of Nottinghamshire-born players would fare in today's Premier League?

1. Steve Ogrizovic - Goalkeeper (Ex-Coventry City)
2. Viv Anderson - Full-back (Ex-Forest / Arsenal / Manchester United)
3. Henry Newton - Full-back / Left-half (Ex-Forest / Everton / Derby County)
4. Chris Fairclough - Central-defender (Ex-Forest / Tottenham Hotspur / Leeds United)
5. Chris Sutton - Striker / Central defender (Ex-Norwich City / Blackburn Rovers / Chelsea / now Celtic)
6. Mark Draper - Midfielder (Ex-Notts County / Leicester City / Aston Villa / Southampton)
7. Gordon Cowans - Midfielder (Ex-Aston Villa / Wolves)
8. Steve Hodge - Midfielder (Ex-Forest / Tottenham Hotspur / Aston Villa / Leeds United)
9. Andy Cole - Striker (Ex-Arsenal / Bristol City / Newcastle United / now Manchester United)
10. Tony Woodcock - Striker (Ex-Forest / Cologne / Arsenal)
11. Garry Birtles - Striker (Ex-Forest / Manchester United / Notts County / Grimsby Town)
    Subs:
12. Darren Huckerby - Striker (Ex-Newcastle United / Coventry City / Leeds United / now Man City)
13. Nigel Pearson - Central-defender (Ex-Sheffield Wednesday / Middlesbrough)
14. Mark Hately - Striker (Ex-Coventry City / Glasgow Rangers)
15. Brian Kilkline - Central-defender (Ex-Notts County / Coventry City)
16. Trevor Morley - Striker (West Ham United)

With the Nottingham-born management team of Peter Taylor and David Pleat at the helm, they could line up in the following, formidable 4-3-3 formation:

I reckon this lot could more than hold their own in the top flight today. It's just a pity the loss to the City of players such as Cole, Huckerby, Sutton and the like, has allowed the 'Nottingham' to all but disappear out of 'Nottingham Forest'.

HAVING accepted the challenge, Big Ron was installed as Forest boss until the end of the season. Whilst finishing off his Caribbean holiday, he'd appointed Peter Shreeves as his assistant and sent him immediately into the City Ground to get on with the job. Forest's next fixture was at home to title contenders Arsenal on Saturday, 16th January and Atkinson wasn't due to arrive in Nottingham until the day of the game. Shreeves was therefore given the task of quickly assessing the Forest squad and putting together a team for the visit of the 'Gunners'.

Having finally jetted in from Barbados, Atkinson met his players for the first time at a Nottingham hotel, just hours before kick off. Naturally, his high-profile appointment attracted massive publicity and when he came out of the players' tunnel immediately prior to the game, he became completely submerged amongst a sea of photographers. And much to the amusement of the watching millions who tuned into Match of the Day that evening, he walked straight past the Forest dugout and took his seat on the Arsenal bench next to their bewildered substitutes and coaching staff. Having eventually realised his error, he had a laugh and a joke with everyone around him and made his way towards the correct dugout. Unfortunately, it wasn't long before the smile had been wiped completely off his face, as defender Martin Keown gave the visitors the lead with a powerful header. And despite a promising display from the 'Reds', this proved to be the only goal of the game and once again Forest were in the record books, having now gone eighteen Premiership games without a victory.

Although the Forest Board hadn't allocated him much in the way of transfer cash, he did however quickly manage to scrape together the princely sum of £1.1 million for the purchase of utility player Carlton Palmer from Southampton. He was drafted straight into the heart of the defence for the trip to Everton the following Saturday, where he was the star performer in a rare Forest victory - their first for more than five long months. Van Hooijdonk scored the only goal of the game, sending Forest's band of travelling supporters home with a smile on their faces at last. Loan signings John Harkes from American club D.C. United and Stale Stensaas from Glasgow Rangers also made their debuts in this game.

A crowd of 30,025 then filed into the City Ground exactly a week later for the visit of League leaders Manchester United. Atkinson had made one or two quips about the prospect of facing first Arsenal and then Man U in his first two home games in charge, but even he couldn't have predicted the outcome of this one, as Forest suffered their most humiliating defeat in decades. It has to be said United were awesome on the day with seemingly every player in their side playing at the very top of his game. There just wasn't a weak link anywhere in the team and all eleven players seemed to have perfected the art of playing football. In contrast to this, Forest just seemed like a team of 'no-hopers' with neither the desire nor the ability to cope with their rampant opposition.

The game proved to be a personal triumph for Ole Gunnar Solskjaer, who came off the bench to score four of United's eight goals in a remarkable thirteen-minute period during the second half. Andy Cole and Dwight Yorke also helped themselves to two goals apiece as United, inspired by the brilliant David Beckham, went on to record the biggest away victory in the history of the Premier League (yet another record involving Forest!). Alan Rogers scored Forest's consolation in this staggering 8-1 defeat.

This had been by far the heaviest defeat during my thirty-three seasons of watching the 'Reds' and in fact, their heaviest since they were on the receiving end of a 9-1 thrashing by Blackburn Rovers way back in 1937. Although many, many thousands of disgruntled and humiliated supporters had left the ground long before the final whistle and, no doubt, retired to the pub, I was determined to hang on in there right to the death. Despite having to endure a humungous amount of piss-taking from the 4,700 United supporters in the stands below us, those of us who did stay until the end, did so out of pride and passion for our Club. I can't say I blame them really for rubbing our noses in it - I'm sure we've done exactly the same thing to others on many occasions in the past - but the fact it was Man U, made it all the more difficult to bear. Their supporters are without doubt, the most arrogant bunch of tosspots around. With their tiresome chants of: *"You've only come to see United"* and *"Part-time supp-ort-ers,"* is it any wonder really that ninety-nine per cent of genuine football supporters in this country detest them intensely? I'd love to see them endure a couple of relegation campaigns followed by a few years in the obscurity of the Nationwide League, then we'd see just how loyal most of them really are? It wouldn't be quite such an attractive proposition for them, getting up so early on a Saturday morning to tackle the two-hundred-mile journey to Old Trafford from their homes all around the country, just to see them pitting their wits against Crewe Alexandra?

It was obvious to Big Ron that more new faces were needed, and very soon former West Ham United winger Hugo Porfirio had been drafted in on loan from Benfica until the end of the season. He was joined by former Tottenham and Glasgow Rangers defender Richard Gough from American side San Jose Clash, and although at 36, very much coming to the end of his career, he was still a class act. Unfortunately, the entire Forest squad now seemed to be suffering from some sort of mental blockage and every game appeared to be lost psychologically before it had even kicked off. They came out onto the pitch looking as if they were already defeated and seemed to lack confidence and co-ordination right from the very first whistle.

The long-suffering Forest supporters did everything they could however to lift their spirits and the atmosphere inside the City Ground couldn't be faulted in any way. Some sections of the crowd may have been justifiably criticised in the past for not getting behind the team, but no-one could question the enthusiastic support the players were getting right at this moment in time. The atmosphere was almost one of defiance; we knew we were going down, but we weren't going to allow a small thing like relegation to dampen our spirits.

Following our annihilation at the hands of United, we went on to lose 2-1 at West Ham the following Saturday and then 3-1 at home to Chelsea in front of 26,351 hearty souls a week later. A 0-0 draw against Charlton at the Valley in our next match was then followed by a 2-1 home defeat by Newcastle United on Saturday, 6th March, at which stage, we were six points adrift at the foot of the table. Then the unthinkable happened - we actually won a game - surprisingly beating Wimbledon by three-goals-to-one at Selhurst Park. It was now over seven months since we'd last won at home, but remarkably City Ground attendances still remained in excess of 20,000, week in, week out.

The victory at Wimbledon proved nothing more than a flash in the pan, and was followed by further defeats at home to Middlesbrough and away to Leeds United, the score-lines being 2-1 and 3-1 respectively. However, despite being eight points adrift at the bottom, the 'Reds' put in a resilient display against Liverpool in front of a City Ground crowd of 28,374 on Easter Monday to earn a share of the spoils. Jamie Redknapp gave the visitors a first-half lead, with Dougie Freedman equalising for Forest. And when Michael Owen restored Liverpool's lead, the score-line had a very familiar look about it, with Forest staring defeat in the face yet again. But a last-minute free kick on the edge of the box gave Pierre Van Hooijdonk the perfect opportunity to level the scores. He placed the ball on the ground, stepped back a few paces, then coolly ran up and despatched it into the top corner of the net - a trademark goal. We knew this wasn't about to save us from relegation, but it was still nice to go home undefeated for a change.

Whilst the loyalty of Forest's support in general was to be applauded, one particular supporter had recently earned his place in the Premier League Hall of Fame and that was Eberhard Kleinrensing of Duisburg, Germany. 'Ebby' as he is otherwise known to the majority of Forest supporters completes a two-day, two-thousand-mile round trip to watch Forest home and away and has been doing so since adopting the 'Reds' as his team during our European Cup winning era back in the late-seventies/early-eighties. His devotion to the Club has cost him his marriage and ended another long-term relationship, with both women eventually deciding they could no longer play second fiddle to Forest. And Ebby has also had to cough up an estimated £14,000 a year to fund his trips to the U.K. All this however, has endeared him to Forest supporters who voted him the Club's number one fan, thereby rightly enabling him to take his place in the FA Premier League Hall of Fans which had been set up within the Hall of Fame.

Joining Ebby as Forest's 'celebrity fan' in the Hall of Fame was golfer Lee Westwood, who was born and bred in Worksop. With the North Nottinghamshire town's close proximity to Sheffield, most of it's footballing population are either Wednesday or 'Blades'' fans, but Lee chose to be different and has thankfully followed Forest since his childhood days. Whilst competing in major golfing tournaments around the world, it is not uncommon for Lee to stop in the middle of the fairway to ask how Forest are getting on. Who knows, one day, many years in the future, when his successes in the game have brought him untold wealth, he may become Forest's very own benefactor along the lines of Jack Walker at Blackburn or Sir Jack Hayworth at Wolves? Well, we can all have our dreams can't we?

Had Forest lost at home to Liverpool and other results gone against us, defeat the following week against the 'Sheep' at 'Shite Park' would have finally consigned us to the First Division. Now, there was no question we weren't about to be relegated, but to be sent down by our sworn enemy would simply have been too much to bear. So it was a huge relief to be heading down the A52 knowing even another humiliating defeat wouldn't finally seal our fate. I hadn't as yet been within ten miles of the 'Sheep's' brand new 'Leggo Land' stadium, vowing never to do so unless it was to watch the 'Reds' in action. In fact I had completely avoided the A52 ever since the ground had first been built. I would sooner undertake a fifty-mile detour across country than drive through the centre of 'Shitesville', such is my loathing for that particular part of the world.

Anyway, with it's close proximity to the ground, we decided Long Eaton would be the perfect place for our pre-match entertainment, so it meant an early dash across from the West Midlands for me that Saturday morning. As I'd arranged to stay in Nottingham the night, I could park the car up and head off into Long Eaton knowing I could happily drown my sorrows if we lost or, dare I say it, have a few celebratory drinks if we won. I met Big Lee and the rest of the gang in the town centre and we embarked on an almighty pub-crawl before jumping into taxis for the short trip to the ground with - as usual - only minutes to spare before kick off.

Now I have to say, even as biased as I am, at first glance, 'Shite Park' really does look the part and I was initially quite impressed. However, taking into account the speed with which the place was built, and the comparatively low cost of construction, I couldn't help but wonder just what a dozen or so harsh winters might do to it's slightly feeble looking exterior. The Executive Stand (recently re-named the Brian Clough Stand of course) down at the City Ground is now twenty-odd-years-old and looks as brand spankingly new as it did way back in the early-eighties. What's more, as the ground has been gradually re-developed over the years at some cost, it has taken on a look of permanence. I can easily imagine it staging matches in another hundred years' time, although I can't say the same for 'Shite Park', which will probably by then have long since fallen down.

Another feeble performance from Forest on the day saw us fall to our twentieth defeat of the season and meant we had to endure an uncomfortable amount of taunting from the majority of the 32,217 crowd. Although there was a reasonable turn out from Nottingham, 28,000-plus versus 3,500 is just no contest, especially when you're as crap as we were at that particular moment in time. I couldn't help wondering though, from where the 'Sheep' had managed to conjure up this new 'army' of fans, especially considering that in recent decades at least, they had been consistently unable to fill the 22,000-capacity Baseball Ground. Perhaps like Middlesbrough before them, the relatively palatial surroundings of their new ground, when compared to the slum-like conditions which they had been used to previously, had managed to tap into the new breed of supporter which the game seems to have attracted in recent years. You know, those very same people who are just as likely to disappear back into the woodwork once the novelty of the new stadium has worn off, or when another more interesting and familiar pass-time such as sheep-shearing becomes fashionable again.

WITH relegation an absolute certainty, winger Steve Stone finally ended his twelve-year stint at the City Ground, when he joined Aston Villa at the beginning of March in a deal worth £5 million. Whilst Stoney had showed a degree of loyalty to the Club over the years by staying put after two previous relegation seasons, it shouldn't be forgotten Forest had also been extremely loyal to him during several low spots in his career. They'd stuck by him on each of the three occasions he'd broken his leg, not to mention his near twelve-month lay-off only two seasons before, following a serious knee injury. They'd also given him massive financial rewards, with a £17,000 per week contract. I couldn't help feeling there was an element of 'the big fish in a little pond' about Stoney and that life away from the City Ground might just condemn him to a period of obscurity - only time will tell. Contract rebel Scott Gemmill had also jumped ship, securing a £250,000 move to fellow strugglers Everton where he'd teamed up with former Forest striker Kevin Campbell, who was there on loan from Turkish side Trabzonspor following a very public falling out with his chairman. I can't say I was sorry to see Gemmill go, and considering he was near to the end of his contract and about to become a free agent, the token quarter-of-a-million transfer fee represented a good piece of business for Forest.

Following another defeat at home the following Saturday - against Tottenham of all people - we travelled to Aston Villa (a home game for me) on Saturday, 24th April, knowing for certain this time, that anything less then a Forest victory would mean relegation once again. Now you'd think, in the circumstances, the players would at least want to go down fighting - after all, teams like Coventry and Southampton do it year after year. But no, yet another pathetic, 'couldn't give a shit' performance from all eleven players, saw us lose by two-goals-to-nil and give away our status as a top-flight club, like it didn't mean a thing. Not that it was any surprise really to the Forest supporters who'd had to witness one gutless performance after another all season. The fact there were barely five hundred amongst the crowd of 34,492 said it all. If there had been even a one per cent chance of us battling it out to the bitter end, half of Nottingham would've turned out for this game. Even Big Ron had had enough of the players' attitude and announced his retirement from the game at the end of the season.

I really don't know what it is about this Club of ours, but it seems to have lurched from one crisis to another since Brian Clough threw in the towel and retired at the end of season 1992/93. Admittedly, he started the rot by getting us relegated in the first place, but considering his awesome achievements at the Club; he could be forgiven for this one minor indiscretion. People outside of Nottingham had always said Brian Clough 'was Nottingham Forest' and without him, the Club would be nothing. Now, whilst acknowledging we would never have become the force in the game which we had under his leadership, I for one could never in the past accept this argument. However, taking into account some of the things I've witnessed down at the City Ground since his departure, I am now beginning to wonder. A look at Forest's record in the Premiership since it's formation at the beginning of the 1992/93 season tells it's own sorry story:

Season	P	W	D	L	GF	GA	Pts	Final Position
1992/93	42	10	10	22	41	62	40	22nd (Relegated)
1994/95	42	22	11	9	72	43	77	3rd
1995/96	38	15	13	10	50	54	58	9th
1996/97	38	6	16	16	31	59	34	20th (Relegated)
1998/99	38	7	9	22	35	69	30	20th (Relegated)
Totals	**198**	**60**	**59**	**79**	**229**	**187**	**239**	

This kind of appalling record would have been unthinkable during Brian Clough's reign and he would have discarded any players who weren't prepared to sweat blood for the Forest cause. Those responsible for the decline of our once-great Club want lining up against a wall and shooting. And although the rot had already set in before Messrs. Scholar and Wray arrived on the scene, they are without doubt the main reason why Forest now seemed destined for a prolonged period of First Division obscurity. Thank goodness the appointment of Eric Barnes as Club Chairman at the end of this forgettable season went some way towards putting 'the Nottingham' back into Nottingham Forest. The subsequent departure of Irvine Scholar also opened up an opportunity for other local businessmen to become involved with the Club.

And thank goodness the bulk of Forest's fan base remains in tact, despite some very lean years during the 1990s. In fact, whilst not wishing to claim the 'Reds' will ever be on a par with the 'big five' of Manchester United, Liverpool, Everton, Arsenal and Tottenham - or even the likes of Leeds, Newcastle or Sunderland for that matter - no-one could argue that the Nottingham public haven't remained loyal to the Club during the 'post Cloughie' era. Our five relatively unsuccessful seasons in the Premier League have attracted the following average home League attendances:

Season	Average	
1992/93	21,866	(Relegation and crowd restrictions due to ground redevelopment)
1994/95	23,625	(Crowd restrictions due to ground redevelopment)
1995/96	25,915	
1996/97	24,586	(Relegation)
1998/99	24,410	(Relegation)

When you consider the ground redevelopments taking place during two of these five seasons and the fact three of them were relegation campaigns from start to finish, an average of 23,620 overall during this period is not bad at all. What's more, I'm convinced that with the Main Stand re-developed, the City Ground would rank as one of the finest stadiums in the country, and with a decent playing staff, prolonged Premiership status, and only a modicum of success, there is enough potential in the City of Nottingham to ensure regular 30,000-plus attendances.

THE ironic thing about this season though, was that having secured their relegation position, the team then went on to win their final three games of the season. It was almost as if they were taking the piss out of we supporters. Was this the same ramshackle bunch of misfits who had managed only four victories in thirty-five previous games and who hadn't won on their own territory since the very first home game of the season? It just goes to show that once the pressure's off, players once again start to do the very things which come naturally to them in the first place and soon start to lose their inhibitions. Confidence is such a big part of the game and without it, even talented players can look very mediocre. You only have to look at the likes of Kevin Keegan in his day and Alan Shearer in more recent times, to see that anyone with slightly above-average ability, who has the correct mental attitude, can go to the very top of the game. Sadly, this is something all too often lacking in British sportsmen and women and why we consistently perform so badly at international level. It would be so refreshing to see all English footballers, rugby-players, cricketers and athletes having belief in their own ability and performing to their true potential. Who knows, we might even manage to beat the Aussies at something then?

Having beaten Sheffield Wednesday 2-0 at the City Ground on Saturday, 1st May - with the previously untested Hugo Porfirio the star of the show - we travelled up to Ewood Park the following weekend to steal a convincing, if rare, 2-1 victory against Blackburn Rovers. This also proved just about the final nail in their coffin and they ultimately dropped out of the Premier League with ourselves and Charlton Athletic - another side seemingly too good for the First Division, but not quite good enough for the top flight.

The season ended on Sunday, 16th May, with a 1-0 victory over neighbours Leicester City at the City Ground in front of 25,353 supporters, most of whom were convinced 'Foxes'' manager Martin O'Neill would shortly be installed as Forest's new supremo. Despite the Club's relegation, there was almost a carnival-like atmosphere inside the ground all afternoon with chants of: *"e's comin' 'ome, 'e's comin' 'ome, 'e's com-in', Mart-in's comin' 'ome!"* ringing out incessantly. Although rumours had been rife in Nottingham for months that O'Neill was a certainty to take over at the end of the season, most football pundits were dismissing this as pure conjecture. "Why would he want to give up his job at Leicester to drop out of the Premiership with Forest?" they asked. Well the answer is simple enough, I would have thought: Forest, as a Club, have always been and always will be, far superior to Leicester City, with a better stadium, much bigger support, and a trophy cabinet which is bursting at the seams. And besides, O'Neill spent many happy years as a Forest player during the most successful period in the Club's history. Anyway, even if there was absolutely no truth whatsoever in the rumours, the Leicester fans certainly looked worried, and in any case, we had a great time taking the piss out of them for the whole of the ninety minutes.

FA PREMIER LEAGUE – FIXTURES

Date	Opposition	Venue	Competition	Score	Attendance
Aug 17	Arsenal	A	League	1-2	38,064
22	**Coventry City**	**H**	**League**	**1-0**	**22,456**
29	Southampton	A	League	2-1	14,942
Sept 8	**Everton**	**H**	**League**	**0-2**	**25,610**
12	Chelsea	A	League	1-2	34,809
15	Leyton Orient	A	LC 2 - 1st Leg	5-1	4,906
19	**West Ham United**	**H**	**League**	**0-0**	**26,463**
22	**Leyton Orient**	**H**	**LC 2 - 2nd Leg**	**0-0**	**6,382**
26	Newcastle United	A	League	0-2	36,760
Oct 3	**Charlton Athletic**	**H**	**League**	**0-1**	**22,661**
17	**Leeds United**	**H**	**League**	**1-1**	**23,911**
24	Liverpool	A	League	1-5	44,595
27	**Cambridge United**	**H**	**LC 3**	**3-3**	**9,192**
	(Forest won 4-3 on penalties after extra time)				
Nov 1	Middlesbrough	A	League	1-1	34,223
7	**Wimbledon**	**H**	**League**	**0-1**	**21,362**
11	Manchester United	A	LC 4	1-2	37,237
16	**Derby County**	**H**	**League**	**2-2**	**24,014**
21	Tottenham Hotspur	A	League	0-2	35,832
28	**Aston Villa**	**H**	**League**	**2-2**	**25,753**
Dec 7	Sheffield Wednesday	A	League	2-3	19,321
12	Leicester City	A	League	1-3	20,881
19	**Blackburn Rovers**	**H**	**League**	**2-2**	**22,013**
26	Manchester United	A	League	0-3	55,216
28	**Southampton**	**H**	**League**	**1-1**	**23,456**
Jan 2	**Portsmouth**	**H**	**FA Cup 3**	**0-1**	**10,092**
9	Coventry City	A	League	0-4	17,172
16	**Arsenal**	**H**	**League**	**0-1**	**26,021**
30	Everton	A	League	1-0	34,175
Feb 6	**Manchester United**	**H**	**League**	**1-8**	**30,025**
13	West Ham United	A	League	1-2	25,458
20	**Chelsea**	**H**	**League**	**1-3**	**26,351**
27	Charlton Athletic	A	League	0-0	20,007
Mar 6	**Newcastle United**	**H**	**League**	**1-2**	**22,852**
13	Wimbledon	A	League	3-1	12,149
20	**Middlesbrough**	**H**	**League**	**1-2**	**21,468**
Apr 3	Leeds United	A	League	1-3	39,645
5	**Liverpool**	**H**	**League**	**2-2**	**28,374**
10	Derby County	A	League	0-1	32,217
17	**Tottenham Hotspur**	**H**	**League**	**0-1**	**25,181**
24	Aston Villa	A	League	0-2	34,492
May 1	**Sheffield Wednesday**	**H**	**League**	**2-0**	**20,480**
8	Blackburn Rovers	A	League	2-1	24,565
16	**Leicester City**	**H**	**League**	**1-0**	**25,353**

SEASON 1998/99

HOME ATTENDANCES

	AGGREGATE ATTENDANCE	HIGHEST ATTENDANCE	LOWEST ATTENDANCE	AVERAGE ATTENDANCE
League:	463,804	30,025	20,480	24,410
League Cup:	15,574	9,192	6,382	7,787
FA Cup:	10,092	10,092	10,092	10,092
All Competitions:	489,470	30,025	6,382	22,248

FINAL LEAGUE TABLE - FA PREMIER

Position	P	W	D	L	GF	GA	Pts
1. Manchester United	38	22	13	3	80	37	79
2. Arsenal	38	22	12	4	59	17	78
3. Chelsea	38	20	15	3	57	30	75
4. Leeds United	38	18	13	7	62	34	67
5. West Ham United	38	16	9	13	46	53	57
6. Aston Villa	38	15	10	13	51	46	55
7. Liverpool	38	15	9	14	68	49	54
8. Derby County	38	13	13	12	40	45	52
9. Middlesbrough	38	12	15	11	48	54	51
10. Leicester City	38	12	13	13	40	46	49
11. Tottenham Hotspur	38	11	14	13	47	50	47
12. Sheffield Wednesday	38	13	7	18	41	42	46
13. Newcastle United	38	11	13	14	48	54	46
14. Everton	38	11	10	17	42	47	43
15. Coventry City	38	11	9	18	39	51	42
16. Wimbledon	38	10	12	16	40	63	42
17. Southampton	38	11	8	19	37	64	41
18. Charlton Athletic	38	8	12	18	41	56	36
19. Blackburn Rovers	38	7	14	17	38	52	35
20. Nottingham Forest	**38**	**7**	**9**	**22**	**35**	**69**	**30**

AWAY ATTENDANCES

	AGGREGATE ATTENDANCE	HIGHEST ATTENDANCE	LOWEST ATTENDANCE	AVERAGE ATTENDANCE
League:	574,523	55,216	12,149	30,238
League Cup:	42,143	37,237	4,906	21,071
All Competitions:	616,666	55,216	4,906	29,365

"I KNOW I AM, I'M SURE I AM, I'M FOREST 'TIL I DIE"

THE RUMOURS linking Leicester City manager Martin O'Neill with the vacant managerial position at Forest continued to gather momentum after the close of the 1998/99 season. However, although he was apparently offered the job by the Forest Board; for the second time during his managerial career, he turned the 'Reds' down flat. One newspaper report even suggested he was dismissive regarding his affinity to the Club, quoting him as saying: "They're just a club I played for during my career and it's more than 17 years since I left them anyway." Somehow, I find this statement very difficult to believe and am convinced O'Neill still holds the Club and the City dear to his heart. Still, it wasn't to be and Forest had to step up their search for the right man.

The recently deposed England manager Glen Hoddle became the Club's next serious target and, whilst many people within the press and the game itself, were casting doubts over his current state of mind, he would certainly have been the ideal man for the job in my book. His creative approach towards the game would have been right up Forest's street, especially after 18 years of the 'Brian Clough' influence down on Trentside. However, suggesting he wasn't yet ready for a return to the limelight, he also politely declined the offer.

With less than two months of the close season remaining, the situation began to grow more and more serious by the day. Many Forest supporters were panic-stricken by some of the names allegedly in the frame - Roy Evans for example. But with six weeks to go before the big kick off, almost completely out of the blue, it was announced that former England captain David Platt had been handed the job.

My own initial reaction to this appointment was one of extreme optimism. Here was a man with the perfect pedigree; someone with all the credentials to become a top class manager. Not only had he played at the very highest level, with Aston Villa, Juventus, Sampdoria, Arsenal and England, but he had been a winner in every aspect of his career. His international career had spanned 62 games and included an impressive tally of 27 goals from midfield. He had also easily adapted to Italian football, one of the most demanding challenges open to any professional footballer, and helped Arsenal to achieve the FA Premier League and Cup double during season 1997/98. The only fly in the ointment to date, was a brief and unsuccessful spell as 'Overall Supervisor' of former club Sampdoria - a career which had lasted only seven weeks and heralded no victories whatsoever.

Money had been made available for new players following the sale of 40 per cent of the Club's shares to Newark businessman and lifelong Forest supporter Nigel Doughty for £6 million. This had been made possible through a successful ballot of the Club's recently acquired shareholders, the overwhelming majority of whom are true Forest supporters and have the best interests of Nottingham Forest at heart; more than can be said for the previous owners Messrs. Scholar and Wray. Mr Doughty was also handed the option of purchasing an additional 15 per cent of the share capital of NFFC for a further £6 million exercisable at any time up to the earlier of 1st July 2002 and six months after the date on which the Club regains Premier League status.

So, with a Board of Directors consisting predominantly of Nottingham-born folk - Chairman Eric Barnes is also a lifelong supporter - a new and exciting young manager in David Platt, and with money to spend; suddenly the future was looking a whole lot brighter for everyone connected with the Club.

And 'Platty' wasn't slow to delve into the transfer market either. In came 30-year-old central-defender Salvatore Matrecano and 29-year-old midfielder Gianluca Petrachi from Italian Serie A club Perugia, for a combined fee of £2.4 million; 36-year-old central-defender Moreno Mannini on a free transfer from Italian club Sampdoria - described by Platt as one of the meanest defenders he had ever played with; followed by 24-year-old defender-cum-midfielder Riccardo Scimecca from Aston Villa for £2.5 million. And with midfielder Andy Johnson having undergone surgery on his damaged Achilles tendon during the summer, and likely to be out for months rather than weeks, this new blood was desperately needed if Forest were to carve out another instantaneous return to the Premiership, following relegation the previous season.

THE season kicked off on Saturday, 7th August, with an unconvincing 3-1 defeat at Ipswich Town - one of the season's promotion favourites - and the Italian trio brought in at such expense by Platt, seemed well out of sorts amongst the rigours of the English game. However, a 3-0 victory over Mansfield Town at home four days later in a League Cup first round, first leg tie, was followed by a 2-1 victory over Grimsby Town at the City Ground the following Saturday, securing Forest their first League points of the season. Carlton Palmer scored a late winner, sending the 17,121-crowd home with a smile on their faces.

The following League fixture at West Brom had been brought forward by one day to Friday,

20th August, to accommodate the Sky Television cameras. Living in Birmingham, this was a 'home' game for me; in fact just a five-minute walk to Acocks Green Railway Station, followed by a twenty-minute journey by train to the Hawthorns. Unfortunately, my life is never quite that simple though and I had to complete a 100-mile round-trip earlier on in the day to pick up Thomas from Nottingham, as he'd decided he was coming with me. Still, that's what dads are for, isn't it?

To get my own back on him, I made sure we left especially early for the game and he had to sit and amuse himself in a pub near the ground for a couple of hours while I enjoyed a few pre-match beers. He was still only fifteen at the time, so had to make do with a pint of Coca-Cola, despite his taste-buds having long since developed a liking for the 'amber nectar'. Forest played quite well in front of a crowd of only 13,202, with Dougie Freedman putting us 1-0 up seventeen minutes into the second half. Unfortunately, the referee was the only person in the ground to completely miss the fact that Albion striker Lee Hughes was at least five yards off-side when he climbed to head home their equaliser in the 76th minute. Yet another two points down the pan, thanks to the incompetence of the man in black.

Having slipped to a 1-0 defeat against the 'Stags' at Field Mill the following Tuesday, David Platt then pulled off one of the moves of the season, bringing in the legendary Ian Wright on a month's loan from West Ham. Despite being almost 36, and retiring from the game at the end of the season, he was just the kind of player Forest needed, both on and off the pitch. Not only was his bubbly personality and extrovert nature sure to bring out the best in the other players, but his presence would also drag a few more of Forest's missing supporters out of their self-imposed retirement.

A crowd of 18,442 watched him in action against QPR at the City Ground on Saturday, 28th August, and although he maintained his record of scoring on every debut, his goal was only enough to earn Forest a 1-1 draw in a largely disappointing contest. And Forest continued their uninspiring form two days later, going down 1-0 to Man City at Maine Road on Bank Holiday Monday. However, things took a turn for the better the following Saturday when Wright was again on the score-sheet in a resounding 4-1 victory over struggling Walsall at the City Ground. Dougie Freedman (2) and Steve Chettle scored the others in front of a disappointing crowd of only 15,081.

A 0-0 draw away to Swindon Town and a 2-1 victory at home to Bristol City in the second round of the League Cup, preceded Forest's second live appearance of the season on Sky Sports 2 against Wolves at the City Ground on Sunday, 19th September - don't you just love those Sunday fixtures with a 1 o'clock kick off! However, the presence of Brian Clough swelled the attendance to a reasonable 20,694, despite Wolves bringing with them probably their smallest away following ever. He'd been invited along by the Forest hierarchy to officially open the re-named 'Brian Clough Stand', formerly the Executive Stand of course. The Board had at long last honoured the great man for presiding over the most successful period in Forest's long history, and although this accolade was long overdue, I'm sure the current Board of Directors would have made this gesture many years earlier had they been in power.

Unfortunately Cloughie's presence failed to inspire ninth-placed Forest and the best they could do was earn a 1-1 draw against a poor Wolves side, who were themselves languishing in 18th position in the table, having accumulated just five points from five games played. Frenchman Bernard Allou scored Forest's goal in his first of only two appearances all season.

On a brighter note, 18-year-old midfielder David Prutton - a product of Paul Hart's very promising Youth Academy - was handed his debut by manager David Platt for the League Cup second round, second leg tie away to Bristol City on Wednesday, 22nd September. He impressed in the 0-0 draw, as did City's 22-year-old Canadian international left-back Jim Brennan, who would shortly become Platt's next big money signing; he was drafted into the Club for a fee of £1.25 million in late October. Prutton had also retained his place in the team for the trip to the Reebok Stadium on Saturday, 25th September, where Forest were edged out in a five-goal thriller. Having led 2-1 with only minutes to go, Freedman and Wright having been on target for the 'Reds', they allowed Bolton back into the game and then succumbed to a dramatic injury time winner from Neil Cox.

I wasn't at the Reebok, having gone over to Northampton for the weekend to see our Graham, who'd moved there with his job the previous September. However, Forest's defeat had been very difficult to swallow, especially as I'd listened to the full match commentary by Darren Fletcher live on Century 106. Although I was aware Century were covering all Forest's games, and of the fact Larry Lloyd hosted a daily phone-in programme on the station, living in Birmingham, I was unable to pick up what is essentially an East Midlands broadcast - or so I thought. Graham had somehow stumbled over the fact that reception was pretty clear in the Northampton area and was convinced I'd be able to pick up the transmission in the West Midlands. I wasn't convinced at all, but much to my delight, upon my return to 'Brum' the next day, discovered I could pick it up loud and clear after all. And, having been totally devoid of information about my beloved 'Reds' for the previous four years, this was an absolute Godsend to me!

Our next live appearance on Sky TV the following Friday evening at a rain-soaked City Ground brought us a much-needed three points, courtesy of a resounding 3-0 victory over Dave

Bassett's much-fancied Barnsley outfit. Our joy was short-lived though, thanks to two unsuccessful visits to the City of Sheffield during the space of only three days. The first of these was to Premiership Sheffield Wednesday in the third round of the League Cup, where we were on the receiving end of a 4-1 thrashing. The second was a controversial 2-1 defeat against Sheffield United at Bramall lane on Saturday, 16th October.

With player-manager David Platt making his League debut for the Club, another display of incompetence on the part of a match official, robbed Forest of all three points. Striker Dougie Freedman had given Forest a late first-half lead and the 'Reds' looked to be cruising through to the half-time whistle. However, when United's Paul Devlin responded to Nigel Quashie's late challenge by flooring the Forest midfielder with a right hook, the large travelling contingent from Nottingham were calling for his head. Remarkably, the referee decided this act of retaliation by the former Notts County striker was deserving of nothing more than a yellow card, whilst Quashie's challenge - nothing out of the ordinary by any means - warranted an instant sending off?

There was uproar at our end of the ground, I can tell you. But things just went from bad to worse from that moment on. First, striker Martin Smith equalised early on in the second half; then the same player put the home side ahead soon afterwards; only for 'Platty' to end up also receiving his marching orders late on in the game for another challenge, which in my book warranted at worst a booking. It was one of those games you'd rather just forget, so me and the rest of the lads, who I'd met up with at Sheffield Station before the game, stayed in the city for a few hours and got absolutely slaughtered, before catching our respective trains home.

Our next away match at Port Vale on Tuesday, 19th October produced probably Forest's best performance of the season to date. The blistering pace of Alan Rogers - rather shrewdly transformed into a left winger by David Platt - was a constant menace to the home side. And up front, strikers Ian Wright - who's loan period had now been extended - and Dougie Freedman, provided all the movement necessary to keep Vale's defence on the back foot throughout the game. Bonelair and Wright were Forest's scorers in a convincing 2-0 victory, and if they'd really capitalised on the amount of possession they'd had throughout, they could have gone on to achieve a substantial victory; one which would have done their confidence no harm at all. The only blight on the whole evening, was an appalling injury to the very influential Matrecano - one which would put him out of action for more than a season.

HAVING sat in the upper tier of the Bridgford Stand since it's completion half-way through the relegation season of 1992/93, I had long since grown tired of the abuse and piss-taking which went on in there between the Forest supporters in the upper tier and the visiting supporters occupying the lower tier below. During six and a half seasons, I had endured no less than three relegation campaigns and had had to suffer the likes of Blackburn Rovers supporters - you know, all three bus-loads of them - taunting us with chants of: "Going down, Going down, Going down," something which I found almost impossible to deal with. The problem is you see: if you stick the knife into Nottingham Forest FC in any way, shape or form, then I bleed profusely.

By the time we'd suffered our third relegation season in 1998/99 - when, I am pleased to say, we were instrumental in taking those arrogant Blackburn wankers down with us in our penultimate game - I'd just about had enough, and was ready for a move. The defining moment for me came during our totally humiliating 8-1 defeat at the hands of Smugchester United, when we were being taunted to the extreme by United's travelling band of supporters. The trouble is, I'm so fiercely proud of my beloved Forest, and such a stubborn git, I refused to leave the ground until the final whistle. And this really was my downfall.

As the abuse intensified, I found myself getting sucked into the war of attrition going on all around me. And what's worse, so was my 15-year-old son Thomas, and all of his mates, who also sat alongside us. I was eventually brought to my senses, by the sight of Thomas and his gang receiving a severe ticking off from an irate policeman, who'd spotted them making offensive gestures towards the visiting supporters, whilst at the same time, completely ignoring the game. "For God's sake," I thought to myself, "I'm 41 years-of-age and acting like a juvenile delinquent." I decided there and then that come the end of the season, I was moving as far away from the Visiting Supporters Section as I possibly could, and, to protect their interests, I was taking Thomas and all his mates with me. And the safest place as far as I was concerned, would be right at the very back of the upper tier of the Trent End.

So season 1999/2000 had heralded a return to my spiritual home - albeit a very different Trent End to the one I'd left behind in the early-1970s. And to say the place had changed for the better is an understatement. Not only is the stand modern and comfortable, with a fantastic view of the pitch, but the facilities which go with it are second to none. When I stand in the refreshment area before the game or at half-time looking out through the glass windows across the Trent and beyond at the wonderful Nottingham skyline, it makes the hairs on the back of my neck stand up. The other bonus of course, is that I no longer have to endure the taunts of visiting supporters, because quite frankly, you can't really hear them that well from high up there in the upper tier of the stand.

Now that brings me nicely onto another matter. During the years I sat in the Bridgford Upper, I was extremely disappointed by the lack of noise emanating from this magnificent new structure at the opposite end of the ground. On anything but the rarest of occasions, you just couldn't hear a song or a chant or an anthem coming from what had historically been one of the noisiest singing choirs in the whole of the Football League. In fact, in it's heyday, it had almost been on a par with the famous Kop End at Anfield, or the Stretford End at Old Trafford. But now, nothing whatsoever seemed to be happening in there on a Saturday afternoon whenever the 'Reds' were in town.

However, having moved over, I found this not to be the case. There is plenty of noise, most of the time; it just seems that most of it disappears in an upwards direction and goes floating off across the West Bridgford skyline, undetected by all other parts of the City Ground. I do have one major problem though with today's Trent Enders: Where's all the wit and originality, synonymous with the Trent End of old, disappeared to? The Trent End of the 1960s/1970s era and the Trent End of today are simply worlds apart. To emphasise this, here are examples of both the old and the new:

TYPICAL TRENT END CHANT - CIRCA 1970

We've travelled far an' wide,
We've bin to Merseyside,
But there is only one place,
I wanna be;

It's at the City Ground,
Where people gather round,
To 'ear the Trent End sound,
We're gonna win today;

Come on an' cheer agen,
Come on an' cheer agen,
For we are 'ere agen,
To see the Forest win;

Come on an' score agen,
With Ian Moore agen,
For we are sure agen,
We're gonna win today;

Come on an' cheer agen....

TYPICAL TRENT END CHANT - YEAR 2000

We 'ate Leicester!...We 'ate Derby!
We 'ate Leicester!...We 'ate Derby!
We 'ate Leicester!...We 'ate Derby!
We 'ate Leicester!...We 'ate Derby!
Ad infinitum...

Where have all the old anthems of yesteryear gone? Back in the sixties and seventies, and to a lesser extent, the eighties, the Trent End's whole 9,000-strong choir would know every song and anthem word for word and would leave the stadium hoarse at the end of every game, having sung themselves into the ground. Originality was the key in those days and virtually every week, a new anthem would appear which, by the end of the game, everyone would know off pat. Nowadays, if we're lucky, we hear one new song per season, and even then it's usually just a silly chant rather than a song or an anthem.

What's more annoying, is the fact that the few old anthems which are still thankfully doing the rounds today, are gradually being ruined because no-one seems to know the proper words to them. And what amazes me, is that whenever there's a word or a line in a song which no-one has quite managed to grasp, it's simply replaced with the rather meaningless sound of *"wooo-ooh"* for example: *"Well I've never felt more like singing the blues, When Forest win, An' Derby lose,* **Oh Baby,** *You've got me singin' the blues!"* has been replaced with: *"Well I never felt more like singin' the blues, When Forest win, An' Derby lose,* **Wooo-ooh-ooh,** *You've got me singin' the blues!"*

Another example, is *'Forest Ever Forest'*, from whence the title of this book originates. Not only has the first verse vanished into thin air, but the second verse is now beginning to receive the dreaded *'wooo-ooh-ooh'* treatment as well. The first verse, which incidentally, in yet another vain attempt on my part to revive it, is: *"Forest ever Forest, All our hopes are with you, True supporters forever, 'til our days are through, La-la-la-la-la,"* should be followed by: *"***Through** *the seasons before us, Down through history, We will follow the Forest, Onto victory, La-la-la-la-la."* However, the Trent Enders of today have, would you believe it, amended it to: *"***Wooh** *the seasons before us, Down through history, We will follow the Forest, Onto victory, La-la-la-la-la."* What next...an entire song made up of *"Wooh-o-oohs?"* God help us, that's all I can say. (For a list of over 100 authentic Trent End anthems of the past and present, turn to 'The A-Z of Trent End Anthems' starting on page 401).

Anyway, now I've got that off my chest (I do go on a bit, don't I!), let's get back to the season in hand.

NOT only was the fact Forest could only manage to draw 1-1 at home with Stockport County on Saturday, 23rd October, a big disappointment, but the fact it was also Ian Wright's last game for the Club, was an even bigger one. When signing him on a permanent basis until at least the end of the season was more than a distinct possibility - he had intimated on more than one occasion just how much he loved the City Ground and that he would be happy to see out his days on Trentside - those who made such things happen, just seemed to be dithering around in the background instead of pulling their fingers out and getting on with the job. And while they were doing exactly that, Celtic manager John Barnes, in a desperate attempt to appease his growing army of critics in Glasgow, stepped in and made him an offer he just couldn't refuse. So he was off up to Scotland in a flash, and who could blame him really?

And when we subsequently went on to draw one and lose four of our next five League games, not only were we looking decidedly lacklustre up-front, but the defence was now starting to leak goals like there was no tomorrow. Following our latest disaster - a 3-0 thumping by John Aldridge's Tranmere Rovers at Prenton Park on Saturday, 20th November - we were sitting in the decidedly uncomfortable position of 16th in the First Division table, having accumulated a total of just 18 points from 16 games. And Forest's long-suffering supporters were now making their feelings known to manager David Platt, both in their attitude towards him down at the City Ground and through Larry Lloyd's nightly phone in programme on Century 106.

Now, as unhappy as I was with the whole situation, I could never take it upon myself to slag the manager off on a phone-in programme, or join in with the anti David Platt chanting which was taking place on the terraces of the City Ground. The negativity about Forest's future was almost reaching fever pitch and many supporters weren't pulling any punches with their criticism of the manager. Supporters of many years standing were suggesting this was the worst Forest side they'd ever seen. And to an extent, I had to agree, although I had no doubts about the quality of the squad. They just completely lacked confidence to my mind and seemed to come out onto the pitch as if already 1-0 down before the game had even begun. I have to say, their performances at this particular moment in time, were definitely the most inept I'd seen in 34 years of watching the 'Reds'.

However, with the benefit of hindsight, I believe that what Platt was doing to the Club, was absolutely necessary and long overdue. With the exception of a couple of good seasons under Frank Clark's leadership, the Club had been in decline since the early nineties and even the great Brian Clough had lost the plot towards the end of his reign on Trentside. Some of the Forest squad - Ian Woan, Steve Chettle and Mark Crossley for example - had been around throughout all three of Forest's disastrous relegation campaigns. Now I'm not suggesting these weren't decent players in their own right, or that they were in any way lacking in their commitment to the 'Reds'. But perhaps it was high time for someone to come along, make some unpopular decisions, clear out some of the deadwood, and start taking the Club forward once again. Perhaps someone completely single minded like David Platt?

Some hope arrived in the form of Trinidad & Tobago striker Stern John, signed at the end of November from American League side Columbus Crew in a £1.5 million deal. Platt had been tracking him for several months, and the fact the 23-year-old had netted no less than 52 times in only 65 appearances for the American outfit, made him the perfect catch for the goal-shy 'Reds'. And he wasted absolutely no time at all in endearing himself to the fans, scoring on his debut with his first touch of the ball in the 2-0 victory over Portsmouth at the City Ground on Wednesday, 24th November. The other goalscorer was Mikkel Beck, who Platt had also brought in on a month's loan from Derby County.

Any optimism gleaned from this victory over 'Pompey' was short-lived, as we lost our next two games, 2-0 at Crystal Palace and 1-0 at home to Ipswich Town, before going on to draw the next two, 1-1 at home to Oxford United in the third round of the FA Cup (on 10th December no less) and 0-0 at home to Fulham. Some hope was restored with a pre-Christmas 1-0 victory over Crewe Alexandra at the City Ground, Stern John grabbing the vital goal. The truth of the matter was, with a very difficult Christmas fixture list looming, we were still well and truly stranded in the wrong half of the table.

THERE was still plenty of movement on the transfer market however, despite Platty having spent many millions of pounds since his arrival at the City Ground the previous summer. No-one could accuse the Forest Board of not providing him with the financial backing necessary to improve the squad and build a side capable of achieving promotion over the short to medium term.

And the manager's cull of players considered surplus to requirements also continued. Club captain Steve Chettle had joined former team-mate Neil Shipperly at Dave Bassett's Barnsley in November, initially on loan, with the move eventually being made permanent a couple of months later. Ricardo Scimeca was appointed captain in his absence. The signing of 24-year-old striker Jack Lester from Grimsby in a £300,000 deal and the capture of on-loan Tony Vaughan, an uncompromising central-defender from Manchester City, followed Chettle's departure. Both of these signings took place at the beginning of February.

Forest's slide down the table had been an alarming one, and by the time they entertained high-flying Manchester City at the City Ground on Saturday, 5th February, on the back of just two victories during their previous eleven games, they were languishing in 18th position in the table. What's more, with just 30 points all season to their credit from a total of 29 games, they were a mere three points above the relegation zone.

A 5,000-plus following from Maine Road swelled the crowd to an impressive 25,836, and despite taking a first-half lead thanks to Chris Bart-Williams' cracking thirty-yard drive, in the end Forest were soundly beaten by three-goals-to-one. One thing which did annoy me intensely during this game though, was the arrogance of the City fans who'd obviously been taking lessons from their equally obnoxious neighbours Manchester United. Their chants of: *"3-1 in your Cup Final, You've lost 3-1 in your Cup Final,"* were about as amusing as they were accurate. Maybe they can get away with such drivel when they're visiting the likes of Tranmere Rovers or Crewe Alexandra, but this was the City Ground, Nottingham, home of the famous Nottingham Forest FC! And boy have I got news for them: When you've seen your team win the League Championship, two European Cups, the European Super Cup, and been with them to Wembley on no less than ten occasions during your lifetime, believe me, Manchester City at home on a cold day in February is no big deal at all. And I'm sure the vast majority of the 20,000-plus Forest supporters inside the City Ground that day would agree with me.

Tony Vaughan made his debut at Walsall the following Saturday in a game which Forest had to win. This was another 'home' game for me, but, as usual, was preceded by a 100-mile round trip to Long Eaton on the Friday evening to fetch Thomas and his mate Scott who were accompanying me to the Bescot Stadium. We caught the 11.20-a.m. train from Acocks Green Station and, following a short stop at Birmingham New Street, arrived at the Bescot Railway Station just yards from the ground at about midday.

Having consulted my copy of the 'Football Fan's Guide' (a must for all fans who travel frequently to away matches) prior to leaving home, we immediately set off in search of the King George V pub on Wallows Lane. And while Tom and Scott amused themselves with a game of pool, I sat and enjoyed a few pre-match pints, whilst reminiscing with some Forest supporters I'd recognised from the old days on Simmo's coaches. The place was absolutely packed with travelling 'Reds' by 1.00-p.m. and so grateful for the extra trade were the Landlord and Landlady, they laid on free sandwiches for everyone in the pub. I had a fantastic lunchtime and was well in the mood for the game by the time we headed back to the stadium at around fifteen minutes to three.

And, as the day wore on, things just got better and better and better. Tony Vaughan looked an absolute rock at the heart of the Forest defence throughout the game - his swashbuckling style reminiscent of Stuart Pearce; and of course, this immediately endeared him to the large travelling contingent from Nottingham. Alan Rogers put us 1-0 up in the first half with a rather fortuitous free kick from out wide, which eluded everyone, including the goalkeeper. And within minutes of coming on as a late second-half substitute, Dougie Freedman had jinked his way majestically through the 'Saddlers' defence before slamming us into a 2-0 lead from six yards out. The travelling 'Reds' went absolutely berserk and as we poured out of the stadium at the end, I genuinely felt we were about to turn the corner.

The train back into 'Brum' was packed with Forest supporters and the mood on board was a happy and buoyant one. When you've had such a disappointing season, so soon after suffering the torment of a third relegation campaign, you're now flirting with relegation to the Second Division; but your travelling support is as good as ever, it makes you realise just what a big Club Forest really are. Never mind the Manchester Cities of this world - not that I'm suggesting for one minute they aren't a massive club - but it would just be nice to see some recognition of Forest's impressive support every now and then in the press. Obviously, we just aren't fashionable enough in most people's eyes.

Despite such an appalling season, we were still pulling in some reasonable crowds: 20,694 against Wolves; 20,821 against Birmingham; not to mention the near-26,000 against City. But still, people continue to question our support - something which not only annoys me, but also baffles me completely. Take for example, a recent conversation our Graham had with a 21-year-old Leicester City supporter at a wedding he was attending in London. The young man in question was slagging Forest's support off, right, left and centre and, laughingly, suggesting Leicester's support was superior to ours. Rather than be drawn into a futile argument, Graham just retreated gracefully, preferring to let the poor inadequate so and so, get on with it. "I just wish you'd been there," he said to me afterwards, "with all your facts and figures."

And you see; the facts and figures are the crucial thing in this argument - or rather the lack of them, on 'Mr Leicester City's' part anyway. What's probably influenced this lad's thinking is this: With a capacity of 30,500, the City Ground looks pretty empty with 20,000 people in it; whilst on the other hand, Leicester's cramped Filbert Street stadium, with it's 22,000-capacity, looks absolutely packed with the same number of folks inside. So, whilst every time he sees a clip of action on the TV from the City Ground, he subconsciously thinks: "That looks a bit empty," every time he sees Leicester on the TV ('cause he quite obviously never goes to see them live!), he probably, on the other hand, thinks: "Packed out again look!" What he obviously fails to do, is spend five minutes on a Sunday morning, poring over the results in the Sunday rags and studying the attendance figures. And that's where him and me differ - because I do!

Now, if he was anywhere near as observant as me; he might just have noticed some of our attendances, whilst we've been struggling in the First Division over the last year or two, in comparison to some of Leicester's, who, during the corresponding period, have been riding high in the Premiership. How about these two, for example:

- **Saturday, 22nd January 2000**
  - Forest, languishing in 18th position in the First Division table, entertained West Bromwich Albion, 19th in the table. Attendance: 19,863!
  - Meanwhile, Leicester City, riding high in the Premiership table (a highly successful season saw them finish in eighth position no less), entertained West Ham United. Attendance: 19,019!

- **Saturday, 5th February 2000**
  - Forest, still languishing in 18th position in the First Division table, entertained Manchester City. Attendance: 25,836!
  - Meanwhile, Leicester City, still riding high in the Premiership table, entertained Middlesbrough. Attendance: 17,550!

No doubt 'Mr Leicester fan' would find some excuse for the 'Foxes'' rather dismal support when compared to that of our own, but the fact is, they're just miles behind Forest in the supporter stakes. I don't doubt for one minute, that once they finally get around to building their proposed new 32,000-capacity stadium not far away from Filbert Street, they, like other clubs before them, will experience a sudden upsurge in support. I like to think of this as 'New Stadium Syndrome', which seems to affect previously unfashionable clubs like Middlesbrough and Derby who, for many years previously, failed to fill their 22,000-ish capacity grounds. Miraculously, the minute the last brick (Lego brick in the case of 'Shite Park') had been laid at the site of their respective new stadiums, another 10,000 fans suddenly crawled out of the woodwork, waving their brand spanking new season tickets in the air and claiming to be lifelong fans. But, just like both of these clubs - admittedly to a greater extent in Derby's case - the novelty will soon wear off and gradually this new-found support will begin to dwindle away again - especially if the current level of performances is not maintained.

THE confidence gained during the 2-0 victory over Walsall carried through to the next game at home to Crystal Palace on Saturday, 19th February, where goals from Alan Rogers and Nigel Quashie ensured another 2-0 success. But what followed a week later at Wolves just about summed up Forest's miserable season to date.

I should have said "no" to our Graham when he invited me to take advantage of his company's corporate hospitality facilities at Molyneux. He works for Scania Trucks and they use these facilities at many stadiums up and down the country to entertain their customers. I've never been comfortable with the 'corporate' scene which has evolved within the game in recent years, despite the fact the company I work for, have only recently ended many seasons of sponsoring Blackburn Rovers. I just can't be doing with going to the match - any match that is - togged up in a suit and watching the game with a bunch of people who know very little about football and certainly contribute nothing to the game financially. I accept it is part and parcel of today's game and it generates massive volumes of money. I just don't want any part of it, preferring to mix with the true supporters on the terraces; the people who really matter within the game.

Anyway, I accepted Graham's invitation on this occasion and we set off for Wolverhampton bright and early, so we could enjoy a couple of pints before the game. Immediately prior to kick off, we made our way through a rather posh-looking restaurant situated within the Billy Wright Stand and out onto a balcony in the middle of the stand, just a few feet above where the 'real' supporters sit in the lower tier. And to say the game degenerated into farce within just a few minutes of the kick off is an understatement.

First of all, Tony Vaughan was floored by a right hook from Ade Akinbiyi, following the most innocuous of challenges on the edge of the box. And as if that wasn't bad enough, with the Wolves fans amazingly baying for his blood, referee Stephen Lodge decided, in his wisdom, to send Vaughan off, whilst administering nothing more than a booking to 'Mike Tyson' himself. And, to cap it all, from the resulting free kick, Ludovic Pollet rose unchallenged to head the home side into the lead.

And worse was to come. As Graham and I were the only two people who didn't jump up out of our seats at the sight of this 'richly deserved' opener for Wolves, it was immediately apparent to the fans in the stand just two foot below us, that we were Forest supporters. This was the signal for some serious abuse, particularly from one particular 'Neanderthal', seated about two or three yards away to our right. He was giving us some serious grief...and it wasn't exactly friendly banter either - he wanted to kill us. And every time a Forest player made a mistake (every three seconds to be precise) he'd turn around and start applauding sarcastically. Within minutes Graham had turned into the 'Incredible Hulk' and was seriously rising to the bait. I talked him out of that course of action, and he proceeded to destroy the brainless looking oaf with some serious abuse of his own. "Wotsupwiya...aren't you allowed to talk at 'ome, or something?" he quipped after yet another torrent of abuse came our way. This brought us a temporary respite as those all around him fell about laughing, while 'Mr Caveman' just stood there scratching his six-inch thick skull and failing miserably to think of anything useful to say in response.

However, this was only a temporary respite until first, Darren Bazeley extended the home side's lead with a tremendous thirty-yard strike, and then once more, Mr. Lodge played his part in farcical situation number two. When Wolves' Lee Naylor went down in a heap in the centre of the field, Forest keeper Dave Beasant sportingly decided to kick the ball into touch to allow him some treatment. However, striker Michael Branch, urged on by the majority of the crowd, raced across to the touch-line to prevent the keeper's tamely-struck kick going out of play. Not only that, he then proceeded to race upfield towards goal - with every other player on the pitch standing still waiting for the trainer to come on - rounded Beasant and slid the ball into an empty net. And amazingly the Wolves fans thought it was fantastic and greeted the 'goal' as if it was the greatest they'd ever seen. And what did Mr. Lodge do about it? Well he allowed it of course...what else would you expect?

As you can imagine, this caused absolute uproar amongst the Forest players - particularly Beasant who tried to strangle Branch, the little runt - those on the Forest bench, and in the Visiting Supporters' Section high up in the Jack Harris Stand away to our right. And of course, this was food and drink to 'Mr Neanderthal', who continued to snarl at us at every opportunity.

This wasn't the end of the controversy either, as first David Prutton was sent off for a second bookable offence - thanks Mr. Lodge - and then the police had to intervene on the touch-line to prevent a pitch invasion by the Forest management. Graham and I were ready to walk out there and then, but we gritted our teeth and tried to encourage nine-man Forest at every opportunity. It was at this point I realised that Molyneux, along with places like Millwall and Stoke is undoubtedly one of the most unpleasant places to visit in the entire Football League. The Wolves supporters are positively vile and without a doubt the most un-sporting bunch of morons I've ever encountered.

The second half passed by without further incident, and not even so much as a murmur from 'Mr Hard-man' below us. And amazingly, there were no more goals, as what was left of the Forest side, defended like Trojans. On reflection, a 3-0 defeat was a good result, given the circumstances. Needless to say, I won't be taking advantage of Wolves' corporate hospitality facilities again in the future.

NOTHING more remarkable than the Wolves fiasco happened between then and the end of the season. Veteran defender Colin Calderwood arrived from Aston Villa in March for a fee of £70,000 and Tony Vaughan's move was made permanent on transfer deadline day - the fee in the region of £350,000. Calderwood then promptly suffered a horrifying fracture of the leg in the 1-0 win at Birmingham City on Saturday, 15th April.

Thankfully Forest managed to find some form, remaining unbeaten over the last seven games and sprinting up to a much more creditable 14th position in the table. They won four and drew the remaining three of these fixtures. And despite this season of woe, the average League attendance at the City Ground was a reasonable 17,195. Not bad for a team which had languished in the bottom half of the table all season. The highest League attendance was the 25,836 for the visit of Manchester City, with the lowest being the 13,841 who turned out for the visit of Portsmouth on Wednesday, 24th November.

And, having been knocked out of the League Cup by Sheffield Wednesday at the third-round stage, we had fared little better in the FA Cup - going down 2-0 at Chelsea in round four on Wednesday, 19th January, after disposing of Second Division Oxford United 3-1 in the third-round replay at the Manor Ground on Saturday, 8th January.

I for one was glad to see the back of season 1999/2000. But still, as the song goes: "I'm Forest 'til I die, I'm Forest 'til I die, I know I am, I'm sure I am, I'm Forest 'til I die!"

SEASON 1999/00 – STATISTICS

FOOTBALL LEAGUE DIVISION ONE – FIXTURES

Date		Opposition	Venue	Competition	Score	Attendance
Aug	7	Ipswich Town	A	League	1-3	20,830
	11	**Mansfield Town**	**H**	**LC 1 - 1st Leg**	**3-0**	**8,300**
	14	**Grimsby Town**	**H**	**League**	**2-1**	**17,121**
	20	West Bromwich Albion	A	League	1-1	13,202
	24	Mansfield Town	A	LC 1 - 2nd Leg	0-1	3,072
	28	**Queens Park Rangers**	**H**	**League**	**1-1**	**18,442**
	30	Manchester City	A	League	0-1	31,857
Sept	**4**	**Walsall**	**H**	**League**	**4-1**	**15,081**
	11	Swindon Town	A	League	0-0	8,321
	15	**Bristol City**	**H**	**LC 2 - 1st Leg**	**2-1**	**5,015**
	19	**Wolverhampton Wanderers**	**H**	**League**	**1-1**	**20,694**
	22	Bristol City	A	LC 2 - 2nd Leg	0-0	8,259
	25	Bolton Wanderers	A	League	2-3	14,978
Oct	**1**	**Barnsley**	**H**	**League**	**3-0**	**15,255**
	13	Sheffield Wednesday	A	LC 3	1-4	15,524
	16	Sheffield United	A	League	1-2	15,687
	19	Port Vale	A	League	2-0	5,714
	23	**Stockport County**	**H**	**League**	**1-1**	**15,770**
	27	**Bolton Wanderers**	**H**	**League**	**1-1**	**15,572**
	30	Barnsley	A	League	0-1	14,727
Nov	6	Norwich City	A	League	0-1	15,818
	14	**Huddersfield Town**	**H**	**League**	**1-3**	**15,258**
	20	Tranmere Rovers	A	League	0-3	6,693
	24	**Portsmouth**	**H**	**League**	**2-0**	**13,841**
	27	Crystal Palace	A	League	0-2	15,920
Dec	**5**	**Ipswich Town**	**H**	**League**	**0-1**	**15,724**
	10	**Oxford United**	**H**	**FA Cup 3**	**1-1**	**8,079**
	15	**Fulham**	**H**	**League**	**0-0**	**14,250**
	18	**Crewe Alexandra**	**H**	**League**	**1-0**	**15,289**
	26	Blackburn Rovers	A	League	1-2	23,604
	28	**Birmingham City**	**H**	**League**	**1-0**	**20,821**
Jan	3	Charlton Athletic	A	League	0-3	19,787
	8	Oxford United	A	FA Cup 3 - Replay	3-1	7,191
	15	Grimsby Town	A	League	3-4	6,738
	19	Chelsea	A	FA Cup 4	0-2	30,125
	22	**West Bromwich Albion**	**H**	**League**	**0-0**	**19,863**
	29	Queens Park Rangers	A	League	1-1	12,297
Feb	**5**	**Manchester City**	**H**	**League**	**1-3**	**25,836**
	12	Walsall	A	League	2-0	8,027
	19	**Crystal Palace**	**H**	**League**	**2-0**	**16,421**
	26	Wolverhampton Wanderers	A	League	0-3	24,444
Mar	**4**	**Swindon Town**	**H**	**League**	**3-1**	**19,748**
	8	**Norwich City**	**H**	**League**	**1-1**	**15,640**
	11	Portsmouth	A	League	1-2	14,336
	18	**Tranmere Rovers**	**H**	**League**	**1-1**	**14,428**
	21	Huddersfield Town	A	League	1-2	12,893
	25	**Blackburn Rovers**	**H**	**League**	**0-1**	**16,823**
Apr	1	Crewe Alexandra	A	League	3-0	7,014
	8	**Charlton Athletic**	**H**	**League**	**1-1**	**20,922**
	15	Birmingham City	A	League	1-0	23,002
	22	**Sheffield United**	**H**	**League**	**0-0**	**17,172**
	24	Fulham	A	League	1-1	12,696
	29	**Port Vale**	**H**	**League**	**2-0**	**15,534**
May	7	Stockport County	A	League	3-2	7,756

HOME ATTENDANCES

	AGGREGATE ATTENDANCE	HIGHEST ATTENDANCE	LOWEST ATTENDANCE	AVERAGE ATTENDANCE
League:	395,505	25,836	13,841	17,195
League Cup:	13,315	8,300	5,015	6,657
FA Cup:	8,079	8,079	8,079	8,079
All Competitions:	416,899	25,836	5,015	16,034

FINAL LEAGUE TABLE - DIVISION ONE

Position	P	W	D	L	GF	GA	Pts
1. Charlton Athletic	46	27	10	9	79	45	91
2. Manchester City	46	26	11	9	78	40	89
3. Ipswich Town	46	25	12	9	71	42	87 *
4. Barnsley	46	24	10	12	88	67	82
5. Birmingham City	46	22	11	13	65	44	77
6. Bolton Wanderers	46	21	13	12	69	50	76
7. Wolverhampton Wanderers	46	21	11	14	64	48	74
8. Huddersfield Town	46	21	11	14	62	49	74
9. Fulham	46	17	16	13	49	41	67
10. Queens Park Rangers	46	16	18	12	62	53	66
11. Blackburn Rovers	46	15	17	14	55	51	62
12. Norwich City	46	14	15	17	45	50	57
13. Tranmere Rovers	46	15	12	19	57	68	57
14. Nottingham Forest	**46**	**14**	**14**	**18**	**53**	**55**	**56**
15. Crystal Palace	46	13	15	18	57	67	54
16. Sheffield United	46	13	15	18	59	71	54
17. Stockport County	46	13	15	18	55	67	54
18. Portsmouth	46	13	12	21	55	66	51
19. Crewe Alexandra	46	14	9	23	46	67	51
20. Grimsby Town	46	13	12	21	41	67	51
21. West Bromwich Albion	46	10	19	17	43	60	49
22. Walsall	46	11	13	22	52	77	46
23. Port Vale	46	7	15	24	48	69	36
24. Swindon Town	46	8	12	26	38	77	36

* Promoted via the play-offs

AWAY ATTENDANCES

	AGGREGATE ATTENDANCE	HIGHEST ATTENDANCE	LOWEST ATTENDANCE	AVERAGE ATTENDANCE
League:	336,341	31,857	5,714	14,623
League Cup:	26,855	15,524	3,072	8,951
FA Cup:	37,316	30,125	7,191	18,658
All Competitions:	400,512	31,857	3,072	14,304

"WE ALL LIVE IN A FLAT IN HYSON GREEN"

HAVING BEEN allocated a substantial transfer kitty by the Forest Board upon his arrival at the Club twelve months earlier, a disappointing 14th position in the table at the end of the season, had led to the cheque book being removed from manager David Platt's office and being locked firmly away in the safe, at least for the time being. Although on paper, his acquisitions to date had all looked the part, they had failed to live up to their reputations where it really mattered - out there on the park.

On a personal note, I wasn't too downhearted by this news, as I firmly believed Forest's miserable campaign had been nothing more than a bedding in period for both manager and players, and that the undoubted potential of the squad would begin to emerge during the course of the new season. To my mind, all that had been lacking to date had been confidence and the players' familiarity with one another.

Like most Forest supporters, I had been delighted by the Board's decision to slash season ticket prices during the summer and happily renewed my seat in the upper tier of the Trent End for the princely sum of £200 - a mere £8.69 per game. What's more, having dreaded the fact I'd be coughing up adult prices for Thomas as well (he was now sixteen); I was positively ecstatic at the news the juvenile age limit had also been extended to 18 years-of-age; and doing cartwheels by the renewal price of only £60 - a staggering £2.60 per game! Can you in your wildest dreams, imagine such a generous pricing structure had Messrs. Scholar and Wray still been at the helm? Not on your life!

Predictably, this unbelievably bold move by the Club led to an increase in sales from 9,700 the previous season, to 12,000 for the current campaign - an increase of 23.71%. Further generous ticket offers planned throughout the course of the season, would also undoubtedly attract more paying customers on a match-by-match basis. At last, we had a Board who cared about the long-term future of the Club and it's supporters - what a refreshing change.

With the purse strings having been understandably tightened, the bulk of the transfer activity during the summer and in the early part of the season, was on an outgoing basis. The long, drawn out saga surrounding goalkeeper Mark Crossley and midfielder Ian Woan, had finally been settled, with 'Big Norm' heading in a north-easterly direction to Premiership Middlesbrough and 'Woany' eventually ending up at Second Division Swindon Town - via Bolton Wanderers and Barnsley - both on free transfers.

Early season casualties included: Nigel Quashie making a £600,000 move to Portsmouth in August (what a shrewd buy he'd turned out to be at a 'mere' £2.5 million!); Dougie Freedman to one of his former clubs Crystal Palace in October for £600,000 (a competent striker in my book - just never given a proper chance at Forest); and, much later in the season, Colin Calderwood on loan to neighbours Notts County.

Not surprisingly, the begging bowl had been very much in evidence as far as incoming transfers were concerned, with 25-year-old midfielder Gary Jones arriving on a 'free' from Tranmere Rovers before the start of the season, Striker Robbie Blake arriving on loan from Bradford City in September, and Ben Olsen on a three-month loan from American club DC United in October. Later on in the season, Francis Benali would also arrive on loan from Southampton.

Despite much criticism from supporters throughout the course of the previous campaign, due to some pretty inept performances by the team, it was apparent that in David Platt, Forest had acquired themselves a manager who had an abundance of self-confidence and someone who was determined to stick to his principles - however unpopular. Some would argue that what we were seeing was in fact arrogance, as opposed to self-belief, but one thing I do find refreshing about 'Platty', is his willingness to throw youngsters into first team action - something sadly lacking at this Club since the days of Clough and Taylor. This policy would see the emergence of potentially top-class players such as Keith Foy, Barrie Roche, Gareth Edds, Gareth Williams, David Freeman, Richard Cooper, Jermaine Jenas and - the jewel in the crown in my opinion - Andy Reid, throughout the course of the season. And with the likes of David Prutton and Chris Doig having already established themselves on the first team scene, the long term prospects for the Club seem very rosy.

Away from the Club, there had also been some significant changes in local radio coverage, not only for Forest, but all the major East Midlands clubs. The already popular nightly phone-in programme on Century 106 had been moved on to another level, with Larry Lloyd making way for the double act of Darren Fletcher and Garry Birtles. 'Fletch' (a Forest fan through and through) had for some time been Century's match-day commentator for all Forest's games home and away, whilst Garry had been performing a similar function for rival station BBC Radio Nottingham. Together, they formed a formidable partnership, with 'Fletch' providing the journalistic input and Garry complimenting this with his vast knowledge of the game.

Their nightly show is compulsive listening and, for those unfortunate enough (or lazy enough) not to attend Forest's fixtures at home or away, their live match-day commentaries are of the highest standard (not that I'm biased in any way of course). Although I still attend every home game, without fail, I'd be the first to admit I don't get to nearly as many away matches as I should do nowadays (too busy writing this damn book, if truth be known!). I have to say though, Darren Fletcher's commentaries on the 'Reds' - particularly for important games - are so enthusiastic; I feel literally drained and exhausted by the end of the ninety minutes. And when you add to this, Garry's technical know-how and deep understanding of the professional game, it goes without saying, Century have indeed come up with a winning formula. What's more, I'm not the only one who sees it this way either; I am reliably informed by Garry that audience figures have already increased by over 10,000 since the pair of them got together - not bad in just one season.

One other positive change for this season, as far as I was concerned, was my own transport arrangements for my Saturday excursions to Nottingham and in particular the City Ground. Having experimented with the train on a couple of occasions the previous season, I had decided to leave my car well and truly parked up each weekend and make my way across the Midlands on the 10.17 from Birmingham's New Street Station. Yes, after several years in exile, Thomas long since able to make his own way down to the ground with his mates, I was going back on the piss with the lads again every Saturday. And boy was I happy! No more sitting there sipping my two pints of lager Shandy in the three hours leading up to the game. No, it was back to the good old days of five or six pints, followed by a mad dash to my seat - via the toilets of course - with only seconds to spare before kick off. It's what going to football matches is all about.

ON Saturday, 12th August, I arrived nice and early at New Street Station to board the train to Nottingham. Not surprisingly, with West Brom providing Forest's opposition on this opening day of the season, this was packed full of 'Baggies' fans. They took little notice of me, despite my Forest T-shirt - one of many I'd been wearing with pride in the Costa Brava during the summer. Most of them seemed to get off at Burton upon Trent and Derby anyway, having obviously decided to indulge in their pre-match refreshments outside Nottingham.

I returned to 'Brum' that evening in a happy (and slightly intoxicated) state, following Forest's 1-0 victory in front of 21,209 people. It was by no means a brilliant performance by the 'Reds', but a first-half header from Jon Olav Hjelde was enough to give them all three points on - surprise, surprise - a hot and sunny day.

The first few weeks of the season were fairly mixed, with draws at Norwich (0-0) and Darlington (2-2) in the League Cup, victories over Crystal Palace (3-2) and Sheffield Wednesday (1-0) also both away, and defeats at home to both Birmingham City (1-2) and Fulham (0-3) and against Blackburn Rovers (0-3) at Ewood Park.

The defeat at home to Birmingham City on Saturday, 26th August not only ended a run of eleven straight League victories over the 'Blues', but remarkably, was the first of eleven defeats they would suffer on home territory during the course of the season, two in the Cup and nine in the League. And although their away form throughout the campaign was impressive enough to keep them within reach of a play-off position, they never really looked like a team capable of holding their own in the Premiership - not without a massive injection of cash anyway.

They won an impressive nine times on their travels, including an excellent 2-0 victory against promotion rivals Birmingham City at St.Andrews on New Year's Day and a competent 3-1 success over Sheffield United at Bramall Lane on Saturday, 10th March. However, every time they put themselves either in, or within spitting distance of a play-off position, they went and blew it in front of an expectant, and at times enormous, City Ground audience. There are many examples I could quote, but perhaps the most significant are the following:

- A 2-0 defeat against fellow promotion contenders Watford on Saturday, 21st October in front of 20,065 fans.
- A 3-1 defeat against bottom-of-the-table Huddersfield Town on Wednesday, 13th December in front of a staggering 28,372 fans.
- A 3-0 defeat against struggling Crystal Palace on Sunday, 14th January in front of 21,198 fans and a watching Sky TV audience of millions.
- A decisive 2-0 defeat against promotion rivals Bolton Wanderers on Saturday, 17th March in front of 22,162 fans.

In their defence, it has to be said that a rake of long-term injuries undoubtedly played a big part in their rather erratic form. The likes of Chris Doig, Alan Rogers, Stern John, Jack Lester, Andy Johnson, Matthieu Louis-Jean, Riccardo Scimeca and (surprise, surprise) John Hjelde, all spent long periods of the season on the sidelines. However, all teams suffer their fair share of injuries during the course of a season and their ultimate fate is very much down to how the fringe players perform in their absence, what tactics are employed by the manager and his coaching staff, and how hungry the squad is as a whole to achieve success? In Forest's case, the answer to the latter would certainly seem to be 'not very'.

Despite ultimately finishing up in a disappointing 11th position, as ever, I've enjoyed myself this season overall and am already looking forward to next. If we can hang onto our best players, particularly the likes of David Johnson, purchased from Ipswich Town for £3.5 million in January, Chris Bart-Williams, Andy Reid, Jack Lester, Alan Rogers, David Prutton, Gareth Williams and Stern John, I'm sure we'll be mounting a serious challenge for the Premiership during 2001/02. In any case, I'd much rather go up as Champions, with a 'feel good' factor about the place and of course, a strong chance of establishing ourselves once again in the top flight.

There are still some things which annoy me about life down at the City Ground though and as a football supporter in general. The lack of atmosphere on Trentside this season has been embarrassing at times, and in stark contrast to the support afforded the team on their travels. It remains an enigma to me? We were never this quiet in the past, so I can only conclude that the lack of inspiration out there on the pitch is the cause. Some would argue the fans have a responsibility to try and lift the team, but there is no doubt in my mind that a crowd responds to good, exciting football. Sadly, that is something we very rarely see down at the City Ground these days, the exception this season being Burnley (5-0), Preston (3-1) and Blackburn (2-1).

The only original thing I've heard all season within the Trent End, was the *"Derby's goin' dairn like a Russian submarine"* chant, which emerged a few months ago. Amusingly, during one game, this prompted a gang of around eight youths who sit several rows in front of me to respond with the following, sung to the same tune (Yellow Submarine, by the way):

We all live in a flat in Hyson Green,
A flat in Hyson Green,
A flat in Hyson Green;

We all live in a flat in Hyson Green,
A flat in Hyson Green,
A flat in Hyson Green;

An' mi mam is on the game,
An' mi dad, is just the same,
An' mi brother's snortin' coke,
An' mi sister - is up the poke!

We all live in a flat in Hyson Green,
A flat in Hyson Green,
A flat in Hyson Green.

(Repeat)

One battle which has raged on in the Trent End all season, has been between supporters in the upper tier and the stewards and centres around the great 'standing versus seating' debate. What I can't quite get my head around is this: if someone who sits on the very back row of the Trent End, decides to stand up at various points throughout the game, and is obstructing the view of absolutely no-one, then what possible harm is he doing? Well obviously in the eyes of the 'powers that be', he's doing something wrong, because at least a dozen times each game, this particular activity prompts hordes of stewards to come racing up to the back of the Trent End (and presumably any other part of the stadium where this 'crime' is being committed) to threaten the perpetrators with everything from being thrown out of the ground, to being thrown in a police cell.

Now this whole situation as far as I'm concerned, is yet another example of bureaucracy gone mad. Just who are these faceless people who make up these nonsensical rules? Having witnessed this game of cat and mouse unfolding game after game (you know, the one where scores of people at the back stand up and try to get the atmosphere going with a bit of chanting, prompting an immediate charge up the steps by the stewards, which in turn inspires the whole stand to rise to their feet chanting: *"Stand up - if you 'ate Derby! Stand up - if you 'ate Derby! Stand up - if you 'ate Derby!"*), I decided to confront one of the stewards during the half-time interval at one game and establish just what the problem was? We had what can best be described as an 'adult' conversation about the whole situation and I was flabbergasted by his explanation. Apparently, this 'offence' is referred to as 'persistent standing' and contravenes rules and regulations laid down by the Local Authority. I wonder how many of these 'geniuses' actually ever attend football matches either at the City Ground, or anywhere else for that matter and have the faintest idea of what being a football supporter is all about? They probably think it's the same as going to the theatre or the ballet, where everyone's that stuck up, they sit there like stuffed ducks throughout the entire performance. Well football isn't like that I'm afraid. It's about passion, emotion, excitement (well sometimes anyway!) and this causes you to jump up and down and to scream and to shout. You wouldn't do it anywhere else, cause nothing else matters as much as football. So why don't they just leave us all alone and let us get on with enjoying the beautiful game unmolested?

As far as I'm concerned, it's high time the terraces were re-introduced in some capacity within the nation's football stadiums. Sports Minister Kate Hoey has raised this matter publicly on several occasions recently, only to be criticised by numerous bodies claiming to speak on behalf of the whole game. Well I'm sorry, but the arguments against are just too blinkered as far as I'm concerned. Terraces alone were not responsible for the Hillsborough tragedy in 1989. My own thoughts on this matter are well documented in Chapter 23, but to re-cap; this was the result of a combination of factors, not least the caging in of football supporters and the incompetence of the police. I'm absolutely convinced there is both a demand and a place for terraces within today's ultra-modern stadiums. Take for example, the lower tier of the Bridgford Stand at our very own City Ground. If the seats were removed and crash barriers installed as appropriate, it would comfortably hold 6 to 7,000 standing supporters (it holds 4,700 seats at present). Provided entrance to this section was by means of tickets only, purchased in advance, crowd control would not be at all difficult and I can't for the life of me envisage safety problems of any description. It would also give today's younger generation of supporters an opportunity to sample this unique experience; something the modern game has so far denied them.

DESPITE the lack of originality on the 'terraces' of the City Ground these days, the loyalty of Forest's support over the last few years is to be commended. How many other Clubs within the Football League (or the Premier for that matter), following a dire season in the First Division (which itself followed an abysmal relegation campaign the season before), would bounce back with the second best average attendances in the division the following season?

Well, at 20,733, Forest's average League gate was second only to Birmingham City's 21,282 - and that was only after a couple of full-houses down at St.Andrews during their final push for a play-off place (unlike Forest, the 'Blues' had occupied a top-six position for virtually the whole of the campaign). For a Club who had hardly set the world alight over the last few seasons, to bring in 13 League attendances in excess of 20,000, was a remarkable achievement and speaks volumes for the often-maligned Nottingham public.

However, Nottingham is an affluent, rapidly expanding City, with a 'feel-good' factor second to none. Everything about the place is buoyant and it's no surprise the game continues to thrive in what remains a traditional footballing stronghold. As the City continues to grow over the next few years, it is essential that Premiership football returns to the banks of the River Trent - and I don't mean on the 'black and white side' either.

The town planners are busily turning Nottingham into a truly European City and the Forest Board have a duty and a responsibility to also bring top class football back into the public domain once again. Outside of London and Glasgow, we already hold the title of 'best provincial centre for shopping' and our famous night-life is unrivalled anywhere else in the country. Since 1995, the number of licensed premises within the City Centre has increased from 209 to a whopping 368, with another 22 new venues set to open shortly. Already, there is the capacity for over 111,000 people to be drinking in town at any one time!

And with the continued expansion of the Lace Market (almost a city within a city), the emergence of the Light Rapid Transit System, the impressive development of Canal side, trendy London Restaurant chains such as Conran Restaurants, Le Petit Blanc, Fish! Yo! Sushi! and Group Chez Gerard all falling over themselves to find premises here; not to mention the ambitious £1 billion redevelopment plans for the 250-acre site along the north side of the river and canal near Trent Bridge, the City is destined to develop still further. 'City living' is all the rage and the population of Nottingham will undoubtedly expand considerably over the coming years as young people are enticed back out of the rural and urban areas both to work and to live in the City. I for one hope some of these people can also be enticed to spend at least ninety minutes of their busy and exciting lives down on Trentside every other Saturday afternoon watching the 'Super Reds' in action.

On a personal note, if my Fairy Godmother were to suddenly appear out of nowhere and grant me three wishes, then they would have to be as follows:

1. A move back to my beloved Nottingham from my miserable exile out here in Birmingham. (I've nothing against Birmingham, by the way, I just love Nottingham too much to ever be happy anywhere else).
2. A fully refurbished City Ground, with the upper tier of the Bridgford Stand extended and arcing round to join a brand new three-tier Main Stand, taking the capacity up to a more realistic 40,000.
3. Forest back in the Premier League (following a barn-storming Championship-winning season in the First Division), boasting a crop of international stars - both English and Continental - regularly challenging for a place in Europe, winning the odd Cup Final at a new national stadium (hopefully and sensibly in the Midlands) and playing to a packed house every week. (That is only three isn't it?).

And the good news is, following a recent return to Nottingham on the job front, by the time this book goes to press, wish number 1 will already have been realised and I will be firmly installed in my new home in Chilwell (there is a God up there after all!). Is it too much to hope that wishes 2 and 3 will also follow in the not-too-distant future? You never know. And that's what makes the game of football so special.

We have had a small taste of success already this season, with the Forest stars of yester-year winning the six-a-side Masters of Britain Grand Final at the Nottingham Arena in October. A squad consisting of Steve Wigley, Gary Mills, Neil Webb, Garry Birtles, Johnny Metgod, Steve Hodge, Bryn Gunn, Steve Sutton, Calvin Plummer and Brian Rice, drew 1-1 with Sheffield Wednesday and beat Arsenal 4-0 at the group stage, to qualify for the Final against Glasgow Rangers. This they went on to win 3-2 in front of a crowd of over 5,000 and a watching live Sky TV audience of millions, with Wigley, Mills and Webb grabbing the all important goals.

I made a point of being over in Nottingham for the weekend especially to attend the competition and enjoyed every minute of it (what a fantastic venue we have in this truly magnificent arena). It was good to see the likes of Birtles and Metgod wearing the famous Garibaldi once again and hopefully their success will rub off on the current members of the squad, inspiring them to greater things?

ALTHOUGH I've now followed Forest for 35 seasons, my enthusiasm remains as intense as ever and, like most football supporters, I am filled with optimism for the future. However, like most people of my age, I am also very nostalgic about seasons gone by and can't help reminiscing about the Club's exploits over the years and in particular the many wonderful players who have pulled on the famous red and white shirt. I've racked my brains to think what my all-time greatest team would be, but with so many gifted individuals having represented this great Club of ours, have found it almost impossible to fathom. Consequently, I have taken the cowards way out and instead put together a twenty-strong squad of my favourite players over the last three and a half decades. And here it is:

Goalkeepers:

Peter Shilton, Hans Van Breukelen

Defenders:

Viv Anderson, Kenny Burns, Larry Lloyd, Des Walker, Stuart Pearce

Midfielders:

Martin O'Neill, Steve Hodge, Roy Keane, Johnny Metgod, Archie Gemmill, John Robertson

Strikers:

Ian Storey-Moore, Joe Baker, Duncan McKenzie, Tony Woodcock, Garry Birtles, Trevor Francis, Stan Collymore

I feel honoured and privileged to have watched these individuals over the years and it would be very difficult to single out any as my absolute all-time favourite. Once again therefore, I'll take the cowards way out and nominate the brilliant trio of Ian Storey-Moore, Duncan McKenzie and Garry Birtles as my collective favourites, each of whom have dazzled me with their sheer brilliance on many occasions over the years. And in complete contrast to this, I would like to nominate Pierre Van Hooijdonk as the number one scumbag of all time down on Trentside, closely followed by a certain Mr. Stanley Collymore (despite him also being in the top-twenty in terms of ability).

THE end of the season brought with it the good news that the already excellent value-for- money season ticket prices have been frozen for yet another year. This is indeed a bold move on the part of the Club, especially when you consider the fact they are losing around £100,000 per week at present. No doubt the wage bill will have to be trimmed during the summer, with the inevitable loss of some of the more high profile players? However, we have some truly promising youngsters at the Club who will surely realise their potential in the not-too-distant future.

I for one will be renewing my seat in the upper tier of the Trent End along with Thomas and his gang, my old mates Jacko and Garry Mason, and my newly-acquired friends in the seats around me such as 'Smudge' and his good lady Sam from Hucknall, Garry Housley from Clowne in Chesterfield, not to mention Rod Symes, who remarkably has been coming to the City Ground week in week out from his home in Cambridge since season 1946/47, and his son Brian (named after 'Cloughie' of course). They'll just have to put up with my ranting and raving for another season at least, because I'm staying put in the Trent End - atmosphere or no atmosphere - until the Main Stand has been redeveloped and is in keeping with the rest of the stadium.

Many thanks for reading this book. Keep on following the 'Reds' and let's cheer them on all the way back to the Premier and beyond!

SEASON 2000/01 – STATISTICS

FOOTBALL LEAGUE DIVISION ONE – FIXTURES

Date		Opposition	Venue	Competition	Score	Attendance
Aug	12	**Ipswich Town**	**H**	**League**	**1-0**	**21,209**
	19	Norwich City	A	League	0-0	18,059
	22	Darlington	A	LC 1 - 1st Leg	2-2	4,724
	26	**Birmingham City**	**H**	**League**	**1-2**	**18,820**
	28	Crystal Palace	A	League	3-2	18,865
Sept	6	**Darlington**	**H**	**LC 2 - 2nd Leg**	**1-2**	**6,530**
	9	Blackburn Rovers	A	League	0-3	18,471
	13	Sheffield Wednesday	A	League	1-0	15,700
	16	**Fulham**	**H**	**League**	**0-3**	**18,737**
	23	Grimsby Town	A	League	2-0	6,467
	30	**Wolverhampton Wanderers**	**H**	**League**	**0-0**	**19,110**
Oct	14	Barnsley	A	League	4-3	14,831
	17	Bolton Wanderers	A	League	0-0	13,017
	21	**Watford**	**H**	**League**	**0-2**	**20,065**
	25	**Burnley**	**H**	**League**	**5-0**	**17,915**
	28	Stockport County	A	League	2-1	6,021
Nov	4	**Preston North End**	**H**	**League**	**3-1**	**19,504**
	12	Gillingham	A	League	3-1	9,884
	18	**Wimbledon**	**H**	**League**	**1-2**	**18,159**
	25	**Tranmere Rovers**	**H**	**League**	**3-1**	**19,678**
	29	**Shefiield United**	**H**	**League**	**2-0**	**17,089**
Dec	2	Burnley	A	League	0-1	17,876
	9	**Portsmouth**	**H**	**League**	**2-0**	**19,284**
	13	**Huddersfield Town**	**H**	**League**	**1-3**	**28,372**
	16	Queens Park Rangers	A	League	0-1	14,409
	23	West Bromwich Albion	A	League	0-3	20,350
	26	**Crewe Alexandra**	**H**	**League**	**1-0**	**20,903**
	30	**Norwich City**	**H**	**League**	**0-0**	**20,108**
Jan	1	Birmingham City	A	League	2-0	20,034
	7	**Wolverhampton Wanderers**	**H**	**FA Cup 3**	**0-1**	**14,601**
	14	**Crystal Palace**	**H**	**League**	**0-3**	**21,198**
Feb	3	Huddersfield Town	A	League	1-1	13,838
	10	**Blackburn Rovers**	**H**	**League**	**2-1**	**24,455**
	17	Fulham	A	League	0-1	17,425
	21	**Sheffield Wednesday**	**H**	**League**	**0-1**	**23,266**
	24	**Grimsby Town**	**H**	**League**	**3-1**	**21,660**
Mar	3	Wolverhampton Wanderers	A	League	0-2	20,291
	7	**Barnsley**	**H**	**League**	**1-0**	**18,788**
	10	Sheffield United	A	League	3-1	25,673
	13	Crewe Alexandra	A	League	0-1	7,916
	17	**Bolton Wanderers**	**H**	**League**	**0-2**	**22,162**
	31	**Queens Park Rangers**	**H**	**League**	**1-1**	**22,208**
Apr	3	Watford	A	League	0-3	13,651
	7	Portsmouth	A	League	2-0	13,018
	14	Preston North End	A	League	1-1	16,842
	16	**Stockport County**	**H**	**League**	**1-0**	**23,500**
	21	Wimbledon	A	League	1-2	10,027
	28	**Gillingham**	**H**	**League**	**0-1**	**20,670**
May	6	Tranmere Rovers	A	League	2-2	9,891

HOME ATTENDANCES

	AGGREGATE ATTENDANCE	HIGHEST ATTENDANCE	LOWEST ATTENDANCE	AVERAGE ATTENDANCE
League:	476,860	28,372	17,089	20,733
League Cup:	6,530	6,530	6,530	6,530
FA Cup:	14,601	14,601	14,601	14,601
All Competitions:	497,991	28,372	6,530	19,919

FINAL LEAGUE TABLE - DIVISION ONE

Position	P	W	D	L	GF	GA	Pts
1. Fulham	46	30	11	5	90	32	101
2. Blackburn Rovers	46	26	13	7	76	39	91
3. Bolton Wanderers	46	24	15	7	76	45	87 *
4. Preston North End	46	23	9	14	64	52	78
5. Birmingham City	46	23	9	14	59	48	78
6. West Bromwich Albion	46	21	11	14	60	52	74
7. Burnley	46	21	9	16	50	54	72
8. Watford	46	20	9	17	76	67	69
9. Wimbledon	46	17	18	11	71	50	69
10. Sheffield United	46	19	11	16	52	49	68
11. Nottingham Forest	**46**	**20**	**8**	**18**	**55**	**53**	**68**
12. Wolverhampton Wanderers	46	14	13	19	45	48	55
13. Gillingham	46	13	16	17	61	66	55
14. Crewe Alexandra	46	15	10	21	47	62	55
15. Barnsley	46	15	9	22	49	62	54
16. Norwich City	46	14	12	20	46	58	54
17. Sheffield Wednesday	46	15	8	23	52	71	53
18. Stockport County	46	11	18	17	58	65	51
19. Grimsby Town	46	13	11	22	43	63	50
20. Crystal Palace	46	12	13	21	57	70	49
21. Portsmouth	46	10	19	17	47	59	49
22. Huddersfield Town	46	11	15	20	48	57	48
23. Queens Park Rangers	46	7	19	20	45	75	40
24. Tranmere Rovers	46	9	11	26	46	77	38

* Promoted via the play-offs

AWAY ATTENDANCES

	AGGREGATE ATTENDANCE	HIGHEST ATTENDANCE	LOWEST ATTENDANCE	AVERAGE ATTENDANCE
League:	342,556	25,673	6,021	14,893
League Cup:	4,724	4,724	4,724	4,724
All Competitions:	347,280	25,673	4,724	14,470

WHY IS it that the supporters of some clubs enjoy a kind of mythical status as passionate, loyal die-hards, whilst on the other hand, others, often unfairly, are labelled as laid back, apathetic or fickle?

Some reputations are of course, well earned. For example, it would be difficult to argue that, in the main, Geordies or Scousers are anything but fanatical and dedicated followers of their respective teams; in the same way it would be hard to dispute that Bradford City's fan base is somewhat lacking, considering both their recent Premiership status, and the size of the local population.

However, what about the Derby Counties, Portsmouths and Wolverhampton Wanderers of this world, who seem to have convinced themselves and the rest of the world, that they are 'big' clubs and that their respective cities represent the 'hot-beds' of English football? Would closer examination of the facts bear this out? I'm not so sure.

As far as I'm concerned, this 'big' club, 'little' club debate is one of the most fascinating in football. But what is it exactly that constitutes a 'big' club? Well, as far as the Manchester Uniteds, Liverpools and Arsenals of this world are concerned, no debate is necessary: they are all 'massive' clubs, with massive support, illustrious histories, and impressive stadiums (the exception being Highbury, which is well past it's prime). But, what about the rest? What is the criteria?

There are 92 clubs within the four divisions of English football, ranging from the 'massive' - such as those previously mentioned - to the 'minnows' such as Wycombe Wanderers or Macclesfield Town, for example. But the only logical way to establish the true status of the rest, is to examine the facts. Only then can a fair and reasonable assessment be made.

So what factors need to be taken into consideration? Well, undoubtedly all of the following:

- Honours achieved throughout the club's history.
- Population size or catchment area.
- Volume of support in the past and the present, and crowd potential for the future.
- Size and quality of the stadium and it's surrounding facilities.
- Number of years spent in the top flight.
- Financial strength, commercial activities and annual turnover.

So, what about Forest? How do they fare in this debate? Well, here are the facts:

Summary of Honours Achieved:
Two European Cups; One League Championship; Two FA Cups; Four League Cups; One UEFA Super Cup; Division One Champions once; Division Two Champions twice; Division Three South Champions once; Football Alliance Champions once; FA Charity Shield winners once; World Club finalists; UEFA Super Cup finalists; Football League Runners-up twice; FA Cup Runners-up once; League Cup Runners-up twice; Division One Runners-up once; Division Two Runners-up once. And, on a lesser note: they have finished third in the top flight on no less than four occasions; and won the Anglo/Scottish Cup, the Simod Cup and the ZDS Cup. (See 'Honours Board' on page 388).

Population:
• With a population of 285,000, the City of Nottingham is the eleventh largest English City (twelfth largest in England and Wales) represented across the four divisions of English football. (See 'English & Welsh Cities' on page 397).
• With a population of 1,031,900, the County of Nottinghamshire is the fourteenth largest English County represented across the four divisions of English football. (See 'English & Welsh Counties' on page 400).
• Forest also attract considerable support from areas of Lincolnshire such as Grantham,

Boston and Skegness; areas of North-West Leicestershire, such as Loughborough and Melton Mowbray; and areas of South-East Derbyshire, such as Long Eaton, Ilkeston, Langley-Mill, Heanor, Ripley, Alfreton and Shirebrook.

Support:

• During their 136-year history (the last 104 of which have been spent at the City Ground), Forest have attracted to the City Ground, no less than 40 attendances in excess of 40,000. The highest of these, was the record 49,946 for the visit of Manchester United on 28th October 1967. (See page 391 'City Ground attendances in excess of 40,000').

• During the same period, they have also attracted no less than 171 City Ground attendances of between 30,000 and 40,000 people. (See page 392 'City Ground attendances of between 30,000 and 40,000'). This is the equivalent of more than ten whole seasons of 30,000-plus attendances!

• Since their promotion to the old First Division in 1957, Forest have spent 35 out of 44 seasons in the top flight. During this period, their average League attendance has topped the 25,000 mark on no less than 12 occasions. At least 4 of these have topped the 30,000 mark. The seasons in question are: 1957/58 - 31,685; 1958/59 - 28,716; 1959/60 - 26,738; 1964/65 - 27,426; 1966/67 - 31,282; 1967/68 - 32,548; 1968/69 - 25,202; 1969/70 - 25,406; 1977/78 - 32,501; 1978/79 - 29,587; 1979/80 - 26,389; 1995/96 - 25,915. (See page 389 - 'Summary of Home Attendances - Seasons 1957/58 to 2000/01').

• Forest's average League attendance in the top flight from season 1957/58 to present is a healthy 24,048! This despite four relegation seasons during this period. (See page 390 - 'Aggregate Top Flight League Attendances - 1957/58 to present').

• No less than 34 of the 40,000-plus attendances and 124 of the 30,000-plus attendances were recorded prior to Brian Clough's eighteen-year reign at the Club!

• No less than 3 of Forest's 40,000-plus crowds and 51 of their 30,000-plus crowds have been recorded whilst the Club was outside of the top flight!

• When Second Division Forest played First Division Newcastle United in the quarter-final of the FA Cup on 6th March 1974, over 14,000 Forest supporters made the journey to St.James' Park! Forest lost this tie 4-3 in very controversial circumstances. (See pages 60 to 64).

• When Forest took on Liverpool in the League Cup Final on 18th March 1978; an estimated 40,000 Forest supporters had made the journey to Wembley! After a 0-0 draw, Forest went on to beat the 'Scoucers' in the replay at Old Trafford four days later. (See pages 100 to 102).

• When Forest took on and beat Malmoe in the European Cup Final on 30th May 1979; a staggering 25,000-plus Forest supporters had made the long journey to Munich! (See pages 123 to 127).

• Over 8,000 supporters made the trip to Amsterdam to see Forest take on Ajax Amsterdam in the second leg of the European Cup semi-final on 23rd April 1980! (See pages 134 to 138). Forest lost 1-0 on the night, but went through to the Final 2-1 on aggregate.

• Over 12,000 supporters made the long journey to Madrid to see Forest take on and beat Hamburg in the European Cup Final on 28th May 1980! (See pages 139 to 149).

• Over 12,000 supporters travelled to St.Andrews on 20th February 1988 to see Forest take on Birmingham City in the 5th round of the FA Cup! Forest won 1-0. (See pages 211 to 212).

• An estimated 14,000 supporters travelled to Highbury on 12th March 1988 to see Forest take on Arsenal in the FA Cup quarter-final! The final score was 2-1 to Forest. (See pages 212 to 214).

• More than 12,000 Forest supporters travelled up to Old Trafford on 18th March 1989 in to see Forest beat Manchester United 1-0 in the quarter-final of the FA Cup! (See pages 224 to 226).

• When Forest triumphed in the Simod Cup Final (a supposedly 'Mickey Mouse' affair) on 30th April 1989, they did so in front of more than 30,000 Forest supporters who had made the journey south to Wembley. Forest's 'illustrious' opponents that day, Everton, brought with them less than 15,000 supporters! (See pages 232 to 233).

• Despite desperate relegation campaigns during seasons 1992/93, 1996/97 and 1998/99, Forest's average League attendances were 21,866 (crowds restricted due to ground redevelopment), 24,586 and 24,410 respectively! (See page 389).

• Following their relegation from the FA Premier League at the end of season 1992/93, Forest still managed to sell 15,500 season tickets during the summer of 1993 and went on to attract average League attendances of 23,050 in the First Division during season 1993/94! (See page 389).

• Having achieved promotion back to the Premiership at the end of season 1993/94, Forest went into the 1994/95 season with over 20,000 season ticket holders! (See page 308).

• Despite being in the bottom third of the First Division (having been relegated from the Premiership for a third time in season 1998/99) throughout the 1999/2000 season, they still managed to attract an average League attendance of 17,195! (See page 389).

• Despite finishing in only 11th position in the First Division Table in season 2000/01, Forest's average League attendance of 20,733 was the second highest in the whole of the Nationwide League! (See page 378).

Stadium/Corporate Facilities:

• The City Ground is one of the most attractive and modern stadiums in England and was selected as one of the venues for the European Championships, held in this country in 1996. The current capacity of the stadium is 30,587.

• There are a total of 36 Executive Boxes situated in the Brian Clough Stand, each including luxury seating for eight guests.

• The Loxley Members' Lounge is also situated in the Brian Clough Stand and includes bar and restaurant facilities. Three-course meals are available prior to the match.

• Situated within the Trent End is the Castle Club, which incorporates 600 seats in one large open plan viewing area, all padded and behind glass.

• The Pitch Diner Restaurant and the Club Museum are also housed within the Trent End complex.

• The Robin Hood Lounge is situated within the Main Stand and has bar and restaurant facilities. A three-course meal is available prior to the match.

• The Sheriff's Lounge is also situated within the Main Stand and provides facilities for match sponsors. Parties of up to ten people can enjoy a champagne reception, five-course silver service meal prior to the game, seats in the Directors' Box, after match buffet, and the opportunity to meet with players and obtain souvenirs and photographs.

• The Lincoln Green Lounge is situated behind the Main Stand and has bar and restaurant facilities available to all Main Stand season ticket holders.

• Forest have one of the finest Youth Academies in English football. The Academy is based on a 24-acre site on Wilford Lane and amongst it's many facilities are two synthetic training pitches, one of which is situated indoors. The outdoor Arena Pitch has floodlights and banking for spectators. The Acadamy has already produced players of the calibre of David Prutton, Chris Doig, Keith Foy, Gareth Williams, David Freeman, Gareth Edds, Andy Reid, Barry Roche, Kevin Dawson and Jermaine Jenas, the majority of whom have featured prominently on the first team scene over the past couple of seasons.

• On Thursday, 12th February 1998, the Club's brand new 2,000 square foot Superstore, situated just behind the Main Stand on Pavillion Road, officially opened for business. A wide range of quality merchandise is available, although prices tend to be a little on the dear side. The shop is very much in keeping with a club of Forest's stature.

Years Spent In Top Flight:

• During their 135-year history, Forest have spent no less than 69 seasons in the top flight of English football!

• Since their promotion to the old First Division at the end of season 1956/57, Forest have spent no less than 35 of the following 44 seasons in the top flight!

<u>Forest Firsts:</u>

- The world's first official local derby took place between Forest and Notts County at the Forest Recreation Ground on 22nd March 1866. The result was 0-0. (See page 176).
- Forest became the first British club to pay £1 million for a player when they brought striker Trevor Francis to the City Ground from Birmingham City on 8th February 1979. (See page 118).
- Forest are the only 'top flight' club ever to go the equivalent of a whole season unbeaten. They remained undefeated in the League from 19th November 1977 until 9th December 1978 - a total of 42 matches! (See page 114).
- Forest were the first club ever to retain the League Cup trophy when they beat Southampton 3-2 at Wembley on 17th March 1979.
- When Forest played Wolves at Wembley on 15th March 1980, they became the first club ever to appear in the Final of a major domestic Cup competition on three successive occasions.
- When Forest beat East German side Dynamo Berlin 3-1 on 19th March 1980, in the second leg of the European Cup quarter-final, they became the first club ever to overturn a first-leg home deficit in the history of the competition.
- Forest are the only club in England to have gone 40 first class matches unbeaten in all competitions. This unbeaten run stretched from 14th March 1978 right up until 9th December 1978. It also included no less than 23 fixtures away from the City Ground (including the League Cup Final against Liverpool at Wembley, the replay at Old Trafford, and the FA Charity Shield against Ipswich Town at Wembley.
- Forest (twice winners) are one of only five British clubs ever to have won the European Cup. The others are: Glasgow Celtic (once), Manchester United (twice), Liverpool (four times), and Aston Villa (once).
- Forest became only the second British club to retain the European Cup when they beat Hamburg 1-0 in Madrid on 28th May 1980. (Well...this is nearly a first!).
- Forest were the first English club to pay £1 million for a black player when they signed Justin Fashanu from Norwich City in the summer of 1981. (See page 161).
- Forest's Nottingham-born full-back Viv Anderson became the first black player ever to play for England at full international level, when he lined up against Czechoslovakia at Wembley on 29th November 1978. (See page 114).
- Forest featured in the first ever live televised English First Division game, when they lost 2-1 to Spurs at White Hart Lane on Sunday, 2nd October 1983. (See page 176).
- Forest also featured in the first ever live televised FA Premiership game, when they defeated Liverpool 1-0 at the City Ground on 16th August 1992. (See page 277).
- Forest were the first club to remain undefeated for 25 games in the FA Premier League, commencing from 21st February 1995 until 18th November 1995. (See page 319). This record was only recently beaten by Manchester United.

Finances – Brief Summary of the Club's Annual Report dated 31st May 1999 (their last season in the FA Premier League):

Profit: (before depreciation, amortisation and player transfer costs) = £ **1,300,000**

| Cash Flow: | Player disposals | = £ | **8,600,000** |
| | Player acquisitions | = £ | **6,800,000** |

Revenue Sources:

Comprising:	Television and radio	= £	6,804,000
	Ticket sales	= £	6,400,000
	Matchday hospitality & catering	= £	1,474,000
	Sponsorship, royalties & advertising	= £	1,448,000
	Merchandising	= £	877,000
	Annual turnover	= £	**17,003,000**

Total Expenses:	Wages and salaries	= £	9,134,000
	Social security costs	= £	977,000
	Pension costs	= £	54,000
	Signing on fees	= £	1,641,000
	Total	= £	**11,806,000**

Persons employed by the Club:

	Playing staff	=	59
	Non-playing staff	=	99
	Total	=	**158**

Assets:	Fixed assets	= £	17,791,000
	Net current assets	= £	1,507,000
	Net assets	= £	**19,298,000**

Capital & reserves:	Called up share capital	= £	11,030,000
	Share premium account	= £	8,378,000
	Profit & loss account	= £	(110,000)
	Equity shareholders' funds	= £	**19,298,000**

• So, there you have all the important facts about Nottingham Forest FC. But don't take my word for it; check them out for yourself over the next few pages. Only then can you answer the question: Nottingham Forest: Big club? Little club? I'll leave you to make up your own mind!

FACTS

DOMESTIC HONOURS

Division One (Pre-FA Premier League)
- Football League Champions 1977/78
- Runners-up 1966/67 & 1978/79

Division Two (Pre-FA Premier League)
- Champions 1906/07 & 1921/22
- Runners-up 1956/57

Division Three South (Pre-FA Premier League)
- Champions 1950/51

Football Alliance
- Champions 1891/92

Division One (Post-FA Premier League)
- Champions 1997/98
- Runners-up 1993/94

FA Cup
- Winners 1897/98 & 1958/59
- Finalists 1990/91

League Cup
- Winners 1977/78, 1978/79, 1988/89 & 1989/90
- Finalists 1979/80 & 1991/92

Charity Shield
- Winners 1978
- Finalists 1959

Anglo/Scottish Cup
- Winners 1976/77

Simod Cup
- Winners 1988/89

Zenith Data Systems Cup
- Winners 1991/92

EUROPEAN HONOURS

European Cup
- Winners 1978/79 & 1979/80

UEFA Super Cup Competition
- Winners 1979/80
- Finalists 1980/81

WORLD HONOURS

World Club Championship Cup
- Finalists 1980

"We've bin to Europe, we've won the cup TWICE!"

SUMMARY OF HOME ATTENDANCES – SEASON 1957/58 TO 2000/01

Season	Division	Final League Position	Highest League Attendance	Average League Attendance	Highest Attendance Overall	Average Attendance Overall
1957/58	Div 1	10th	47,804	31,685	47,804	32,016
1958/59	Div 1	13th	44,971	28,716	44,971	30,540
1959/60	Div 1	20th	42,335	26,738	42,335	26,821
1960/61	Div 1	14th	37,248	24,624	37,248	23,132
1961/62	Div 1	19th	40,875	23,517	46,218	24,482
1962/63	Div 1	9th	34,171	22,086	37,120	23,452
1963/64	Div 1	13th	41,426	22,497	41,426	22,697
1964/65	Div 1	5th	43,009	27,426	43,009	27,478
1965/66	Div 1	18th	34,750	23,724	34,750	23,724
1966/67	Div.1	2nd	47,188	31,282	47,510	32,675
1967/68	Div.1	11th	49,946	32,548	49,946	32,533
1968/69	Div.1	18th	41,892	25,202	41,892	25,148
1969/70	Div.1	15th	42,074	25,406	42,074	24,943
1970/71	Div.1	16th	40,692	23,322	40,692	22,626
1971/72	Div.1	21st	42,750	21,433	42,750	20,665
1972/73	Div.2	14th	18,082	10,016	19,168	11,010
1973/74	Div.2	7th	29,962	14,415	41,472	16,619
1974/75	Div.2	16th	25,013	13,000	25,361	14,365
1975/76	Div.2	8th	19,757	12,805	31,525	13,224
1976/77	Div.2	3rd	31,004	17,978	38,284	17,132
1977/78	Div.1	1st	47,218	32,501	47,218	32,298
1978/79	Div.1	2nd	41,898	29,587	41,898	30,446
1979/80	Div.1	5th	32,266	26,389	33,277	26,343
1980/81	Div.1	7th	33,900	24,419	34,796	24,483
1981/82	Div.1	12th	26,327	19,889	26,327	19,245
1982/83	Div.1	5th	25,554	17,851	25,554	17,429
1983/84	Div.1	3rd	29,692	17,703	34,084	18,318
1984/85	Div.1	9th	25,902	16,776	25,902	17,071
1985/86	Div.1	8th	30,171	16,815	30,171	16,496
1986/87	Div.1	8th	35,828	19,090	35,828	18,694
1987/88	Div.1	3rd	31,061	19,264	31,061	18,900
1988/89	Div.1	3rd	30,092	20,796	30,092	20,417
1989/90	Div.1	9th	26,766	20,609	30,044	20,732
1990/91	Div.1	8th	27,347	22,138	28,962	21,966
1991/92	Div.1	8th	30,168	23,720	30,168	23,045
1992/93	FA Premier	22nd	26,752	21,866	26,752	21,318
1993/94	Div.1	2nd	27,010	23,050	27,010	21,880
1994/95	FA Premier	3rd	28,822	23,625	28,822	22,208
1995/96	FA Premier	9th	29,263	25,915	29,263	24,126
1996/97	FA Premier	20th	29,181	24,586	29,181	23,252
1997/98	Div.1	1st	29,302	20,583	29,302	19,647
1998/99	FA Premier	20th	30,025	24,410	30,025	22,248
1999/00	Div.1	14th	25,836	17,195	25,836	16,034
2000/01	Div.1	11th	28,372	20,733	28,372	19,919

• Not only did Forest win the League Championship Trophy in season 1977/78, but they were also Runners-up in seasons 1966/67 and 1978/79 and finished in third position in seasons 1983/84, 1987/88, 1988/89 and 1994/95!

AGGREGATE LEAGUE ATTENDANCES IN THE TOP FLIGHT
- SEASON 1957/58 TO PRESENT

No.	Season	Aggregate League Attendance	Number of Games Played
1.	1957/58	665,388	21
2.	1958/59	603,055	21
3.	1959/60	561,501	21
4.	1960/61	517,124	21
5.	1961/62	493,861	21
6.	1962/63	463,809	21
7.	1963/64	472,445	21
8.	1964/65	575,951	21
9.	1965/66	498,221	21
10.	1966/67	656,925	21
11.	1967/68	716,056	21
12.	1968/69	554,449	21
13.	1969/70	533,546	21
14.	1970/71	489,782	21
15.	1971/72	450,105	21
16.	1977/78	682,524	21
17.	1978/79	621,330	21
18.	1979/80	554,181	21
19.	1980/81	512,805	21
20.	1981/82	417,684	21
21.	1982/83	374,878	21
22.	1983/84	371,772	21
23.	1984/85	352,311	21
24.	1985/86	353,122	21
25.	1986/87	400,904	21
26.	1987/88	385,285	20
27.	1988/89	395,125	19
28.	1989/90	391,578	19
29.	1990/91	420,636	19
30.	1991/92	498,137	21
31.	1992/93	459,194	21
32.	1994/95	496,128	21
33.	1995/96	492,391	19
34.	1996/97	467,148	19
35.	1998/99	463,804	19
	Totals	**17,363,155**	**722**

• Average League attendance in top flight between seasons 1957/58 to 1998/99 (35 seasons) = **24,048**

CITY GROUND ATTENDANCES IN EXCESS OF 40,000
SEASON 1898/99 ONWARDS

No.	Date	Opposition	Competition	Score	Attendance
1.	01-03-30	Sheffield Wednesday	FA Cup 6	2-2	44,166
2.	19-01-52	Notts County	Division 2	3-2	40,005
3.	28-09-57	West Bromwich Albion	Division 1	0-2	41,825
4.	12-10-57	Manchester United	Division 1	1-2	47,804
5.	26-10-57	Blackpool	Division 1	1-2	41,586
6.	29-01-58	West Bromwich Albion	FA Cup 4 – Replay	1-5	46,455
7.	15-03-58	Wolverhampton Wanderers	Division 1	1-4	40,197
8.	27-08-58	Manchester United	Division 1	0-3	44,971
9.	27-12-58	Newcastle United	Division 1	3-0	40,057
10.	24-01-59	Tooting & Mitcham	FA Cup 4 – Replay	3-0	42,320
11.	28-02-59	Bolton Wanderers	FA Cup 6	2-1	44,414
12.	19-04-60	Wolverhampton Wanderers	Division 1	0-0	42,335
13.	23-09-61	Tottenham Hotspur	Division 1	2-0	40,875
14.	27-01-62	Sheffield Wednesday	FA Cup 4	0-2	46,218
15.	19-10-63	Manchester United	Division 1	1-2	41,426
16.	01-09-64	Everton	Division 1	3-1	40,382
17.	26-12-64	Tottenham Hotspur	Division 1	1-2	42,056
18.	16-01-65	Manchester United	Division 1	2-2	43,009
19.	01-10-66	Manchester United	Division 1	4-1	41,854
20.	14-01-67	Leeds United	Division 1	1-0	43,849
21.	04-02-67	Tottenham Hotspur	Division 1	1-1	41,822
22.	18-02-67	Newcastle United	FA Cup 4	3-0	45,962
23.	25-02-67	Leicester City	Division 1	1-0	47,188
24.	11-03-67	Swindon Town	FA Cup 5	0-0	45,878
25.	27-03-67	Burnley	Division 1	4-1	41,586
26.	08-04-67	Everton	FA Cup 6	3-2	47,510
27.	15-04-67	Aston Villa	Division 1	3-0	41,468
28.	22-08-67	Coventry City	Division 1	3-3	44,950
29.	28-10-67	Manchester United	Division 1	3-1	49,946
30.	31-03-69	Manchester United	Division 1	0-1	41,892
31.	14-03-70	Derby County	Division 1	1-3	42,074
32.	13-04-71	Arsenal	Division 1	0-3	40,692
33.	27-12-72	Arsenal	Division 1	1-1	42,750
34.	27-01-74	Manchester City	FA Cup 4	4-1	41,472
35.	26-12-77	Liverpool	Division 1	1-1	47,218
36.	02-01-78	Everton	Division 1	1-1	44,030
37.	27-02-78	Queens Park Rangers	FA Cup 5 – Replay	1-1	40,097
38.	19-08-78	Tottenham Hotspur	Division 1	1-1	41,223
39.	11-04-79	1FC Cologne	ECSF – 1st Leg	3-3	40,804
40.	28-04-79	Liverpool	Division 1	0-0	41,898

• The crowd of 49,946 for the League fixture with Manchester United on 28th October 1967 is Forest's record all-time attendance at the City Ground!

• The average of all the City Ground attendances in excess of 40,000, is 43,156!

• The City Ground capacity was reduced to 36,000 upon completion of the brand new Executive Stand (now the Brian Clough Stand) during season 1979/80!

CITY GROUND ATTENDANCES OF BETWEEN 30,000 AND 40,000
SEASON 1898/99 ONWARDS

No.	Date	Opposition	Competition	Score	Attendance
1.	28-01-1899	Aston Villa	FA Cup 1	2-1	32,070
2.	25-02-1899	Sheffield United	FA Cup 3	0-1	33,500
3.	26-12-1911	Derby County	Division 2	1-3	35,000
4.	15-10-21	Leicester City	Division 2	0-0	30,000
5.	27-12-26	Portsmouth	Division 2	1-0	30,616
6.	01-02-28	Derby County	FA Cup 4 – Replay	2-0	35,625
7.	18-02-28	Cardiff City	FA Cup 5	2-1	30,570
8.	25-01-30	Fulham	FA Cup 4	2-1	31,250
9.	19-02-30	Sunderland	FA Cup 5 – Replay	3-1	31,106
10.	31-01-34	Chelsea	FA Cup 4 – Replay	0-3	37,187
11.	26-01-35	Manchester United	FA Cup 4	0-0	32,862
12.	16-02-35	Burnley	FA Cup 5	0-0	34,180
13.	02-09-36	Aston Villa	Division 2	1-1	35,122
14.	22-01-38	Middlesbrough	FA Cup 4	1-3	39,055
15.	06-10-45	Derby County	League South	1-1	30,516
16.	05-09-46	Newcastle United	Division 2	0-2	32,758
17.	26-10-46	Leicester City	Division 2	2-0	30,077
18.	23-11-46	Manchester City	Division 2	0-1	32,194
19.	26-12-46	Burnley	Division 2	1-0	31,484
20.	08-02-47	Middlesbrough	FA Cup 5	2-2	32,000
21.	07-04-47	Tottenham Hotspur	Division 2	1-1	30,656
22.	04-10-47	Cardiff City	Division 2	1-2	30,618
23.	15-11-47	Birmingham City	Division 2	0-2	33,364
24.	28-02-48	Leicester City	Division 2	1-0	32,123
25.	21-08-48	West Bromwich Albion	Division 2	0-1	32,110
26.	08-01-49	Liverpool	FA Cup 3	2-2	35,000
27.	09-04-49	Leicester City	Division 2	2-1	30,774
28.	03-12-49	Notts County	Division 3 South	1-2	37,903
29.	27-12-49	Norwich City	Division 3 South	0-1	31,932
30.	04-11-50	Millwall	Division 3 South	2-0	33,472
31.	22-08-51	Southampton	Division 2	3-0	32,470
32.	25-08-51	Cardiff City	Division 2	2-3	31,776
33.	08-09-51	Leicester City	Division 2	2-2	37,642
34.	06-10-51	Luton Town	Division 2	2-0	31,257
35.	15-12-51	Rotherham United	Division 2	4-2	31,091
36.	26-12-51	Sheffield Wednesday	Division 2	2-1	39,530
37.	29-12-51	Birmingham City	Division 2	0-1	34,316
38.	15-03-52	Coventry City	Division 2	3-1	31,096
39.	11-10-52	Leicester City	Division 2	1-3	39,282
40.	03-01-53	Notts County	Division 2	1-0	38,002
41.	06-04-53	Sheffield United	Division 2	1-1	30,630
42.	10-10-53	Notts County	Division 2	5-0	30,559
43.	07-11-53	Derby County	Division 2	4-2	31,397
44.	23-01-54	Leicester City	Division 2	3-1	34,423
45.	25-09-54	Notts County	Division 2	0-1	30,348
46.	07-03-57	Birmingham City	FA Cup 6 – Replay	0-1	36,486
47.	16-03-57	Stoke City	Division 2	4-0	32,444
48.	30-03-57	Leicester City	Division 2	1-2	39,750
49.	01-05-57	Notts County	Division 2	2-4	32,046
50.	24-08-57	Preston North End	Division 1	2-1	33,285
51.	07-09-57	Manchester City	Division 1	2-1	37,191
52.	09-11-57	Arsenal	Division 1	4-0	34,366
53.	23-11-57	Aston Villa	Division 1	4-1	30,382
54.	26-12-57	Newcastle United	Division 1	2-3	32,509
55.	28-12-57	Sheffield Wednesday	Division 1	5-2	31,903
56.	15-02-58	Tottenham Hotspur	Division 1	1-2	32,334
57.	01-03-58	Leicester City	Division 1	3-1	38,341
58.	13-09-58	West Ham United	Division 1	4-0	30,307

No.	Date	Opposition	Competition	Score	Attendance
59.	04-10-58	Blackpool	Division 1	2-0	31,934
60.	11-10-58	Luton Town	Division 1	3-1	30,337
61.	25-10-58	Preston North End	Division 1	0-1	33,583
62.	08-11-58	Manchester City	Division 1	4-0	31,154
63.	06-12-58	West Bromwich Albion	Division 1	1-1	34,784
64.	28-01-59	Grimsby Town	FA Cup 4	4-1	34,289
65.	18-02-59	Birmingham City	FA Cup 5 – Replay	1-1	39,431
66.	04-04-59	Arsenal	Division 1	1-1	32,708
67.	26-08-59	Arsenal	Division 1	0-3	32,536
68.	31-10-59	Chelsea	Division 1	3-1	30,268
69.	12-12-59	Manchester United	Division 1	1-5	31,816
70.	28-12-59	West Bromwich Albion	Division 1	1-2	34,755
71.	12-03-60	Tottenham Hotspur	Division 1	1-3	35,291
72.	20-08-60	Manchester City	Division 1	2-2	30,133
73.	01-10-60	Sheffield Wednesday	Division 1	1-2	30,223
74.	15-10-60	Tottenham Hotspur	Division 1	0-4	37,248
75.	31-12-60	Arsenal	Division 1	3-5	30,040
76.	19-09-61	Wolverhampton Wanderers	Division 1	3-1	32,506
77.	04-10-61	Valencia	ICFC 1 – 2nd Leg	1-5	36,158
78.	22-09-62	Aston Villa	Division 1	3-1	32,434
79.	13-11-62	Everton	Division 1	3-4	31,610
80.	01-12-62	Burnley	Division 1	2-1	34,171
81.	29-01-63	Wolverhampton Wanderers	FA Cup 3	4-3	34,976
82.	19-03-63	Leeds United	FA Cup 5	3-0	37,120
83.	08-10-63	Leicester City	Division 1	2-0	30,990
84.	10-10-64	Chelsea	Division 1	2-2	35,320
85.	06-02-65	Leeds United	Division 1	0-0	36,596
86.	27-02-65	Leicester City	Division 1	2-1	32,985
87.	24-08-65	Manchester United	Division 1	4-2	33,744
88.	07-09-65	Arsenal	Division 1	0-1	30,540
89.	27-12-65	Everton	Division 1	1-0	34,750
90.	15-10-66	Liverpool	Division 1	1-1	32,887
91.	26-12-66	Everton	Division 1	1-0	36,227
92.	28-01-67	Plymouth Argyle	FA Cup 3	2-1	34,005
93.	18-03-67	West Ham United	Division 1	1-0	31,426
94.	01-04-67	Southampton	Division 1	3-1	37,731
95.	02-05-67	Manchester City	Division 1	2-0	33,352
96.	26-08-67	Arsenal	Division 1	2-0	33,977
97.	05-09-67	Liverpool	Division 1	0-1	39,352
98.	09-09-67	Newcastle United	Division 1	4-0	30,151
99.	23-09-67	Chelsea	Division 1	3-0	34,871
100.	14-10-67	Sheffield Wednesday	Division 1	0-0	37,983
101.	31-10-67	FC Zurich	ICFC 2 – 1st Leg	2-1	32,896
102.	11-11-67	Wolverhampton Wanderers	Division 1	3-1	36,522
103.	16-12-67	Sheffield United	Division 1	1-0	30,501
104.	26-12-67	Stoke City	Division 1	3-0	37,577
105.	06-01-68	Manchester City	Division 1	0-3	39,581
106.	20-01-68	West Bromwich Albion	Division 1	3-2	34,298
107.	27-01-68	Bolton Wanderers	FA Cup 4	4-2	37,299
108.	16-03-68	Tottenham Hotspur	Division 1	0-0	37,707
109.	19-03-68	Leicester City	Division 1	2-1	30,403
110.	10-08-68	Burnley	Division 1	2-2	30,298
111.	24-08-68	Leeds United	Division 1	1-1	31,126
		(Game abandoned due to Main Stand fire)			
112.	25-02-69	Leeds United	Division 1	0-2	36,249
113.	08-04-69	Chelsea	Division 1	1-2	30,413
114.	16-08-69	Leeds United	Division 1	1-4	34,290
115.	11-10-69	Manchester City	Division 1	2-2	30,037
116.	26-12-69	Arsenal	Division 1	1-1	38,91
117.	31-01-70	Liverpool	Division 1	1-0	30,838
118.	31-03-70	Manchester United	Division 1	1-2	39,228

No.	Date	Opposition	Competition	Score	Attendance
119.	26-09-70	Leeds United	Division 1	0-0	31,475
120.	14-11-70	Manchester United	Division 1	1-2	36,373
121.	28-11-70	Derby County	Division 1	2-4	30,539
122.	30-10-71	Derby County	Division 1	0-2	37,170
123.	22-04-72	Manchester United	Division 1	0-0	35,063
124.	17-02-74	Portsmouth	FA Cup 5	1-0	38,589
125.	01-01-76	Peterborough United	FA Cup 3	0-0	31,525
126.	29-01-77	Southampton	FA Cup 4	3-3	38,284
127.	08-03-77	Notts County	Division 2	1-2	31,004
128.	17-09-77	Aston Villa	Division 1	2-0	31,016
129.	15-10-77	Manchester City	Division 1	2-1	35,572
130.	12-11-77	Manchester United	Division 1	2-1	30,183
131.	26-11-77	West Bromwich Albion	Division 1	0-0	31,908
132.	21-01-78	Arsenal	Division 1	2-0	35,743
133.	24-01-78	Manchester City	FA Cup 4	2-1	38,509
134.	22-02-78	Leeds United	LCSF – 2nd Leg	4-2	38,131
135.	02-03-78	Queens Park Rangers	FA Cup 5 – 2nd Replay	3-1	33,950
136.	04-03-78	West Ham United	Division 1	2-0	33,924
137.	14-03-78	Leicester City	Division 1	1-0	32,355
138.	25-03-78	Newcastle United	Division 1	2-0	35,552
139.	01-04-78	Chelsea	Division 1	3-1	31,262
140.	15-04-78	Leeds United	Division 1	1-1	38,662
141.	18-04-78	Queens Park Rangers	Division 1	1-0	30,339
142.	29-04-78	Birmingham City	Division 1	0-0	37,625
143.	13-09-78	Liverpool	European Cup 1 – 1st Leg	2-0	38,318
144.	01-11-78	AEK Athens	European Cup 2 – 2nd Leg	5-1	38,069
145.	04-11-78	Everton	Division 1	0-0	35,515
146.	13-12-78	Brighton & Hove Albion	LC 5	3-1	30,672
147.	26-12-78	Derby County	Division 1	1-1	34,256
148.	17-01-79	Watford	LCSF – 1st Leg	3-1	32,438
149.	26-02-79	Arsenal	FA Cup 5	0-1	35,908
150.	07-03-79	Grasshopper Zurich	European Cup 3 – 1st Leg	4-1	31,949
151.	16-04-79	Leeds United	Division 1	0-0	37,397
152.	18-04-79	Manchester United	Division 1	1-1	33,074
153.	26-12-79	Aston Villa	Division 1	2-1	32,072
154.	22-01-80	Liverpool	LCSF – 1st Leg	1-0	32,220
155.	26-01-80	Liverpool	FA Cup 4	0-2	33,277
156.	02-04-80	Manchester United	Division 1	2-0	31,417
157.	09-04-80	Ajax Amsterdam	European Cup SF – 1st Leg	2-0	31,244
158.	19-04-80	Derby County	Division 1	1-0	32,266
159.	27-12-80	Aston Villa	Division 1	2-2	33,900
160.	24-01-81	Manchester United	FA Cup 4	1-0	34,110
161.	07-03-81	Ipswich Town	FA Cup 6	3-3	34,796
162.	23-11-83	Glasgow Celtic	UEFA Cup 3 – 1st Leg	0-0	34,084
163.	26-04-86	Everton	Division 1	0-0	30,171
164.	04-10-86	Manchester United	Division 1	1-1	35,828
165.	01-01-87	Liverpool	Division 1	1-1	32,854
166.	28-12-87	Coventry City	Division 1	4-1	31,061
167.	15-02-89	Bristol City	LCSF – 1st Leg	1-1	30,016
168.	27-03-89	Manchester United	Division 1	2-0	30,092
169.	17-01-90	Tottenham Hotspur	LC 5	2-2	30,044
170.	11-01-92	Notts County	Division 1	1-1	30,168
171.	06-02-99	Manchester United	FA Premier	1-8	30,025

• The average of all the City Ground attendances in excess of 30,000 (but less than 40,000) is 33,607!

• No less than 51 of Forest's attendances in excess of 30,000 (but less than 40,000) have come whilst the Club has been outside the top flight!

POPULATION SIZES – ALPHABETICAL ORDER

FA PREMIER LEAGUE: SEASON 2000/2001

	Name of Club	Name of Town/City	City or Town	Population	County / Metropolitan Area	Population	No. of Clubs in Town/City
1.	Arsenal	London	City	6,679,700	Greater London	6,679,700	13
2.	Aston Villa	Birmingham	City	1,220,000	West Midlands	2,637,300	2
3.	Bradford City	Bradford	City	357,000	West Yorkshire	2,105,700	1
4.	Charlton A.	London	City	6,679,700	Greater London	6,679,700	13
5.	Chelsea	London	City	6,679,700	Greater London	6,679,700	13
6.	Coventry City	Coventry	City	303,000	West Midlands	2,637,300	1
7.	Derby County	Derby	City	218,800	Derbyshire	944,800 *	1

(* Population of the City of Derby included, although now a separate Unitary Authority)

8.	Everton	Liverpool	City	481,800	Merseyside	1,376,800	2
9.	Ipswich Town	Ipswich	Town	113,000	Suffolk	649,500	1
10.	Leeds United	Leeds	City	424,000	West Yorkshire	2,105,700	1
11.	Leicester City	Leicester	City	295,700	Leicestershire	888,400 *	1

(* Population of the City of Leicester included, although now a separate Unitary Authority)

12.	Liverpool	Liverpool	City	481,800	Merseyside	1,376,800	2
13.	Manchester C.	Manchester	City	402,900	Greater Manchester	2,499,400	2
14.	Manchester U.	Manchester	City	402,900	Greater Manchester	2,499,400	2
15.	Middlesbrough	Middlesbrough	Town	146,000	Teesside	323,000	1
16.	Newcastle U.	Newcastle	City	274,000	Tyne & Wear	1,095,200	1
17.	Southampton	Southampton	City	207,100	Hampshire	1,213,600 *	1

(* Populations of Cities of Southampton and Portsmouth included, although both now separate Unitary Authorities)

18.	Sunderland	Sunderland	City	183,200	Tyne & Wear	1,095,200	1
19.	Tottenham H.	London	City	6,679,700	Greater London	6,679,700	13
20.	West Ham U.	London	City	6,679,700	Greater London	6,679,700	13

FOOTBALL LEAGUE DIVISION ONE: SEASON 2000/2001

1.	Barnsley	Barnsley	Town	75,100	South Yorkshire	1,298,000	1
2.	Birmingham C.	Birmingham	City	1,220,000	West Midlands	2,637,300	2
3.	Blackburn R.	Blackburn	City	106,000	Lancashire	1,424,000 *	1

(* Includes populations of Blackburn and Blackpool, although both separate Unitary Authorities)

4.	Bolton W.	Bolton	Town	210,000	Greater Manchester	2,449,400	1
5.	Burnley	Burnley	Town	74,700	Lancashire	1,424,000	1
6.	Crewe Alex.	Crewe	Town	63,400	Cheshire	978,100	1
7.	Crystal Palace	London	City	6,679,700	Greater London	6,679,700	13
8.	Fulham	London	City	6,679,700	Greater London	6,679,700	13
9.	Gillingham	Gillingham	Town	92,100	Kent	1,551,300	1
10.	Grimsby Town	Grimsby	Town	89,400	N.E. Lincolnshire	164,000	1
11.	Huddersfield T.	Huddersfield	Town	119,000	West Yorkshire	2,105,700	1
12.	Norwich City	Norwich	City	172,600	Norfolk	768,500	1
13.	Nottingham F.	Nottingham	City	285,000	Nottinghamshire	1,031,900	2
14.	Portsmouth	Portsmouth	City	189,300	Hampshire	1,213,600 *	1

(* Includes populations of Cities of Portsmouth and Southampton, although both now separate Unitary Authorities)

15.	Preston N.E.	Preston	Town	126,100	Lancashire	1,424,400	1
16.	Queens P.R.	London	City	6,679,700	Greater London	6,679,700	13
17.	Sheffield U.	Sheffield	City	501,200	South Yorkshire	1,298,000	2
18.	Sheffield W.	Sheffield	City	501,200	South Yorkshire	1,298,000	2
19.	Stockport C.	Stockport	Town	130,800	Greater Manchester	2,499,400	1
20.	Tranmere R.	Birkenhead	Town	93,100	Merseyside	1,376,800	1
21.	Watford	Watford	Town	110,500	Hertfordshire	975,800	1
22.	West Brom.	West Bromwich	Town	144,700	West Midlands	2,637,300	1
23.	Wimbledon	London	City	6,679,700	Greater London	6,679,700	13
24.	Wolves	Wolverhampton	City	256,100	West Midlands	2,637,300	1

POPULATION SIZES – ALPHABETICAL ORDER
FOOTBALL LEAGUE DIVISION TWO: SEASON 2000/2001

Name of Club	Name of Town/City	City or Town	Population	County / Metropolitan Area	Population	No. of Clubs in Town/City
1. Bournemouth	Bournemouth	Town	160,900	Dorset	673,800 *	1

(* Includes the populations of the Towns of Bournemouth & Poole, although both now separate Unitary Authorities)

2. Brentford	London	City	6,679,700	Greater London	6,679,700	13
3. Bristol City	Bristol	City	374,300	Bristol Unitary Auth.	516,500 *	2
4. Bristol Rovers	Bristol	City	374,300	Bristol Unitary Auth.	516,500 *	2

(* Formerly County of Avon, which was abolished in 1996)

5. Bury	Bury	City	62,600	Greater Manchester	2,499,400	1
6. Cambridge U.	Cambridge	City	117,000	Cambridgeshire	686,900	1
7. Colchester U.	Colchester	City	96,100	Essex	1,577,500	1
8. Luton Town	Luton	Town	181,400	Bedfordshire	554,400 *	1

(* Includes the population of the Town of Luton, although now a separate Unitary Authority)

9. Millwall	London	City	6,679,700	Greater London	6,679,700	13
10. Northampton T.	Northampton	Town	192,400	Northamptonshire	594,800	1
11. Notts County	Nottingham	City	285,000	Nottinghamshire	1,031,900	2
12. Oldham A.	Oldham	Town	102,300	Greater Manchester	2,449,400	1
13. Oxford United	Oxford	City	121,000	Oxfordshire	590,200	1
14. Peterborough U.	Peterborough	City	139,000	Cambridgeshire	686,900	1
15. Port Vale	Stoke-on-Trent	City	254,200	Staffordshire	1,056,300 *	2

(* Includes the population of the City of Stoke-on-Trent, although now a separate Unitary Authority)

16. Reading	Reading	Town	131,000	(Formerly Berkshire - abolished 1998)		1
17. Rotherham U.	Rotherham	Town	154,000	South Yorkshire	1,298,000	1
18. Stoke City	Stoke-on-Trent	City	254,200	Staffordshire	1,056,300 *	2
19. Swansea C.	Swansea	City	182,100	(Formerly W.Glamorgan – abolished 1996)		1
20. Swindon Town	Swindon	Town	170,000	Wiltshire	594,600 *	1

(* Includes the population of the Town of Swindon, although now a separate Unitary Authority)

21. Walsall	Walsall	Town	172,600	West Midlands	2,637,300	1
22. Wigan A.	Wigan	Town	84,700	Greater Manchester	2,449,400	1
23. Wrexham	Wrexham	Town	123,500	(Formerly Clwyd – abolished 1996)		1
24. Wycombe W.	High Wycombe	Town	62,500	Buckinghamshire	468,700	1

FOOTBALL LEAGUE DIVISION THREE: SEASON 2000/2001

1. Barnet	London	City	6,679,700	Greater London	6,679,700	13
2. Blackpool	Blackpool	Town	153,600	Lancashire	1,424,000 *	1

(* Includes the populations of Blackpool and Blackburn, although both now separate Unitary Authorities)

3. Brighton & H.A.	Brighton & Hove	City	248,000	East Sussex	730,800 *	1

(* Includes the population of Brighton & Hove, although now a separate Unitary Authority)

4. Cardiff City	Cardiff	City	306,500	(Formerly S.Glamorgan – abolished 1996)		1
5. Carlisle United	Carlisle	City	72,400	Cumbria	490,200	1
6. Cheltenham T.	Cheltenham	Town	91,300	Gloucestershire	549,500	1
7. Chesterfield	Chesterfield	Town	71,900	Derbyshire	944,800	1
8. Darlington	Darlington	Town	100,600	Durham	593,500 *	1

(* Includes population of the Town of Darlington, although now a separate Unitary Authority)

9. Exeter City	Exeter	City	107,000	Devon	1,058,800	1
10. Halifax Town	Halifax	Town	91,100	West Yorkshire	2,105,700	1
11. Hartlepool U.	Hartlepool	Town	90,400	(Formerly Cleveland – abolished 1996)		1
12. Hull City	Hull	City	265,000	(Formerly Humberside – abolished 1996)		1
13. Kidderminster H.	Kidderminster	Town	54,600	Worcestershire	699,900	1
14. Leyton Orient	London	City	6,679,700	Greater London	6,679,700	13
15. Lincoln City	Lincoln	City	80,300	Lincolnshire	605,600	1
16. Macclesfield T.	Macclesfield	Town	69,700	Cheshire	978,100	1
17. Mansfield Town	Mansfield	Town	71,100	Nottinghamshire	1,031,900	1
18. Plymouth A.	Plymouth	City	257,000	Devon	1,058,800 *	1

(* Includes population of Plymouth and Torquay, although both now separate Unitary Authorities)

19. Rochdale	Rochdale	Town	138,000	Greater Manchester	2,449,400	1
20. Scunthorpe U.	Scunthorpe	Town	74,700	N.Lincolnshire	153,000	1
21. Shrewsbury T.	Shrewsbury	Town	64,200	Shropshire	419,900	1
22. Southend U.	Southend-on-Sea	Town	171,000	Essex	1,577,500	1
23. Torquay U.	Torquay	Town	59,600	Devon	1,058,800 *	1
24. York City	York	City	174,800	North Yorkshire	698,800 *	1

(Includes population of City of York, although now a separate Unitary Authority)

ENGLISH & WELSH CITIES REPRESENTED ACROSS THE FA PREMIERSHIP & FOOTBALL LEAGUE DIVISIONS ONE, TWO & THREE - IN ORDER OF POPULATION SIZE:

No.	Name of City	Population Size	Name of Club/s
1st	London	6,679,700	1. Arsenal
			2. Charlton Athletic
			3. Chelsea
			4. Tottenham Hotspur
			5. West Ham United
			6. Crystal Palace
			7. Fulham
			8. Queens Park Rangers
			9. Wimbledon
			10. Brentford
			11. Millwall
			12. Leyton Orient
			13. Barnet
2nd	**Birmingham**	**1,220,000**	**1. Aston Villa**
			2. Birmingham City
3rd	Sheffield	501,200	1. Sheffield United
			2. Sheffield Wednesday
4th	**Liverpool**	**481,800**	**1. Everton**
			2. Liverpool
5th	Leeds	424,200	1. Leeds United
6th	**Manchester**	**402,900**	**1. Manchester City**
			2. Manchester United
7th	Bristol	374,300	1. Bristol City
			2. Bristol Rovers
8th	**Bradford**	**357,000**	**1. Bradford City**
9th	Cardiff	306,500	1. Cardiff City
10th	**Coventry**	**303,000**	**1. Coventry City**
11th	Leicester	295,700	1. Leicester City
12th	**Nottingham**	**285,000**	**1. Nottingham Forest**
			2. Notts County
13th	Newcastle-upon-Tyne	274,000	1. Newcastle United
14th	**Hull**	**265,000**	**1. Hull City**
15th	Plymouth	257,000	1. Plymouth Argyle
16th	**Wolverhampton**	**256,100**	**1. Wolverhampton Wanderers**
17th	Stoke-on-Trent	254,200	1. Port Vale
			2. Stoke City
18th	**Brighton & Hove**	**248,000**	**1. Brighton & Hove Albion**
19th	Swansea	232,000	1. Swansea City
20th	**Derby**	**218,800**	**1. Derby**
21st	Southampton	207,100	1. Southampton
22nd	**Portsmouth**	**189,300**	**1. Portsmouth**
23rd	Sunderland	183,200	1. Sunderland
24th	**York**	**174,800**	**1. York City**
25th	Norwich	172,600	1. Norwich City
26th	**Peterborough**	**139,000**	**1. Peterborough United**
27th	Oxford	121,000	1. Oxford United
28th	**Cambridge**	**117,000**	**1. Cambridge City**
29th	Exeter	107,000	1. Exeter City
30th	**Blackburn**	**106,000**	**1. Blackburn Rovers**
31st	Colchester	96,100	1. Colchester United
32nd	**Lincoln**	**81,900**	**1. Lincoln City**
33rd	Carlisle	72,400	1. Carlisle United
34th	**Bury**	**62,600**	**1. Bury**

ENGLISH & WELSH TOWNS REPRESENTED ACROSS THE FA PREMEIRSHIP & FOOTBALL LEAGUE DIVISIONS ONE, TWO & THREE - IN ORDER OF POPULATION SIZE:

No.	Name of Town	Population Size	Name of Club/s
1st	Bolton	210,000	1. Bolton Wanderers
2nd	**Northampton**	**192,400**	**1. Northampton Town**
3rd	Luton	181,400	1. Luton Town
4th	**Walsall**	**172,600**	**1. Walsall**
5th	Southend-on-Sea	171,000	1. Southend United
6th	**Swindon**	**170,000**	**1. Swindon Town**
7th	Bournemouth	160,900	1. Bournemouth
8th	**Rotherham**	**154,000**	**1. Rotherham United**
9th	Blackpool	153,600	1. Blackpool
10th	**Middlesbrough**	**146,000**	**1. Middlesbrough**
11th	West Bromwich	144,700	1. West Bromwich Albion
12th	**Rochdale**	**138,000**	**1. Rochdale**
13th	Reading	131,000	1. Reading
14th	**Stockport**	**130,000**	**1. Stockport County**
15th	Preston	126,100	1. Preston North End
16th	**Wrexham**	**123,500**	**1. Wrexham**
17th	Huddersfield	119,000	1. Huddersfield Town
18th	**Ipswich**	**113,000**	**1. Ipswich Town**
19th	Watford	110,500	1. Watford
20th	**Oldham**	**102,300**	**1. Oldham Athletic**
21st	Darlington	100,600	1. Darlington
22nd	**Birkenhead**	**93,100**	**1. Tranmere Rovers**
23rd	Gillingham	92,100	1. Gillingham
24th	**Cheltenham**	**91,300**	**1. Cheltenham Town**
25th	Halifax	91,100	1. Halifax Town
26th	**Hartlepool**	**90,400**	**1. Hartlepool United**
27th	Grimsby	89,400	1. Grimsby Town
28th	**Wigan**	**84,700**	**1. Wigan Athletic**
29th	Barnsley	75,100	1. Barnsley
30th	**Burnley**	**74,700**	**1. Burnley**
31st	Scunthorpe	74,700	1. Scunthorpe United
32nd	**Chesterfield**	**71,900**	**1. Chesterfield**
33rd	Mansfield	71,900	1. Mansfield Town
34th	**Macclesfield**	**69,700**	**1. Macclesfield Town**
35th	Shrewsbury	64,200	1. Shrewsbury Town
36th	**Crewe**	**63,400**	**1. Crewe Alexandra**
37th	High Wycombe	62,500	1. Wycombe Wanderers
38th	**Torquay**	**59,600**	**1. Torquay United**
39th	Kidderminster	54,600	1. Kidderminster Harriers

ENGLISH & WELSH COUNTIES/METROPOLITAN AREAS REPRESENTED ACROSS THE FA PREMIERSHIP & FOOTBALL LEAGUE DIVISIONS ONE, TWO & THREE - IN ORDER OF POPULATION SIZE:

No.	Name of County/ Metropolitan Area	Population Size	Name of Club/s
1st	Greater London	6,679,700	1. Arsenal 2. Charlton Athletic 3. Chelsea 4. Tottenham Hotspur 5. West Ham United 6. Crystal Palace 7. Fulham 8. Queens Park Rangers 9. Wimbledon 10. Brentford 11. Millwall 12. Leyton Orient 13. Barnet
2nd	**West Midlands**	**2,637,300**	1. **Aston Villa** 2. **Coventry City** 3. **Birmingham City** 4. **West Bromwich Albion** 5. **Wolverhampton Wanderers** 6. **Walsall**
3rd	Greater Manchester	2,499,400	1. Manchester City 2. Manchester United 3. Bolton Wanderers 4. Stockport County 5. Bury 6. Oldham Athletic 7. Wigan Athletic 8. Rochdale
4th	**West Yorkshire**	**2,105,700**	1. **Bradford City** 2. **Leeds United** 3. **Huddersfield Town** 4. **Halifax Town**
5th	Essex	1,577,500	1. Colchester United 2. Southend United
6th	**Kent**	**1,551,300**	1. **Gillingham**
7th	Lancashire	1,424,000	1. Blackburn Rovers 2. Burnley 3. Preston North End 4. Blackpool
8th	**Merseyside**	**1,376,800**	1. **Everton** 2. **Liverpool** 3. **Tranmere Rovers**
9th	South Yorkshire	1,298,000	1. Barsnley 2. Sheffield United 3. Sheffield Wednesday 4. Rotherham United

FACTS

No.	Name of County/ Metropolitan Area	Population Size	Name of Club/s
10th	**Hampshire**	**1,213,600**	1. **Southampton** 2. **Portsmouth**
11th	Tyne & Wear	1,095,200	1. Newcastle United 2. Sunderland
12th	**Devon**	**1,058,800**	1. **Exeter City** 2. **Plymouth Argyle** 3. **Torquay United**
13th	Staffordshire	1,056,300	1. Port Vale 2. Stoke City
14th	**Nottinghamshire**	**1,031,900**	1. **Nottingham Forest** 2. **Notts County** 3. **Mansfield Town**
15th	Cheshire	978,100	1. Crewe Alexandra 2. Macclesfield Town
16th	**Hertfordshire**	**975,800**	1. **Watford**
17th	Derbyshire	944,800	1. Derby County 2. Chesterfield
18th	**Leicestershire**	**888,400**	1. **Leicester City**
19th	Norfolk	768,500	1. Norwich City
20th	**East Sussex**	**730,800**	1. **Brighton & Hove Albion**
21st	Cambridgeshire	686,900	1. Cambridge United 2. Peterborough United
22nd	**Dorset**	**673,800**	1. **Bournemouth**
23rd	Suffolk	649,500	1. Ipswich Town
24th	**Worcestershire**	**629,900**	1. **Kidderminster Harriers**
25th	Lincolnshire	605,600	1. Lincoln City
26th	**Northamptonshire**	**594,800**	1. **Northampton Town**
27th	Wiltshire	594,600	1. Swindon Town
28th	**Durham**	**593,500**	1. **Darlington**
29th	Oxfordshire	590,200	1. Oxford United
30th	**North Yorkshire**	**556,200**	1. **York City**
31st	Bedfordshire	554,800	1. Luton Town
32nd	**Gloucestershire**	**549,500**	1. **Cheltenham Town**
33rd	Bristol Unitary Authority	516,500	1. Bristol City 2. Bristol Rovers
34th	**Cumbria**	**490,200**	1. **Carlisle United**
35th	Buckinghamshire	468,700	1. Wycombe Wanderers
36th	**Shropshire**	**419,900**	1. **Shrewsbury Town**
37th	Teesside	323,000	1. Middlesbrough
38th	**Cardiff Unitary Authority**	**306,500**	1. **Cardiff City**
39th	Hull Unitary Authority	265,000	1. Hull City
40th	**Swansea Unitary Authority**	**232,000**	1. **Swansea City**
41st	North East Lincolnshire	164,000	1. Grimsby Town
42nd	**North Lincolnshire**	**153,000**	1. **Scunthorpe United**
43rd	Reading Unitary Authority	131,000	1. Reading
44th	**Wrexham Unitary Authority**	**123,500**	1. **Wrexham**
45th	Hartlepool Unitary Authority	90,400	1. Hartlepool United

All population figures taken from Hutchinson's 'The Encyclopedia of Britain'.

Note: A new population census is scheduled for the year 2001.

THE A TO Z OF TRENT END CHANTS AND ANTHEMS

BELOW IS a list of over 100 authentic Trent End chants and anthems which have been popular during the last three decades or more. There are many, many others around, which have not been included, for one reason or another, for example, too violent, too many swearwords, and to be honest, I've just about run out of space.

My advice to any Trent Enders under the age of 25 who may be reading this (thousands of you hopefully!) is: Get reading and learn something, then perhaps we'll get away from this inane, non-stop chanting of: *"We hate Leicester - We hate Derby"* throughout games, which hardly creates the kind of atmosphere necessary to lift the players and inspire them to greater things.

Take it from me, a 7,500-strong Trent End choir, bellowing out the full version of *'Forest Ever Forest'* (not just the second verse folks, which, on it's own, is meaningless), would not only give the players an immediate adrenaline rush; but would also frighten the opposition to death. And at the same time, it would make the hairs on the back of your neck stand up in a way you have never experienced before.

Let's get back to the days when the wit and enthusiasm of the Trent End, created a 'Fortress City Ground' atmosphere and gave the lads a goal-start before they even came out onto the pitch. *Cum on u Red uns!*

1. All I want is a walkin' stick, An 'and grenade and a buildin' brick, A Derby fan to kick, Oh wuddennit be luvv-erly! (See page 171 - Not a very pleasant one this to start the list off; but nevertheless an example of the rather violent tendencies of the Trent End of the early-seventies).

2. 'ang yer boots up, 'ang yer boots up, 'ang yer boots up - Emlyn Hughes! 'ang yer boots up, 'ang yer boots up, 'ang yer boots up - Emlyn Hughes! (See page 157 - Forest fans taunting old Liverpool adversary 'Crazy Horse' Emlyn Hughes, during the 4-1 demolition of Wolves at Molineux on Boxing Day 1980).

3. An' it's Hi-Ho, We 'ate Derby, Everywhere we go there's aggro; I see the Pop-side runnin', To gerraway from us, Oh it's obvious! (A Trent End version of the hit song Hi-Ho Silver Linin', popular amongst the Skinhead fraternity and sung mainly along to this record at discotheques in and around Nottingham during the early-seventies).

4. An' it's Nott-ing-ham Forest, Nottingham Forest FC; We're by far the greatest team, The world 'as ever seen! (Repeat). (See pages 60 & 228 - not by any means unique to Forest this one - most other clubs have a similar version. However, it has been around for many years).

5. An' now yer gonna believe us, An' now yer gonna believe us, An' now yer gonna believe us, We're gonna win the League! (See page 95 - the supporters of most clubs have sung this one (most very optimistically) from time to time. This was adapted by Forest fans to: *"We're gonna win the lot!"* during the highly successful season of 1988/89 - see page 221).

6. 'appy days are 'ere agen, An' we're only 'ere for the beer agen, An' the Popside's turned all queer agen, 'appy days are 'ere agen! (See page 171 - One of my favourites this one and again goes right back to the early-seventies).

7. Are ya watchin', Are ya watchin', Are ya watchin' Jimmy Greaves? (See page 170 - reserved especially for those who have publicly criticised the Club in any way or predicted their downfall - in this case the unfortunate Mr Greaves being the guilty party).

8. 'ark now 'ear, The Trent End sing, The Der-by ran away; An' we will fight, For evermore, Because of Boxing Day! (See Page 115 - although this was subsequently adapted by many other clubs, it definitely originated on Trent-side prior to Christmas 1978, with the Trent End eagerly awaiting the visit of their 'much-loved' neighbours!).

9. 'arry Roberts is our mate, Is our mate, Is our mate; 'arry Roberts is our mate, 'e kills coppers! (This rather nasty little ditty was very popular with the Trent Enders of the late-sixties, who constantly fought running battles with the police on the terraces. Harry Roberts was an infamous cop killer of that era - See page 37).

10. Aye-Oh, Aye-Oh, It's off to Mexico, With Ian Moore an' 'en-er-y', Aye-Oh, Aye-Oh, Aye-Oh, Aye-Oh! (This was the Trent End's prediction that both Ian Storey-Moore and Henry Newton would be in the England squad for the 1970 World Cup in Mexico. As it turned out, neither of them made the final squad).

11. Aye-Oh, Aye-Oh, We are the Trent End boys, Aye-Oh, Aye-Oh, We are the Trent End boys; We are the best team in the land, This no-one can deny, We will follow the For-est! (See page 64 - one of our best and most popular anthems, this has been around for as long as I can remember and is still popular to this day).

12. Bertie Mee sez to Bill Shankley, 'ave you 'eard of the North bank - Highbury? Bill sez no - I don't think so, But I've 'eard of the Trent End Boot Boys! La-la-la-la-la-la-la-la-la, La-la-la-la-la-la, La-la-la-la-la-la, We are the Trent End - Boot Boys! (See page 39 - another throwback to the Skinhead days of the early-seventies this one - the whole of the Trent End would bounce up and down during the chorus - fantastic!).

13. Blue moon, You started singin' too soon, An' now your dreams 'ave all gone, Cos Roy Keane's made it two-one! (See page 266 - one of the best piss-takes of all time this one, after Roy Keane had put us 2-1 up at Spurs in the second leg of the League Cup semi-final on 1st March 1992).

14. Brian Clough's a football genius! (See page 254 - need I say more?).

15. Bring back, Bring back, Oh bring back our Duncan to us - to us! (See page 77 - rumours were rife that former Trent End idol Duncan McKenzie was on his way back to Forest from Leeds United in April 1976. When he turned out for the 'Reds' in Sammy Chapman's testimonial

401

match on 26th April, the Trent End made their feelings on the matter abundantly clear with this one).

16. City Ground, Oh mist rolling in from the Trent, My desire, is always to be here, Oh City Ground; Far have I travelled, And much have I seen, Goodison, Anfield, The places I've been, Maine Road, Old Trafford, Still echo to the sounds, Of the boys in the red shirts, At the City Ground; City Ground, Oh mist rolling in from the Trent, My desire, is always to be here, Oh City Ground. (See page 97 - I would like to shake the hand of the man who put these lyrics together during our Championship-winning season of 1977/78 - absolutely brilliant!)

17. Come on without, Come on within, You'll not see nothing like the Mighty Jim! (See page 18 - the Trent End greeting a wonder goal from Jim Baxter during season 1967/68).

18. Dave Mackay runnin' dairn the wing, You will 'ear the Trent End sing, Ya-Fat-Bastard, Ya-Fat-Bastard, Ya-Fat-Bast-ar-ard! 'ear worra say now! (See page 25 - the Trent End showing just how much they 'love' everything 'Derby County!').

19. Derby, Derby, 'ave ya gorra puff? Yes sir; yes sir, Brian Clough! Derby, Derby, 'ave ya gorra queer? Yes sir; yes sir, John O'Hare! Derby, Derby, 'ave ya gorra woman? Yes sir; yes sir, John McGovern! Derby, Derby, 'ave ya gorra queen? Yes sir; yes sir, Lesley Green! (See page 25 - one of the many anti-Derby songs of the 1969/70 season - long before three out of the four individuals mentioned in the song joined the 'Reds' of course!).

20. Derby's goin' down like a Russian submarine, A Russian submarine, A Russian submarine! (See page 377 - good God, some wit from the Trent End of the current era at last! Although I have heard Man U fans singing the same song about their 'nearest and dearest' from across the other side of Manchester).

21. Dun-can, Dun-can, Dun-can, Dun-can, Born is the Ki-ing of the City Ground! (The standard Trent End greeting for hero Duncan McKenzie).

22. Ee-Aye, Ee-Aye, Ee-Aye-Oh, Up the Football League we go, When we get promotion, This is what we'll sing, We are Forest, We are Forest, Clarky is our King! (First sung during the promotion season of 1993/94 when Frank Clark was boss. Since amended to 'Bassett is our King!' (1997/98 promotion season) and 'Platty is our King!' during this latest season of 2000/01).

23. 'ello-'ello, Forest are back, Forest are back, 'ello-'ello-'ello! (See page 228 - first sung during the League Cup Final victory over Luton Town at Wembley stadium on 9th April 1989 - Forest's first trophy since season 1979/80).

24. 'ello-'ello, Forest reject, Forest reject, 'ello-'ello-'ello! (See page 118 - famously sung to Southampton's Terry Curran during Forest's League Cup Final victory at Wembley Stadium on 17th March 1979 - but sung to any ex-Forest player turning out for the opposition, with the exception of Des Walker or Stuart Pearce).

25. Forest boys, we are 'ere, Woo-ooh, woo-ooh, Forest boys, we are 'ere, Woo-ooh, woo-ooh; Forest boys, we are 'ere, T' shag your women, An' t' drink your beer! Woo-ooh-ooh, woo-ooh-ooh. (See page 75 - this song emerged in the early-seventies and would always be sung at away matches by the invading 'Red & White Army').

26. Forest ever Forest, All our hopes are with you, True supporters forever, 'til our days are through, La-la-la-la-la-la; Through the seasons before us, Down through history, We will follow the For-est, Onto victory, La-la-la-la-la! (See page 10 - the undisputed number one Forest anthem, which emerged during the sixties. However, to my eternal frustration, no-one ever sings the first verse anymore - except me!).

27. Fo-o-o-rest, Fo-o-o-rest, We'll support you evermore, We'll support you evermore! (See page 46 - this is a song of defiance, usually a favourite when times are hard down at the City Ground. This has been around for as long as I can remember).

28. Forest 'til I die, I'm Forest 'til I die, I know I am, I'm sure I am, I'm Forest 'til I die! (See page 372 - this is a fairly recent song which has emerged over the last two or three seasons. The first set of supporters I heard singing it were 'Pompey' fans in 1998/99, although their version isn't of course dedicated to the 'Reds'!).

29. Forever an' ever, We'll follow our team, We're Nottingham Forest, We rule supreme; We'll never be mastered, By you (insert any of the following: Cockney / Brummie / Yorkshire / Geordie / Derby) Bastards, We'll keep the red flag, Flyin' 'igh! (See page 188 - suitable for most occasions; this song 'welcomes' visiting supporters to the City Ground and first emerged in the early-eighties).

30. Gary Charles, Gary Charles, Gary-Gary Charles, When 'e gets the ball, 'e scores a goal, Gary-Gary Charles! (See page 303 - this was a tribute to the former Forest full-back who, whilst playing for our enemy - the 'Sheep' - scored a crucial own-goal in the promotion battle between the two clubs at the 'BBG' on 27th April 1994. Forest won this encounter 2-0 and went on to achieve promotion back to the Premiership at the first attempt).

31. Give it to Moo-oo-re, Give it to Moo-oo-re, 'e will score, 'e will score! (Popular chant during the late-sixties about the goal-scoring prowess of hero Ian Storey-Moore).

32. Ian Moore runnin' dairn the wing, You will 'ear the Trent End sing, A sensation, A sensation, A sensa-tio-on, 'ear worra say now! Ian Moore, Viva Ian Moore! Ian Moore, Viva Ian Moore! Viva, viva, Ian Moore, Viva! (When sixties hero Ian Storey-Moore was in full flight down that left wing, it was indeed a sight to behold...something which was not lost on the Trent Enders!).

33. If I 'ad the wings of a sparrow, If I 'ad the arse of a crow, I'd fly over Derby tomorrow, And shit on the bastards below, below! (Originally a rugby song, this was adapted by the Trent End during the late-sixties, in order to welcome our 'friends' from down the A52 into the First Division).

34. If y'all 'ate Derby clap yer 'ands, If y'all 'ate Derby clap yer 'ands, If y'all 'ate Derby, All 'ate Derby, All 'ate Derby clap yer 'ands! Sheep-sheep-sheep-shaggers! Baaaaaaaaaaaaah! (See page 25 - as above really, but the sheep noises tagged onto the end are most impressive and always make me fall about laughing!).

35. In Nottingham fair city, Where the girls are so pretty, I first set my eyes on sweet Molly Malone; As she wheeled her wheel-barrow, Through the streets broad and narrow, Crying: Joe-Joe-Joe-Ba-ker! Joe-Joe-Joe-Ba-ker! (See page 13 - one of many Joe Baker anthems sung in the mid-to-late-sixties. Joe Baker was the undisputed 'King' of the Trent End).

36. I was bo-orn, Under a Trent End goal, I was bo-orn under a Trent End goal; Boots are made for kickin', A razor's made to slash, I've never seen a Derby fan, I didn't want to bash! I was bo-orn, Under a Trent End goal, A Trent End, Trent End goal. (See page 27 - yet another anti-Derby anthem; once again reflecting the rather violent tendencies of the Trent Enders of the late-sixties/early-seventies).

37. Joe Ba-ker, Joe Ba-ker, Is it true what the Trent End sing? You are our King, Oh yeah, oh yeah! (Another 'Joe is King' anthem of his era).

38. My old man, Said be a Derby fan, I said: Fuck off, Bollocks, You're a ct, And a twat!** (Another 'charming' little ditty; sung exclusively by those Forest supporters born in Derbyshire, but who have nevertheless rather wisely chosen to follow the 'Reds').

39. Na-na-na-na, Na-na-na-na, He-he-hey...Peter Cormack! / We 'ate derby! (See page 30 - take your pick with this one. You can either hail latest signing Peter Cormack (season 1969/70), or once again, tell the 'Sheep' how much you love them!).

40. No-one likes you, No-one likes you, No-one likes you - Collymore! Greedy Bastard, Greedy Bastard,

Greedy Bastard - Collymore! (See page 327 - the City Ground welcomes the 'highly-popular' Mr Collymore back to Nottingham on 23rd March 1996. To cap it all, Forest beat Liverpool 1-0 and 'Stan the man' was substituted during the second half, leaving the pitch to 'rapturous applause' from the Forest faithful!).

41. *Not-Not-Not-Not-Nottingham, Nottingham, Nottingham!* (See page 118 - again, this one's been around since the early-seventies and sounded particularly good echoing around Wembley Stadium on League Cup Final Day, 17th March 1979, during the 3-2 victory over Southampton).

42. *Oh I do like to be beside the sea-side, Oh I do like to be beside the sea, Oh I do like to walk along the prom-prom-prom, As the brass band plays: Fuck off West Brom!* (This 'tribute' to the 'Baggies' first came to prominence during the late-seventies and always gets a blast whenever Forest are at the Hawthorns).

43. *Oh Nottingham, Oh Nottingham, Is full of fun, Is full of fun, Oh Nottingham is full of fun; It's full o' tits, Fanny an' Forest, Oh Nottingham, Is full of fun!* (See page 225 - this anthem definitely originated on Trentside during the mid-eighties, although it has been copied since by many other clubs, particularly Manchester United supporters).

44. *Oh, we're better than United, An' we're louder than the Kop, We're second in the League, An' we should be at the top! La-la-la-la, La-la-la-la-la...* (See page 18 - first sung during the 1966/67 season when the 'Reds' were battling it out at the top of the First Division with Manchester United. Everyone used to bounce up and down in unison during the chorus!).

45. *Oh wi come from Nottingham Forest, With a shotgun on our knee, Oh wi come from Nottingham Forest, An' it's time for you to flee; Oh Derby County, It's time for you to run, Cos wi come from Nottingham Forest, With a fuckin' grett shotgun!* (See page 75 - another of the never-ending bank of anti-Derby songs which emerged in the late-sixties - yet again with rather violent undertones).

46. *Old Macdonald 'ad a farm, Ee-aye, ee-aye-oh, An' on that farm 'e 'ad a nod, Ee-aye, Ee-aye-oh; With a nod-nod 'ere, An' a nod-nod there, 'ere a nod, there a nod, Everywhere a nod-nod; Old Macdonald 'ad a farm, Ee-aye, ee-aye-oh!* (See page 37 - this was a classic Trent End piss-take of the late-sixties/early-seventies - and I loved every minute of it!).

47. *One Garry Birtles, There's only one Garry Birtles, One Garry Bir-tles...There's only one Garry Birtles!* (See page 110 - a regular chant during the Birtles era - once again, sounded particularly splendid echoing around Wembley Stadium after Garry's second goal went in against Southampton on League Cup Final Day, 17th March 1979).

48. *One Greedy Bastard! There's only one Greedy Bastard! One Greedy Bastard! There's only one Greedy Bastard!* (See page 328 - it's the 'loveable' Mr Collymore again and his City Ground re-union party on 23rd March 1996).

49. *One team in Europe, There's only one team in Europe, One team in Europe; There's only one team in Europe!* (See page 320 - when Forest were the last remaining English Club competing in Europe during the 1995/96 season, Forest supporters made sure they let everyone know about it at every conceivable opportunity!).

50. *Ooh-Ah-Franzie-Carr, Say Ooh-Ah-Franzie-Carr!* (See page 201 - a much-copied chant which had it's origins at the City Ground during the Franz Carr era of the late-eighties).

51. *Psycho's gonna get ya, Psycho's gonna get ya, La-la-la-la, La-la-la-la!* (Kick a Forest player at your peril - 'cause Stuart Pearce would always be around to demand retribution. And the Trent End were always quick to jump on this bandwagon!).

52. *She wore, she wore, She wore a scarlet ribbon, She wore a scarlet ribbon, In the merry month of May; An' when I asked her, Why she wore that* ribbon? She sez it's for the Forest fans, Whose gooin' to Ger-man-y! Ger-man-y, Ger-man-y, Oh we're all pissed up, An' wi gonna win the Cup, Ger-man-y, Ger-man-y! (See page 111 - despite Forest having to take on the national press, as well as the opposition, during the European Cup competition of season 1978/79, the Trent End at least were in no doubt that we were going all the way to Munich!).

53. *Shit on the Derby, Shit on the Derby tonight...Shit on the Derby, Shit on the Derby tonight...Shit on the Derby, Shit on the Derby tonight...Everybody shit on the Derby, Cos the Derby are shi-i-ite!* (See page 325 - again, been around for a long time this one, but sounded particularly impressive in the Hofbrauhaus Bier Keller in Munich on 5th March 1996, sung with great gusto by about 1800 Forest supporters, ably supported by the resident Um-pa band!).

54. *Show them the way to go 'ome, Oh they're tired and they want to go to bed, Oh they're only arf a football team, Compared to the boys in red!* (A regular chant during the late-sixties/early-seventies whenever Forest had the upper-hand in a game on Trentside).

55. *Sign on, sign on, With a pen, in yer 'and, And you'll ne-ver work, agen, You'll ne-ver work agen, Sign on, sign on!* (Aimed at either Liverpool, Everton or Tranmere supporters, this is of course a spoof version of the Kop's famous *'You'll never walk alone'* anthem. This has been around since the early-eighties and the 'Scousers' are probably as sick of hearing it, as we are of hearing their version!).

56. *Six foot two, Eyes of blue, Sammy Chapman's after you, La-la-la-la, La-la-la, La-la!* (See page 77 - an earlier equivalent of the 'Psycho's gonna get yer' song, but obviously this time the 'hero' is the swashbuckling Sammy Chapman of the late-sixties/early-seventies era).

57. *Tell mi mam - mi mam, I don't want no tea - no tea, (Why not?) We're goin' t' Wem-ber-ley! Tell mi mam - mi mam.* (See page 92 - absolutely brilliant and totally original Trent End anthem of the 1977/78 season. The shame is this has subsequently been 'borrowed' and adapted by so many other clubs, not least Everton, Leeds and Middlesbrough. I'm certain they would also try and lay claim to it, given half a chance).

58. *Tell mi mam - mi mam, To put the champagne on ice, We're goin' t' Wembley twice, Tell mi mam - mi mam!* (See page 99 - the creativity of the Trent End was probably at an all-time high during the Championship-winning season of 1977/78, and as we progressed further and further into both domestic Cup competitions, the above anthem was just amended accordingly).

59. *There's a circus in the town, In the town, Robert Maxwell is a clown, Is a clown; An' Arthur Cox, 'as got the fuckin' pox, An' Derby County's gooin' down, Gooin' down!* (See page 208 - a little bit heavy on the bad language front this one, but nevertheless, it is another perfect example of the contemptuous manner in which the 'Sheep' are held by those on Trentside).

60. *Those were the days my friend, We thought they'd never end, We'd sing an' dance, Forever an' a day; We'd live the life we choose, We'd fight an' never loose, Those were the days, Oh-yes, those were the days; La-la-la-la-la, La-la-la-la-la...* (A famous hit by Mary Hopkins during the late-sixties, the lyrics perfectly summed up Forest's demise at the time and the song was adopted largely for it's nostalgic value).

61. *Tiptoe through the Popside, With a razor, An' a sawn-off shotgun, Tiptoe through the Popside, With me!* (See page 25 - yet another example of the rather violent tendencies of the Trent Enders of the late-sixties/early-seventies. First appeared during season 1969/70 before what was our first trip to the 'Sheep-dip' in many decades).

62. *T' Mun-ich, T' Mun-ich, La-la-la-la-la-la, La-la-la-la-la-la!* (See page 122 - yet again, the Trent End confidently predicting that Munich and a European Cup Final place is beckoning for the 'Reds' during season 1978/79. How right they were, bless 'em!).

63. *To 'ell with Leeds United, To 'ell with Liver-*

pool, We'll fight-fight-fight for the Fo-o-rest, 'til we win the Football League! (A defiant Trent End, swearing their allegiance to the cause during the late-sixties/early-seventies).

64. Tottenham - we always beat Tottenham, We always beat Tottenham, We always beat Tottenham! (See page 240 - we appear to have become something of a bogey team to Spurs over the last couple of decades, as we are always quick to remind them. Mind you, they usually have the last say on the matter, with their standard reply of: "Wembley-Wembley '91, Wem-bley '91!" Touche!)

65. Twenty quid - and you're 5-2 down, Twenty quid - and you're 5-2 down! (See page 348 - Charlton Athletic supporters were incensed (and rightly so!) when charged the standard £20 admission fee at the City Ground during the reign of the 'Cockney spivs' in season 1997/98. This was after all, only the First Division. They were even more incensed when Forest supporters suggested to them, with the score 5-2 in Forest's favour, this may not quite have been the best £20 they had ever spent! Mind you, they eventually had the last laugh, by charging us £20 to get into the Valley later on in the season, and by whooping us 4-1 in the FA Cup and 4-2 in the League. He, who laughs last, laughs loudest!).

66. United-United, Can you swim? United, Can you swim? (See page 11 - the Trent Enders of the mid-to-late-sixties, kindly asking the visiting Manchester United supporters whether they would like to engage in some recreational activities on the banks of the River Trent after the game?).

67. We all agree; Nottingham Forest are magic! We all agree; Nottingham Forest are magic, Are magic, Are magic! (Rather irritating chant from the Championship-winning season of 1977/78. Died out many years ago...thank God!).

68. We all agree; Walker is worth more than Derby! (See page 250 - same tune, much better lyrics! The 'Travelling Trickies' take the piss out of the 'Sheep' at the 'BBG' on 24th November 1990, with Forest having recently turned down a £5 million bid for 'Dessie' from Italian giants Juventus).

69. We are the boys in the red an' white, We love to sing an' we love t' fight...So let's fight! So let's fight! (Another Trent End 'bovver boy' song from the late-sixties/early-seventies).

70. We are the greatest fans in the land, We carry broken bottles in our 'ands, If you think that we are doin' wrong, We'll walk dairn Arkwright Street an' sing this song! Ooh-ooh-ooh-ooh-ooh-ooh-ooh-Nottingham! (Repeat). (Blimey - were the Trent End really this violent during the 'bovver boy' days, 'cause this is yet another one from that era? Makes today's Trent Enders seem like pussy-cats dunt it!).

71. We are the Nutters, The Nutters from Notts! (See page 75 - proud boast of Forest's notorious hooligan element on their away excursions during the mid-seventies).

72. We 'ate Der-by, An' we 'ate Der-by, We 'ate Der-by, An' we 'ate Der-by, We 'ate Der-by, An' we 'ate Der-by, We are the Der-by 'aters! Sheep-sheep-sheep-shaggers! Baaaaaaaaaaaaaaah! (Another all-time favourite of Forest supporters, which has been around forever, and is similar to No.34 - 'If ya'll 'ate Derby clap yer ands', particularly the farmyard impressions at the end!).

73. We 'ate Leeds United, We 'ate Liverpool too (and Leicester!), We 'ate Derby County, But Forest we love you, Altogether now... (The Trent End's own version of the famous 'Altogether now...We hate Nottingham Forest' anthem, which was sung by virtually every club in the land during the nineteen-seventies (and still is by some) and is hated by Forest supporters!).

74. We don't care we're Forest fans, Doo-da, doo-da, We don't care we're Forest fans, Doo-da, doo-da-day! On the piss all night, On the piss all day, We don't care we're Forest fans, Doo-da, doo-da-day! (Always sung by Forest supporters in the face of adversity i.e. when the team are gerrin' a right good thumpin', and has been around since the late-sixties).

75. We don't carry 'ammers, We don't carry lead, We only carry 'atchets, T' bury in your 'ead; We are true supporters, Fanatics every one, We 'ate Derby County, Spurs an' Everton! Nottingham-Boot-Boys! Nottingham-Boot-Boys! (See page 39 - what...more threats of violence from the Trent End 'bovver boys' of the early-seventies!).

76. We'll be back, We'll be back, We'll be back agen next year, We'll back agen next year! (See page 133 - Forest supporters in defiant mood after the 1-0 League Cup Final defeat against Wolves at Wembley Stadium on 5th March 1980. This was later adapted to: "We'll be back as Champions!" after Forest were relegated from the Premiership at the end of season 1992/93 - see page 284).

77. We'll be runnin' rairnd Wembley wi' the Cup, We'll be runnin' rairnd Wembley wi the Cup, We'll be runnin' rairnd Wembley, Runnin' rairnd Wembley, Runnin' rairnd Wembley wi' the Cup; Singin' aye-aye-Ian-Storey-Moore, Singin' aye-aye-Ian-Storey-Moore, Singin' aye-aye-Ian, Aye-aye-Ian, Aye-aye-Ian-Storey-Moore! (Started during the famous FA Cup-run of 1966/67 season and became the unofficial FA Cup anthem thereafter until Moore eventually left the Club in March 1972).

78. Well I never felt more like singin' the blues, When Forest win, An' Derby lose, Oh- baby, You got me singin' the blues! Sing! Sing! Sing! (See page 351 - started in earnest in Yates' Wine Lodge in town on Sunday evening, 25th April 1998, after we'd just beaten Reading 1-0 to secure our return to the top flight. Leicester had gone to 'Shite Park' that same afternoon and slaughtered the 'Sheep' 4-0 - a game we watched live on the tele in the Aviary straight after our game had ended. It just doesn't come any better than this!).

79. We'll see you all outside, We'll see you all outside, We'll see you all, We'll see you all outside; We'll see you all outside, We'll see you all outside, We'll see you all... We'll see you all outside! (The Trent Enders arranging to meet the opposition outside the City Ground for a 'friendly chat' after the game. This is yet another from the late-sixties and was always sung when we were losing...which incidentally was quite often!).

80. We you love you Forest, we do, We love you Forest, we do, We love you Forest, we do, Oh Forest we love you! (See page 192 - a song we originally 'borrowed' from Sheffield Wednesday supporters in 1985 and which has been around ever since!).

81. We're all goin' t' Wem-bley, We're all goin' t' Wem-bley, La-la-la-la, La-la-la-la! (Popular chant when on the FA Cup or League Cup trail and has it's origins in the early-eighties).

82. We're gonna win the European Cup! (See page 133 - throwback to the glory days of seasons 1978/79 and 1979/80, when the Trent End were in confident mood about our likely end-of-season accomplishments!).

83. We're on the march wi' Cloughie's ar-my, We're all goin' t' Wem-ber-ley, An' we'll really shake 'em up, When we win the FA Cup, Cos Forest are the greatest football team! (See page 70 - Cloughie's first match in charge on 8th January 1975, saw Second Division Forest achieve an unlikely FA Cup victory away at First Division Spurs. The Trent End had to quickly adapt one of their oldest anthems 'Who's that team they call the For-est' (See no.94) in order to celebrate this achievement!).

84. We're sick and tired of you - Fashanu, Fashanu! (See page 165 - Forest supporters tell Justin Fashanu just what they think of him, shortly before the local derby with Notts at Meadow Lane on 12th April 1982. Wasn't impressed with this one really at the time, as it is my view that no matter how badly he may be playing, you should never boo any player wearing the famous Red Garibaldi!).

85. We've bin to Europe; We've won the Cup twice! (See page 152 - started out as a quite legitimate boast back in 1980, but now smacks just a little bit of 'we know we're crap now, but we 'ant always bin!' What's more, half of those chanting it nowadays, weren't even born at the time we won the damn thing anyway!).

86. We've got you on the run, We've got you on

the run, *We've got you on the run!* (See page 118 - I loved this one, which was sung during our halcyon days of the late-seventies, when we used to give just about everyone - including the 'Scousers' - the run-around! Sounded particularly impressive when we were takin' the piss out of Southampton in the League Cup Final at Wembley on 17th March 1979).

87. *We've travelled far an' wide, We've bin to Merseyside, But there is only one place, I wanna be; It's at the City Ground, Where people gather round, To 'ear the Trent End sound, We're gonna win today! Come on an' cheer agen, Come on an' cheer agen, For we are 'ere agen, To see the Forest win; Come on an' score agen, With Ian Moore agen, For we are sure agen, We're gonna win today! Come on an' cheer agen...*(See page 368 - what an absolute classic this one is from way back in the late-sixties - and not so much as a swear-word in sight. I'd like to drag the scribe who penned this one out of retirement and transport him back down to the City Ground in order to give the Trent Enders of today some much-needed lessons in lyric writing!).

88. *What a waste o' twenty quid, What a waste o' twenty quid!* (See page 348 - Charlton fans gettin' it in the neck again (see no.65) re. the extortionate price they'd had to pay to see their team get whooped by the 'Super Reds'! We weren't picking on them particularly; every team that got beaten down at the City Ground that season got exactly the same treatment).

89. *What's it like? What's it like? What's it like to be outclassed? What's it like to be outclassed?* (This particular chant came to prominence during season 1977/78, when the players took the piss out of the opposition out there on the pitch and we did the same to their supporters on the terraces. Oh happy days!).

90. *When Derby g' dairn agen, agen, We'll sing, we'll sing, When Derby g' dairn agen, agen, We'll sing, we'll sing; When Ian Moore scores a goal, Ya can shove yer 'ector up yer 'ole, An' we'll all go mad, When Derby g' dairn agen!* (See page 27 - this is by far the most common 'we hate Derby' anthem on the terraces of the City Ground. Like most others, it first arrived on the scene back in season 1969/70 and is still sung in most parts of the ground on most match-days to this day - it's even rumoured some of the supporters in the upper tier of the Brian Clough Stand once got so excited during a game they started singing it, although personally, I find this very hard to believe!).

91. *Whenever yer sad, Whenever yer blue, Whenever the Forest are playin'; If we're out o' luck, We fight like fuck, T' keep the Trent End swayin'! Ooh, Ooh, Ooh, Ooh, Ooh, Ooh, Ooh, Ooh, Ooh, Ooh, Ooh!* (See page 22 - very popular Trent End anthem of the late-sixties/early-seventies era. Perfectly sums up the undying loyalty of the Trent Enders!).

92. *When I'm strollin', just strollin, By the light of the silvery moon; I don't envy the rich, In their automobiles, A motor car is phoney, I'd rather shag a pony; When I'm strollin', just strollin'...* (Don't ask me? This was a very popular anthem on the Trent End terraces of the late-sixties, although I haven't the foggiest idea what it's all about or in what way it's connected to the Club or it's supporters?).

93. *When I was just a little boy, I asked my mother: What will I be? Will I be Derby? Will I be Reds? Here's what she said to me: It's Forest-Forest, It's got to be Fo-o-rest, It's got to be Fo-o-rest, It's Forest, Forest!* (See page 204 - another 'Derbyshire Reds' anthem sung by those who would otherwise have had the misfortune to spend their Saturday afternoons chewing a cud in the fields outside 'Shite Park' with the rest of the inadequates!).

94. *Who's that team they call the For-est? Who's that team we all adore? Oh they play in red an' white, An' they fight with all their might, An' they're out t' show the world the way to score!* (What no swearwords? Another popular one this from the mid-to-late sixties).

95. *Who's yer father? Who's yer father? Who's yer father - Referee? You ain't got one - you're a bastard!*

You're a bastard - Referee! (This was the normal terrace chant in the sixties and seventies whenever the Ref' was wearing the number 12 shirt for the opposition. This has now given way to: *"Who's the bastard in the black?"* or *"The Referee's a wanker!"*).

96. *With a bow-legged chicken, An' a knock-kneed 'en, We ain't 'ad a fight, Since we don't know when; We don't give a wiggle, An' we don't give a wank, We are the Trent End - Boot Boys! La-la-la-la-la-la, La-la-la...* (Once again, no idea what this one from the early-seventies is all about, but it was very popular amongst the Skinhead fraternity within the Trent End. Also accompanied by lots of bouncing up and down during the chorus).

97. *Worra dump, Worra dump, Worra dump! Worra dump, Worra dump, Worra du-ump! Worra dump, Worra dump, Worra dump; Worra dump! Wo-rra dump!* (See page 265 - the first time I heard this particular chant, was back in season 1991/92, when we were congratulating Leicester City on the 'quality' of their 'luxurious' Filbert Street 'stadium'! They didn't look too pleased for some reason!).

98. *You are my Forest, My only Forest, You make me 'appy, When skies are grey; You'll never notice, 'Ow much I love you, Please don't take, My Fo-rest away! La-la-la-la-la, La-la-la-la-la...*(See page 103 - another one which emerged during the Championship-winning season of 1977/78 - have I mentioned we won the Championship that year? - and was subsequently copied and adapted by most other clubs).

99. *You'll never beat Des Walker! You'll never beat Des Walker!* ('Dessie' quickly inspired this particular chant on Trentside following his debut back in 1984. Has stuck with him ever since).

100. *You never close your eyes anymore, When I kiss your lips, And there's no tenderness, Like before in your fingertips; You're tryin' hard not t' show it, baby, But baby, baby I know it; You've lost that lovin' feelin', Woo-ooh, that lovin' feelin', You've lost that lovin' feelin, Now it's gone, gone, gone...woo-oo-oo-ooh!* (I haven't got the foggiest where this came from (other than the Righteous Brothers of course!) or what it's connection, if any, is with our beloved 'Reds'; but it first came to prominence in the early-nineties and is still very popular today. Sounded particularly good with over 30,000 'Trickies' singing it at Wembley Stadium on 29th March 1992 when we beat Southampton 3-2 in the ZDS Final!).

101. *You're goin' in the Trent, You're goin' in the Trent, You're goin' in the Trent!* (See page 11 - this popular chant from the notorious Trent Enders of the late-sixties must have sent a shiver down the spine of every visiting supporter during the pre-Lady Bay Bridge days. A loud chorus was always struck up at about twenty to five, in the full-knowledge that the police would be escorting the visitors along the Trent Embankment just behind the Trent End immediately after the game).

102. *Zigger-Zagger, Zigger-Zagger, Joe-Ba-ker! Zigger-Zagger, Zigger-Zagger, Joe-Ba-ker! Zigger - Joe! Zagger - Joe! Zigger-Zagger, Zigger-Zagger, Joe-Ba-ker!* (See page 318 - this was the number one 'Joe Baker' chant of the mid-to-late-sixties, which echoed around the Trent End before, during and after every game. Sounds particularly good in a pub crowded with drunken 'Reds'!).

103. *I could just go on...and on...and on...but I won't.* Take it from me however, there are dozens and dozens more which could also have been included. So if any opposition supporters ever give you the old: *"One song - you've only got one song!"* routine (although Everton supporters seem to be the main recipients of this particular chant), you've got more than enough ammunition to throw back at them!

By the way, if you can think of any other decent ones, not in the above list, why not drop me a line at: Tricky Red Publications, P.O. Box 6729, Nottingham, NG1 3JE. Who knows, the next little project might just be a book of Trent End anthems?

SOURCES OF REFERENCE

WRITTEN MATERIAL:
- My entire collection of Forest programmes which comprises seasons 1966/67 to 2000/01 respectively.
- My own diaries in which I have maintained a meticulous record of fixtures, results and attendances during my 35 seasons of supporting the 'Reds'.
- 'Forest - The First 125 Years - The Official Statistical Record of Nottingham Forest Football Club' - by Ken Smales. (All attendances quoted in this book up to and including season 1990/91 are gleaned from Mr Smales' publication. Although some may differ from those quoted in the Official Match-day programmes, they are considered to be the most accurate available. All attendance figures quoted from season 1991/92 onwards are from my own personal diaries and the Official Forest Review magazines).
- 'Football Fan's Guide' - by Janet Williams & Mark Johnson - updated version for season 1996/97.
- 'The Hamlyn A-Z of British Football Records (Revised Edition)' - by Phil Soar.
- 'The Breedon Book of Football Records - 1871-2000' - by Gordon Smailes
- 'The Official History of Nottingham Forest' - by Phil Soar.
- 'The Garibaldi Reds' - by Keith Mellor.
- 'Forest - 1865-1978' - by John Lawson.
- 'Forest - The 1979 Season' - by John Lawson.
- 'Forest - The 1980 Season' - by John Lawson.
- 'Nottingham Forest Annual 1979' - by Dave Horridge.
- 'With Clough - By Taylor' - by Peter Taylor.
- 'Is there a book inside you?' - by Dan Poynter & Mindy Bingham.
- 'The Oxford Everyday Dictionary and Guide to Correct English'.
- Hutchinson's - 'The Encyclopedia of Britain'.

COMPUTER SOFTWARE:
- Microsoft - Encarta 98 Encyclopedia.

OFFICIAL FOREST VIDEOS:
- 'Forest Video 1986' - by Nottingham Video Productions.
- 'That Championship Feeling' - by Andrew Dolloway.
- 'League Cup Final - Nottingham Forest v Southampton - 1978/79' - by The Video Collection.
- 'Nottingham Forest - The Official Review of Barclays League Division One - 1988/89' - by CBS Fox Videos.
- 'Wembley, Wembley - The Official Nottingham Forest FC Season 1988/89' - by Watershed Pictures/Castle Communications PLC.
- 'The Official History of Nottingham Forest FC' - by Watershed Pictures/Castle Communications PLC.
- 'The FA Cup semi-final - Nottingham Forest v West Ham - Sunday 14th April 1991' - by Watershed Pictures Ltd.
- 'Nottingham Forest - The Official Season Review 1993/94' - by PolyGram Video.
- 'Nottingham Forest - The Golden Goals Collection' - by PolyGram Video.
- 'Nottingham Forest - Season 1994/95' - by Tele Video Productions.
- 'Nottingham Forest - The Official Season Review 1995/96' - by Televideo.
- 'Champions! Nottingham Forest - Season Review 1997/98' - by Disc Distribution.

PERSONAL FOREST VIDEO COLLECTION: - Footage of the following televised games:

- Watford v Forest - FA Cup 5th Round - Vicarage Road - 19th February 1989.
- Manchester United v Forest - FA Cup 6th Round - Old Trafford - 18th March 1989.
- Forest v Luton Town - League Cup Final - Wembley Stadium - 9th April 1989.
- Forest v Everton - Simod Cup Final - Wembley Stadium - 30th April 1989.
- Forest v Liverpool - FA Cup semi-final - Old Trafford - 7th May 1989.
- Tottenham Hotspur v Forest - League Cup quarter-final replay - White Hart Lane - 24th January 1990.
- Forest v Coventry City - League Cup semi-final 1st Leg - City Ground - 11th February 1990.
- Coventry City v Forest - League Cup semi-final 2nd Leg - Highfield Road - 25th February 1990.
- Forest v Oldham Athletic - League Cup Final - Wembley Stadium - 29th April 1990.
- Forest v West Ham United - FA Cup semi-final - Villa Park - 14th April 1991.
- Forest v Tottenham Hotspur - FA Cup Final - Wembley Stadium - 18th May 1991.
- Notts County v Forest - Football League Division One - Meadow Lane - 24th August 1991.
- Tottenham Hotspur v Forest - League Cup semi-final 2nd Leg - White Hart Lane - 1st March 1992.
- Forest v Manchester United - League Cup Final - Wembley Stadium - 12th April 1992.

AND...LAST BUT NOT LEAST:
- The thousands of memories I have clogging up my brain-cells in respect of my own personal experiences over 35 seasons of following the 'Reds' through thick and thin. Reference to all the above programmes, books and videos etc. has enabled me to recall these experiences in a clear and chronological order, rather than the confused, patchwork manner in which they would have otherwise been re-produced!

SUBSCRIBERS LIST

Many, many thanks to each of the following for subscribing to this book:

1. **John & Amy Webster,** Long Lane, Shirebrook, Mansfield, Notts.
2. **Peter Kerry (Senior),** Greenland Crescent, Chilwell, Beeston, Nottingham.
3. **Gary Taylor,** Charlton Grove, Chilwell, Beeston, Nottingham.
4. **John Farley,** Lambourne Gardens, Woodthorpe, Nottingham.
5. **Dean Farley,** Lambourne Gardens, Woodthorpe, Nottingham.
6. **Malc & Chris Hall,** Trent Road, Beeston Rylands, Nottingham.
7. **Mick Bench,** High Road, Chilwell, Beeston, Nottingham.
8. **Peter Kerry (Junior),** Greenland Crescent, Chilwell, Beeston, Nottingham.
9. **John Baxter,** Stanley Road, Forest Town, Mansfield, Notts.
10. **Neal Baxter,** Wentworth Close, Forest Town, Mansfield, Notts.
11. **'Biff',** Egerton Close, Mansfield, Notts.
12. **Andy Hallam ('The Worm'),** Pierrpont Road, West Bridgford, Nottingham.
13. **Stephen Bentley,** Blake Crescent, Ravensdale, Mansfield, Notts.
14. **Janet O'Connor & Richard Panter,** Old Way, Hathern, Leicestershire.
15. **Martin Auckland,** Paget Crescent, Ruddington, Nottingham.
16. **Stephen Ford,** Central Park, Halifax, West Yorkshire.
17. **Gary Hall,** Y Fron, Nant Parc, Johnstown, Wrexham.
18. **Martyn Soar,** Cecil Avenue, Dronfield, Derbyshire.
19. **Alan Carroll,** Southbridge Road, Croydon.
20. **Roger Brumpton,** Sunnymede Cottages, Ray Mill Road East, Maidenhead, Berkshire.
21. **Chris Clifford,** Thorpe Road, Lyddington, Rutland.
22. **Peter Gibson,** Little Breck, South Normanton, Derbyshire.
23. **Steve Adcock,** Cheltenham Close, Toton, Beeston, Notts.
24. **Rupert Bellamy,** Lark Close, Littleover, Derby.
25. **Keith Shillingford,** Beales Road, Great Bookham, Nr.Leatherhead.
26. **Mark Jackson,** Eltham Road, West Bridgford, Nottingham.
27. **Stuart Holland,** Church View Close, Belton, Doncaster, South Yorkshire.
28. **Antony Neale,** Hilton Close, Belton, Doncaster, South Yorkshire.
29. **David Neale,** Hilton Close, Belton, Doncaster, South Yorkshire.
30. **Alan Hazzledine,** Charlotte Grove, Beeston, Nottingham.
31. **Bev Hazzledine,** Charlotte Grove, Beeston, Nottingham.
32. **John Cooper,** c/o Charlotte Grove, Beeston, Nottingham.
33. **Nick Ayers,** Gorsy Lane, Morton, Southwell, Notts.
34. **Shaun Morley,** South View Road, Carlton, Nottingham.
35. **Peter Castledine,** Church Street, Granby, Nottingham.
36. **Mark Dilloway & Family,** Dudley Road, Grantham, Lincolnshire.
37. **Susan Jackson,** Beresford Road, Mansfield Woodhouse, Notts.
38. **Stefen McKay,** North Avenue, Sandiacre, Nottingham.
39. **Steve Maltby,** Central Avenue, Chilwell, Beeston, Nottingham.
40. **Neil Dwyer,** Offerton Road, Torkington, Hazel Grove, Cheshire.
41. **Robert Shepherd,** Rufford Road, Edwinstowe, Mansfield, Notts.
42. **Rich Fisher,** Fernleigh Avenue, Mapperley, Nottingham.
43. **Christopher Haywood,** Templar Road, Beeston, Nottingham.
44. **Gillian Haywood,** Templar Road, Beeston, Nottingham.
45. **John ('Cosmo') Sisson,** Wadham Road, Woodthorpe, Nottingham.
46. **Andrew Smith,** Foden Close, Shenstone, Lichfield, Staffordshire.
47. **T.C. Bakewell,** Forest Road, Annesley Woodhouse, Kirkby-In-Ashfield, Notts.
48. **Barry Baker,** Bridge End Road, Grantham, Lincolnshire.
49. **Jaymes Mayne,** Cornish Road, Chipping Norton, Oxon.
50. **Dominic Chien,** Stag Hill Court, University of Surrey, Surrey, Guildford.
51. **Robert Martinson,** Bruce Drive, West Bridgford, Nottingham.
52. **Richard Danbury,** Heath lane, Bladon, Woodstock, Oxfordshire.
53. **Kevin Daybell,** Sharrard Close, Underwood, Nottinghamshire.
54. **David & Nick Long,** Smugglers Lane North, Highcliff, Christchurch, Dorset.
55. **Martin Holodynsky,** Tudor Road, West Bridgford, Nottingham.
56. **Dave Brown,** Charlton Road, Crownhill, Plymouth, Devon.
57. **Micheál Spain,** Hillside Park, Rathfarnham, Dublin 16, Ireland.
58. **Pat Elliott,** Church Road, Snitterfield, Stratford Upon Avon, Warwickshire.
59. **Hannah Dexter,** Mallard Hill, Brickhill, Bedford.
60. **Bernard Davis,** Haddon Crescent, Chilwell, Beeston, Nottingham.
61. **Ian Taylor,** George Avenue, Beeston, Nottingham.
62. **George Tucker,** Coronation Avenue, Sandiacre, Notts.
63. **Janet Baldwin,** Ashworth Avenue, Heanor, Derbyshire.
64. **Ivor Garton,** Leyburn Road, North Hykeham, Lincoln.
65. **Trevor Fermie,** Rufford Road, Ruddington, Nottingham.
66. **Rod Symes,** Picknage Road, Barley, Nr.Royston, Herts.
67. **Ann Hilton & John Conniss,** Norman Road, Thorneywood, Nottingham.
68. **John Kelvey,** Chilwell, Beeston, Nottingham.
69. **Jeff Bunting,** Leamington Drive, Chilwell, Beeston, Nottingham.
70. **Paul 'Tank' Cassidy,** Dylan Thomas Road, Bestwood, Nottingham.
71. **Alan C. Sims,** Allendale Avenue, Aspley, Nottingham.
72. **Martin Clarke,** Naseby Road, Clipston, Market Harborough, Leics.
73. **Chris J. Fensom,** Hope Street, Beeston, Nottingham.
74. **Jan Wilcox,** Bakersfield, Crayford Road, Holloway, London.
75. **Sean Kieron Smith,** Wyvern Avenue, Long Eaton, Nottingham.
76. **Stephen Purdy,** Ruffs Drive, Hucknall, Notts.
77. **David Wildgoose,** Annesley Road, Hucknall, Notts.
78. **Wayne C. Watson,** Dundas Close, North Sherwood Street, Nottingham.
79. **Andy Widdowson ('Sherwood The Bear'),** Honeysuckle Grove, Bingham, Notts.
80. **Bryn Pryse-Jones,** Selby Road, West Bridgford, Nottingham.
81. **Richard Tebb,** Westborough Lane, Long Bennington, Newark, Notts.
82. **Philip Doorly,** Eggington Close, Cantley, Doncaster.
83. **Andy Ibbett,** Windsor Street, Stapleford, Nottingham.
84. **Emma Sparks,** North Street, Asfordby Valley, Melton Mowbray, Leics.
85. **Jeffrey Pinkett,** Deepdale Road, Long Eaton, Nottingham.
86. **Kevin Carter,** Sevenfields, Highworth, Swindon, Wilts.
87. **Neil David Harrison,** Staple Lane, Balderton, Newark, Notts.
88. **Ivy Joan Trussell,** Wirksworth Road, Kirk Hallam, Ilkeston, Derbyshire.
89. **Mark Trussell,** Ditchfield Road, Penketh, Warrington, Cheshire.
90. **Robert Phillips,** Cromwell Road, Caversham, Reading.
91. **Jason McLoughlin,** Pen-Y-Fai, Bridgford, Cardiff.
92. **Tom Clough,** Mountbatten Way, Chilwell, Beeston, Nottingham.
93. **Stuart Chadwick,** Big Barn Lane, Mansfield, Notts.
94. **Martin Pullon,** St.Hilary, Cowbridge.
95. **Matt Walton,** Runswick Drive, Wollaton, Nottingham.
96. **Francis Eizens,** Rotherham Road, Swallownest, Sheffield.
97. **Anthony Smith,** Keats Close, Horsham, West Sussex.
98. **Donald Barton,** Hermit Street, Lincoln, Lincs.
99. **John Dobney,** Winchester Road, Grantham, Lincolnshire.
100. **Alan Spencer,** Queens Court, Kings Parade, Holland On Sea, Clacton On Sea, Essex.
101. **Andrew John Weightman,** Cromford Meadows, Broughton Astley, Leics.
102. **Keith Peat,** Sycamore Road, East Leake, Loughborough, Leics.
103. **Chris Cupit,** The Chine, Broadmeadows, South Normanton, Alfreton, Derbys.
104. **Amy Hill,** Ludgate Drive, East Bridgford, Nottingham.
105. **Michael Hollingsworth,** Minster Crescent, Leicester.
106. **John Parke,** Greenway Road, Taunton, Somerset.
107. **Chris Dorey,** The Hornet, Chichester, West Sussex.
108. **Alan Sinden,** Canterbury Way, Exmouth, Devon.
109. **Darren Fee,** Thorneywood Rise, Thorneywood, Nottingham.

110. **Ian Whyte,** Queenscourt, Wembley, Middlesex.
111. **Dr. George W. Waterhouse,** Brainton Road, Tallington, Stamford, Lincolnshire.
112. **Margaret Brownett,** Trent Lane, Castle Donington, Derby.
113. **Rob Haynes,** Chapmans, Hemingford Abbotts, Huntingdon.
114. **Darrell Bowser,** Greenhills Road, Eastwood, Notts.
115. **Chris ('Tiff') Humphries,** Hartwood Drive, Stapleford, Nottingham.
116. **Bernard Blount,** Morpeth Arms, Millbank, Westminster.
117. **Jenny Snow,** Cornford Park, Pembury, Tunbridge Wells, Kent.
118. **Alan Robinson,** Latimer Drive, Bramcote Moor, Nottingham.
119. **Dr. Andrew Holman,** Lambourne Close, Bury St.Edmunds, Suffolk.
120. **Stephen Rawlinson,** Warden Avenue, Harrow, Middlesex.
121. **Martyn Allen,** Nottingham Road, Toton, Beeston, Nottingham.
122. **Adam Williams,** Park Road, Calverton, Nottingham.
123. **Kevin Reidy,** Woodfield, Barna Road, Galway, Ireland.
124. **Ian & Marie Kirkland,** Melbourne Court, Sawley, Long Eaton, Nottingham.
125. **Alan Springthorpe,** Moseley Road, Annesley, Notts.
126. **Alan Maplethorpe,** Wilson Road, Chaddesden, Derby.
127. **Guy Smith ('Smudge'),** Oakenhall Avenue, Hucknall, Nottingham.
128. **Frank & Zel Swinscoe,** Field Lane, Chilwell, Beeston, Notts.
129. **Andrew Cook,** Redstart Road, Chard, Somerset.
130. **Ian Whyte,** Queenscourt, Wembley, Middlesex.
131. **Andy Webber,** Blenheim Road, Taunton, Somerset.
132. **Simon Litchfield,** Glenridding Close, Gamston, Nottingham.
133. **Barry & Jake Clarke,** Morley Street, Sutton-In-Ashfield, Nottinghamshire.
134. **Graham & Dawn Broughton,** Cottesbrooke Gardens, East Hunsbury, Northampton.
135. **Ian Copping,** Exchange Road, West Bridgford, Nottingham.
136. **A.Redhead,** Ribble Way, Melton Mowbray, Leicestershire.
137. **Don White,** Reydon Drive, Whitemoor, Nottingham.
138. **Rose O'Carroll,** Woodlands Farm Close, Hucknall, Nottingham.
139. **Andrew Basford,** Long Lane, Attenborough, Nottingham.
140. **Adam Perczynski,** Torvill Drive, Wollaton, Nottingham.
141. **David Gravener,** Red Lodge Road, Bexley, Kent.
142. **Darren Stoppard,** Tichfield Street, Warsop, Mansfield, Notts.
143. **Nigel Newbold,** Slade Road, Ilfracombe, Devon.
144. **Danny Webster** (Bsc Hons.), Long Lane, Shirebrook, Mansfield, Notts.
145. **Scott Davies,** Letchworth Crescent, Chilwell, Beeston, Nottingham.
146. **Ian Marriott,** Deepdale Park, Sutton In Ashfield, Notts.
147. **Alan Hill,** Joyce Avenue, Toton, Beeston, Nottingham.
148. **Gerald Adkins,** Rosecroft Drive, Edwards Lane Estate, Nottingham.
149. **Garry Housley,** Church Street, Clowne, Chesterfield, Derbyshire.
150. **Dave Shaw,** Near Meadow, Long Eaton, Nottingham.
151. **Stuart Kaye,** Hotpsur Drive, Colwick, Nottingham.
152. **Grenvill Sisson,** Main Road, Underwood, Notts.
153. **Dr. James P. Kingsland,** Cambridge Road, Wollaton Park, Nottingham.
154. **Mr. & Mrs. F. Stimpson,** Gedling Road, Arnold, Nottingham.
155. **Joseph Dobson,** St.Hughs Drive, Langworth, Lincoln.
156. **Matthew Dobson,** St.Hughs Drive, Langworth, Lincoln.
157. **Philip Ridley,** Campion Street, Arnold, Nottingham.
158. **M.F. Holford,** Digby Avenue, Mapperley, Nottingham.
159. **Steven Keeling,** Daisy Farm Road, Newthorpe, Nottingham.
160. **Stephen Crean,** Robinson Road, Tooting, London.
161. **Carl Barker,** Newtons Lane, Cossall, Notts.
162. **Robin Morris,** Lime Close, Prestbury, Cheltenham, Gloucester.
163. **Grace Fyles,** Repton Road, West Bridgford, Nottingham.
164. **Phil Wilson,** Cologne Road, Bovington, Wareham, Dorset.
165. **Douglas Bowen,** Windsmoor Road, Brinsley, Notts.
166. **John Grain & Sandra Clifford,** Eastcote Avenue, Bramcote, Nottingham.
167. **Philip Colcomb,** Orchard Way, Balderton, Newark, Notts.
168. **Ian Arslan,** Coledale, West Bridgford, Nottingham.
169. **Anthony Balchin,** Coledale, West Bridgford, Nottingham.
170. **Janet Spittle,** Coledale, West Bridgford, Nottingham.
171. **Lee Spittle,** Coledale, West Bridgford, Nottingham.
172. **Alan Balchin,** Coledale, West Bridgford, Nottingham.
173. **Malcolm Woodhead,** Audon Avenue, Chilwell, Beeston, Nottingham.
174. **Steve Jamison,** Westerlands, Stapleford, Nottingham.
175. **Steve Williams,** Minerva Street, Bulwell, Nottingham.

176. **'Eli' Ellis,** Minerva Street, Bulwell, Nottingham.
177. **Nick Payne,** Westerdale Road, Grantham, Lincolnshire.
178. **Walter Madden,** Sunninghill Drive, Clifton, Nottingham.
179. **Simon Cook,** Melrose Street, Sherwood, Nottingham.
180. **Ian McGlashan,** Kent Street, Seddlescombe, Battle, East Sussex.
181. **Mark Williams,** Blachford Road, Ivybridge, Devon.
182. **Gary ('Eddie') Edwards,** Maori Avenue, Hucknall, Nottingham.
183. **Peter Jenkin,** Steyning Lane, Swineshead, Boston, Lincolnshire.
184. **Geoffrey Raynor,** Highwray Grove, Clifton, Nottingham.
185. **Matt Whitmarsh,** Brentnall Court, Kirk Close, Chilwell, Beeston, Nottingham.
186. **Julian Brenton,** Farm Drive, Alvaston, Derby.
187. **Sean Stevenson,** Wharfedale Gardens, Mansfield, Notts.
188. **Robert Stevenson,** Wharfedale Gardens, Mansfield, Notts.
189. **Antony Pennington,** Wharfedale Gardens, Mansfield, Notts.
190. **Lee Dunville,** Wharefdale Gardens, Mansfield, Notts.
191. **Barrie Fell,** Fletcher Street, Heanor, Derbyshire.
192. **Idris Hall,** The White Hart, Station Road, West Hallam, Derbys.
193. **Gareth Hall,** Seaburn Road, Toton, Beeston, Nottingham.
194. **Raymond Bonsor,** The Woodthorpe Inn, Coupe Lane, Old Tupton, Chesterfield.
195. **Wayne Allcoat,** St.Peters Avenue, Kettering, Northants.
196. **Scott Ulke,** Shelby Close, Lenton, Nottingham.
197. **Steven Bacon,** Western Avenue, Kirkby-In-Ashfield, Notts.
198. **Will Mather,** Willow Road, West Bridgford, Nottingham.
199. **Richard Kirk,** Marshalswick Lane, St.Albans, Herts.
200. **Paul Burrows,** Park Road, Chilwell, Nottingham.
201. **Stuart Simms,** Park Road, Chilwell, Nottingham.
202. **Jason Cranidge,** Goldsmith Road, Balderton, Newark, Notts.
203. **Brian Cranidge,** Goldsmith Road, Balderton, Newark, Notts.
204. **Tony Kirk,** c/o Latimer Drive, Bramcote Moor, Nottingham.
205. **Nick Gaywood,** Oldmills, Fochabers, Morayshire.
206. **Dave Chambers,** Tipnall Road, Castle Donington, Derby.
207. **Mel Hart,** Monza Street, Beeston, Nottingham.
208. **Nigel Guthrie,** Honeysuckle Grove, Bingham, Nottingham.
209. **Graham Grant,** Clarence Street, Market Harborough, Leics.
210. **Peter Bardens,** Long Lane, Attenborough, Nottingham.
211. **Craig Taylor,** Long Lane, Attenborough, Nottingham.
212. **Stuart Crossland,** Acacia Crescent, Carlton, Nottingham.
213. **Arthur Preston** F.E.C., Brandish Crescent, Clifton, Nottingham.
214. **Chris Rigby,** Walnut Close, Brighton, East Sussex.
215. **Adam Cook,** Church End, Hillesden, Buckingham.
216. **P.S. Richardson,** Sherwin Road, Stapleford, Notts.
217. **Michael Downes,** Old Tollerton Road, Gamston Village, Nottingham.
218. **Mark Campbell Donaldson,** Hambleton Close, Leicester Forest East, Leicester.
219. **Kirk Donaldson,** Shorwell Road, Dales Estate, Bakersfield, Nottingham.
220. **David Bruce,** Lichfield Road, New Invention, Willenhall, West Midlands.
221. **S.M. Gleave,** Moore Close, Claypole, Newark, Notts.
222. **Graham Bowden,** Belvedere Close, Spalding, Lincolnshire.
223. **Garry Mason,** Thomas Avenue, Radcliffe-On-Trent, Nottingham.
224. **Phil Colver,** Temple Meadows Road, Churchfields, West Bromwich.
225. **Nigel Smallwood,** Westacre Drive, Church Gresley, Swadlincote, S.Derbyshire.
226. **Steve Wilson,** Hannah Crescent, Wilford Village, Nottingham.
227. **John Yates,** Manor Close, Station Road, Rolleston, Nr.Newark, Notts.
228. **Nigel Inovskis,** Wallace Street, Gotham, Nottingham.
229. **Stuart Harrison,** Derby Road, Draycott, Derbys.
230. **Robert Banks,** Goldswong Terrace, Nottingham.
231. **Andrew Marshall,** C/O The Barbers, Attenborough, Nottingham.
232. **Mike Neal,** C/O The Barbers, Attenborough, Nottingham.
233. **David Cook,** The Tiger Inn, Tamworth Road, Long Eaton, Nottingham.
234. **David Dethick,** Devonshire Avenue, Long Eaton, Nottingham.
235. **Simon Coll,** C/O The Barbers, Attenborough, Nottingham.
236. **Mick Coll,** C/O The Barbers, Attenborough, Nottingham.